EDEN TO ARMAGEDDON

EDEN TO ARMAGEDDON

The First World War in the Middle East

Roger Ford

Weidenfeld & Nicolson

LONDON

To my wife, Michèle,
without whom none of this would have happened

First published in Great Britain in 2009
by Weidenfeld & Nicolson

1 3 5 7 9 10 8 6 4 2

© Roger Ford 2009

A CIP catalogue record for this book
is available from the British Library.

ISBN 978 0 297 84481 5

Typeset by Input Data Services Ltd,
Bridgwater, Somerset

Printed in the UK by CPI William Clowes Beccles NR34 7TL

The Orion Publishing Group's policy is to use papers
that are natural, renewable and recyclable products and made
from wood grown in sustainable forests. The logging and
manufacturing processes are expected to conform to the
environmental regulations of the country of origin.

Weidenfeld & Nicolson

The Orion Publishing Group Ltd
Orion House
5 Upper Saint Martin's Lane
London WC2H 9EA

An Hachette UK company

www.orionbooks.co.uk

Contents

List of Maps

List of Illustrations

Sultan Abdul Hamid II
Ismail Enver Pasha
Ahmed Jemal Pasha
Mehmet Talaat
Hans Freiherr von Wangenheim
Colmar Freiherr von der Goltz
Brig.-Gen. Walter Delamain
Lt.-Gen. Sir Arthur Barrett
Maj.-Gen. Sir Charles Townshend
Lt.-Gen. Sir John Nixon
Lt.-Gen. Sir Percy Lake
Lt.-Gen. Sir Fenton Aylmer VC
Maj.-Gen. Sir George Gorringe
Sir Frederick Maude
Sir William Marshall
Halil Pasha and staff
Rt. Hon. Winston Churchill and Sir John Arbuthnot Fisher
Rear-Adm. John de Roebeck
Rear-Adm. Rosslyn Wemyss
Maj.-Gen. Aylmer Hunter-Weston
Mustafa Kemal
Lt.-Gen. Sir Frederick Stopford
Lt.-Gen. Sir Bryan Mahon
Sir Ian Hamilton and Gen. Henri Gouraud
Gen. Henri Gouraud and Gen. Maurice Bailloud at Gallipoli
Maj.-Gen. Beauvoir de Lisle
Lt.-Gen. Sir Julian Byng
Lt.-Gen. Sir William Birdwood
Nikolai Nikolaevich Yudenich
Feisal ibn Hussein
Gen. Sir Edmund Allenby
Captain T.E. Lawrence
Kaiser Wilhelm II

David Lloyd George, Vittorio Orlando, Georges Clemenceau and Woodrow
   Wilson
The *Bab-i Ali*
Bashi-Bazouks
SMS *Goeben*
Riverine hospital ship
Turkish ski troops
Dunsterforce advance party
Towing landing parties to ANZAC Cove
Australian troops aboard HMS *Prince of Wales*
ANZAC wounded
Steam drifters
Australian troops charging at Gallipoli
The Royal Naval Division rehearsing an attack
Australian sniper and observer at Quinn's Post
ANZAC dugouts giving onto terraces
ANZAC Outpost No. 2 inland from North Beach
Steele's Post at ANZAC Cove
Sénégalese at Gallipoli
75mm field gun in action
V Beach at Cape Helles
British machine gunners, Gallipoli
Bathing at Helles
Kiretch Tepe
Turkish field artillery
Australian dressing station
Suvla Point
HMS *Cornwallis*
Playing cricket to deceive the Turks
The Hureira Redoubt
Turkish machine gunners on the Gaza-Beersheba Line
Gen. Kress von Kressenstein inspecting Turkish stormtroopers
Turkish infantry north of Jerusalem
Australian Light Horse entering Damascus
Greek forces at Smyrna, 1919

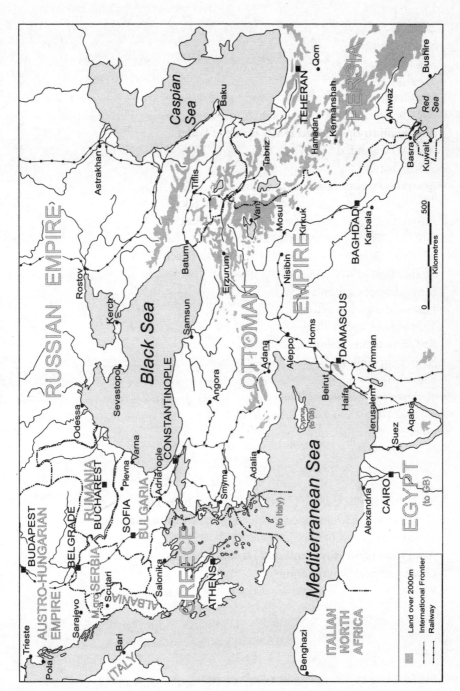

1. *Eurasia in 1914*

OVERTURE

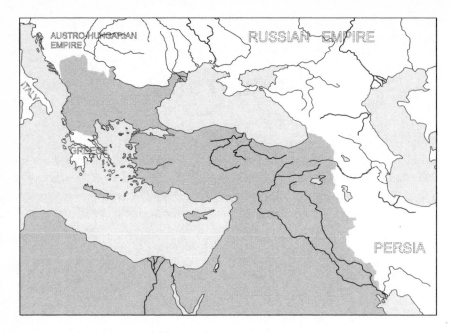

2a. The Ottoman Empire in 1875

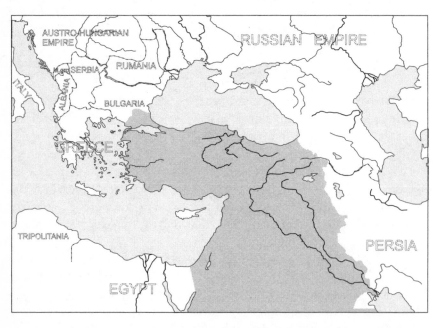

2b. The Ottoman Empire in 1914

1

The Route to War

The Ottoman Empire was a dominant force in world affairs for over half a millennium. At its height it had spanned three continents, reaching from the Persian Gulf to modern-day Algeria,[1] and from the borders of Austria east to the Caspian and south to the Sudan. By the early years of the nineteenth century, however, terminal decay had set in; the Sublime Porte[2] had already lost anything more than nominal control over its North African provinces, and its grip on the remnant of its European territory in the Balkans was being prised loose, thanks largely to the efforts of the power which had been its implacable enemy since the closing years of the seventeenth century and would remain so until her own fall in 1917: Russia.

Russia was a force to be reckoned with in the Balkans thanks to her self-appointed status as defender of the Christian faith, a role she had assumed following the fall of Byzantium on 29 May 1453. Despite forceful Turkish proselytising, two-thirds of the population of the Balkan provinces remained Christian, and provided the Russians with an adequate working mass. Dissidence flared up and was more or less put down[3] on a regular basis, but in 1875 something altogether more serious began to take shape.

By that year, thanks largely to the Industrial Revolution having passed it by and left it with a balance-of-payments disaster,[4] the Ottoman Empire was indebted to European banks to the tune of £200 million.[5] Amortisation and the interest on the debt amounted to £12 million, half of Turkey's gross annual national product, and the Porte, nowhere near able to raise such a sum, reneged on its commitments.[6] This immediately shut off all sources of credit, of course, and desperate for money, it levied swingeing new taxes in a forlorn attempt to raise it. Already the taxation situation was weighted heavily against non-Muslims (who were deprived of at least 40 per cent of their incomes); the new demands further exacerbated that, and the Russians wasted no time in exploiting the resulting unrest.

The Porte expected a backlash, no doubt, but it had every confidence of being able to weather it; that was a sorry miscalculation. Protests began in June 1875 – in Bosnia-Herzegovina, as it happened, but could have broken out in any one of a half-dozen virtually identical locations – and were put down swiftly enough, but the Turks failed to stamp out the embers completely, and they were blown into life again the following year, this time in Bulgaria. By the spring of 1876 the Russian-inspired dissidents were ready to act, but the Ottomans, forewarned by an excellent intelligence-gathering apparatus, beat them to it and decided to make an example of them *pour encourager les autres*. By 25 April the Porte had unleashed its weapon of choice: irregulars known as bashi-bazouks,[7] who settled the matter in their own inimitable fashion while the Turkish Army looked on. By mid-May the tragic affair was over. No attempt was made to separate the guilty from the innocent, and the most vulnerable suffered inordinately. There are no clear historical data for the number of people killed, and estimates range from 3,000 to ten times that, with 12,000 being generally accepted; 80 towns and villages were burned to the ground, and perhaps 200 more sacked.

The Turkish government's miscalculation was to underestimate just how badly a reversion to almost mediaeval standards of repressive behaviour would play in the West, and after the smoke, both literal and metaphorical, had cleared it found itself isolated and friendless (and with a new sultan at its head, Abdul Aziz having paid the ultimate price[8]). Russia was always ready to force any such moment to its crisis; the events were a more than adequate *casus belli*, and the government in St Petersburg orchestrated events so that it was able to go to war against the Turks in the Balkans and the Caucasus the following year as an injured party-by-proxy. (For those who are interested in keeping score, this would be for the tenth time in almost exactly two centuries.[9]) They met unexpectedly stiff resistance at Plevna (Pleven) in Bulgaria,[10] but within months the tsarist forces were at the very gates of Constantinople, and were only restrained from entering the city by the combined efforts of the other Great Powers, Disraeli's government, sticking to established Palmerstonian principles, taking a prominent part.[11] An armistice was reached, and followed by a conference at San Stefano, where Istanbul's international airport now stands; the resulting treaty saw Bulgaria granted her independence and awarded Northern and part of Eastern Thrace and most of Macedonia.

The other Great Powers (and they were not alone) were not amenable to what was seen as a move towards pan-Slavism, and convened the Congress of Berlin to reopen the matter in July 1878. While the resulting treaty watered down the effects of Russia's victory substantially, it left the Ottoman Empire in Europe in tatters, with Constantinople in possession only of a band of territory stretching from the lower Adriatic to the Black Sea. The rest of the Balkan states – Serbia, Rumania (that is, Wallachia and Moldavia), Montenegro and the northern part of Bulgaria[12] – gained their independence, while Austria-Hungary took control of Bosnia-Herzegovina and Russia held on to what it had taken in the Caucasus. It also cost the Turks Cyprus, annexed by the British to act as a gatehouse to the Suez Canal,[13] as the price of Britain's support at Berlin; that was to be the last time Britain took Turkey's part, thanks largely to the position adopted by the Grand Old Man of nineteenth-century British politics, William Ewart Gladstone. Gladstone's relentless revulsion at the Turks' behaviour in Bulgaria knew no bounds, and when he returned to power in 1880 at the head of a Liberal government he ensured that his antipathy became official policy.[14] His opinion was to inform that of subsequent British administrations; it was still reverberating (in that of David Lloyd George) well into the 1920s.

This was a considerable departure from previous practice, for Britain's relationship with the Ottoman Empire had traditionally been almost paternal. When Ottoman interests wished to adopt western ways of doing business – in the creation of a National Bank, for example – they had naturally looked to London for expertise and the required capital (though there was a good deal of French money at work in the Empire, too, and not just in the Levant, which Paris considered its own sphere of interest). Now they did not, and the British financiers who suffered in consequence blamed Gladstone's campaign of vilification; as the military correspondent of *The Times*, their newspaper of choice, had it:

> ... under the magnetic touch of Mr Gladstone's withering oratory the cause of Turkey in England crumbled to dust ... The question for us has always been whether Turkey would be on our side or on the side of our rivals and potential enemies. Mr Gladstone and the Liberal party, unwarned by any British Moltke,[15] decided the question in the latter sense. The warm and generous sympathy of our people with suffering races overbore the cold and calculating prudency of diplomacy which weighs beforehand the consequences of its acts.
>
> For Germany the Turkish alliance was an excellent *trouvaille*. Magnificently placed astride three continents, inveterately hostile to Russia, whose overwhelming numbers lay upon the soul of the German strategist like a nightmare, embittered with England on account of the atrocity campaigns and the loss of Cyprus and of Egypt, and capable of serving as a weapon against Russia, Austria or England at will, the warlike Empire of Othman appealed with irresistible force not only to the soldier-heart of a military state but to the common-sense of German statesmen and to the pocket of the German merchant.

This was polemic journalism, of course, but not too far wide of the mark for all that, and did indeed reflect a radical shift in alignments. Unified only in January 1871, after Prussia had invaded France and defeated her in a campaign which lasted barely six months, Germany's main strategic impetus was to supplant her as the dominant power in continental Europe. The *Dreikaiserbund* (the 'League of the Three Emperors'), which allied Germany with Austria-Hungary and Russia from 1872, was the mainstay of that policy. When that alliance fell apart, following German efforts (at the Congress of Berlin) to thwart Russian ambitions to rearrange the Balkans, German interests were free to court the Turks, and fell to it with a will. Trade ties were forged, and slowly Berlin took on a new importance in Constantinople, a timely and welcome alternative to perfidious, sanctimonious London and crafty, self-righteous Paris. Coincidentally, during that same period Bismarck, in whom the real power in the nation was vested still, was persuaded to relax his policy of restricting his nation's interests to Europe,[16] and this gave new strength to voices preaching expansionism.

Those in Germany, intellectuals and academics for the most part, advocating expansion into the Near East, received a boost when the old emperor died in 1888. Wilhelm II[17] ascended the throne, and with him came an end to Bismarck's restraining influence; new voices had the kaiser's ear, among them Graf Paul von Hatzfeld, a long-time ambassador to Constantinople, who was instrumental in convincing him that Germany should make haste to step into the shoes England and France had worn for so long. Others came to be heard more publicly; amongst them were those who saw the Lower Danube and the Black Sea littoral as desirable target-territories, and others who looked even further afield, to the old 'fertile crescent' encompassing Syria and Mesopotamia, now fallen on hard times through centuries of mismanagement but capable, perhaps, of being returned to its former glory by the capacity for hard work and ingenuity which Germans possessed in considerable quantity. That resulted in a new set of policies and attitudes: the *Drang nach Osten*, the 'drive to the east' in search of territory into which to expand, a radical updating of the mediaeval *Ostsiedlung*, was stretched to include not just Eastern Europe but also the Near and Middle East,[18] where Bismarck had been reluctant to tread for fear of upsetting British, French and Russian sensibilities.

It would be wrong to say that there was anything like an obsession with the Ottoman Empire in Germany, but there was certainly an undercurrent of feeling within the business community that no opportunity to penetrate the fabric of Turkish society should be missed, and that took the form of what we may call commercial colonialism, with German banks, particularly the relatively junior but very aggressive and fast-growing Deutsche Bank, taking considerable risks to secure business there, handsomely undercutting the interest rates offered by institutions in London and Paris. In 1882 Germany's arms and munitions industry received a boost when the sultan requested that a new military mission be sent from Berlin to advise on the modernisation of the Ottoman Army; under its guidance German arms manufacturers including Mauser, Loewe/DWM and Krupp received massive contracts to re-equip it. The young emperor played his part, too, he and his empress visiting Constantinople in state in 1889 (over opposition from Bismarck and to tremendous public acclaim), repeating the exercise in 1898 and proceeding as far as the Holy Land – where his triumphalist entry into Jerusalem on horseback was not quite so well received by the populace – and again in 1917.

It would be wrong, too, to suggest that British and French interests were not still well represented in Constantinople. The Turkish National Bank was (still) funded from the City of London, and all its senior executives, from its chairman down, were British. The French, too, were extremely active, and not only in Constantinople but also in Syria. However, by the time of the emperor's first visit, German commercial interests had achieved a great deal in the way of opening up new markets in the Ottoman Empire, and in the process they had expanded their horizons: now they were looking not just to individual deals but to 'infrastructure projects', to shape the country's still-primitive economy. They were relative latecomers to this sphere, but when they did take a hand, it was an impressive one, for they soon proposed a scheme which would provide the empire with a rail network linking Hay-derpaşa station, across the Bosporus from Constantinople, with Mecca, by way of Damascus and Amman, and also with Baghdad, with the promise of an extension to the Persian Gulf.[19] The railway was a keystone of German expansionist aspirations – and it is interesting to speculate upon the outcome, had it been completed prior to October 1914 – but it was not the *casus belli* between Britain and Germany that some have tried to make it out to be, for the simple reason that the British government possessed the means to thwart Berlin's efforts at every turn. The dispute between Britain and Germany – which centred on, but was not limited to, the former's fear that the latter wished to develop a major port at the head of the Persian Gulf – was settled in Britain's favour in March 1914.

By the last years of the nineteenth century the Ottoman Empire was at the very limit of its endurance, and displayed the classic signs of a regime ripe for old-style revolution. Its wafer-thin upper crust was not just accustomed to uncountable wealth and unaccountable power but was literally ignorant of any other condition, while Sultan Abdul Mejid's largely banal reforms of half a century earlier had finally succeeded in producing a thinking officer/middle class, one which had a sense of purpose, and perhaps even one of direction.

The first cracks in the façade had appeared in 1889, when a reform movement began in the rather unlikely setting of the military medical college and soon spread to other institutions in Constantinople and among the important expatriate Turkish community in Cairo, always a hotbed of dissent. Understandably, it was a painfully slow process, but clandestine groups grew stronger and better organised, and eventually (though not until 1906) associated themselves into a body calling itself the Ittihad ve Terakki Cemiyeti (Committee of Union and Progress; CUP), widely known as the Young Turks.[20] Wisely they based themselves not in Constantinople but in Salonika (Thessaloniki), away from the direct and determinedly prying gaze of the Sublime Porte.

One telling factor in the rise of the CUP was the attitude of the army. The sultanate was invulnerable while it retained its loyalty, but unfortunately for Abdul Hamid, from 1890 onwards increasing numbers of its officers, particularly those on the staff of III Army Corps in Salonika, began to ally themselves with the reformists' cause. The émigrés held a congress in Paris in 1902, and a second, five years later, at which the Young Turks, now at last with a formal structure, issued a declaration calling for the overthrow of the sultan. In the first days of July 1908, two young officers from III Army Corps, Niyazi Bey and Enver Bey, organised a small rising of their own, taking to the hills above Salonika with a small body of men. Sultan Abdul Hamid ordered them arrested, only to find their comrades unwilling to act against them; he sent a small force from Constantinople under Şemsi Pasha, who was shot and killed soon after he arrived on the scene, on 7 July. Two weeks later matters came to a head with the despatch of a telegram to the sultan announcing the army's intention to depose him unless he restored the limited constitution he had briefly put in place in 1876.

Abdul Hamid was unable to garner enough support to put down the threatened insurrection, and capitulated on 24 July; in elections which followed the CUP swept the board. However, the forces of reaction were not beaten yet. On 15 April the following year, inspired by a religious organisation known as the Mohammedan Union, which reviled the liberalisation which had followed from the transfer of power, and whipped up by students from the *madrassas*,[21] the rank and file of I Army Corps, based in Constantinople, mutinied and staged a counter-coup which returned Abdul Hamid to absolute rule. It proved a brief restoration, for III Corps, with Mahmud Şevket in command (and the twenty-seven-year-old Lt.-Col. Mustafa Kemal as his Chief of Staff), now styling itself the Liberation Army, entrained for Constantinople, arriving on 24 April 1909, and the reactionaries wilted before it. Before that day was out the sultan had been deposed, and within three more he was aboard a train to Salonika, to be replaced, but strictly as a figurehead, by Mehmet V Reşat, the next in seniority of his surviving brothers.

Mehmet V was sixty-four years old when, on 27 April 1909, he ascended the still-luxurious but by now very rickety throne. He had spent his adult life confined to the *Kafes*[22] and was totally unworldly as a result, but since he would not be expected (indeed, was absolutely forbidden) to play more than a ceremonial role in affairs of state, that was actually of little moment. Real power in the Ottoman Empire was shared between Mahmud Şevket Pasha[23] as head of the army, and the Committee of Union and Progress, which controlled parliament and nominated the sultan's ministers from the Grand Vizier down.

The Young Turks were essentially inward-looking: their principal objective was to establish a principle of united Turkishness in a loose agglomeration of individual ethnic communities where no pretence, even, of unity existed. Their foreign policy was informed by a single reality: the Empire was sickeningly vulnerable now, and not just to its *bête noire* for the past two centuries and more, Russia – fast recovering from the setback she'd received so unexpectedly when she'd blithely gone to war with Japan and been mauled, and now allied with Britain and France in the Triple Entente – but also to its own ex-vassals in the Balkans. Their only hope for survival, they believed, lay in rekindling the sort of patronage which had shielded the empire during the previous century, and they had begun trying to forge a protective alliance in the hope of staving off the would-be predators – with a complete lack of success, it must be said – when they were attacked, quite out of the blue, from a completely unexpected quarter.

Italy was another latecomer to the notion of empire, but had already shown that she had muscles to flex, grabbing the lion's share of Somalia in the 1880s and following it up with Eritrea in 1890. She had been eyeing up the Ottoman province of Tripolitania (the coastal region of modern-day Libya) for some time, and in late September 1911, she pounced. By the year's end, all the coastal settlements were in Italian hands.[24] In May 1912, the Italians went a step further, and occupied the Dodecanese islands off Turkey's coast, the (mostly ethnic Greek) inhabitants of which had conveniently proclaimed their independence from Constantinople just weeks earlier.

By the end of September the Turks had been largely defeated in Libya,[25] and were anxious to see the matter closed, for other predators had awakened, and a fresh conflict in the Balkans was brewing up. The capitulation was formalised by the Treaty of Ouchy on 15 October. Libya became Italian territory; the Dodecanese were to have been returned to Turkish rule, but in the event they were not.

The Balkan storm broke when Montenegro went to war with Turkey on 9 October 1912, and in quick succession Bulgaria, Greece and Serbia all joined in, each one keen to grab as much territory as possible for itself in the process of clearing the Turks out of Europe once and for all. That which followed was to be a most peculiar war, characterised solely by the mutual enmity in which the Christian 'allies' held the Turks; it should not be assumed for one moment that the three had anything like amity for each other.

The Montenegrins had focused their attentions in the west, the Bulgarians descended on Thrace, the Serbs invaded Macedonia, and the Greeks[26] moved north to meet them. The latter fought the Turks at Elasson, in the Vardar Valley, and beat them; their next objective was Monastir (Bitola), but they were distracted by a Bulgarian advance on Salonika, the prize Sofia coveted most, marched eastwards to head the Bulgars off, and in the process fought the Turks at Venije Vardar, Kastoria and Banitsa; by 5 November the Greeks had prevailed, and occupied Salonika, and by that time the Turks retained only Adrianople, Yannina (Ioannina) and Scutari (Shkodër, in modern-day Albania), and had been driven back to the permanent defensive positions of the Chatalja (Çatalca) Lines running between the Black Sea and the Sea of Marmara, almost within sight of Constantinople itself.

An armistice was agreed early in December, and a peace conference convened in London, but talks broke down in mid-January, and ten days later the Young Turks overthrew the government[27] and repudiated the armistice,

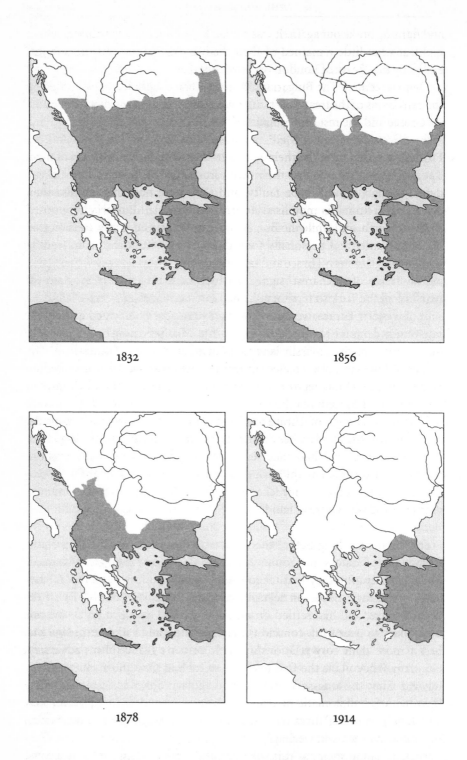

1832

1856

1878

1914

3. The Western Limits of The Ottoman Empire

and fighting broke out again. It was a mistake; within a few months the Turks had lost what little remained of their territory in Europe and the war was ended by the Treaty of London on 30 May 1913.

Or so it seemed. The Bulgarians, however, had other ideas. Dissatisfied by the provisions of the treaty, particularly the settlement of most of Macedonia on Greece and the rest on Serbia, and their failure to secure territory giving them direct access to the Mediterranean, bypassing the Bosporus and the Dardanelles, they attacked their erstwhile allies without warning on 16 June. The Bulgarian estimate that their own forces were superior and the others' deficient soon proved to be faulty, and they were first checked and then driven back. Rumania mobilised its army and invaded Bulgaria unopposed from the north, and while the Bulgars were thus engaged, Enver Pasha seized his opportunity and personally took charge of the Turkish forces, leading them through eastern Thrace and taking back Adrianople. Peace was restored by the Treaty of Bucharest, signed on 10 August 1913, which left Bulgaria bereft of all the Turkish territory she had managed to seize save for a narrow slice of western Thrace, west of the River Evros (Maritsa), which did at least satisfy her demand for direct access to the Mediterranean, even if it was limited to a stretch of marshy land without a port worthy of the name.[28] The Treaty of Bucharest also created an independent state of Albania including Scutari, which Montenegro had been forced to relinquish, and confirmed the division of Macedonia. Enver's dash to Adrianople allowed the Empire to hold on to enough of Thrace to give it control of the Gallipoli Peninsula, and thus over the Dardanelles Straits. That completed the restoration of the CUP's fortunes, and had there been time to consolidate their position, the party's strong men might have been able to revitalise their nation, despite the enormous problems they faced, but time there was not, for much more momentous events were at hand.

From the outset, long before the Italians and the Balkan Christian states emerged as predators, the Young Turks had been very much aware that the dilapidated empire they had taken over was enormously vulnerable. They had pinned their hopes on securing a protective alliance with one of the Great Powers, and had settled on an approach to Great Britain as the one most likely to bear fruit, conscious that the ruler they had overthrown had had a more than cosy relationship with Britain's likely future adversary, Germany. They made the first overture as early as November 1908, and Sir Edward Grey, the long-serving Foreign Secretary, declined the offer, telling them with few diplomatic niceties that Britain wasn't buying into any new alliances. The Young Turks tried again, after the unsuccessful counter-coup the following year, and were again rebuffed, this time in plainer terms, Grey impressing upon them, as if it were not self-evident, that if they could not maintain their position without outside assistance, then they were probably doomed. They tried once more at the end of 1911, when the war with Italy was at its height, and once more were rebuffed. During the hiatus in the Balkans War, in January 1913, Grey was approached yet again, and this time dismissed them out of hand, Britain's ambassador to the Porte, Sir Louis Mallet, noting that 'an alliance with Turkey would, in present circumstances, unite Europe against us', while Grey opined that such an arrangement would, in any event, not put Turkey on her feet, but would simply go towards allaying her fears and allow her 'to resist efforts at reform and play off one Power against the other'.

It seems clear, then, that there was a well of low esteem in which the Young Turks were generally held in London, and one quite separate from that into which their predecessor regime had fallen, but if so, whence did it spring? Inasmuch as the making of government policy can ever be attributed to a functionary, it seems to have been born of the mindset of one man, and a relatively obscure one at that: Gerald Fitzmaurice.[29]

Fitzmaurice 'had lived half a lifetime [in Turkey] and was the Embassy's official go-between and native authority. He knew everything and was feared from end to end of Turkey', according to T E Lawrence. At the time of the 1908 *coup d'état* he had been the British Ambassador's First Dragoman for nine months. This curious position – most embassies had one; the Dragoman was nominally an interpreter and facilitator, but Fitzmaurice was very much more than merely the ambassador's ears and mouth – allowed him to exercise considerable sway over Anglo-Turkish affairs at a very delicate time, and his antipathy towards the Young Turks made him ill-suited to the task. That might not have mattered if the ambassador himself had been a strong figure, but neither Fitzmaurice's first chief, Sir Nicholas O'Conor, nor his replacement, Sir Gerard Lowther – a protégé of Sir Charles Hardinge, the Permanent Under-Secretary at the Foreign Office – was that. When Lowther arrived to take up his post (after a four-month hiatus following O'Conor's sudden death, during which Fitzmaurice had had rather too free a hand), at the end of July, a week after the Young Turks had demanded that the sultan restore the constitution or face insurrection, it was to find Fitzmaurice in a position of pre-eminence.

For all his expertise, Fitzmaurice had formed an imperfect understanding of the background and aims of the Committee of Union and Progress. He believed it to be dominated by Jews and freemasons, and as a dedicated Catholic fundamentalist – he was born in Howth, near Dublin, and trained initially for the priesthood at the so-called French College established in 1860 by a Paris-based ultra-conservative Catholic order known as the Congregation of the Holy Ghost and of the Immaculate Heart of Mary – he despised both. He 'regarded [the CUP] as the devil', according to Lawrence, 'and threw the whole influence of England over to the unfashionable Sultan and his effete palace clique. Fitzm. was really rabid ... and his prejudices completely blinded his judgement. His prestige, however, was enormous and our Ambassador and the F.O. staff went down before him like nine-pins.

Thanks to him, we rebuffed every friendly advance the Young Turks made.'

In fact, while the Young Turks were willing to use freemasonry to further their cause, and would co-operate with Jewish organisations when it suited them, they were essentially secular ultra-nationalists, and had little regard for the non-Turkic ethnic groups, including Greeks, Kurds, Arabs and Armenians, who together made up a majority of the population of the Ottoman Empire. In a sense, their ideology was similar in nature to that which developed and rose to pre-eminence in Germany in the 1930s; like the German National Socialists they were elitist, and derived much of their 'authority' from the 'scientific' theories of racial superiority which gained currency in European circles in the latter part of the nineteenth century, their main intellectual influences being the fundamentally racist social psychologist Gustave Le Bon and the 'Grandfather of Sociology', Auguste Comte. Their objective was to create a strong nation without undue reference to outside influences, and there was a faction which wished to re-establish Turkish control over the territory which had been lost to her during the previous century in the southern Caucasus. That faction would gather strength when Enver Pasha emerged to lead it, and he was convinced that the route to it was by way of an alliance with Germany.[30] However, that is not to say that Enver controlled substantial aspects of Turkish policy, at home or abroad; there were others potentially as powerful as him who were at least as interested in continuing to explore avenues other than the one which led to Berlin.

By May 1910, when Ambassador Lowther submitted a lengthy report on the situation in Turkey to Hardinge at the Foreign Office, he had adopted the Fitzmaurice gospel and had gathered and contributed further 'evidence' of his own to substantiate the estimation; it was that derogatory report – he called the CUP 'the Jew Committee of Union and Progress' – which seems to have coloured and informed the British government's corporate opinion of the Young Turks, and its biased position can perhaps be said to have been the biggest single factor in the Asquith government turning down their pleas for a protective alliance in 1911 and 1913.

Still, the Turks had not yet given up hope of cementing some sort of agreement,[31] and a final, rather oblique, approach was made to the French,[32] Jemal Pasha raising the matter with a relatively lowly official, Pierre de Margerie, the Director of Commercial Affairs at the French Foreign Ministry, when he attended the annual review of the French fleet in Toulon on 14 July 1914. The suggestion was evaluated, we may imagine – though there are some who suggest that actually, it was not – at considerably higher level, for at that time the French premier, René Viviani, was himself acting as Foreign Minister, and was turned down.

That was the last such approach, for war broke over Europe just weeks later and by that time there was another, and absolutely insurmountable, obstacle to friendly relations between the Triple Alliance and Turkey, and this time it was the unaided work of Winston Churchill.

Thanks to Abdul Hamid II's paranoia,[33] when the CUP came to power Turkey had no functioning navy, a peculiar state of affairs for a nation which boasted a coastline thousands of kilometres long and which had both overseas possessions and a plethora of islands in her home waters. The Young Turks' Minister of the Marine, Jemal Pasha, soon announced an ambitious naval construction programme, but funds were short and nothing came of it. Then, in 1910, the Greeks purchased a modern armoured cruiser from the Italians; the Ottoman government promptly reconsidered, and the outcome was that most ponderous of maritime manoeuvres, a naval race, between the two rivals for control of the Aegean.[34]

In June the following year the Turks ordered two state-of-the-art 'superdreadnoughts' from British yards. One was to come from Vickers at Barrow-in-Furness, the other from Armstrong Whitworth of Elswick, Newcastle-upon-Tyne. The contracts had been won at the last minute, in the face of very stiff competition from a German consortium led by Krupp. Unusually there was no 'up-front' money, and the builders had to bear the cost of sourcing the materials themselves. This made them extremely cautious, and when the first Balkan War broke out in October 1912, and the Turks failed to meet a demand for an improved guarantee of payment, the yards suspended work on the ships. Armstrong's later broke *Reshad-i-Hamiss* up on the slip to recoup their outlay, but Vickers restarted work on the *Resad V,* and she was launched, as the *Resadiye,* on 3 August 1913.[35]

The Greeks responded rather half-heartedly in July 1912 by ordering the *Salamis,* a second-class battleship, from the AG Vulcan yard in Hamburg.[36] While *Salamis* would have been no match for *Resadiye,* her presence would undermine the Turks' efforts at regional domination, and when, a year later, they were suddenly presented with the means to forge ahead once more, they jumped at it. On 6 August 1910, the Brazilian government – engaged in a naval race of its own, this one involving Argentina and Chile – had ordered a superdreadnought from Armstrong's, and she had been laid down in September the following year at the Elswick yard on the Tyne as the *Rio de Janeiro.* By July 1913, Brazil's differences with her neighbours were in the process of resolution, and she let it be known the ship might be for sale. There was competition for her from Italy and Greece, but on 29 December, thanks to a loan raised from a French bank at a usurious rate of interest, which was applied to a downpayment, the Turks were able to announce that they had acquired the biggest battleship in the world – she wasn't, quite, by the accepted rules, though she *was* the longest at 671 feet 6 inches (204.7m) overall – delivery to coincide with that of *Resadiye* in six months' time.

This was a step too far for the already overstretched Turkish economy. The cost of the second dreadnought, on top of other commitments – including completely re-equipping the army in line with recommendations made by a

German military mission which arrived in November 1913 – was more than the Treasury could meet, and the shortfall was funded by every means possible: extra taxes on such everyday commodities as bread, wool and tobacco, and the December 1913 salaries of every public servant in the empire. And it was still not enough. Collecting boxes appeared throughout the empire, and it is said that every man, woman and child in Anatolia contributed a coin of some sort. It is fair to say that *Sultan Osman I*, as the second ship was to be known, and *Resadiye* carried more than just the aspirations of the Ottoman navy: they were emblematic of national pride.

By the end of June 1914, *Resadiye* was lying almost complete at Barrow, and *Sultan Osman I* had proceeded under tow down the Tyne to the berth where her guns would be mounted. During the last days of July the Turkish steamer *Neşid Paşa* arrived with a delivery crew; everything was set for a 2 August hand-over and immediate departure for Constantinople. On 1 August the thirteenth 12-in gun was mounted, with the last to follow the next morning, just before the ceremony. That evening a company of British infantrymen was sent to the dockyard with orders to prevent the Turkish crew from going aboard. The First Lord of the Admiralty, Winston Churchill – ironically, the only remotely Turkophilic member of the British Cabinet – had decided, unilaterally and quite illegally, to seize the ships for the Royal Navy. *Resadiye* and *Sultan Osman I* were duly taken up by the Royal Navy and renamed HMS *Erin* and HMS *Agincourt*.

Churchill's detractors were to claim that his actions in seizing the two ships pushed Turkey into the arms of the Central Powers, and that is the version which has entered the canon. Whether they were correct is moot, for by the time it knew the ships had been seized, the Turkish government – or at least, the part of it which really mattered – had already espoused the Central Powers. Churchill's supporters, on the other hand, and with rather more reason, claimed equally vociferously that he could have taken no other course of action; that to deliver two state-of-the-art battleships to a country with which the British government had no meaningful relationship and had done nothing to cultivate, and which would, in consequence, be at best neutral in the coming war, would have been unthinkable, for war with Germany was imminent, and the balance of capital ships – twenty-four to the Royal Navy, seventeen for the Kaiserliche Marine – was too close for comfort.

By then war had been declared and was about to become pan-European, and the spark which set it off was indeed 'some damned foolish thing in the Balkans', just as Bismarck had warned in 1898: the assassination of the heir to the throne of the Austro-Hungarian Empire, Archduke Franz Ferdinand, in the course of a visit to the Bosnian capital, Sarajevo, on 28 June.

The Austrians blamed the Serbs, of course. The assassin, 18-year-old Gavrillo Princip, was certainly succoured and supplied by a Serbian secret society, the Black Hand,[37] which was composed largely of disaffected army officers hostile to the civilian government in Belgrade; however, the investigation which followed found the Serbian government itself to be free of blame, which, theoretically at least, left the Austrians without a target for their wrath. Their reaction was typical: they simply ignored the facts, and proceeded as they wished.

Berchtold, the Austrian Foreign Minister, having decided that the time had come 'to settle with Serbia once and for all', formulated a series of demands which violated Serbian independence, content that the likely response would provide the *casus belli* he sought. The very carefully worded ultimatum containing them was presented on 23 July, and, when Serbia rejected them, eventually led to war, firstly between Austria-Hungary and Serbia, on 28 July. Austria-Hungary's ally Germany declared war on Serbia's ally Russia four days later, and on France, Russia's treaty-partner, on 3 August, whereupon Great Britain declared war on Germany. From that point on the status of nations allied with varying degrees of conviction to the two main groupings becomes both very complicated and rather unnecessary to define absolutely.[38]

In Constantinople the situation appeared grim; with war between the Great Powers just days away, the Ottoman Empire stood alone, with no one to take its part, facing a very real prospect of dismemberment or worse if a greedy – or needy – victor decided to focus its attention upon it. In desperation, the Young Turks turned, reluctantly, to the one remaining potential patron, and opened negotiations with Germany.

That is one view of the situation: that Turkey was driven into participating in the Great War on the side of the Central Powers more or less against her will. There are alternative explanations, of course: firstly, that she was manoeuvred into the alliance by the Young Turks; secondly, that she was dragged into it by Germany.

The truth is a combination of those scenarios. On 22 July, when Enver was authorised to try his luck at the German Embassy, he got precisely nowhere, and his advance was rejected out of hand.[39] There are two starkly different reasons put forward for Wangenheim's rejection. The first is altruistic: that he was far from convinced that an alliance with Germany, and thus assured enmity with Russia, as well as Britain and France, was in Turkey's best interests. The second is altogether more realistic: it stemmed from his view that the Ottoman army was weak, the government had no money to spend on improving it, and anyway, its leaders were incompetent; as a partner, Turkey would be a liability.

To Enver Pasha, this rebuff came as a severe and unexpected blow; he had bided his time until all the other – and to him, undesirable – avenues had been explored, and now he had been rejected by his esteemed Germany and was left with nowhere else to go. He need not have feared. Thirty-six hours later, with his customary readiness to exercise his God-given right to interfere in the workings of his government, Kaiser Wilhelm II took a personal hand.

Informed of Enver's approach to the ambassador, and the reaction to it, he ordered a volte-face, and the next day negotiations started between Wangenheim, now operating under the direct instruction of Chancellor Theobald von Bethmann Hollweg, and the Ottoman Grand Vizier, Said Halim. On 28 July a draft treaty was cabled to Berlin. Bethmann Hollweg was not overly impressed by its terms, and on 31 July ordered Wangenheim not to sign unless he was sure the Turks would bring something useful to the alliance; specifically, that they would take some action against Russia, upon whom he was poised to declare war. Wangenheim seems to have been out-manoeuvred; the Turks gave no such undertaking, nor even implied one,[40] but obtained their treaty anyway, on 2 August.

It was a concise document, as treaties of friendship go; the (second) clause which contained the meat of the agreement stated:

> In case Russia should intervene with active military measures, and should thus bring about a *casus fœderis* [a cause to go to war by reason of alliance] for Germany with relation to Austria-Hungary, this *casus fœderis* would also come into existence for Turkey.

No mention was made of any other party. Effectively it obliged Turkey to go to war with Russia (*only* with Russia, we should observe, though we should not neglect the nature of the pact which established the Triple Entente, and note that if Turkey committed an aggressive act against Russia, Russia's allies would be bound to declare war on *her* ...) if Germany did by reason of Austria-Hungary having done so (ignoring the fact that Germany had *already* declared war on Russia the previous day and that Austria-Hungary had yet to do so).

Written into the pact was a clause binding the parties to secrecy. Both assiduously observed it, but what could not be concealed was the mobilisation of the Empire's armed forces, ordered on 3 August.[41] To the Triple Entente's envoys in Constantinople, Said Halim represented the mobilisation as a natural reaction to events in Europe, and assured them that it was motivated primarily by fears of a surprise attack from Bulgaria. Bulgaria was indeed in the Turks' thoughts, but not as a potential adversary, for as early as 1 August, Wangenheim and the head of the German military mission to Turkey, Gen. Otto Liman von Sanders, had begun the task of convincing Enver of the benefits of entering into a pact *with* Bulgaria, with a view to mounting a combined assault on Russia's southern extremities (they were unsuccessful, though a treaty of mutual defence was agreed on 19 August).

In the course of these discussions a new factor was introduced: the offer of a powerful naval force, to be stationed in the Black Sea to support the joint Bulgaro-Turkish operations. Germany had just such a thing conveniently to hand: the modern Moltke-class battlecruiser SMS *Goeben* and her companion, the Magdeburg-class light cruiser *Breslau,* under the overall command of Rear-Admiral Wilhelm Souchon, in the Mediterranean since November 1912, when they had been ordered there to safeguard German interests during the Balkan War. *Goeben* was not in perfect order – though not two years in commission, the water tubes of her boilers were defective, and though most had been replaced, she could not quite attain full power as a result – but even so, with her ten 28-cm guns, capable of throwing a 300kg armour-piercing shell out to a range of almost twenty kilometres, she would be far superior to anything in Russia's Black Sea Fleet, at least until the three dreadnoughts of the Imperatritsa Mariya class, then completing at Nikolayeva, entered service.

Goeben left Pola, the Austro-Hungarian navy's base at the head of the Adriatic, on 30 July, and met up with *Breslau* at Messina. From there the two ships sailed for Cap Blanc on the coast of Tunisia. Very early on 4 August, France having now declared war on Germany, they parted company and bombarded the Algerian ports of Philippeville (Skikda) and Bône (Annaba), where troop ships were loading. As he turned away, hurrying to join up with *Breslau* once more, Souchon contemplated new instructions he had just received, ordering him to head for Constantinople.

The British Mediterranean Fleet, under the command of Vice-Adm. Sir Archibald Berkley Milne, made a bungled attempt to intercept the two ships, only the light cruiser HMS *Gloucester* actually getting within range,[42] and *Goeben* and *Breslau* arrived off the entrance to the Dardanelles at five o'clock in the afternoon on 10 August. Turkish destroyers emerged and signalled the ships to follow them. Three days later they cleared the Sea of Marmara, left the Blue Mosque, Hagia Sophia and the Topkapi Palace on their hilltop to port and dropped anchor off the Golden Horn, with the city of Constantinople rising up before them in the dusty morning sunlight.

Most accounts suggest that Germany subsequently offered *Goeben* and *Breslau* to Turkey as replacements for the seized *Resadiye* and *Sultan Osman I*. In fact, the proposal to transfer them came from the Turks, ostensibly as a way of circumventing the necessity to intern them. On 16 August, Jemal Pasha formally received them into the Turkish navy as *Yavuz Sultan Selim* and *Midilli*, whereupon their crews were enlisted into the Ottoman navy.[43] Suddenly, the two ships had real value again, for *Goeben* alone, while she could not have stood long against the Allies' capital ships in the Mediterranean, gave Turkey control of the Black Sea.

Having acquired their protector, and secured the services of modern ships and a very competent German admiral to go with them, the Young Turks did not, as the Berlin government hoped and expected, then come out openly in its support, but instead seem to have begun to ask themselves just how far a careful policy of studied prevarication might take them,[44] and they showed every sign of continuing to wish to remain neutral.

Churchill, for one, was not moved. Indeed, by the start of September he had become convinced of their enmity, and had begun to plan counters to it. On 2 September, even though there was no state of war between the two nations, he received permission from the Cabinet to sink Turkish naval vessels if they sortied into the Mediterranean in company with *Goeben* and/or *Breslau*, and later instructed the commander of the Dardanelles Squadron[45] to turn back Turkish warships if they issued by themselves. On 26 September a Turkish torpedo boat – with German matelots among its crew – did just that, and was indeed turned back. The German commander of the Turkish forts controlling the entrance to the Straits, Gen. Weber, retaliated on his own authority by closing them,[46] ordering the gaps in the mine barrages filled and the lighthouses extinguished. The government in Constantinople seemed to be willing to compromise under pressure from ambassadors, but it was soon obvious that powerful factions within it had no wish to reverse the process. Far and away the biggest loser was Russia, of course, for Turkey's obduracy both prevented her from exporting her wheat harvest and thus earning precious foreign currency, and also isolated her, for with the Baltic already under German control her only remaining accessible ports in European waters were Archangel and Murmansk in the White Sea, and they would soon be closed by ice.

And still there was no overt support from the Sublime Porte. To Wangenheim, Enver explained his government's reticence as emanating from a faction led by Said Halim and including Talaat and Jemal and most of the notables in the Cabinet, and there were indeed dissident voices even within the army, amongst them that of Mustafa Kemal Bey. In unofficial exile following a series of disagreements with his political master, serving as military attaché to the Bulgarian government in Sofia, Kemal had tried to dissuade Enver from entering into the August treaty, pointing out that the likely outcome would be disaster: if Germany won the war, Turkey would be reduced to the status of satellite;[47] if she lost, as he supposed she would, Turkey would lose everything along with her.

Enver was content to shelter behind his fellow-triumvirs and bide his time, still not quite sure that he had made the right choice, by some accounts; by others, perhaps more credible, hoping to improve his position still further. The brilliant German victory at Tannenburg, at the end of August, perhaps swayed him, but within days that was offset by the failure of the German army in France to take – or even threaten – Paris following its defeat at the Marne. Then the pendulum swung again, Hindenburg driving the Russians clean out of East Prussia ...

By the first week in October Enver had made up his mind that it was time to act, before Germany brought Russia to her knees, forced her into making a separate peace, and removed the legal basis for Turkey to go to war with her, for that would deprive her of anything in the way of spoils, particularly the Caucasian provinces he wanted so badly. On 9 October he told

Wangenheim that he had managed to bring Talaat around to his way of thinking, and that Jemal, too, showed signs of shifting. What he needed now, he told the German ambassador, was money to pay the increasingly restive troops. On 12 October the German government despatched twenty million marks (£1m; anything up to half a billion pounds in modern values, depending upon the criteria used) in gold to Constantinople, by train, and repeated the exercise five days later,[48] and Enver duly announced that Jemal had come on side. However, no sooner was the gold in a Turkish vault, on 21 October, than Talaat seemingly reneged on his promise and rejoined the neutralists. Enver shrugged that off; so long as he retained the support of Jemal, he told the Germans, that did not really matter. He did not, however, tell them precisely *why* he needed the support of his colleague at the Marine Ministry.

All became clear when Constantinople awoke on the morning of 28 October and discovered one of its landmarks missing. Tired of trying to finesse his partners in government into declaring war on the Triple Entente, Enver had decided to employ a blunt instrument to achieve the same result in reverse. He convinced Jemal to co-operate, and without informing their colleagues, to order Souchon to take *Yavuz Sultan Selim* and *Midilli* out into the Black Sea, giving him *carte blanche* to proceed as he chose. In company with Turkish destroyers he steamed up to the Crimea and, early on 29 October, with no warning, bombarded Sevastopol, Odessa and Novorossisk, setting oil storage tanks on fire, sinking a Russian gunboat and six merchant ships, and killing civilians. 'I have thrown the Turks into the powder keg and kindled war between Russia and Turkey,' the German admiral wrote to his wife.

It took time for news of the affair to reach London, but when Churchill learned of it on 31 October he immediately ordered the Royal Navy to commence hostile operations against Turkey; the following day an armed yacht believed to be laying mines was sunk off Smyrna, and on 3 November ships of the Dardanelles Squadron plus two French battleships bombarded the forts on Cape Helles at the tip of the Gallipoli Peninsula. In the excitement, no one in either London or Paris (or even Petrograd, as the Russian capital had become in August, St Petersburg being deemed to have a too-German sound to it) had actually thought to declare war on Turkey, but the oversight was rectified by the Russians later that day, and the British and French followed on 5 November.

I
MESOPOTAMIA

4. *Mesopotamia Theatre of Operations*

2

To the Garden of Eden

Mesopotamia – 'the land between the rivers' – was the name given to the lowland regions of the joint basin of the Rivers Euphrates and Tigris. Flat and featureless, the Tigris at Baghdad, some 560 kilometres from the sea, is at a mean elevation of under 40 metres. Its drainage system was destroyed, along with most of the rest of the historic infrastructure, by Hulagu Khan, grandson of Genghis and brother of Kublai, at the head of the Mongol horde in 1258CE[1] – without this, the lower reaches of the system turned into marshland with extensive areas of standing water for as much as half the year.

The climate, too, is one of extremes. The hot weather, when daytime temperatures seldom fall below 37°C and frequently reach well over 50°C, lasts from May to October; in contrast, night-time temperatures during the cold season are often below freezing. When it rains sand and dust turn into a sea of glutinous, clinging mud; when it does not, and the wind blows, those same materials are raised into a thick, opaque curtain and are carried into every crack and orifice, and even when the skies are clear, visibility is routinely impaired by mirages which transform objects in the landscape most grotesquely, and make it impossible to trust one's own eyes.

And as to the social climate in 1914, Brig.-Gen. FJ Moberly, the author of the British Official History of the Mesopotamia Campaign, wrote: 'Tribal law and customs reign ... and the Turkish administration was wont deliberately to foster tribal jealousies from sheer inability to exercise effective control ... The Arab is used to continual warfare of a guerilla type. He frequently commits acts of treachery and is generally ready to rob or blackmail a weaker neighbour.' A complete lack of sanitation meant that the region was 'a hotbed of ravaging diseases. Plague, smallpox, cholera, malaria, dysentery and typhus, if not actually endemic, are all prevalent.' Things had clearly changed somewhat since the expulsion of Adam from the Garden of Eden, which, tradition has it, was located where the Tigris and the Euphrates met, to become the Shatt al Arab at Qurna.

Mesopotamia and neighbouring Persia were of little account to the British until the latter part of the nineteenth century,[2] when the Baron Julius de Reuter, Belgian by birth but British by naturalisation, and the founder of the news agency which still bears his name, was granted, by the poverty-stricken but monumentally greedy Persian ruler Nasserudhin Shah, the right to

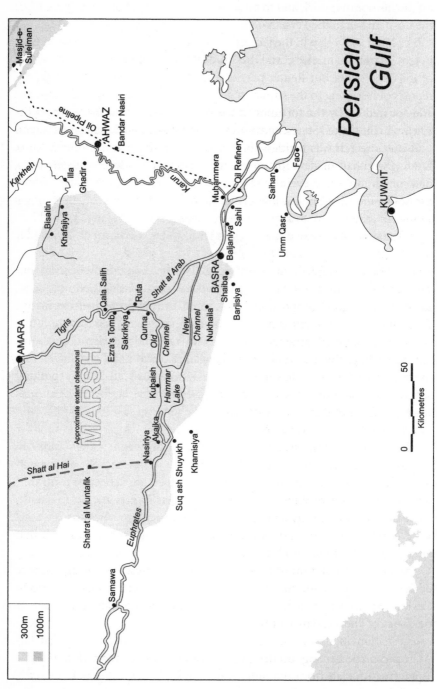

5. *Mesopotamia – Amara to the Gulf*

exploit all his realm's mineral reserves with the exception of gold, silver and precious stones; to establish a bank; to set up and operate a customs service on the European model, and to build and run a rail network extending from the Caspian Sea to the Persian Gulf.

The latter was a slap in the face to the Russians, who harboured ambitions in that quarter themselves,[3] and they forced Nasserudhin to rescind elements of the concession, but Reuter persisted in the search for oil, stimulated by reports of it seeping to the surface naturally in the south-west of the country and spurred on by the fortunes which were already being made from petroleum in the United States, and by developments around Baku in Azerbaijan.

Reuter's search was fruitless, but in 1901 another Briton, William Knox D'Arcy, who had made a fortune in the Australian goldfields, negotiated a new concession. After several false starts, on 26 May 1908, his engineer, George Reynolds, found oil in commercial quantities near Masjid-e-Suleiman, in Arabistan (Khuzestan, today), close to the head of the Persian Gulf.

By the time war broke out in August 1914, events had taken an important turn for the Anglo-Persian Oil Company, as the concessionaires now styled themselves: they were about to be bought out by the British government.[4] The decision to invest public funds in the enterprise was not a simple commercial one: a good proportion of its output would go to fuel the British fleet,[5] and that transformed APOC, and its operations in Arabistan, into a concern of national strategic importance. Of obvious significance was APOC's refinery, which stood on the Persian island of Abadan, which forms the northern shore of the lower reaches of the Shatt-al-Arab. Strictly speaking it was of no real importance to the Ottoman Empire, whose energy needs were met from coalfields near the coast not far from Constantinople,[6] and by oil from Baku, shipped across the Black Sea.

As soon as it became clear that the Ottoman army was being mobilised, in the first week of August, parties at the civil/military interface in London and in Delhi,[7] the government of India having responsibility for the Persian Gulf region, had begun working up contingency plans in case the Turks should come out openly for Germany, and it had been decided as early as the third week of September to send land forces (from India) to the region in that event,[8] to safeguard oil production.[9]

The first manifestation of heightened British interest was the appearance of the Royal Navy's gunboat HMS *Espiègle*, summoned from Colombo in Ceylon (Sri Lanka), which joined her sister-ship HMS *Odin* on station at the head of the Persian Gulf on 29 September. That caused considerable consternation in Basra, and it increased when she entered the Shatt-al-Arab and made her way up the channel to drop anchor in the Karun River separating Abadan from the independent sheikhdom of Muhammera, the ruler of which was friendly to the British. Worse was to come: soldiers, with orders to land and secure the entire area to protect British interests.

The force Sir Beauchamp Duff, Commander-in-Chief of the Army of

India, selected for the expedition was the Indian Army's 6th (Poona) Division, under the command of Lieutenant-General Sir Arthur Barrett. It was designated Indian Expeditionary Force D,[10] and its 16th Infantry Brigade[11] was ordered to move to the Gulf region immediately; its 18th Brigade,[12] together with divisional troops and HQ, was to be prepared to follow at short notice, with the 17th Brigade[13] to make its own move some weeks later.

Ottoman forces in the region were both scant and makeshift. Following the Balkan War, two understrength Army Corps – XII, which comprised the 35th and 36th Divisions, and XIII, with a single division, the 37th – had been allocated to the region as the Sixth Army. Like those of the rest of the land forces of the Ottoman Empire, their officer corps had undergone a profound purge when Enver Pasha was appointed War Minister (he dismissed or retired around 1,300 senior officers). Under the Turkish Primary Campaign Plan adopted in September, they were deactivated, their troops reassigned to other regions (the 35th and 36th Divisions to Syria, and the 37th to Armenia) and responsibility transferred to a newly created Iraq Area Command, which was to comprise a single newly constituted infantry division, the 38th, plus Frontier Guards and nine Jandarma (militarised police) battalions. On the outbreak of hostilities the 38th Division, which relied heavily on local recruitment, and was thus largely Arab in character, was still in the throes of formation, with just six (of nine) battalions in being. Discipline was poor, the men's loyalty to the Constantinople government questionable, and their equipment deficient. The British believed the Turks' strength around Basra to be over 8,000 infantry and 500 cavalry, with 58 guns and six machine guns, which was roughly double the true number.

The 16th Brigade left Bombay (Mumbai) on 16 October and reached Bahrain on 23 October. It was ordered onward (and the 18th Brigade was readied to move up to join it) after the news of the attack on Russian Black Sea ports reached London, and arrived at the mouth of the Shatt al Arab on 3 November. Three days later, companies from three of the 16th Brigade's battalions, together with a detachment of Royal Marines from HMS *Ocean*, the convoy's guardship, landed against light opposition and occupied a telegraph station and the adjacent fort at Fao.[14]

On 13 November the 18th Brigade, together with the divisional staff, arrived in the Shatt al Arab and Barrett assumed command of the expeditionary force. Delamain's brigade fought an action at Saihan on the morning of 15 November, driving the Turks back towards Sahil with little effort. Two days later Delamain, now reinforced by Fry's brigade, attacked again, and this time the British inflicted a significant defeat on the Turks, killing or wounding 1,500 or more by the their estimate, before advancing on Basra.

The sole effort the defenders had made to impede the British progress proved to have been an unsuccessful attempt at blocking the Shatt al Arab near Baljaniya by sinking shipping, including the SS *Ekbatana* of the Hamburg-America Line, across the channel, and Basra was found to be empty of Turkish forces. It was occupied without resistance, the 16th and 18th Brigades, colours flying and bands playing, making a ceremonial entry on 23 November.

The Turks had fallen back to Qurna, and two days later a naval flotilla comprising *Espiègle* and *Odin*, the small steamer *Miner*[15] and the tugboat *Mashona*, was despatched to investigate. After some misadventures, *Miner* alone reached Qurna and bombarded it. Late on 3 December the British set out to occupy the town. They landed the next morning on the left bank, some eight kilometres below the confluence; the advance thereafter was somewhat hesitant, but eventually, on 8 December the Tigris was crossed, and the following day the garrison at Qurna surrendered. Forty-two Turkish officers and around a thousand troops were taken prisoner, together with eight guns, but many more managed to escape.[16] British troops of the 17th Infantry Brigade, brought up later to garrison the town, were not overly impressed, a disgusted Tommy opining that it would have required no angel with a flaming sword to have kept *him* out of the Garden of Eden.[17]

Enver Pasha responded by ordering the 35th Infantry Division back to Iraq, and other substantial troop movements were also rumoured. He also appointed a new commander in Lower Mesopotamia, Lt.-Col. Suleyman Askeri Bey. Askeri was a former head of *Teşkilat-i-Mahsusa*, the Ottoman army's intelligence organisation – which also carried out guerrilla warfare, espionage, counter-espionage, and propaganda operations – in which capacity he had made something of a name for himself in Bulgaria, two years earlier. He took up his post on 2 January 1915.

From the first days of 1915, Turkish troops were reported gathering above Qurna. On 10 January Barrett sent two additional battalions to the town, then set about planning a response. The Turks were encamped at Sakrikiya, on the right bank, and were assembling at Ruta, on the left bank ten kilometres above the confluence; their total strength was put at three to four battalions. Barrett ordered an offensive operation involving most of the Qurna garrison, supported by *Espiègle*, *Mejidieh* and *Miner*. It met with a good measure of success, and left him regretting a decision to stop short of Ruta Creek.

Queried by Delhi, on 22 January Barrett reported himself confident in maintaining the status quo (but unable to go onto the offensive) with the troops at his disposal, but only four days later, warned that Turkish forces were advancing towards the Karun River from Amara, he revised his opinion and requested reinforcement. Reluctantly – for it depleted the forces on the North-West Frontier – a composite infantry brigade, the 12th, was assembled[18] and ordered to be ready to move from India within a week, with a second, the 33rd, to follow. In the meantime Barrett responded to the threat on the Karun by sending the steam yacht *Comet* and the tug *Shaitan*, with half a platoon from the Dorsets, quite literally to show the flag, and moved a half-battalion of Indian infantry from Qurna to Muhammerah.[19]

The Viceroy, Lord Penshurst (Charles Hardinge), arrived in Basra on 4 February for a tour of inspection and took back with him to India a somewhat over-optimistic impression of the overall position there, but also a warning from Barrett that the situation in Arabistan could worsen rapidly. His caveat was timely; within days of Hardinge's departure reports arrived in Basra of the Turks having reached a point not forty kilometres from Ahwaz on the Karun, and of further tribal groupings normally loyal to the Sheikh of Muhammera, the Bawi and the Cha'ab, rallying to them, cutting the pipeline and destroying some of the well-head gear. Worse, the Turkish garrison at Sakrikiya was reported now also to be bound for Ahwaz. Barrett ordered two battalions of infantry, two troops of cavalry and a mixed unit of mountain and field guns, under the leadership of Brig.-Gen. CT Robinson, his Commander, Royal Artillery, to reinforce the small detachment of Dorsets. In fact, even while the force was still en route, levies loyal to the Sheikh suppressed the insurgency, and by the time Robinson's troops arrived and set up camp near Ahwaz the tension seemed to have eased. That was an illusion; in fact the situation was about to deteriorate.

Unrest in Arabistan was not the only matter giving Barrett cause for concern. From the end of January there had been minor clashes with mounted Arabs near a British encampment at Shaiba, west of Basra, and on 9 February a more serious engagement near Nukhaila. On 19 February an expedition to drive them out found Turks in prepared positions there, and in far greater strength than earlier reports had suggested. Outnumbered, the British retreated to Basra. On 2 March Barrett issued orders to renew the attempt, and this time Arab horsemen got in amongst an artillery battery and only the officers' and NCOs' revolvers saved them from being overrun. The British managed to extricate themselves, but at the cost of twenty-five casualties.

Meanwhile the situation in Arabistan had deteriorated too, with reports of four thousand Turkish troops camped along the Karkeh River near Illa acting as a focus for Arab irregulars. If true, this threatened a serious attempt to outflank the British at Basra and cut their lines of communication with the outside world. Robinson, not having sufficient numbers to take on the Turks, decided to disperse irregulars gathering at Ghadir, fifteen kilometres north-west of Ahwaz, before the two bodies could link up, his attack planned for the morning of 3 March.

British forces moved out of their own encampment at 0200, and were in position an hour before sunrise; as soon as conditions allowed, two 18-pounders of the Royal Field Artillery opened up at a range of six thousand yards (5.5km), and within minutes it was clear that they had stirred up a hornet's nest. Arabs poured out of the encampment, and Robinson, in danger of being surrounded, was soon obliged to withdraw; only the discipline of the Dorsets prevented a rout, and at that British losses amounted to sixty-two dead, including six officers, and one hundred and twenty-seven wounded, and they also lost a field gun and a mountain gun.

Just days later a decision to increase the size of Force D further was made in London, over grumblings from Delhi. On 7 March Barrett was informed that the 33rd Brigade,[20] together with a howitzer battery, would leave India directly, and three days later that it would be joined by the 30th Infantry Brigade,[21] then in Egypt. Together with the 12th, which had arrived in Basra during the first week of February, they would make up the 12th Indian Division, under the command of Maj.-Gen. George Gorringe.[22] The force now constituted a corps, and on 18 March Lt.-Gen. Sir John Nixon was appointed to command it.

Before the end of the month the Turks went onto the offensive, with sporadic artillery fire aimed at Qurna. The shelling continued for ten days, but then the focus shifted abruptly to Shaiba, and cavalry patrols reported the enemy in large numbers some six kilometres west of the camp, at a scrubby area referred to as Barjisiya Woods, on 10 April. Suleyman Askeri – directing operations from his bed, having been wounded in Barrett's raid on Ruta – had achieved a degree of tactical surprise and was preparing to move on Shaiba as a precursor to attacking Basra itself. The British, not completely ignorant as to his intentions, had meanwhile brought their forces at Shaiba up to most of two brigades of infantry and one of cavalry, with a field artillery brigade and other divisional troops including engineers and pioneers. Defensive positions were established occupying a roughly semicircular front some two kilometres in length, backing on to flooded terrain which stretched all the way to Basra.

The expected offensive opened at dawn on 12 April, but effective counter-battery fire soon silenced the dozen guns employed, and the infantry assaults which followed were ineffectual. Late that afternoon Nixon, who had been in theatre just three days, instructed Melliss to reinforce the Shaiba garrison further, and he took charge of the defence the following morning. Repeated attempts by the Turks to penetrate the perimeter in both the northern and southern sectors were beaten off at little cost, and by the early afternoon he felt confident enough to send Delamain's 16th Brigade on a wide sweep outside the defensive perimeter to the west and south, to clear the front and seize abandoned Turkish guns.

The following morning, after the two remaining battalions of his 30th Brigade had come up from Basra, Melliss went onto the offensive, committing seven battalions of infantry from the 16th and 18th Brigades and most of his field artillery. The South Mound, a slight rise outside the British perimeter, was soon occupied, and from that vantage point it became clear that a line of Turkish trenches extended along the edge of the Barjisiya Woods. Melliss' decision to deploy his advancing troops in echelon – which some had questioned – now paid off, for he was able to reorient the entire force to the right without losing cohesion or contact. He was, however, not able to gain much ground, and slowly but surely the attack began to stall until, in mid-afternoon, Melliss reluctantly decided to abandon the attempt, and began to draft a plan to retire. He had actually sent runners to summon unit commanders to an orders group when news reached him of what became known as the Miracle of Shaiba: a charge by the 2nd Dorsets which drove the Turks from their trenches over a wide front.

Melliss, hardly daring to believe his good fortune, took the prudent course; once the wounded were gathered in, he ordered his men to retreat to the safety of their own defensive perimeter. When he sent out patrols the next morning, they returned with news of stands of arms and stocks of ammunition left abandoned, and 'clothing, even their cooked food, left untouched'; the Turks had fled, to Nasiriya. This so depressed Suleyman Askeri, we are told, that he shot himself.[23]

With his Basra base now secured, Nixon was able to turn his attention to the protection of the oilfield and the pipeline connecting it to the Abadan refinery, and he instructed Gorringe to take two brigades to clear Western Arabistan of enemy forces and threaten an advance on Amara. He was unable to bring the Turks to battle, and had to content himself with driving them off and destroying grain stocks and seizing animals at Khafajiya (Susangerd).

As soon as Gorringe had left Basra for Arabistan, Nixon's thoughts turned to matters of strategy. His orders were unequivocal enough:

> Your force is intended to retain complete control of the lower portion of Mesopotamia, comprising the Basra *Vilayet* and including all outlets to the sea and such portions of the neighbouring territories as may affect your operations.
>
> So far as you may find feasible without prejudicing your main operations you should endeavour to secure the safety of the oil-fields, pipeline and refineries of the Anglo-Persian Oil Company.
>
> After acquainting yourself on the spot with the present situation you will submit:
>
> (i) A plan for the effective occupation of the Basra *Vilayet*
>
> (ii) A plan for a subsequent advance on Baghdad.
>
> In all operations you will respect the neutrality of Persia ...

Nixon decided that in order to comply with the first requirement he would need to occupy Nasiriya and Amara, and he made the case for both most strongly, stressing the need to act quickly, before the Turks could regroup. Lord Crewe, the Secretary of State for India, had the last word and he prevaricated, saying that he would sanction a move against Amara only if the Indian government supported such an operation. It was 17 May before Nixon responded, sending to Delhi an appreciation which described how the majority of the Turkish regulars engaged at Shaiba had decamped from Nasiriya to Kut, and thence to Baghdad, to regroup. The lack of appropriate shallow-draught craft, promised in March, had forced him to postpone his planned advance on Nasiriya, even though the three battalions the Turks had left there were insufficient to hold it. He was, however, even then preparing an attack on Ruta to clear the way for an advance on Amara. He would not, he said, require reinforcements. On 23 May Hardinge signalled Crewe that he was prepared to sanction the advance on Amara. Crewe dithered again, then, on 27 May, in the wake of the fall of Asquith's Liberal government due to the 'shell crisis',[24] was relieved of the responsibility for the decision when he was replaced by Austen Chamberlain. It appeared that the whole process of obtaining approval would have to begin again when Chamberlain signalled to Hardinge on 28 May that he could not give further instructions 'till . . . [he knew] what force Nixon considers necessary for [Amara's] garrison during summer and how generally he proposes to distribute his troops . . .', but Hardinge had had enough of the prevarication and was prepared to exploit Chamberlain's weaknesses as a newcomer in post. He responded by stressing that permission to advance on Amara had already been given; Chamberlain conceded.

Sir Arthur Barrett, a sick man, returned to India on 10 April, to be replaced at the head of the 6th Division by Maj.-Gen. Charles Townshend, who was reckoned an astute tactician, energetic, ambitious, and resourceful, but above all lucky. Townshend arrived in Basra on 23 April, and had hardly settled in before Nixon ordered him to begin planning an advance on Amara. He went up to Qurna to see the situation on the Tigris for himself, and found something akin to desolation, for the entire region around the town – itself a sea of mud, more serious flooding kept at bay by leaking dykes – was inundated to a depth of over a metre, with only isolated features visible above the surface.

It was clear that the operation would have to be an amphibious one. The orders for the advance up the Tigris were issued on 11 May; boats were assembled, and as many as possible were provided with rudimentary armour consisting of iron plates (which proved to be an encumbrance; the shields would be dumped before the advance entered its second day), while barges and rafts were outfitted as floating gun and machine gun platforms and as water-borne ambulances and casualty clearing stations.

A dress rehearsal of a sort took place on 28 May, and went well, and as soon as darkness fell on 30 May the attacking force assembled, with the 17th Brigade, eager to quit the place after almost six months of miserable garrison duty, as the primary assault force, and the 16th Brigade and some units from the 18th in reserve. The offensive opened with an artillery bombardment at 0500; it lifted after an hour, and the infantry battalions began their leap-frog advance, taking One Tree Hill, Norfolk Hill and One Tower Hill in quick succession. Before 1130 they had reached Gun Hill – well forward of the day's objective, Barbukh Creek – whose garrison promptly surrendered. By now the heat was intense, and Townshend called a halt. British casualties were very light indeed (just eleven wounded), but significant numbers of Turks were killed and wounded and substantial numbers of prisoners taken, though many more, having abandoned their positions at the first sign of trouble, succeeded in escaping northwards.

The following morning at 0530 the artillery barrage recommenced, this time against Abu Aran, some five kilometres upstream. Suspicions that there was no one on the receiving end were confirmed by a reconnaissance flight;[25] a general advance as far as Ezra's Tomb was ordered, and Townshend's Regatta, as the riverine fleet had become known, set out again.

In the event, Townshend decided to push on past Ezra's Tomb. The armed tug *Shaitan* soon came up with a *mahaila* packed with Turkish troops who begged to be taken prisoner rather than left to the Arabs, and soon after with the half-submerged wreck of the Turkish steamer *Bulbul*. Sheltering in the lee were two lighters she had been towing, and they, too, were packed with Turkish troops. When *Shaitan* dropped anchor in the gathering darkness she had taken some two hundred prisoners, and captured three guns.

As soon as the moon had risen high enough to give useful light, Townshend ordered the advance to continue. The flotilla soon came up with a pair of Turkish river steamers, the *Marmaris*[26] and the *Mosul*, both aground and abandoned by their crews. *Marmaris* was destroyed, and *Mosul* was taken as a prize. Navigation in vessels as large as the sloops was becoming increasingly difficult, and the command party transferred to the much smaller steam-yacht *Comet* and continued upriver with *Lewis Pelly*, *Shaitan* and *Sumana*.

The flotilla passed the night at anchor near Qala Salih, some thirty kilometres short of Amara, and continued very early the next morning, meeting no resistance. At about 1400 on 3 June, rounding the last bend below the town, *Comet* was presented with the sight of a boat-bridge across the river, troops picking their way across it towards a loading steamer. As they approached, the steamer hastily cast off, and the bridge opened for her to pass through. *Shaitan* steamed full ahead, crashing through the gap, firing on the steamer as she went. Along both banks were large numbers of men. They seemed taken aback at the sudden appearance of an enemy vessel in their midst, and *Shaitan*'s commander reacted rapidly, rounding up as many as he could by dint of threats, and holding them under his guns.

Townshend and Cox went ashore later in the afternoon, and took the surrender of the Governor, Aziz Bey. By that time Turkish captives numbered many hundreds; they were marched aboard lighters which were taken out to the middle of the river and moored there under the guns of the British vessels.[27] The British contingent – just some fifty strong and top-heavy with senior officers – passed an uncomfortable night, wondering when the Arabs would realise just how few they were in number. A shoot-on-sight curfew proved effective until just before dawn, when looting broke out, but before it could take a serious hold a steamer arrived carrying a company of men from the Norfolk Regiment, who speedily restored order.

There is no good – or even rough – estimate of Turkish losses over the five days it took to secure the Tigris from Qurna to Amara; bodies were left where they lay – or floated – and nature took its course. We do know how many British troops died, however: just four, almost incredibly, with twenty-four more wounded.

Securing Amara satisfied two conflicting requirements; those elements which wished to press on up the Tigris to Baghdad – and they were gathering adherents – saw it as an essential step in the right direction, while the more conservative justified it as necessary for the protection of the pipeline. Both were right, but it still constituted what we would now call 'mission creep', and what came next was more of the same: the long-postponed advance on Nasiriya.

Nasiriya, on the Euphrates, lay at the southern end of a partially canalised waterway known as the Shatt al Hai, which ran off from the Tigris at Kut; this was believed to be a viable, navigable route (in fact it was quite useless for the purpose, but Nixon was ignorant of that), and Nixon wished to block it. The Indian General Staff disagreed, but was overruled by Duff, who wished to keep his options open.

Gorringe's 12th Division[28] was ordered to advance to Nasiriya on 23 June, just as the very hottest season of the year was beginning. It would be supported by such ships and boats of Nunn's naval force[29] as could still navigate the fast-lowering waters. Its route would take the flotilla from Qurna by way of the old channel of the river to Kubaish, across Hammar Lake to the Akaika Channel – where an irrigation dam blocking the waterway would have to be destroyed – and thence to rejoin the main course of the Euphrates north of Suq ash Shuyukh.

It set off westwards on 27 June. Negotiating the lake was far from straight-forward, seemingly promising channels petering out into shallows without warning. On entering the Akaika Channel, the flotilla was confronted by two Turkish gunboats – launches supplied by the British firm Thorneycroft, each armed with two one-pounder Maxim 'pom-poms' – above the irrigation dam, but they were soon driven off by gunfire. Sappers and pioneers laid a sixty-pound explosive charge which, after three false starts, eventually breached the dam, but the torrent of water which issued proved beyond the meagre power of the stern-wheelers. It was 30 June before the first boats had been hauled up the artificial rapids and four days more before the flotilla had traversed the twenty-kilometre-long channel and stood poised to re-enter the Euphrates proper. Reconnaissance had shown that it could expect opposition from Turkish troops with two guns in a date-palm grove on the right bank of the Euphrates opposite the entrance to the Akaika Channel, and from the two gunboats which had first made their presence felt above the irrigation dam; it had also revealed the existence of command-detonated mines both in the channel and in the river beyond.

At 0400 on 4 July landings were made on both banks of the channel. The men attempted to push out from the waterway but were soon stalled, the impasse continuing for twenty-four hours until a drive by the 76th Punjabis up the left bank, with the support of the guns of the *Shushan*, eventually subdued the resistance and they were able to cross the river in boats. It took a further eight hours for the navy to clear the mines from the channel, and it was late that evening before the transports could be brought up and the troops re-embarked.

The advance was now able to continue to within ten kilometres of Nasiriya, but was brought up short by a strong defensive position at a bend in the river. Melliss' brigade was now down to no more than about 1,500 men, and this was clearly nowhere near enough to take positions which extended on both banks, protected by earthworks and fronted by creeks. Gorringe ordered his reserve brigade, Lean's 12th, plus the 67th Punjabis from the 33rd Brigade, up from Basra, but that proved insufficient, and more men, from the 6th Division's 18th Brigade, were sent up to join him. It was 24 July, with the British ration strength now up to around 6,300 officers and men – not all of whom, by any means, were entirely fit for duty – before he felt strong enough to launch another frontal assault, with Lean's 12th Brigade leading on the left bank and Melliss' 30th on the right. The British artillery, now mounted on barges and rafts towed by shallow-draught steam launches, made a telling difference; around mid-afternoon the Turkish defence began to show signs of breaking up, and soon men could be seen fleeing northwards in increasing numbers through the marshes towards their reserve position at Sadanwiyah and then, faced with an impromptu assault from the river, all the way back to Nasiriya itself. Nunn's naval flotilla gave chase, *Shushan* demolishing one of the Thorneycroft launches with her 12-pounder gun despite it having broken away from much of its mounting, whereupon the other surrendered.

Turkish losses in the final phase of the assault were considerable: at least 500 killed and over a thousand prisoners taken, along with seventeen guns, five machine guns and 1,500 rifles; those who succeeded in escaping – and there were many, once again – headed north up the Shatt al Hai. Nunn, aboard the *Shushan*, reconnoitred the Euphrates as far as Samawa, a hundred and twenty kilometres above Nasiriya; he was welcomed there, but Nixon declined to garrison the town.

Even while the battle for Nasiriya was still being played out, the Turks had begun pushing troops down the Tigris from Kut. Their primary objective was to create a diversion, but they wished also to regain some influence over indigenous tribes who had drifted towards the British after the fall of Amara.

They reoccupied Kumait, but gave it up when Nasiriya fell, and Nixon ordered Brig.-Gen. Delamain – in command, absent Townshend, who had fallen victim to fever and had returned temporarily to India – to push troops on up the river, but only as far as Ali Gharbi, some 130 kilometres above Amara. The nearest Turks were reported to be at Shaikh Sa'ad, fifty kilometres further upstream.

In fact, Nixon had been developing justifications for an advance on Kut in signals to India since mid-June, and he summed up his arguments in a memorandum which reached Lord Hardinge's desk on 6 July, concluding by noting that, since the Basra *vilayet* extended almost to Kut itself, he could not be said fully to have discharged his duty of controlling the whole of it, as his original orders specified, until Kut was in British hands ... The question of advancing to Baghdad – which was occupying many minds now, not just in Mesopotamia but also in Delhi and London – he did not address, save for remarking that should the Turks advance on Nasiriya by way of the Euphrates, a British presence at Kut would 'expose Baghdad to a counter-stroke from there'.

On 27 July Hardinge lent his weight to Nixon's argument, and suggested that an additional infantry brigade, the 28th, then at Aden, should be transferred to Force D, just for the time it would take to capture Kut, whereupon it would be returned to its rightful owners in Cairo. Kitchener would have none of that, but Chamberlain was enthusiastic in general, and accepted the proposition with a single – and to him routine – caveat: that sufficient force must be kept available to safeguard the oil supply. Chamberlain's approval reached Hardinge on 20 August, and two days later the Viceroy passed it on to Nixon; he in turn drafted an executive order to Townshend, who would command the operation.

Charles Townshend had returned to Basra only the previous day, and was still settling back into his routine when he received his orders. 'Your mission,' they began, 'is the destruction and dispersal of the enemy ... who are prepared to dispute your advance; and the occupation of Kut al Amara, thereby consolidating our control of the Basra *vilayet*.' He says in *My Campaign in Mesopotamia* (published in 1920) that he told Nixon that if he routed and stampeded the Turks in the coming battle, he 'might follow them into Baghdad'. Apparently General Nixon raised no objection and told General Townshend in such an event to telegraph, 'as he might be able to enter Baghdad with him', as if it were of no more moment than arranging to meet for drinks at the United Services Club in Pall Mall.

The Turkish defences before Kut were located about twelve kilometres east of the town, as the crow flies, and extended out on both sides of the river, with the strongest and most heavily populated positions on the left bank; it was there that Townshend had decided to strike, having first feinted to the right in the hope of convincing Nurettin Bey that that was where the blow would fall. By 11 September the entire 6th Division was assembled at Ali

Gharbi, together with Melliss' 30th Brigade, which would take on the responsibility of policing the lines of communication.

The 6th Division's infantry arrived at Sannaiyat, the assembly point for
the assault, on 16 September, and the transports were unloaded and returned
to Amara to bring up guns and howitzers. Over the previous two days 30
Squadron, Royal Flying Corps, as the aviation section had by now become,
had flown aerial reconnaissance missions, which allowed a rough map of the
area to be compiled. The defensive line on the left bank was some twelve
kilometres long and very robustly built, with brick-lined gun emplacements
linked by communications trenches wide enough to allow guns to be moved
from one to another, and covered by barbed-wire entanglements and land
mines. It spanned two areas of marsh and was divided into three sections:
the most northerly, which rested on three redoubts, lay between the southern
limit of the Ataba Marsh and the Suwada Marsh and extended for almost five
kilometres; the centre section covered the 1,500m gap between the Suwada
and a horseshoe-shaped marsh which had once formed part of the river's
course, and the third stretched the same distance to the left bank of the river,
where it terminated in gun emplacements which commanded a boom of
barges and cables. The Turks had failed to extend the northern section to
keep it anchored on the wetlands as they receded, and Townshend had
identified that as the serious weakness it was. The defensive line on the
right bank commenced with gun positions overlooking the river boom and
stretched over five kilometres in a south-easterly direction to Es Sinn, following the line of one of a pair of ancient canals running between banks
six metres high in places, the 'Sinn Banks', which provided an excellent
observation platform and clear fields of fire.

On 25 September the riverine transports returned, bringing Nixon himself,
to observe and 'in case questions of general policy had to be settled as a result
of the battle'. By that evening Townshend's forces included three and a half
brigades of infantry – he had incorporated two battalions of the 30th Brigade
into his plans, the Turks' positions having proved more extensive than he
had thought – three and a half squadrons from the 7th Lancers and the 16th
Cavalry combined into a single command, with eighteen field guns, six heavy
guns and four howitzers, and the 48th Pioneers.

The Turkish positions on the left bank were believed to be occupied by six
battalions from the 35th Division, and those on the right by six battalions of
the 38th; four more battalions formed a reserve, located some eight kilometres
upstream on the left bank, near a point where a bridge of boats crossed the
river, and there were two regiments of cavalry and one of camelry present,
plus large numbers of mounted Arab irregulars of questionable reliability.

Townshend had decided to send Delamain, with the majority of his forces,[30]
to advance up the right bank with a flank guard on the far side of the river,
and Fry to disembark on the left bank at a village named Nukhailat, where a
pontoon-and-boat bridge was to be thrown across the river out of sight of

the Turkish positions. That bridge was in place by 1600 on 26 September. Early on 27 September, Fry's infantry battalions advanced slowly on an extended front, preceded by an artillery bombardment; by midday they were within two kilometres of the enemy's positions, and there they dug in. During the course of the morning half of Delamain's 17th Brigade moved up to within rifle-shot of the enemy's southernmost positions at Es Sinn and put on a demonstration there before retiring to the camp established downstream. His cavalry and field artillery crossed the river by way of the pontoon bridge during the afternoon, and the infantry fell back from its encampment, leaving its tents standing and fires burning, and followed after nightfall.

By midnight Delamain's force had joined with its flank guard at the southeastern extremity of the Suwada Marsh. Solid ground separated the Ataba Marsh from the larger Suwaikiya, to the east, and this would be the route which the cavalry would take to fall on the enemy's rear echelons from the north, while a substantial part of Delamain's infantry – under the command of Brig.-Gen. A Hoghton, who had taken over the 17th from Dobie – wheeled to the left, to pass south of the Ataba Marsh and attack the northernmost point of the defensive line from its flank. Delamain himself led a much smaller force of infantry (the Dorsets and half the 117th Maharattas, the remainder having been detached to guard the rear echelons) and would make a frontal assault between the Ataba and the Suwada Marshes.

The deployment began before first light, the cavalry preceding Hoghton's infantry north from the jumping-off point,[31] but within an hour the latter had lost its direction, and instead of passing south of the Ataba Marsh found itself between it and the Suwaikiya. Delamain ordered Hoghton to stop and retrace his steps, but Hoghton replied that he was by then so far north that to continue was a more practical course. In the event the detour did not affect the outcome of the battle, though it did oblige Delamain to attack the positions between the Ataba and the Suwada Marshes without direct support on his right. The northern and central redoubts proved to be lightly held, however, and were in his hands by soon after 0830, by which time Hoghton's column had dealt with another strongpoint, previously unsuspected, which lay further north.

A necessary delay while artillery was brought up gave the Turks time to regroup in and around the southern redoubt; Delamain's men could get no closer than eight hundred metres to it, and it was well past noon before the artillery and the brigade's machine gun battery had worn the defenders down to the point where an assault was even feasible. The unexpected tenacity of the Turks in the southern redoubt had a knock-on effect on Fry's attack on the enemy positions south of the Suwada Marsh. His 18th Brigade had left its trenches at 0600 with orders to advance slowly on the enemy positions some two kilometres to their front, under cover of artillery, the final assault to be made in concert with that of Delamain. By 0830 the men had covered roughly a quarter of the distance when Townshend, belatedly having received news of the delay Hoghton had imposed on Delamain, ordered Fry not to commit his men to the assault until he could see clear signs that Delamain was engaged. The 18th duly went to ground, and remained in place for the next four hours and more.

In the meantime Hoghton had been fighting his way southwards. Around noon Delamain had called him to a conference to reassess the situation, and had told him to keep on pushing towards the river in order to join up with him, but he made slow progress, and was still three kilometres short of the river when he came under accurate artillery fire and was forced to retreat.

Meanwhile Delamain had advanced to a point within (rather extreme) striking distance of his objective when enemy reinforcements appeared in considerable strength on his right flank, and he had no alternative but to turn and face them. This was the remainder of Nurettin's reserve, which had belatedly been sent back across the river; they were relatively fresh – much more so, anyway, than the exhausted soldiers facing them, who had been marching and fighting almost non-stop for over twelve hours – and should have made a considerable impact upon them, but did not. Instead, their four field-guns were quickly silenced by counter-battery fire as Delamain's small force advanced on them with bayonets fixed, driving them into the gathering darkness and occupying the positions they had held. Meanwhile, Fry had launched his attack on the original positions north of the horseshoe marsh; deprived of the support he had expected from Delamain, and with night now upon him, his men were unable to get closer than five hundred metres to the enemy's line, and there they dug in.

The next morning at first light, reconnaissance flights revealed that the Turks had abandoned their positions on both sides of the river, and the naval flotilla easily breached the boom and pressed on as far as Kut, arriving off the town at 1000. Reports told of the Turks having made off upriver aboard steamers, and the naval flotilla gave chase but came under fire from mountain guns and dropped back down to Kut, which Townshend had in the meantime sent the 16th Brigade to occupy. Fry's 18th Brigade was later sent upriver aboard steamers as far as Aziziya, while Hoghton's 17th began the grisly task of policing the battlefield, assembling the dead for burial and evacuating the wounded.

The battle for Kut cost the Turks around four thousand men, of whom 1,153 were made prisoner, together with fourteen guns and a large quantity of stores. British losses were just ninety-four killed, but over 1,200 were hospitalised.[32] This large number of wounded put a severe strain on the medical teams operating with the army, and even more on the scant resources allocated to evacuating the injured men to Basra and the single hospital ship available there.[33]

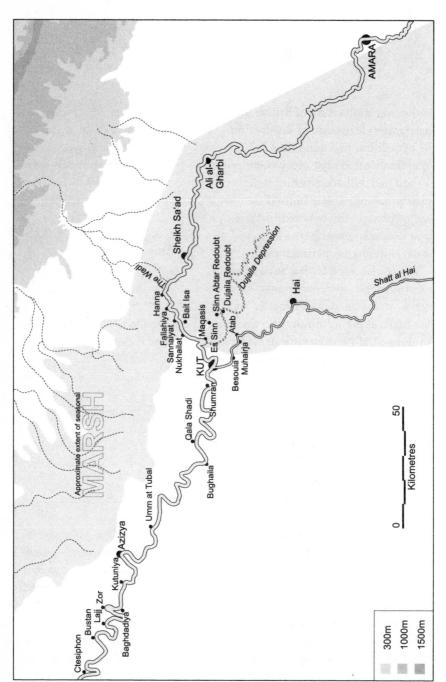

6. Mesopotamia – Ctesiphon to Amara

3

Besieged at Kut

As the first anniversary of British intervention in Mesopotamia approached, there was a clear sense of satisfaction in both London and Delhi at the way the expedition had gone thus far. That was entirely justifiable; with minor exceptions, on almost every occasion the expeditionary force had met the Turks it had inflicted crushing defeats on them, and Sir John Nixon had every reason to congratulate himself on having discharged his duty with just the sort of panache he believed himself to exemplify. Now, he felt sure, it was time to take the next step – to secure the region's capital, Baghdad – and he began agitating for permission to do so.

Slowly the appetite for such a venture grew. Those who resisted were uncomfortable, in general, only with projections of the manpower requirements, and ultimately the matter was put to a study group drawn from the War Staffs at the Admiralty and the War Office. It came down in favour of a (prolonged, if necessary) destructive raid on the city, rather than its occupation. The outcome was a compromise, the War Council deciding to permit an advance to Baghdad so long as provision was made for the troops to be withdrawn rapidly if they came under threat from a superior force, for example from Turkish troops released from the Gallipoli front. And to do so, despite earlier reluctance, Force D *would* be further reinforced, it was decided, albeit temporarily, by the 'Emergency Force', two hastily assembled composite brigades from India, the 34th and 35th,[1] with the prospect of the two Indian infantry divisions sent to France in 1914 as part of Force A – the 3rd and the 7th – which had suffered badly during the previous winter, being withdrawn to join it if and as required.

As early as 4 October Townshend submitted an outline plan for the advance. With the water level in the river too low to permit of reliable navigation, he proposed to assemble his forces at Aziziya and march to confront the Turks at Ctesiphon – thirty kilometres short of the capital, where the enemy had been preparing a defensive position for some months – by way of the left bank of the Tigris. Nixon gave his broad approval.

By his own (later) account Townshend was already having second thoughts about advancing on Baghdad, his intelligence reports now indicating that Nurettin's forces probably outnumbered his own. Nixon too was warned of the imminent arrival of Turkish reinforcements, and of the veteran German Field Marshal Colmar Freiherr von der Goltz, to command the Turkish Sixth Army. In fact, the 51st and 52nd Infantry Divisions (previously known as the

1st and 5th Expeditionary Forces (see Chapter 7) were on their way from
Armenia; they would not begin to arrive at Baghdad until mid-November,
but that would mean they would be in good time to confront a British
advance, and Nurettin had also raised a new formation locally, the 45th
Division, around a core of around 4,000 Jandarma, and that was now combat-
ready.

On 24 October Nixon received the despatch sanctioning the advance on
Baghdad, but it was four days before he passed orders on to Townshend,
telling him he wished the advance to begin by 14 November. By that date the
build-up at Aziziya, begun on 5 October with the landing of the 18th Brigade,
was complete. Townshend's force now numbered approximately 13,500
including engineers and rear-echelon personnel, with thirty-five guns, and
was supported by a new gunboat, HMS *Firefly*,[2] together with *Comet*, *Shaitan*
and *Sumana*, and horse-barges mounting 4.7-in naval guns and 5-in howitzers, towed by *Shushan* and *Mahsoudi*. The expedition's advanced guard
had by now occupied Kutuniya and reconnaissance parties had gone on to
Baghdadiya and Zor. On 15 November Townshend moved more men up to
Kutuniya, and by 19 November his entire main force had reached Zor.

Ctesiphon, near the modern town of Al Madain, was little more than a mark
on the map in 1915, but in earlier times it had been a significant place; indeed,
it is said to have been the biggest city in the world in the sixth century, when,
as the seat of the Sassanids, it extended to perhaps thirty square kilometres.
There were (and are still) remnants of its glorious past to be seen, most
significantly the Arch of Khosrow – a vaulted structure over thirty metres
high which, with a length of decorated wall, was all that was left of the
imperial palace – and, some three kilometres south-east of there, a section
of what was known as the High Wall, a right-angle of ridges or mounds some
hundreds of metres in length, rising to a height of fifteen metres in places
and eighty metres thick at the base.

This latter structure marked the approximate centre of the Turkish defensive line on the left bank. That line, anchored on the river, ran for some ten
kilometres roughly north-eastwards, and consisted of fifteen redoubts spaced
at four- to six-hundred-metre intervals, linked by deep trenches, the whole
covered by wire entanglements and twenty guns and manned by the 9,500
men of the Turkish 38th (to the south) and 45th Divisions. The two redoubts
which formed the northern end of the defensive line, which were constructed
on low mounds, were particularly strong. On the far side of the river, where
the 3,500-strong 35th Division was stationed with ten field and three heavy
guns, the defences ran in a dog-leg for a kilometre and a half.[3] There was a
secondary line of defence on the left bank, in front of Qusaiba, some three
kilometres back from the primary line – much less well fortified, though it
used a low ridge to good advantage – behind which the 51st Infantry Division
was being held in reserve. The terrain on the left bank was generally flat, with

some scrub, which had been cleared in front of the defensive positions. The river, which ran parallel to the Turks' left-bank front at a distance of about a kilometre for almost four kilometres, was obstructed near the downstream end of that reach by an impenetrable barrier of sunken vessels and tethered mines, covered by the heavy guns on the right bank.

Townshend divided his force into four columns: A, B, C and a 'Flying Column', keeping no divisional reserve. Column A – the 'Principal Mass' – was under the command of Walter Delamain (freshly promoted to major-general) and comprised five and a half battalions of infantry (3,650 men), a field battery and the howitzer battery. Column B – the 'Turning Force' – was under Hamilton and comprised four battalions (2,700 men) and a field battery. Column C, under Hoghton – the 'Minimum Force' – comprised three and a half battalions and the pioneers (2,400 men), a squadron of cavalry, a field battery and some heavy guns. The Flying Column, under Melliss, comprised one battalion of infantry, the bulk of the cavalry, their guns, the Maxim battery, a motor machine gun section mounted on two lorries, and two armoured cars.

Townshend intended to feint both frontally and in a hooking movement round to the right, and then deliver the decisive attack on what he termed the Vital Point, the redoubts forming the northern end of the defensive line. Hoghton's Column C, on the left, was to advance to within range of the enemy; when it was engaged, Hamilton's Column B and Melliss' Flying Column, pre-positioned well to the north, were to advance, the cavalry rounding the secondary defensive line. Then, with what could be construed as a pincer movement under way, Delamain's Column A was to assault the Vital Point (henceforth, VP), with all guns switching to give converging fire upon it.

The preparatory barrage began at around 0700. By about 0715, Hoghton's men had advanced through the mist to within long rifle shot of the Turkish position, but failed to draw fire from them. At 0745 Townshend ordered Hamilton forward, Melliss conforming. Column B had covered perhaps two kilometres when Nurettin sent two battalions from the local reserve out into open ground to meet it, while more men were sent to reinforce VP, which had by now come under effective artillery fire.

Delamain, believing the moment had arrived though the preconditions had not yet been met, asked for and received permission to launch his own assault. His men advanced at walking pace to within a thousand metres of the Turkish line and then continued in hundred-metre rushes, the brigaded machine guns wide on the right and a half-battalion of riflemen on the left adding their weight to the artillery which had given supporting fire throughout. They were brought up some forty metres short of their objective by wire entanglements but made their way through them, taking heavy casualties in the process, and by 1000 were in the Turkish positions. The entire operation had been carried out in textbook fashion but at very considerable cost.

The next step should have been to roll up the main Turkish line from its left, but instead more than half of Delamain's men, under the command of Col. Climo, set off westwards intent on capturing eight guns left unmanned, and Townshend was forced to order Hoghton to move his men across the face of the defence to the right and assault the positions between VP and Water Redoubt. He did so, with the assistance of Delamain's last reserves, driving the defenders back into Ctesiphon village, but only at considerable cost, and when the Turks counterattacked – employing two battalions of the 51st Division and a battalion which had earlier crossed over from the right bank – could not hold them and was forced to retire. Climo's ill-judged advance was also halted in its tracks and driven back, and then it was the turn of Hamilton's column, which had been stalled since that morning. Meliss' column could do nothing to assist.

Townshend, his own account tells us, realised at that moment that a shortage of manpower was going to cost him the battle of Ctesiphon. His only course was to reorganise, and with darkness falling he issued instructions to all units to break contact with the enemy and fall back. It was his intention to resume the offensive the following morning, but even as the exhausted men were retiring, and a tally of the dead and wounded was being made, he realised that that was beyond their capabilities.

When the British disengaged and retired, the Turks, no less exhausted, did likewise, some to the shelter of Ctesiphon village, some to the secondary defensive line. They were not, however, demoralised – or in any event, their commander Nurettin Bey was not – and by around 2100 he had made a positive appraisal of the situation. He reorganised his army into two corps, XIII, made up of the 35th and 38th Divisions, and XVIII, comprising the 45th and the 51st, and ordered most of those units of the 35th still on the right bank to cross over, leaving behind the three heavy guns, which had done such valuable work against the gunboats during the day, with a battalion of infantry to protect them. By daybreak on 23 November he was ready to re-engage if conditions looked favourable.

Aerial reconnaissance, flown at first light, reported the Turks in retreat to the Diyala River, fifteen kilometres away to the north-west. This was exactly what Townshend wished to hear, of course, but it was entirely false, and far from the defenders having retired, the last two battalions of the 51st Division had now come up from Baghdad to join them. Turkish intelligence was more accurate, reporting that the British had evacuated the area north and north-east of VP. This convinced Nurettin to renew his counterattack, and with the benefit of hindsight, it is only surprising that he left it until mid-afternoon to put the plan into effect. Had he moved earlier, he might have enjoyed more success, but as it was he ran out of daylight before he had gained his objectives, and though he continued to feed more men into the attack until after midnight he was unable to break through.

Early the next morning Nixon concluded there was nothing more he could do at Ctesiphon, and retired to Lajj with his staff, while Townshend began to weigh the (military) merit of a withdrawal against the 'political' benefits of remaining in place. At 1130 he swayed towards the former, and telegraphed his decision to Nixon, who concurred, but by 1220 he had changed his mind, and announced that he was going to stay put, and order all the shipping up to Bustan, under naval escort. Nixon reminded him that even the gunboats alone had been unable to get as far as Bustan; Townshend was not to be deterred, however, saying 'it will have a much better political effect not to retire, both [sic] here, India, and at home', and eventually Nixon acquiesced.

Around 1600, Delamain led a mixed force of infantry back out to the north of VP, to screen his right wing's withdrawal to High Wall. This convinced Nurettin that the British were preparing a counterattack of their own. Uncertain of his enemy's strength, he decided that after all, discretion might just be the better part of valour, and gave orders to his men to withdraw behind the Diyala River. The withdrawal started at 0400 on 25 November, the Iraq Cavalry Brigade remaining behind to screen it. At first light it reported that the British had in fact now evacuated VP, and were not behaving at all aggressively; it seems to have taken several hours for the Turkish commander to convince himself that he had acted precipitately, but by about midday his men had reoccupied the Ctesiphon positions.

When Townshend learned that the Turks were returning, he changed his mind once more, explaining to Nixon – who had already decamped to Aziziya – that 'it is always fatal ... if political reasons are allowed to interfere with military reasons'. The British withdrawal began after dark that evening. The back-markers reached Lajj by 0100, and there the men rested. They set out for Aziziya, thirty-five kilometres away, on the morning of 27 November, the stragglers stumbling in twenty-four hours later, and that same day the Turks reached Lajj and the first German aircraft to arrive in Mesopotamia made its maiden reconnaissance flight,[4] reporting the situation to Nurettin and Halil Bey, who had by now come up from Baghdad.

Townshend spent two days at Aziziya (losing *Shaitan*, which ran aground and opened a seam trying to get off) before setting off once more for Umm at Tubal. There the Turks caught up with him, and he was obliged to fight a brief rearguard action in which the principal casualties were *Firefly*, which took a direct hit on her boiler, and *Comet*, which tried to take her in tow but went aground and was soon set ablaze. Nunn ordered both vessels stripped of essential machinery and equipment[5] and abandoned. Townshend now resolved not to allow a halt before Qala Shadi, forty-two kilometres from Umm at Tubal, and more than halfway to Kut. The head of the column reached the destination at around 2100, but the tail did not arrive until the early hours. The exhausted men slept where they halted, fitfully, for the cold was intense, and at daybreak resumed their march. The head of the column reached Shumran (Shamam), some way short of Kut, where food had been laid out, as dusk fell on 2 December. By midnight the last stragglers were in, and the next morning the men – just under 10,400 in all, of all arms[6] – entered the town they would come to know and hate over the months which followed. 'I mean to defend Kut like I did Chitral,' Townshend promised Nixon, referring to his management of the siege of that town on the North-West Frontier which had made his name, a decade earlier.

By the time Townshend arrived at Shumran, Nixon had left Kut for Basra, leaving Sir Percy Cox, together with Brig.-Gen. JC Rimington, who had been in command of the garrison there, to await Townshend. Rimington, who had no confidence in Kut as a defensive position, rode out to meet him and tried to persuade him to continue on to Es Sinn. Townshend rejected that, saying his men were too exhausted to march further than Kut, and that in any event, it would be impossible to move the vast quantities of stores and ammunition stockpiled at Kut before the Turks arrived. Two days later, with the Turks just twenty-four hours away, he was telling Nixon 'I am making Kut into as strong an entrenched camp as possible in the given time ... I have shut myself up here reckoning with certainty on being relieved by large forces arriving from Basra.'

'Every effort is being made to relieve you as soon as possible,' Nixon replied, 'and it is hoped to do so within two months.'

'"Within two months" is serious,' Townshend replied. 'I hope we can be relieved by a month. My rations for British troops are only one month,[7] and fifty-five days Indian troops. I shall have to reduce scale of rations.[8] Am commandeering all bazaar supplies.'[9]

By 6 December, the day he sent away the bulk of his cavalry and much of his transport – supernumeraries including Cox and Rimington had already departed – he had changed his mind about holding at Kut, and proposed withdrawing after all, and not just to Es Sinn, but to Ali Gharbi. Nixon told him that Younghusband's 28th Brigade and the Cavalry Brigade would be at Ali Gharbi and Shaikh Sa'ad 'within next week'. Townshend took his word for it, and was placated. That same day, however, the General Staff in India decided that the situation was graver than they had been led to believe. 'Taking into consideration the various advantages and disadvantages of holding on to Kut, [they] arrived at the conclusion that the risk ... out-weighed the advantages; and they considered that Kut ought to be evacuated if it were still possible to do so,' they reported to Duff.

Duff chose not to pass that message on verbatim to Nixon, but simply hinted that Townshend should quit Kut. It was too late in any event. The following day Townshend reported that 'his position had been turned'. Kut was invested, and evacuation of the town was no longer an option.

In broad strategic terms Kut had a singular importance: it gave the British command of the Lower Tigris and thus barred the way to Basra at a point sufficiently far away from the latter to permit the invaders adequate room to manoeuvre. By holding there, Townshend was buying time for Nixon – who, despite the setback, had not abandoned his ambition to take Baghdad – to strengthen the British position in Mesopotamia. However, as the location for a major defensive position, Kut had nothing to recommend it save that it was situated at the apex of a sharp bend in an unfordable river. When Townshend arrived actual defensive installations were almost non-existent, consisting of a mud-walled 'fort' – really little more than an enclosure – three kilometres due north and downstream of the town, on the bank of the river where deep water close in had made it possible to construct a dock of sorts, linked by a simple barbed-wire fence to a point on the riverbank two kilometres upstream of the town. Along that line there were four inadequate isolated blockhouses. The line was far too far out from the town, and thus longer than it needed to be, but its position had been determined by that of the fort, which could not be given up because it was adjacent to the dock and held much of the supplies and stores, which could not be moved because all the able-bodied men were needed to dig trenches to create a proper defensive line.[10] There was a further anomaly in the way the position had been laid out: across the river from Kut, near the mouth of the Shatt al Hai, lay Yakasub, which the British called Woolpress Village; there much of the force's locally obtained grain was stored, and this, too, had to be defended, at least until it could be removed, which meant something like two kilometres more of trenches to be dug and manned. Adjacent to the fort a boat-bridge had been hastily thrown across the river, but as soon as the cavalry and transports had crossed, it was dismantled and reassembled two kilometres upstream. It was usable again by the evening of 8 December, but it soon became obvious that it would be more of a danger than an advantage to retain it, and the following night it was destroyed by explosive charges.

Nixon enquired as to the status of his reinforcements (and made an attempt to secure more, saying that there might be as many as eight enemy divisions opposing him within as little as two months). He was told that the despatch of British troops to Salonika, in reply to Bulgaria entering the war, and the requirements of evacuating Gallipoli had caused the supply of shipping to dry up, and that the 3rd Division was still encamped at Marseilles, but that the greater part of both it and the 7th Division was likely to be at Basra by the end of the year. In an aside to Hardinge – in his weekly letter – Chamberlain added that Nixon could not count on getting further reinforcements from Europe, and raised again another possibility which had been under consideration: sending untried British soldiers – who, in any event, would not be combat-ready for some months – to India to act as garrison troops and thus free seasoned men for service in Mesopotamia. Hardinge had been holding out against that, but on 18 December he accepted the proposal; if Kitchener sent him twelve battalions, he would agree to the 34th and 35th Brigades remaining in Mesopotamia after the 3rd and 7th Divisions arrived, and would add a third, the 36th Brigade,[11] to make a fifth division for service there.

The first serious attempt to break into Kut had come on 9 December, and was aimed at the defences in the north-west sector. Two more attempts were repulsed before the Turks adopted a calmer approach; von der Goltz had by this time arrived and taken personal command, and had ordered more conventional siege tactics employed, including the digging of saps to threaten the fort. By 17 December the sap-heads had got so close to the fort's walls that it was decided to mount a raid to disrupt the work and to check that mining was not in progress. The men sortied just before dawn, under the cover of an artillery and machine gun barrage; forty Turks were killed in hand-to-hand fighting and eleven prisoners taken, at the cost of just one man lightly injured, and no mines were found. The Turks resumed work almost immediately the raiders had returned to their own positions.

The next attempt to take Kut by storm came on 24 December, apparently on Nurettin's orders while von der Goltz was occupied elsewhere. First, artillery started pounding the fort. 'Bit by bit the walls crumbled,' says Cecil Aspinall-Oglander in the Official History, 'leaving large gaps ... and by 11am little remained of the north-eastern wall or the northeastern bastion, and large sections of the northern wall were in ruins.' When the bombardment ceased, and Turkish infantrymen emerged from their trenches, they were driven off by furious rifle and machine gun fire and a hail of bombs. The second phase of the attack began at 2000, and was more determined. More than once it appeared that the assault must succeed, but each time the Turks were driven back; around midnight they withdrew but only to regroup, for at 0230 on Christmas Day they came on again, and were repulsed once more. That was the last time the Turks attempted to take Kut by assault; from now on they would follow von der Goltz's orders, and wait the British out while preventing the relieving force from reaching the besieged garrison.

The first elements of the relieving force – the headquarters and the 51st Sikhs of Maj.-Gen. Sir George Younghusband's 28th Brigade,[12] part of the 7th Division which had not gone further than Egypt – arrived in Mesopotamia on 2 December, and were rushed aboard steamers and sent on their way upriver the same day. Battalions of the 34th and 35th Brigades were similarly treated as they began to arrive later in the month (though some of the former went to Nasiriya instead).

Lt.-Gen. Sir Fenton Aylmer[13] reached Basra from India a few days after Younghusband, and was despatched upriver to Amara to take command. By the time he arrived on 12 December the force totalled nine battalions of infantry, thirteen squadrons of cavalry, sixteen guns and some support troops, spread between there and Ali Gharbi, with another battalion and a half of infantry and a cavalry regiment at Basra under orders to join him. His task was complicated by a lack of trained and experienced staff officers and changes in the command structure[14] did not help the situation, but perhaps more serious was the composite nature of the force, none of its elements having fought or trained together. The acute shortage of transport created huge problems too, those responsible for moving troops and supplies vying with each other for the available craft.[15]

By the first week of January the force concentrated at Ali Gharbi amounted to a full division. On the morning of 4 January it set out for Shaikh Sa'ad, and by the evening of the fifth had reached a point some five kilometres downstream from where Turkish forces, thought to number around 2,500, with two guns, were entrenched a similar distance below Shaikh Sa'ad. They were, in fact, at least four times more numerous than Younghusband estimated, with many more guns.

Younghusband's plan was to engage the Turkish forces on the left bank the following morning, pinning them in place with the reinforced 35th Brigade while the 28th drove the enemy force on the right bank back into the loop of the river where the village lay. He had no doubt that the Turks would retire as soon as they appreciated his superior strength. During the evening of 5 January he received a signal from Aylmer telling him to hold where he was, doing no more than was necessary to force the enemy to show his hand, until he himself arrived with the rest of the corps the following evening. Younghusband decided that the plan he had already worked up fulfilled Aylmer's new instruction, and went ahead with it.

The offensive was launched into thick mist at 0900 on 6 January. It soon became clear that the Turkish positions on both banks stretched further than Younghusband had thought, and by the end of the day little real progress had been made. When Aylmer came up the following morning, Younghusband told him he still proposed to follow his original plan, and fight a holding action on the left bank while pushing through on the right and then bringing enfilading fire to bear across the river, but Aylmer switched the main emphasis of the attack to the left bank, where Younghusband himself was to take charge and was to be reinforced by the 19th and newly arrived 21st Brigades.

Younghusband decided to keep the 21st in reserve, and, without adequate reconnaissance – in fairness, he had little time in which to make one – ordered the 35th to remain in place and the 'light' 19th Brigade to 'sweep round and roll up the enemy's left flank'. It soon became clear that there were strong Turkish positions out to the right, and when the 19th ran into them it stalled. Younghusband sent up two battalions of the 21st to assist, but they made no difference to the situation; he sent the other two, to no better effect, and by nightfall on the second day of the battle had still made no real progress, and casualties had been heavy, at an average of around 350 men per battalion.

On the right bank, Kemball's 28th Brigade had fared better, and by 1600 the advancing line had got to within about three hundred metres of the

Turkish trenches; the men rushed them and, fatally, the defence faltered. The first and second lines were occupied, but as night fell it proved impossible to advance further over ground cut by drainage ditches.

Aylmer, heartened, urged Kemball on the next morning, and told Younghusband to hold back until he had broken through. When Kemball began to advance again, however, he met stiff resistance once more, and reconnaissance suggested that at least five thousand Turkish troops still lay between him and Shaikh Sa'ad. He made little progress, and throughout the day Younghusband could but sit on his hands.

The ninth of January dawned in mist and continuing rain. Flying was out of the question, but cavalry patrols reported that the positions on the right bank were empty, and Kemball at once ordered them occupied. By 1100 the left bank positions, too, had emptied, and by 1130 Aylmer was able to order a general advance towards Shaikh Sa'ad along both banks. By 1400 the town was occupied, and cavalry patrols had been pushed out into the countryside beyond, while gunboats pressed on upstream.

The Battle of Shaikh Sa'ad was a pyrrhic victory for the British; they had driven the enemy back before them, admittedly, but only for a short distance, and at the cost of 30 per cent of their strength. As at Ctesiphon, the arrangements made to care for the wounded were wholly inadequate, and once again badly wounded men suffered, lying exposed in the open for days, their wounds dressed on the battlefield, if they were lucky, but most untreated, most without even a blanket, awaiting evacuation. Many died before help came.

On the morning of 11 January it was possible to fly a reconnaissance mission; the results it brought back were not comforting to Aylmer, for they revealed that the Turks were present in significant numbers – 11,000, his staff estimated – behind a watercourse known simply as the Wadi. Aylmer decided to send the bulk of his forces in a flanking movement around to the right, leaving two infantry brigades to hold the Turks in place. Believing himself outnumbered, all he could fall back on was the hope that the Turks would suddenly revert to the incompetence they had shown a year earlier, and there was precious little chance of that, for the men he was fighting now were cast in a very different mould, and had a new and very ambitious commander, Halil Bey having replaced Nurettin Bey in consequence of his having retired at Shaikh Sa'ad.

Aylmer allocated the 19th, 21st and 35th Brigades, temporarily constituted as the 7th Division,[16] to the flanking force and the 28th, with the 9th in reserve, to the frontal position, the Cavalry Brigade to screen the flanking movement. The 7th Division was to move out under cover of darkness to an assembly point some twelve kilometres north-north-west of Shaikh Sa'ad, then, at 0630, move west to cross the Wadi at a point about three kilometres 'upstream' from the Turkish positions, advance to take the Turks in enfilade, and roll up their line. The night was clear, the moon giving some light. The 7th Division moved off at 2130, and by 0230 was at its assembly point; the 28th Brigade crossed the river at dusk, and occupied the positions the 19th and 21st had just vacated, ready to move forward when the planned artillery barrage drove the Turks from advance positions centred on a walled enclosure known as Chittab Fort, east of the Wadi.

Dawn on 13 January brought the customary mist, but it lifted rapidly, and the 7th Division's deployment was delayed by only an hour; the bombardment of the Chittab positions had the desired effect, and by noon they were in the hands of the 28th, the 9th – substantially under strength still – following up into the overnight positions. The crossing points over the Wadi proved to be poorly chosen, the banks high and steep; this was not too much of an obstacle to the men, who were all across by 1000, but the guns had to be manhandled, and that took until 1300. The infantry columns marched their prescribed distance westwards and then wheeled towards the river, coming into action progressively, beginning with Brig.-Gen. Norie's 21st Brigade. It soon became clear that Aylmer's plan had failed to take account of a defensive line extemporised on that of a drainage ditch which ran at right-angles to the Wadi and brought the advance up short.

With the entire 21st Brigade committed, Younghusband sent the 19th Brigade to extend the line still further westwards, in the hope that its right wing would reach the riverbank and establish a cordon around the defenders. When it failed he sent in the 35th Brigade and the Cavalry Brigade to prolong the line still further. By 1840 – some two hours after he had committed the last of his reserves – Younghusband was convinced that he was within striking distance of the river and a significant victory; he was never close to either.

Aylmer, having been informed that the Turks had been shifting men out of the line along the Wadi and sending them to oppose Younghusband, ordered Kemball forward at around 1600, his advance covered by a barrage from the heavy guns and the gunboats on the river. Five hundred metres out from the Turkish line they emerged from scrub; just as they had done at Ctesiphon, the defenders had burned it off and driven in stakes to act as ranging markers. As they crossed the open ground, controlled by interlocking beaten zones of machine gun fire, more and more of the attackers went down. In all the brigade took 648 casualties including three of its four battalion commanders, leaving Kemball no alternative but to withdraw.

Once again, the Turks pulled back in the darkness, this time to prepared positions across the mouth of the Hanna defile. Once again they had bought time, evaded a decisive defeat, and cost the British dearly in the process.

Aylmer contemplated attacking the Hanna positions directly, but the troops were in no fit condition to do so, and instead 14 January was taken up with reorganisation, policing the battlefield and evacuating the wounded, a task which was not completed that day. The weather, unsettled for more than a week, took a distinct turn for the worse during the afternoon, with heavy rain and high winds. Despite prodigious efforts, all attempts to establish a new boat-bridge had failed, much material being lost in the process in what the Official History calls the 'boisterous yellow flood' the Tigris had now become.

On the night of 16 January Aylmer telegraphed Nixon telling him that he proposed to send the 3rd Division[17] across as soon as the bridge was completed, in order to outflank the Hanna defile, and also suggested that it might be time for Townshend to use such boats as he had to ferry his able-bodied men to the right bank and march them around the Es Sinn position, west of which he would meet them and bring them in. 'The opportunity is now favourable and may cease directly enemy sends troops down right bank, which may be very soon ... If Townshend thinks this possible, I shall issue orders for him to do so,' he concluded.

Nixon would have absolutely none of that. What we might now call 'his legacy' was under threat, and even seriously ill as he was (he was awaiting the arrival of his replacement, Lt.-Gen. Sir Percy Lake, lately Duff's Chief of Staff, who arrived in Basra to take over on 19 January), Townshend breaking out in order to withdraw had no place in his plans. 'The course you now propose,' he said melodramatically, 'would be disastrous from every point of view – to Townshend's force, to the whole of the forces in Mesopotamia and to the Empire, and I cannot sanction it.'

And still it rained, the storms repeatedly breaking up the still incomplete boat-bridge across the Tigris. Aylmer had so far been able to ferry across the river only a few guns – one section of 'S' Battery RHA's 13-pounders and four 10-pounder mountain guns – and that was nowhere near sufficient to produce the sort of enfilade bombardment necessary to support a frontal attack on a position as deep as the Turks had established. A superhuman effort on 19 January saw a battery of the 19th Brigade RFA's 18-pounders and two 4.5-in howitzers ferried across the rapidly rising river that night, while the 93rd Infantry, one of four battalions now established on the right bank, moved up to a point opposite the Hanna positions. The 7th Division's troops – no more than 3,500 all told, and Younghusband had broken up the 21st Brigade and distributed its personnel between the other two – moved up, too, to within five hundred metres of the enemy positions.

They consisted of a continuous double line of trenches from the river-bank to the limits of the marsh, the entire frontage covered by barbed-wire entanglements. The systematic nature of the defences proved very effective during the artillery bombardment which followed, according to Turkish prisoners; when shells fell on the forward line, they were able to retreat quickly to the secondary, and vice versa. That and the quality of the positions themselves – they were two metres deep and well furnished with shelter recesses and dugouts – meant that casualties were light. When the 35th

Brigade advanced it was unable to get closer to the Turkish trenches than a hundred metres.

Aylmer had no idea the attempt to take the front-line positions had failed, for he had, as usual, no communication with the 7th Division's assault units. Believing that the attack was going as planned, he ordered the 28th Brigade, the general reserve, to begin to advance to support the 19th. Eventually, reports of the impasse reached him; he called for a further intense ten-minute artillery bombardment on the Turkish front line, and instructed Younghusband to push his men forward once more in its wake. It commenced at 1250, but had little effect, and by then heavy rain was falling once more, accompanied by a biting wind; soon the mud was glutinous again. Those who did try to take advantage of the renewed artillery bombardment found themselves stuck in it and the remains of the wire, horribly exposed to enemy small-arms fire.

The Turks made no attempt to harass the men as they withdrew, or to follow up. However, as reports of the numbers and condition of the men came in, it became clear that any thought of renewing the offensive the following morning was out of the question. The First Battle of Hanna was over; once again the British had suffered well over two thousand casualties, and some of their combat units had been reduced to no more than a shadow of their established strength. And perhaps more significantly, this time they had failed to drive the enemy from his ground.

Townshend had become convinced – by reason of the troop movements observed around Kut – that Aylmer was facing less than 4,500 Turks at Hanna, and the news of his defeat there came as a great shock to him. When Aylmer suggested again – on 21 January, the obstacle to this course of action having been removed with the departure of Nixon – that he should 'sortie on a large scale', this time to 'endeavour to defeat what is in front of you, returning on to Kut again', he replied that he was prepared to make an attempt to break out, but only definitively, not to return. When Aylmer learned of that he cabled Lake to support Townshend's suggestion, saying that he did not believe he could relieve Townshend 'even after reinforcements now on their way arrive', which was a most serious admission and perhaps sowed in Lake's mind the seeds of doubt as to Aylmer's reliability.

Townshend may have been actively considering breaking out of Kut, but he was hedging his bets. On 21 January – when his effective strength was '6450 bayonets' – he signalled that, down to fourteen days' rations, he was finally ready to acknowledge the scale of the problem by cutting them in half and by making serious attempts to locate food caches[18] in private hands. Three days later he sent a much improved estimate of his endurance: having found large stocks of wheat and *atta* (coarsely ground flour) in the homes of the civilian population and in the Lynch Bros. warehouse, together with almost twenty tons of *ghee* (clarified butter); having reappraised the amount of barley in his granaries (and discovering that he still had over nine hundred tons) and being about to give the order to begin eating the division's three thousand horses and mules (which, he said, 'he had not brought forward till then ... [thus] rendering the division inefficient for service in the field, until Aylmer had told me he did not think he could relieve me'), he found that he could now hold out for at least a further fifty-six days ...

It is difficult to imagine how Aylmer took this news. He had been pushed into fighting three battles in quick succession in the belief that Townshend's division was a few weeks away from starvation, and now he was told it could hold out for months to come.

By the beginning of February, Aylmer had a total of around 12,000 infantry, 1,300 cavalry and forty-six guns, distributed roughly two-to-one across the board in favour of the left bank; another 12,000 men were on their way from Basra to join him (and a recent decision to augment the force by a further three brigades from India[19] – negotiated between Hardinge and Chamberlain, on the same 'raw troops for seasoned men' basis as previously – would give him perhaps eight thousand more, though it would inevitably put extra pressure on the already overloaded logistical system). By British estimates the Turks had around 12,000 men and thirty guns at Hanna, 1,000 infantry and a brigade of regular cavalry at Es Sinn, and perhaps 4,000 men around Kut.

On paper at least, then, Aylmer would soon have numerical superiority, and he had developed a new plan to exploit it: he would advance up the right bank of the Tigris with as big a force as his transport could support – as many as twelve thousand, if the supply column carried only one day's rations in addition to those the men carried themselves, the remaining men being left to hold the line before Hanna – and attack the Turkish positions at Es Sinn; if he were successful he would then cross the Shatt al Hai, recross the river at Shumran, confront the encircling forces and relieve Kut. He would commence as soon as the new drafts arrived from Basra – they were promised for around 15 February – and his engineers had established a boat-bridge.

Lake approved the plan, but then heard from Duff that the Chief of the Imperial General Staff (CIGS), Sir William Robertson, had offered Maj.-Gen. Stanley Maude's 13th Infantry Division – which had fought at Gallipoli, had sustained a 50 per cent casualty rate and was still rebuilding – together with a mountain artillery brigade, both of them then in Egypt, as extra reinforcements for Mesopotamia, in addition to the three new brigades from India, if Lake could 'receive and maintain' them. He could, he replied, and on 7 February Duff asked that they be sent as soon as possible. That put a different complexion on the matter in the minds of men in both London and Delhi. Townshend having said he could hold out at least until the end of March, there was reduced urgency; if the operation Aylmer was now planning was held back until further reinforcements had arrived, and if significant numbers of additional Turkish troops had not arrived in the meantime, it might be possible to secure an overwhelming advantage.

Lake felt delaying was too great a risk, but Duff was intransigent. He had consulted the CIGS, he said, and their joint recommendation was that Aylmer should await all the reinforcements he could get, provided that Townshend's situation did not change materially. Lake had no grounds to object, for where previously the CIGS's opinion would have been no more than advice, it would very soon have authority, for on 3 February it had been proposed, and on the tenth it was accepted, that the conduct of the war in Mesopotamia, as in all other theatres, should become the responsibility of the CIGS under the authority of the Secretary of State for War, though in this case his orders would pass through the Commander-in-Chief of the Army of India, who continued to administer the forces in the theatre.[20]

Aylmer maintained a steady bombardment of the Turkish positions without much effect. A new boat-bridge across the Tigris, about a kilometre upstream of the mouth of the Wadi, was completed eventually, on 11 February, and that simplified troop movement considerably, but Aylmer's efforts at reconnaissance were hampered by his having lost air supremacy, his aircraft now having to contend with more capable German machines which began a bombing campaign. News from elsewhere was heartening, however, especially that coming from the Caucasus – of Erzurum having fallen to the Russians on 17 February[21] – and from south-western Persia, where Baratov, pressing on, with the objective of drawing Turkish forces away from Kut, had reached Kermanshah (see chapter 7). Elsewhere in Persia, however, things had taken a distinct turn for the worse, the elusive Wilhelm Wassmuss having proved sufficiently troublesome that an additional battalion of troops had been sent from Basra, and active consideration was being given to raising a separate force to operate in the region.[22]

Thanks to the delay the weather imposed on him, Aylmer had had plenty of time to refine his plan, and had decided to attempt to break through on the right bank, focusing on what was known as the Dujaila Redoubt, in a bend of the depression of the same name, an ancient course of the river. The operation, which was to be carried out by two-thirds of the 24,000 infantry he now had available, would involve a ten-mile night approach march on a compass bearing. The attacking force was to be divided into three groups, the first, with three brigades, under Kemball, the second consisting of the Cavalry Brigade, led by Brig.-Gen. RC Stephen, and the third three brigades under the command of Maj.-Gen. Keary. A fourth group, consisting of the 35th Infantry Brigade, would remain in reserve. The force was to assemble at a point known as the Pools of Siloam, north of the Umm al Baram Marsh, as soon as darkness fell on 7 March, and be in position by 0615, with Kemball's brigades south of the Dujaila Redoubt and one of Keary's brigades east of there, another east of the Sinn Abtar Redoubt, three kilometres north, and the third in local reserve. Townshend had undertaken to sortie from Kut with two brigades of his fittest men when he saw Aylmer's turning attack coming round to the south of the Dujaila Redoubt. Kemball, though he did not receive a copy of the plan in advance, had had some warning of what would be required of him, and didn't like the timetable. He appealed to Gorringe – now serving as Aylmer's chief of staff; he was incapacitated by a wound he had received some weeks before, and took no active part in the operation – who overruled him.

Ideal conditions prevailed on the night of 7 March, but even so there was considerable confusion and delay at the rendezvous point and the head of the leading column did not move off until 2220. It reached the 'point of divergence', where the column would split into its component groups, at about 0230, but instead of continuing after a brief halt, Kemball elected to try to separate his transport echelon from the rest of the column; as a result it was 0400 before it moved off again, and 0510 before it crossed into the Dujaila depression, with five kilometres still to cover to its attack position, and barely a half-hour of darkness remaining. To Kemball, it seemed that any chance of achieving surprise had already been lost.[23]

In the event, even though it was 0700 before the last units of his column reached the depression, a direct assault on the redoubt would almost certainly have succeeded; a reconnaissance by one of Aylmer's intelligence officers, disguised as an Arab, revealed it to be very lightly held. Unfortunately, no one took the initiative to give the order.

At 0730 Kemball signalled to Aylmer that his assault forces – the 9th, 28th and 36th Brigades, that last under the semi-independent command of Brig.-Gen. G Christian, were moving into position, but they did so desperately slowly, and by the time they began to advance Halil Bey had deduced the main thrust of Aylmer's plan, and had begun to move his reserves up. Kemball's men then came under attack themselves, and thus were never able to give their full attention to assaulting the redoubt, with predictable results.

By midday, Kemball's control over his sector of the battlefield had slipped, his brigade commanders contributing by passing him situation reports which contained egregious inaccuracies and were often wildly optimistic, but it was around 1530 before Aylmer realised that the attack was going nowhere. He was still ignorant as to the reason why, however, and instructed Keary to send the 8th and 37th Brigades – which, up until this point, had taken no part in the fighting – to assault the Dujaila Redoubt from the east (leaving the reserve 7th Brigade still uncommitted), ordering Kemball to co-operate with a renewed assault by the 28th Brigade.

It was no more successful than the earlier attempts. By now, significant numbers of fresh Turkish troops had reached the redoubt and the trenches fronting it. The 8th Brigade's advance went well enough until the men crossed into the depression, but then they came under very heavy fire. Despite sustaining heavy casualties, the leading troops – the Manchesters, in the main, with some men of the Indian formations – actually succeeded in breaking into the redoubt itself, but were driven back. The 28th and 37th Brigades did not even reach the outlying trench line.

As darkness fell Aylmer accepted that he had failed, and instructed the entire force to withdraw to the artillery park. Kemball had great difficulty in complying, thanks to the sheer number of casualties his battalions had sustained – the majority of the British total of almost 3,500. It was far into the night before all of them had been recovered, and not until 0500 that the columns set off back the way they had come.

Predictably (and reasonably) enough, Lake blamed Aylmer for the defeat at Dujaila, and immediately requested his recall; on 11 March he was replaced as the commander of the Tigris Corps by Lake's chief of staff, Sir George Gorringe, promoted temporarily to the rank of lieutenant-general. The force he inherited comprised the 3rd Division, on the right bank of the Tigris, the 7th Division in front of the Hanna position on the left, with remaining corps troops – which included a cavalry brigade and two of infantry – mainly in the Wadi camp. The advance guard of the 13th Division,[24] which had reached Basra on 27 February, had begun to arrive at Shaikh Sa'ad. On the river were five gunboats plus *Flycatcher*, the Thorneycroft launch captured from the Turks at Nasariya and put into British service as an armed despatch boat; *Gadfly* and *Dragonfly* remained below the boat-bridge, while *Mayfly* and *Sandfly*, together with the first of a new, much bigger, class, HMS *Mantis*,[25] operated upstream of it. Some improvements had been made to the transport situation, but still only three hundred tons of supplies were being delivered to the front as a daily average, when the requirement was for almost five hundred.

At Kut, the men's morale plummeted when it became clear that the attempt to turn the Es Sinn line had failed. On 9 March Townshend informed Lake that he was killing off eleven hundred more animals, and hoped now to be able to sustain the garrison until 7 April, later adding another week to that estimate. The following day Halil Bey wrote to him suggesting he surrender. Townshend telegraphed Gorringe and Lake, asking their opinion as to whether he should enter into negotiations. Lake told him he believed it would be pointless. He also asked the Senior Naval Officer if it was practicable to fit a tug with armour plating and use it to run barges upriver at night. Capt. Nunn told him it was not.

Gorringe began planning a new campaign to relieve Kut as soon as he took command of the Tigris Corps, but without any overt sense of urgency – it was twenty-four days before he actually put it into effect – which begs some questions, given that he must have been acutely aware that with the river rising daily, speed was of the essence. He estimated the Turkish strength at around 9,000 on the left bank, the majority of them at Hanna, and 12,000 on the right bank. He had even fewer options open to him than Aylmer had had a month earlier, and he chose the straightforward approach: a massive blow against the Hanna position, using all the forces at his command, to be followed immediately by a push through the reserve positions at Fallahiya and Sannaiyat, and then by an advance on the Es Sinn positions across the river, the operation to be wound up within six or seven days of its projected start on 1 April. With the 13th Division he would be able to field around 30,000 infantry and over a hundred and twenty guns, but the viability of his plans ultimately rested on the right bank being passable, and that was by no means assured, as a survey undertaken on 18 March demonstrated.

On 30 March Gorringe decided that his attack would have to be postponed, thanks to the delay in bringing up extra heavy artillery. In the event, torrential rain on the night of 31 March would have made it impossible anyway, and it was late on 4 April before conditions improved enough to allow it to proceed. At 0455 the next morning the troops of the 13th Division, which had taken over from the 7th three days earlier, and had been specially trained for the operation, took the positions at Hanna easily, the Turks, fearing inundation, having withdrawn most of their force during the night. They were found to stretch back two and a half kilometres towards Fallahiya. Later that morning, troops of the 8th Brigade took the Abu Ramman positions on the right bank; the Turks threatened to counter-attack there in the afternoon, but were driven off. At 1915 the artillery began to bombard Fallahiya; as soon as the barrage lifted, at 1930, the 13th Division's 38th and 39th Brigades moved forward over a front nine hundred metres wide. They met stubborn resistance but comfortably outnumbered the defenders, and by 2130 the position was in British hands. In just one day the 13th Infantry Division had advanced six kilometres on the left bank, through two extensive defensive positions, and the 3rd had made significant gains on the right.

Gorringe pressed straight on, the task of taking the now unmasked Sannaiyat positions allocated to the 19th and 28th Brigades, the attack to be made before dawn the following morning, 6 April. The operation began to go awry even in the assembly phase, as the troops moving up in the darkness became mixed up with the men of the 13th Division moving back with their wounded, and was further delayed during the passage through the Fallahiya position, with its complex system of cross-trenches. When the order came for the men to deploy into line, they were still well short of the Turkish trenches, and day was breaking; though at the limit of effective machine gun fire, they were horribly exposed. The moment had passed, but instead of retiring they were ordered on, advancing over open ground and taking many casualties as they neared the Turkish positions until, at a distance of about seven hundred metres, funnelled into a front no more than nine hundred metres wide, they were brought to a halt; some managed to retire, but the rest dug in as best they could. On the following two days Gorringe ordered pre-dawn attacks, with no more success. By 8 April even Gorringe, as stoical as anyone in the face of mounting casualties, had despaired of a straightforward assault succeeding.

The alternative, though, was to sap forward and gain more ground with short nocturnal advances, and this would bring him hard up against the deadline beyond which Townshend could not hold out. When he presented his conclusions to Lake, who had finally come up from Basra, the commander-in-chief instructed him to change tack, and try a further offensive on the right bank. It was perhaps a sign of his pessimism that the following day he informed Townshend that it was extremely unlikely that he would be relieved by 15 April. Townshend responded by cutting the ration further, extending the deadline to 21 April. The Official History reports that 'Lake then made arrangements for the Air Force to drop a certain amount of food supplies into Kut.'[26] The total amount delivered in this way seldom reached the ton a day which would have been necessary to have satisfied demand, but perhaps it gave Townshend heart, for four days later he reported that he could now hold out, *in extremis*, until 29 April, though at that the men would have been surviving on a meat-only diet (from the slaughtered animals) for the best part of a week.

It was early afternoon on 11 April before Gorringe was able to issue an operations order for the right-bank offensive. The following morning the 3rd Division would take the enemy's outpost line south of Bait Isa; after a reorganisation of forces, the 13th Division's 38th and 39th Brigades would then cross the river by means of a pontoon bridge newly completed at Fallahiya and occupy those positions, while the 3rd pushed on to take a trench line east of the Sinn Abtar Redoubt by the morning of 13 April. Preparations were well in hand that evening when the weather took a decided turn for the worse, over an inch of rain falling onto ground which could absorb no more, and before 2200 Gorringe had ordered a twenty-four-hour postponement.

By now the floods on the right bank were almost contiguous, leaving just a strip of dry ground which became known as the Narrows, where engineers were frantically building up a causeway. Beyond it lay a feature named Twin Pimples, which Gorringe believed to be the key to the Bait Isa position, and he ordered Keary to take it. Keary decided the 7th Brigade, supported by the 9th, would push towards the objective on the night of 13 April and either dig in close to it, prior to an assault early on 15 April, if it met significant opposition, or rush the position, if it did not. Simultaneously, the 8th Brigade would push westwards and southwards with the 37th Brigade in support, enlarging the salient in the process.

Reconnaissance reported the Twin Pimples position too strongly held to make the risk of an impromptu assault worthwhile, and Keary reverted to the more orthodox plan, the 7th and 9th Brigades to advance across four hundred metres of open, scrubby ground on an eight-hundred-metre front, the operation to commence at 0445. At 0300 a violent thunderstorm broke, cutting the already poor visibility to almost nothing. The troops moving up to their starting positions were delayed by it, and some lost their way, leaving uncomfortable gaps in the line. However, despite the confusion, and heavy artillery fire from Bait Isa, the enemy positions were taken soon after daybreak on 16 April, and were held against a counterattack later in the morning. A subsequent advance by the 8th and 37th Brigades was less successful initially, but reached its objective eventually, the men wading through knee-deep water and thick mud to reach the Turkish outpost line. That night Keary pushed his artillery further forward, preparatory to an assault on the Bait Isa positions themselves.

The Turkish trench line in front of Bait Isa ran south from the riverbank for about six hundred metres, following the west bank of the most easterly of seven canals, before curving back to the west where the waterway turned south-east. It then ran on towards the Sinn Banks, crossing a second line running from halfway between Bait Isa and the Chahela Mounds to the Sinn Abtar Redoubt in the process. Behind it lay six parallel irrigation canals, the first of which uniquely turned south-east to pass the Twin Pimples position at a distance of around six hundred metres from the canal which lay outside the defences. It was between these first two canals that the assault would come, the objective being to break through the Turkish line to gain control of all the waterways lying behind it, to prevent them from being used to flood the approaches to the Es Sinn positions, and as a precursor to assaulting the Chahela trenches and taking the mounds beyond, from which point the crossing the Turks were using at Maqasis would be vulnerable to artillery fire.

The barrage began just before dawn on 17 April, and ten minutes later the infantry formations stepped out to cover the kilometre to their objective. By 0800 the attacking force had swept right through the Turkish lines, taking hundreds of prisoners and eight machine guns, and had taken up positions to the west of the canal system, facing the trenches running south from Chahela at a distance of a thousand to fifteen hundred metres. The surprise achieved gave the men that crucial few minutes in which to consolidate; by the time the Turks rallied and counterattacked their chance had gone, and they were driven off by machine gun and artillery fire.

Once again there was to be no further offensive action that day; instead, Gorringe ordered Maj.-Gen. Maude to move his 13th Division's brigades into the positions those of the 3rd Division had occupied, to allow Keary to reorganise his men prior to a fresh advance in the direction of Sinn Abtar the following morning, and in preparation for that he told Keary to send his fourth brigade, the 37th, together with a field artillery battery, to the vicinity of a position known as the Triangle, 1,200 metres south of Twin Pimples, to form the left flank. Maude was also ordered to prepare a plan for a supporting offensive against fifteen hundred metres of the Chahela trench line to his front, and selected the 38th and 39th Brigades, keeping the 40th, which had now also crossed the river, in reserve.

Halil Bey, however, was not content to let matters rest, and as the light was fading, and they began making preparations to hand over to men of the 13th Division, the 7th and 9th Brigades came under attack. The first to come into action was a small group of Gurkhas, who had captured two Turkish guns a few hundred metres in front of the main line, who were soon engulfed. The main bodies of the 1/1st and 1/9th Gurkhas behind put up a spirited fight but soon began to run short of ammunition, and by 1900 the Turks had broken through.

A kilometre to the rear, at Twin Pimples, where the 9th Brigade had its headquarters, its reserve battalion – the 1st Highland Light Infantry – rallied. Supported by the machine guns of the 8th Brigade to the south, and field artillery firing over open sights, they channelled the Turkish advance northwards. Carey's 27th Punjabis were the leftmost unit of the 7th Brigade; at the first sign that something was amiss, he ordered his support company to dig in on the left flank, facing south. This was sound thinking, but time was not on the Punjabis' side; they had barely begun digging when they were engulfed by a mass of fleeing Gurkhas and men of the 93rd Infantry. Two more companies of the 27th and the 128th Pioneers to their right, who were moving to support them, were also drawn in, and the tide of retreating soldiery soon swamped the 7th Brigade's headquarters, the men in full flight now and heading for the river. The next battalion in the line was the Connaught Rangers; they held, and when Lt.- Col. WA Hamilton, their commanding officer, managed to pull his machine gun company across from his right flank to his left, they held the Turks, too.

Keary, informed of the early developments as they happened, asked Maude to push his brigades forward in support. That was perhaps the turning point. In any event, before midnight Keary had managed to reorganise his forces, and the addition of Maude's men was beginning to tell. Halil had by now reoriented the thrust of his attack, focusing on the 8th Brigade's positions, and would continue to try to shatter its resistance until first light, without success. By 0530, the Turks could be seen withdrawing under artillery and machine gun fire. The Battle of Bait Isa was over, and once again it remained only to consolidate the position, police the battlefield, and recover the wounded and the dead. In purely tactical terms, it was a Turkish defeat of a sort, the British having gained some ground, but strategically it was a different story. At the cost of between three and four thousand dead and wounded, the Turks had effectively killed off any chance the British had of advancing along the right bank of the Tigris, and with the situation at Sannaiyat, on the left bank, still stalemated, that meant that any hope of relieving Kut before the garrison there reached starvation point was almost certainly gone.

Gorringe arrived at Keary's headquarters at around 0600 on 18 April, and immediately began issuing orders for a resumption of the offensive. There was no question of sending the 3rd Division straight back into battle after twenty-four hours of almost non-stop fighting, yet it was on the front which it occupied that Gorringe wished to concentrate, and that required another complicated set of manoeuvres to put the relatively fresh 13th Division into the northern sector and shift the 3rd to the south. In the event it was well into the night before the required reorganisation was completed, and at 0710 the following morning the 39th Brigade advanced ponderously across what was now no more than a bog, the Turks having let yet more water in; the men got not even halfway across no-man's-land before they were driven back by heavy gunfire. The attempt was repeated again and again over the next few days with no greater degree of success.

Long before then, however, Gorringe had transferred his attention back to the left bank, and the Sannaiyat positions, though flooding had been extensive there, too, the river and the marsh joining forces to create what seemed to be an impassable obstacle. However, patrols reported that there was a wide median strip where the water was no more than ankle-deep; Younghusband proposed sending his two forward brigades through this gap side by side, and Gorringe agreed, the attempt being scheduled for the morning of 20 April. Before Younghusband could begin to put his plan into effect, however, the weather intervened once more; the wind strengthening and shifting to the north, blowing sheets of water from the Suwaikiya Marsh towards the river, inundating a much wider area and flooding the 7th Division's trenches, forcing the 21st Brigade, on the right, to abandon their positions and Gorringe to postpone the operation. When the ground was reconnoitred again, on the morning of the twentieth, the shallow area was now found to be twenty centimetres deep in water, with as much soft mud again beneath it.

The last British attempt to relieve Kut began at 0620 on 22 April, with a forty-minute barrage; five minutes later Brig.-Gen. Norie told Younghusband that the terrain over which his 21st Brigade was to advance was impassable, and he reverted to a contingency plan which called for the 19th alone to attack on a narrower front. At 0700, as planned, the artillery barrage intensified on the defenders' forward positions and the troops set off to cover the five hundred metres of boggy ground towards the Turkish lines.

As the barrage lifted the 19th's composite Highland battalion, with the 92nd Punjabis to their right, pushed through the first-line trenches and on into the second. Both were full of water, and the intervening ground was churned by artillery fire into deep slurry. The men floundered, sinking to their armpits; their clothing, their boots, even the barrels of their rifles filled with mud.

With the 19th Brigade fully engaged, Norie asked for assistance from the 21st, and Younghusband ordered the 'Norsets' – a composite battalion formed from the Norfolks and the Dorsets – to comply. Even as they were moving up the Turks counterattacked from their third-line positions; the British resisted desperately, many of the infantrymen, unable to fire their clogged weapons, fighting hand to hand. Supported by massed machine guns on the far side of the river they stemmed the tide and as the leading elements of the Norsets arrived in support of the Punjabis, the Turks gave ground once more. It soon became clear, however, that the main body of the composite battalion had strayed too far to the north; they encountered deep water and stalled, coming under murderous machine gun fire from the Turkish left wing. The order to withdraw was given (by an officer whose identity was never discovered), and they fell back, exposing the Punjabis' right flank. They too were obliged to retire, in consequence, and with that the cohesion of the line, such as it was by that time, was lost; the Highlanders too were ordered to break off and withdraw, an instruction with which many were disinclined to comply until the impossibility of the situation was brought home to them.

Gorringe arrived at Younghusband's forward HQ at around 0900 and ordered a renewal of the artillery bombardment, but the consensus was that it would be impractical to resume the offensive. At 1120, without warning, the Turks raised two Red Crescent flags, and began to move stretcher-bearers forward to recover their wounded; the British promptly raised Red Cross flags and began to do the same, though were prevented from proceeding past the second line of trenches, the Turks claiming the men lying wounded there as prisoners of war.

By the end of the day Gorringe had finally become convinced that any further effort to relieve Kut was futile, and told Lake so; Lake instructed him to keep up his efforts on the right bank, but it is clear from both official and personal signals he sent to Sir Beauchamp Duff that night that he was of the same mind. The following day, Townshend, having been told of the situation, asked Lake if the time had not now come to try to open surrender negotiations with the Turks. Lake forwarded his query to London and Delhi (where, on 4 April, Lord Hardinge of Penshurst had been succeeded as Viceroy by Lord Chelmsford, Frederic Thesiger) with a rider of his own, saying that he was prepared to try again to force the situation but that in the event of his failing, surrender seemed the only course. His telegram to London crossed with one from the CIGS which also enquired whether the time to consider surrender had not now come.

Lake had one more shot in his locker. Ten days earlier naval artificers had begun armouring the side-wheel paddle-steamer *Julnar*, and now he asked the Navy to put a plan to push her through to Kut into effect. She cast off at 1900 on 24 April, laden with around 270 tons of supplies, enough to keep the garrison going for a further month. Gorringe ordered a general artillery bombardment to cover the noise she made, but it was to no avail; despite the conditions being near-perfect, with the sky heavily overcast, she was spotted before she was past the Sannaiyat positions. Making only six knots (12km/h) against the current, she was hit repeatedly, and near Maqasis an artillery round demolished her bridgeworks, killing her commander and fatally wounding his first lieutenant and the helmsman. She struck a cable, swung around and went aground. All efforts to get her off failed, and she was captured, along with the surviving members of her crew.

Lake reported the failure to London; he would make a last attempt to break through, he said, if Kitchener insisted, but had no faith at all that it would succeed. Just over twenty-four hours later he received a reply from Kitchener: unless he had good reason to change his mind, the Secretary of State told him, he was authorised to open negotiations. The attempt to relieve Kut was over.

It had been a very expensive failure, the casualty rate amongst the ranks of the Tigris Corps extremely heavy: a total of something over 46,500 men had taken part, and on 25 April the corps' effective strength was 23,450. Maj.-Gen. Sir George Younghusband's 7th Division, which had been in contact with the enemy throughout, had suffered the worst, and could now muster no more than 5,200 men. As for the 6th (Poona) Division of the British Army of India, it now numbered just over 13,300 men, including 3,250 non-combatant camp followers, 1,450 of whom were sick or wounded. In the course of the siege, 1,500 had been killed or died of wounds, 721 had died of disease (including some who had poisoned themselves eating plants they found; Brig.-Gen. Hoghton was among them) and some were posted missing.

Townshend and Lake had little to offer the Turks, and in something like desperation they tried to buy their freedom. Townshend himself first raised the possibility on 23 April, suggesting that the British government offer to defray any 'expenses' that Halil might incur in allowing the garrison to march out of Kut, and very soon it became a mainstay of Lake's negotiating policy. A figure of a million pounds was suggested in a signal sent in the early hours of 26 April, together with the offer of negotiators with 'special qualifications for such work': Capt. Aubrey Herbert, MP, and Capt. TE Lawrence of the Cairo Intelligence Staff, together with Lake's own head of intelligence, Lt.-Col. WH Beach.

Later that morning Townshend wrote to Ali Nejib Pasha, who commanded the blockading forces surrounding Kut, with a request that he inform Halil Pasha that he had been authorised to open negotiations. He asked for six days' armistice, during which food could be sent up to the garrison, together with negotiators, and implied that he expected the Turks to permit the 6th Division to leave Kut with side-arms and belongings intact.[27] Halil was unmoved.

There is little reason to drag the account of the 'negotiations' out, for there was to be no last-minute twist, and a summary will serve. Halil and Townshend met the following morning. The Turkish general demanded unconditional surrender, as a precursor to which he insisted that the garrison move out of Kut into a tented encampment, though when Townshend mention money he held out a slender hope, saying he would have to put the matter to Enver Pasha. On top of the money Townshend offered him his guns and to free a number of Turkish prisoners equal to that of the garrison if his men were permitted to return to India having given their word not to take up arms against the Turks again. He also asked that Beach, Herbert and Lawrence be permitted up to Kut, having been told by Lake that he declined to take over the negotiations himself, as Townshend would have preferred. Halil gave him short shrift in reply the following day. He had received a communication from his War Minister, he said; Enver would permit only Townshend himself to be released on parole 'avec son sabre', and then only if all the weapons and warlike stores in Kut were given up intact. In an aside to one of Townshend's staff officers he also made it clear that a cash payment would not be acceptable, since the Turks 'had already lost 10,000 men over Kut'. Townshend's response was to ask Lake to double the money, to £2,000,000; he would ask London's permission, said Lake, but in the light of Enver's refusal of the first offer, he held out little hope.

It was too late. Townshend's men had not eaten at all for three days, and in their already weakened state could hold out no longer. Throughout that night Townshend destroyed what he could of his weapons and military stores, and at 0600 on 28 April he wrote to Halil surrendering unconditionally, asking only that the sick and wounded be allowed to go downriver in exchange for a like number of Turkish prisoners. When Beach, Herbert and Lawrence arrived on the scene later that day it was only over these points that they were able to negotiate; eventually, 1,136 men were evacuated, and 345 more were later sent downriver from Baghdad.

Both Townshend and the next most senior officer, Melliss, were sick when the Turks entered Kut on 29 April, and it fell to Delamain – who had led the first force ashore in Mesopotamia, almost eighteen months earlier – to surrender Kut to the Turkish divisional commander. For the rest of that day and most of the next the prisoners were marched to Shumran, where eventually they were given food in the shape of barely edible 'hard-tack' biscuits.[28] There was no shelter of any kind, and no blankets; by 6 May, when they set out to march to Baghdad, almost three hundred more had died of starvation or exposure, but long before then Townshend had left the scene in some comfort aboard a river steamer, bound for Constantinople and incarceration under extremely favourable conditions.

The starving men, ragged and for the most part barefoot, goaded all the way by Arabs wielding whips and sticks, reached Baghdad on 15 May. Here they were allowed some rest, and Delamain was able to arrange some minimal medical care for the worst cases, but soon they were packed aboard trains in batches for the short journey to Samarra, whence they were marched some six hundred kilometres to Ras al Ain. There many of the Indian troops were to remain, put to work on extending the railway from Constantinople, while the rest and all the British were transported to other points along the incomplete line and put to work there. It soon became clear that they were in no fit state for hard labour, and instead they were taken to pestilential camps in central Anatolia. Many died along the way; many more died in confinement, but some were exchanged and a few even escaped.[29] Of the 2,900 'white' troops who went into captivity, fewer than 1,200 survived. Townshend did not just survive, but prospered,[30] and could even be said to have made himself useful in the end, as we shall see when we come to examine the way the war against the Ottoman Empire was concluded.

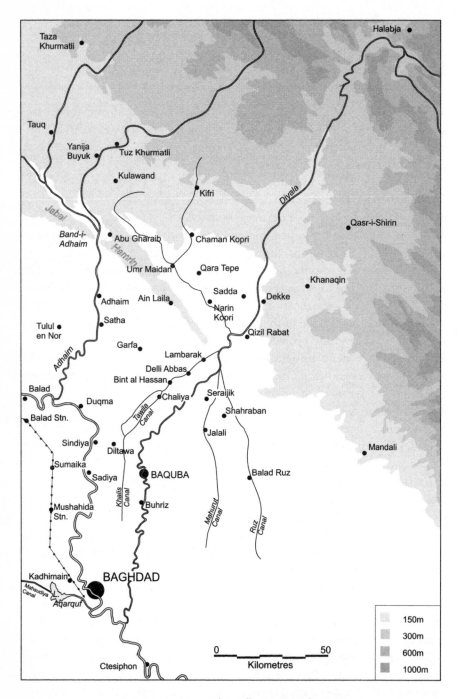

7. Mesopotamia – The Adhaim/Diyala Basin

4

To Baghdad and Beyond

With the failure to relieve Kut al Amara before Townshend was forced to surrender, the British Tigris Corps and the Turkish Sixth Army were left facing each other in impotence at Sannaiyat and east of Bait Isa, each exhausted by their recent efforts.

In the despatch he sent authorising Sir Percy Lake to open negotiations for the surrender, Kitchener laid down guidelines for him to follow thereafter: broadly, he was to take up a defensive posture, not retreating, but keeping his forces in place as far as possible, in order to discourage the Turks from sending troops to confront the Russian expeditionary force which had reached the Persian frontier, north of Baghdad. Lake replied that he would encourage Gorringe to act aggressively wherever possible, which prompted the CIGS to issue a clarification (to Duff). It began: 'At present ... we do not attach any importance to the possession of Kut or to the occupation of Baghdad. ... Lake would probably be directed to fall back to Amara, or even to Qurna, if no other consideration were involved ...'[1]

As Moberly says in the Official History, 'the description of the British campaign for the seven or eight months following the surrender of Kut is mainly a narrative of efforts to put matters on a proper footing.' Those efforts began with changes to the order of battle, which saw the 35th, 36th and 37th Brigades constituted as the 14th Division,[2] and the 12th, 34th and 42nd Brigades constituted as the 15th (on the Euphrates front, at Nasiriya and Khamisiya).[3] The 41st Brigade, now made up of four weakened battalions,[4] was at Basra. Detachments were located at points on the Tigris from Qurna to Ali Gharbi, the strongest contingent being at Amara.[5] There was a small force in Arabistan, and two and a half battalions at Bushire. The return of the 13th Division to Egypt, for redeployment to France, was discussed, but the proposal was eventually dropped.

Later the overall command structure was modified, Lt.-Gen. Sir Stanley Maude (as he became; the promotion was a temporary one, but was made substantive as a reward for his success in taking Baghdad) taking over from Lt.-Gen. Sir George Gorringe[6] as commander of the Tigris Corps on 11 July. On 28 August Maude assumed overall command in Mesopotamia in succession to Sir Percy Lake. Maj.-Gen. Walter Cayley took over command of Maude's 13th Division, while Maj.-Gen. Alexander Cobbe succeeded Sir George Younghusband in command of the 7th. Maude reorganised his force into two corps on 15 November, Cobbe taking over

I Indian Army Corps,[7] with Maj.-Gen. Vere Fane succeeding him in command of the 7th Division, and Lt.-Gen. William Marshall, who was then commanding the 27th Division at Salonika, taking over III Indian Army Corps.[8] A group of logistics experts were drafted in at brigadier level to run supply and transport operations.

On a more exalted level, Gen. Sir Charles Monro replaced Gen. Sir Beauchamp Duff as Commander-in-Chief in India when the latter was recalled to London to give evidence before the Mesopotamia Commission (see page 93), and at an even higher level, David Lloyd George was appointed Secretary of State for War on the death of Kitchener[9] on 5 June.

Additional combat and support units, including three British and six Indian battalions raised to replace those which had formed the infantry component of the 6th Division – they retained the same designations as the originals (but were not brigaded in the same fashion), and were employed as replacements for depleted formations – arrived in theatre during the course of the summer and autumn, and some troops were rotated back to India.[10] By mid-July the authorised establishment of the expeditionary force stood at some 41,500 British and 54,500 Indian personnel (and there were over 32,000 Indian camp followers present), though by no means all of them were combat troops. *Their* numbers stood at around 60,000 infantry and 4,600 cavalry as of late October, and by then there were about 225 guns in theatre,[11] plus those aboard the naval flotilla. In order to hold stores and lodge personnel in transit, the area around Basra protected from inundation by earth berms now extended to around 123km (48 square miles), with accommodation for 15,000 and hospital facilities for 7,000 (and there were places for twice that number of sick and wounded at Amara).

Reshuffling and reorganising to one side, there was to be little movement on the ground. On 19 May reconnaissance revealed that the Turks had pulled back on the right bank, leaving the Bait Isa and Chahela positions unoccupied. In the event, the Sinn Abtar and Dujaila Redoubts also proved to have been abandoned, and by the morning of the twenty-first the British front on the right bank had been pushed up to a line following that of the depression from the latter to Maqasis, allowing the heaviest guns to control the Turkish crossing point on the Shatt al Hai. The position on the left bank remained unchanged. Elsewhere, on the Euphrates front all was quiet save for sporadic mischief. In Arabistan the Bakhtiari were firmly in control of the region through which the pipeline ran, and oil was flowing at an ever-increasing rate. There was, however, still unrest further east, in southern Persia, which required a strong garrison at Bushire and considerable efforts on the part of Sir Percy Sykes' South Persia Rifles to contain, though the situation there improved as the year progressed.

Above all, the hiatus in activity gave Maude – a very much more competent soldier-manager than any of his predecessors – the time to develop a conceptual plan for the war in Mesopotamia where none had existed before beyond the ambition to capture Baghdad and the dire necessity to relieve Kut.

There was some apprehension in Maude's headquarters when rain fell on 6 December, but it came to very little, and did not upset his plan to go onto the offensive within days. His strike, he had decided, would fall on the right-bank positions, and the troops he would employ would be from Marshall's III Corps, its 14th Division already occupying the area west of Sinn Banks–Dujaila Redoubt and its 13th Division on the way up from Amara, plus Keary's 3rd Division.

The operational plan was straightforward: the 6th and 7th Cavalry Brigades, now organised as a division, would loop around to the east of the Dujaila Redoubt, secure the Hai crossing at Basrugiya, and then move northwards to a point opposite Shumran. III Corps' infantry would advance to the Shatt al Hai, clear its left bank of hostile troops as far as Kala Haji Fahan, just short of the (very extensive) main Turkish positions opposite Kut, and bridge the waterway north-west of Basrugiya. By way of diversion, I Corps would launch a feint attack against the left-bank positions at Sannaiyat. Maude would then confront the Turks on both sides of the water-way, and target the enclave downstream at the Khudhaira Bend. The advance to and across the Hai went according to plan during the early hours of 14 December, and by the morning of 18 December the infantry were in contact with the Turkish defensive positions

The following day Maude sent a strike force comprising the 35th, 37th and 40th Infantry Brigades, with five field batteries, sappers and No. 2 (Mobile) Bridging Train, to advance to the Husaini Bend above Kut, to cut the enemy's lines of communication. The operation was abandoned after some eight hours. No one above the rank of brigadier was involved, and it may actually have been a feint, albeit with the hope of achieving success by surprise.

There was no question of trying to take the Khudhaira Bend position by direct assault, but instead it would be necessary to sap up to it. Work began on 26 December, but that day it started to rain in earnest, and it continued almost unremittingly until 6 January. Despite the bad weather, considerable progress had been made with the saps, and Keary's 3rd Division was assembled to assault the enemy's right, over a front extending to around fifteen hundred metres. The Hai Salient, Shumran and Sannaiyat positions were to be bombarded to cover his intentions; Marshall, opposite the two former, was to push his infantry forward if conditions allowed.

Zero hour was fixed for 0845 on 9 January; it came in heavy mist (which persisted until well into the afternoon), and by 0900 the entire sector, through to the second-line trenches, was in British hands. Then the Turks counter-attacked in strength around their centre, and the position was reversed, and by 1500 the Turks had regained all but about four hundred metres of their first-line trenches. However, after darkness fell the Turks evacuated their first line and some of the second, and by the morning of 10 January the Khudhaira position had been reduced to little more than half its previous size. That night Maude ordered renewed efforts to clear it; the 8th and 9th Brigades were unsuccessful at first, but over the next seven days the Turks were slowly driven back into a small pocket on the left of their original position, and during the night of 18 January they retired across the river.

Maude asked Marshall for proposals for clearing out the Hai Salient on 10 January, believing that the offensive against the Khudhaira Bend positions would be speedily concluded. Marshall pushed forward the next day on both banks of the waterway but met stiff resistance. Lacking artillery, which was committed to bombarding the Khudhaira pocket, he could but suspend his operation until it was released to him, but then heavy rain intervened, and it was 25 January before he was able to go onto the offensive once more.

The 13th Division was to spearhead the attack, the 39th Brigade on the west bank, and the 40th, on the east, advancing along the line of the Hai under cover of a creeping artillery barrage from a total of over a hundred guns and howitzers, the 38th Brigade on the right flank, and the 35th (of the 14th Division) on the left 'shooting them in' and standing ready to advance themselves. The 39th made some progress initially but was then driven back to its starting point. The 40th Brigade fared better, and by nightfall it was in possession of the Turkish first-line positions across a front fifteen hundred metres wide.

During the night the 14th Division's 36th Brigade, held in reserve, relieved the depleted 39th. It attacked at 1040 the next morning, and within ten minutes had stormed its objective and held it against repeated counterattacks. By nightfall it had increased the area the British held on the west bank of the Hai, and made still more gains during the night. There was little action on the east bank that day, but bombing parties from the 40th Brigade made inroads on their right, and broadened the front.

By the start of the third day, Turkish resistance on the west bank of the Hai was beginning to show signs of faltering; the 36th Brigade, supported by massed artillery, was able to gain a significant amount of ground at comparatively little cost in a three-phase attack, while on the east the 40th, though it continued to extend to the right, made less headway. The following day, however, the balance was redressed, and proportionately greater gains were made on the east bank; by nightfall on 28 January the first- and second-line trenches there were in British hands, and the Turks had fallen back to create a new perimeter approximately six hundred metres back from the original, their troops on the west bank, where the front was much narrower, being driven back until they were not quite level with them. Marshall, conscious that the men on the east bank would be vulnerable to defenders in Woolpress Village and across the Tigris in Kut if they advanced further, decided to concentrate his efforts to the west of the Hai, and spent the next two days repositioning his forces.

The defensive positions in the entire salient, but particularly on the west bank, were tightly packed – between the first line and that which was to be the objective on 1 February, when the offensive was renewed, there were no less than eight lines of fighting trenches, linked by communications trenches and littered with strongpoints – and in consequence much of the fighting was at close quarters, which both caused severe congestion and limited the support the assault troops could expect from machine guns and artillery. In the event, the advance on the west bank stalled, two Sikh battalions suffering very heavy casualties in the process,[12] while that on the east made unexpectedly good progress. During the night the 38th and 40th Brigades on the east bank were relieved by the 8th, and crossed over the Hai to broaden the front towards the Shumran Bend, uncommitted formations of the 13th Division also being brought up.

Mist and fog persisted throughout 2 February, and it was not until daybreak on the third that the advance restarted. The main force on both banks of the Hai immediately made good an advance to the Turkish picket line and those on the far left made inroads into the less heavily defended area to the west. The advance was most successful on the east bank, and before daybreak the next morning the entire zone was found to be clear of defenders, and was speedily occupied. There was a withdrawal on the right bank of the Hai, too, but not the complete evacuation of the salient which Maude had hoped to see, and by nightfall on 4 February the Turks' front line ran due west across the Dehra Bend from Woolpress Village towards the apex of the Shumran Bend; the line was continuous for perhaps the first three kilometres, but then petered out into isolated posts. Maude, having lost over eight and a half thousand men killed, missing and wounded since the Kut offensive started on 13 December, adopted a cautious approach, and halted his infantry while the artillery redeployed and its guns were re-registered.

On 9 February the decisive operation to clear the Turks out of the Dehra Bend commenced with an attack on the front immediately west of Woolpress Village. The two Lancashire battalions of the 38th Brigade in the forefront made heavy going of it, but had taken their objectives by the end of the day, while to their left the 39th Brigade made better progress against less heavily manned positions, advancing in a north-westerly direction towards the river (though the cavalry, to its left, was thwarted by a combination of entrenched infantry and floodwater from reaching the river upstream of the Shumran Bend). Fresh units were brought into the front line and the following day the Turks were driven out of their position west of Woolpress Village; by nightfall the right bank of the Tigris for a kilometre and a half upstream from the mouth of the Hai was in British hands, and that night the Turks withdrew to shorten their line. Even though their position was by now theoretically untenable, the defenders were very tenacious indeed, holding their ground in the face of repeated attempts by the British infantry to penetrate their positions, and inflicting heavy casualties, and it was not until 16 February that all resistance was extinguished and the right bank of the Tigris to a point upstream of the Shumran Bend was in British hands.

With that it was possible to bridge the river upstream of Kut and force the Turks to retire or risk envelopment. By 24 February the last of them were leaving Kut; HMS *Mantis* landed a party of matelots the following morning, and the Union Flag was raised over the ruins of the town once more. The Second Battle of Kut was the decisive engagement in the theatre; from then on the Turks were never able to offer the same degree of sustained, long-term resistance. It is intriguing to speculate what would have been the outcome if an alternative strategy – that no effort should have been spared to prepare more favourable defensive positions nearer to Baghdad, that the entire Kut position, including Sannaiyat and Shumran, should have been evacuated in favour of them, and all available Turkish forces in the region, then numbering around 30,000 combatants and set to rise, concentrated there – had been adopted, as some, Kazim Karabekir amongst them, had suggested.

Be that as it might have been, the surviving Turks were actually retreating in fairly good order, most of their guns and *matériel* having been recovered intact. The rearguard was well handled, and kept the advancing British off the main body while it passed through Imam Mandi and Qala Shadi. The Cavalry Division failed to make any real impact, though it did keep the enemy – who, by the evening of the twenty-sixth, had reached the Nahr al Kalek Bend, some fifty kilometres, as the crow flies, upstream from Kut – in sight. More effective were the gunboats of the Royal Navy; on the morning of 27 February Maude asked Capt. Nunn to take a flotilla[13] upstream and inflict as much damage as possible on the enemy, and Nunn complied with a will. It began passing stragglers by about 1400, and soon came up with the captured *Firefly* (now renamed *Suliman Pak*, the name by which the Turks knew Ctesiphon[14]) and the *Pioneer*. The former gave a good account of herself, hitting *Mantis* and severely damaging *Moth*, but was eventually run ashore and abandoned, as were *Pioneer*, *Basra* and the captured tug *Sumana*.

More importantly, perhaps, the flotilla then came within sight (and shot) of the Turks' main body, which lost its discipline as a result, 'turning the orderly retreat ... into a panic-stricken flight, as was clear from the spectacle that met our aircraft and advancing troops next morning', as the Official History has it. A Turkish source says that Halil Pasha arrived in Baghdad that day, having already abandoned all hope of holding the city, and had signalled Ali Ihsan to retire from Persia (see Chapter 9) with all speed.[15]

The British advance slowed then, Maude being concerned that the combat troops would outpace the supply train. He allowed III Corps and the Cavalry Division to proceed no further than Aziziya after the Turks evacuated it on 28 February (and subsequently moved his advanced headquarters there), while I Corps, having in the meantime policed the battlefields around Kut and secured the line of communications, concentrated at the Nahr al Kalek

Bend. Then he ran into a net of political/strategic wrangling surrounding the advisability, or not, of attempting to occupy Baghdad, reminiscent of the arguments which had raged in the autumn of 1915, the CIGS doubting his ability to hold the city with the troops at his disposal, while Monro in India wished him to press on regardless, and give the Turks no opportunity to reorganise for its defence, which view Maude reinforced in his own despatches. Robertson reappraised the situation reports, changed his mind and gave his approval on 3 March.

Maude's advance continued on 5 March, the Turks falling back before it. By the following morning they had reached the Diyala River, where the 51st and 52nd Divisions were joined by the 14th, which had begun arriving in the theatre from the Caucasus in mid-February, and which had by now absorbed the remnants of the 45th. With its arrival the 52nd Division was sent across to the right bank of the Tigris.

Halil had wasted days on trying to recondition the defensive positions downstream of the Diyala before accepting that they could not be made good, and it was 1 March before he had ordered trenches dug on the far bank of the river. By the sixth the line extended for some twelve kilometres from the river's confluence with the Tigris, but unconvinced that it would hold, Kazim Karabekir, XVIII Corps' commander, decided that it was to be employed as a forward position only, and began preparing another defensive line five or six kilometres to the rear, anchored on the Tigris at Qarara. The outcome was unavoidable: when Maude's forces appeared at the Diyala on 7 March, the defensive positions were incomplete and the river itself proved to be the biggest obstacle. Ferrying men across in pontoons against active opposition, even under cover of darkness, proved very expensive, and by the morning of 9 March little more than a hundred were across; they survived repeated attempts to overrun them, however, and the following night – by which time they were running very short of ammunition – were joined by two complete battalions, with sappers and pioneers. An enlarged bridgehead was secured by 0600, and by 1000 the British perimeter had been pushed out by fifteen hundred metres, with patrols extending beyond that. Some two hours later a bridge was completed near the river's mouth, and the remainder of Cayley's 13th Division crossed. By then the Turks had transferred most of their men to the right bank of the Tigris, and on the left had withdrawn to the secondary positions running north-eastwards from Qarara.

There had also been considerable discord concerning the siting of defences on the right bank, the line selected by the Turks – it was that which they had employed in 1915, when Townshend threatened the city, and followed the Umm at Tabul sandhills from Lake Aqarquf[6] to the Karada Bend of the Tigris – being rejected by a German specialist as being too close to the city. He decided on another, five kilometres further south, which required ten kilometres of trench to be dug. Something over half its length, eastwards from a disused railway embankment at Tel Aswad, had been completed by

7 March, when Kazim ordered work on the Umm at Tabul line restarted to provide a fall-back position.

Maude sent the 14th Division's 35th Brigade across the Tigris by steamer, at a point near Bawi, on the evening of 7 March. Brig.-Gen Thomson advanced during the night, and by daybreak was opposite the mouth of the Diyala. By that time No. 1 Bridging Train had arrived at Bawi, and threw a pontoon-bridge across; it was in commission by 1430. The Cavalry Division was then sent over, followed by the 7th Infantry Division. The cavalry followed the riverbank for ten kilometres as darkness fell, and then struck out to the west, aiming to hit the Mahmudiya–Baghdad road near the Shawa Khan ruins; its maps were inaccurate, and in the dark it soon lost its way. At daybreak it was surprised to find itself approaching a line of sandhills which, a patrol reported, hid an entrenched defensive line; the Turks appeared not to be aware of the British presence. There was a proposal to charge the line to disperse the enemy, but the divisional commander, Brig.-Gen. SF Crocker, vetoed it, and ordered a move westwards, to locate the enemy's right flank. This revealed its existence to the Turks, and the entire force, save one squadron left to screen the infantry, hastily withdrew to the Tigris; Crocker, who commanded the 6th Brigade, was replaced as divisional commander by Brig.-Gen. LC Jones of the 7th the following day.

By that time the 7th Infantry Division's vanguard unit, the 28th Brigade, had reached the vicinity of Shawa Khan. The Turkish positions extended much further than its commander had estimated, however; the flank was not located, and when Fane, the divisional commander, came up, at around 1300, he found the situation deadlocked. He ordered more men up, but that failed to get the advance going again, and as night fell he ordered the battalions to dig in. He had been out of contact with Cobbe, by now himself established at Shaikh Aswad, for much of the day, but communications were restored around 2000. The corps commander asked him if he needed further reinforcements; Fane asked him for an additional brigade and a howitzer battery, and to instruct the cavalry to act vigorously on the left the following day.

At around 0500 on 10 March reports of the Turks falling back from the Tel Aswad line to the Umm at Tubal sandhills began to reach Fane's headquarters; Cobbe had instructed him to press the enemy if he showed signs of retiring, and he ordered his brigades to advance along the line of the disused railway embankment, the 19th on its far side, the 28th on the near with the 35th to its right, and the 21st in reserve. Against them the Turks numbered around 5,300, Kazim having brought the 51st Division from the left-bank positions overnight, with its seven battalions holding the line between the railway and the Tigris, and the 52nd (six battalions) on the far side of the embankment, with a battalion in reserve at Tel Ataf, three kilometres to the north. The defenders deployed thirty guns, including modern German 12-cm and 15-cm howitzers.

Fane received reports from aerial reconnaissance at about 1000, and decided that the Turks meant to make a stand at the positions he was approaching. He rethought his dispositions, and ordered the 28th Brigade to fall back and become the divisional reserve, the 35th to extend to cover the area between the embankment and the river, the 19th to cover the sector between the embankment and the operating railway line (which had by now been cut by cavalry patrols), and the 21st to cross it and deploy with the intention of rounding the Turkish right flank. All the while the wind from the south was getting up, and by noon had become a veritable storm, the dust reducing visibility to a hundred and fifty metres and often much less. This, and almost constant artillery fire, hampered Fane's redeployment, and it was not completed that day.

By sunset on 10 March, despite the poor visibility, Fane's intentions were obvious to the Turks. There was discord in their headquarters, Halil having seemingly convinced himself that he must at least make an effort to defend Baghdad, while Kazim and the commanders of the 51st and 52nd Divisions dissented, arguing that if driven back, they would have to retreat through the streets of the city itself. Better, they argued, to break off and withdraw now, while they still had some freedom of choice ... After a short internal debate, Halil agreed, and issued orders accordingly: the 51st and 52nd Divisions were to withdraw up the right bank of the Tigris to Samarra, the 14th up the left (though in the process a force would be detached to proceed to Baquba, to cover the withdrawal of Ali Ihsan's XIII Corps from Khanaqin), while a detachment at Musayib on the Euphrates, and the reserve at Tel Ataf, would retire on Falluja, some sixty kilometres west of Baghdad. The withdrawal, while confused and disorganised, went undetected by the British until around 0200 on 11 March, some hours after the rearguard had departed. At 0900 that morning, the men of the 1/5th Buffs (the East Kent Regiment) entered Baghdad, and one of its company commanders planted the Union Flag on the citadel.

Since the Turks had abandoned Baghdad precipitately, they had been forced to leave a vast stockpile of *matériel* and goods, and in the few hours between them pulling out and the British arriving, Arabs and Kurds looted extensively, destroying or despoiling much of what they could not carry away, and the first priority was to restore order. Equally, however, there were urgent military requirements to be met, organising the defence of a city which had no natural exploitable features and pushing troops forward, both to co-operate with the Russians in Persia, should that prove possible, and to harry the Turks and prevent them from demolishing the flood defences on the Euphrates or Tigris. Aerial reconnaissance soon identified large bodies of enemy troops on the right bank of the latter within around thirty kilometres of Baghdad, and on 13 March Cobbe's I Corps, less the 3rd Division, was sent to confront them. He was hindered by inaccurate maps and spotty intelligence, but his cavalry patrols located the Turks at breakfast time the following day, five kilometres south of Mushahida Station.[17] Their positions were found to be over ten kilometres long, stretching westwards from the Tigris to a low, conical mound, later known as Bhopal Hill, which lay just beyond the railway line, the 51st Division to the right, the 52nd to the left; the main strength was in the centre, where they occupied a triple line of trenches with excellent fields of fire across open ground.

Cobbe instructed Fane to advance a brigade each side of the railway. He placed the 21st, with two battalions of the 19th in support, to form the divisional reserve, on the western side; the men were to cross the line surreptitiously, by way of the numerous culverts beneath it, and deploy on a front four hundred metres wide. The 28th Brigade was to advance up the eastern side of the line, the troops to form up some two and a half kilometres short of the Turkish positions. It took some considerable time for the five battalions to cross the line, and it was not until 1520 that the 21st Brigade began its advance, and 1600 before it came up to the 28th's line. Both brigades soon came under heavy fire, the 21st getting the worst of it, and the advance slowed; the field artillery was brought up to operate at shorter range, but still the defenders clung to Bhopal Hill, and it was not until sometime after 1830 that the positions upon it, and eastwards to the railway, were taken. With their right flank thus turned, the Turks could but fall back from their main defensive positions.

Night was falling by this time, and the subsequent advance on Mushahida Station, across broken ground, was slow. Once again, it was the spearhead units of the 21st Brigade which reached the objective first, at around 2330. By first light the following morning, the entire area from the station to the river was in British hands, at a cost of just over five hundred casualties. The Turks were believed to have suffered perhaps twice that number, but the remainder escaped; aerial reconnaissance put the main body of them some forty kilometres to the north by the morning of 16 March. The 21st Brigade, plus an artillery battery and a company of sappers, were left to secure the area, and the rest of the corps returned to Baghdad.

Meanwhile, Maude had instructed Marshall to push a brigade group up towards Falluja, having been informed that north of the town the embankment closing the Sakhlawiya Canal – which linked the Euphrates with Lake Aqarquf, and thus with the Tigris – was to be breached, threatening the entire area with inundation (the embankment was indeed breached; only a barrier hastily thrown up between the Tigris north of Khandimain and the Mahsudiya Canal prevented the resultant floods from reaching Baghdad). On 19 March the 7th Infantry Brigade, with support troops, reached Falluja; the Turks had trenches covering the town, but declined to stand, and the town was occupied by mid-afternoon.

On the Persian front, Maude had but scant intelligence. From reports he received from the liaison officer with Baratov's Cavalry Corps (by way of

Tiblisi, Petrograd, London and Delhi; he later received permission to communicate directly with the Cossack's headquarters, but the link was never good) he knew that the Turkish 2nd Infantry Division, part of the force sent to confront the Russians, was retreating down the road from Kermanshah, making for Khanaqin, and expected its arrival by about 20 March, but of the 6th Division which had preceded it he had no news; it could conceivably be waiting to fall on Baratov's flank, or it could simply be making for the border itself. On 12 March he sent a troop of armoured cars to reconnoitre the road to Baquba; they exchanged fire with enemy infantry at the town, and then withdrew. A lorry-mounted infantry battalion followed two days later; there was a delay while scouts determined just how many enemy troops were in the area and where they were located, then they crossed the Diyala under cover of darkness some way to the south of the town, near the village of Buhriz. By nightfall on 18 March Baquba was in British hands, and a bridge across the river had been completed.

Maude now made preparation to send a substantial force – most of Keary's 3rd Division, less the 7th Brigade, plus the 7th Cavalry Brigade and two brigades of field artillery and a howitzer battery – towards Khanaqin.[18] The column reached Jalali, where the bridge across the Mahurut Canal had been destroyed, by nightfall on 21 March. Keary was under pressure from Maude to make haste to confront the retreating Turks who, he believed, were intent on crossing the Diyala and making for Kirkuk by way of Kifri. 'You should get in touch with the enemy and act vigorously so you can pin him to his ground,' Maude exhorted. Keary did his best to comply. Two companies of Sikhs were ferried across to protect a bridging operation, and the advance was able to continue the following morning.

Reconnaissance revealed the Turks to be entrenched before Shahraban in sufficient numbers to dissuade him from a frontal assault, but Maude sent him a re-run of the previous day's sharp signal, adding that it looked very much as if the Turks had been slipping away across the Diyala all night (which in fact they had not), and he changed his mind. That night he sent two infantry battalions forward; when they reached Shahraban they found the Turks had decamped. Keary pursued, but was checked by artillery at the Haruniya Canal.

The next day he resumed his advance. A couple of kilometres beyond lay the southern extremity of the Jabal Hamrin – an isolated ridge at its southern extremity, then a rampart forming the western wall of a fertile plateau, running over two hundred and fifty kilometres from south-east to north-west into Kurdistan – which nowhere rose higher than about two hundred metres but which provided excellent cover with first-rate fields of fire over the exposed plain below. While Keary judged that he outnumbered the Turks by perhaps three to two, this was certainly no place to mount a frontal assault, and he decided instead to hold them in position with something under half his force while trying to turn their left flank with the rest, rolling them up towards the Diyala as they advanced. Though in the course of it British troops reached the foothills of the Jabal Hamrin, the attempt eventually failed, and by the evening of 25 March Keary's men had retired to the line of the canal.

Maude, furnished at last with an effective wireless network, had a tendency to interfere in the management of fairly small engagements when he wasn't otherwise engaged, and this was no exception.[19] Having been kept informed of the situation, he sent Keary a series of quite unnecessary 'advisory' signals, the first telling him to go onto the defensive if he could not prevail, a second questioning the need to withdraw. Keary replied that he had met 'the spirit and scope' of Maude's instruction to pin the enemy to his ground, but that the Turks had proved too strong for him. Only late that night did Maude reply that he was satisfied with Keary's actions. They had cost the lives of 122 men, with 316 more missing in action, and 727 wounded.

That same day the Cavalry Division had been ordered to penetrate between the Diyala and the Khalis Canal to the north, with the objective of seizing the bridges over the latter at Delli Abbas and Lambarak and blocking any southerly/westerly Turkish movement in that sector. The 7th Brigade encountered Turks in strength – perhaps two and a half thousand infantry, with ten guns – on the right bank of the river near Avashik; it broke off and withdrew, to bivouac some ten kilometres away, where it was joined by the 6th Brigade. It was not clear whether these enemy troops were men of the 6th Infantry Division, retreating from Persia, or of the 14th who had withdrawn up the Diyala when Baghdad fell. Aerial reconnaissance showed that the Turks were also holding the line of the Adhaim (Al Uzayim) River (another left-bank tributary of the Tigris, further north), and were present east of it in numbers, too; these were men of XVIII Corps who had crossed the Tigris after being pushed north from Mushahida. Maude feared an attempt by these forces to link up with those on the right bank of the Diyala in order to attack Brig.-Gen. Lewin's 40th Infantry Brigade, which had occupied Diltawa and Sindiya on 24 March.

The left of Lewin's line came under artillery fire early on 27 March, as did gunboats on the river near Sindiya, and Maude instructed Marshall to assemble a force to deal with the threat while the cavalry and Keary's column continued to pin the enemy troops they confronted. By nightfall on 27 March Marshall had moved up the rest of Cayley's 13th Division, with a view to launching an attack on the twenty-ninth. The 'Affair of Duqma', as it became known, occupied the 13th Division for the day, its 39th and 40th Brigades stemming the Turkish advance. When they came to push on the following morning, they found the Turkish positions empty.

Meanwhile, more and more troops from Ali Ihsan Pasha's XIII Corps were arriving from Khanaqin; Maude received information that the regiment which had opposed Keary on the Jabal Hamrin had crossed the Diyala, to be replaced by another, and that the main body of the corps could be expected momentarily, and would also cross the Diyala, to line up on the left of XVIII Corps. He estimated the Turks' total strength at around 13,000 infantry with at least 60 guns, half of them on the Jabal Hamrin, on both banks of the Diyala, the rest between that river and the Tigris, with concentrations near Mara and in the Chaliya/Lubi region, to the west.

The Cavalry Division continued to operate between the Diyala and the Khalis Canal, encountering only small groups of Turkish troops moving northwards. By nightfall on the twenty-eighth it had become apparent that the expected surge of troops through that area to join up with XVIII Corps had not materialised, those men having opted to make for Kifri, on the road to Kirkuk, instead, though the Jabal Hamrin positions were still occupied. The following day the cavalry occupied Delli Abbas and the 13th Infantry Division regrouped at Diltawa. Intelligence reports revealed that the Turks had completed a bridge across the Diyala at Dekke, south-west of Khanaqin, and that units remaining north of the Jabal Hamrin were using it to retreat to Kifri, where Halil Pasha had now set up his headquarters, instead of being forced to traverse the Jabal Hamrin ridge in order to cross by way of the bridges on its southern side. It soon became clear that the troops facing Keary were retreating along the ridge, perhaps in the hope of escaping by the same route. That same day there were reports of Russian forces from Kermanshah having arrived, at long last, at Qasr-i-Shirin, having been held up for ten days at the Pai Tak Pass by the Turkish rearguard. The latter, and those who had held the Jabal Hamrin positions against Keary, undoubtedly saved XIII Corps from being caught between two Allied forces and enabled it to fight another day.

Though the Russians were physically poised to enter the Mesopotamia theatre, they were reluctant to do so, Gen. Radatz, in local command, believing his mission to have been limited to clearing the Turks out of Persia. Maude communicated this to Robertson, who wrote to his Russian counterpart, Alexeyev, asking him to confirm that he would co-operate. Alexeyev replied asking for material assistance (Maude sent forty-six lorryloads of supplies to Qasr-i-Shirin; the convoy came under artillery fire at Qizil Ribat (As Sadiyah), and sixteen vehicles had to be temporarily abandoned, but were later recovered), acknowledged that discipline in the Russian Army was breaking down and suggested that it would be some time before it was restored.[20] Robertson read between the lines and told Maude not to expect much of the Russians, pointing out that if they collapsed completely, Turkish forces then in the Caucasus might well be diverted to Mesopotamia. He also reconfirmed his mission in the light of these developments: as instructed (on 28 February) Maude was to 'establish British influence' over the Baghdad *vilayet*, which stretched east to the Persian border to a point some thirty kilometres north of Khanaqin, north to beyond Tikrit on the Tigris, west to Ana on the Euphrates and south, following a line roughly parallel with the river's course (beyond which there were no major settlements for hundreds of kilometres), to Nasiriya.

Maude's private opinion, expressed in letters, was that a great opportunity had been lost; had the Russians been able to make a last push, the Turks, short of rations and ammunition, would have retreated to Mosul before the spring of 1917, with all that would have meant for the campaign. The premise was that the Turks in the theatre were so diminished that even a fairly minor offensive on their left flank would have seen them in retirement. The reality was rather different: XIII Corps, reinforced, if that is the right word, by the 14th Division, amounted to 11,000 rifles, 1,350 sabres and 60 guns; its rearguard had held off Radatz's column for ten days and its vanguard had done the same to Keary in the Jabal Hamrin. Russia's I Caucasian Cavalry Corps was worn out and demoralised, while its VII Caucasian Corps was snowbound hundreds of kilometres away, and unable to assist even if *its* commanders wished to (and there is no evidence that they did). Even if the February Revolution had not occurred, it is doubtful whether the Russian forces in Persia – who had been living off the land since the previous spring, in an area not noted for its productivity – could have performed as Maude wished.

The Russians aside, Maude's imperative was to deal with the Turkish XVIII Corps, and do so before it could be reinforced, as intelligence reports suggested it soon would be, by 6,000 Turkish troops who had passed through Aleppo on their way to Mosul in mid-March, and were expected at Samarra any day.[21] Maude put the corps' strength at 4,300 infantry and 28 guns on the Adhaim, 3,200 infantry and 16 guns near Balad, on the right bank of the Tigris, and 2,200 infantry and 10 guns at Samarra, forty kilometres upstream. He ordered two columns formed, each with an infantry division, cavalry and artillery, a bridging train and a flight of aircraft. Marshall was to command that on the left bank, Maude himself that on the right, with Fane as his man on the spot. Marshall's right flank, potentially vulnerable to Ihsan's XIII Corps, was to be covered by the Cavalry Division.

By nightfall on 5 April, the head of Maude's column had reached Sumaika, on the Baghdad–Samarra railway[22] (though the bulk of its troops, of Fane's 7th Division, were still guarding the lines of communication north of Baghdad, awaiting relief by elements of Keary's 3rd Division brought back from Shahraban); Marshall's column, which chiefly comprised Cayley's 13th Division, was still in the process of assembling. By the next night Maude's column had closed up on Sumaika, and Marshall's had reached a point north of Duqma. On 7 April Maude issued an operations order: the right-bank force would advance to a line from Balad Station to a point opposite the mouth of the Adhaim; the left-bank force would drive the enemy back across the Adhaim but would not itself cross the river, and the Cavalry Division would contain the Turks behind a line from Delli Abbas to Garfa. The right-bank force advanced as planned, but was brought up five kilometres short of

Balad Station by an entrenched defensive line spanning the railway tracks and stretching, on the left, as far as the Dujail Canal, rather more than a kilometre distant, and flanked on the right by a strip of broken ground. Fane pushed the 28th Brigade forward up the line of the railway, favouring the eastern side. The advance was checked momentarily when it came within rifle range, but the 51st Sikhs made skilful use of the broken ground and outflanked the defenders; some managed to make good their escape, but, pinned in their trenches, many prisoners were taken (and so, later, were thirty very valuable railway wagons), and by 1430 the station was in British hands. The following morning, 9 April, Fane advanced to Harba, which was as far as the supply line could then reach; it was reported that the defending Turks had retreated to prepared positions at Istabulat, twelve kilometres further up the line.

The previous day Marshall had asked Maude to allow him to cross the Adhaim. Maude refused, and proved to have been prescient: on the morning of the ninth, patrols reported the threat to the right flank materialising, and in some strength. The cavalry did its best to hold it in check, but by 1030 a large formation of infantry, plus around five hundred regular cavalry, were advancing across a five-kilometre front. Around noon they halted, and began to consolidate their position, north of Bint al Hassan. That afternoon, Maude issued an estimate of the number of troops Marshall faced: 6,000, with 32 guns, on the right flank, and 4,300, with 28 guns, on the line of the Adhaim River. He announced that he would deal first with the threat on the right – the 2nd and 14th Divisions advancing from the north-east – and ordered Marshall to redistribute his forces accordingly, O'Dowda maintaining a brigade group (the 38th) on the Adhaim line while Cayley marched south overnight with the remainder of the 13th Division and a cavalry detachment, in order to be in position to launch a flanking attack on the Turks on the morning of 11 April. The nature of the terrain meant that the march of around twenty kilometres took seven hours, but by 0500 Cayley's column had crossed the railway line, and there he called a rest-halt, sending his cavalry on ahead to reconnoitre.

They found the Turks at around 0530: they were on the move in a south-westerly direction along the Delli Abbas–Diltawa road. Cayley sent the 40th Infantry Brigade forward to occupy a line of mounds west of Chaliya, facing roughly east, with the 39th Brigade echeloned out to its left and the 66th Field Artillery Brigade in support, and by 1000, by which time the Turks had reached Shaikh Muhammad Ibn Ali, they were in position; they achieved complete surprise, and the 39th Brigade, advancing, forced the Turks' right wing to fall back. Their left was unaffected, however, and was soon in contact with the Cavalry Division, reinforced by the 1/2nd Gurkhas, which, following orders, promptly withdrew. Seeing the cavalry retire (leaving the Gurkhas isolated, with around three kilometres between them and the right of the 40th Brigade), Cayley assumed they had been pushed back by the Turks.

Fearing a wheeling movement to turn his right flank, he extended in that direction.

In the meantime, Marshall[23] had received somewhat garbled reports of the way the action was developing (he knew nothing of Cayley's redeployment), and had become convinced that the Turks were trying to work around both of Cayley's flanks. At 1140 he had ordered Brig.-Gen. Thomson – who was holding a defensive line some five kilometres to the west, from the Diyala to Sindiya by way of Abu Tamar – to advance with all available forces. Thomson complied, arriving at Cayley's headquarters at 1500, by which time the enemy infantry had withdrawn out of machine gun range, and the battle had settled down into an artillery duel. With fresh troops on hand, Cayley soon went back onto the offensive, Thomson's men being sent forward on the right together with the 1/2nd Gurkhas to straighten the British line, driving the Turks back before them. By the time night fell they had taken Shaikh Muhammad Ibn Ali, and the British position extended north-westwards from there as far as the railway.

The next morning, cavalry patrols reported that the Turks had withdrawn some way, but, it soon became clear, only to consolidate their position, which now stretched north-westwards from Bint al Hassan, across the Sindiya–Delli Abbas road, at which point the line curved round to the north; some ten kilometres separated the Turkish and British lines. It proved difficult to pinpoint the enemy's location, and Cayley decided to reconnoitre before committing himself; it was early afternoon before he was confident of the situation, and two hours more before the 35th Brigade, on the right, and the 40th, on the left, began to advance. By 1800 they had reached a point level with the junction of the Khalis and Tawila Canals, and had come under artillery fire; as darkness fell the order to halt and dig in was given, the advance to continue at 0530 the following morning. During the night the 40th Brigade's 5th Wiltshires and 4th South Wales Borderers moved forward a further kilometre, the 55th Field Artillery Brigade moving up behind them. When the time came to resume the advance they were pinned down by gunfire; however, the 35th, on the right, made some progress after initial delays in front of Bint al Hassan, taking its outposts just before noon, and that allowed the British guns to be brought up and the effectiveness of counter-battery firing to be improved. By nightfall on 13 April the British line had come within long machine gun range of the Turkish positions, and there the men dug in once more.

During the morning of 14 April Maude told Marshall that he had good reason to believe that the Turks would hold their position during the day but then, with the coming of darkness, fall back into the Jabal Hamrin; he proposed to follow only as far as the line they abandoned and then to turn his attention to crossing the Adhaim, confronting the remnants of XVIII Corps and improving the resupply position of Fane's 7th Division at Harba so that it could advance on Istabulat. His information proved accurate; when the troops moved forward once more, they encountered no opposition, and at 0800 the next morning they occupied the Turkish line. However, patrols found the Turks still occupying Delli Abbas; if Maude thought their withdrawal a precursor to a retreat on Kifri and Kirkuk, he was mistaken.

Maude instructed Cayley to consolidate, withdrawing Thomson's 35th Brigade and the 1/2nd Gurkhas but leaving him 16 squadrons of cavalry. His task was to slow the advance of XIII Corps should they return, and he could call on the support of the 37th Infantry Brigade and its attached cavalry and artillery, which was drawn up at Baquba and along the line from there to Sindiya. The remainder of Marshall's column – the 35th and 38th Brigades, plus cavalry and a mixed bag of 40 guns and howitzers – was to cross the Adhaim and drive back the Turkish forces on the right bank, and occupy what was known as the Barura Peninsula – a long spit of land formed by the Tigris having doubled back upon itself – where Fane's bridging train was to construct a crossing of the Tigris. The first phase, which saw two battalions ferried across by pontoon, and a third utilising a ford some way upstream, was completed by 0800 on 18 April, and a bridge across the Adhaim was finished by noon. By 1400 the whole of the Kabaj Peninsula, as the area between the Adhaim and the Tigris upstream of its mouth was known, was in British hands, and troops were advancing against meagre opposition along the line of the old Nahrwan Canal, taking considerable numbers of prisoners. Long before nightfall the Barura Peninsula had been sealed off, and the entire Turkish 40th Regiment was in captivity.

By now Cobbe had arrived at Harba to take command of the right-bank force, and had begun to put together a plan to drive the Turks back from their positions at Istabulat. He originally estimated that the positions were held by close on ten thousand Turkish infantry, but later reduced that by a quarter, and subsequently further still; it was suggested that the reduction in numbers there indicated that men from XVIII Corps were being pulled back to Samarra, perhaps with the intention of transferring them to operate alongside XIII Corps.

An essential precursor to that attack was the construction of a Tigris crossing to allow Marshall's column to reinforce Cobbe's at need; work began early on 19 April, and a pontoon-bridge 250m in length was completed at Sinija by that evening. By that time Cobbe's force had advanced to within four kilometres of the Turkish lines at Istabulat, and was ensconced behind a high earth bank (the remains of an ancient wall) from the Jibbara Mounds, on the riverbank, to a point south of Al Khubn, on the canal. To the left of the canal the terrain was flat and featureless and, worst of all, very stony, making it next to impossible to dig in,[24] though to the right, closer to the river, it was more practicable. It was here, on the north side of the canal, that the main force of the attack would fall, Cobbe decided, even though the topography would push the assault force into a narrow front – and one controlled by two large redoubts – by the time it reached the enemy lines.

The attack was timed for the morning of 21 April, and in preparation for it, a force in brigade strength would push forward during the early hours of 20 April and occupy an advance line astride the canal, 1,500m forward of the main position, in order to facilitate the establishment of gun emplacements. That preparatory advance proceeded according to plan, and by the morning of 20 April everything was in place.

There was, however, a potential problem, not before Istabulat but along the Adhaim and the Diyala, the threat coming from XIII Corps. For some days Maude had been receiving intelligence reports of Turkish troops massing at Band-i-Adhaim ('Gates of the Adhaim'; a topographical feature rather than a settlement), and now it seemed they were moving south along the river towards Satha, while the garrison at Delli Abbas had been more than doubled, to around 2,400 infantry and three squadrons of cavalry, and was showing renewed signs of wishing to advance towards Diltawa.[25] Maude's reaction was to order Marshall to go onto the defensive, while Cobbe took on XVIII Corps and then came to his assistance.

Cobbe's plan called for the 7th Infantry Division to launch a straight-forward frontal attack on the Turks' left, supported by all available artillery. The 21st Brigade would spearhead it, securing the canal bridges as it advanced[26] on its northern side, with additional troops from the 19th Brigade poised south of the canal to exploit the 21st's success. At 0505 on 21 April, after a short artillery bombardment, the 21st Brigade advanced. They soon overran the Turkish outposts, but by 0535 were coming under heavy rifle and machine gun fire from the main defensive positions. On they pressed, taking first the northern and then the southern redoubts, whereupon the trenches between the two fell. In the process all three battalions had taken heavy casualties, and the reserve was sent to reinforce them. Meanwhile, the 19th Brigade's 92nd Punjabis had begun to advance on the far side of the canal, along the line of the railway; they took Istabulat Station at around 0645 and then advanced to within 800m of the main defensive line and dug in as best they could under heavy small-arms fire. There they were to remain for the rest of the day, securing their brigade's left flank, and were later joined by the 8th Brigade's 56th Rifles. Behind them the main body of the brigade set out to advance more than three kilometres across the open plain. Though they came under heavy fire they did not waver, the 1st Seaforth Highlanders taking seven hundred metres of the enemy front-line trenches south from the canal bank.

Fane ordered all his artillery switched to the far left, hoping that the 21st Brigade would succeed in penetrating the enemy line between canal and river; it was soon evident that the positions were too strongly held, however, and the attempt was abandoned before it had begun. Later in the afternoon the Turks made a determined attempt to take back Istabulat Station but were repulsed. Throughout the night the men of the 19th and 21st Brigades, assisted by sappers and pioneers, worked to improve their positions, while new gun emplacements were constructed to allow the artillery to be brought up to focus its attention on a ridge in front of the trench line the 19th now occupied, where many machine guns were sited. Further support would come from artillery from a column under Brig.-Gen. Thomson which Marshall had sent to find enfilading positions on the left bank. In the event, such preparations proved unnecessary, for by 0330 patrols were reporting the Turks to be withdrawing from their positions north of the canal. They appeared to be holding to the south, but in time that area, too, was reported free of enemy troops. By 0930 on 22 April, Fane's two forward brigades had advanced through the enemy positions, and had reached a line some two kilometres to the rear. At that point Fane halted them and sent the reserve 28th Brigade through their lines, the revamped formation continuing through the Istabulat ruins. They had come under sporadic artillery fire as they had advanced, but at around 1315, having reached a line some twelve kilometres on from the previous morning's starting point, they began to take rifle and machine gun fire from entrenched positions along a ridge some fifteen hundred metres away. Fane called a halt while reconnaissance patrols went out and the guns were brought up.

During the course of the morning, cavalry sent across from the left bank on the eve of the battle had embarked on a wide circling sweep out to the left, as far as the Aj Jali Canal, and had then followed its line northwards. By noon it had come into contact with the Turks on the ridge and had withdrawn just out of gunshot, and had sent back a rider to inform Fane of the situation; he returned with orders – to close up to the 28th Brigade – at 1515, and Lt.-Col. Cassels, the column's commander, complied immediately, sending his guns into action while patrols searched for the Turks' right flank. Meanwhile, the advance by Thomson's column on the left bank of the Tigris had kept pace with that of Cobbe's infantry, and had now arrived at a point within sight of the left of the Turkish line, where it was anchored on the river. Unobserved, the guns were worked forward to high ground, and began to pour shells into the Turkish positions. Fane's own artillery had also come up, and it, too, now opened fire. Under cover of the bombardment four hundred metres of trench were taken, with over 300 prisoners and two machine guns. Through the late afternoon the Turks counterattacked strongly, and it was after 1700, with barely an hour and a half of daylight left, before the positions could be said to have been consolidated. Despite Maude urging him to make all haste, Cobbe understood that he was unlikely to gain further ground that day and called a halt. Once again, when the British advance recommenced the following morning, the Turkish positions were found to be empty. The lead units reached Samarra Station by 1000. It had been torched, and attempts had been made to destroy the sixteen locomotives and much rolling stock left there,[27] but in their haste, the Turks had been clumsy, and several locomotives and around 60 per cent of the trucks were salvageable, and were soon back in service, easing enormously the supply situation up the Tigris beyond Baghdad.

The main body of XVIII Corps was found to have withdrawn all the way to Tikrit, fifty kilometres north of Samarra, where a defensive line was formed on both banks of the river. Their numbers there were put at around 5,000 rifles, with 24 guns. However, a strong detachment – around 2,400 infantry, with ten guns – had been left on the right bank some twenty kilometres north of Samarra, near Daur (Ad Dawr[28]). Samarra itself – an important settlement since at least 5500BCE, and once the Abassid Caliphate's capital, but by now very much reduced – was occupied on 24 April, and four days later the pontoon-bridge erected at Sinija was dismantled and moved up. With its rail link to Baghdad and its dominant position close to the point where the Tigris issued on to the Mesopotamian plain, this was a logical place for the British to set up an advanced base. The 7th Infantry Division was quartered there and two more infantry brigades of the 3rd Division were located between there and Baghdad Station along the line of the railway, the 8th with its headquarters at Balad, and the 9th with its at Kadhimain.

Maude's ambition to destroy XVIII Corps as a fighting force before it could link up with XIII Corps had not been achieved, but forcing it back up the Tigris had a similar effect, at least for the moment, by dramatically increasing the distance between the two groups, and he was now free to return his attention to the Turks advancing down the Adhaim and the Diyala Rivers. Reports from Gen. Radatz suggested that the Turkish rearguard facing him across the Diyala had been reduced to less than three thousand men; those who had left had moved towards Band-i-Adhaim, where around 5,000 infantry were expected to be assembled, and there were over two thousand more – what remained of the 14th Division – at Tulul en Nor, halfway to the Adhaim's confluence with the Tigris, and moving south.

When Maude issued a new operations order to Marshall, on 23 April, it was that latter force on which he focused, telling him to despatch troops sufficient to deal with it immediately. Marshall pleaded for time to re-assemble his assets – chiefly to recover the column Thomson had led up the left bank of the Tigris to support Cobbe, which was now at Kadisiya – and Maude agreed to a twenty-four-hour delay; the following day he 'suggested' that perhaps Cayley's force was unnecessarily strong, and Marshall ordered it reduced by two infantry battalions (of the 39th Brigade), half its artillery and some cavalry, which were to march to join him.

That evening Marshall left two battalions of infantry and some field guns to defend the Barura Peninsula, and another battalion and a section of guns near the mouth of the Adhaim, and the rest of his force moved north towards Dahuba. His main force would make a night march on a compass bearing to a *nullah* thought to be about fifteen hundred metres south-west of the Turks' prepared positions, in time to launch a frontal attack the following morning, while Thomson's column marched to threaten the right flank. The 7th Cavalry Brigade was to loop around to the right to cut the Turks' lines of communication and prevent reinforcements from coming up from Satha.

Marshall's maps were unreliable, and the 38th Brigade, in the lead, found itself in contact with enemy troops as soon as it became light. Marshall told O'Dowda to await the arrival of Thomson's column (which had gone even further astray, and was by now some three kilometres *north* of the Turkish forces), but when reports from the cavalry indicated that the Turks were withdrawing, Marshall changed his mind and told O'Dowda to press on. He brought a third battalion up, and together they pushed forward under heavy but erratic rifle and machine gun fire and the cover of their own artillery, driving the Turks before them and occupying their positions, while a fourth battalion moved up the right bank of the Adhaim and half of a fifth kept pace on the left. By about 0800, the 7th Cavalry came into contact with the head of a Turkish column moving south-west from Tulul en Nor. 'V' Battery, Royal Horse Artillery, was in the process of unlimbering its guns when Turks – the 14th Division, in retreat – appeared from the south and began to form up in close order, offering excellent targets. Something close to panic ensued when they were engaged, and the Turks fled for the river, and it was only the appearance of Turkish reinforcements from the north which prevented their complete annihilation.

By now – around 1100 – the temperature had already climbed well above 40°C, and Marshall called a halt while his men regrouped and recovered from twelve hours' virtual non-stop marching and fighting. There was no shade on the open plain, but for once, due to the proximity of the Adhaim, they had adequate supplies of drinking water. When Marshall reported the situation to Maude, he told him to press on as soon as possible, re-engage with the 14th Division before it could recover, and then deal with the rest of XIII Corps' troops in that sector.

As the afternoon wore on, there were signs of unrest in the Turkish lines, and that, combined with intelligence sent from Army headquarters, suggested that the Turks' 2nd Division would not stand at Tulul en Nor, but would retreat towards the Jabal Hamrin that night. Maude told Marshall he was sending extra artillery up to the left bank of the Adhaim (from Baquba by way of Sindiya), and detaching the 40th Brigade from Cayley's command to join him (by way of the Barura positions), and Marshall began to prepare an order for the next day's operations, essentially, to pursue the enemy as closely as possible, to prevent him from regrouping. In the event he was forestalled; at around 1830 he received aerial reconnaissance reports that the Turks were already on the move. With his own assets still fairly widely distributed, there was no question of him pressing them closely. Maude did not hector him for once, saying 'there is no object on calling on troops for unusual exertion', but added: 'But you are to move as early as practicable and secure Band-i-Adhaim. . . . Report when you are ready to move.'

In fact, the next morning's departure was fairly leisurely – the main body of the column moving off at 0930, following an advanced guard comprising the 7th Cavalry and the 35th Infantry Brigade – and so was the day's progress; the column bivouacked for the night of 25 April at Tulul en Nor, having covered no more than fifteen kilometres, with lengthy rest stops. The following day the column advanced no further than Satha, but during the night and the early hours of 27 April, the 35th Infantry Brigade, together with cavalry, field artillery, a howitzer battery and one of 60-pounder guns, moved up four or five kilometres further, Thomson occupying positions in sight of the Turks' own, on both sides of the river near the village of Adhaim. His instructions were to familiarise himself with the terrain and register his artillery.

Thomson's reconnaissance suggested that the left (eastern) side of the Adhaim – little more than a stream except when in spate, the river meandered in a bed two to three kilometres wide, fringed by bluffs and cliffs up to ten metres high – was marginally more attractive than the right, which was dominated by an encroaching spur ('the Boot', so called because its eastern extremity opened out to a transverse ridge). On the left the Turkish line was anchored on a hillock ('the Mound'), whence it stretched to the riverbank cliff, with secondary positions and gunpits to the rear. On the right it ran from the Boot to a ridge of high ground about three kilometres away, once again with supporting positions and gunpits to the rear. In all the Turkish defensive line was some six kilometres in length and was, all agreed, skilfully placed and provided excellent fields of fire. It was manned, Marshall estimated, by around 6,000 men, the 2nd Division holding the west bank, the 14th on the east.

During the daylight hours of 27 April there was little activity beyond the occasional Turkish shell, but after dark two battalions of the 38th Brigade crossed the river and moved up to join the men Thomson had sent across. The following day registration of the guns commenced; it was hindered by poor visibility, but that allowed the newly arrived 40th Brigade to be pushed forward in relative safety to relieve the mixed bag from the 35th and 38th, and during the night additional artillery was brought up. Attempts to complete registering the guns the following day were hampered once more by high winds which kicked up thick clouds of dust and grounded the aircraft.

By nightfall the 40th Brigade was lined up around two kilometres short of the Turkish positions on the east bank across a front about two kilometres wide, stretching to a feature known as 'Three Ridges', with four batteries of field artillery, most of the cavalry and the reserve 38th Brigade to the rear. As soon as it was fully dark, the 38th Brigade was to take up a position northeast of Three Ridges, facing west. On the other side of the river, the 35th Brigade, plus two Gurkha battalions from the 37th, were drawn up at and west of an isolated mound in the river bed ('the Island'), three kilometres back from the Turkish line, across a rather wider front.

Throughout the night there was to be a general artillery bombardment which, at 0500, was to be concentrated for 36 minutes on the east-bank trenches. The 40th and 38th Brigades would converge under cover of that bombardment and take the positions. The 38th took the Mound with little opposition, but discovered that it was not the key redoubt it had been thought to be, but more in the nature of a masking position; having taken it, the three forward battalions came under very heavy fire from a trench line to the north and from a series of mounds to the west, which separated them from the 40th Brigade. That brigade's lead battalions – the 4th South Wales Borderers and the 8th Cheshires – carried their primary objectives easily, too, and by 0540 the latter had reached and passed the second line, advancing into the village and driving the Turks before them. However, instead of stopping then, and consolidating, as their orders had specified,[29] they set off in pursuit of the fleeing enemy. To their right the Borderers also overran the second line, or so they thought; in fact, by the purest chance they had found a wide gap in it, and had bypassed the positions themselves. Seeing the Cheshires well ahead, they then hurried to catch up.

Around 0615, Turkish guns started to shell these now isolated battalions, and massed machine guns located along the transverse 'foot' of the Boot joined in. The Cheshires and the Borderers, caught in the open, took such cover as they could, some in firing positions facing west, others in the gulleys and watercourses running down to the river. They had long outrun their communications wire, and it was not until around 0700 that the 40th Brigade's headquarters learned of their predicament; straight away, Brig.-Gen. Lewin ordered his two reserve battalions, the 5th Wiltshires and the 8th Royal Welch Fusiliers, to push forward to support them but not to advance beyond the village. By now the wind had got up again, and visibility was much reduced by dust and sand, and the Turks had taken full advantage of that, sending a regimental-sized force from the 2nd Division to cross the Adhaim to the north. They looped around to the east, and came upon the scattered and disorganised British infantry from the right and rear, forcing them to withdraw in the direction of the village, capturing many during hand-to-hand fighting in the process. Eventually, exhausted and almost out of ammunition, the survivors reached the relative safety of what had been the Turkish second line. Owing to the poor visibility, artillery support had been withdrawn, and was not reinstated until some time after 0900, when the guns took the village under fire and forced the Turks there to withdraw. In the meantime, the 38th, ignorant of the 40th's plight, had managed to make very little headway against the positions to the north of the Mound and had also come under fire from the Turks sent to take the Borderers and Cheshires in the rear; when Marshall instructed O'Dowda to push his battalions on towards the village, he replied that he was unable to comply.

On the west bank, the 35th Brigade's initial task had been limited to adopting a defensive posture lest the Turks should counterattack, save for the

102nd Grenadiers, who had worked their way along the foot of the cliff towards the Boot. Later the 2/9th Gurkhas came up on their right, to the meagre shelter of a linear mound, but could proceed no further due to the sheer weight of fire coming from the positions along the 'calf' of the Boot. Those positions were subjected to a heavy artillery bombardment which lasted from 0700 to 1000 but seemingly had little real effect, though under cover of it a second Gurkha battalion, the 2/4th, was sent up to extend the line further to the right. As the morning progressed, there was no reduction in the weight of rifle and machine gun fire coming from the Boot, or from artillery posted north of there and of the Mound. Soon after midday the wind began to drop, however, and as the dust settled large numbers of Turkish infantry were seen to be moving north-eastwards. Fearing this was the pre-cursor of a further attack on the left-bank positions, which were much weakened by the losses the Cheshires and the South Wales Borderers had sustained, Marshall ordered one of the Gurkha battalions still in reserve on the right – the 1/2nd – across the river, together with the howitzers. The move was completed by 1500, but in the event, no attack materialised. As night fell the situation remained unchanged, and Marshall began making preparations for a night-time assault on the Boot; it proved to be unnecessary for the Turks withdrew into the Jabal Hamrin under cover of darkness. By AJ Barker's reckoning, this had been the bloodiest engagement of the entire Mesopotamia Campaign, in terms of losses as a proportion of those committed.

The Battle of the Boot, as it became known, was the last in the offensive cycle which had commenced with the advance on Kut, on 14 December. It had been an expensive campaign, costing the British some 18,000 battle casualties (and well over twice that number hospitalised due to illness in March and April alone), but now it was time to call a halt. As the spring progressed and became summer, so the temperatures rose still higher, until by July the daytime norm in Baghdad stood at around 50°C, and locals 'proclaimed it the hottest season in the memory of man'. With the hinterland of Baghdad cleared, and the city secured, there was no appetite in such conditions for chasing the Turks into the mountains; that could wait for autumn.

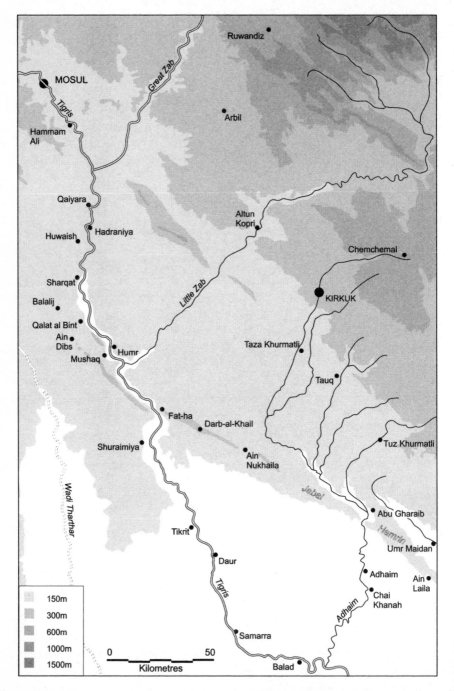

8. Mesopotamia – Mosul to the Adhaim

5

On to Mosul

In the spring of 1917 there was widespread satisfaction in British government circles that the gamble taken in appointing the relatively inexperienced Stanley Maude to command in Mesopotamia had paid off so well. However, that there was good news from that theatre now did not mean there was not still the price to be paid for earlier malpractice, and come mid-May, the sky above Westminster was suddenly dark with proverbial chickens – loosed at Kut the previous year – coming home to roost.

Prime Minister Asquith resisted calls for publication of the relevant papers during a debate in the House of Commons on 20 July 1916, citing the need to maintain unity, but was ultimately forced to announce he would set up an inquiry; he envisaged a parliamentary select committee, made up exclusively of members, which he could expect to control, but in the event was forced to accept a Special Commission, which would allow the enlistment of non-parliamentarians.

The Commission interviewed one hundred witnesses and deliberated for months, and its report (one member, Josiah Wedgwood MP, dissenting;[1] he presented a minority report) was delivered to the War Cabinet on 17 May 1917. It found the campaign necessary, but ill-run from the outset, especially the division of responsibilities between Delhi and London (which had by then been resolved, of course), singling out the 'untoward advance' on Baghdad in October 1915 as 'an offensive movement based on political and military miscalculations, and attempted with tired and insufficient forces, and inadequate preparation', and blamed Nixon, Hardinge, Duff, Barrow (the Military Secretary at the India Office[2]) and Chamberlain, in that order, plus the entire War Cabinet which had 'made decisions on the principle that they should decide military policy'. It then went on to criticise virtually every aspect of the handling of the campaign in some detail, particularly supply, transport, reinforcement, medical facilities and the maintenance of troop morale. Corrosive criticism, but in a real sense this was all water under the bridge anyway, for those named had already been removed: Nixon had long been replaced by Lake, who had himself been replaced by Maude; Hardinge had given way to Chelmsford and Duff had been supplanted by Monro. (Chamberlain, the one survivor, resigned as Secretary of State on 17 July 1917, during the debate on the report in the House of Commons, after taking all the blame upon himself. He was replaced by ES Montagu.) Eventually it was accepted that, since they had been granted immunity from prosecution by the Commission's enabling legislation, the civilians could not be hauled before the courts; Hardinge got off scot-free, and the fate of Nixon and Duff, together with that of the three senior army medical officers, Babtie, MacNeese and Hathaway,[3] was put into the hands of the Army Council. It deliberated, considered how courts-martial could be constituted, and then, when it was pointed out that the enabling legislation gave these men immunity too, dropped the matter and demanded 'reasons in writing' instead. As a consequence Nixon was officially exonerated (but never recovered from the shame he felt, and died just a few years later), as were Babtie and MacNeese, while Hathaway, the junior of the three surgeons-general, was called upon to resign. Duff submitted no reasons for his actions but took matters into his own hands instead; he took his own life on 20 January 1918.

The events of March 1917 in Petrograd had come as a bombshell, of course. There were attempts to convince the Russians to remain active in Persia over the spring and summer, based on a series of tentative proposals to fund their operations there, but ultimately they came to very little. On 30 September, the British liaison officer with Przevalski's headquarters, Lt.-Col. A P Wavell,[4] summed up the situation in a signal to Maude: 'British gold may keep the Russian troops in Persia, but it will not make them fight. The old Russian Army is dead, quite dead. Our efforts, therefore, to resuscitate it stand useless.' He failed to take into account the fact that revolution in Russia was not yet a fait accompli; the existence of counter-revolutionary forces within the Russian ranks in Persia meant there *would* be further efforts, and they would even pay minor dividends, but he was right in as far as the campaign in Mesopotamia was concerned. There, Britain was now well and truly alone, and would be until hostilities ceased late in 1918.

With or without the Russians to fight alongside him, Maude needed to know what he was likely to face when hostilities recommenced. The Turks *could*, his intelligence staff reckoned, conceivably have eleven extra infantry divisions at Mosul by the end of September, each with twenty-four field guns and four heavy guns (though whether they had transport for them, and could support them, was another matter). Add that to the number of troops thought to be in theatre already, and the total came to almost 100,000 rifles and over 450 guns, 10,000 of whom (the 46th Division at Ruwandiz) were still focused exclusively on the Russians. Against that Maude had five divisions at and around Baghdad (the 15th having been brought up from Nasiriya[5]), and with further reinforcements either on their way or promised, he would have 75,000 infantry and 284 field and heavy guns available by the autumn. If the Russians continued to sit on their hands – or, worse still, decamped – the shortfall would have to be made up ... Maude had been reluctant to ask for substantially more men,[6] but faced with facts as stark as these (and reports that Turkish troops were already leaving the Caucasus and moving south), his hand was forced. He could not take the risk of being outnumbered, and needed an additional division, he told Robertson. The CIGS agreed, as did Monro, and preparations to constitute one, as the 17th Infantry Division,[7] were put in hand in India. In September it was also decided to send a further composite cavalry brigade – one British and two Indian regiments – to the theatre (it was constituted as the 11th Cavalry Brigade, but was not up to strength until the year's end; it would be commanded by Cassels, now promoted to brigadier) and at the end of that month it was decided to send yet another infantry division, to be formed as the 18th, also from new recruitment in India, to Mesopotamia early the following year. During the summer hiatus Maude also received additional armoured car units,[8] more Stokes mortar batteries[9] and machine gun companies, an additional anti-aircraft section, and ten motor transport companies: six equipped with vans and lorries, two with ambulances and two more with artillery tractors. In addition to these reinforcements, there had been some modification to the composition of individual units, particularly within the artillery, and the total number of guns Maude would have available when hostilities recommenced was 324.

On a local level, Maude's main concern during the summer of 1917 was to rest his men,[10] while consolidating his perimeter positions,[11] especially along the Jabal Hamrin, and building up stockpiles of supplies. He saw to the men's welfare by constructing tented encampments close to the rivers, with as much in the way of recreational facilities as could be obtained (and some 20,000 all-ranks were sent out of the country on leave). In order to make real progress towards improving his supply position he had to look to his infrastructure, and that meant constructing railways, improving roads and building bridges: by September there were seven over the Diyala, one over the Adhaim, five over the Tigris at and above Baghdad, and three on the Euphrates at and below Falluja.

Only once during the period 1 May–31 July did Maude embark on a military operation.[12] On 5 July, he announced his intention of occupying Dhibban, up the Euphrates from Falluja, as a precursor to rebuilding the embankment closing the Sakhlawiya Canal, and decided to go a step further and launch a raid on Ramadi, thirty kilometres further west, 'to surprise and drive away its garrison, taking as many prisoners and as much booty as possible', though there was actually a second and perhaps more valid objective: to win over the local Anaiza and Dulaim Arabs in the hope that they would interfere with Turkish lines of communication with lower Syria, as followers of Sherif Hussein of Mecca, whipped up by the likes of TE Lawrence, were doing in the Hejaz. If the result was little short of a disaster, it was only because relatively small numbers of men were involved, and that apart, the most interesting aspect of the operation was its use, for the first time in that theatre, of motor vehicles to carry troops into battle.

*

In the sense that they were fighting the same enemy, there was to be a degree of co-ordination (at General Staff level in London) between Maude's endeavours in Mesopotamia and those of Allenby in Palestine, but there was no co-operation. Thus, when Allenby was unable to return to the offensive until October, instead of September as planned, it was unnecessary for Maude to change his plans.

He made his first move on 20 August, sending a brigade group under Brig.-Gen. Thomson to occupy Shahraban; the Turks fell back before it, offering very little resistance and withdrawing into the Jabal Hamrin. That, however, was an isolated manoeuvre, designed to clear the way for a link-up with the Russians on the Diyala north of the Hamrin ridge if they reappeared, and it was not until the second week of September that he made his next, to take Ramadi.

That decision was taken in the light of sustained (though unconfirmed) reports of Turkish reinforcements being assembled in the vicinity of Aleppo to descend the Euphrates[13] and congregate at Hit, just above Ramadi, with the intention of retaking Falluja and then Baghdad. The responsibility for implementing it was given to Brooking and the 15th Infantry Division. Its 50th Brigade was already at Falluja, but moving the rest of the division there from the vicinity of Baghdad, and then the entire ensemble on upriver to Madhij, chosen as the assembly area for the attack, was far from straight-forward, the road in very poor repair,[14] and it was 26 September before the force was concentrated there. Aerial reconnaissance showed the Turks holding the Mushaid Ridge only lightly, and that their main lines of defence were on its far side, to the east and south-east of the town, stretching as far as the Aziziya Canal. Brooking deduced from this that the Turks expected a re-run of the abortive attack in July, and worked towards encouraging that belief in making his dispositions. In fact his intention was to push his cavalry brigade, with 'V' Battery, RHA, and reinforced by four armoured cars, in a wide flanking movement out to the west of the town to take up a blocking position astride the road to Hit, while two infantry brigades crossed the Euphrates Valley Canal out of sight of the enemy positions (having first taken Mushaid Ridge), advanced across the face of the defensive line and turned to attack from the south.

When the offensive opened, early on 28 September, the ridge and the outlying hillocks south-east of it were taken easily, despite some little con-fusion between the 12th Brigade and the 42nd as to which was supporting and which was taking the lead. The forward Turkish positions were on the Aziziya Ridge, to the south of Ramadi, and Ramadi Ridge, to the south-east. The defence was certainly competent, and though both ridges were taken that day, in the face of artillery from the main positions further back the Aziziya Ridge had to be evacuated before nightfall.

By then, the main body of the cavalry, with a horse battery and armoured cars, had arrived to the west of the town and were occupying the line from the Euphrates across the Hit road. They came under attack just after the moon set, at 0300, and replied with massed machine guns (twelve Vickers and forty-eight less effective Hotchkiss guns), together with the guns of 'V' Battery, at a range of little more than 200 metres.

At 0615 elements of the 12th Brigade began advancing towards the Aziziya Ridge once more; despite some initial setbacks, by 0700 they were pressing on to the western end of the Shaikh Farajah Ridge beyond, from which they believed they could control the only bridge over the Aziziya Canal. In fact, that was not the case, and it was necessary to fight their way along the canal and take the bridge, which was secured at some cost. By 0930 the Turks had begun to surrender in significant numbers, and by 1100 the capitulation had become complete. In all, 3,456 prisoners were taken, together with ten guns, three 1-pounder pom-poms and twelve machine guns.

While Brooking was still assembling his force at Madhij, north of Baghdad Maude ordered Brig.-Gen. Norton to occupy Mandali, on the right flank, with the 7th Cavalry Brigade, both to cut the Turks off from the agricultural produce of the area and as the precursor of a much larger operation to drive them out of the southern end of the Jabal Hamrin. Though Mandali was important to the Turks, there were only small numbers of troops present, and they retreated when the British horsemen rode into view, early on the morning of 28 September.

On 7 October he issued orders to Marshall to begin the second stage, and occupy the ridge up to the line of the left bank of the Diyala River, which bisected it.[15] Marshall's plan hinged on a frontal assault on the Turks' prepared positions around Delli Abbas, to hold them while he developed a flanking attack on their left. He divided his forces into three columns, the left (Cayley) and the right (Egerton) fairly evenly balanced in terms of infantry – eight and seven battalions respectively – but with the latter markedly stronger in cavalry and artillery, and the centre (Thomson) with just four infantry battalions but a strong artillery contingent including both 60-pounder and 6-in guns. Once again, the force would be partially mechanised, with almost 800 Ford vans as well as armoured cars.

Concentration of forces began on 16 October, and on the eighteenth the left group moved into positions north of Delli Abbas, with its right flank curved around to connect with the centre group's left; the right group had a brigade at Shahraban, another south of Tel Ibara and the 7th Cavalry Brigade at Mandali, and over the following night its infantry redeployed east of Tel Ibara as far as the small settlement of Chahriz, at the very tip of the ridge. Just before dawn on 19 October, the 37th Brigade, with the 7th Cavalry on its right and leaving the 36th as a reserve, skirted the tip of the ridge and began to advance towards Qizil Ribat, encountering no opposition. By midday, and now due south of the town, it established contact (by heliograph) with Thomson's 35th Brigade, which had in the meantime crossed the Ruz Canal and gained the heights of the ridge near the Diyala Gorge. It, too, had been unopposed. The 38th Infantry Brigade, part of Cayley's force, had meanwhile occupied Mansuriya village, and was coming under artillery fire from the foothills of the ridge to the north, from positions secured by entrenched infantry; with over six hundred metres of flat, open ground to cross before those trenches, Marshall called a halt until nightfall. In fact, it was dawn before the advance came, and was unopposed, the Turks having withdrawn in the meantime. By midday on 20 October all Marshall's objectives had been achieved, and in addition Cayley's men were occupying the right bank of the Diyala from the village of Mujariyin, west of Mansuriya, to a point some two kilometres north of there. The 7th Cavalry had reached Qizil Ribat and found it, too, empty of Turks, while the armoured cars which had reconnoitred the road towards Khanaqin for ten kilometres also reported the Turks gone. Over the course of the next weeks it became clear that Turkish forces had been withdrawn north of a line Narin Köpri–Shaikh Baba.

As the Turkish XIII Corps was withdrawing, XVIII Corps on the Tigris was advancing, in an attempt to relieve the pressure on it. On 22 October, patrols from the outpost north of Samarra encountered large bodies of infantry moving south on the right bank of the Tigris; they reached the vicinity of Huwaislat that evening, when another, smaller, column on the left bank reached Eski Baghdad. Maude responded by instructing the Cavalry Division to assemble around Sindiya and sent a brigade from the 17th Division up to Balad, and Cobbe ordered the 3rd Division's 8th Infantry and 4th Field Artillery Brigades up to Samarra. Maude suggested to Cobbe that he should attack straight away, before the Turks had time to deploy into a defensive position, but Cobbe disagreed, preferring to wait twenty-four hours for his reinforcements. When he did go onto the offensive, early on 24 October, it was to discover that the Turks had retired, their attempt to draw off British troops from the Jabal Hamrin having backfired thanks to Maude's very considerable local superiority in numbers.

In fact, the attempt rebounded with considerable force, for having moved additional infantry and artillery brigades up to Samarra, Maude now decided to capitalise on that, and press on up the Tigris to confront the Turks on the right bank, across from Daur, and at Auja and Tikrit with the object of driving them north by fifty kilometres, to the vicinity of Fat-ha (Al Fathah), at the northern extremity of the Jabal Hamrin, where it came down to the Tigris, and destroying or capturing anything of military value they left behind. He believed these positions to be held by a total of around six thousand infantry and forty guns. He issued an operational order on 28 October, the attack on the positions across from Daur to commence at dawn on 2 November.

The Turkish positions opposite Daur were arranged in two tiers, the first line forming a marked salient following a dry watercourse and then the edge of a plateau of higher ground before descending, on the left, into the floodplain across from the village itself, while the main positions ran west to east some three kilometres to the rear of the salient's point, before tailing round to the north as they, too, descended to the river. The ground to the south-west of the positions, from which direction the infantry attack would come, was open and undulating, and on average some twenty metres above the level of the floodplain.

The infantry's night march to the assembly point south-west of the Turks' positions – under the light of a full moon – went off without a hitch, but the Cavalry Division missed its mark and halted short of its allotted location; when it tried to rectify the mistake, just after first light, it came under heavy fire and was unable to support the assault. In the event, it mattered little; the 28th Brigade, in the lead, was soon through the Turkish first-line trenches, and though there was more resistance from the second line, it, too, was penetrated by 0930, when the leading battalions were advancing towards the river with the defenders in full retreat.

Around mid-afternoon Cobbe signalled Maude that he proposed to withdraw to Samarra, but the commander-in-chief, convinced that the Turks would not stand, instructed him to remain in place until he had established whether that was the case; if not he could withdraw, but otherwise he was to proceed to Tikrit and destroy any military stores he found there, and Cobbe ordered the men to bivouac in place. The following morning, while the 19th Infantry Brigade occupied Auja, Cobbe's cavalry pushed on towards the town and found it held in strength. Cobbe gave orders to return to the previous night's positions, intending to return to Samarra the following morning, 4 November.

At 0710 he received a despatch from Maude telling him to remain where he was 'in consequence of certain developments on the whole front' – by which he seems to have meant Allenby's convincing victory over the Turks at Beersheba on 31 October – and report his dispositions. At midday he signalled once more, saying he had received confirmation that the Turks would retire, and that they were already moving *matériel*, and suggesting that the cavalry moved to a position north-west of the town and the infantry and artillery moved into an attacking position under cover of darkness. Cobbe replied that he would be in position to attack at dawn the following day. Maude told him to proceed, but to take more time if he needed it.

The units designated for the assault were in place an hour before sunrise, with the 8th Infantry Brigade in the lead, poised to occupy a deep wadi about two kilometres back from the enemy trench line, with the 4th Field Artillery Brigade in close support. Cobbe's plan of action called for Maj.-Gen. Fane, the 7th Infantry Division's commander, to produce a detailed operational plan even as events were unfolding, using information coming back to him from his spearhead units. He was able to do that by 0900, the 47th Sikhs leading the 8th Brigade having by then established themselves in broken ground within rifle-shot of the defenders. He ordered the 8th to attack over a five-hundred-metre front under a barrage from all available guns, and brought the 19th Brigade up in support as far as the lip of the wadi.

The Turks put up strong resistance, their artillery being particularly effect-ive, and it was over two hours before Fane's own guns had been properly co-ordinated and the infantry assault could begin. The 8th Brigade's three attack battalions stormed through the Turkish positions, finding them only lightly held but taking heavy casualties from artillery fire and enfilading machine guns from a strongpoint on the left, and were soon in the third-line trenches; the reserve battalion was sent up just in time to fight off a counterattack, and three battalions of the 19th Brigade arrived in support, and together they worked to strengthen their position. At this point, Fane had intended the 19th Brigade to pass through the 8th and push on northwards, but the latter was so heavily engaged that this was impractical. A second counterattack was repulsed in mid-afternoon, but the enfilading fire was still taking a toll, and it was not until 1645, after a fifteen-minute artillery barrage, that men of the Seaforth Highlanders and the 125th Rifles were able to take the strongpoint from which much of it was emanating, and then press on further northwards.

Throughout the day so far, the 7th Cavalry, off to the infantry's left, had had little to do save act as a deterrent, but seeing the strongpoint taken, its commander decided to intervene in order to screen the 19th Brigade's left flank. He sent two squadrons of the 13th Hussars forward to locate the first-line trenches and they did so unopposed, but then espied three or four hundred Turkish infantry a kilometre away to their left, and turned to charge them. The Hussars achieved little by their action, and were very lucky not to have been savaged by machine gun fire, especially on their return journey.

As darkness fell, the infantry consolidated its gains, patrolling in strength and meeting little opposition; by 0100 an east–west line as far as the river, some way to the north of Tikrit, had been secured and by daybreak it was clear that the remaining Turks had abandoned their positions, destroyed what stores they could not move (including the *Julnar*, captured at Kut) and withdrawn; it was later established that they had in fact retreated as far as Fat-ha, as Maude's intelligence had predicted. However, there had never been any intention of occupying Tikrit permanently at that stage, and by the morning of 10 November most of the British troops had been pulled back to Samarra, with the rest to follow, the cavalry proceeding to Sadiya.

Eight days later, Lt.-Gen. Sir Stanley Maude died, of cholera. His sudden death left the army in Mesopotamia in disarray, for in addition to having had a penchant for interfering in relatively minor matters, Maude had been extremely secretive as to his plans and intentions, and had written nothing down and confided in no one; his death had an effect 'analogous to the sudden shut-down in the power-house controlling a large electrical scheme', in the words of A J Barker. Marshall, selected to replace him (he was succeeded as corps commander by Egerton; Thomson moved up to command the 14th Division), was thus left in limbo, and it is perhaps fortunate that Maude's death did not occur in the middle of an active campaign. Robertson, the CIGS, who was instrumental in selecting Marshall just as he had been in Maude's case, wrote to him on 22 November to restate the instructions he had given his predecessor, taking the opportunity to stress the defensive nature of Marshall's task and asking him to consider how his forces could be reduced[16] since the Turks were believed to be in no position to attack him.

As Maude lay dying, a rather more momentous event occurred in Russia: the Bolshevists finally overthrew Kerensky's Provisional Government and immediately signalled their intention to withdraw from the Triple Entente. This put a different complexion on matters both in Persia and in the Caucasus, but in the event had only a very limited effect in the other theatres of the war in the Middle East, since Enver elected not to withdraw troops from the Caucasus in large numbers (see Chapter 9).

During the last week of November, sure, now, that he would have to secure the Persian border area himself, Marshall planned an offensive aimed at clearing the Turks out of the Jabal Hamrin once and for all. He put their total numbers in the region at no more than about 3,500 rifles with around 25 guns, the majority of them in the high ground of the ridge and along the western bank of the Diyala north of it, and planned to drive them out by an advance northwards on a broad front from Suhaniya to Qizil Ribat, to converge on Qara Tepe, combined with a movement up the Adhaim by a cavalry column which was to cut the lines of communication between Qara Tepe and Kifri (it found it impossible to penetrate the Turks' defensive positions on the Adhaim and withdrew, as Marshall had instructed if that were the case, on the morning of 3 December).

Egerton's plan called for a general advance during the night of 2/3 December. The 14th Division's 35th and 37th Brigades were to cross the Diyala below and above Qizil Ribat respectively, a detachment of Cossacks under Col. Lazar Feodorovitch Bicherakhov – which had been sent south by Baratov some weeks earlier to disperse a column of Persian gendarmes, and had then continued, to link up with the British – advancing as far as Kishuk, where it would be joined by elements of the 12th Cavalry; the right wing would then fold inwards, containing the Turks' left flank. The 13th Division's 38th and 40th Brigades would move up to an east–west line south of Abu Zenabil during the night, then advance towards Suhaniya and the Sakaltutan Pass. The second phase of the operation would see the 35th and 40th Brigades – with Cayley, more experienced at handling a division than the newly elevated Thomson, in overall command – advance on Qara Tepe by way of Narin Köpri, the former north, and the latter south, of the Narin River, while the 37th and 38th consolidated the gains made so far.

Only with some difficulty were the 14th Division's brigades able to cross the Diyala, the fords being few and far between and suitable bridging sites proving elusive. Battalions of both came under fire in the process, and the delays allowed the Turkish forces on the far side to retreat in good order. The situation did not improve materially when they had crossed the river either, the going being very difficult. By mid-afternoon the 37th Brigade was still short of its objective, Tel Baradan, and since the 35th had been ordered not to push forward from the riverbank until it had reached that location, it, too, was stalled. In the event, the 37th got no further than Tel Baradan that day, and the 14th Division bivouacked for the night with many of its men still within sight of the Diyala.

To the south of the Jabal Hamrin, the 13th Division's brigades found conditions easier until they reached the foothills of the ridge, and then they, too, slowed as they came to terms with the broken ground, the field artillery, in particular, finding it very difficult to locate routes and being forced to make long detours from the direct line. By dusk, the 38th Brigade had reached a line running north-east from a point just beyond Suhaniya, and settled there for the night, while to the left the 40th Brigade had made rather better progress, and were within sight of the Sakaltutan Pass, where they were stopped by well-sited machine guns and obliged to withdraw.

The next day, 4 December, proved to be generally more productive. The 40th Brigade found the Sakaltutan Pass free of Turks and occupied it, and elements of the 12th Cavalry passed through their positions, forded the Narin, and linked up with the rest of the regiment and the Cossacks advancing from Kishuk; they then made a looping march to the north of Qara Tepe, intending to cut the road to Kifri, but met solid opposition. In the late afternoon the Russians, both men and horses weakened by their march through famine-ridden Persia, withdrew to Kishuk; the British cavalry also retired, to rejoin the 35th and 40th Infantry Brigades which had by then converged on Narin Köpri and had bivouacked. With that, the first phase of the operation could be said to have been concluded, and that night Egerton issued orders for the second – to drive the enemy from the hills immediately to the north of Qara Tepe – to begin the following morning.

The 35th Brigade skirted Qara Tepe to the east, the 40th to the west. The defensive line was some two kilometres north of the town; after offering solid resistance initially the Turks suddenly crumbled and ran, the British declining to pursue. In terms of the amount of damage inflicted on the enemy, the operation was somewhat disappointing, but the territorial gain, though small, was significant, the British now holding a line from Khanaqin to the Sakaltutan Pass.

By the beginning of December, the newly recruited 18th Division had arrived at Baghdad.[17] By Robertson's reckoning that gave Marshall more men than he could conceivably need,[18] and on 4 December the CIGS asked him to choose an Indian division – other than the 17th or 18th – to be transferred to Palestine. He selected Fane's 7th, and it left for Egypt before the month's end, its place in I Corps being taken by the 17th Division. Later that month the

11th Cavalry Brigade came up to full strength, the 7th Hussars and 'W' Battery, RHA, having arrived in theatre, and by the end of the year the heavy artillery had been reorganised, each corps now having six batteries each, in two groups of one heavy and two siege batteries, with another of the latter being allocated to each of the 15th and 18th Divisions.

Having driven the Turks north from Qara Tepe, Marshall stuck firmly to the terms of reference Robertson had set out for him, and, with one exception, did not engage in further offensive operations until early March. By mid-way through January, his dispositions, in outline, were as follows: III Corps occupied the region east of the Tigris, the 14th Division east of the Diyala – with a brigade group spread out across the area between Qasr-i-Shirin and Mirjana, north of Qizil Ribat, another on the Kurdarra River and the remainder at Shahraban – and the 13th Division to the west of the Diyala, with a brigade group in the Jabal Hamrin and the remainder between Delli Abbas and Sindiya. I Corps occupied the region west of the Tigris, centred on Samarra, less one brigade temporarily attached to the 18th Division. The 15th Division was on the Euphrates, with a brigade at Ramadi, another at Madhij and the third at Falluja. The 18th Division, not yet at full strength but with the 52nd Brigade of the 17th attached, was at Baghdad. The Cavalry Division was based at Sadiya, but had detached one regiment to I Corps and two more to III Corps, while the 11th Cavalry Brigade was at Baghdad. Those dispositions remained largely unchanged until March, when, in response to a request from the Chief of the Imperial General Staff – Sir Henry Wilson, who replaced Sir William Robertson on 18 February[19] – Marshall gave up a second infantry division – Hoskin's 3rd – to the campaign in Palestine, its place in I Corps being taken by the 18th. At the beginning of March a third squadron of the Royal Flying Corps,[20] No. 72 Squadron, arrived in Mesopotamia.

Even as the Mesopotamia Expeditionary Force was in the throes of reorganisation, events of much greater global importance were unfolding in the neighbouring theatre to the north, in the Caucasus. During the first week of November, by British reckoning, the sociopolitical fire which had been burning in Russia since the overthrow of the tsar in the spring finally exploded into the promised inferno, when the Bolsheviks seized power. Almost immediately the war against the Turks ground to a halt, Russian soldiers, singly and in entire units, 'self-demobilising' to be thrown on their own resources, the process being exacerbated when news of the agreement which would evolve into the Treaty of Brest-Litovsk filtered down. The almost ubiquitous run of success the Russians had enjoyed in Armenia had worked to the direct advantage of the British in Mesopotamia, but now there was a very real danger of a dramatic turnaround, and the likelihood of additional Turkish divisions being sent south into Mesopotamia to halt Marshall's advance up the Tigris. And worse was in prospect, too: a threat to invade Persia, and not (just) as an avenue to launch a flanking attack from the east, through the Zagros Mountains, but as the precursor to a march on Afghanistan to threaten the very gates of India itself, an ambition Enver Pasha had long been known to cherish.

Far-fetched as either might actually have appeared – the Turks had, after all, been very comprehensively beaten in their own back yard, so to speak, and it would require a massive influx of (largely non-existent) men and *matériel* to put them back on their feet – so appalling was the latter prospect, as viewed from London and Delhi, that immediate steps were necessary to develop a strategy to combat it. This would be no simple matter. Firstly, there was no obvious source of manpower for such an endeavour, and secondly, it was by no means clear that the situation in Persia – where there was no sort of political stability and certainly no form of centralised control, and where famine and disease were rife – would be amenable to the deployment of a force of the size required, even if one could somehow be conjured up. There was a solution in prospect, however, and a fairly elegant one at that: in theory, at least, it was feasible to establish a blocking force west of the Persian border, employing Christian forces inimical to the Turks – Armenians, Georgians and even Russians opposed to the revolutionaries – led, equipped and, perhaps most important of all, paid by the British. There was good precedent for such a stratagem in India, in the North-West Frontier region and elsewhere, and it was there that the man who was to lead the British Mission to the Caucasus, Brig.-Gen. Lionel Dunsterville, was to be found.

In the event, the fear of Enver leading a Turkish army eastwards out of the Caucasus proved groundless, and Dunsterforce, as the expedition was to become known, after an extremely arduous progress to the Caspian Sea, found itself engaged in an ugly and ultimately unsuccessful little war-within-a-war for control of the oil-rich Apsheron Peninsula and the city of Baku. Though the force was supplied from Mesopotamia, and was under Marshall's control, its links to Baghdad were actually fairly tenuous; its activities are better to be understood against the backdrop of the culmination of the war in the Caucasus, and are thus to be found in that context, in Chapter 9 below.

The establishment and deployment of Dunsterforce was a very minor affair, at least at the outset, and even as it was set in motion, Marshall's attention was elsewhere, on the Euphrates. It had been Marshall's intention to move on Hit, chiefly in order to gain control of nearby bitumen deposits, around mid-March, but on 8 February he learned that the Turks had abandoned their positions in the Broad Wadi, just to the north of the town, and also at Sahiliya, ten kilometres further upstream, and he decided to act forthwith. On 18 February a detachment from the 42nd Brigade was moved to a position some fifteen kilometres downstream from Hit, Khan Abu Rayan being occupied in the process. Hit was occupied virtually unopposed the following day, some stores and around a hundred *shakturs* awaiting breaking-up for return to Jerablus were captured, and on the tenth Sahiliya was taken too, the Turks taking casualties in air raids as they fell back in the direction of Khan Baghdadi. Brooking subsequently moved the 15th Division's headquarters to Hit, stationing one of his brigades there, one at Sahiliya and another half-way to Khan Abu Rayan. In order to secure the area, Marshall instructed Brooking to prepare plans for an offensive to drive the Turks back upriver, out of the positions they now occupied at Khan Baghdadi and conceivably as far as Haditha or even Ana, the operation to begin on 24 March.

Marshall tried to hide his intentions from the Turks, ordering work at Hit and Sahiliya designed to make it appear that the troops were settling in there for the summer, and also launching diversionary operations above Samarra and in the Jabal Hamrin. Together they seemed to have had the desired effect. Brooking estimated the Turks to have one understrength division – the 50th, which had originally been intended to form part of the Yildirim Group, but had been detached and sent to the Euphrates front, where it had been largely inactive – confronting him, with perhaps 3,000 men and a dozen guns at Khan Baghdadi and 1,500 and around twenty guns at Haditha or Ana. He himself had three infantry brigades (less six companies, which would be left to garrison Hit and Sahiliya) plus a machine gun company; the 11th Cavalry Brigade plus reinforcements and three LAMBs; a total of forty-eight guns and howitzers; engineers and pioneers, including a mobile bridging train, and four flights of aircraft and a Kite Balloon section.

The attack came on the morning of 26 March, the assault force divided into five groups. Information extracted from prisoners indicated that the Turks were present in somewhat greater strength than had been thought, and were concentrated in the first-line trenches, about two kilometres south-east of Khan Baghdadi and extending westwards for six kilometres, the fall-back or reserve positions, some way to the north-west of the village, being only lightly held.

Brooking instructed 'Andrew's Group' (the 50th Infantry Brigade plus a field artillery brigade, a cavalry squadron and pioneers) to attack on the right flank, while Lucas advanced his group (the 42nd Infantry Brigade plus a reduced field artillery brigade) to his left to give support. As Andrew's brigade began to move, the Turks retired, and he was able to occupy their positions with little opposition, taking over a hundred prisoners before setting off in pursuit. He was finally checked at around 1300, at a line running south-westwards from Khan Baghdadi itself, some two kilometres short of the Turks' reserve positions. As Andrew's and Lucas' brigades began to advance again, at 1730, across a front around a kilometre wide, the artillery began bombarding the Turks' positions at ranges no greater than 2,500 metres, the machine gun company joining in with indirect fire. The gunfire built in intensity as the infantrymen closed in, and proved so effective that the 42nd and 50th Brigades were unchecked, and suffered remarkably few casualties. As darkness came, the reserve positions were occupied, the 6th Jats leading the way with a charge which overwhelmed a machine gun nest.

Meanwhile, Cassels' cavalry and armoured cars had circled the enemy positions, and were now drawn up roughly along the line of the Wadi Haurah, some ten kilometres north-west of Khan Baghdadi, with their left flank on the road to Haditha. They were deployed across a front some five kilometres wide to begin with, but in response to messages telling him of the Turks having begun to retire, Cassels extended his left out towards the Euphrates in the hope of covering all avenues of retreat. In the event, when the attempted breakthrough came, at around midnight, it took place precisely where he was at his strongest, and after less than an hour the Turks, with nowhere to go, began to surrender.

At 0630 on 27 March Brooking issued orders for the pursuit. With the armoured cars in the lead, Hogg's mechanised column (two companies of lorry-mounted infantry) was to proceed in the direction of Haditha; when it was secured, Cassels' cavalry, now resting near the apex of the Alus Bend, was to move through it and go on towards Ana, about sixty kilometres further upstream. The operation went exactly according to plan. At Haditha and on the road to Ana hundreds more prisoners were taken, including the 50th Division's commanding officer and his staff and the commander of the Ana garrison. In all, at a cost of 36 killed or missing and about 120 more wounded, Brooking's division took 5,254 prisoners (including a dozen German communications specialists), twelve guns and forty-seven machine guns, as well as huge quantities of ammunition. With its objectives entirely achieved, the force occupied Haditha and Khan Baghdadi (but later withdrew downriver to shorten the lines of communication; Haditha and Ana were subsequently reoccupied by Turkish troops).

In early April, Marshall turned his attention to his right flank once more, and began contemplating an operation to drive the Turks out of the region north of Qara Tepe, through Tuz Khurmatli and Kifri, with the intention of securing the route into Persia, the situation there becoming more important and Dunsterville's mission gathering strength. Egerton's III Corps would face light opposition, he believed, the bulk of the Turkish Sixth Army being located on the Tigris above Fat-ha (XVIII Corps) and around Kirkuk, where XIII Corps now had its headquarters. Egerton was instructed to draw up a plan of action, and delivered it on 12 April. He would feint towards Qara Tepe and Kifri, he decided, but in fact aim to take control of a wider area, making his real attack along the Abu Gharaib–Tuz Khurmatli axis. Since this was a large area – it was something of the order of fifty kilometres from the northern end of the Sakaltutan Pass to Abu Gharaib, a hundred more to Tuz Khurmatli, and fifty kilometres from Band-i-Adhaim to Kifri – the force employed would be considerably larger than the enemy could be expected to deploy, and mechanised to an unprecedented degree to allow it to move rapidly. By way of a bonus, the region was largely fertile tableland, and it was envisaged that loss of control over it, just prior to the harvest, would be a heavy blow to the Turks.

Under Maj.-Gen. Sir Walter Cayley's direct command, the attacking force was to be divided into four groups, the most powerful of which would be further subdivided. Column A, under the command of Brig.-Gen. Holland-Pryor, consisted of the 6th Cavalry Brigade and the 13th Hussars from the 7th, plus two LAMBs, artillery and a small detachment of mechanised infantry. Its objective was to drive the Turks north from Tuz Khurmatli and nearby Yanija Buyuk. Column B, which was subdivided, had two full infantry brigades and an additional battalion, elements of the 12th Cavalry, and artillery and support troops; the bulk of its foot-soldiers would be carried in over a thousand Ford vans. B1 (the 38th Brigade Group, under Brig.-Gen. O'Dowda) was to be in a position to destroy enemy forces driven out of Abu Gharaib; B2 (the 40th Brigade Group, under Brig.-Gen. Lewin) was to perform the same function in relation to Qara Tepe. Column C was a smaller mixed force, with two battalions of infantry, a cavalry squadron, two field and one siege battery. Its function was to act as a beater, driving Turkish troops out of Qara Tepe onto the guns of Column B2. Column D was made up of the 14th Lancers, 'V' Battery, RHA, and a section of armoured cars. It, too, was to drive enemy troops before it, this time from Abu Gharaib. Each column had attached aircraft, two flights of three each to the first two, one to the others, with two more available as required. The concentration of these troops was somewhat delayed by heavy rain, but by 24 April they were in position, with Columns A and B north of Delli Abbas, Column C at Mirjana, upstream of Qizil Ribat on the Diyala, and Column D at Satha, on the Adhaim.

The advance-to-contact was delayed by poor weather, but by the evening of the twenty-sixth Column A had reached a point about five kilometres north of Umr Maidan, with B1 around the village itself; B2 was at Narin Köpri, and had bridged the river there. Column C had advanced only to Sadda, as per Egerton's orders, while Column D was actually in contact with the enemy south-west of Abu Gharaib. The columns continued their advance through the night, and it soon became clear that the Turks were retreating before them, quitting both Qara Tepe and Abu Gharaib (for Kifri and Tur Khurmatli) before daybreak, just as Egerton had hoped they would.

Pursuing them, Column A came under artillery fire about eight kilometres south of Kulawand at around 0815. Having pushed the rearguard back, Holland-Pryor sent the 13th Hussars and the 21st Cavalry straight for the main enemy positions, with the 22nd Cavalry in support on the left, and his armoured cars to loop around to the right; his intention was to force the Turks to reveal themselves, whereupon the cavalry would back off and work around their right flank. In the event, the vehicles were unable to negotiate boggy ground, and the cavalry, too, ran into a swamp as it came under fire. As ordered, the Hussars extended to their left, but as they did so Turkish reinforcements were seen moving forward from Tuz Khurmatli. A squadron was detached to hold them off, and the rest of the Hussars and the 21st Cavalry were withdrawn some distance and, together with the 22nd, resumed their movement to the left, out of rifle-shot of the Turks' trenches. They were on solid ground now, drawn up in a line facing north-east, some three kilometres from the right-hand end of the enemy positions, and at 1230 the brigadier gave the order to advance at the walk, and for the supporting artillery and machine guns to begin barrage fire. Fifteen hundred metres out the horsemen broke into a trot, and at five hundred, a gallop. Many Turkish infantrymen left their positions and made for a dry watercourse to their right; their rifle fire proved ineffective, and they were ridden down, the cavalrymen using their swords to considerable effect,[21] killing over a hundred and fifty and taking 565 prisoners, though some among the defenders were able to make their escape into broken ground to the north. British casualties numbered just fourteen men and thirty-six horses. Holland-Pryor subsequently attacked Tuz Khurmatli, but found it strongly held, and withdrew as darkness fell, bivouacking six kilometres south of Kulawand, where there was both water for the horses and abundant grazing.

During the course of the day Column C had begun to move northwards towards Kifri, and by the evening had reached Chaman Köpri; it bivouacked there for the night, under orders to occupy Kifri as early as possible the next day (and did so, without opposition; the coal workings there – the reason for the town's relative importance; there were also 'oil springs' in the vicinity – were found to be flooded but otherwise undamaged). During the afternoon Egerton ordered a reorganisation of his main force, recombining the two components of Column B and adding Column A and the armoured cars of Column D, the remainder of which was to remain at Abu Gharaib. Thus equipped, with nine battalions of infantry, siege and field batteries, a strong detachment of armoured cars and cavalry fresh from a notable victory, Cayley was to take both Tuz Khurmatli and Yanija Buyuk, six kilometres to the west along the Aq Su River.

The following morning, the cavalry column approached the objectives and found both occupied in strength. O'Dowda's 38th Brigade Group then advanced up the Abu Gharaib road, making for a point west of Kulawand (and when it arrived there, pushed its artillery up to within range of Yanija Buyuk), and Lewin's 40th Brigade Group moved to Kulawand. At 1725 Cayley issued the next day's operational order. Before dawn the cavalry column would cross the Aq Su at Khasradala and cut the road between Tuz Khurmatli and Tauq, the 40th Brigade would attack along the line of the Kulawand–Tuz Khurmatli road, and the 38th would cross the Aq Su at the ford, which would by this time have been made usable by the artillery, and attack Yanija Buyuk from the west, pushing on to Tuz Khurmatli when opposition there had been suppressed.

The cordon was in place by daybreak, by which time all three of its elements were in contact with the enemy. Lewin's men found the defensive positions astride the road to Tuz Khurmatli strongly held; a second battalion was ordered in to climb to the crest of the ridge and clear out the enfilading defensive positions. This proved no easy task, the ridge being dominated by a high point where four guns and four machine guns were sited. Eventually, after a third battalion had been committed, the strongpoint was captured and the ridge, as far as the Aq Su, was in British hands by 0900.

O'Dowda's brigade had a marginally easier task, the terrain being more in its favour, and by 0700 Yanija Buyuk was in its hands. The Lancashire battalions now advanced on Tuz Khurmatli, a distance of around five kilometres, the divisional field artillery keeping pace on the left bank of the river. Resistance here was lighter, and by 0900 it, too, was in British hands, together with many prisoners.

Earlier large bodies of Turkish troops were seen making for the high ground north of Tuz Khurmatli, and the three cavalry regiments had given chase; once again, large numbers of prisoners were taken, and by 0900 the area had been cleared of defenders.

Even as reports of the successful conclusion of the affair were reaching Marshall, he was being forced to consider extending the operation further into Kurdistan, having received a signal from the War Office on 29 April requesting that he strike in the direction of Kirkuk and Sulaimaniya with the objective of forcing XIII Corps' commander to request reinforcement and thus draw off Turkish troops from the Caucasus which, it was believed, were then being readied to push into Armenia, Azerbaijan and north-western Persia. He replied immediately with an analysis of the situation. Broadly, he proposed sending a mobile column north from Tuz Khurmatli to advance by way of Tauq and Taza Khurmatli and a second from Tikrit to Kirkuk by way of the Ain Nukhaila Pass, deploying a brigade to secure it; by this means, he said, he could drive the Turks from Kirkuk (cutting the only road to Sulaimaniya in the process). Securing Sulaimaniya, however, would be a much more difficult task, thanks to the nature of the terrain, and he suggested instead sending a mobile force to Halabja to establish a cordon sanitaire in the border region south of there.

Told to proceed, he began by reorganising the forces he now had at Tuz Khurmatli into two commands; Lewin would take responsibility for maintaining the security of the lines of communication (which were established through Narin Köpri, Qara Tepe and Kifri) with the 40th Infantry Brigade, two squadrons of cavalry, two field batteries and a machine gun company, while Cayley would command the striking force which would advance on Kirkuk by way of Tauq and Taza Khurmatli. When Cayley began his advance, on 4 May, he would be supported by a column sent north from Samarra to take and occupy the Ain Nukhaila Pass and secure his left flank from an attack from the direction of Fat-ha. Reconnaissance patrols ran into opposition near Taza Khurmatli, but when the main force appeared there on 6 May it disappeared. Contact was made again briefly that afternoon, about four kilometres outside Kirkuk, in very heavy rain which persisted all night and into the morning, making both communications and the advance difficult. However, when the advanced element of the force reached Kirkuk, it found the town deserted of enemy troops, who had clearly spent some time preparing to withdraw, for they had emptied the granaries and other food stores and slaughtered all the livestock, leaving the civilian population half starved, most without a roof over their heads. Atrocious weather prohibited reconnaissance north of the city until 10 May, but then the cavalry and a battery of armoured cars reconnoitred in the direction of Altun Köpri, on the Little Zab River. British troops began withdrawing from Kirkuk on 11 May, leaving a small mobile column as a garrison; this, too, withdrew on 24 May. By the end of the month the British had withdrawn to the Diyala, leaving advanced posts at Tuz Khurmatli and Kifri. Turkish forces subsequently reoccupied Kirkuk in substantial numbers, and maintained an outpost at Tauq.

The operation, Marshall reported to London on 12 May, while it had 'liberated' Kirkuk and driven back the Turks' 2nd Division, had been only a limited success, for the enemy had retired in preference to calling in reinforcements from further north. In order to achieve that, he suggested, it would be necessary to advance up the Tigris from Tikrit, and confront XVIII Corps at Fat-ha. However, daytime temperatures had already risen to the point where combat operations were virtually impossible, and he urged that nothing be undertaken before mid-September, when the weather would start to cool down, and that in the intervening period the railway be extended to Tikrit.

Just as Maude had done the previous year, Marshall used this opportunity to reorganise his forces. The Cavalry Division had ceased to exist in April, its brigades becoming independent commands with the 6th Brigade attached to III Corps and the 7th and 11th Brigades attached to I Corps. The heavy artillery was organised into three brigades – 38th, 74th and 101st – which were attached respectively to III Corps, the 15th Division and I Corps. In response to the demand for replacements for the heavy casualties infantry battalions were taking in France,[22] each of the sixty Indian battalions in Mesopotamia gave up a company, their numbers being made up by recruits from India.[23]

At the beginning of the summer hiatus, Marshall had estimated the Turkish strength in Mesopotamia at something less than 2,000 cavalry, 17,000 infantry and 130 guns, grouped at and about Ana on the Euphrates (750/1,500/9), at and above Fat-ha on the Tigris (100/7,000/63), around Altun Köpri and Kirkuk (450/3,000/22), at Sulaimaniya (50/1,000/4), around Ruwandiz and Lake Urmia (150/2,500/12) and at Mosul (300/2,000/24). The troops were said to be somewhat demoralised and experiencing severe logistical problems. The situation in the Caucasus was anything but clear, but British Intelligence estimated that there were seven (much depleted) Turkish divisions in the region, and that they were intent on advancing on Baku and into Persian

Azerbaijan. There were also reports of German troops having landed at Potì and occupied Tiflis (T'bilisi), and of fears that up to 80,000 Turkish prisoners of war had been repatriated from Russia.[24]

Marshall went on leave to India on 1 August, and on his return it was clear that the situation had been in a state of flux in his absence. Overall command of the Turkish Sixth Army had passed to Ali Ihsan Pasha, Halil having been transferred to the Caucasus front in April. Turkish troop strength was unchanged on the Euphrates – where Marshall's staff saw no threat materialising – but infantry numbers at Fat-ha and Kirkuk had halved, had been reduced significantly at Sulaimaniya and Ruwandiz, and the Turks had almost disappeared from Mosul.

Combined with Allenby's successes in Palestine, these troop reductions were enough to promote a feeling in London that Turkish 'influence' in both theatres was about to collapse, and that bred a determination to exploit the situation, specifically with regard to gaining control over those regions of Upper Mesopotamia where oil was known to exist, the terms of the Sykes-Picot Agreement (see page 399–400) notwithstanding.[25] With this in mind, Marshall was asked to produce a proposal for an advance up the Tigris, and also for mounting a cavalry raid up the Euphrates, in order to attempt to draw troops away from the Palestine front.[26] In a cable of 4 October he dismissed the latter as both impossible (due to most of his transport being occupied in operations in Persia) and ill-considered, since it was unlikely to assist Allenby in any material way. However, the former he considered entirely feasible, and promised a proposal in short order.

He produced it the following day, outlining an advance by I Corps reinforced by two cavalry brigades with the Little Zab River as the first objective. He warned, however, that the necessity to pre-position supplies and the collection of transport would mean that he would be unable to commence the operation for at least ten days. The next day the War Office approved the plan.

The main obstacle in the way of an advance to the Little Zab was the Fat-ha Gorge, where the Tigris had cut a path through the Jabal Hamrin and where the Turks had been preparing defensive positions for almost eighteen months. Despite the apparent reduction in their numbers there over the preceding four months, this would still be a very formidable obstacle even if only lightly defended, and Marshall would have preferred to have circumvented it by means of an advance on Mosul by way of Kirkuk, but time pressure and the lack of adequate transport removed that option.

By now the intelligence estimates were suggesting there were 2,600 infantrymen at Fat-ha, with 28 guns (lighter calibres; the heavier pieces had been sent to Aleppo), with around 2,900/14 further back at Ain Dibs, at Humr and on the Little Zab (around thirty kilometres from the Fat-ha positions), and around 2,250/30, some of whom might be on the way to the Tigris, around Kirkuk. Cobbe, who had operational command, decided to concentrate on the left bank of the river, with a force on the right to give support. He was hampered by the men at his disposal being inexperienced, and also by the arrival in their ranks of an influenza epidemic, the advanced guard of that which would sweep Europe the following year and by some estimates kill more people than the entire war had done; it, and malaria also was present in the ranks of Allenby's army in Syria.

His supply dumps – seven days' worth – were in place by 18 October, and that day the Ain Nukhaila and Darb-al-Khail Passes were occupied.[27] His plan was for the 7th Cavalry Brigade to cross the Jabal Hamrin by way of the Darb-al-Khail Pass and loop around to attack the Turkish left-bank positions from the rear while the 18th Infantry Division made a frontal assault, supported by fire from the 17th Infantry Division on the right bank and by all available artillery, the operation to commence on the evening of 23 October. Prior to that the 11th Cavalry Brigade was to have crossed the Jabal Hamrin by way of the Ain Nukhaila Pass, then advance as far as the Little Zab at a point some forty kilometres upstream from its confluence with the Tigris, while Lewin advanced from Tuz Khurmatli and occupied Tauq with a mixed force, advancing further as necessary to secure Cobbe's right flank from attack from the direction of Kirkuk. On the right bank, a mechanised column consisting of armoured cars and lorry-mounted infantry was to make a wide loop to the west, and arrive at Hadr (Al Hadhar), a desert city some sixty kilometres from Sharqat (Esh Sharqat), by the evening of the twenty-fourth. It was then to occupy itself raiding lines of communication and cutting the line of retreat while being prepared to co-operate with Cassels' cavalry, which had been warned to be ready to cross the Tigris if necessary.

It all proved unnecessary. When the 55th Infantry Brigade advanced on the left bank at moonrise on 23 October, under cover of an artillery barrage, they found empty positions. On the right bank there was sporadic firing until about 0330, and then nothing; patrols reported the trenches empty, and they, too, were occupied by 0500. By daybreak on 24 October the entire defensive position was in British hands. Thereafter the British – after having rebuilt the roads through the Fat-ha Gorge which the Turks had destroyed as they retired – chased the Turks northwards on the right bank of the Tigris by fits and starts, the terrain favouring the retiring defenders. They quit the left bank on the twenty-fourth, destroying the bridge at Humr as soon as the last units had crossed, and made a stand south of Mushak, along the spine of the Jabal Makhul ridge, their positions extending north as far as Ain Dibs. There, assisted by considerable confusion, particularly in communications and the transmission of orders, and some supply problems in the British camp, they succeeded in holding the British until the morning of 27 October, but then they withdrew once more, falling back all the way to Sharqat and establishing a defensive line south of the town.

By now Cassels' 11th Cavalry Brigade had made a long flanking march, forded the Tigris well north of the town, near Hadraniya, and joined up with the mechanised units sent north by way of Hadr. The force sat astride the Turks' escape route towards Mosul at Huwaish, twenty kilometres from Sharqat, where the road crossed the Wadi Muabba, and a picket line running north from there had been established. It had fought a brief engagement with enemy infantry some three kilometres south of its main position during the afternoon of 27 October, and was in contact with a force around four hundred strong, advancing from the direction of Mosul and then some twenty kilometres to the north. The 11th Brigade was to be joined at Huwaish by the 7th Cavalry Brigade, which had been withdrawn temporarily to the reserve positions at Shuraimiya, on the right bank, south of the Fat-ha Gorge, and by an infantry column under Brig.-Gen. GAF Sanders, which had been despatched up the left bank.

By the morning of 28 October Sanders' column, having marched all night, had reached a point opposite the 11th Cavalry's position (bringing with it much-needed ammunition for Cassels' field batteries), and the two were in contact and a ferry had been established. The cavalry's northern pickets reported the enemy infantry still advancing, and seemingly trying to outflank them to the west, while those to the south soon reported the force Cassels had held off the previous afternoon now advancing determinedly, with its right flank on the river. Cassels ordered his own artillery to open fire on the approaching troops, and asked Sanders to co-operate. This slowed, but did not stop, the advance, and neither did an audacious flanking attack by the 7th Hussars, and by mid-morning it had become clear that perhaps as many as three thousand Turkish infantry were moving northwards from Sharqat. Cassels asked Sanders to send an infantry battalion across the river, and he despatched the 1/7th Gurkhas.

At around 1400, two additional field batteries, sent up by Fanshawe from the Little Zab line, arrived at Sanders' position, and were joined by a section of 6-in howitzers an hour later. Though large numbers of Turkish troops were now in contact with Cassels' force, the expected attack did not materialise, and the situation eased somewhat at 1615 with the arrival of Brig.-Gen. Norton, whose men immediately began to cross at the Hadraniya ford.[28] Cassels directed them to extend his line back to the river on the northern side.

Meanwhile, Leslie had detached two columns to push on up the right bank as the advanced guard of his 17th Infantry Division. Wauchope's column was ordered forward just after dawn on 27 October, when the Mushak positions had been discovered to be empty; the other, Coningham's, a smaller force, had formed the left flank during the attack on Mushak, and was thus well placed to continue its advance. Neither made rapid progress across very broken ground, but by that evening had reached Qalat-al-Bint and Balalij respectively, with orders to press on to Sharqat the following morning. Wauchope moved his men out long before dawn and began to close on the Turkish positions some eighteen kilometres away. By 0700 he had covered less than half the distance, and detached the 112th Infantry with a mountain battery to push out to the left. It was 0825 before Coningham, at Balalij, received orders to advance and form Wauchope's left flank, and news that a second infantry battalion (the 45th Sikhs) was being sent up to reinforce him.

Wauchope's advance was painfully slow, the going very difficult, and it was early afternoon before he closed with the defensive line, which ran west for some three kilometres from the Jabal Khanuqa, bordering the river, to the road, around five kilometres south of the town of Sharqat. The first units were in the front-line trenches by 1330, and half an hour had taken the second, together with around two hundred prisoners and a dozen machine guns. During the afternoon the 51st Infantry Brigade – which had left its bivouac position at 0200 – came up, and Leslie ordered a halt.

At this point the remains of the Turkish Tigris Force probably amounted to no more than four thousand men, and they were caught between two brigades of infantry and a very considerable quantity of guns to the south (Leslie), an infantry brigade and more artillery to the south-east (Fanshawe), most of another infantry brigade and yet more guns to the north-east (Sanders) and two cavalry brigades with more artillery and an infantry battalion to the north. To the west lay open desert, with no significant source of water for perhaps fifty kilometres. Their performance south of Sharqat seemed to indicate that their morale was deteriorating rapidly, but it was clear that they intended to try to fight their way out of the corner in which they found themselves.

Cobbe's fear was for the security of Cassels' column. He proposed to deal with that by pushing Leslie's 17th Division forward as soon as the moon rose, at around 0130, and he so ordered at 2035. Leslie, conscious that his men were close to exhaustion, asked to be allowed to delay execution until daybreak, but Cobbe refused. In the event, the night passed relatively quietly for Cassels' men, the Turks unwilling to make any real effort to break through. Nonetheless, he asked Sanders to send him an additional artillery battery and another infantry battalion, and ready a third. At around 0430 the 1/39th Gahrwalis began to cross, together with a machine gun company. The capacity of the ferry was limited, and it would be 0700 before enough men had crossed to make them an effective fighting unit.

Of more pressing importance was the fact that the infantry detachment which had approached from the north had grown to the equivalent of at least two battalions,[29] and had taken up residence at the southern end of a thirty-metre-high bluff about a kilometre north of Norton's main position and commanding the ford. Norton had positioned the 13th Hussars directly south of the nose of the position, and he ordered them to advance at the gallop, dismount in the dead ground at the foot of the slope and continue on foot, the assault to be supported by 'V' Battery, RHA – which was still on the far bank of the Tigris, but in an advantageous location – and every

Sultan Abdul Hamid II prior to his abdication in 1909; he returned to Constantinople in 1912 from exile in Salonika, and died there six years later

Ismail Enver Pasha was the youngest of the Young Turks' ruling triumvirate, aged just thirty-three when he led his country to war in November, 1914. He served as War Minister throughout the conflict, then fled first to Germany, later to Russia, where he died in 1922

Mehmet Talaat was the only member of the Young Turks' ruling triumvirate not to come from a military background – he was an official in the post office – but was believed by many to be the most influential. He served as Minister of the Interior until 1917, and then as Grand Vizier; he was assassinated by an Armenian in Berlin in 1921

Ahmed Jemal Pasha was perhaps the least significant of the Young Turk triumvirs, having been sidelined by his colleagues soon after the opening of hostilities and despatched to govern Syria. Like Talaat he was assassinated by Armenians in revenge for the part he played in what they considered to be an attempt at genocide

(right) Hans Freiherr von Wangenheim was Germany's ambassador to the Sublime Porte from 1912 until October, 1915; under the guidance of Chancellor Theobald von Bethmann-Hollweg he negotiated the German-Ottoman Alliance which brought Turkey into the Great War on the side of the Central Powers

Colmar Freiherr von der Goltz first served in Turkey after the disastrous Russo-Turkish war of 1877-8, remaining as head of a military mission until 1896. He returned to Constantinople in 1915, to serve under von Sanders

Brig.-Gen. Walter Delamain commanded the 16th Infantry Brigade, the first British troops to land in Mesopotamia; he was later promoted to major-general and played a pivotal role at the First Battle of Kut and at Ctesiphon

Lt.-Gen. Sir Arthur Barrett commanded Indian Expeditionary Force D, sent to Mesopotamia on the outbreak of war with the Ottoman Empire in November, 1914. He was relieved of his command – for health reasons – the following April

Maj.-Gen. Charles Townshend succeeded Barrett in command of the 6th Indian Division; after some initial success he was defeated at Ctesiphon and retreated to Kut, where he was forced to surrender on 29 April, 1916

Lt.-Gen. Sir John Nixon acceded to command in March, 1918. His determination to take Baghdad with inadequate resources led to Townshend's defeat at Ctesiphon and the 6th Indian Division's subsequent retreat to Kut

Lt.-Gen. Sir Percy Lake was appointed to command British forces in Mesopotamia on the recall of Sir John Nixon. He was unsuccessful in his attempts to relieve Kut, and was replaced by Maude, in July, 1916

Lt.-Gen. Sir Fenton Aylmer VC. He was sent to Mesopotamia in December, 1915, was subsequently given command of the Tigris Force and tasked with relieving Kut. He failed, and was replaced by Gorringe in March, 1916

Maj.-Gen. George Gorringe commanded first the 12th Indian Division and later, in succession to Aylmer, the Tigris Force in Mesopotamia. Like Aylmer he failed to re-take Kut, and his career then stagnated

Sir Frederick Maude took over from Gorringe as commander of the Tigris Corps. By then commander-in-chief in the theatre, having replaced Lake, he died of cholera in Baghdad on 18 November, 1917

Like Maude, Sir William Marshall, then a major-general, commanded a division at Gallipoli, and later moved to Mesopotamia to command III Corps. In November, 1917, he succeeded Maude as commander-in-chief

Halil Pasha (seated) and his staff; Halil – Enver's uncle – first took a division to the Caucasus and then shifted to Mesopotamia; despite being beaten convincingly in every battle from that which saw the ultimate fall of Kut, he remained in command in the theatre until April, 1918, when he returned to the Caucasus

Rear-Adm. John de Roebeck took over command of naval operations in the Dardanelles on 15 March, 1915; it is he who must bear the brunt of the responsibility for the Royal Navy's lamentable refusal to continue the effort to force the straits after the near-disastrous events of 18 March, 1915

As First Lord of the Admiralty, the Rt. Hon. Winston Churchill (left) had a stormy relationship with the professional head of the Royal Navy, Sir John Arbuthnot Fisher (right)

Rear-Adm. Rosslyn Wemyss was Adm. de Roebeck's second-in-command at the Dardanelles, leading the battle squadron and supervising the naval side of the evacuation. He went on to hold the highest rank in the Royal Navy

Maj.-Gen. Aylmer Hunter-Weston commanded the 29th Infantry Division (and briefly, promoted temporarily to lieutenant-general, VIII Corps) at Gallipoli; he was invalided home in the latter half of July 1915

Mustafa Kemal (left), then a colonel, commanded the Turkish 19th Division at Gallipoli with panache and determination

(above left) Lt.-Gen. Sir Frederick Stopford had never commanded men in battle, but was called out of retirement to lead IX Corps at Suvla thanks to Mahon's refusal to serve under a nominally inferior officer; his efforts were entirely insufficient, and any chance of breaking through the Turkish defences was lost due to his complacency

(above right) Lt.-Gen. Sir Bryan Mahon, who commanded the 10th Infantry Division at Suvla Bay. It was largely through his intransigence that the totally unsuitable Stopford was given command of IX Corps

(left) Sir Ian Hamilton, the commander-in-chief at Gallipoli, with the commander of the French contingent, Gen. Gouraud

The two French commanders at Gallipoli, Gouraud (right) and Bailloud; despite being badly wounded (when he was replaced by Bailloud) Gouraud survived to become the French military supremo in the Middle East, and expelled the Hashemite Feisal from Syria

Maj.-Gen. Beauvoir de Lisle succeeded Hunter-Weston in command of the 29th Division at Cape Helles during the first week of June, 1915; he took over temporary command of IX Corps at Suvla in mid-August from Stopford

Lt.-Gen. Sir Julian Byng had a sterling reputation, gained on the Western Front, when he took over command of IX Corps at Gallipoli from de Lisle on 23 August, 1916

Lt.-Gen. Sir William Birdwood was given command of the Australia and New Zealand Army Corps in November, 1914, and took overall charge of Allied forces at Gallipoli, succeeding Hamilton, a year later. He is shown here (in the paler uniform) presenting his officers to FM Lord Kitchener during the War Minister's visit to the operational theatre

Nikolai Nikolaevich Yudenich, the commander of Russian troops in the field in the Caucasus theatre and arguably one of the best Russian military leaders of his generation. From Sarikamiş, at the end of 1914, to the disintegration of the Russian war effort following the revolutions of 1917 he hardly put a foot wrong

The Hashemite Feisal ibn Hussein, whom the British installed as King of Iraq after the French had kicked him out of Syria; his brother Abdullah was made ruler of Trans-Jordan, and proved a more successful dynasty-builder

Gen. Sir Edmund Allenby, known as 'The Bull' by reason both of his stature and brusque manner, commanded Allied forces in Palestine from the end of June, 1917, having replaced Murray after his failure at the Second Battle of Gaza. He was raised to the rank of field-marshal in 1919, and created Viscount Allenby of Megiddo

T E Lawrence was perhaps always as much about style as he was about substance... His collaboration with the equally ambitious American film-maker and photojournalist Lowell Thomas brought him fame if not fortune, but he was also well regarded in official circles and there is no knowing what he might have achieved had he not met a premature death in 1935

Kaiser Wilhelm II visited Constantinople for the third and last time in 1917; he is shown here during his visit, wearing the uniform of a field-marshal ('Mushir') in the Ottoman Army

The 'Big Four' at Versailles: David Lloyd George ('The Welsh Wizard'), the British Prime Minister; Vittorio Emmanuele Orlando ('The Weeper'), his Italian counterpart; Georges Clemenceau ('The Tiger'), the Prime Minister of France; and US President Woodrow Wilson, the academic and flawed idealist

available machine gun. The first attempt was made at 0815, but was abandoned almost immediately, and more artillery brought up. Throughout the course of the morning heavy fire was poured into the Turkish positions, and at 1320 the Hussars broke cover and galloped forward. They met heavy machine gun fire, as was to be expected, but it proved wildly inaccurate, and they reached their objective without a single man being hit. Under the cover of the steep slope they dismounted and began to climb, their colonel in the lead, while every gun and machine gun at Norton's command fired just above their heads, not lifting until they were bare metres from the lip. So accurate and effective was the supporting fire that they incurred no casualties in the scramble up the slope, and but seven in the course of taking the position, together with about 730 prisoners and twelve machine guns; a considerable achievement for a force which numbered just 239 officers and men.

The additional field-artillery battery Cassels had requested was in position by 1130, and soon after Sanders informed him that he was pushing infantry and supporting machine guns to the left bank of the Tigris, opposite what appeared to be the main Turkish position, about five kilometres south of Cassels' line, and asked him if he wanted the third infantry battalion sent across. Cassels replied that he did, and the 1/3rd Gurkhas began to cross, the operation being completed at around 1715.

The 17th Division had set out from the positions south of Sharqat as ordered at 0145, but had made slow progress, and by dawn its vanguard was still only about five kilometres north of the town, and well short of Cassels' position, the remaining Turks falling back in relatively good order, using the terrain to their advantage to slow the advance still further. Throughout the day Cassels looked for signs of their arrival, but was consistently disappointed. Not in direct contact with Leslie, he had to depend on reports passed by the 18th Division headquarters and, as throughout this operation, communications proved unreliable. Most of his information regarding the broader situation came from messages dropped by aircraft, which channel of course closed before dusk. The last he received, at 1620, reported the situation unchanged, with the 17th Division still well short of his position and continuing to bombard the Turks. At 2200 he received a signal from Cobbe's headquarters. Leslie's men had not made the sort of progress expected of them, he was told, and the situation would be unlikely to improve before the following morning.[30]

Improve it did then, and with a vengeance, for as day broke, white flags were to be seen right across the Turkish positions; the commander of the Turkish Tigris Group, Ismail Hakki Bey, having become convinced that there was no escape and with his ammunition running out, surrendered personally to the commanding officer of the 112th Infantry at 0730. Throughout the rest of the day more prisoners were taken on the road north to Mosul, over twelve hundred of them at and about Qaiyara, where a river steamer and a large quantity of *matériel* was also seized. In all, between 18 and 30 October, Cobbe's forces captured 11,322 prisoners, 51 guns and 130 machine guns.

Cobbe, briefed as to the need to be in control of as much territory as possible when an armistice was declared, launched his cavalry brigades on an expedition northwards, with the 54th Infantry Brigade to follow as soon as supply difficulties were overcome. Cassels' cavalry and armoured cars arrived at Qaiyara only at nightfall on 31 October; the following morning they continued their advance and were met by Turkish troops displaying a white flag at Hammam Ali, twenty kilometres short of Mosul.

The officer in command told Cassels that an armistice had been signed, and had come into force at noon the previous day (and that was confirmed at 1430 by a message dropped to him from an aircraft). Cassels then pushed on in a car, and ran into a Turkish infantry regiment astride the road, ten kilometres south of Mosul. Its commanding officer asked him to return to Qaiyara, and Cassels refused, but withdrew to Hammam Ali while a political officer accompanying the force proceeded to Mosul to make contact with Ali Ihsan and deliver a letter from Cassels explaining that he had orders to occupy the regional capital, and requesting that all Turkish troops be withdrawn eight kilometres north of the city. Ali Ihsan refused. After some to-ing and fro-ing a deal was negotiated whereby Cassels' force would approach within three kilometres of the city, while the Turks remained there. When informed of this, Marshall told Cassels that the occupation had been ordered by the War Office in London, citing the appropriate articles of the armistice agreement.[31] Cassels communicated this to Ali Ihsan, who tried valiantly to manoeuvre around the (woefully inexact) wording of the agreement and ultimately fell back on *force majeure* and told him he was unable to comply until he received instructions from his own government. Later that day (4 November), Fanshawe arrived at Cassels' headquarters, and took over from him.

The government in Constantinople duly objected to the occupation of Mosul on the same grounds that Ihsan had cited[32] (to Admiral Calthorpe, who had signed the agreement on behalf of the Allies). Calthorpe reported to the Admiralty, and was told (on 6 November) that the only concession possible was to allow Ihsan to withdraw his forces from the city, rather than surrendering them, but that the occupation must go ahead, by force of arms if necessary. This telegram was copied to Marshall (who received it only on 8 November). By that time he had arrived at the headquarters outside Mosul in person, and had already issued orders to Ihsan to evacuate the town beginning on 8 November, the operation to be completed by 15 November. Ihsan agreed under protest, but on 9 November received orders from Constantinople that he was to comply, whereupon he resigned his command and left for Nisibin. On 10 November the British occupied Mosul, and with that, belatedly, the war in Mesopotamia was over. Immediate efforts were made to locate the men captured at Kut and elsewhere, some of whom were believed to have been held in Upper Mesopotamia, where they had been made to work on extending the railway from Nisibin to Mosul; sadly, rough graves were all that was found.

II
THE CAUCASUS, ARMENIA, ANATOLIA AND PERSIA

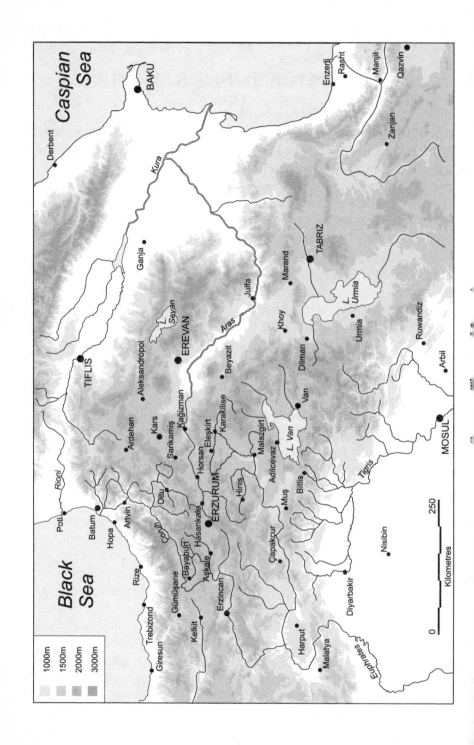

6

Sarikamiş Faciasi[*]

When Turkey went to war in the autumn of 1914, her generalissimo, Enver Pasha, had only two locations in the entire Ottoman Empire in mind for aggressive, offensive action: one was the Suez Canal; the other was the Caucasus. The latter was not well suited, topographically, for his purposes; indeed, its lack of roads and narrow valleys, simple to transform into choke points which all too easily became killing grounds, had enabled the Turks to limit Russian incursions there, even during the disastrous war of 1877–8. However, Enver's primary regional war aim required the Turkish forces to cross the frontier established in 1878 to take back the prizes it had lost then[1] before going on to invade the Greater Caucasus beyond and occupy the fertile Rioni and Kura Valleys as a precursor to an even grander design.

Enver's instrument was no more suitable than his choice of territory: the Turkish Third Army, under the command of Hasan Izzet Pasha. It consisted of IX Corps, based at Erzurum, together with Army headquarters and a Fortress Command; X Corps at Sivas, and XI Corps at Harput (Elaziğ). On the outbreak of war X and XI Corps were ordered to Erzurum, each leaving one of its three divisions to garrison the Çoruh and upper Murat-Su (Eastern Euphrates) valleys at Ispir and Tutak respectively. Izzet had fallen out of favour with Enver Pasha – whom he had taught at the Imperial Military Academy – and the War Minister had failed to take him into his confidence regarding his plans for the region. As a result, when he learned that war was imminent he was still working to an outdated general plan, a purely defensive strategy which envisaged meeting an invading Russian army east of Erzurum, and, if necessary, retreating before it in order to draw it into the strongest fortress in all of the Ottoman Empire east of the Bosporus and defeat it there. It came as a considerable surprise to him, then, when, on 2 November, Enver ordered him to advance east from Erzurum, cross the 1878 border and invade Russia.

On the other side of the frontier, while the topography and climate were similarly unforgiving, there was at least a semblance of modern order. This had been the one area where the Tsarists had made gains during the Crimean War of the 1850s, and since then a programme of building roads to military standards and requirements had been under way. More recently, after the gains made during the 1877–8 war, that network had been supplemented –

* The Disaster of Sarikamiş

10. Caucasus. Erzurum to Kars

thanks to the growing importance of the oilfields on the Caspian and the necessity to transport the product to markets in the West – by a railway linking Baku with Batum, which had sprouted a branchline to Sarikamiş ('Yellow Reeds'), to serve the frontier settlements and defensive lines of the Lesser Caucasus. The military advantage this logistical system gave the Russians over the Turks was enormous, of course; where the Turks had to bring supplies of all kinds from the nearest railhead, many hundreds of kilometres away, by cart or pack animal, and march their men in on their own two feet, the Russians simply loaded up a train and sent it on its way, to arrive at its destination just a few hours later, even in the depths of winter.

Hasan Izzet's opponent-to-be was the elderly General Bergmann, a favourite of Tsar Nicholas II, who commanded Russia's I Caucasian Army Corps from an advance position at Sarikamiş, an isolated, modern, mountain town – a Turkish village within living memory – on the old caravan route from Erzurum to Tiflis, and now some thirty kilometres back from the frontier. Bergmann had no field experience; neither did Count Illarion Ivanovich Vorontsov-Dashkov, the regional viceroy and commander-in-chief of the Army of the Caucasus, to whom he answered, or his deputy, a retired history professor from the Imperial Military Academy named Alexander Myshlayevski. The real responsibility lay with the Army's Chief of Staff, Nikolai Nikolaevich Yudenich.[2] Thanks to the decision of the Stavka, the Russian High Command, to strip the Army of the Caucasus of half its manpower and send it to Poland and East Prussia on the outbreak of war, Bergmann's force was badly undermanned; its chief asset was the 39th Infantry Division, supplemented by two brigades of the 20th, together with a division of Cossack cavalry and the 1st Kuban Plastun Brigade.[3] Further east, towards Beyazit, at the border with Persia, was a mixed force under the command of Gen. Oganovski: a brigade of the 66th Division (the others were dispersed in the coastal region), the 2nd Kuban Plastun Brigade, the 2nd Caucasian Cossack Division and the Transcaspian Cossack Brigade.[4] In general reserve at Tiflis was II Turkistan Army Corps, made up of the 4th and 5th Turkistan Rifle Brigades and the Siberian Cossack Brigade.[5] In all, Russian forces in the Caucasus, including a sizeable detachment which had been occupying Tabriz, in western Persia, for some years, amounted to 100,000 infantry, 15,000 cavalry and 256 guns.

At dawn on 2 November,[6] on orders from the Stavka, Bergmann sent his forces across the frontier into Turkish territory. The two forward units – the 155th Kubinski Regiment and the 156th Elizavetpolski Regiment – advanced from their starting positions at Karaurgan and Mecinkirt, the former bound for Zivin and the latter for Horsan (Horasan) on the Aras River (the Araxes of classical times). Simultaneously the two reserve units in quarters at Sarikamiş – the 153rd Bakinski Regiment and the 154th Derbentski Regiment – moved up behind them. Fifty kilometres away to the north, and separated from the main force by a mountain known as Çakir Baba, General Istomin was ordered to lead his brigade from the 20th Infantry Division, plus a regiment of Cossack cavalry, from its quarters at Oltu through Nariman (Narman) up to the vicinity of Id. The Cossacks, led by Gen. Nikolai Niko-laevich Baratov (or Baratashvili), quartered at Kağizman, were sent down the right bank of the Aras River as far as Yuzveran, south-west of Horsan, at the lower end of the Pasin Valley. Przevalski's 1st Kuban Plastun Brigade, also at Kağizman, was despatched across the Ağri-dağ to Karakilise (Karaköse) in the Eleşkirt Valley. By the morning of 5 November the 39th Division occupied a line Sanamer–Horsan, and was hard at work fortifying it, while Istomin, to the north, and Baratov, to the south, occupied flanking positions forward of it. If there was a serious weakness in this disposition it lay in the distance between Istomin – who was effectively isolated – and the main force, but in any event the ridge of the Çakir Baba mountain was the latter's real flank guard.

At that point, Bergmann had fulfilled his instructions to the letter. Then, that evening, things took an unexpected turn: his scouts reported the village of Köprüköy empty of Turkish troops, and Bergmann sent his main force to occupy it.

Unfortunately for him, Izzet's advance had by that time itself reached Hasankale, and at dawn on 6 November, in response to ill-tempered orders from Enver to press ahead more vigorously, and just as the four Russian regiments were departing the Sanamer–Horsan line, he ordered the two infantry divisions of XI Corps, under Galip Pasha, to make their best speed eastwards along the last stretch of the road to Köprüköy, while the two divisions from IX Corps, under Ahmet Fevzi Pasha, moved up on their left.

XI Corps and I Caucasian Army Corps met, head-on, at Köprüköy on the late afternoon of 6 November. Sustained fighting continued throughout the night, and against the odds the next morning found the Russians in pos-session of the village. Bergmann signalled his success to Army Headquarters in Tiflis, expecting, no doubt, to be congratulated on having used his initiative to buy an early victory cheaply, but the news was met with consternation. Yudenich, through Myshlayevski, replied sharply that he should seek author-ity before making any further advance.

A congenital tendency to disregard orders was something like endemic within the upper reaches of the Tsarist army, and Bergmann was no excep-tion – one historian observed of him that he 'was merely blindly obstinate where he thought to show strength of character' – and the next morning, perhaps reasoning that his actions wouldn't constitute an advance so much as a consolidation, he did precisely what he had been instructed not to do, and sent six battalions of infantry to take the settlement of Badicivan, ostensibly in order to strengthen his right flank.

Badicivan occupied a commanding position on the slopes of Çakir Baba; it had become the centre of IX Corps' operations and was temporary home to its headquarters, and thus not only to a large force of infantry, but also to artillery, and Bergmann's advance was both futile and costly. Undeterred, since obstinate invariably does as obstinate will, he ordered the exercise repeated the next day, with similar results.

At first light on the morning of 11 November it was Izzet Pasha's turn to go onto the offensive. The two divisions of IX Corps pushed forwards across the lower slopes of the Çakir Baba, putting them in a position to turn the Russian right; Bergmann could but retreat and did so, accepting heavy losses but avoiding being outflanked. By the evening of 12 November he was back where he'd been a week before, on the Sanamer–Horsan line.

Crucially, however, whether it was due to its commander's shortage of real commitment, as Enver seems to have believed, or to other, more mundane, factors such as terrain and logistical support, Izzet's offensive lacked something. Bergmann was able to hold his main defensive line, and on 15 November his situation improved markedly with the arrival of the Turkistan Rifles, sent up from Tiflis, who were immediately committed on the Russian right. Now it was Izzet's turn to weigh the balance of forces, and he decided to withdraw IX Corps' 29th Division, which retreated on Portanos. Coincidentally Przevalski's Kubans arrived from Karakilise and changed the situation dramatically along the Aras, driving the Turks back on Yuzveran and, on the morning of 17 November, retaking the village. They went no further, however, and through the course of the day the fighting simply petered out.

One factor in that was the weather, which had already begun to deteriorate. Before winter's grip could harden further and make movement difficult Yudenich acted to straighten his line. He met with mixed fortunes. Pushing through the coastal region towards Artvin, an infantry column sent to protect the important copper workings near Borchka was cut to pieces by Turkish irregulars, leading to the abandonment of the entire lower Çoruh Valley. South-east of Sarikamiş, Oganovski's 2nd Caucasian Cossack Division was more fortunate; it met no meaningful opposition, advancing to link up with Baratov's men at Tahir, on the descent into the Eleşkirt Valley, and finding winter quarters south of Karakilise.

In the course of that opening battle of the war on the Caucasian front Bergmann lost close to 7,000 men, well over 20 per cent of his force, really quite needlessly and to little purpose. As for the Turks, they lost a similar percentage of their strength (which amounted to rather more, in terms of numbers) but, crucially, demonstrated that they could take on a substantial invading force, stop it in its tracks and then drive it back. Their morale rose – and that of the Russians fell – accordingly.

By his thirty-third birthday, 22 November, Enver's plan to lead a winter offensive into the Lesser Caucasus personally had hardened. Several factors combined to fuel his belief in a favourable outcome, among them the inferior performance of Bergmann's troops and the manner of the Russian withdrawal from the lower Çoruh Valley, and not least that he could field a comfortable numerical superiority. When he presented his proposal in outline to Otto Liman von Sanders, however, not only did the head of the German military mission not admire its ambitious strength and well-rounded, far-reaching audacity, but he did not even take it entirely seriously.[7]

The key to the first stage of Enver's plan was Sarikamiş, with its rail link to Kars, Aleksandropol (Gyumri) and Tiflis. The town stood on the old road from Erzurum to Kars at the point where a track from Karakurt in the Aras Valley crossed it, and continued on through the saddle, across the Bardiz Pass, and into the Oltu Valley to the north. Beyond the village of Bardiz that track split, the western fork crossing into Turkish territory and running along the northern side of Çakir Baba through Çatak and Portanos to Köse, on the road from Hasankale to Oltu. It was impassable to wheeled traffic but practical under normal conditions for men on foot and mules, even mules carrying mountain guns capable of being broken down into manageable loads, for that, we are told, was how it had got its unlikely name: *Top Yol*, the 'Cannon Road'.[8]

In all, the distance from Köse to Sarikamiş was some sixty kilometres, and the track nowhere dropped below two thousand metres. It was exposed from every direction, though that was said to have the dubious merit of scouring it clear of snow in the winter. This was the missing piece in Enver's puzzle, the back door to the Russians' key location, and he did not hesitate, brushing aside warnings of the route's impracticability. By the time he left Constantinople on 7 December, it had become the cornerstone of his strategy, and he had decided on the disposition of his forces.

IX Corps, comprising the 17th, 28th and 29th Infantry Divisions, less their field artillery but with their mountain batteries intact, nominally some 30,000 men but in fact no more than 21,000,[9] would make the approach march by way of the *Top Yol* and descend directly on Sarikamiş.

X Corps comprised the 30th, 31st and 32nd Infantry Divisions. Its 28,000 men would be sent north from the regional capital to the vicinity of the village of Tortum. From there it would split, take three separate routes and recombine at Oltu. Once the Turkish garrison there was overcome, X Corps would be available to exercise its main (dual) functions of reinforcing IX Corps' attack on Sarikamiş and acting as a stopping force both to prevent reinforcement and to block the Russians if they should attempt to fall back on Kars.

XI Corps, comprising the 18th, 33rd and 34th Infantry Divisions totalling just over 22,000 men, and reinforced by three battalions of Frontier Guards and four battalions of Jandarma,[10] and with IX Corps' field artillery, would keep Bergmann's force in the Pasin Valley pinned in place.

Simultaneously, elements of the 3rd Division of 1 Army Corps from Eastern Thrace – just two infantry battalions and two artillery batteries, under the command of a German artilleryman, Major Stange – were to be transported by sea to the small port of Hopa, south of Batum (Batum'i), to advance on

Ardahan by way of Artvin and Ardanuch. Further south, the 37th Infantry Division of XIII Corps, transferred from Mesopotamia before the British landed there, had arrived at Tutak in the upper Eastern Euphrates Valley, and was thus to hand as a reserve formation. Including these peripheral units and troops left to garrison Erzurum, Enver's force numbered some 120,000 men,[11] though the total number he was able to commit to the battle for Sarikamiş did not exceed 76,000.

Against Enver, Bergmann, whose losses of early November had been made up, and who had been reinforced by elements of II Turkistan Corps and the 2nd Kuban Plastun Brigade from the Eleşkirt Valley, still disposed of no more than 50,000 infantry and 4,000 cavalry, spread out along an extended line running almost forty kilometres across the Pasin Valley from a spur of Çakir Baba at Kocut, through Maslahat and across the Aras to Ardi, on the breast of the Dram-dağ to the south. In addition he had perhaps 8,000 more infantrymen and a few squadrons of cavalry at Id and Oltu, and other reserves, largely Armenian levées, further south, on the road to Eleşkirt, giving a total of perhaps 65,000. There were also 14,000 men at Kars – though sending substantial numbers of them to the Sarikamiş front would denude its fortress – another 2,000 at Ardahan, and more significant numbers in the general reserve at Tiflis and beyond.

When Enver arrived in Köprüköy on 13 December, and revealed his plan to Hasan Izzet Pasha, the Third Army's commander-in-chief was considerably less than enthusiastic. Over the next few days he presented a series of arguments why the operation should not go ahead in the depths of winter but should wait for spring. None of them came even close to convincing Enver, for his Grand Design was by now burning a hole in his imagination. On 18 December things came to a head. As reported by Kazim Bey (first assistant to Colonel Friedrich Bronsart von Schellendorf, the chief of the Turkish General Staff, and Enver's brother-in-law[12]), the War Minister accused Izzet of having failed in his duty. Had Hasan Izzet not been his teacher at the Imperial Military Academy, he told him, he would have had him executed, but settled for sacking him instead, as he had surely intended all along. He made replacements at subordinate levels also: command of IX Corps passed from Brig.-Gen. Ahmed Fevzi Pasha to Col. Ali Ihsan Bey, who had previously commanded the 34th Infantry Division. Command of X Corps – perhaps the most important element of the three, certainly the one with the most complex task – passed from Brig.-Gen. Ziya Pasha to Col. Hafiz Hakki Bey,[13] and that of XI Corps passed from Brig.-Gen. Galip Pasha to Col. Abdul Karim Bey.

By way of a parting shot, Fevzi Pasha[14] told Enver what he did not want to hear: that the chances of the encirclement operation by way of the *Top Yol* being successful at this season were, at best, very questionable. Such a march, he said, would only be practical for specially trained troops with adequate winter equipment, supported by pre-positioned supply dumps. His men were neither appropriately trained nor properly equipped; many had only sandals to their feet, and none had winter clothing. That carried no weight with Enver; indeed, according to a report from a German source – though whether he did so with Enver's encouragement or even his knowledge is unclear – Fevzi's replacement, Ihsan, even ordered the men of IX Corps to leave behind their greatcoats, blankets and packs in the interests of speed and manoeuvrability, permitting each to keep only his small haversack with a minimal supply of the flat bread which was all that was issued in the way of rations. And that same day the first really heavy snowfall of the winter came.

On 22 December news reached Tiflis from the Stavka headquarters at Baranovichi (Baranowice) in Belorussia (Belarus) that Enver Pasha himself was at Erzurum. Combined with reports from Istomin, of Turks having been spotted at Cucurus, a border post not ten kilometres north-west of Oltu, this convinced Yudenich that a major offensive was about to begin, and he made preparations to move to Mecinkirt to assess the situation at first hand, taking along Myshlayevski – who complained bitterly at being forced to leave the comforts of Tiflis – to give him the authority to replace Bergmann if need be.

That afternoon, Istomin's forward positions at Id came under attack, and he withdrew to Oltu. As a foggy, grey dawn broke on 23 December, he came under attack there,[15] and was forced eventually to give ground. He used his artillery to cover his retreat, falling back – in good order – to Avçali, on the road to Ardahan. The Turks were in control of Oltu by midday and diverted themselves by looting it.[16] During the course of the afternoon Enver arrived, and it was there that he spent the night.

There was a further heavy snowfall the next day; this made movement difficult both in the valleys, which were rapidly becoming clogged with snow (and men), and on the mountain paths. By nightfall the 29th Division had reached the shelter of Bardiz, the Russian border guards giving way before it and retiring towards Kizilkilise, but the 17th, following behind, had taken the full force of the blizzard in an extremely exposed position east of Çatak, and was now strung out over about eight kilometres of mountain track, while the 28th Division, which had joined the line of march by way of a track from Nariman, was stuck on the steep, north-facing slopes below the *Top Yol.* Somehow Enver himself reached Bardiz that night. Despite the terrible conditions, he was in high spirits and issued very optimistic orders for the following day: 29th Division was to move directly into Sarikamiş which, he had been informed by a Russian prisoner, had only a skeleton garrison of rear-echelon troops and no artillery. It would be followed in close order by the 17th, which was hopelessly unrealistic given that the division was actually still some distance short of Bardiz and was unlikely to arrive there in any fit state to proceed immediately. The 28th, when it arrived, was also to move straight on without pause, taking a second, more westerly, route from Bardiz, via the Hana Pass to cut the road west of Sarikamiş at Yeniköy and establish the Turkish right flank. Meanwhile, Hafiz Hakki's X Corps was to cross the lower slopes of the Allahüekbar Mountains and descend a track which skirted the northern side of the Turnagel-dağ above Sarikamiş and led down to the valley linking the town with Kars, thus forming the left flank.

Responding to reports of troop movements on Çakir Baba, Bergmann despatched a battalion of Dovgirt's 18th Turkistan Rifles north to Yeniköy; when they reported increasing numbers of Turks in the vicinity he ordered the regiment's two remaining battalions, together with a gun battery, to join them. This was the only significant repositioning of troops Bergmann carried out, despite the increasingly bleak reports he was receiving, and his staff officers were becoming extremely anxious.

During the morning of 24 December Yudenich and Myshlayevski arrived at Sarikamiş and there parted company. Yudenich, sensing the urgency of the situation, took personal command of II Turkistan Corps in the Pasin Valley, preparing to fight a defensive battle before Sanamer with at most ten battalions. Despite the numerical disadvantage, he was relatively optimistic; the primary fear he had was of Myshlayevski's (very) limited competence as a fighting commander, coupled with his strong instinct for self-preservation, leading him to make poor tactical decisions.

Myshlayevski, meanwhile, had gone to Mecinkirt, to Bergmann's headquarters, to discover that he believed the loss of Oltu was not significant,[17] and instead of a withdrawal to shorten and strengthen the defensive line, proposed a general offensive in the direction of Köprüköy. Senior staffers sensed an immediate danger to Sarikamiş, and they began pressing Myshlayevski to take personal control. That was the last thing the old man wanted, and he prevaricated, making changes to Russian troop dispositions which were no more than cosmetic while allowing planning for Bergmann's advance in the Pasin Valley to continue. That changed dramatically when he returned to Sarikamiş later that morning and received reports of large numbers of Turks making their way along the *Top Yol*. This finally convinced him that Bergmann's staff officers had been right, and he sent orders to him to call off the planned offensive and withdraw troops from the Pasin Valley to defend Sarikamiş from an attack from the north.

Myshlayevski was unused to confusion, and by now his morale was eroding rapidly. When, on his way back to Mecinkirt from Sarikamiş the following morning, his car came under fire from a Turkish patrol, he panicked. Now even regrouping to defend the town was not an option, he decided, and a withdrawal on Kars was called for before the entire Caucasian Army was cut off. When he arrived back at Bergmann's headquarters he immediately began issuing orders for a general retreat.

The withdrawal was to begin that night, with the majority of the units which made up I Caucasian Army Corps instructed to bypass Sarikamiş to the south, by way of a poor track to Karakurt, and to follow the Aras River in the direction of Kağizman and thence to Kars. By the following morning, baggage and supply trains were streaming away while three regiments of the 39th Infantry Division and the 1st Kuban Plastun Brigade remained in the front line, ready to pull out in their turn. Yudenich, subordinate as he was to Myshlayevski, was powerless to intervene.

In Sarikamiş the situation was calmer, as if the retreat order itself had somehow passed the town by. On the morning of 25 December there were rather less than two thousand armed men at hand: two squadrons of Frontier Guards, two extended companies of militiamen, about a thousand railway-men and some odds and ends of rear-echelon personnel. Save for the Frontier Guards, who had the bolt-action Mosin-Nagant magazine rifle, they were armed with the obsolete single-shot Berdans with which their grandfathers had fought the war of 1877. Quite by chance (and contrary to the intelligence Enver had received) they did, however, have two modern field guns, which had been set up in the main square. The presence of these two guns – for which a range card to the most likely targets had been prepared by an artillery officer passing through to the front some days before – was to be a crucial factor in the coming days.

The morale of the Russians defending Sarikamiş was to be another. Few in number they might have been, but they were quite ready to take the fight to the enemy. Before dawn on 26 December, Frontier Guards and railwaymen marched from the town and climbed the road towards the Bardiz Pass. Three hard hours out they crossed the col and began the descent towards Kizilkilise; some way below the crest they halted, dispersed, secreted themselves in the snow and brushwood which covered the slopes, and settled down to await the Turks.

They were in action by mid-afternoon. Unsure of the numbers which faced them, the Turks deployed into an attacking formation; eventually they managed to threaten the dispersed snipers, who promptly fell back just far enough to repeat the exercise, and continued to do so until dusk fell and they were able to disappear into the gathering darkness. The Turks bivouacked where they were, still ten kilometres short of their objective, to spend their fourth night in the open.

When 27 December dawned, the surviving troops of the 29th Division struggled to their feet and began to move forward as best they could, leaving hundreds of their number frozen to death in the snow. It was late in the morning before at last they saw Sarikamiş in the distance, and by then Enver had arrived at the head of the column to supervise the impending battle himself. He deployed four of his twelve mountain guns in an exposed pos-ition; before they had time to get off more than ranging shots the Russian field-pieces in the square below replied, putting three of the four out of action. It is fair to say that Enver was nonplussed by the presence of Russian artillery; he had set great store by the prisoners' intelligence, and when it proved to be faulty he had no fallback position. All he could think of doing was call a halt to proceedings, go to ground and wait for the 17th Division to

arrive. Its first regiment appeared early in the afternoon, and Enver immediately committed it to the attack, its men and those of the 29th stumbling
down the slope. The snow reduced the attackers' advance to a plodding
crawl; they were cut to pieces by the defenders' Maxims and artillery as they
staggered through the drifts, and the survivors withdrew as best they could,
having achieved nothing. Even when the third division, the 28th, began to
arrive before Sarikamiş, just as it was beginning to get dark, Enver had
nowhere near enough fit men to mount an assault on the town.

At this juncture he desperately needed X Corps, and it was conspicuous
by its absence. On 24 December Hafiz Hakki had been ordered to detach a
unit of sufficient size to pursue and harry Istomin, and to proceed with the
rest of his corps from Oltu to Bardiz, to arrive there by the evening of 25
December and then advance on Sarikamiş. Instead, Hafiz took his 30th and
31st Divisions off in pursuit of Istomin's depleted brigade, leaving the 32nd
at Oltu.

At some point on 25 December, in the afternoon or evening, a messenger
from Enver caught up with him near Merdenik, and handed over a despatch
ordering him in no uncertain terms to leave off his unauthorised pursuit and
proceed towards Sarikamiş by the most direct route, to link up with IX Corps
and launch a joint attack upon the town. That direct route would lead him
straight across the Allahüekber Mountains by way of a pass 3,000 metres
high ...

Hakki sent word for the 32nd Division to move to Bardiz via Kop, as per
the original plan, while the 30th and 31st – save for one regiment, detached
to occupy Merdenik – took the track southwards towards the village of
Beyköy, whence they could take either the Eşek-Meydan Pass to arrive on the
reverse slopes of the Turnagel near Kizilkilise, or descend by way of Divik
and Çatak towards Yağbasan in the Kars Valley. Hakki's first mistake was to
believe his map when it told him that Beyköy lay less than twenty kilometres
south of the Merdenik road (it was over thirty-five), which led him to
conclude that he could reach the village in a forced march of five hours. His
second was in failing to take into account that there was a high pass to cross
en route.

As the men set out the skies cleared, causing temperatures to fall dramatically, and the cold itself became their worst enemy. Over twenty hours
had passed before the first of them stumbled into Beyköy. Some units were
to leave almost 90 per cent of their entire strength on the mountainside;
by the next morning, of the 15,000 or so men of the two divisions which had
set out to cross the mountain, only about 3,400 had arrived, and most of
them were in no fit state to go a step further, let alone straight into
battle.

Hakki knew nothing of this when he himself reached Enver's headquarters
at Bardiz on the evening of 26 December, by which time his 32nd Division
had already arrived. Despite having come by an easier route, it was still in no

fit state to be committed to the attack on Sarikamiş, and was instead held at Bardiz in reserve. Thus, only the single much reduced regiment of the 17th Division which had been left to garrison the village was released to strengthen the assault force.

Late that same afternoon the Turks had suffered what seems at first sight to have been another potentially serious setback, when the chief of staff of the 28th Division was captured by a Cossack cavalry patrol on the slopes of the Yağmurlu above Upper Sarikamiş. He had in his possession a copy of the order of the day, which clearly set out Enver's entire strategy for the capture of Sarikamiş. In fact, of course, the orders reflected a most unreal situation, and, taking no account of the depredations they had suffered, portrayed the Turks as fielding over 75,000 men. When this order was brought to Myshlayevski, the academic, as skilled in military theory as he was unskilled in its practice, had no trouble at all in translating it into a clear but entirely misleading picture of the situation, with the Turkish XI Corps poised for a frontal attack on the defensive line across the Pasin Valley, IX Corps massed to the north-west of Sarikamiş and X Corps moving into a position on its left flank, whence it would advance to cut off the Russians' line of retreat towards Kars and threaten to complete the envelopment of Sarikamiş.

In fact, the situation in Sarikamiş was much improved. The 80th Kabardinski Regiment had arrived from the west, and its commander, Col. Barkovski, had taken over command; during the morning of 27 December the 155th Kubinski Regiment and the 15th Turkistan Rifles also moved into the town, and further reinforcements in the shape of Przevalski's 1st Kuban Plastun Brigade were on their way. The Russians needed all the reinforcements they could get, for the surviving Turkish *askers* of IX Corps had begun to get their second wind, and fighting before Sarikamiş had become more intense. During the course of the day Upper Sarikamiş would change hands twice, and the Turks would establish themselves in a rocky outcropping known as the Eagle's Nest, which allowed them to pour direct fire from mountain guns and machine guns into Sarikamiş for the first time. During the afternoon a Turkish attack on the outskirts of the town was held and driven back at the road to Kars; however, soon afterwards news arrived that Turkish troops had descended on the railway station at Selim.

Apart from the very real effect of cutting Sarikamiş's direct communications with Kars, this had a secondary consequence: it confirmed to Myshlayevski everything he had read into the orders captured the day before, and announced that an enveloping movement was imminent.[18] That was the last straw, and he reacted in the worst possible way, taking flight by car to Kars and thence to Tiflis by train. On the way he ordered Oganovski, who commanded the troops in the Eleşkirt Valley, and Chernozubov, who had led an invasion force into Persian territory some years before and remained there, to do likewise. Oganovski simply ignored him, but Chernozubov showed less fortitude, and ordered a general withdrawal. (That caused considerable temporary confusion but no real lasting damage, for though Tabriz was soon occupied by irregulars, the Turks were not able to channel men into the region in sufficient numbers rapidly enough to hold it.) By the time Myshlayevski arrived in Tiflis he had convinced himself that not just the battle for Sarikamiş but the entire war in the Lesser Caucasus was lost. He shared his view with anyone who would listen; unrest soon spread to the streets, and within hours the citizens were running for their lives.

It took some time for order to be restored in Tiflis and over two months for Myshlayevski to be called to account for his actions, but early the following March he was dismissed from the service. Thus he was out of the picture before the last chicken he had sent scurrying in the dying days of 1914 came home to roost, for it was his abject pessimism, communicated to the Tsar, which stimulated the Russian government to beg their allies, in early January 1915, to do anything in their power to divert Turkish attention – and manpower – away from the Caucasus. In the event the imagined danger had passed, but no one thought to rescind the request for assistance. The result was the plan to force the Dardanelles, which in turn became the ill-fated Anglo-French invasion of Gallipoli.

For the Turks, 28 December was a day of uneasy rest, Hafiz Hakki having succeeded in convincing Enver that this would allow the stragglers of his 30th and 31st Divisions to be collected, nurtured and brought back to something like operational readiness. It had the desired effect to some extent, but the respite for X Corps had a deleterious effect on the men of IX Corps, who spent another day and night out in the open on the slopes of the Turnagel. By the next morning – the decisive day of the Battle of Sarikamiş, as it was to turn out – after the worst night of the campaign so far, in terms of the weather, the entire corps could field no more than 6,000 men, not even 30 per cent of its nominal roll.

Towards dawn on 29 December the depleted combat units of X Corps began to move into position east of Sarikamiş. 31st Division was to line up on the eastern slopes of Turnagel, facing roughly south-west, with its left flank at Yağbasan, on the Kars River. It had poor communications with IX Corps, to its right, by way of a network of snowy tracks and paths on the northern side of the mountain. On the left, its line slewed round to the right, the 30th Division occupied the area from Yağbasan as far as Alisofu, on the far side of the valley. The 32nd Division remained in reserve at Bardiz. IX Corps' 17th Division was on the right of the 31st, the 29th to its right and the 28th occupying the western slopes of the Turnagel and across the track leading up to the Bardiz Pass, their line some three kilometres north of the railway. That day Gen. Przevalski[19] arrived in Sarikamiş and assumed command, his Kuban Cossacks altering the balance of power (though it was still weighted in the Turks' favour). They met the Turkish 30th Division when it attacked; the Turks were halted, and withdrew northwards, across the railway line, leaving it entirely in Russian hands. In the process they exposed the flank of the 31st Division, which had itself advanced along the axis of the permanent way, and forced it, too, to halt. In the confusion a battalion of the Cossack infantry also managed to scale the heights of the Eagle's Nest and recapture it.

It is a measure of the surge in Russian confidence and numbers that they were able to fight on two fronts on 29 December. Even as the Kubans were driving the Turks back in the east, Bukretov had led a force six battalions strong to attack their right flank in the west, to retake Upper Sarikamiş and to drive across the Ahardahar beyond, and up the slope which gave access to the road towards the Bardiz Pass. When darkness came he had failed in his primary objective, and the Turks were still in control of the village, but they were effectively cut off, for men of the 15th Turkistan Rifles had bypassed it, advanced up the slope and cut the road within sight of the pass itself, denying it to Turkish reinforcements.

Elsewhere, Bergmann's intransigence was still creating problems. On 27 December he had halted his retreat at Yudenich's insistence, but the following day he resumed – not entirely without good reason; it is fair to say that the withdrawal of Przevalski's 1st Kuban Plastun Brigade to Sarikamiş had left his left flank exposed – and by that night his rearguard was at Çermuk, about twelve kilometres south-west of Mecinkirt. Yudenich was determined to give no more ground until attempts to take the Hana Pass and menace Bardiz had either been successful or had to be abandoned, and was able to persuade him to call a halt there, but he in turn was forced to order a retreat in his own sector to straighten the line, which now ran from north-west to south-east through Hoşap. Happily for him, early on 30 December the 18th Turkistan Rifles occupied the summer pastures above Bardiz, and Bergmann agreed, albeit reluctantly, to hold his line for forty-eight hours while he threatened the village itself.

Before the evening was out Bergmann went back on his word, and Yudenich learned that he intended to resume his withdrawal as planned. He sent one of his staff officers to explain the situation; after what one commentator was to describe as 'a dramatic interview', Bergmann agreed to halt the 39th Division at the pre-war frontier and leave it and the 4th Turkistan Division under Yudenich's command while he, with the 154th Derbentski Regiment, proceeded to Sarikamiş.

That was probably as much as Yudenich could have hoped for, and he made plans to straighten his line once more. The final piece slotted into place on the afternoon of 30 December, with the arrival at Selim of Col. Voronov at the head of three battalions of infantry and a squadron of cavalry, despatched from Kars on the initiative of the commander there; this opened the way for additional reinforcements from the east, and boosted Yudenich's confidence still further. Now he believed not just that he would prevail in his own sector, but that the troops he was shielding would defeat the Turks to the north of Sarikamiş convincingly, and even wipe them out, if Enver did not move fast to effect their withdrawal.

Enver was indeed moving, quitting his command post at Çerkezköy for Bardiz and then decamping to Abdul Karim's headquarters at Köprüköy, having given Hafiz Hakki command of the remnants of IX and X Corps, consolidated into what he called the Left Wing. It is clear that by this time his self-confidence had evaporated, that he had accepted the situation of much of the Third Army was little short of desperate. His nightmare was to be some days in the fulfilment, and by then IX Corps was finished as a fighting unit, its original complement of 21,000 by now whittled down to little more than a tenth of that. It ceased to be, in any real sense, on 4 January, when the ring of Russians closed around it, the *coup de grâce* coming that afternoon when Ali Ihsan Bey, his chief of staff Lt.-Col. Şerif[20] and his entire headquarters were cut off and forced to surrender.

By the morning of 2 January the Russian repositioning was completed, and Yudenich could order them onto the offensive. He had reckoned without Bergmann, however, who had determined that the counterattack was his to command, and promptly brought all his characteristic incompetence to bear upon it. On 3 January he gave orders for an operation aimed at cutting the Turkish 30th and 31st Divisions' lines of retreat. It was mounted chiefly by Baratov's Cossacks, and came to nothing as a result of its author's misreading of the situation and Baratov's lackadaisical approach to carrying out his orders. Far from outflanking the Turks and getting ahead of them to establish a blocking force, the Russians arrived late on the scene and actually fell on the Turks' main body, and were severely punished. The episode did have one good consequence, however: it finally convinced Vorontsov-Dashkov to dismiss Bergmann.

By now the situation in Sarikamiş itself was easier; the threat to the town from the north had been dissipated, while that from the west was rapidly wearing itself out and would soon grind to a halt. Perhaps the most convincing sign that the battle was nearing its conclusion was the departure of the Turkish commander-in-chief. Enver Pasha left Köprüköy for Erzurum on 8 January, calling down the blessings of Allah on his men and reminding them that He (if not he himself) was with them at all times. His final act was to install Hafiz Hakki in his place as head of the Third Army. The following morning he left Erzurum to return to Constantinople; he would never again take command of an army in the field.

That was not, however, the end of the story; the Battle of Sarikamiş, though decided, was not yet over, and there were many lives, the majority of them Turkish, still to be lost. At this point, as far as can be estimated there were something less than 30,000 Turkish troops still capable of bearing arms in the theatre, around 10,000 of them at Bardiz, where the remnants of the 31st Division had now joined those of the 32nd. It is suggested by some that the dead and wounded were outnumbered by deserters, and if one included in that last category men who were incapable of going on, and who had sought such shelter as they could to give themselves a chance to weather the storm and recover, with whatever end in mind, then that may well have been the case. It is said that Enver became convinced that Armenians in the ranks of the Third Army had deserted en masse – and indeed, that many had actually gone over to the enemy – and used that as an element of justification in the revenge he was to extract from their community for his defeat.

All that remained now was for the Russians to sweep up as many of the remaining Turkish troops as possible. Yudenich chose Baratov to deal with those in and around Bardiz and allocated him just six battalions – about four thousand men – with which to carry it out, which seems questionable but proved realistic.

Baratov may not have been entirely reliable, but he knew his trade and didn't lack determination. He assembled his forces in the area between Kizilkilise and Çerkez, and divided them into three columns. Conditions were atrocious and movement slow, but by 9 January Bardiz had been taken, along with around 4,000 prisoners.

In the meantime, measures had been taken to deal with the force which, under the German, Stange, had occupied Ardahan. Elements of the Siberian Cossack Brigade, under General Kalitin, set out from Tiflis on 26 December and reached their objective four days later. An artillery barrage convinced Stange that he faced a superior force, and by the time Kalitin ordered the assault the Turks were already streaming out of the town westwards, along the road to Ardanuch. Istomin, revitalised, then led his brigade towards Ardanuch and Artvin, reoccupying the lower Çoruh Valley, while Kalitin moved on towards Merdenik and Oltu.

He reached Merdenik on 7 January, just as the advance guard of the impoverished Turkish 30th Division, which had recrossed the Allahüekber Mountains, reached the Merdenik–Oltu road. There they turned westwards and moved into a sheltered position near Penek in order to recover from their protracted ordeal. Kalitin bided his time, and on 9 January he was reinforced by Caucasian Cossacks and two battalions of infantry which had pursued the Turks. The Turks, exhausted by their efforts of the past weeks, had little stamina left; by the evening of 11 January the 30th Division had virtually ceased to exist as a fighting force. The following day Kalitin reoccupied Oltu, with orders to continue on through Nariman and block the retreat of the survivors of the 31st and 32nd Divisions who had managed to escape from Bardiz by way of the *Top Yol*. He was only partially effective this time. In the fighting which followed, a further 3,000 Turks were made prisoner, but many managed to escape and eventually reach Erzurum and temporary safety.

On 10 January Yudenich had turned his attention towards Abdul Karim's XI Corps. His troops were as exhausted as the Turks they faced, but they rallied and gave Yudenich a platform from which to launch a flanking attack on the Turkish centre, specifically on Zivin, and he gave the job to Dovgirt. The conditions his men encountered were even worse than those at Bardiz, with snow to their chests, and they were able to make barely five kilometres a day. By 15 January Yudenich had given them up for lost, but that afternoon they appeared in Abdul Karim's rear, inspiring the Turks to retreat to the positions they had occupied a month earlier, and with that, the Battle of Sarikamiş finally drew to a close.

Despite its role in defining the entire war in the Caucasus, despite the enormous losses sustained, even by conservative estimates, outside Turkey the first major engagement of the Caucasus campaign is little known. Most reports of it are seemingly based on the work of Ali Ihsan's chief of staff, Lt.-Col. Şerif (Köprülü), as quoted by Larcher in *La Guerre Turque dans la Guerre Mondiale*, published in Paris in 1926, which had it that 90,000 Turks died in the course of the fighting, that 40,000 to 50,000 more were taken prisoner and most died in captivity, and that just 12,400 escaped and lived to tell the tale. These estimates – irreconcilable as they are with the Third Army's strength at the start of the battle – have become widely accepted, perhaps due to the extra dramatic weight their magnitude adds. They are contradicted by the official account of the Third Army's (German) chief of staff, Lt.-Col. Felix Guse, who reported that 30,000 of its men died and 7,000 went into captivity. WED Allen and Paul Muratoff take a middle line in their *Caucasian Battlefields*, stating that Turkish losses due to all causes amounted to 75,000. Russian numbers and losses are harder to ascertain. Allen and Muratoff put their dead and wounded at 16,000, with another 12,000 incapacitated, mostly as a result of frostbite, and that seems uncontentious.

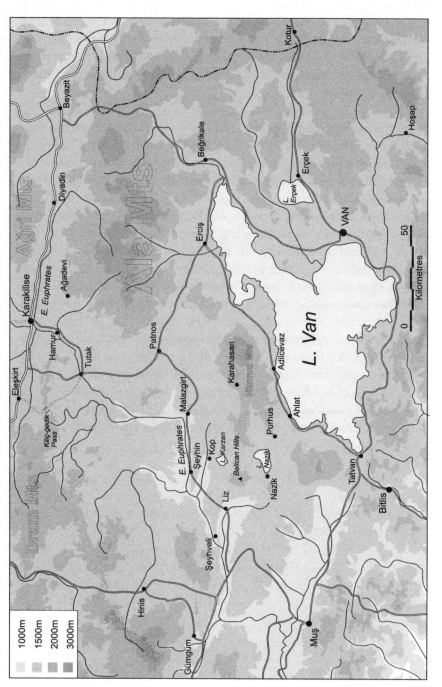

11. *Caucasus – The Upper E. Euphrates Basin*

The Turks Fight Back

As the last act of the tragedy of Sarikamiş was being played out, Enver Pasha retreated to Constantinople, and into denial. Once re-established in the War Ministry he tried everything he knew to play down the magnitude of the defeat[1] and the likely effects of it. Thanks to poor internal communications and the Young Turks' control of the means of disseminating information, he was largely successful to begin with. Eventually, however, German officers who had witnessed events in the Caucasus for themselves began to return to the capital, and the truth started to come out. Enver then began to search for a scapegoat and was to find one, not in an individual but in the entire Armenian people; they were the root of the rot in his army, he declared, and commenced what would become a sustained, vengeful campaign against them.

In the war zone itself, Hafiz Hakki, the newly appointed commander of the decimated Third Turkish Army, had no time to waste on either public relations exercises or recriminations, for now the Russians posed a very real threat to the key city of Erzurum, and he had few enough resources with which to resist them. In addition to the troops who had managed to escape from Sarikamiş he had perhaps 40,000 fresh men in reserve, but this was nowhere near enough to man the fortresses ringing the city, and he cast around frantically for local sources of recruits.

In the event, the attack Hakki feared did not materialise. The Russians were actually in no fit state to launch a major offensive, and Yudenich, still subordinate to the sedentary, unimaginative Vorontsov-Dashkov, had to content himself with local actions designed to consolidate the Russian position rather than trying to improve his situation materially, while frantically trying both to make up his losses and prevent the Stavka from denuding his army of entire formations to bolster those further west, in which latter campaign he was, inevitably, a great deal less than successful.[2]

Specifically, having secured the defensive line in the Sarikamiş sector approximately upon that of the pre-war frontier, he gave free rein to his commander in the area to the north, Gen. Lyakhov, who had eight battalions of regulars and units of Georgian militia, together with a gun battery, at his disposal. The Black Sea littoral is dominated by the Pontic Alps, their steep-sided valleys running directly across the Russian line of advance. It was home to aggressive Muslim communities, and with a competent force of regular Turkish troops at large under a determined German commander,

Lt.-Col. Stange – which remained a threat despite having been driven out of Ardahan – Lyakhov made little progress initially. Eventually, however, with some support from ships of Eberhardt's Black Sea Fleet, which supplied both gunnery support and transport for landing parties in the more remote coastal regions, in the course of a three-month campaign he was able to secure the entire area, including the lower Çoruh and lower Oltu Valleys, the small but important port of Hopa, and Artvin, together with the copper workings at Borchka.

In southern Armenia the situation was rather different. While the main thrust of his Caucasian campaign was to have been made through Sarikamiş, Enver had also laid plans to push eastwards from Lake Van into Persian Azerbaijan, as a precursor to a hooking drive northwards into the Eastern Caucasus. However, the only forces he had available locally were lightly armed Jandarma, essentially militarised police, based in the city of Van, and while such units were composed of picked men, they were not equipped to mount an invasion. Nonetheless, sometime around 13 December Enver had ordered them forward, and they crossed into Persia near the undistinguished border town of Kotur – Turkish until 1878, when Russian influence had seen it ceded to Persia, and still home to many ethnic Turks – where they dug in to await events.

The Jandarma battalions' reinforcements were to come from Thrace. There the First Army – I, II, III, and IV Corps, each of three infantry divisions, most of them up to full strength, and with a further two divisions in the course of formation – and the Second Army – V and VI Corps, also of three divisions each – faced a phantom enemy in defence of the capital. No matter that there was nothing for them to do, and little prospect of change in that situation any time soon, the perceived threat to Constantinople from the west was so great that reducing their numbers substantially required considerable courage. Lower Mesopotamia was deemed not to be worth the risk, despite the loss of Basra, but satisfying Enver's pan-Turanian ambitions was another matter, and before he left for the Caucasus front on 7 December, he ordered the redeployment of some of the troops from Thrace to the Persian frontier.

IV and V Corps were ordered to relinquish men to make up what was to be known as the Halil Bey[3] Division, and on 11 December the new force – three infantry regiments and three battalions of cavalry, with a dozen mountain guns and a machine gun unit in support – left Haydarpaşa station, on the Asian side of the Bosporus, on the first leg of its journey on 11 December. It faced a 1,500-kilometre trek by rail and on foot[4] which was expected to take at least three weeks. On 26 December, hardly past Adana, and already haemorrhaging men,[5] it was redesignated the 5th Expeditionary Force.

The day the Halil Bey Division entrained, Enver ordered a second, smaller, force constituted. Made up chiefly from elements of II Corps in Adrianople and commanded by that corps' intelligence chief, Lt.-Col. Kazim Bey,[6] it too was nominally a division, but actually amounted to two infantry regiments, with proportionately reduced cavalry and mountain artillery detachments, with the promise of a third to join it en route. It left Haydarpaşa on 19 December, bound initially for Aleppo in northern Syria. Like the Halil Bey Division, the Kazim Bey's journey east was only partially conducted by train. Arriving at Adana it was redesignated the 1st Expeditionary Force; it then continued on foot, coming under fire from the Royal Navy[7] where the road followed the shores of the Gulf of Iskenderun.

The 5th Expeditionary Force reached Diyarbakir on 10 January, by which time the situation in the Caucasus had been transformed out of all recognition. The following day Halil Bey learned that his orders had been revised: he was now to make for Erzurum, to reinforce the garrison there. In all he brought with him around nine thousand men, of whom perhaps 75 per cent were combat-fit, and received a warm welcome. However, he also brought something far less acceptable: spotted typhus. It ran through the garrison like wildfire, and Hafiz Hakki was an early victim; he died on 12 February, to be replaced in command of the Third Army by Mahmut Kamil Pasha, who retained the German, Guse, as his chief of staff.

The 1st Expeditionary Force arrived at Aleppo on 10 January. There it too received orders for Erzurum. With Halil Bey's division strung out directly across its line of march, clogging up the one road worthy of the name and picking the land clean of supplies as it went, there was no question of it heading directly towards its objective, and instead it was routed far to the east, to Mosul. That stage of the journey, in the course of which it picked up a third infantry regiment, took no less than two months, and it was 12 March before the last of its stragglers arrived in the city. The following day, events having taken several turns in the meantime, it was ordered to the region around Van, where Christian Armenian rebels were taking full advantage of the absence of the Jandarma who normally garrisoned the city, massing and threatening open revolt.

We left those Jandarma at Kotur in mid-December, facing elements of the substantial Russian force – it comprised the 2nd Caucasian Rifle Brigade and the 4th Caucasian Cossack Division, with a full complement of 24 guns, under Chernozubov – which had occupied Persian Azerbaijan with the approval of the government in Teheran when the Kurds in the region had renewed their perennial campaign for independence in 1910. The lightly armed Turks had little rational prospect of breaking through the Russian defensive line, and even less of advancing on Khoy (Khvoy) and Tabriz if they did, and had settled down to await events. They were well rewarded, for during the last days of 1914, following Myshlayevski's panic attack and his order to Chernozubov to withdraw his forces and fall back on Tiflis, the Russians disappeared, and the gendarmes were left unopposed while Kurdish tribesmen began plundering towns and villages across the region, even seizing control of Tabriz on 14 January. Yudenich, once he assumed command, lost no time in ordering Chernozubov to reoccupy the area and re-establish

Russian control; he moved quickly, and order soon returned to Tabriz, but spring was well advanced before the province was entirely back under Russian rule.

As soon as it became clear that the Russians were not going to move on the Erzurum front for some time, Enver detached Halil Bey to take command of the 36th Division, which, together with the 37th, had been sent to the area south of Lake Van with orders to be ready to advance eastwards. He was to be thwarted afresh by Yudenich who, despite losing further significant formations of experienced troops to the European theatre, had managed to regroup sufficiently well to reassert his authority over the border area. That regrouping had had the effect of moving the Russian centre of mass to the south, out of the Aras Valley and across the Ağri Mountains, which tempted Yudenich into formulating a plan for an expedition towards Malazgirt, employing Oganovski's IV Caucasian Army Corps, a fresh force which had wintered south of Karakilise and had not yet seen action.

First of all, however, he had to deal with Halil Bey, who had advanced past Başkale, crossed the ill-defined border into Persian Azerbaijan, taken the town of Urmia and then turned north to round the lake of the same name, heading for Dilman and Kotur and threatening Tabriz. On 29 April Halil attacked Dilman, which was held by a single Russian battalion; Chernozubov responded by ordering his subordinate commander in the area, the Armenian Gen. Tovmos Nazarbekov, to counter him. He rapidly assembled six battalions of infantry and two regiments of Cossacks from Julfa (Culfa) and Khoy, and drew them up north of the town. When Halil attacked, on 1 May, he held him, despite the Turks' superiority in numbers, killing over a thousand. At that the Kurdish irregulars who had accompanied Halil deserted him, and overnight his numerical advantage disappeared; he withdrew across the border, back towards Van, leaving the field to Nazarbekov, who – much to Yudenich's irritation – declined to pursue him.

The internal political situation in Armenia had changed very dramatically by that time. Ever since the Jandarma battalions had quit Van, the city's largely Christian population had become increasingly restive and by late March the Armenian nationalist movement, the Dashnaktsutiun, was openly challenging for control.

During non-stop street fighting over the first weeks of April they slowly overcame the Turks, and by 14 April the city was in their hands and unrest had spread right across the region. Kazim Bey, who arrived at Van the next day with both regular soldiers and gendarmes, could do no more than throw a cordon around it and establish what proved to be a rather ineffectual state of siege. As far as Yudenich was concerned, this merely pinned Kazim in place, and he was content to allow the situation to mature, though he did alter his plans for the offensive to come, to allow for elements on his left flank, a mixed force of Cossacks and Armenians under Trukhin, to advance down the eastern shore of Lake Van with the none too urgent object of lifting the siege and taking control of the city.

It would, however, be some weeks before he put the plan into effect. First he moved to re-establish the Russians as the controlling force in Persian Azerbaijan, sending the Caucasian Cavalry Division and the 3rd Transbaikal Cossack Brigade, under the overall command of Gen. Charpentier, to Tabriz by rail. Six-thousand-strong, they swept across the countryside east and north of Lake Urmia on a broad front, taking the old trade route through Khoy to Van as their axis, routing the Kurds wherever they found them. Having completed their mission very much to Yudenich's satisfaction (and perhaps rather to his surprise; he had no high opinion of Charpentier's military acumen, and later events were to prove him right), they rested at Dilman, and then moved slowly north to round Lake Van and join up with elements of IV Corps, arriving at Adilcevaz, halfway along the northern shore of the lake, only towards the end of June.

Yudenich released Trukhin to begin his sweep south from Beyazit towards Van early in May, but even in springtime the route across the Ala Dağ was arduous, and it was three weeks before he reached Beğrikale, little more than halfway to his destination. The going got easier from then on, however, and the occasional Turkish patrols he had encountered disappeared, Halil Bey having withdrawn the 36th Division to Bitlis, taking care not to become involved in the siege of Van in the process. That affair had never shown much promise for the Turks and now, as the Russians neared, Kazim Bey, too, withdrew along the southern shore of the lake, leaving the city to the Armenians, who greeted Trukhin and his men with open arms on the last day of the month. That same day, at Hoşap, Trukhin's patrols linked up with the advance guard of Nazarbekov's force, which had finally come up from Dilman by way of Başkale. Nazarbekov's tardiness, coming on top of his having allowed Halil Bey to escape a month earlier, perhaps decided Yudenich that he was unsuited for independent command, and he ordered his force broken up, assigning some of his units to Chernozubov, and the 2nd Caucasian Rifle Brigade and 4th Plastun Brigade, as a semi-independent formation with the general still at its head but subordinate to Oganovski, to join IV Caucasian Army Corps in the area north of Lake Van.

The Armenian rising at Van was the last straw to Enver. As we have noted, in the aftermath of Sarikamiş he had sought a scapegoat, and had settled on the Armenians, and now the full weight of his wrath landed on their community. All Armenians, civilians as well as those serving in the Army (Christians had only been eligible for military service since the General Staff reforms of 1908), were disarmed and the latter, said to number around 40,000, were transferred to labour battalions. That proved to be a sentence of death, for they were systematically subjected to a brutal regime of overwork and deprivation. Then, at Enver's prompting, Talaat, the Ottoman Minister of the Interior, went further, and promulgated the 'Tehcir Law', which came into force on 1 June 1915. This legislation enabled the Ottoman government to round up all Armenians, estimated at between 1.25 million and at least twice that number, throughout the empire, wherever they were to be found, and concentrate them in camps prior to 'resettling' them in the extremely inhospitable desert areas of Syria and northern Mesopotamia – a textbook example of what we have come to call ethnic cleansing. Many – some say, 800,000 – died in the process, some brutally but relatively quickly, others after prolonged, systematic ill-treatment. Many were enslaved; many, particularly very young boys, were taken from their parents and forcibly converted to Islam.

There is a very considerable body of evidence of the massacres, some of it in great detail,[8] but is there, as the Armenians continue to insist, any real proof that the campaign was one of *deliberate* genocide against their people? Or were they 'simply' victims of collateral damage – casualties of a civil-war-within-a-war – as the official Turkish line still maintains? In the absence of anything which documents intent on the part of the Turks – something analagous to the infamous Wannsee Protocol, perhaps – it is difficult to imagine how this impasse will ever be entirely resolved, save by an admission of guilt which is extremely unlikely to be forthcoming, so deeply entrenched is the tradition of denial within the Turkish establishment.

1915 was more than half over before the Russians and the Turks met in another set-piece battle, and when they did, west of Malazgirt[9] in mid-July, the clear advantage the encroaching tsarists had had over the defenders ever since they had driven the Third Army from the field at Sarikamiş had dwindled, thanks to the Russians' ranks having been thinned by the demand for fresh bodies for the European Front.

Even without the benefit of hindsight it would be clear that compared to the events on the European Front, the campaign in the Caucasus was a minor affair, and that the Russian High Command was right to denude its army there of troops. However, we should not neglect the fact that by mid-spring the Turks were fighting on four fronts, having crossed Sinai to attack the Suez Canal and being engaged at Gallipoli, and suggest that had Yudenich been able to strike at the end of April, when the Turkish High Command was looking the other way and before the Third Army had been brought up to the sort of strength it had reached by July, the outcome might have been very different. Had he been able to drive the Turks back on Muş, the road to Diyarbakir – and, potentially, to the Mediterranean coast at Alexandretta – would have been open to him, with all the consequences that would have had for the Turks in Syria, Palestine and Mesopotamia when they were cut off from Anatolia and unable even to communicate effectively with Constantinople.

Oganovski left his winter quarters around Hamur, twenty kilometres south-west of Karakilise, and followed the Eastern Euphrates south towards

Tutak. His much under-strength IV Caucasian Army Corps – it comprised just the 2nd Caucasian Cossack Division and the 66th Infantry Division – met no opposition when it pushed on towards Malazgirt; he took the important town easily on 17 May, and there he halted, advancing his left towards Adilcevaz, on the northern shores of Lake Van. Four weeks later, having waited in vain for Charpentier and Nazarbekov to join him as ordered, he turned his attention on Kop, twenty kilometres to the west. This he took after a brief fight, the three battalions from the Turkish 37th Division which held the town retreating in good order to the Belican Hills, where a stronger defensive position had been established. These hills, an isolated massif some fifteen kilometres in diameter, running down to the Euphrates in the north,[10] the southern of its two summits climbing to 1,000 metres above the surrounding countryside,[11] formed a natural barrier running north–south, to the east of two small lakes, Haçli, to the south of Kop, and Nazik. Further south still, the land ran flat down to Lake Van, and, some twenty kilometres east of Adilcevaz, the village of Ahlat.

Charpentier's progress around Lake Van to Adilcevaz had been painfully slow, and it was 26 June before he arrived, by which time Oganovski had grown impatient. Yudenich had instructed him to carry out a simple consolidation, a straightening of his line to take in the Belican Hills, and he sent Charpentier on directly, to take Ahlat as a precursor to an assault on the enemy positions in the hills themselves. Oganovski believed he was facing a single division on the Belican Hills; on 10 July he ordered the 66th Infantry Division moved up from Kop, and two days later began a two-pronged assault, around the northern flank, down the eastern slope and directly across through the saddle separating the two summits. He met stubborn resistance, but when Nazarbekov's four recently arrived Plastun battalions and two of his Caucasian Rifle Regiments were thrown in on the southern flank, he prevailed. By 16 July he was in control of the heights, but the picture revealed from there was disquieting: Turkish reinforcements in significant numbers, advancing along both banks of the Euphrates and threatening to outflank him in his turn, and also across the plains to his front. However, the next day he received news that Trukhin, who had advanced from Van, had gained ground on the south side of the lake, and he ordered Charpentier to take two of his dragoon regiments to Tatvan, to link up with him. He succeeded, and was joined by the third of Nazarbekov's infantry regiments, the 7th Caucasian Rifles; but things had already begun to go seriously wrong in the area west of the Belican Hills. It was soon clear that the Turks had vastly greater resources at their disposal than Oganovski had estimated.

Yudenich was working on faulty intelligence, having failed to exploit the enormous advantage his access to a sympathetic indigenous population gave him. The estimates he had of the size of the Turkish Third Army opposing him were perhaps as much as two months out of date. Since May it had increased from under forty thousand to considerably over fifty thousand men, and its centre of mass had shifted southwards even more markedly than had his own, for Erzurum had been stripped of every nonessential soldier in order to form a task force to be known as the 'Right Wing Group', with Abdul Karim Pasha – independent of Mahmut Kamil Pasha and working directly to orders from Constantinople – in command. It was a formidable formation, including IX Corps – which had received the bulk of the new drafts of men after Sarikamiş,[12] and had been transferred to Hinis, roughly halfway between Erzurum and Lake Van, in late May or early June to complete its retraining; its 17th and 28th Divisions had subsequently moved south, to the area east of Muş – together with the 1st and 5th Expeditionary Forces, now redesignated yet again as the 51st and 52nd Divisions. It also encompassed the 36th and 37th Divisions and the Jandarma battalions, now near Bitlis. Instead of three divisions, the Russians were facing eight, albeit not at full strength, and they had nothing like enough men to take them on, as Oganovski was about to discover.

The Turkish counterattack began near the village of Liz, west of the main massif of the Belican Hills, on 20 July, and with an infantry-versus-cavalry engagement on the far bank of the river to the north. Neither was decisive, but the Turks persisted, and when the Plastun battalions, on the left of the main force and trying to maintain contact with Nazarbekov's 5th and 6th Caucasian Rifles, also came under attack, it was clear that a dangerous situation was developing. In fact that latter development was something of a feint, and the main attack, when it came on 22 July, saw the 17th and 28th Divisions of IX Corps committed alongside the expeditionary groups and launched directly at Oganovski's main force, centrally and simultaneously on both flanks.

By nightfall Oganovski had been outflanked on his right. He had no reserves to throw in, save for the Cossack infantry of the Don Foot Brigade, who were little more than raw recruits; when, early on the morning of 23 July, they came under sustained and fierce attack, they broke and ran, leaving the road to Kop and Malazgirt open. Oganovski now had no choice but to retire as best he could over the Belican Hills; with Nazarbekov's 6th Caucasian Rifles and Charpentier's Tverski Dragoon regiment as its rearguard, the 66th Infantry Division began its withdrawal in the direction of Malazgirt.

The Plastun battalions to the south of the main force now came under more sustained attack, and in the confusion, instead of fighting as a single block, three of the four edged to their left, maintaining their link with the 5th Caucasian Rifles but leaving the other to face the entire strength of the Turkish right. Nazarbekov disengaged and refused to become involved again, withdrawing to the south of Lake Nazik instead. The Turks ignored him and smashed the one remaining Cossack battalion aside, opening a second road to Malazgirt, between Lakes Kazan and Nazik.

Oganovski ordered Charpentier to quit Tatvan and fall back and join him at Malazgirt, but when his dragoons arrived, on 25 July, they were too late; the Turks were already in the outskirts. Charpentier, on his own responsibility, turned around and made for Adilcevaz instead, where he was joined the next day by Nazarbekov's six infantry battalions. Further south Trukhin, on hearing that Charpentier had abandoned Tatvan, made a volte-face of his own and retired along the southern shore of Lake Van. He reached the city on 29 July, just in time to participate in its evacuation; by 4 August he was on his way to Dilman, across the frontier in Persia, and the following day Van was reoccupied by the Turks, who lost no time in revenging themselves on such of its Christian population as had unwisely stayed on.

His entire left flank having disappeared, and his other units badly mauled, short of supplies and very weary after a fortnight's non-stop fighting, Oganovski had only now come to grasp fully how serious the situation was. With certainly no more than fifteen thousand men – mostly infantry, with just one regiment of Charpentier's dragoons – to confront at least five Turkish infantry divisions and another of cavalry, he could but hope that retreat did not turn into rout. He abandoned Malazgirt on 26 July and began the long trek north to the Eleşkirt Valley, his dispirited soldiers vying for space on roads congested with terrified Armenian civilians. The 66th Infantry Division's supply train was lost along the way, though almost miraculously its artillery was saved. When Gen. Tomilov, Yudenich's quartermaster, sent to Malazgirt to report on the situation, and Gen. Mdivani – sent from Kars to replace Oganovski's Chief of Staff Ryabinkin when Yudenich received Tomilov's despatch informing him just how bad things were – tried to organise resistance at the Kiliç-gedik (Fenç) Pass, an alternative route into the Eleşkirt Valley west of Karakilise, they failed. In headlong retreat and with its morale plunging, IV Caucasian Army Corps was fast coming undone.

Understandably, Abdul Karim Pasha was jubilant, and so, when he telegraphed news of his victory to Constantinople, was Enver. The War Minister, quick to see a chance to revive his moribund pan-Turanian strategy, urged him to press the retreating Russians closely, and rapidly worked up an ad hoc plan to capitalise on it by driving the enemy out of the Eleşkirt Valley and the Ağri Mountains, clear back to the Aras. Even under fairly cursory examination, it is clear that his scheme had multiple shortcomings. To begin with, every day's march would not only stretch Abdul Karim's lines of communication but require him to open new ones, and entail him dominating an ever-larger area, the loyalty of the population of which was far from certain, in order to secure them. That would swallow up much of his numerical advantage over Oganovski, and he had little in the way of reserves to throw in. Secondly, he lacked adequate intelligence as to the size, readiness and location of forces which the Russians could be expected to commit in order to save the situation.

Karakilise, an important station on the old caravan route from Erzurum to Beyazit and thence to Teheran, and now the key to the situation south of the Ağri Dağ, stands at the junction of four valleys. The Eastern Euphrates, the Murat-Su, arrives from the east, from the direction of Dayadin, and makes a sharp turn, flowing south-west towards Tutak and Malazgirt, and this latter, and the Kiliç-gedik Pass to the west, were the Turks' routes towards the town. To the north a road climbs into the Ağri Mountains and gives access to the Aras Valley east of Kağizman, while to the east the River Şarian descends steeply from the direction of Tahir and Eleşkirt.

Yudenich had maintained two strong divisions on the extended front west of Sarikamiş to guard against the possibility of a renewed Turkish offensive down the Pasin and upper Oltu Valleys. He thus had a firm base from which to push forces to the left across the Aras and into the Eleşkirt Valley from the north, by way of Tahir, where the 153rd Bakinskis were stationed. This opened up the possibility of taking the Turks on their left flank.

Abdul Karim arrived at Karakilise on 2 August, by which time Oganovski's main force had crossed the Ağri Dağ by way of the Ahtalar Pass. Karim sent a mixed force of infantry and cavalry after him, but not until the following day, and when it caught up with him, on 4 August, it did not attack immediately. That was a tactical error, for it allowed the Russians enough breathing-space to reform. Meanwhile a Turkish infantry division, sent west towards Eleşkirt, took up a position south of the town but made no attempt to take it. These two events combined convinced Yudenich that Abdul Karim had turned cautious, and he immediately ordered the counteroffensive he had been planning ever since 30 July – when he had been forced to recognise that Oganovski would not stop short of the Ağri Mountains – put into effect.

Oganovski had pestered him for reinforcements, but Yudenich, not prepared to allow fresh troops to be caught up in a retreat and risk their being demoralised, had consistently turned a deaf ear to his pleas. Instead, he built up reserves to launch an entirely separate and self-contained counterattack, and chose Tahir as its locus, reasoning that if it turned out that he had been fooled, and the Turks were using Abdul Karim's pursuit of Oganovski as a cover for an offensive against the Pasin/Oltu Valley front, he would be able to reorient them rapidly. He sent in a significant force – Baratov, with the newly formed 14th Caucasian Rifle Division and the 1st Caucasian Cossacks plus the 13th Turkistanskis, moving the 156th Elizavetpolskis up to Velibaba, and the 17th Turkistanskis to Basköy, to support them – to reinforce the 153rd Infantry Regiment already positioned there and, playing his cards characteristically close to his chest, kept his other commanders completely in the dark as to his intentions and timetable. Oganovski was told merely to fight a delaying rearguard action if he were attacked, retreating on the Aras Valley as necessary. He also sent orders to Charpentier, who had by now reached Daydin, and Nazarbekov, who was some days behind him, to make haste for the upper Eastern Euphrates Valley.

Over the twenty-four hours which followed, Yudenich, who had by now moved his headquarters up to Karakurt, came under considerable pressure to justify his actions, and resisted it all. He issued orders to Baratov to be ready to send infantrymen forward to the Kiliç-gedik Pass at a moment's notice and cavalry to cross the Sarian Dağ to the south, towards Tutak, where they would be in a position to cut Abdul Karim's likely line of retreat. He gave the executive order on the evening of 4 August, and by the next morning the 13th Turkistanskis had made contact with the Turks near Çeruk, south of Eleşkirt, and had pushed them back towards Karakilise.

It was twenty-four hours before fighting became widespread, with the 13th Turkistanskis having been joined by the 14th Caucasian Rifle Division. Oganovski was now back on the offensive and making headway, while Charpentier, who had arrived on the eastern edge of the battlefield that morning, was advancing on Karakilise. By the afternoon, reports that the Turks were withdrawing from the town were starting to come in from cavalry patrols. That may have been so, but Abdul Karim had certainly not decided on a full-scale retreat at that juncture, and was in fact planning a fresh offensive, deploying the 29th Division of IX Corps, still at Hinis and fresh, on the very left of his front, towards the Mirgemir Pass to the west of the Şarian Dağ. By that route they would be able to take Baratov's advance on its right flank and head off reinforcements for the battle which was developing at the Kiliç-gedik Pass.

Yudenich had held reserves for just such an eventuality as the incursion of the Turkish 29th Division, and as soon as he received news of it he despatched the Elizavetpolski and 17th Turkistanski Regiments to confront them. They had been held too far back, perhaps; the Turkistanskis made a forced march of almost forty kilometres across the mountains to get to the combat zone, and it was almost midnight on 7 August before they arrived, in a state of extreme fatigue. Their commander, Col. Kruten, understood the importance of an immediate strike, however, and sent them into the attack at once. Weary they may have been, but their night assault was an overwhelming success, and by first light, when the Elizavetpolski arrived to reinforce them, the Turks had abandoned their positions and retreated to the south, leaving the Mirgemir Pass in Russian hands. That proved to be the key to the entire battle. The Turks put up a spirited defence at the Kiliç-gedik Pass but on the morning of 8 August it crumbled under sheer weight of numbers, and they retreated down the pass towards Tutak, where they were joined by those retiring in not particularly good order from Karakilise.

With the discovery that there were Cossacks at Tutak the retreat became even more disorderly, and soon showed every sign of turning into a rout. However, Abdul Karim rallied enough of the men streaming out of Karakilise to make a defensive stand on a line running across the valley south of the town, from Hamur east to Ağadevi. Baratov was slow in confronting him and Charpentier, who had been advancing for two days with his customary laxity, also failed to show up in time to have any effect, and he bought perhaps as much as forty-eight hours for his retreating army. That, and the fact that his deployment had itself been dispersed, ensured that Baratov's Cossacks were never in a position to surround him, and reduced his losses dramatically. Nonetheless he had been forced to abandon all his supplies at Karakilise, as well as a good deal of his artillery. His ill-considered expedition into the Eleşkirt Valley cost him at least 10,000 killed and wounded, and 6,000 prisoners, which, coincidentally, was very close to the losses Oganovski had suffered in his advance from Malazgirt. Honours, however, were far from even, for mid-August found the Russians back in control of the entire area north of Lake Van as far west as Adilcevaz, and of the whole eastern shore, including Van and Vastan, while the Turks controlled the southern, and disputed, Malazgirt.

And thus the situation in the Lower Caucasus and Armenia was to remain throughout the rest of 1915, chiefly because events in other theatres over-shadowed the region, and both Turkish and Russian forces were starved of men and *matériel*. Across the entire region there was only skirmishing activity, much of it directed at suppressing the ingrained Kurdish habit of raiding any location left unprotected. Persian Azerbaijan was relatively quiet, too, but further east the German Minister at Teheran, Prince Henry of Reuss, and the newly appointed Military Attaché there, Count Kanitz, were very actively encouraging dissident elements, of which there was no shortage, to form a rival government to that of the eighteen-year-old Ahmad Shah with the objective of bringing the country into the war on the side of the Central Powers. Kanitz had an armed force drawn largely from the Persian gendarmerie, which had been established in 1910 with assistance from Sweden,[13] together with volunteers from the German community in Persia, Austro-Hungarian PoWs who had escaped from camps in Turkistan and made their way there, and pro-German Persians. The British, who were, of course, actually occupying a small but vital area of Persian territory in Arabistan, and who feared the consequences of a pro-German *coup d'état*, asked the Russians to intervene.

That request coincided with the arrival of a new overall commander in the region, the Grand Duke Nicholas,[14] sent to replace the never satisfactory Count Vorontsov-Dashkov as commander-in-chief of the Army of the Caucasus. The Grand Duke brought with him Gen. Bolhovitinov as his chief of staff, but retained Yudenich as his field commander, which many feel to have been the best single move he made. However, his first instructions to Yudenich, when he arrived in Tiflis on 24 September, were to prepare an expeditionary force to be sent to Persia, depriving him of yet more seasoned men and undoing, at a stroke, virtually all the rebuilding he had been able to accomplish over the course of the summer. The expedition was to be under the Grand Duke's direct command.

Yudenich selected two regiments of Frontier Guards as the infantry for the Persian expedition, together with the equivalent of two battalions of

Armenian militia, a force some six thousand strong. To this he added the Caucasian Cavalry Division, with Prince Beloselski appointed to replace the unfortunate Charpentier, plus the 1st Caucasian Cossack Division and the equivalent of two Kuban Cossack regiments made up of individual squadrons, eight thousand horsemen in all, with sixteen horse-drawn guns, twelve mountain guns and two 120mm howitzers, these last mostly for show. Not entirely spoiled for choice among senior officers, he selected Baratov for overall command.

Baratov's force was transported by ship from the Russian Caspian ports to Enzeli (Bandar-e Anzali) from mid-November, with instructions to occupy Qazvin, and did so by the month's end with the 1st Caucasian Cossacks, while the Kuban squadrons penetrated as far as Karaj and patrolled the area west of Teheran. The pro-German faction had anticipated the arrival of the Russians; the day Baratov's staff embarked for Enzeli, 12 November, the staff of the German, Austro-Hungarian and Ottoman Embassies quit Teheran together with those deputies of the *Majlis* (parliament) and civil servants who were sympathetic to the Central Powers, some for Hamadan, others for Qom, travelling under the protection of the gendarmerie.[15] Meanwhile gendarmes in the southern city of Shiraz took over the British Consulate in the city, and occupied – and emptied the vaults of – the branch of the Imperial Bank, as well as the telegraph office and other government buildings, taking all the British residents captive; similar action was taken in all the other important cities across the south of the country.

Baratov, his infantry still lagging behind, advanced one of his cavalry brigades from Qazvin to Hamadan in the first week of December, and occupied the city after a brief fight with gendarmes at the Sultan-bulak Pass, roughly halfway from Qasvin. Two weeks later another brigade was sent to Qom, and this time the city was abandoned by the rebels, and occupied without opposition. At the first sign of the Cossacks, Kanitz and his followers had quit Hamadan in favour of Kermanshah, closer to the border with the Ottoman Empire. Baratov set out to confront them there, fighting a minor engagement at the Asadabad Pass on the way. By then the veteran Field-Marshal Colmar Freiherr von der Goltz had arrived in Baghdad to command Ottoman forces in Mesopotamia, and had become convinced that a show of force was necessary across the border to the east. He sent a battalion of Turkish troops with a battery of mountain guns to Kermanshah; no sooner had they arrived, during the second week of January 1916, than news came that Baratov was at Kangavar, and they advanced to meet him in the company of an unknown number of Kanitz's followers. They were badly advised, for Baratov very comfortably outnumbered them, and dispersed them with heavy losses (including Kanitz himself, perhaps, for he was never heard of again).

Baratov retired to Hamadan, where the bulk of his troops were assembled, but there he found orders from the Viceroy to advance on Kermanshah once more, a more substantial body of Turkish troops – four battalions of infantry, plus artillery, under German command – having been sent to augment the Persian gendarmes and irregulars who had gravitated there. On paper their combined force was as strong as Baratov's in terms of numbers – each had around ten thousand – but in reality the gendarmes and irregulars in particular were no match for the Cossacks. When they failed to join up with the Turks and Baratov met them at Nihavend, on the road east from Kangavar, on 8 February, he dispersed them easily. On 22 February he brought the Turks to battle at Sinna (Sanandaj), and routed them too, and four days later entered Kermanshah, setting up advance posts to watch the border crossings into Mesopotamia and establishing what was effectively a cordon sanitaire to prevent the Turks sending more troops to stir up trouble in Persia.

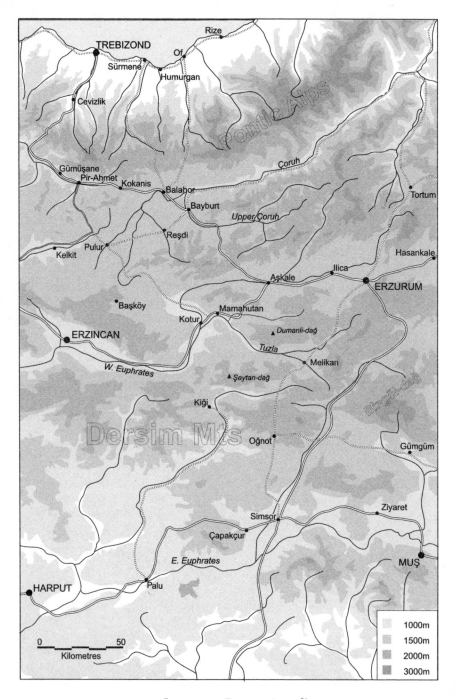

12. Caucasus – Eastern Anatolia

Anatolia Invaded

By the end of October 1915, Nikolai Nikolaevich Yudenich had become convinced that the Allied offensive in Gallipoli was doomed to failure, probably within a month, as a consequence of the Turks having been able to bring new heavy artillery into action. That would release troops for transfer to the Caucasus front, which would tip the balance there most decisively in the Turks' favour. However, given the weaknesses of Turkey's inadequate railway system, he believed it would be at least three months before the extra divisions could be relocated and become effective in the east, and had evolved a plan to counter the threat: a pre-emptive strike to cause such damage to the Turks' infrastructure that a meaningful counteroffensive would be rendered impossible. To stand any realistic chance of success, this would mean taking Erzurum, and in the depths of winter.

Yudenich was constrained by the simple necessity of playing to his own strength: the presence of the first-class logistical route provided by the railway from Tiflis into the Lesser Caucasus by way of Kars and Sarikamiş, which he had extended to Karaurgan the previous spring.[1] That dictated a direct frontal assault with Köprüköy, near the front's geographical centre, as the immediate objective. However, he rejected the direct approach by way of the Pasin Valley, for there the Turkish defences were three lines deep and well engineered; instead, and despite the obvious risks inherent in such a choice, he would approach the village from the north-east, by way of Çakir Baba, the same mountain Enver had chosen as his back-door route into Sarikamiş.

It was clear to Yudenich from the start that everything hinged on having an inch-perfect plan and commanding strict obedience to it. From mid-December, munitions and supplies were brought forward surreptitiously. By way of demonstration, troops were very obviously marched off to the rear, only to be returned under cover of darkness (though one unit, the 13th Caucasian Rifles, was ostentatiously transferred to Julfa, in Persian Azerbaijan, and agents there were ordered to buy up grain and fodder to stockpile against the arrival of other Russian units, who, they said, would winter in the region), and all this seems to have lulled the Turks into a false sense of security.

In all, the forces Yudenich would deploy would amount to approximately eighty thousand infantry, in eighty-five battalions, plus appropriate cavalry and artillery. They were divided into three blocks. On the right, Przevalski[2] commanded II Turkistan Corps: eight infantry regiments and three Plastun battalions, plus the Don Cossack Foot Brigade with Voloshinov-Petrichenko in command, and now virtually made over since its poor showing at Malazgirt, with the Siberian Cossack Brigade in reserve at Oltu. On the left stood Kalitin's I Caucasian Corps: the 39th Infantry Division, eleven *druzhiny* of Armenian militia and two infantry regiments, with another and the 1st Caucasian Cossack Division in reserve at Sarikamiş. Between them stood the three regiments of the 4th Caucasian Rifle Division, drawn from the strategic reserve, which was to operate as an independent force under Vorobyev.

The Turks were spread even more thinly than Yudenich believed. After the winter and summer campaigns, the entire Third Army, which manned a line from the Black Sea coast to Bitlis and beyond, probably amounted to no more than seventy thousand men in eleven under-strength infantry divisions.[3] Perhaps as a result of Yudenich's deception, it was missing its leader at this critical time, for Mahmut Kamil Pasha was on leave in Constantinople, and command had passed temporarily to Abdul Karim Pasha, the commander of XI Corps; and to make matters worse Kamil's influential chief of staff, Lt.-Col. Guse, a pivotal figure, had returned to Germany to convalesce after an attack of typhus. Quite how important Kamil's absence was is debatable, but Guse's was certainly to be regretted.

The Third Army's central front was divided into three sectors. From a point north of Lake Tortum to the ridge of the Çakir Baba-dağ the line, some seventy kilometres in length, including the Oltu and Sivri Valleys, was manned by X Corps' 30th, 31st and 32nd Infantry Divisions, XI Corps' 34th Division and a mixed force of Frontier Guards and Jandarma. From the heights of the Çakir Baba to the Aras River – thirty kilometres – the centre was covered by XI Corps' 18th and 33rd Divisions, and from the Aras to the Dram-dağ – a further thirty kilometres – the right was manned by the 28th and 29th Divisions of IX Corps plus elements of the 37th Division, with some Kurdish irregulars on the southern flank. The strategic reserve consisted only of the remaining division (the 17th) of IX Corps, positioned near Hasankale (Pasinler). From the dispositions it is not clear that the most heavily defended sector was in fact the centre, where the so-called Lines of Köprüköy had carefully sited machine gun and artillery positions covering extensive fields of barbed wire.

Yudenich had decided that the ridge line of the Çakir Baba, where the central and left sectors met, was the vulnerable point. His offensive was planned to begin on 10 January, last for six days, and would consist of three phases. On Days One and Two, II Turkistan Corps would launch an assault from the direction of Oltu, by way of the Ak-dağ and Kara-dağ; it was not envisaged that they would proceed far beyond a line Lake Tortum–Id. On Days Three and Four, I Caucasian Corps' 39th Division was to advance along both banks of the Aras; this, too, was in the nature of a feint, in the hope of drawing in any reserves not already committed further north. Then, on Day Five, the real blow would fall: Vorobyev would advance across the southern slopes of the Çakir Baba, parallel with the ridge line, and on the following morning, having broken through on a narrow front between Koziçan and Çilligül, would be in a position to strike at Köprüköy itself.

The first phase went poorly for the Russians. The Turkistanskis failed to achieve tactical surprise, and their leading units were cut to pieces by machine guns in fortified positions. Only on his left did Przevalski meet with a measure of success, when a force almost two regiments strong (Treskin), having managed to penetrate for some distance up the Oltu Valley, made contact with a column (Voloshinov-Petrichenko) which had advanced along the flank of the Çakir Baba, and had positioned itself to take the shoulder below the Koziçan-dağ which was to be the northern 'door-post' of the breakthrough corridor.

The second phase, Kalitin's offensive in the Aras Valley, seemed to go even less well when it was launched on Day Three. The Russians were held on both banks of the river, while on the right the 155th Kubinski Regiment, tasked with securing the southern 'door-post' of the breakthrough corridor, the spur of the Çakir Baba known as Çilligül-dağ, was inexplicably not provided with artillery support and failed. However, the true objective was achieved, for Abdul Karim became convinced that the Russians would continue to apply pressure there, and the following day he did as Yudenich had gambled, and threw in his reserves, moving the 17th up to a position near Azapköy.

Meanwhile, Vorobyev, fearful that the extreme conditions on the Çakir Baba, where the snow lay chest-deep, would prevent him from keeping to Yudenich's strict timetable, had ordered his 16th Caucasian Rifle Regiment forward ahead of schedule. That could have given the game away but proved to be fortuitous, and by nightfall he was in touch with Voloshinov-Petrichenko, whose men were making slow but steady progress north of the Çakir Baba ridge and were poised to take the all-important Koziçan shoulder.

All in all, Yudenich concluded that night at his headquarters at Karaurgan, he had experienced disappointments, chief amongst them the failure to take and hold the Çilligül-dağ, but no major setbacks, and ordered the main thrust of his attack to go ahead as planned the next morning. Voloshinov-Petrichenko took the Koziçan shoulder soon after dawn, threatening the fortified heights of the Koziçan-dağ, and the northern 'door-post' was secured. Then Vorobyev pushed his regiments forward towards Alakilise, towards Maslahat and neighbouring Elimi; by 1100 his objectives were taken, and the Turkish 18th and 33rd Divisions were in retreat. By that evening advance units of the 4th Caucasian Rifles had possession of the village of Hisar-dere[4] on the western extremity of the Çilligül-dağ, from which a well-trodden path led to Pazarçor and there joined a good track to Köprüköy, just fifteen kilometres further on, and though the summit of the Çilligül-dağ itself was still in Turkish hands, it now posed little danger.

Day Six was to prove the decisive one of the battle. It took most of the day, but eventually Voloshinov-Petrichenko's men – the revitalised Don Foot Brigade in the van – fought their way to the summit of the Koziçan-dağ, which gave them access to the western portion of the *Top Yol*, leading to Portanos and Köse (on which village Treskin was already advancing). Meanwhile, the main body of the 4th Caucasian Rifles had rounded the northern flank of the Çilligül-dağ – making slow progress, because there was only one passable track – and were approaching Pazarçor, well to the rear of the Turks' second line of defence in the plains running down to the Aras. However, in the Aras Valley itself, every metre the Russians advanced brought them into contact with more, and better-organised, defenders, and by nightfall that advance had ground to a halt. That setback made it imperative for the men pushing westwards on the slopes of the Çakir Baba to outflank Azapköy and allow the Russians the chance, at least, of encircling the static defensive positions in the Aras Valley and cutting their avenue of retreat.

It was not to be. On the evening of 16 January Abdul Karim gave the order to retire, and his weary men lost no time in obeying, abandoning large stockpiles of *matériel*. Katilin's men were too fatigued to be able to pursue them with anything like the necessary enthusiasm, and as a result Turkish losses during the evacuation of the Aras Valley were less than they might otherwise have been. Vorobyev, though still hampered by the terrain, was less hesitant; the following morning he descended to Badicivan, and by the end of the afternoon he had occupied Köprüköy. The following day the Siberian Cossack cavalry advanced within a few kilometres of Hasankale, where the Turkish rearguard made a stand; it fell early on 18 January, leaving the way to Erzurum clear.

The Turks paid a high price for their failure to maintain sufficient numbers of troops to mount an adequate defence. In addition to precious territory and an expensively constructed defensive position before Köprüköy, they lost perhaps as many as 25,000 dead, wounded and missing, and it is estimated that significantly less than 40,000 managed to make their way back to Erzurum. Russian losses were smaller, perhaps 10,000 dead and wounded, which meant that Yudenich still had perhaps 75,000 effectives with which to mount the second phase of his operation.

Yudenich had a firm belief that the Turks had nowhere near enough men to defend the fortress complex around the regional capital, and his reconnaissance operations – which included the use of scout aircraft for the first time on the Caucasus front[5] – soon reinforced that view, reporting that no new Turkish troops had arrived in the region, and that no attempt had been made to recover the considerable quantity of stores which had been abandoned in the headlong retreat from Küprököy. Col. Maslovski, his intelligence officer, who oversaw the operations and who had considerable influence over him, came down in favour of an offensive campaign, and on

23 January the theatre commander put the case for it to the Viceroy. He was rebuffed, Nicholas making much of the fact that just eight million rounds of rifle and machine gun ammunition remained in the strategic reserve in the arsenal at Kars.[6] Nicholas did not have the final say, however, and the matter was referred to the Russian Chief of Staff, Alexeyev, and the tsar himself. The Viceroy, who had suffered a loss of prestige as a result of his demotion, was overruled, and on 23 January gave his formal approval for an operation to take Erzurum.

Yudenich tried and failed to persuade the Stavka to release fresh additional units to him, and was forced to borrow units from elsewhere in the theatre, principally IV Caucasian Corps (at the head of which he had installed Gen. de Witt in place of Oganovski, replaced after his poor performance in southern Armenia), which gave up the 6th Caucasian Rifles, and the expeditionary force in Persian Azerbaijan, which ceded the 4th Plastun Brigade (unnecessarily, as it turned out, for it failed to arrive at Erzurum in time to see action), together with the 13th Caucasian Rifles which he had sent to Julfa as a decoy and now brought back to the front. He also ordered de Witt and Chernozubov to begin offensive operations in order to tie down the maximum number of Turks.

In particular, de Witt was to take Hinis, a key point on the route between Erzurum and the Muş/Bitlis region, in order to prevent the Turks from reinforcing the fortress from that direction. De Witt sent the 8th Rifles and the Cossacks by way of Malazgirt, occupying that town, and then taking Hinis from the south-east without encountering serious opposition. Chernozubov, wintering in the area west of Lake Urmia, split his Van–Azerbaijan Force, sending units around Lake Van to north and south. By early in February they were advancing on Ahlat and Tatvan respectively, threatening the weak Turkish garrisons of Bitlis and Muş and reducing their capacity for offensive action to virtually zero, and with that Yudenich deemed his left flank adequately protected.

Just as he had at Köprüköy, Yudenich intended to deploy II Turkistan Corps along a north-east/south-west axis, and I Caucasian Corps from roughly due east, with Vorobyev's 4th Caucasian Rifle Division and Voloshinov-Petrichenko's Don Foot Brigade to advance between them. This time, however, they would be the decoy, and the real offensive would come from Przevalski's Turkistanskis. While he was probably frustrated at the slow pace which was all the latter could manage against the continuing dogged resistance of X Corps – Yussuf Izzet, not having conformed to the general headlong retreat, was fighting a rearguard action through Tortum – there was little he could do about it, and much to be done elsewhere. In I Caucasian Corps' sector, from the slopes of the Palandöken in the south-east round to the Deve-boyun Ridge, his troops were in position by 23 January, and that same day Vorobyev was ordered to occupy the southern heights of the

Kargapazar to his right. His men met Turkish troops on the same mission; after desperate fighting the Russians prevailed, and thereafter the Turks made no further effort to control what was to be a key feature. Even though weather conditions were extreme – the men could work in shifts of only a few hours at a time – before a week had passed gun emplacements had already taken shape and artillery was being manhandled into place to overlook Erzurum.

This somewhat lackadaisical, even passive, attitude to possession of the heights of Kargapazar seems to sum up the Turkish approach to the defence of Erzurum, and can perhaps be attributed to an unreasonable confidence that the Russians could not launch an attack before the spring thaw.[7] That proved to be a fatal error of judgement, for Yudenich had no intention whatsoever of waiting until the advantage had swung towards the Turks.

On the surface, the Turks had good reason to be confident. The city had withstood a Russian siege during the war of 1878, and since that time had been extended and extensively modernised. British military advisers drew heavily on the work of the Belgian military architect, Henri Brialmont, and when German advisers took over from them in the 1890s, most of the updating was already completed, and they suggested the addition of but two forts, in the outlying southern flanking positions, on the Palandöken-dağ. Now, in the dying weeks of 1915, the complex was very formidable indeed: fifteen individual forts, eleven grouped closely and more or less mutually supporting, and two each in flanking positions north and south.

The defences had a ruinous weakness, however: their equipment. The forts were furnished with a total of only 235 guns of all calibres, few of them larger than 90mm (3.5in) and most of them antiquated, instead of the thousand modern pieces which the planners had envisaged. Even with the Third Army's own field artillery the total only added up to around 350 guns in all, including small mountain pieces; and machine guns – invaluable in this sort of situation – were in short supply, many having been lost or abandoned at Köprüköy. The complex needed a bare minimum of 75,000 to man its defences; the Turks could not field more than 50,000, and perhaps a third of those were raw, untrained conscripts. With the number of guns and defenders so reduced, the entire fortress strategy was put at risk, because while the individual forts may have been invulnerable to artillery – or at least, to the sort of artillery Yudenich had at his disposal in the first weeks of 1916 – undermanned and undergunned as they were, they could be taken by storm.

Unsurprisingly the Russian High Command had invested a considerable amount of time, money and energy in gathering intelligence about the fortress complex, had a very good idea of its layout, and save in one respect, considerable regard for it. That caveat was a suspicion that both British and German engineers had overlooked the significance of the Kargapazar-dağ – or had simply overestimated its value as a barrier – and Yudenich decided that it was from there, and in the defile north of it in which ran the road to

Tortum, where the forts were not entirely mutually supportive, that the main thrust of his attack would come.

By the start of the second week of February, somewhat alarmed by intelligence reports that Turkish reinforcements were on their way,[8] Yudenich was ready to put his plan into effect. On the eighth he summoned his commanders to dinner and, without preamble, informed them that the offensive would begin two days later. There was widespread consternation at the short notice, and he agreed to delay the start by twenty-four hours.

While he had nowhere near enough artillery to hope to reduce the Erzurum forts by bombardment, he did have an advantage, for he could move guns around to obtain local superiority. On 11 February he had them concentrated upon the outer ring forts in the north-eastern sector – Çoban-dede, Dalangöz and Uzunahmet – and at noon he gave the order to commence firing. They kept up a sustained barrage until 2000, and when it lifted, Russian infantry moved up in the darkness. A battalion of the 153rd Bakinskis succeeded in getting right up to the walls of Dalangöz undetected, and two companies penetrated the fort itself. Hand-to-hand fighting continued through most of the night, and several times the outcome was in doubt, but eventually the Russians prevailed; the first of Erzurum's forts had fallen, for the loss of no more than a few hundred men. Meanwhile, the 156th Elizavetpolskis had been in action at neighbouring Çoban-dede, and while they had not succeeded in breaching the fort's defences, they had taken and managed to hold the high ground south-east of it, which gave the Russians a position from which to pour in plunging fire.

Przevalski's Turkistanskis made steady progress in the broken ground of the Gürcü-boğaz defile and on the slopes of the Kara-göbek, where the most northerly of the outlying forts was located, and when the village below the fort was taken, by the 18th Turkistanskis in mid-afternoon, he concentrated all his available artillery there. Just hours later his gunners were rewarded by a substantial explosion, which they took to be the result of a shot hitting the magazine; it was indeed the magazine going up, but it had been fired by the defenders as a precursor to evacuating the position, and when the fort's guns fell silent and Russian infantry advanced they found it abandoned.

On the Turkistanskis' left, the Don Foot Brigade was fighting its way through deep snow across the Kandil-dağ, and was making very slow progress, while on its left the 4th Caucasian Rifle Division was having an easier time of it in the descent of the western slopes of the Kargapazar. Both arrived at the critical area of the battlefield, the Gürcü-boğaz defile, late on 13 February, by which time the defenders had rallied noticeably and had all but stopped the Russian advance. That revival of Turkish spirits was not to last; the following day the fort at Tafet, the second of the northern outliers, came under attack from three sides and fell, and that opened the way for a breakthrough in strength into the plains of the Kara-Su south of the Gürcü-boğaz defile, which spelled *finis* for Erzurum. That evening Mahmut Kamil made the decision to withdraw from the city while he still had the chance to do so in some semblance of order, and next morning Russian aerial reconnaissance revealed soldiers and civilians streaming away to the west.

At 0940 on 16 February Yudenich signalled to Przevalski to 'march on the city and take it from the north'. However, he reckoned without a line of defence his spies had not been able to reveal to him in detail: a system of trenches and interlocking wire, installed in that sector at the suggestion of a German specialist, in the aftermath of Sarikamiş. It did no more than slow the advancing Russians, but that allowed the Turks to conduct a fighting retreat, and as a result the loss of Erzurum was not quite as painful as it might have been, all but perhaps 5,000 escaping. However, the amount of *matériel* the Russians took was enormous, and included virtually every piece of artillery installed there. Most of the few smaller pieces which the Turks managed to take with them were later abandoned or lost along the way, and fell into Russian hands anyway.

Over the four weeks which followed Yudenich harried the Turks struggling westwards, and by mid-March only at Bayburt, in the upper Çoruh Valley, did a body from X Corps, supported by Frontier Guards and Laz irregulars, continue to offer any sort of meaningful resistance. Elsewhere, Yudenich had ordered de Witt to occupy Muş and Bitlis with assistance from the Van–Azerbaijan Force. The Turks' resistance was patchy, Muş falling without a fight on 16 February, Bitlis at bayonet and sabre point after a spirited night attack, which saw 1,000 prisoners and a score of guns taken, on 3 March.

In the north, along the Black Sea coast in Lazistan, Lyakhov had a harder time of it, chiefly because the terrain was so difficult, and had elected for an amphibious campaign, the obsolete battleship *Rostislav* and the gunboats *Kubanetz* and *Donetz*, together with four destroyers and two armed steamers, having been put at his disposal (albeit reluctantly) by Admiral Eberhardt, and assembled at Batum. The Turkish forces – equivalent to a reinforced brigade, with eight guns – were drawn up west of the Arhavi River, and on the morning of 5 February the naval task force began bombarding them. Over the next twenty-four hours it inflicted large numbers of casualties, and by noon the following day the Turks had abandoned their positions. The same exercise was repeated at Vice, fifteen kilometres further west, ten days later, with similar results, and was followed by a Turkish retreat to the mouth of the Büyük River, near the small town of Atina (Pazar), where a strong defensive position was constructed in the shadow of overhanging cliffs which gave some protection from naval gunfire. This time Lyakhov decided on a true amphibious operation. Commandeering two steamers built to accommodate local coastal conditions – ships of around 1,500 tons which, unusually for that period, had their accommodation and machinery well aft, drew considerably less water forward, and could thus approach the beach closely, bows-on[9] – he loaded each with a Plastun battalion, with the intention of putting them ashore in the rear of the Turkish position. They approached without lights under cover of darkness, and arrived at the landing beaches before dawn; within forty minutes the men were all ashore, and not until the ships were retiring did the Turks wake up to their presence and lob a few shells in their general direction, achieving nothing except to betray their battery's exact position. When the *Rostislav* appeared around a headland and began bombarding them with her secondary 6-inch guns they fled into the mountains without firing another shot. Lyakhov later occupied the important small port of Rize, on 8 March, after another brilliantly executed amphibious landing, and there he rested, just fifty kilometres from the real prize, Trebizond.

Enver's first reaction to a second catastrophic defeat in the Caucasus was to sack Mahmut Kamil as commander of the Third Army and replace him by Mehmet Vehip Pasha,[10] Kamil's protestation that he had been expected to hold far too long a front with far too few men falling on deaf ears. Secondly he ordered Mahmut Fevzi Pasha to take the 9th and 13th Infantry Divisions and move east immediately to combine with the 10th Division to form V Corps. This placed severe additional strain on the already creaking railway system, for eleven divisions were already in, or planning for, transit across Anatolia, and the result was protracted delays, with some units taking as much as eight weeks to complete the journey from Constantinople. Then, on 10 March, Enver added a further contingent, the newly formed XVI Corps, initially two divisions strong, to the mix.

It was clear that the Third Army's headquarters could not cope with such a degree of enlargement, even under a new, ambitious and promising leader, and Enver split military responsibility for the theatre in two, sending Second Army headquarters, under the command of Ahmet Izzet Pasha,[11] from Thrace to Diyarbakir, to take charge of the majority of the reinforcements already on their way[12] and assume responsibility for the southern segment of the front, below the Bingöl massif. In these circumstances it would have been normal to appoint a superior commander, at army-group level, to co-ordinate Izzet's actions with those of Vehip, but Enver did not; it was a serious mistake.

When Vehip Pasha arrived in theatre on 16 March he found the Third Turkish Army in disarray bordering on chaos. Not only was it reduced to no more than 25,000 effectives, with just 67 machine guns and 84 mainly small-calibre artillery pieces, but with the fall of Erzurum it had lost its logistical base, with everything that implied for its organisation. His first priority was to rally his troops in Lazistan and somehow organise an effective defence of Trebizond, but he reckoned without Yudenich's dynamism, for the Russian commander was already considering how best to take the town. On 20 March he met with Admiral Eberhardt at Batum, the latter agreeing to provide transportation and escorts – for a short and limited period – for a sizeable amphibious operation which was to be mounted by two Plastun brigades the

Stavka had finally agreed to release from the Crimea. However, hardly had the admiral committed himself before highly-coloured reports, originating in the Greek coastal communities, started to come in of strong contingents of fresh Turkish infantry having arrived at Trebizond by sea, together with five thousand Germans and, worst of all, of German submarines operating in coastal waters. In fact, the reports were largely the creations of certain fertile imaginations; there were a few fresh troops (from the 10th Division), but certainly no Germans (though there *was* at least one U-boat[13]). The rumours soured the optimistic atmosphere at Lyakhov's headquarters and turned it from one of confidence to one of anxiety; news of the presence of submarines had an even more profound effect on Eberhardt, and he began to have second thoughts as to the virtue of deploying a fleet which had very little in the way of anti-submarine warfare capability.

The Turks facing Lyakhov were mostly the same men he'd already seen off the battlefield on more than one occasion. Following their ignominious retreat from the Büyük River they had regrouped on higher ground west of the coastal town of Of, twenty-five kilometres from Rize. From Of a track rose into the mountains and led, eventually, to Bayburt; Lyakhov became convinced that the Turks would use it to try to turn his flank, and wasted days in establishing a defensive position, only to see the Turks fall back a further dozen kilometres to Sürmene, whereupon he advanced himself, to Humurgan, at the mouth of the Mezra Dere River, some nine or ten kilometres short of their lines. The force facing Lyakhov was soon reinforced by four battalions of the 10th Division from Trebizond, and amounted to around twelve thousand, considerably more than he had at his own disposal. Even more concerned at the possibility of being outflanked and less certain of his ability to best the defenders, even with naval fire-support, he began clamouring for reinforcements, overstating the danger he was in in the process.

The 1st and 2nd Plastun brigades, with their artillery and supply train, embarked at Novorossiysk on the night of 4 April and, the next morning, the invasion fleet – ten transports and twelve elpidiphores, shepherded by two light cruisers, four destroyers and two steamers adapted as seaplane carriers[14] – set sail for Rize. Twenty-four hours later they came up with the main body of the Russian fleet, which fell in as an escort. Yudenich himself arrived at Rize on the morning of 7 April. He was met by Lyakhov, who had by this time become convinced that the Turks would fall on him at any moment, and in his turn convinced Yudenich to alter the plans he had agreed with Eberhardt, and land one of the two brigades at Humurgan, where they would be available to support him immediately. When Yudenich transmitted this request to Rear-Admiral Homenko, who commanded the transport flotilla and had caught Eberhardt's own anxiety, he was met by a point-blank refusal. His orders were for Rize, said Homenko, and to Rize he would go. Yudenich then appealed to Eberhardt, who had that morning received proof-positive (in the shape of the crumpled bow-plates of the destroyer *Strogi*, which had rammed *U 33* without sinking her two days earlier) of the existence of at least one U-boat in the area. He refused to countenance any change of plan save that, as soon as the troops were safe ashore, the entire escorting force would be returning to Sevastopol at full speed, lest it come under attack, leaving Lyakhov without the naval gunnery support which had proved vital earlier in the campaign.

With time of the essence, and his only recourse an appeal to the distant Stavka,[15] Yudenich decided to go it alone. As soon as the 2nd Plastun Brigade was ashore at Rize, he had the men crammed aboard the pair of elpidiphores Lyakhov had at his own disposal there. That night they set sail, escorted by the single armed steamer which had brought Yudenich from Batum, and early the following morning were ashore at Humurgan. The five thousand extra men he now had under his command improved Lyakhov's morale, and when, two days later, the second of the Plastun brigades arrived on foot from Rize, he began to marshal his assets for an attack on the Turkish positions. His preparations were interrupted briefly when *Breslau* appeared, and lobbed some 10.5-cm shells into the Russian ranks, but the attack was not pressed home, and little damage was done. It was enough to convince Eberhardt to revoke his earlier decision to leave the soldiers to fend for themselves, though, and early on the morning of 14 April the *Rostislav*, in company with the *Pantelimon* (ex-*Potemkin*) and four escorting destroyers, arrived and began bombarding the Turkish positions with their secondary armament. By early in the afternoon the Turks were on the run, heading for Trebizond.

Lyakhov pursued the retreating Turks in an almost leisurely fashion the next day, calling down naval gunfire on would-be hold-outs whenever they halted to slow his progress. By the afternoon of 16 April he had reached a line some twelve kilometres short of Trebizond, and there he rested his troops while the ships returned to Batum to replenish their magazines. On the morning of 18 April a delegation from the town's Greek community appeared, and told him that the Turkish forces had left Trebizond during the course of the previous night. He immediately sent a column to round the town to the south, in a belated attempt to intercept them. It cut the road to Gümüşane at Cevizlik, twenty kilometres south of Trebizond, but by that time the enemy's main body had passed, and a skirmish with elements of the rearguard was all it had to show for its considerable efforts.

The fall of Trebizond was a serious blow to the Turks. Now not only did the Russians control the only port with good direct access, via a paved road, to the interior of eastern Anatolia, but they had also opened up a second front in the theatre, with forces equal to around two divisions as those formations now mustered. That inevitably diluted the value of the reinforcements sent to the Third Army by increasing the size of the disputed area it sought to control, and also stretched its internal lines of communication. This latter, it was soon clear, was actually a major problem in its own right, and in mid-April Vehip attempted to solve it by subdividing his command into three operational regions. The First Region stretched from Diyarbakir north to the Bingöl massif, and was to be occupied by XVI Corps, under the command of Mustafa Kemal. This was essentially an interim arrangement, for the region had been assigned to the Second Army, and when that became more than a phantom force, Ahmet Izzet would take it over. The Second Region, north to Bayburt, comprised the old Third Army – XI Corps in reserve, with IX Corps covering Erzincan and X Corps to the north – and the Third, from Bayburt to the Black Sea coast, was made up of V Corps plus the remnants of the Lazistan detachment. The entire strength available to Vehip at that point amounted to around 65,000, about three-quarters of whom were infantry; more were arriving every week, but at a much slower rate than the new commander wished.

XVI Corps' 5th Division reached Diyarbakir around the time that reorganisation was announced. Mustafa Kemal established his headquarters, and when the division reached its operational area, at Siirt, south of Bitlis, it immediately began aggressive patrolling. It was soon in regular touch with the enemy but Kemal failed to work up a plan which seemed to offer him any real chance of taking the city. Some three weeks later the 8th Division arrived, and was deployed towards Muş with similar consequences. The third division, the 7th, arrived in theatre in early June and based itself at Palu, on the Murat-Su between Muş and Harput, where Izzet had set up his own headquarters.

V Corps, too, was now all present, with one of its divisions stretched out between the small port of Tirebolu, some seventy-five kilometres west of Trebizond, and Ardasa, fifty kilometres inland on the Harşit River, covering the Zigana Pass, where the road south from Trebizond crossed the mountains, another between Ardasa and Gümüşane, and the third between there and Bayburt.

Thus Vehip at least had a defensive line of a sort in place; common sense probably dictated that he hold on, waiting for the rest of his reinforcements to come up, but instead he suddenly went onto the offensive at Mamahatun, west of Erzurum.

It seems likely that the motivation for that surprise attack came from the usual source: Enver Pasha himself. The War Minister arrived at Erzincan in the second week of May and demanded to know how Vehip planned to use his new resources. Vehip talked of a probe into the territory held by I Caucasian Corps, to the west of Erzurum, where he believed the Russians were weak, and by the time Enver and his entourage left, to move on to Izzet's headquarters, he found himself committed.

The Russians were indeed weak in that sector; the 39th Division, which had been in combat since the outbreak of war and had often been in the very thick of things, was at Mamahatun in the valley of the Kara-Su, at the apex of a bend which almost reverses the course of the river. It was in something of a salient, and was badly in need of rest and replenishment, having suffered at Köprüköy and again at Erzurum. The units to be left behind when it was withdrawn – the 15th Caucasian Rifle Regiment and the 1st Transcaucasian Rifle Brigade, which had been a militia unit until recently, together with the Don Foot Brigade, which was itself due for relief – were either not trained to a high standard or were stretched far too thinly. Throughout the second half of May Vehip made sure his patrols kept in touch with the situation, and when he learned that the 39th was in the process of being withdrawn from the line, he struck.

Employing the three divisions of IX Corps, with elements of XI Corps in support, he launched a three-pronged surprise attack on the Mamahatun sector on the morning of 29 May. The brunt of it fell in the centre, where the 29th Division easily broke through the 15th Caucasian Rifles, taking Mamahatun itself and advancing up the paved highway towards Aşkale and Erzurum, while to the south the 17th Division drove the Transcaucasians before them up the valley of the Tuzla River, a tributary of the Kara-Su. To the left the Turks made slower progress, the Don Foot Brigade making a stubborn fighting retreat from Barnakaban. As chance would have it, the 4th Plastun Brigade, which was to have occupied its positions, had already arrived at the front, and Yudenich immediately threw it into the fight, stopping the Turkish advance dead. In the centre he ordered the four veteran regiments of the 39th Division to halt their withdrawal and turn and face the Turks once more, the Derbentskis and the Elizavetpolskis on each side of the road to Erzurum, the Kubinskis and the Bakinskis to their left in the valley of the Tuzla. Along the highway, to the north of the Dumanli-dağ, the Turks were held, and only in the southern sector did they continue to make progress, largely due to the presence of cavalry to support their infantry. It was only after a dogged stand by the Bakinskis on 4 June that the advance was halted there, with very heavy casualties on both sides.

With that the fighting stopped, as if the Turks had abruptly run out of steam. They held Mamahatun and the road to Erzurum a good way towards Aşkale, the Dumanli-dağ which separated the road from the Tuzla valley, and the valley itself as far as the Zazlar defile, which gave them access to tracks which led into the Bingöl massif, to Oğnot, and thence to Hinis and Muş. Had Vehip been able to pour more troops into the sector, he might have shown an even greater profit from his adventure, but he was distracted at the vital moment.

Some weeks earlier the Russians had landed a fresh infantry division, the 127th – 15,000 men in four three-battalion regiments and an artillery section – at Trebizond. This had been a considerable undertaking, requiring up to thirty transports and a sizeable escort force, and had gone off without incident, the troops embarking at Mariupol in the Sea of Azov and disembarking in the Bay of Kovata, to the east of Trebizond. Now, on 4 June, Vehip learned that a second division, the 123rd, had followed and that it, too, was safely ashore, an attempted attack by a late-arriving German submarine (possibly

U21) having been driven off. That altered the complexion of the situation most significantly, and Vehip returned to Erzincan to consider his options.

These fresh divisions were two out of the forty or so which had been raised in the wake of the great retreat (across Poland and Galicia) of the previous year. Most, of course, went to the European front, and provided the manpower for the Brusilov Offensive, the massive surprise attack, made without preliminaries across a front five hundred kilometres wide, in which the Russian South-Western Army Group would rip through the Austrians, destroying their Fourth Army and routing their Seventh.[16] That had kicked off that very day, but the Stavka, acknowledging at last the importance of his victories at Erzurum and along the Black Sea coast, threw Yudenich this scrap. He had requested the additional resources for a very clear purpose: another pre-emptive strike. This time he intended to hit the Turks on their left, between Erzurum and the sea, before they could assemble the troops they needed to hit him on *his* left, along the Muş–Bitlis axis. It was partly in preparation for that that he had been reorganising his forces around Mamahatun. Vehip's attack there had come as something of a surprise, and caused him to reappraise the situation, but in the long run it made very little difference, chiefly because the Third Army had hit the buffers again, and had simply run out of men.

Things might have been very different if Vehip had co-ordinated his actions with Izzet, but there seems to have been no attempt, even, to establish any direct contact, let alone link the two armies up, and this was where Enver's failure to appoint an army-group commander to oversee the activities of the two began to tell. True, Izzet had yet received only half of the forces allocated to him, but that amounted to five divisions, of which only XVI Corps' two originals were at all involved with the enemy. Had he struck north sometime around mid-June with the object of linking up with Vehip's right in a sector where I Caucasian Corps' zone of responsibility abutted against that of IV Caucasian Corps, somewhere between Oğnot and Hinis, where Yudenich was arguably at his weakest, leaving Kemal to block the Muş–Bitlis axis, he might have been able to change the course of events significantly.

The Russians' advance through Lazistan had presented the Turks with a small but important asset: the front was now lodged in territory which was predominantly Muslim, not Christian, and the local population was sympathetic to Vehip, not Yudenich. Thus the former's intelligence-gathering was simplified, and the latter's complicated. The picture Vehip's staff pieced together seemed to indicate that the vulnerability in Yudenich's formation lay at the point where V Caucasian Corps (Lyakhov's original detachment plus the two Plastun brigades landed at Humurgan and the two divisions landed at Kovata Bay) abutted against II Turkistan Corps. As it happened, that junction point was north of Balahor, on the road from Bayburt to Gümüşane, where two reasonably practical tracks left it, running north. One was that which Lyakhov had feared would facilitate his envelopment at Of; the other descended to Sürmene.

Vehip moved quickly to capitalise on what he saw as a golden opportunity to cut off V Caucasian Corps, surround it and, with any luck, push it back into the sea. He moved the two southernmost divisions of his own V Corps (the 9th and 13th) to Balahor, added selected units from X Corps and detachments of Frontier Guards, and sent the force northwards along the two tracks across the mountains. On 26 June they ran into the 19th Turkistanskis at the Madur-dağ, and despite their considerable numerical advantage fought their way through them only after two days of heavy combat.

Then, three days later, rather than responding to the specific threat they posed, Yudenich trumped their efforts, ordering a general offensive he had already planned down to the last detail to open across the entire area.

Yet again he opted for a straightforward central frontal assault, with the heaviest weight to fall between the Çoruh and the Kara-Su, focused on Bayburt and intended to split the Turkish Third Army in two along a line Erzurum–Erzincan. In all he would throw thirty-four battalions, most of them from II Turkistan Corps, into a front not thirty kilometres wide, principally between the Upper Çoruh (confusingly, a tributary of the main river, not its upper reaches) and the Çoruh proper, just to the east of Bayburt. V Caucasian Corps was expected to hold the line – which paralleled the intended Russian line of advance – to the north, and form the right flank, while elements of I Caucasian Corps attacked through Mamahatun and the Tuzla Valley and formed the left flank, which was anchored on the mountains to the south.

The offensive began on 2 July with an attack on X Corps. The Russians made some progress in the north, against the 30th Division, less in the near-impenetrable mountains between the two rivers east of Bayburt against the 32nd, and very little south of the Upper Çoruh against the 31st, though on the latter's right, the Kuban Plastun brigades under Kruten succeeded in driving a division of XI Corps back, retaking Barnakaban but being held on the second defensive line at Sapdiran. Vorobyev's 4th Caucasian Rifle Division broke through decisively at Dencik and reached the main road to Bayburt on 4 July. This unmasked X Corps' right flank, and it began to retreat in disorder, losing significant numbers of men and guns in the process, and the infection soon spread to other sectors. By 8 July Vehip had lost control of his centre and the Turks were in full retreat across the entire front. Bayburt was surrounded on 14 July, and the following day the 17th Turkistanskis entered the town; already Russians were probing westwards along the roads to Gümüşane and Kelkit in significant numbers.

On the Turkish left only the newly opened salient at Madur-dağ saw heavy fighting, the division of V Corps which had penetrated the 19th Turkistanskis' position coming under attack from the Plastun brigades which had landed at Humurgan. The Russians pushed them back slowly but surely until the

Turks heard of the presence of Cossacks on the road between Bayburt and Gümüşane, whereupon they disengaged smartly and withdrew, rather than risk envelopment themselves, the Turkistanskis and the Cossacks hot on their heels.

In contrast, on Yudenich's left the fighting in front of Mamahatun, on the Dumanli-dağ and in the Tuzla Valley, where the three divisions of XI Corps faced I Caucasian Corps, with Lyakhov now in command, developed into a battle in its own right. The Turks' defensive positions were formidable, and for the first time they had modern German howitzers; numbers were about even. Lyakhov, 'a tempestuous and ambitious man, impatient to fight and indifferent to losses', rather than awaiting the results of the operation against Bayburt, sent his forces in on the night of 5 July, the Elizavetpolskis following the line of the road, the Kubinskis to their right, across the Akbab-dağ, and the Bakinskis on the eastern face of the Dumanli-dağ itself, with two Cossack regiments to the south, maintaining contact with the Transcaucasian Brigade in the Tuzla Valley. None made significant progress, and the following day the Turks counterattacked strongly, winning back most of what the Russians had gained, and continued to press forward throughout 7 July. Lyakhov was compelled to commit the Derbentskis, his last reserves, and planned a night assault on the Akbab-dağ, which he saw as the key to the position.

In the event, and due largely to the fortitude of his men rather than his own good generalship, his somewhat desperate measure paid a very good dividend. The Kubinskis and the Derbentskis threw the Turks off the mountain and sent them fleeing to Mamahatun with heavy losses, and as they withdrew the 27th Division exposed the flank of the 17th, to the south, and the Bakinskis and the Cossacks threw them back, too. The Derbentskis took Mamahatun on 10 July, with the Elizavetpolskis at Peçeriç and the Bakinskis at Çerme, and by then the Turks were in full retreat right across the front, desperate to reach the bridge across the Kara-Su at Kotur before they were cut off.

Reach it they did, five somewhat demoralised regiments of IX and XI Corps establishing a defensive position on the hillsides above the river. Desperate, they presented a serious obstacle, the approaches to their positions not allowing an assault on a wide front. Lyakhov reined in his impatience on this occasion. He selected the Bakinskis and the Kubinskis to make the attack, on the night of 13 July, and by the next morning many Turks lay dead, many more were in captivity and the rest had melted away towards Erzincan. In all, the Russians had destroyed or captured fully a third of the Turkish Third Army – the units lined up against Lyakhov alone lost 12,000 – and that defeat broke it as a fighting force. Now Yudenich need have no fear of it intervening on the left when he had to face Izzet's Second Army, as he knew he must in the weeks to come. His line was consolidated across the Pontic Alps from the Black Sea coast west of Trebizond to the Eastern Euphrates, and he was able to despatch the 5th Caucasian Rifle Division, which he had held in strategic reserve at Erzurum, to fill the gap between I and IV Caucasian Corps, south of the Tuzla Valley, towards Oğnot.

Thus, that 15 July Yudenich had much to be thankful for, but the operation in north-eastern Anatolia was not over yet. It soon became evident that the confusion in the Turkish ranks had extended to V Corps; it made no attempt to defend Ardasa, the two divisions which converged there retiring in opposite directions, leaving a gap which was, quite literally, big enough to drive a brigade through. The 1st Plastun Brigade, advancing from the north with V Caucasian Corps, obliged, while other elements of the northern force advanced on its flanks, driving all before them and themselves on to Gümüşane, which fell to them on 18 July. The Turks not having even considered being forced to retreat so far and so quickly, had had no time to destroy the large quantity of stores and *matériel* there, all of which fell into grateful Russian hands.

And still the rout continued. That same 15 July the 17th Turkistanskis had moved through Bayburt and had begun advancing along the road to Gümüşane, to link up with V Caucasian Corps. In combat for almost a fortnight by now, they made no great haste, and it was four days before they came up with the Turkish rearguard at Balahor. The Turks had no fight left in them, and ran, with the Russians, who had by now found their second wind, in pursuit. They chased them through Kokanis, and the following day the unlucky fugitives arrived at the crossroads near Pir-Ahmet, where a road from the south meets that from Bayburt to Gümüşane, just as the 2nd Plastun Brigade and the 19th Turkistanskis, approaching from the west, caught up with their own quarry – the remnants of V Corps – there. There was considerable confusion which was not calmed by the arrival from the east of the 17th Turkistanskis. Those Turks who survived took to the mountains, hoping to reach Kelkit, forty kilometres away to the south, before the Russians got there. Meanwhile the 18th Turkistanskis had been pursuing the remnants of the Turkish 32nd Division westwards from Bayburt by way of Reşdi. They caught them there, and the Turks turned and fought, giving a good account of themselves until they were taken in the flank by the 4th Caucasian Rifle Division. They broke and ran then, but were soon overtaken by Cossack cavalry; those who did not die on the spot were eager to surrender to the following infantry. The Russians continued westwards as fast as tired legs and aching feet could carry them. They caught up with another band of fugitive Turks west of Pulur, and then continued to Kelkit, taking the town, which was of considerable strategic importance since it commanded a route westwards into central Anatolia, on 23 July.

The real prize, Erzincan, went to the veterans of the 39th Division, and together with the 4th Plastun Brigade they moved out of their positions east of Kotur on 19 July. First of all, however, they had to negotiate the Euphrates, already a major waterway though still many thousands of kilometres from its mouth, the retreating Turks having succeeded in blowing the bridge which had spanned it since mediaeval times. In the interim, Russian engineers had worked night and day to throw a temporary wooden bridge across the chest-deep waters of the fast-flowing river, and had achieved a near-miracle. Still, it took three full days for the infantry, the artillery and the division trains to cross – and at that, fully half the men had had to ford the stream as best they could – and a further three to cross the fertile upland plain in which the city stood. On the morning of 25 July, the advance units of the 39th Division came in sight of the city and halted, waiting for the artillery to catch them up and begin the long process of bombarding it into submission. It proved unnecessary. Vehip Pasha had already evacuated his forces, and had begun regrouping twenty-five kilometres away to the west, in the hope of holding the Russians if they attempted to break through towards Sivas or Harput.

By midday on 25 July Erzincan was in Russian hands, the Derbentski Regiment, the first troops in from the east, having been joined by the 17th Turkistanskis who had arrived from the north. As more and more men poured in, Lyakhov began to test the mettle of the Turkish rearguards, and met stubborn resistance from desperate men well provided with artillery. He managed to drive them back a short distance by 28 July, but by that time Yudenich had decided that enough was enough, and began to consolidate his gains, conscious that all too soon he would have to face a new adversary in the south, to the west of Lake Van.

During the Çoruh Campaign, as this series of interlinked battles became known to the Turks, it is estimated that Vehip lost seventeen thousand men killed and wounded, and an equal number taken prisoner, plus, once again, an unknown number, certainly thousands more, who had simply turned their backs on their comrades and deserted. On paper, his Third Army still consisted of fifteen divisions; in reality, he had the remnants of four or five, none of them actually stronger than a regiment, strewn across the countryside west of Erzincan; what was left of X Corps, probably no more than 5,000 men in all, west of Kelkit, and two much reduced divisions of V Corps near the coast well to the west of Trebizond. As the dismal summer wore on, desertion increased still further; it is thought that by September, absconders outnumbered those still in the ranks by perhaps two to one.

When Enver had conceived the notion of establishing a second army in eastern Anatolia, in the weeks after the fall of Erzurum, and opening a second front there, the Russian front line ran from the Eleşkirt Valley south to Malazgirt, west from there to Hinis, and around the Bingöl massif; north of there it ran to the west of Erzurum and the east of Bayburt, and in the coastal strip Lyakhov's forces had reached a point some fifty kilometres from Trebizond. That established the parameters for the counteroffensive Enver contemplated, and for which he briefed the new army's commander, Ahmet Izzet. Essentially, Vehip was to hold the Russians in place while Izzet struck north, along the axis Muş–Hinis–Köprüköy, take Yudenich in his left flank, cut the Russians' lines of communication, retake Erzurum and then advance to the Black Sea coast.

Though it was certainly ambitious, given the Turks' generally poor performance in the region so far, there was nothing wrong with such a plan in principle; the problem arose from the fact that no one, least of all the generalissimo, made allowance for any further progress Yudenich would make before it could be put into effect. By the time the Second Army was powerful enough to attempt to implement it, it was irrelevant; in particular the Bingöl massif now protected the Russians' flank, not the Turks', and any advance to the north would have to cross it, or the equally uninviting Dersim (Mergan) range immediately to the west.

Enver had instructed Izzet to set up his headquarters at Diyarbakir, but he opted for Harput (Elaziğ) instead, for not only was it closer to the railhead, by a good road via Malatya, but it also had better links to Erzincan, where Vehip was quartered. As we have noted, the first units allocated to his command began arriving in theatre in March, but it was May before it amounted to a corps, June before it could muster two, and late July before it was up to anything like full strength, with II, III, IV and XVI Corps mustering nine infantry divisions[17] and one of cavalry, plus five battalions of artillery, most of their guns unsuitable for mountain warfare.

While spring turned to dusty summer, and Vehip Pasha's Third Army was being ground down inexorably, Izzet's Second was growing in size, and organising and distributing its formations seems to have consumed all his energy. For two months he turned a deaf ear to Vehip's increasingly desperate cries for help, steadfastly refusing to send him reinforcements – which is perhaps understandable – or even mount a meaningful diversionary offensive, which is not, and with hindsight, this must be considered a serious strategic error. By waiting until Yudenich had finished with Vehip before launching his own campaign, he allowed the Russian to move troops – tired troops, perhaps, but men with a solid string of victories under their belts – to oppose him, and in the process lost any advantage he may have had, numerical, strategic or tactical. Worse, when he did finally commit them, he divided his forces, splitting them into three corps-sized groups and fighting them independently of each other, which proved to be disastrous.

The Bingöl/Dersim massif, the range which separates the Eastern from the Western Euphrates basins, is a formidable obstacle by any standard. While it exceeds three and a half thousand metres in height in only a few isolated spots, its central spine seldom falls below two and a half thousand, and in the early twentieth century there were very few even half-satisfactory routes through it, none east–west, and few enough north–south. There were few enough centres of population worthy of the name, too, amongst them Gümgüm (Varto), thirty kilometres west of Hinis on the road from Köprüköy to Muş; Oğnot, sixty-five kilometres west of there, on the road from Diyarbakir to Erzurum, and Kiği, in what was essentially a dead-end valley, sixty kilometres west again.

It was the weakest of the three operational groups Izzet created, comprising the 14th, 47th and 48th Infantry Divisions plus the 3rd Cavalry Division, of only limited value in such country, which was given the task of moving north towards Kiği. The remote mountain town was linked to Palu, east of Harput, where the group had assembled after its long journey from Thrace, by barely practicable tracks, and to the north conditions deteriorated still further, and there were nothing more than rough, poorly defined shepherds' paths across the spine of the massif and down into the Endres Valley beyond. Inexperienced troops such as those of the 47th and 48th Divisions, not adapted to the rigours of mountain warfare, would be very vulnerable indeed to hardened uplanders in such terrain.

The second group comprised the 1st, 11th, 12th and 49th Infantry Divisions; they would march east from Palu to Çapakçur (Bingöl) and Simsor, and would then turn left for Oğnot, fifty kilometres further on, up the valley of the river of the same name. From Oğnot the track became progressively more difficult as it crossed the mountainous spine, but then descended into the valley of the Endres (which debouched in turn into that of the Tuzla) and provided a practicable, though never easy, route to Erzurum.

The third operational group, the 5th, 7th and 8th Infantry Divisions plus a ragbag of auxiliary units and irregulars, under the command of Mustafa Kemal, would concentrate on the south-eastern sector, specifically the target cities of Bitlis and Muş. The 5th and 8th Divisions, which had been the first fresh units to arrive in the theatre, were concentrated around Siirt, to the south of Bitlis on the road to Diyarbakir, while the 7th Division was based at Simsor, some sixty kilometres east of Palu, where the Diyarbakir–Erzurum road crossed that from Harput to Muş.

Izzet began pushing formations from his first and second groups forward in late June, by which time elements of Kemal's 8th Division had established themselves only ten kilometres from Muş, on the Kurtik-dağ. Yudenich, alerted by increased patrol activity in the southern valleys of the Bingöl/Dersim chain, began to feed troops of his own into the upper valley of the Oğnot, and also ordered the Turks dislodged from their position south of Muş. That was achieved by a night assault on 13 July, at a cost to the Turks of over a thousand prisoners, and with the immediate threat to the key city removed, Yudenich redeployed some of the brigade he had sent there to carry out the operation. They – three regiments of the 66th Infantry Division – arrived in the plain of Gündemire, west of Gümgüm and some forty kilometres from Oğnot, and linked to it by good tracks, and there they were to be joined by the 5th Caucasian Rifle Division, which had been held in reserve at Erzurum. Two more regiments – the 5th and 6th Caucasian Rifles – were sent to Ziyaret, twenty kilometres north-west of Muş in the valley of the Murat-Su, whence they were to advance towards Çapakçur. This would bring them into conflict with the Turkish 7th Division – by now moved up to the Boğlan Pass, which crossed a spur of the forbidding Şerefeddin-dağ separating Ziyaret from Gündemire – if it advanced on Muş.

Yudenich ordered his men forward into contact with the Turks on 29 July, the day after he had decided to advance no further west than Erzincan. They met the Turkish 12th Division at Oğnot, and at first made little progress, but on the afternoon of 1 August they broke through the centre of the Turkish defences and took the town itself, whereupon the Turks withdrew down the valley, but in good order, giving up only a handful of prisoners. The two regiments at Ziyaret, the 5th and 6th Caucasian Rifles, had also begun to move westwards, towards the Boğlan Pass, and looked set to run into the 7th Turkish Division, but Izzet now ordered that latter to retreat, to stay in line with the 12th and join up with it, rather than risk creating a weak salient. That same day he instructed Kemal to advance on Muş and Bitlis from the south, from the direction of Siirt, with the 5th and 8th Divisions. He also ordered the three remaining divisions constituting the Oğnot group to move up with all speed, to be ready to commence a counteroffensive in the Oğnot valley in two or three days' time, and the 47th and 48th Divisions of the Kiği force to begin advancing on their primary objective.

Yudenich responded to that latter development by ordering elements of IV Caucasian Army Corps, the 1st and 2nd Transcaucasian Brigades – now constituted as the 6th Caucasian Rifle Division, with the enterprising Voloshinov-Petrichenko promoted to command it – to move to Melikan in the Endres Valley, on the far side of the Şeytan-dağ, the Devil's Mountain, north-east of Kiği, to act as a blocking force should the Turks succeed in crossing the ridge. There it would be joined by the Don Foot Brigade, a brigade of Cossacks and two battalions of the 4th Plastun Brigade, moving up the valley of the Tuzla from Mamahatun. He also ordered the intrepid Col. Kruten, at the head of his four Kuban Plastun battalions, to set out on a two-hundred-kilometre forced march from Erzincan directly to Kiği, keeping away from highways and thus from the attention of informers.

Kemal's divisions opened their offensive against Muş and Bitlis on 2 August. In front of Bitlis Nazarbekov had the 7th and 8th Caucasian Rifles in prepared positions, supported by field artillery and howitzers, with a battalion of the 6th Caucasian Rifles in reserve. However, he feared being outflanked on his right by way of Mutki and tracks over the Nimrud-dağ, and on his left by way of the valley of the Güzel, which offered a route to Lake Van itself, and under cover of darkness that night withdrew to the village of Basan, five kilometres the other side of Bitlis, near the head of the Bitlis valley, where he felt more secure. The following morning the Turks walked back into Bitlis unopposed.

Before Muş, the Russians – the 261st Akhulginski Regiment, under Col. Potto, which had recaptured the Kurtik heights on 13 July – continued to occupy those positions. Heavily outnumbered by the 8th Division, but with artillery support which was denied to the Turks by virtue of the terrain, they resisted throughout the first three days of the offensive, causing disproportionate Turkish casualties, but on 5 August their defences were penetrated; with no strength in depth, Potto was obliged to retire to positions well beyond the city, and like Bitlis, Muş fell to the Turks without further resistance.

Retaking both Bitlis and Muş boosted Turkish spirits considerably, not only within the ranks of Kemal's XVI Corps, but throughout the Second Army, and damaged Russian morale even though the losses incurred in the process had been small. However, forces deployed in the Oğnot Valley continued to push the Turkish 12th Infantry Division back, until on 6 August, Yudenich, fearing that his spearhead units were over-exposed, ordered the advances down the Oğnot and towards the Boğlan Pass halted, and warned the five regiments involved to be ready to withdraw to the eastern slopes of the Şerefeddin-dağ. He gave the executive order for the withdrawal the following day. It is fair to say that had Izzet been more enterprising, he could have inflicted severe pain on the retreating Russians, but where he should have hurried he tarried. The 7th Division pursued the 5th and 6th Caucasian Rifles in a fairly leisurely fashion as far as Ziyaret, but no further, halting instead, and linking up with the left wing of the 8th Division, north-west of Muş, while the 1st and 49th Divisions, which arrived at Oğnot well after the regiments of the 66th Division had pulled out, failed even to pursue them out of the valley, but contented themselves with patrolling and reconnaissance towards Boran and Bingöl-kale. There they met the advance guard of the 5th Caucasian Rifle Division, then arriving in the upper Endres Valley from Erzurum, and backed off in the face of superior numbers.

The 5th was not the only formation Yudenich had directed into the upper Endres Valley; the Siberian Cossack Brigade was on its way there from Erzurum, and was to be followed by the 4th Caucasian Rifle Division, which had now reached the regional capital after a five-day forced march from Kelkit. With their arrival, Russian forces north of the Şeytan-dağ would be equivalent to around four divisions. Izzet could perhaps have stolen a march on Yudenich, quite literally, by pushing forces forward to and through Bingöl-kale, and on to Çatak, as early as 6 or 7 August, but he did not; he waited a full week, and by that time he had lost both the initiative and the numerical superiority he needed. He almost prevailed anyway, however, for the lead Russian unit, the 5th Caucasian Rifle Division, was a new formation lacking combat experience, and was driven back with heavy losses, but then the Siberian Cossacks and the 2nd Plastun Brigade arrived to bolster it, and reversed the pattern. When they descended into the upper Oğnot Valley, the Russians had numerical superiority and effective cavalry – which the Turks lacked – and soon drove them back on to the town; with no reserves left to throw into the battle, Izzet was probably beaten by 16 August, but he failed to realise it and withdraw his forces, the result being far heavier losses than he need have sustained.

The 47th and 48th Divisions had been ordered to keep pace with those of the Oğnot group, but had failed, and by the time they did set out for Kiği, on 5 and 6 August, they were already well behind schedule; not so their adversaries-to-be, for Voloshinov-Petrichenko had proved as reliable as ever, and had his 6th Caucasian Rifle Division in place at Melikan in good time, his cavalry patrolling the Devil's Mountain in strength. Voloshinov-Petrichenko enjoyed Yudenich's full confidence for good reason, and had no hesitation in anticipating his wishes, and when his cavalry declared Kiği free of Turkish troops he ordered his men to cross the mountains and occupy it. Thus, the Turks, when they approached Kiği on 15 August, found themselves having to fight for territory they had assumed they would simply be able to occupy. They had a small superiority in numbers, but lacked effective artillery, having found it impossible to drag their field guns up the valley, and Russian mountain batteries created havoc in their ranks as they were forced to bunch at choke-points. Nonetheless, they persevered, taking serious losses, for several days, and while they made only slow progress, they were still going forward, and the Russians seemed powerless to hold them.

Reversal came with Col. Kruten and his Kuban Plastuns, on 20 August. These men had marched two hundred kilometres from Erzincan, much of it over trackless mountainsides where few Kurdish shepherds, even, ever set foot, in little over a fortnight, and their remarkable feat, which took the Turks completely by surprise as Yudenich had desired, gave Voloshinov-Petrichenko the numerical superiority he needed to go onto the offensive. Initial Russian optimism was short-lived, however, for the terrain was better suited to defence than offence, and over the next ten days a dour scenario was played out, neither side gaining any significant advantage, until September, when the Turks were reinforced by the 14th Infantry Division, and compelled the Russians to give ground once more. Then, some days later, it was the Russians' ranks which were strengthened again, this time by the arrival of the 156th Infantry Regiment, who had also marched from Erzincan but by a more roundabout, easier route. Alas, even the addition of a veteran, battle-hardened formation such as the Elizavetpolskis was insufficient to tip the balance, and by 10 September the situation was clearly stalemated, with the Turks holding the line of the Horhor stream, and the Russians facing them south of Temran, almost exactly where they had been almost a month earlier.

To the east, in the Oğnot Valley, by 18 August Vorobyev had completed a concentration of forces north of the town and launched a three-pronged offensive. The Turks threw in their reserve 11th Division; the Russians suffered serious losses on both flanks, but eventually, after six days of heavy fighting, the column in the centre broke through and outflanked the outflankers, and within twelve hours the Turks were in full retreat, and did not stop until they reached Elmali, fifteen kilometres south of Oğnot. Yudenich, kept up to date by Vorobyev regarding his intentions, ordered the 5th and 6th Caucasian Rifles and the 66th Infantry Division to resume their offensive simultaneously with his advance on Oğnot, and over the next two days the Caucasians reached and took (intact) the important bridge over the Murat-Su north of Muş while the 66th met the Turkish 7th Division near Ziyaret and drove them back in disorder, pursuing them through Boğlan and Haraba and linking up with the forward elements of Vorobyev's left wing in the Oğnot Valley in the process. With the right flank of his central – Oğnot – group thus unmasked, Izzet had no choice but to order it to withdraw, and by 1 September it was back almost exactly at the point from which it had jumped off.

On the Russian right, after retreating from Bitlis and giving the town up without argument, Nazarbekov had subsequently fallen back still further, firstly from Basan to Tatvan, and then to Ahlat. As news of Russian gains further north and west – and, more significantly, perhaps, that the Turkish 5th Division had withdrawn from Bitlis in favour of a stronger position south-west of the town – reached him he reversed that last withdrawal, but at Tatvan he stuck, his numbers so depleted by now, after many months of isolated campaigning without replenishment, that any attempt to drive the Turks still further back would have been near-suicidal.

And thus the situation deadlocked on all three fronts, and the early onset of winter – it snowed for the first time on 26 September – translated stand-off into impasse, leaving the Turks with very little to show for a six-or-more-week campaign which had cost them at least 30,000 killed and wounded out of a total strength which had probably never exceeded a hundred thousand. By any standard, this was a disaster; not quite the catastrophe which had befallen Vehip's Third Army, perhaps, but nonetheless a calamity, and one which effectively spelled the end of Turkish offensive campaigning in the Caucasus. The final blow to Turkish morale fell before September's end, when Kemal ordered his 8th Division to pull back from Muş, and the Russians retook the city as easily as they had given it up.

As they went into poor winter quarters, the Turks were staring defeat in the face, and defeat would almost certainly mean the invasion of Anatolia . . .

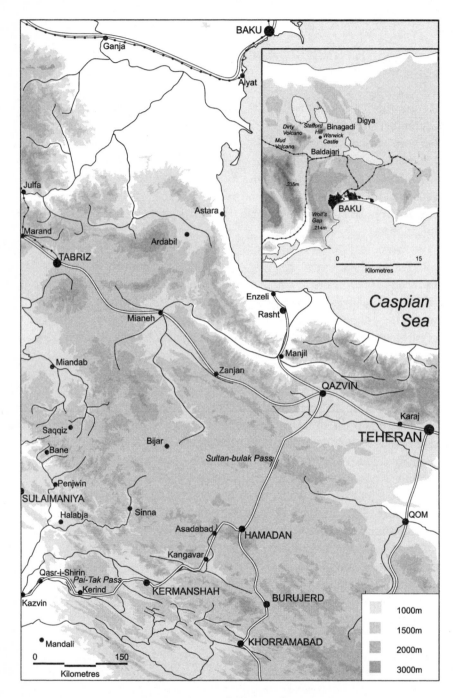

13. *Caucasus – Azerbaijan and W. Persia*

Armenia, Azerbaijan and Persia

As the third bleak winter of the Great War set in, prematurely, in late September 1916, the Turks' position in Armenia and eastern Anatolia was between parlous and perilous. Over the course of just nine months they had lost perhaps a hundred thousand men of the Second and Third Armies while failing to stop the Russians from overrunning tens of thousands of square kilometres of territory, including the region's most important fortress and its only sizeable port. A further Russian progress westwards seemed inevitable.

At this point, almost two years into a war which was now being fought on four fronts,[1] there was no realistic prospect of filling out the depleted units by means of recruitment, and instead War Minister Enver Pasha approved a massive reorganisation. Vehip Pasha set to work on the Third Army, which was in the poorer state, on 10 September. At a stroke V, IX, X and XI Corps ceased to exist, being recombined into two Caucasian Corps, the First, under Yussuf Izzet Pasha, and the Second, under Mustafa Fevzi Pasha. The result was an army of seven infantry divisions, each established at around six thousand men. The three operational regions into which Vehip had divided his zone of responsibility were redrawn too, with the First Region being eliminated and the other two split into six, each with a 'resident' infantry division, with the last (the 49th) in reserve. By mid-December, when the reorganisation was complete, the Third Army had an effective strength of around 36,000 men, little over a third of the number it had mustered when it had first gone to war, two years earlier, but at least it was a cohesive whole once more, with a table of organisation that was actually reflected by its formations on the ground.

The Second Army, too, was in need of restructuring, its strength having dropped from around 100,000 to perhaps two-thirds of that number. The approach Ahmet Izzet (with the assistance of Mustafa Kemal, who replaced him in March 1917) adopted was somewhat less draconian than that of Vehip, but nonetheless reduced it to three two-division corps.

The arrival of spring 1917 failed to bring the expected burst of activity in the theatre, for in March Russia had erupted into revolution. Though it did not take Russia out of the war, as many had hoped and expected, it did bring with it significant changes in the way it was prosecuted, including the removal of Grand Duke Nicholas as Viceroy in the Caucasus and his replacement as commander-in-chief there by Nikolai Nikolaevich Yudenich. However, in the process Yudenich lost any degree of independence that his promotion might have been expected to give him, his command being subject to review by the Special Transcaucasian Committee appointed by the new government. Its restraining influence was the cause of the failure to launch any form of offensive in 1917.[2]

As the year wore on, and Russia's domestic situation deteriorated, so did the morale of her armies. Events took a very dramatic turn for the worse on 7 November (25 October by the Julian calendar), when the Bolsheviks turned on their erstwhile allies in the government, now led by Kerensky, and seized power for themselves; the military situation finally dissolved into chaos when the new government, led by Vladimir Ilyich Ulyanov – Lenin – reached a separate peace with the Central Powers at Brest-Litovsk, in a treaty agreed in principle on 15 December.

The day after the armistice was agreed, the Caucasian Army Group was de-activated, the Second Army reduced to a single token division, and the majority of its units reallocated to the Third Army, which got the 5th, 11th and 12th Infantry Divisions, as well as the remnant of the now disbanded 8th. Only the 1st Infantry Division was reassigned to another theatre, Syria. Under other circumstances, one might have expected the reallocation of precious resources to have gone further; that they did not is perhaps an indication that Enver Pasha was already planning to go back onto the offensive in the Caucasus, this time against other factions with ambitions in the region: the Armenians and the Georgians, who had every intention of using this opportunity to establish independent states of their own, either together or separately, and with or without the Azeris, to the east.

The members of what would become the Transcaucasian Federation began by making peaceful overtures to the Turks; they responded positively, and by the end of January 1918 an agreement had been reached that a conference should take place at Trebizond, early in March. Before it could convene, however, the Federation's proto-parliament, known as the Sjem, met in Tiflis, on 10 February, in an attempt to formalise – indeed, to formulate – the alliance's standing. Twelve days later it proclaimed its existence as an independent 'Federative Republic' within the Russian Soviet Federative Socialist Republic, and followed that, on 1 March, by calling for a return to the pre-1914 frontiers. That was not acceptable to the government in Constantinople, whose attitude to the Federation now began to harden.

While there was no sentiment in either camp that they were actually at war with each other, Vehip had already been in action against Armenian elements; on 12 February, approaching Erzincan, I Caucasian Corps had confronted an organised defence for the first time: three Armenian volunteer infantry battalions, the self-styled Erzincan Regiment, with some guns and a squadron of cavalry, under the command of a Russian colonel named Morel. Decisively outnumbered, Morel offered only token resistance while organising a general retreat; he fell back on Erzurum, his men shielding a large column of panic-stricken civilian refugees as best they could from attacks by Kurdish tribesmen out for loot and blood. The Turks occupied Erzincan, then Bayburt and Mamahatun, and II Caucasian Corps began to advance eastwards along the coast and through the Pontic Alps, taking control of Trebizond and Gümüşane from the Georgians before the month's end.

Erzurum was garrisoned by two 'regiments' of Armenian Infantry who, when reinforced by Morel's men, amounted to perhaps 3,000, under the command of a partisan leader named Andranik Ozanian. Andranik had come to prominence as one of the leaders of the Armenian irregulars who took Van in May 1915. He made a token stand at Ilica, but his forces were soon outflanked, and it became clear that resistance would probably result in a massacre; on 11 March he gave orders to evacuate the city (during which it seems clear that his men performed a massacre of their own; official Turkish sources state the bodies of 2,127 Turkish males were found when it was reoccupied the following morning).

The ease with which their forces were able to advance into Armenia convinced the Constantinople government that there was no need to negotiate further with either the Transcaucasian Federation or the Russians, and when the Federation's representatives arrived in Trebizond for the conference, on 8 March, they left them cooling their heels while they revised their position. On 10 March Vehip telegraphed the overall leader of the Transcaucasian alliance's forces, the Russian General Lebedinski, that he would accept nothing less than an immediate evacuation of all the territory ceded to Turkey by Russia under the terms of the Treaty of Brest-Litovsk.[3] On 14 March, when the Turkish delegation deigned to put in an appearance at the conference, the Transcaucasians rejected the Turkish demands, protesting that they were not signatories of Brest-Litovsk, and were thus not bound by its requirements. From a strictly legal standpoint, that may have been the case, but under the circumstances it was an extremely naive position to have adopted. Over the next weeks, while the Turks' advance continued (they took Malazgirt on 23 March, Karaurgan on 30 March, and Bardiz and Karakurt the next day; Sarikamiş, surrounded on three sides, was evacuated on 5 April), the Transcaucasian Federation vainly put forward a succession of alternative proposals, none of which was accepted. They succeeded only in stretching the patience of the Turks, and on 6 April it snapped. The disputed districts were to be evacuated, the Federation's delegates were informed in a telegram emanating from Constantinople, by 10 April.

The delegation in Trebizond took a realistic view of the overall situation and began urging acceptance of the Turks' terms soon after they had become known. The Sjem, by now in almost constant session in Tiflis, first prevaricated, then accepted the inevitability, and on the day the ultimatum came into effect, 10 April, telegraphed its acceptance. The message was apparently never received, and two days later Vehip Pasha, whose II Caucasian Corps was pushing towards Batum, demanded the surrender of the garrison there not later than the next day. Almost incredibly, the Sjem decided that Vehip issuing a modified ultimatum, instead of moving to implement the original, constituted a sign of weakness on the part of the Turks, and withdrew its acceptance of the offer! Thus, on 14 April a state of war existed between the Ottoman Empire and the Transcaucasian Federation.

The first confrontation came on 19 April at Selim, on the road from Sarakamiş to Kars, where around ten thousand men of the Armenian National Army confronted three times that number of Turks, and were driven back peremptorily in an action lasting less than twelve hours. Three days later the provisional government of the Transcaucasian Federative Republic formally proclaimed its independence from the Russian Soviet Federative Socialist Republic. It is not recorded whether there was dancing in the streets of Tiflis, but there was scant celebration in Kars, for the Turks were but days away. Vehip demanded its immediate surrender. Nazarbekian (as Nazarbekov was now calling himself; he had somehow acceded to command of the Armenian National Army despite a well-deserved reputation for laziness and general incompetence) wished to defend the city but the newly appointed War Minister, the Georgian General Odishelidze, ordered him to negotiate. The Turks refused to moderate their demands, and on 26 April the Armenians capitulated. The first phase of the Ottoman reoccupation of the Lesser Caucasus was complete.

On 11 May the peace conference, now transferred from Trebizond to Batum, resumed, and after the obligatory initial sparring was out of the way, Vehip Pasha dropped a fresh bombshell: the Turks no longer felt themselves bound by the agreement of 10 April, since the Armenians and Georgians had abrogated it, and compelled Turkey to take the territory in question by force of arms ... Now they would be satisfied with nothing short of the regions around Akhaltzikhe (Akhalts'ike), Akhalkalaki (Akhalk'alak'i), both of them Armenian enclaves in Georgian territory, and Aleksandropol, together with control of the railway line running from the latter south and east to Nahçivan (Naxcivan), Julfa and Tabriz, as well as free use of the Transcaucasian railway linking Batum with Baku by way of Tiflis. If the first and second claims were comprehensible – the former for straightforward territorial reasons, the latter since it would allow the easy passage of troops into northern Persia – the third was harder to fathom, until one recalls the gleam which perhaps returned to Enver Pasha's eye when it dawned on him that the end of Russian control of the Greater Caucasus opened the mythical road to pan-Turania once more, and that the first staging post along that road was the terminus of the railway line in question, Baku ...

He would, of course, need more troops, and selected the 15th Infantry Division, which had returned from the Rumanian front the previous autumn and had meanwhile regrouped and re-equipped in Thrace, ordering it to assemble in Constantinople to await transportation by sea to Batum. He also selected two trusted commanders for his new adventure. One was his half-brother, Ferik Nuri Pasha, who had taken Van on 7 April and then joined Şevki Pasha at Kars. The second was his uncle, Halil Pasha, who was now handily placed at Mosul.

While Enver's actions caused some consternation in German circles in Constantinople, Berlin had little interest in Enver's pan-Turanian ambitions. However, it did have an interest in the Caucasus: Baku's oilfield, the production of which it desperately needed in order to feed its massive war machine, and which was at long last accessible. Even while Enver was still plotting, German forces were already moving in that direction, pushing into the eastern Ukraine – they had reached Kharkov by 20 April – and slowly taking control of the northern littoral of the Black Sea, entering Sevastopol and securing the Crimea, and occupying Rostov, at the mouth of the Don, soon afterwards. They were working the military-political axis too, and sent Gen. Otto von Lussow, the chief of the German military mission to Turkey, to the Batum Conference as a delegate, and Gen. von Kressenstein – who had been removed from his post as commander of the Turkish Eighth Army in Palestine after his defeat at the Third Battle of Gaza, and was no longer in much favour in Turkish Army circles – to 'liaise' with the Georgian members of the Transcaucasian government in Tiflis, accompanied by Count Friedrich-Werner von der Schulenberg. The latter had cultivated a wide circle of friends there during his time as Consul-General in Tiflis, pre-war, and the pair immediately began to intrigue, their objective being to place a barrier in Enver's way and open the road to Baku to German interests instead. They did so by mobilising all men of German origin – ex-prisoners of war, in particular, but also peasants from numerous pre-war German settlements – into a foreign legion to serve under the Georgian flag; it was never a significant force, but it served a function important out of all proportion to its size, for it allowed Germany to 'support' the Georgian Army against its own ally, Turkey, should that ally prove to have an agenda substantially different from its own.

Vehip gave the Federation very little time for deliberation, for he had come to understand the value of immediate action. When he presented the delegates at Batum with a new ultimatum, on the evening of 14 May, he gave them just twenty-four hours to withdraw their army forty kilometres east of Aleksandropol. In fact, even that was a deception, for the following morning, without waiting for the ultimatum to expire, he pushed his forces across the Arpa River, threatening the city. The Armenians, still massively outnumbered and now very short of supplies, had the choice of standing and dying, or retreating; they fled eastwards. Nazarbekian himself had not lingered in Aleksandropol, but had set up his headquarters in Karakilise (Vanadzor), fifty-five kilometres to the east. It was a much stronger location, strategically, at the point where the railway turned north to Tiflis and near the the important junction at Amamli (Spitak) where a paved road, which skirted the

4,000-metre-high Mount Alagöz to the east before running down to Erevan (Yerevan), left the highway for Delijan and Baku.

Nazarbekian tried to hold the Turks short of Karakilise – west of Amamli and at Güllü-bulak, below the Karakhach Pass on the Aleksandropol–Tiflis road – and also sent eight volunteer battalions to Erevan, the Armenians' historic capital city, to reinforce the 'regular' units under Gen. Silikian located there. The Turks dispersed the Armenians – though not as easily as they might have liked at Amamli, and with even greater difficulty when they regrouped, halfway to Karakilise – who were driven back to Delijan.

As well as advancing on Karakilise from Aleksandropol, the Turks also moved against Erevan: from Kağizman down the Aras valley; across the Ağri mountains out of the Eleşkirt valley, and down the western flank of the Alagöz Dağ along the railway from Aleksandropol. When Amamli fell, opening up the possibility of a Turkish advance down the eastern side of the Alagöz Dağ too, Silikian's prospects looked bleak. His response was to send a thousand picked men under the local partisan leader 'Dro' (Drastamat Kanayan) to take up positions at Baş-Abaran, where the road from Amamli ran in a defile, stripping his regular units of many of their machine guns with which to equip them. It proved to be a sound decision, for when Dro's men did come under attack they were able to keep the Turks at bay.

By then, Silikian himself had scored a notable victory, too, against both the odds and the run of events. On 20 May the Turkish 12th Infantry Division, advancing down the right bank of the Aras, occupied Iğdir. The following day the Armenian main force shielding Erevan west of the city came under attack from the rest of the 11th Caucasian Division. Silikian first held them, then, on 23 and 24 May, launched a series of skilful counterattacks, pushing them back beyond Sardarabad. This enabled him to free up first cavalry then additional infantry to assist Dro, who was also able to throw the Turks back, and the start of the last week of the month saw the Turkish offensive against the Armenian capital stalemated and then halted, when the Turks turned their attention to the Georgians and signed a treaty of friendship with the Armenians.

On 27 May the situation changed abruptly, when Kressenstein and Schulenberg played the hand they had been assembling so assiduously over the previous month, and the Georgian members of the Transcaucasian government in Tiflis proclaimed Georgia an independent republic.[4] Berlin, forewarned, immediately announced that it was offering the fledgling state its formal protection. In Batum, the Turks greeted the announcement with blank consternation which quickly turned to rage, Vehip warning the Georgians that this development changed nothing, and that the ultimatum of 14 May remained in force. Turkish troops would, he said, move on the coastal city of Potì and Kutaisi, inland, in three days' time.

Vehip was already making plans to march on Tiflis, and advanced his troops as promised. On 10 June the vanguard of the Turkish 9th Caucasian

Infantry Division came into contact with Georgian troops at at Vorontsovka, on the newly created frontier. Within the Georgian ranks there were German volunteers, but also, and probably unbeknown to the Turks, two companies of regular German troops. The Turks overran the defenders and took prisoners; among them were German soldiers. The following day the German General Staff telegraphed its counterpart in Constantinople threatening to withdraw *all* German support for the Ottoman Empire – including all troops and officials – if they were not released immediately. The Turks could but comply, and their advance into Georgia halted, not to be renewed.

When Enver had been informed of the developments in Tiflis, he had dropped everything in his haste to get to the region. Accompanied by the German General Hans von Seeckt, who had by now taken over as chief of the Turkish General Staff from Friedrich Bronsart von Schellendorf, he took ship from Constantinople for Batum on 5 June, to take personal charge of the situation. He arrived in Batum to find the whole furore building nicely, and acted in his usual impetuous manner. Faced with the need to refocus his strategy, within forty-eight hours he had torn up the Turkish order of battle in the Caucasus yet again, and had created an entirely new force at army group level, the Eastern Army Group, with Vehip promoted to command it. (His new standing was short-lived; within a fortnight he was recalled to Constantinople and a job on the General Staff. He was replaced by Enver's uncle Halil Pasha, who was conveniently on hand for the purpose; one might speculate that Enver welcomed the opportunity to make the substitution, but it is also significant that Halil enjoyed German confidence and Vehip, by this time anyway, did not.) He replaced Vehip as the commander of the Third Army, now reduced to the size of a corps, with his brother Esad Pasha, who had also made a name for himself in the Gallipoli campaign. To fill out the Eastern Army Group's order of battle Enver created a new force, the Ninth Army, with Yakup Şevki Pasha in command. No additional troops were made available to Esad or Şevki; they simply divided up the old Third Army between them. The Ninth Army was to push south-eastward into Persian Azerbaijan, with Tabriz as its immediate objective, while the Third Army would drive eastwards towards the Caspian and Baku. Most of Esad Pasha's forces were located to the west of the region, but one of his divisions, the 5th Caucasian Infantry, was by now in the vicinity of Delijan, and was earmarked to become the core unit of an autonomous 'Army of Islam', which was to be filled out with ten to twelve thousand (Azeri) Tartar irregulars.[5] It was to form at Ganja (now Gäncä, sometimes known as Elizavetopol and Kirovabad) on the Tiflis–Baku railway, in late June, under the command of Nuri Pasha. It was to stay out of Georgia but cross Armenian territory to operate within the Republic of Azerbaijan, which had come into being on 28 May 1918, the Azeri Tartars being extremely eager to be revenged on the expatriate Armenian community in their new nation, following the events of late March in Baku.

*

By the start of the Great War, Baku, on the Apsheron Peninsula which juts into the Caspian Sea, was a city of more than a quarter of a million people, far and away the most prosperous in the entire Caucasus by virtue of the oil industry established chiefly by the Nobel brothers[6] and the Rothschilds from the 1870s. Just prior to the October Revolution, a group of Muslim Azeri nationalists calling themselves the Musavat Party[7] came to power in the city. Their control was short-lived, for the Bolsheviks, knowing that the revenue from the region's oil production would be vital to Soviet Russia's economy, soon seized it from them. Events came to the first of a number of heads on 30 March 1918, when what amounted to a Bolshevik-sponsored civil war in miniature broke out, the Red Guards, the only (para)military force on hand that was in any way organised, turning a blind eye to ethnic Armenian Dashnaks[8] running amok, killing Muslim Azeris at will and dealing a severe blow to the rump of the Musavat Party in the process. Estimates put the death toll over four days at around three thousand, very few of whom were Christians.

In the aftermath many of the able-bodied men amongst the Azeri population made for Ganja, and the growing ranks of what would become the Army of Islam, very hungry indeed for revenge, while the Christians – their own ranks swollen by refugees from as far away as Erzincan, amongst whom there were considerable numbers who had fought with the Russian Army – consolidated. By the beginning of June they formed a rough army of perhaps fifteen thousand men, in thirty battalions, and set out to confront the Azeris. By 5 June they had reached Hajikabul, on the railway, some fifty kilometres south-west of Baku. Co-ordination was poor, or perhaps there were command-and-control problems in a force where a disinclination to follow orders was endemic, and they achieved very little, though their presence did guarantee the temporary safety of the small Christian communities spread out across the lower Kura valley.

On 26 June reports arrived of a large body of regular Turkish troops – it was the 5th Caucasian Infantry Division – advancing along the railway line from Ganja to Ujari. The Armenians offered some resistance but were soon driven back, but on 5 July their situation took a very decided turn for the better when the Cossack General Lazar Fedorovich Bicherakhov landed at Alyat, south of Baku, from Persia, with twelve hundred seasoned, disciplined men supported by four British armoured cars.

In order to explain Bicherakhov's sudden appearance from a very unlikely direction, we have to jump well over two years back along the narrative path to trace the activities of the force Baratov led into Persia during the winter of 1915–16.

We left them in Kermanshah on 26 February at comparative ease, having accomplished everything which had been expected of them – they had put paid to a German attempt to mount a *coup d'état* in Persia and seen off

Turkish attempts to establish a presence there – well-placed to prevent any further incursion by Turkish troops. Baratov may have believed his contribution complete, but there were others elsewhere who soon began to develop plans for his further employment, and they were to be found not with the Stavka in Mogilev or at the tsar's court in Petrograd, but in London, amongst those casting around for anything which might draw Turkish attention away from Kut, where Townshend's 6th Division had been besieged since 7 December.

Throughout March the possibilities were discussed in Petrograd, and on 1 April Baratov received orders to advance towards Baghdad. Even as he began to draw up a plan, von der Goltz, now in command in Mesopotamia, was moving to pre-empt him, despatching four battalions of troops to the border town of Khanaqin. By 10 April they had crossed into Persia and established an advanced position at Karind, with a reserve base, manned by the remnants of the units Baratov had defeated six weeks earlier at Sinna, at Qasr-i-Shirin. Baratov was preoccupied with supply problems, and it was 20 April before he set out from Kermanshah, nine days more before he confronted the Turks at Karind and threw them back, and 1 May before he ejected them from Qasr-i-Shirin and drove them out of Persian territory entirely. That same day he received news that the garrison at Kut had surrendered to the Turks, which effectively removed the objective of the mission he had been handed. However, he did not withdraw to Kermanshah, even though his supply situation dictated that as a sensible course, and his remaining presence on the border with the Ottoman Empire, whether it represented a real threat or not, was soon to become an irritation to Enver Pasha, who had himself arrived in Baghdad just days earlier.

The prime purpose for Enver's visit was to map out a strategic plan for the furtherance of the war in Mesopotamia. Halil Pasha, in command of the Sixth Army, made it clear that he wished to launch a campaign to push the British back down the Tigris with all the forces at his disposal. However, while they amounted to five divisions on paper, none were anything like up to establishment, and were in no fit state to go onto the offensive. It was clear that though three fresh divisions were on their way to make up the numbers in the theatre, there would have to be a period of recovery and retrenchment, and in the interim, Enver decided, his cherished pan-Turanism still tugging at him, an expeditionary force would be deployed to Persia, to confront Baratov, but with the long-term objective of proceeding towards Afghanistan in the hope of stimulating a popular uprising against the Amir and threaten the British hold on the North-West Frontier of India itself.

Leadership of the force he entrusted to Ali Ihsan Pasha (Sabis),[9] who commanded XIII Corps, to whom he allocated two of the fresh infantry divisions: the 2nd, from I Corps, which had already reached Mosul and was expected in Baghdad in a matter of weeks, and the 6th, from II Corps, which was due in theatre by the end of the month.

Of Ihsan's own troops, the 38th Division, now little more than a skeleton, was to be disbanded, and the 35th and 52nd were to be transferred to join the 45th and the 51st in XVIII Corps, which was to remain in Mesopotamia and rebuild its strength.[10] Ihsan was also to have an additional independent cavalry brigade and the 'assistance' of the 4th Division, also from II Corps, which was to be based at Sulaimaniya, in Kurdistan, plus a gaggle of zealously nationalistic expatriate Persians, which, Enver supposed, would grow into a veritable army as Ihsan advanced into their homeland.

Ihsan began assembling his troops in the last week of May 1916, and was on the move by the month's end; he brushed off an ill-conceived foray from Baratov (at Khanaqin) on 3 June, forced him to retreat to Qasr-i-Shirin then to Karind, and chased him from Kermanshah at the end of the month. Baratov attempted to organise a defensive position at Hamadan, but it soon became clear that the Turks were too strong for his now much-depleted force, and on 9 August he continued his retreat. Within ten days he had recrossed the last natural obstacle, the Sultan-bulak Pass, and there, his reconnaissance patrols reporting that the Turks seemed to be in no hurry to follow, he halted, to await events.

Though they were significantly stronger than the Russians numerically, the advance across the Zagros Mountains had taken its toll on the Turkish troops, and Ihsan – who had long been of the mind that his long-term mission was neither feasible nor even strategically desirable – called a halt to their progress at Hamadan, restricting his activities thereafter to patrolling south of the Sultan-bulak Pass. The reports he sent to Baghdad never ceased to stress the length of his supply lines (he was almost six hundred kilometres from Baghdad) and the poor overall condition of his men. XIII Corps was allowed to remain in place, making no further real contribution to the Turkish war effort beyond the threat that an army-in-being always represents, until ordered to withdraw back to Ottoman territory in February of the following year, after Maude had driven Halil Pasha from Kut.

Over the remainder of the year Baratov's depleted forces recovered their strength, receiving reinforcements as a precursor to going back onto the offensive. At an inter-allied conference at Petrograd in January 1917, it was decided that his command, now (somewhat misleadingly, for it had large numbers of infantrymen in its ranks) redesignated I Caucasian Cavalry Corps, and another of similar size under Chernozubov, located south of Tabriz at Saqqiz and Bijar, and now designated VII Caucasian Corps, would co-operate with British forces, which were advancing up the Tigris again. However, that was as far as the matter went at the highest level, and it was left to theatre commanders – Grand Duke Nicholas and Lt.-Gen. Sir Stanley Maude – to decide exactly what form that co-operation should take.

There was a very obvious obstacle in the way of any combined operation: the Zagros Mountains, which were frequently impassable to large bodies of troops in winter. They rendered impossible any immediate expedition in the direction of Mosul by VII Caucasian Corps, as the British urged, and it would in all likelihood be April, at the earliest, before Chernozubov's force could be brought into play. Baratov's Cavalry Corps could conceivably be sent south immediately, at least as far as Hamadan, though it was acknowledged that that would be little more than a gesture since progress beyond that point would be unpredictable until the thaw came.

The objectives for the Spring Offensive were discussed between the British and the new Provisional Government in Petrograd in April, by which time Baratov's men had appeared in force at Khanaqin. It was agreed that I Caucasian Cavalry Corps and VII Caucasian Corps (with Vadbolski in command in place of the too reactionary Chernozubov; Pavlov briefly replaced Baratov at the head of the Cavalry Corps, but was deposed by a vote of the men; field command went to his deputy, Radatz) were to continue in the roles originally allocated to them, the former to take part in the offensive along the Diyala River, alongside British troops, the latter to advance into Kurdistan, on Sulaimaniya and Ruwandiz, with Mosul as its ultimate objective.

Neither of these tasks were easy ones; the sector allocated to Radatz was defended in depth by Ihsan's XIII Corps, supported by German artillery, while the defences in the Kurdistani passes had also been reinforced. The renewed offensive opened in the first week of May, and Maude made it fairly clear that he expected little of the Russians, and that future planning would have to discount them. Sure enough, as 1917 progressed the cohesion of those forces disintegrated, men – individually, and in whole units – 'self-demobilising', turning away from the enemy, drifting northwards without orders from Petrograd, simply trying to return to their homes, the break-up becoming more pronounced and rapid after the second revolution. The British went to considerable lengths to try to persuade individual Russian commanders to remain in place, and offered to meet their 'expenses', often by subterfuge such as purchasing road-building materials they claimed to have accumulated, but it soon became clear that none of these quasi-mercenary units was worth its salt, save perhaps for Bicherakhov's Cossacks, who had by now settled at Kermanshah. And even they were in danger of falling apart unless some meaningful role could be found for them.

By the autumn of 1917, there were renewed fears in London of a Turkish attempt to exploit the prevailing chaotic atmosphere in Persia and send an expedition eastwards from the Caucasus. The first instinct was to send a blocking force to north-west Persia, but that would require divisions, and it was by no means clear where the personnel were to be found. Instead another possibility was mooted and accepted: a military mission to forge a relationship with the Georgians and Armenians,[11] bringing them funds to sustain them, and weapons if necessary, and a cadre of experienced men to help with their training.

The officer chosen to lead the mission was Brig.-Gen. Lionel Dunsterville, then serving as a brigade commander in India. Dunsterville – a friend of Rudyard Kipling since their school days at the United Services College at Westward Ho in Devon, and immortalised by him as the eponymous hero of *Stalky & Co.* – was an officer of some standing in the Indian Army; he was chosen for this mission largely because he spoke Russian, though he had built a 'can do' reputation on the North-West Frontier, in Waziristan, and in China during the Boxer rebellion. Summoned from Peshawar to Delhi for orders on 24 December 1917, he arrived in Baghdad on 18 January to take command of what was then known locally as 'The Hush-Hush Army' and later became Dunsterforce,[12] but which was officially the British Mission to the Caucasus. Promoted temporarily to major-general, and provided with a skeleton staff – the officers and NCOs who would become his personnel were still in the process of recruitment, and would follow when they arrived in theatre – he left nine days later for Enzeli on the Caspian, hoping there to take ship for Baku as a prelude to pushing on to Tiflis. His journey, over eight hundred kilometres across the Zagros Mountains and the highlands of western Persia in a convoy of Ford Model T motor cars[13] in the depths of winter, was an arduous one, but the mission arrived at its destination intact on 17 February, having encountered Bicherakhov at Kermanshah and Baratov at Hamadan along the way.

At Enzeli Dunsterville was confronted by a group organised as a Revolutionary Committee. He was refused permission to proceed to Baku and threatened with arrest, and left to return to Qasvin on 20 February. By 25 February he was back in Hamadan, where he was to remain, with the exception of a brief excursion to Teheran – 'a nasty place', in Dunsterville's opinion, with 'an atmosphere of lilies and languor and love in the air . . . full of Russian officers who drink and gamble for huge sums at the Imperial Club with Persian noblemen and any bounder with money to be squeezed' – for the next three months.

Only weeks after he arrived at Hamadan, the new Chief of the Imperial General Staff, Sir Henry Wilson (he took over from Robertson in mid-February), amended Dunsterville's orders. He was not to attempt to push on to the Caucasus – which was now on the brink of chaos, with the Turks playing cat-and-mouse with the Transcaucasian Federation – but was to remain in Persia under Baghdad's orders, and was to receive armoured cars and cavalry as soon as the road to Kermanshah could be reopened. Asked for his recommendations as to how to proceed immediately, Dunsterville asked for money – £20,000 per month – to support famine relief work, and this was approved on 23 March, as was a request for funds to pay the living expenses of Bicherakhov and his men, Dunsterville having convinced the Russian leader to remain in Persia until replaced by British troops if this were the case. Long before then, however, London had been forced to acknowledge that the situation was deteriorating rapidly, and Marshall, in command in Baghdad since Maude's untimely death, was instructed to send additional men to join Dunsterville immediately, on foot if necessary. A platoon from the 1/4th Hampshire Regiment was duly sent up to Karind on 16 March, reached Kermanshah eight days later and then continued towards Hamadan, and a second platoon arrived at Kermanshah before the month's end; by that time detachments had been positioned at five points along the road from Qasr-i-Shirin. In addition, the British consul in Kermanshah,[14] Col. Kennion, had recruited tribesmen to patrol the road between Qasr-i-Shirin and Asad-abad. The situation further north had improved slightly, too, the revitalised Bicherakhov having moved north to Qasvin to keep out Jangali tribesmen who had been threatening the city.

By mid-April the hundred and fifty officers and three hundred NCOs who had volunteered to serve with Dunsterville when the call had gone out in January (the majority of whom were from Empire units; the choice to recruit 'colonials' was that of Brig.-Gen. Byron, Dunsterville's chief of staff, who had been impressed by their performance during the Second Boer War) had begun arriving at Baghdad. By the end of the month thirty-five officers and forty other ranks had moved up to Hamadan (together with a squadron from the 14th Hussars and three Rolls-Royce armoured cars of the 6th Light Armoured Motor Battery, which were sent on to Qasvin), and the rest fol-lowed in May. It was Dunsterville's intention that his cadre of officers and NCOs should lead locally recruited irregulars[15] and operate, guerrilla-style, across the probable lines of advance of the newly formed Army of Islam, should it penetrate into Persia.

The CIGS, pressured by politicians alarmed at the progress the Turks were making through the Caucasus, then began to press Marshall to augment the force in Persia beyond the one battalion of infantry and one regiment of cavalry which the commander-in-chief in Baghdad claimed was all he could keep supplied with the assets at his disposal. The minimum requirement, Wilson maintained, following Dunsterville's own assessment, was for a cavalry regiment and an infantry brigade, but Marshall was adamant. With the seven mechanical transport companies to hand, he insisted, he could only guarantee to keep the smaller force supplied, and then only as far as Hamadan. Three additional infantry battalions would require ten more transport companies, and he simply did not have them. There was an alter-native, however: with Kirkuk taken, and operations in southern Kurdistan suspended until the autumn, he could allocate all his available motor vehicles to Dunsterforce. Supported by sixteen armoured cars and a flight of aircraft, this would form a flying column which would be able to control the road between Hamadan and Enzeli more effectively than a much larger force strung out in penny packets along it, he maintained, and eventually the CIGS agreed. In the event, Marshall's premise would prove unworkable, but for reasons beyond his control.

The force, half of it drawn from the 1/4th Hampshires, the other from the 1/2nd Gurkhas, set out in the last week of May, and began arriving in Qasvin

on 17 June. It soon became evident that Marshall's notion of establishing a
flying column had been overambitious, for after a journey of eight hundred
kilometres on what were roads in name only, many of the vehicles were fit
for little but the scrap heap. However, Dunsterville would soon have enough
additional personnel at his disposal in north-western Persia to allow him to
release Bicherakhov and his men to proceed to Baku, as he had agreed with
the Russian (and with Marshall) in late May. On 26 June he went to Enzerli
himself, and was relieved to find that the Revolutionary Committee now
raised no objections to the Cossacks taking ship for Azerbaijan, especially
since they would be sailing under the red flag of the revolution, Bicherakhov
having been accepted into the fold with open arms upon declaring for the
Bolsheviks, and even named as commander-in-waiting of the Red Army in
the Caucasus. Bicherakhov and his men, together with four Austin armoured
cars provided by Dunsterville, under the command of Capt. Crossing, and
many of the Red Guards assembled there,[16] plus Russian-speaking British
liaison officers, embarked at Enzerli on 3 July, and arrived at Alyat two days
later. And with that the clumsy time-loop we were obliged to create upon the
Cossacks' sudden appearance in Azerbaijan is closed, and we may return, as
it were, to the present.

On 7 July the War Office indicated that it would be happy to see Dunsterforce
proceed to Baku after all. Dunsterville made a flying visit to Baghdad to
clarify the situation, and some days after his return to Qasvin he learned that
he could now ready a battalion, plus a field battery and any available
armoured cars, to be sent to Baku, Baghdad having learned from the British
Vice-Consul there, Ranald MacDonell, that a *coup d'état* had seen the Bolsheviks of the Baku Commune, in power since mid-April, ousted, and
replaced by a coalition of political factions – Armenian Dashnaks, Social
Revolutionaries and Mensheviks, styling themselves the Centro-Caspian Dictatorship – which had voted in favour of asking for British assistance to
combat the advancing Turks.

An advance party, a platoon of 1/4th Hampshires, arrived in Baku on 4
August to initial consternation; the city's population expected a British army,
and expressed its collective disappointment quite vocally when just a handful
of men arrived. More troops followed later that same day, with Col. Robert
Keyworth of the Royal Field Artillery, Dunsterville's brother-in-law, in overall
command. More men (of the North Staffordshire Regiment), two armoured
cars and two more machine gun sections followed two days later, and by 10
August Keyworth had the equivalent of about half a battalion of infantry at
his disposal. On 15 August he sent Dunsterville a long and unambiguous
report in which he made clear the difficulties involved in holding an unwired,
unentrenched front, twenty kilometres long, with less than six thousand men,
the vast majority of them unreliable, undisciplined and largely untrained. The
situation, he said, was exacerbated by the military commissar, Grigory Petrov,

still the de facto leader of the Red Army faction, insisting that his men would not take up arms to support one imperialist group against another, but would instead retire, taking all their weapons and ammunition with them,[17] and it would require a division of British troops to hold Baku, contradicting Dunsterville's repeated assertions that a brigade would suffice. Though Keyworth did not say so, one of the factors contributing to the weakness of the defence was the absence of Bicherakhov's Cossacks. Bicherakhov had become increasingly alarmed at the Red Army's leaders' intrigues against him – and their denying him ammunition from their prodigious stock – while he was providing the only really effective defensive force Baku had, and had taken his men north to Derbend on 4 August. Dunsterville later stated that he had come to see that withdrawal as a grave mistake, and attributed to it his inability to hold the city,[18] but it is hard to see what else Bicherakhov – who was coming under increasing internal pressure to lead his men towards their homes on the steppe north of the Greater Caucasus – could have done.

Dunsterville had nothing like the division Keyworth wanted at his disposal, of course, but knew he had to act immediately if he was to make any attempt to save the city. He had already commandeered transportation in the shape of the *President Kruger* (and the smaller *Kursk* and *Abo* had been taken over too, and were lying at Baku, ready to help with an evacuation, should it prove necessary) and had transferred his headquarters into her. He set sail for Baku late the next day – 'A British General on the Caspian, the only sea unploughed before by British keels, on board a ship named after a South African Dutch president and whilom enemy, sailing from a Persian port, under the Serbian flag,[19] to relieve from the Turks a body of Armenians in a revolutionary Russian town', as he was to put it later – with the remainder of the North Staffords, a field battery and three more armoured cars, arriving after a wearisome eighteen-hour passage.

Baku, Dunsterville tells us, 'lay in a crater-like cup, the ground on the west and north rising gradually for about two miles [3km] till it reached the line of cliffs, whence it fell precipitously for over 500 feet [over 150m] to the bottom of the desert valley'. The morning following his arrival he set out to see the situation for himself. He found the North Staffords well dug in on the left, their flank at the sea, and next to them an Armenian detachment which had followed their example to some degree. The line then ran northwards for ten kilometres, following the cliff-top, then dropped to cross the railway line and rose again to cross the flanks of Mud Volcano and Dirty Volcano to the north before dropping again to the shores of the Masazir Salt Lake. From the far shore of the lake there were no organised defences; Bicherakhov had held that area, but after he decamped no move was made to replace his men, and as a consequence the Turks and particularly their Tartar allies, many of whose homes lay in the area, had infiltrated and occupied the network of small villages across the Apsheron Peninsula to the north and east of Baku.

The first attack had come on 5 August. The defensive line had been driven back but not breached, and though the defenders had lost six hundred killed and wounded, the Turks had suffered more heavily, and left sixteen machine guns behind when they retreated. This was not the easy victory the Turks had expected, and it was only towards the end of the month that they attacked in strength again. A weak company of the North Staffords – five officers and 135 men – had by now moved on to the northern slopes of Dirty Volcano, and it was they who bore the brunt of the assault, by two Turkish battalions supported by artillery, on 26 August. The North Staffords repulsed four attacks, but during the fifth the Turks turned their flank; they lost all their officers and almost eighty men killed or wounded, and were forced to retire to the foot of the hill. There they rallied, assisted by the dismounted machine guns from Duncars, but the position was untenable, and they were forced to pull back still further. The Turks contented themselves with having taken the hill, and made no attempt to continue their advance. Throughout the action, three Armenian battalions to the North Staffords' right had looked on, playing no part.

British reinforcements – more North Staffords and half a company of the Royal Warwickshire Regiment – came up belatedly and established defensive positions south and east of Dirty Volcano on a line Binagadi–Digya, anchored on the left on high ground christened Stafford Hill; they were further reinforced by a gun battery and a company of the Worcestershire Regiment, who linked up on the right to Armenians with more of the Royal Warwicks in reserve. This, of course, had the effect of shortening the defensive line, but it was still horribly porous, gaps in those stretches held by local troops opening up with appalling regularity. Before dawn on 31 August the Turks attacked again, concentrating on Stafford Hill, and in a three-hour firefight in the Binagadi oilfield, amongst the derricks and pumping gear, eventually forced the troops there to give ground. The North Staffords were found to have lost almost half their strength when they regrouped at a point known as Warwick Castle.

That position, too, soon came under attack; Armenians on the flank fled on hearing the opening shots, and fearing encirclement, the British infantry withdrew once more. It was clear to Lt.-Col. Faviell of the Worcesters, who was in command on the spot, that he had insufficient numbers to put up any meaningful resistance where he was, and he fell back still further as soon as darkness came, to the railway embankment linking Baladjari with the Beyuk salt marsh. The defensive line was by now just a few kilometres from the outskirts of Baku, roughly following the line of the railway.

By midday on 1 September it had become clear to Dunsterville that the situation was irrecoverable. At 1600 he met with the five leaders of the Centro-Caspian Dictatorship, and informed them that he considered that Baku could not be saved from the Turks. British troops had hitherto done all the fighting, he told them, and the local troops had consistently failed to assist or support them. Accordingly, he said, he was about to give orders to his men to withdraw from the line, and suggested they fill the gaps which would be left with their own men, but make terms with the enemy at once. In parting he urged them to take immediate action, and not to waste time in making speeches and passing resolutions.

That was a forlorn hope. He left them for an hour, but when he returned it was to find angry men arguing with each other and no conclusion reached. He left them to deliberate further, but when he returned after a further hour had passed, he found the situation unchanged. Dunsterville was a compassionate man who lived by the Christian values of his class and time. He understood that in the absence of effective leadership, he could not simply leave the people of Baku to their fate, and told the Dictators (sic) so. The gist of their reply was that, in any event, British troops would only be permitted to evacuate the city on the same terms as their own forces, and after the evacuation of such noncombatants as wished to leave.

That same day Marshall arrived back in Baghdad from two months' leave, and though he had other, bigger, fish to fry (the temporary unofficial armistice in Upper Mesopotamia was about to come to an end) he nonetheless became involved in the affairs of Dunsterforce, deciding that preparations to evacuate the city should begin. His signal crossed one from Dunsterville telling him that he could not hold the city. Dunsterville had also received a signal from Bicherakhov, who said he had taken Petrovsk, well to the north of Derbend, and promised to send a thousand men to Baku within a week (in fact he sent half that number, and very valuable they proved during the last days of the siege). This gave him heart once more, and he sent Marshall a further, contradictory, signal, asking him once again to send the rest of the 39th Infantry Brigade from Persia and promising to hold Baku if he did. Marshall was unmoved. No more troops would be sent, he replied and Dunsterville's orders remained unchanged.

Just to confuse matters further, on 9 September Marshall received other signals Dunsterville had sent on 4, 5 and 6 September, all of them by now out of date and presenting further contradictions. He reacted sharply, telling Dunsterville that while he did not pretend to understand fully the situation in Baku, he (Dunsterville) did not seem to be attempting to carry out his orders, and that as a result, operations elsewhere in Persia were in danger of being compromised. And at that point, another ponderous figure, Gen. Sir Charles Monro, who was by now Commander-in-Chief of the Indian Army, added his weight to the argument. Actually, he opined in a telegram to the War Office the next day, Dunsterville seemed to be holding his own and even improving his position. He did not understand Marshall's signal – which had been copied to Delhi as a matter of course – and questioned his assertion that other Persian operations (for some of which, notably Sykes' South Persian Rifles, he had ultimate responsibility) would be compromised.

And of course, Monro's signal coincided with others from Dunsterville to

Marshall. One of them stated that the tactical situation in Baku was entirely due to the delay in sending him the troops he had asked for; the second that evacuation was impossible in any event, for the Centro-Caspian Dictatorship still controlled the sea-lanes with its pair of gunboats and would not permit his men to leave. He then went on, at considerable length, to try to improve Marshall's understanding of the situation, describing reduced Turkish morale, the arrival of some men from Bicherakhov, reports of Georgians rising against the Germans. And at that point – 11 September – the War Office weighed in too, responding to a signal which had originated on 7 September and had been forwarded to London by Marshall, the work of Lt.-Col. Clutterbuck, lately Bicherakhov's liaison officer and invalided back to Enzeli with fever the previous day. Clutterbuck had painted an optimistic picture: there had been rumours of Turkish withdrawals from the Baku perimeter, and patrols had found no sign of them within five kilometres of the defensive line, which seemed to bear that out. Loaded troop-trains had been seen moving west. The Baku government had received a letter from that in Moscow with an undertaking from Berlin that German, not Turkish, troops would occupy Baku. All this the War Office found seductive; Baku should be held, it decided – on the basis of an appreciation which was at least five days out of date – and the British forces in north-west Persia increased.

By the time that order was issued, the situation on the Apsheron Peninsula had changed yet again, of course. As Clutterbuck had reported, the Turks had indeed withdrawn from their positions due north of the city, but it was, Dunsterville soon discovered, a case of *reculer pour mieux sauter*; they had done so only to prepare a major assault, timed to take place, an Arab officer who had defected from the Turkish ranks informed him, on the night of 13 September. His information proved to be largely correct; the attack – by the Turkish 5th Caucasian Division – came, under cover of darkness, in the north of the Wolf's Gap sector, west of the city. As day began to dawn further attacks were launched in the Baladjari sector by the 15th Infantry Division, and there was renewed fighting to the west. By 1000 on 14 September the British troops in both zones had been forced back by over a kilometre. Turkish artillery was now bombarding the city centre and the port area, and there was no real prospect of reversing the trend; Keyworth, in tactical command, concluded that evacuation was the only alternative to annihilation. Dunsterville concurred, and informed the Dictators of his decision.

The general retreat towards the wharves where the waiting ships were drawn up began as darkness fell. Throughout the evening, while the North Staffords held the perimeter around the dock area, sick and wounded men were embarked on the *Kursk* and the *Argo*, guns and munitions were loaded aboard another commandeered ship, the *Armenian*, and the main body of the force, with Dunsterville and his staff, boarded the *Kruger*. *Argo* and *Kursk* left first; the North Staffords came aboard and *Kruger* was just about to slip her moorings when two members of the Dictatorship appeared and ordered

Dunsterville to return his men to the defensive line. He refused. They told him that his ships would be sunk by their gunboats if they ventured out of the harbour. He told them to do their worst. *Kruger* cast off, followed by the *Armenian*; both came under desultory fire from the guardship out in the bay, but escaped without serious mishap. As they sailed away, the Azeri Tartars began to take their revenge on Baku's Armenians; the Christian quarter of the city was turned into a charnel house, with at least six thousand dead. There are suggestions that the Turkish Army delayed its entry into Baku until the following day in order to allow the Tartars more time to conclude their self-appointed task.

Only a small amount of *matériel* had to be left behind in Baku, which speaks highly of the way the withdrawal had been planned and was carried out, and that was destroyed. The animals were handed over to Bicherakhov's men, who withdrew in the direction of Derbend. By the evening of 15 September, the remnants of Dunsterforce which had occupied Baku for just a month had landed at Enzeli, and the Turks had taken over the city. That same day Dunsterville received a signal relieving him of his command and ordering him to Baghdad, where he arrived, having proceeded without much urgency, ten days later. 'Everybody very nice, but a general sort of feeling that I have been a naughty boy and ought to be put in the corner,' he commented in his diary.

By the time Dunsterville left Baku, the situation in north-west Persia seemed to have taken a distinct turn for the worse, the Turks at Tabriz – the 11th Infantry Division had taken the city on 23 August – having advanced as far as the Kuflan Kuh Hills, halfway to Zenjan. However, there they stuck, and in early October they began to retire, from there and from the areas to the south, around Bijar and Sinna. At the time of the Armistice they held a line from Astara, on the Caspian, to Mianeh and south-west to Sulaimaniya, though that is not to say they controlled all the territory north of it by any means.

The situation in Azerbaijan and across the Caucasus had likewise changed, with the arrival at Baku of Nuri Pasha, who now garrisoned the city with most of three infantry divisions. In mid-September, Marshall's headquarters received a report from 'a reliable source' that Enver had ordered Nuri to reduce the force at Baku to a single regiment, send another to confront Bicherakhov in Daghestan, where he was whipping up anti-Turkish sentiment, and transfer command of the other five to Halil, who was to advance on Enzeli. That order may well have been given, but carrying it out was another matter. While Baku itself, and a corridor along the railway back to Ganja, were under Turkish control, the rest of the hinterland – the rest of Azerbaijan, even – was not; and in particular a very significant number of Armenians – admittedly, men who were of dubious value as a body, but who were armed and determinedly anti-Turkish – lay across Halil's proposed line of march. And for the major part of the maritime fleet which had been at Baku having followed Dunsterville's example and decamped to Enzeli, a movement by sea was not an option. In the event, Turkish forces got no further south on the littoral than Astara, and occupied the territory north of a line from there to Mianeh.

Frustrated, Halil returned to Constantinople soon after the armistice, while Nuri Pasha, who first tried to confuse matters by declaring himself commander-in-chief of the Army of Azerbaijan, then set off north into Daghestan in fruitless pursuit of Bicherakhov, occupying Derbend and Petrovsk. Bicherakhov had long moved further north and had begun to recruit amongst the Terek Cossacks for Denikin's White Army, while Przevalski had begun to do likewise around Baku.

The Royal Navy began to (re)establish its presence in the Caspian Sea, as a precursor to the reoccupation of Baku, in October, and the city was reoccupied by British troops – elements of the North Persia Force led by Maj.-Gen. WM Thomson – on 17 November. The 27th Indian Division was later sent to the region, and British troops moved into towns and cities right across the Caucasus, including Tiflis and Batum – which became an important base both for them and for a naval flotilla – and controlled both the trans-Caucasian railway and the oil pipeline from Baku to the Black Sea.

III
THE DARDANELLES
AND GALLIPOLI

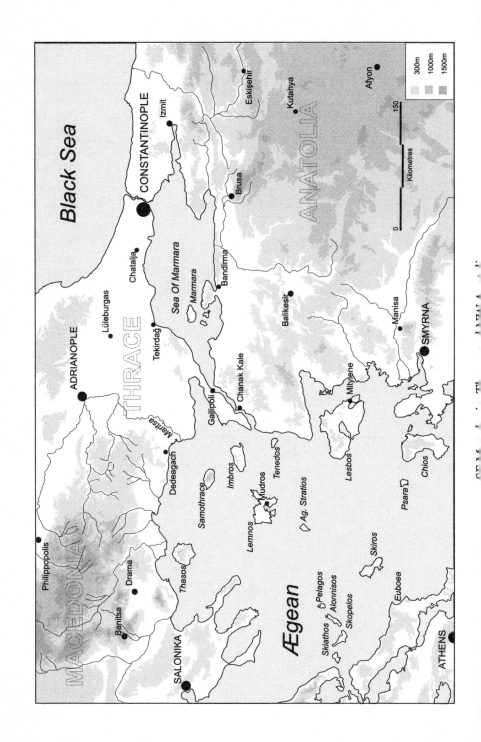

To Constantinople!

On 19 August 1914 Sir Louis Mallett, Britain's ambassador to the Sublime Porte, cabled Winston Churchill, the First Lord of the Admiralty, suggesting that in the event of war with Turkey he consider a naval operation to force the Dardanelles and threaten Constantinople. This was not a novel proposal; Adm. Sir John Duckworth had done it in 1807[1] (at considerable cost), but though it had been considered on no less than five subsequent occasions, no further attempt had ever been sanctioned. However, Elefthérios Venizélos, the Prime Minister of Greece, had coincidentally offered to put the Greek Army and Navy at the disposition of the Allies, and on 31 August Churchill and his counterpart at the War Office, Lord Kitchener,[2] agreed to form a joint committee to evaluate the proposal. The Director of Military Operations, Maj.-Gen. Charles Callwell, was asked for his opinion and wrote a few days later saying it was feasible – the Greeks having available the 60,000 men he thought the minimum requirement – though it would be a very difficult undertaking.

By the time of the first meeting of the War Council, on 24 November, Churchill had become convinced of the desirability of mounting such an operation, and suggested that to do so would offer the best protection possible for the Suez Canal (by the simple expedient of taking Turkey out of the war). He did, however, throw in a caveat, repeating Callwell's opinion that it would be a difficult undertaking and require the involvement of at least 60,000 soldiers as well as warships, and by now it was clear that the Greek offer would not be accepted for political reasons.[3] In stepped the Secretary of State for War, Lord Kitchener. There was no question of sending that number of troops – any number of troops, in fact – to the Eastern Mediterranean with the situation in Northern France seemingly on a knife-edge, he pronounced, and with that Churchill withdrew his proposal.

No more was heard of it until the new year. By Christmas the Russians and the Turks were locked in battle at Sarikamiş; faced with what he believed to be a successful envelopment; the most senior Russian officer in the theatre, the incompetent Alexander Myshlayevski, panicked, and that resulted in a false appreciation of the situation there being made at the headquarters of the Stavka, the Russian High Command (see Chapter 6). The outcome was a request from Grand Duke Nicholas, the Russian commander-in-chief, that Britain launch some sort of diversionary activity.

Kitchener received that request on the morning of 2 January 1915, and

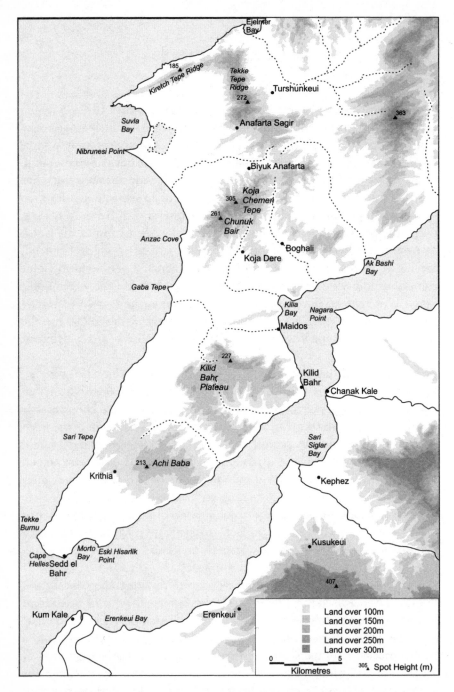

15. Gallipoli and The Dardanelles

immediately sent a copy over to Churchill; later in the day the two met to consider their response. Churchill once more brought up the subject of a 'descent' on the Dardanelles from Egypt, and Kitchener accepted that it was one viable possibility, but stressed that he had no troops to spare for it. In the event, Kitchener replied to the Grand Duke that 'steps will be taken to make a demonstration against the Turks', but carefully avoided specifying where or when it would take place, or what form it would take, and ended by saying that he didn't believe it would have the desired effect anyway. In fact, by the time the telegram reached Russia the Battle of Sarikamiş was effectively over, the Turks decisively beaten and the need for a diversion gone, but the Russians did not see fit to withdraw the request for a diversion, and by that time the notion had developed an impetus of its own.

The next morning Adm. of the Fleet Lord Fisher, the First Sea Lord (the professional head of the Royal Navy), aware of the existence of the correspondence, chipped in with a wild proposal of his own. He advocated stripping Sir John French's British Expeditionary Force in France of all Indian and 75,000 British troops (they were to be replaced by Territorials from Britain on the basis that 'anyone could stand in a trench and hold a gun') and sending them off to land at Besika Bay, just south of the Dardanelles on the coast of Anatolia. Simultaneously, troops from Egypt would feint at Haifa and land at Alexandretta with the objective of marching on 'the oil fields of the Garden of Eden, with which by rail it is in direct communication' (which, of course, it was not), while the Greeks landed their army on the Gallipoli Peninsula, the Bulgarians advanced on Constantinople and the Russians, the Servians (sic) and the Rumanians went for Austria. Finally, Vice-Adm. Doveton Sturdee would force the Dardanelles with obsolete Majestic- and Canopus-class battleships[4] which were scheduled for disposal anyway, and threaten Constantinople with bombardment.

Churchill does not record how long it took him to discount most of Fisher's plan, but he fastened onto the last element as entirely sensible, and it became a central plank of his own strategy. The very same day he cabled Vice-Adm. Sackville Carden, the commander of the squadron blockading the Dardanelles, asking his opinion of the merits of such a scheme. Carden took two days to reply, and then was cautiously supportive. 'I do not consider the Dardanelles can be rushed,' he said, adding, 'They might be forced by extended operations with large numbers of ships.' Well, like the original Jingoists, Churchill had the ships ... He had no less than forty-three such otherwise-largely-useless ships, in point of fact, and if that proved insufficient, France had at least a dozen more ... With those sorts of numbers to hand, he could have lined them up side by side and ploughed through the Straits in a phalanx ...[5]

Churchill kept his own counsel at a meeting of the War Council that afternoon, save for reading out Carden's terse telegram; it generated considerable interest. When he returned to the Admiralty he sounded out senior staffers, and found them unanimously favourable, and the following day he asked Carden to elucidate.

Carden delivered a proposal for a four-phase naval operation on 11 January,[6] and Churchill wasted no time in circulating it, to general enthusiastic approval. Only in one particular was an amendment suggested: to employ the new 'superdreadnought' Queen Elizabeth[7] to bombard the forts, something she could achieve from well outside the range of their own guns.[8] The just completed ship was, as luck would have it, actually under orders to proceed to the Mediterranean for gunnery trials; why not kill two birds with one stone?

Churchill circulated the proposal on 12 January, and the War Council met next day and unanimously[9] accepted it, resolving 'That the Admiralty should ... prepare for a naval expedition in February to bombard and take [italics added; the point was not lost on the Dardanelles Commission[10]] the Gallipoli Peninsula with Constantinople as its objective.'

The First Lord now wrote to his counterpart in Paris, Augagneur, to acquaint him with the outline of the plan; Augagneur offered four obsolete battleships. Churchill also wrote informing Grand Duke Nicholas and asking him to ensure that the Russian Black Sea Fleet would co-operate by initiating an action off the northern entrance to the Bosporus (and that an army would be brought to the Crimea, ready to be transported to the Turkish capital in the event of the operation succeeding; Nicholas did that, depriving Russian forces on the Caucasian front of sorely needed reinforcements for many months).

'Up to about January 20 there seemed to be unanimous agreement in favour of the naval enterprise against the Dardanelles,' wrote Churchill later. He was mistaken, however; there was a dissenter: Fisher. The First Sea Lord had never been fully convinced that a purely naval operation, without a landing, could achieve the desired result; he had remained silent previously, but now he made his doubts known and opposed the plan with the only means at his disposal, demanding the withdrawal of the Queen Elizabeth[11] in the belief that without her it could not go ahead. Churchill declared that the operation did not depend on the presence of one ship, and eventually Asquith intervened on his side; Fisher threatened to resign, but was convinced to remain by Kitchener reminding him of his duty.

By 15 February, the ships earmarked for the operation were assembled in Mudros' spacious harbour, the island of Lemnos having been made available by the Greek government, and two battalions of marines from the Royal Naval Division, which were to supply the personnel for landing parties should they be required, joined them. That day Adm. Sir Henry Jackson, who was then attached to the Admiralty specifically to advise on matters concerning the war in Germany's overseas colonies, but was also consulted on matters relating to Turkey, wrote a new memorandum underlining the need to send a military force 'to assist in the operation or, at least, to follow it up immediately the forts are silenced'. Kitchener capitulated, and at the War Council the next day it was resolved to send the 29th Division, plus forces from Egypt if required, to Mudros at the earliest possible date.

At the Council's next meeting three days later – the day the bombardment of the outer forts commenced – Kitchener announced that he had changed his mind; that he could not consent to the despatch of the 29th Division (he had been influenced by his own General Headquarters, by Churchill's account; by the French, according to the Official History[12]). Churchill protested; Kitchener held firm. The only concession he would make was to authorise the employment of 'the Australasian Army Corps' (ANZAC[13]) to aid the fleet. Churchill appealed to the Prime Minister once more, but he did not dare overrule Kitchener for fear that he would resign in protest, and could only attempt to persuade him. Something did, but it wasn't the Prime Minister.

Kitchener had sent Lt.-Gen. Sir William Birdwood, ANZAC's GOC, whom he knew well and trusted, to Mudros to assess the situation for himself, and on 5 March Birdwood reported 'I am very doubtful if the Navy can force passage unassisted.' On 10 March Kitchener did a volte face, telling the War Council 'he felt the situation [in France] sufficiently secure to justify the despatch of the 29th Division [to the eastern Mediterranean]' (though only as a loan).[14] The operation would have its military component brought up to the level thought to be required, even if no one – least of all Gen. Sir Ian Hamilton, who was appointed to command the Mediterranean Expeditionary Force on 11 March[15] – had the vaguest idea how it was to be deployed.

Before proceeding we should perhaps look at the physical features of the Dardanelles Strait, the Hellespont of ancient times. It is just seventy kilometres in length from their mouth to the Sea of Marmara; at the mouth it is little more than four kilometres wide, from Sedd el Bahr (Seddülbahir) to Kum Kale, and at the Narrows, between Kilid Bahr (Kilitülbahir) and Chanak Kale (Çanakkale), only 1,400 metres separate Europe from Asia. The average depth of water is fifty-five metres, increasing to a maximum of around ninety. The Strait have counter-currents; that on the surface runs from the Sea of Marmara towards the Aegean, but the deep current runs in the opposite direction; both run at four to five knots. There is no tide to speak of.

By the time the German military mission under Otto Liman von Sanders arrived in Turkey at the end of 1913, plans developed during the wars with Italy and in the Balkans for strengthening the Strait's naval defences were already being put into effect, with forts reconstructed and to a limited extent rearmed with modern guns. Over the autumn and winter of 1914/15 a German coastal defence specialist, Vice-Adm. von Usedom, oversaw repairs and improvements to the forts and to the communications infrastructure linking them with spotting positions. Many additional guns were brought in, including a regiment of modern 15-cm field howitzers, which were installed in dead ground, and by February there were eighty-two operational guns in fortress emplacements, and 230 in field emplacements. There were also torpedo installations commanding the Narrows at Kilid Bahr. Out in the Straits a total of ten lines of mines – around 370 in all – had been laid by then, the mines anchored at around four and a half metres below the surface at intervals of a hundred to one hundred and fifty metres. However, many had been in place for six months, and their condition was uncertain. Nets had been deployed to deter submarines.[16]

The naval bombardment of the four outer forts began at 0951[17] on 19 February. In all, one hundred and thirty-nine shells were fired, to little effect. For the next five days the weather intervened, and no bombardment was possible. It resumed on the twenty-fifth, and in the light of experience gained on the first day, when it had been difficult to determine which ship had fired which shell, just four ships participated, *Agamemnon* targeting Cape Helles, *Queen Elizabeth* Sedd el Bahr and then switching her fire to Cape Helles, while *Irresistible* fired on Orkanie and *Gaulois* on Kum Kale, on the Asiatic shore. *Queen Elizabeth* knocked out the Cape Helles battery after eighteen rounds had been fired, and *Irresistible* eventually achieved a similar result at Orkanie; thus all four of the Turks' long-range guns were eliminated. This allowed the ships to approach, and their fire to be more effective. That evening and the following day the entrance was swept for mines – none were found – and on the afternoon of the twenty-sixth three ships entered the Strait and continued the bombardment, coming under fire themselves from the intermediate defences and field artillery batteries. Later, demolition parties with marine escorts were landed, and over the following four days, as the weather permitted, forty-eight still-serviceable guns in the outer forts were destroyed.

As February turned to March the weather deteriorated still further, and operations often had to be suspended. The trawlers deployed as sweepers got a foretaste of what was to come in trying to clear the mine barriers on the night of 1 March, when they were driven back by gunfire.

The weather eased on 4 March and though the next four days were fine, and the ships used every opportunity to continue their bombardment, very little progress was made in suppressing the intermediate defences (and there was no sign that any would be, any time soon, largely due to the absence of effective radio-equipped spotter aircraft, a situation which would not be rectified until the end of March). Meanwhile, attempts to sweep for mines continued, and were routinely abandoned, the civilian crews of the trawlers being extremely reluctant to work under fire. On 10 March[18] Carden's chief of staff, Cmdr Roger Keyes,[19] personally led the minesweeping flotilla. It was greeted by searchlights (which HMS *Canopus* vainly tried to extinguish) and artillery fire; two pairs of trawlers passed over the first barrier without lowering their 'kites' (as the simple board-like paravanes were known), and one of the remaining couple hit a mine herself and blew up. Keyes tried again the following night, dispensing with the battleship. The trawlers turned away and fled, and this time it was the commodore's turn to blow up, at least metaphorically. Disgusted at what he thought abject cowardice,[20] he called for naval volunteers to crew the trawlers. On the night of 13 March he led them out again, with the elderly light cruiser HMS *Amethyst* in attendance, and once again they were illuminated by batteries of searchlights and showered with shells; they stuck to the task until four of the boats had been put out of action and the cruiser damaged, and for the first time the operation met with a measure of success, many mines cut free from their moorings drifting down the Straits and being destroyed by small-arms fire.

By now there was agitation to land troops as an alternative (in Jackson's words) to 'advancing with a rush over unswept minefields and in waters commanded at short range by heavy guns, howitzers and torpedo-tubes', which, as Churchill pointed out, no one had ever suggested. Kitchener counselled caution. No land operations on a large scale should be attempted until the 29th Division could participate, he wrote, on 13 March (the first elements would leave British ports on 16 March, the remainder following over the next week[21]). Astoundingly, with significant (if largely obsolete) naval assets and five infantry divisions[22] now committed to the theatre, there was still no plan of action in existence beyond Carden's, and that was rapidly proving itself unworkable.

Its author was close to breaking point. Unable to eat or sleep and suffering from recurring stomach ulcers, anxiety at his failure to obtain significant results was rapidly sapping his will, and on 15 March he met with Rear-Adm. John de Roebeck,[23] his second-in-command, and Roger Keyes and told them he could not continue. The following morning a senior medical officer pronounced him unfit. Churchill learnt of this while visiting Sir John French's headquarters in France and touring the Flanders battlefield ('two days' holiday' he called it), and appointed his deputy de Roebeck to succeed him, even though he was junior in the Navy List to Rear-Adm. Rosslyn Wemyss[24] who commanded at Mudros (who volunteered to stand aside, recognising the logic of maintaining continuity in the fighting force).

De Roebeck stuck to Carden's plan, which was to send ten battleships into the Strait, holding six back in reserve.[25] First, the four most modern ships (*Queen Elizabeth, Agamemnon, Lord Nelson*[26] and *Inflexible*, in that order from the left) were to steam in line abreast and engage the forts at the Narrows at 14,000 yards (12,800m) while *Triumph* and *Prince George* on their flanks and some way astern engaged the intermediate defences. When the forts showed signs of weakening, the French squadron (*Gaulois* and *Charlemagne*,[27] *Bouvet*[28] and *Suffren*,[29] in that order from the left) was to pass through the first line and engage the forts at 8,000 yards (7,300m); they would later retire, to be replaced by *Vengeance, Irresistible, Albion* and *Ocean*, in that order from the left. When the forts had been reduced, the minesweepers would come up and clear a channel 900 yards (825m) wide through the first five belts of

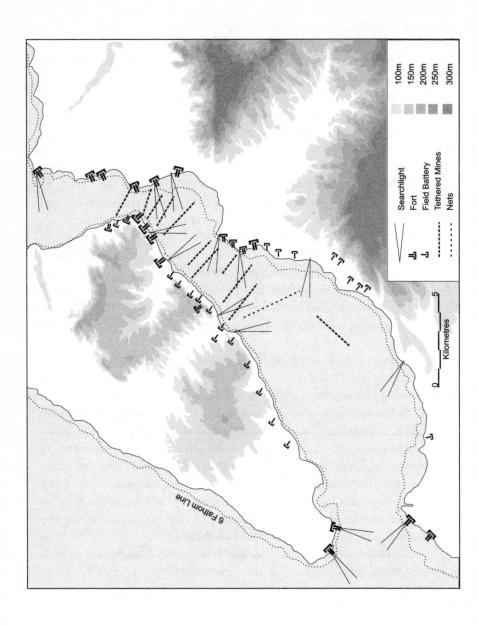

6 Fathom Line

Searchlight
Fort
Field Battery
Tethered Mines
Nets

100m
150m
200m
250m
300m

0   5

Kilometres

mines, the last of which ran north-west from Kephez Point. Under the protection of the two remaining reserved ships, *Cornwallis* and *Canopus*, the sweeping operation was to continue through the night, and the next morning the fleet would advance into the Narrows and demolish the forts at close range. The remaining five lines of mines would then be swept, and the fleet would advance up the Strait and enter the Sea of Marmara.

The ships in the first line entered the Strait at about 1030 on the morning of 18 March, when the haze had cleared sufficiently to reveal their targets. They steamed steadily up the channel, coming under fire from the massed howitzers and guns on both banks, reaching their station at around 1130. They then steamed back and forth along fixed lines. *Queen Elizabeth* engaged two forts adjacent to Chanak Kale, on the Asian side, while the others engaged three forts near Kilid Bahr, on the European side. Their guns replied, failed to reach the ships, and fell silent; other guns continued to fire, hitting the ships but doing no significant damage. At 1150 the magazine at the more northerly of the forts at Chanak exploded. Ten minutes later de Roebeck, aboard *Queen Elizabeth*, called up the French squadron, and Rear-Adm. Guépratte led his ships forward to a line about 3,500 yards ahead of the British line. Within minutes, all eight were firing every gun they had, the lighter pieces engaging individual targets of opportunity and the main batteries continuing to target the Narrows forts, while all serviceable Turkish guns replied. The duel continued for over an hour, first Fort No. 13, south of Kilid Bahr, and then No. 8, south of Kephez, falling silent. By 1330 the rate of fire from the defences had dropped markedly, and by 1445 it had almost ceased. De Roebeck now ordered the minesweepers forward, and asked Adm. Guépratte to retire, intending to bring up the reserve squadron in place of his vessels. Each ship turned ninety degrees to starboard and moved off towards the Asian shore, and made a second ninety-degree turn to starboard as she crossed the six-fathom line. At 1354, just as she came abreast of HMS *Inflexible*, *Bouvet*, the second ship in line, suffered a massive explosion below the starboard 10.8in gun turret; it was assumed she had been hit by a large-calibre shell. The explosion set off another in a magazine, and within two minutes, still travelling at a fair speed, she had capsized and sunk, with the loss of all but sixty-six men of her crew of over seven hundred.

In fact the *Bouvet* had hit a mine, one of a string of more than twenty laid (at right-angles to the other lines) on the night of 8 March across the mouth of the shallow Eren Keui Bay by the Turkish steamer *Nousret* after Allied ships had been observed passing through that location on 6 and 7 March during bombardment operations. By chance, three of those mines had been swept on the night of 16 March, but were assumed to have drifted down from the Narrows.

Queen Elizabeth and *Lord Nelson* were still firing on forts in the Narrows, while the four ships from the reserve squadron passed through the line to close with them and engage. When they did, firing from the forts and field positions resumed, and the Turks kept it up for another hour, their guns falling silent again at around 1600. At 1611 HMS *Inflexible*[30] reported that she had struck a mine. She was ordered to leave the line of battle and retire and did; like *Gaulois*[31] – hit by artillery below the waterline earlier in the afternoon by gunfire, and shipping large quantities of water – she made for the island of Tenedos (Bozcaada), and reached safety, anchoring in shallow water. Just minutes later *Irresistible* was seen to be listing. It was some time before it was confirmed that she, too, had suffered an underwater explosion, and at that point, convinced that the Turks had released free mines which had floated down with the current to his position, de Roebeck decided to break off the action and give orders for a general retirement, and for *Ocean* to assist *Irresistible*. Keyes, who went in to supervise the operation aboard a destroyer, ordered *Ocean's* captain to take the crippled ship in tow; he refused, saying there was insufficient depth of water. Minutes later *Ocean*, too, struck a mine, and almost immediately her steering gear was hit by gunfire and put out of action. Her crewmen were taken off by destroyer; both ships sank during the night.

In London, Churchill reported the losses to the War Council the following morning,[32] adding that five additional ships[33] had received orders for the Dardanelles and de Roebeck had been instructed to renew the attack if he thought fit. He did, reporting to Churchill on 20 March that he was fitting out eight Beagle-class destroyers as minesweepers, and six of the older River class and four torpedo-boats as minehunters (to search for drifting mines); in all, he said, he would soon have fifty minesweepers available, all of them manned by naval volunteers, and planned to recommence operations within three to four days. His optimism was not shared by Sir Ian Hamilton, who had told Kitchener in a cable sent late on 19 March that, having seen for himself the latter part of the action on the previous day, he no longer believed the Strait could be forced by a naval operation, but that it would require a deliberate advance by his whole force, to open the passage to the fleet.

On 22 March de Roebeck and Wemyss met with Birdwood and Hamilton aboard *Queen Elizabeth*; Hamilton repeated the opinion he had given Kitchener and it is clear that his disquiet affected de Roebeck and converted him to the same view. A full-scale amphibious operation would be required to secure passage through the Strait, he reported to Churchill in a cable that night, adding that that would not be possible before 14 April. The First Lord was aghast at the thought of the Turks having three weeks in which to further strengthen their defences, and for their German and Austro-Hungarian allies to send submarines to the region, and incredulous that the naval plan 'on which hitherto all our reasoning and conclusions had been based' was now to be abandoned. Losses in naval personnel had been small, and only one ship of importance (*Inflexible*, which would be out of action for only six weeks; the others, we should recall, were scheduled for scrapping anyway) had been damaged; so 'why turn and change at this fateful hour and impose upon the Army an ordeal of incalculable severity?' He put before the Admiralty War Group a cable he proposed to send to de Roebeck, ordering him to continue the naval operation, and was met with solid resistance from Fisher, Wilson and Jackson – the First Sea Lord, delighted that his own preferred course of action was at last to prevail, flatly refusing to go against 'the man on the spot'. Churchill took the matter to Asquith and Balfour, who agreed with him in principle but refused to overrule the professionals, and he was reduced to sending a long, cajoling cable to de Roebeck, telling him the forts, desperately short of ammunition,[34] were vulnerable now more than ever, and restating the case for continuing the naval operation, to no avail whatsoever. De Roebeck, very grateful for the opportunity to bow out and pass the responsibility to the army, would not budge.

There were to be several critical points in the Dardanelles/Gallipoli campaign; this was surely the most significant of them, and with hindsight it is clear that the Royal Navy should have been compelled to continue with the attempt to force the Strait, no matter what the fall-out from its senior commanders. Churchill, analysing this aspect of the affair later, claimed it characterised a rift (he called it 'two schools of thought') within the highest echelons of the Royal Navy at that time. Was its function 'to carry the army to where they wanted to go, to keep open the sea communications, and to be ready in overwhelming strength to fight the enemy's main Fleet should it ever accord them an opportunity', or was it 'a gigantic instrument of offensive war, capable of intervening with decisive effect in general strategy, and that it must bear its share of the risks and sufferings of the struggle'? There was no doubt where his own views lay. 'Such [latter] is the true spirit of the Navy, which only gradually liberated itself from the shortsighted prudent housewifery of the peace-time mind,' he wrote.

Be that as it may have been, the navy's senior commanders' abject, pusillanimous abdication of responsibility in mid-March marked the turning point in the Dardanelles operation. What had been conceived as a maritime affair would now become terrestrial, whether the army liked it or not. (There was a third way, of course; it would still have been perfectly possible to stop the whole thing in its tracks, and send the ships and men away, but the loss of face that would entail was just too great to contemplate.) That the British and French were sublimely ignorant of the dangers they faced in invading Gallipoli – even the *numbers* they faced – was entirely irrelevant; there was an imperative to go ahead now, and no other course of action would do.

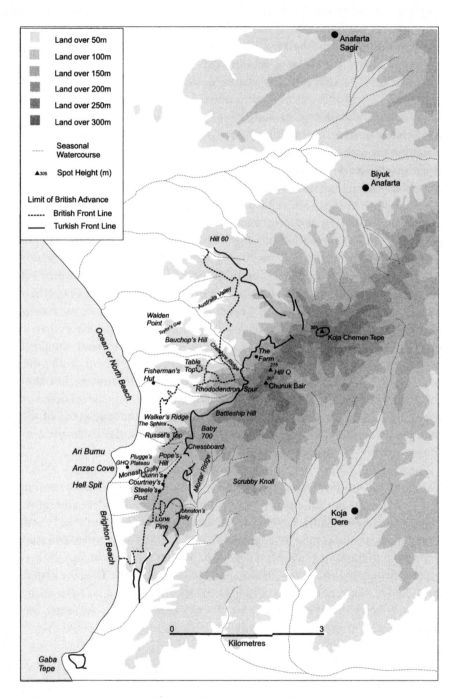

Anafarta
Sagir

Biyuk
Anafarta

Hill 60

Australia Valley

Walden
Point
Taylor's Gap

Bauchop's Hill

Chailak Ridge

305
Koja Chemen Tepe

Table
Top

The
Farm

275
▲ Hill Q
261

Fisherman's
Hut

Rhododendron Spur

Chunuk Bair

Ocean or North Beach

Walker's Ridge
The Sphinx

Russel's Top

Battleship Hill

Baby
700

Chessboard

Ari Burnu

Plugge's
GHQ Plateau

Pope's

Hill

Anzac Cove

Monash Gully

Quinn's

Hell Spit

Courtney's

Steele's
Post

Morter Ridge

Scrubby Knoll

Koja
Dere

Johnston's
Jolly

Lone
Pine

Brighton Beach

0   3

Kilometres

Gaba
Tepe

17. Gallipoli – The Anzac Cove Positions

Landings and Stalemates

Enver Pasha's response to the bombardment of Cape Helles and Kum Kale was to tinker with the structure of the defensive forces around Constantinople, much to the disgust of Otto Liman von Sanders, who urged him to address the threat of Allied troops landing on the peninsula directly. It was not until 24 March that he ordered the Fifth Army activated for the defence of Gallipoli, and asked Sanders to relinquish command of the First in order to take it over. Had the British been able to land prior to that date, they would have been opposed by only two divisions, with a smaller force on the Asian side of the Straits.

The Turkish Fifth Army was to comprise III Corps (Esad Pasha), with the 7th, 9th and 19th Infantry Divisions; the newly formed XV Corps (Weber), with the 3rd and 11th Infantry Divisions taken from I Corps and IV Corps, plus the 5th Infantry Division (von Soderstern) from II Corps and a cavalry brigade, which remained as independent commands. III Corps, with its headquarters close to Sanders' Army HQ at Gallipoli, had responsibility for the peninsula, with the 7th Division (Remsi Bey) holding the isthmus and the Bulair Lines, and the 9th (Khalil Sami Bey) holding the sector from just south of Suvla Bay to Cape Helles, with two battalions of Jandarma spread thinly between them, and with the 19th (Mustafa Kemal Bey) in reserve at Boghali (Bigali), north of Maidos/Aji Abad (Eceabat). XV Corps at Kum Kale had responsibility for the Asian side, with the 3rd Division (Nicolai) at Kum Kale and the 11th (Refet Bey) at Besika Bay, opposite Tenedos.[1]

A short detour from the historic narrative is necessary in order to describe the physical aspects of the Gallipoli Peninsula (Gelibolu Yarimadasi). It juts south from Thrace near its eastern limit, running north-east to south-west; less than five kilometres wide at its narrowest point, near its base, and just over twenty kilometres wide at its broadest, it is some eighty-three kilometres long from the head of the Gulf of Saros (Saros Körfezi) to Cape Helles (Ilias Burnu). It is a hilly region, though nowhere does it exceed 375m in height; large areas are uncultivated, often covered in pines or densely packed chest-high scrub. A noteworthy exception is the area known as the Anafarta Plain, around the seasonal salt pan/lake inland from Suvla Bay, but there are (and were) other extensive areas of cultivated land including olive groves and orchards in the valleys formed by seasonal rivers, notably the Maidos Valley which spans the peninsula three-quarters the way down its length. The peninsula receives only sixty to seventy centimetres of rain a year, almost none of it in the summer months, much of it coming in short, sharp storms which frequently cause flash flooding and have carved out abundant deep, steep-sided gullies. At other times there is little surface water to be found, though the porous rock forms aquifers.

The only maps available to the British were derived from a French survey carried out at the time of the Crimean War. That was translated into a one-inch to the mile (1:63360) map in 1908, and formed the basis for an enlargement to 1:40000, in three sheets, hastily made in Egypt in 1915.

No army in the modern era had ever attempted an opposed amphibious landing on anything like the scale of that required at Gallipoli; there were no textbooks on the subject, and little or no doctrine, though the problem had formed a (very minor) part of the curriculum at the Staff Colleges at Camberley and Quetta. Thus, in essence Hamilton and his staff made up the rules as they went along, guided largely by instinct.

The planning process proper began only when they arrived in the theatre on 17 March. Superficially, once the beaches had been cleared, it was not too complex a task, given that the objective of the expedition – to take and hold Kilid Bahr, and thus control the Narrows – was straightforward, but it was apparent from the beginning that the devil would most certainly be in the detail.

A landing on the Asian shore had already been ruled out. Besika Bay or Yukyeri Bay, further south, perhaps looked attractive at very first sight but soon became markedly less so, for by even the most direct route Chanak Kale was well over fifty kilometres away.

The Gulf of Saros was soon dismissed as impractical, both for its distance from the objective and its proximity to Bulgaria, still an unknown quantity. The beaches west of Bulair had a certain superficial attraction, but only because the isthmus was at its narrowest there, and possession of it seemed to offer the promise of cutting the Turks on the peninsula off from supplies and reinforcement.[2] However, an invading force would find itself under attack from both sides, and still facing a forty-kilometre unsupported advance before it even approached the forts defending the Narrows. The next candidate was Suvla Bay, and the flat area immediately to the south of it, but the seasonal salt lake behind the bay was full of water at this time of year, and impassable, and the adjoining area to the south faced the difficult rampart terrain of the Sari Bair Ridge (more correctly, Koja Chemen Tepe (Kocaçimentepe)). Further south, towards Gaba Tepe, the terrain offered possibilities, even though the routes towards the Maidos Valley looked poor. South of Gaba Tepe the beaches and immediate hinterland were perfect for the task and could be presumed to be particularly heavily defended. That left just three small beaches close to the tip of the peninsula, one facing west, north of Cape Tekke (Tekke Burnu), and two facing south, one between Cape Tekke and Cape Helles, the other between Cape Helles and Sedd el Bahr.

Though none of the three was extensive, they were close enough together to form a beachhead surrounded on three sides by the sea.

In the event it was decided to split the force, and utilise the beaches near Cape Helles and the area immediately north of Gaba Tepe. The British 29th Division would land at Cape Helles, with the French Corps Expéditionnaire d'Orient (CEO)[3] to remain offshore in reserve, to be landed there as required, while ANZAC's two divisions[4] would disembark north of Gaba Tepe. The decision to land at two locations twenty-three kilometres apart came about as a means of maximising the number of men who could be put ashore in a given period; it was felt that since communications between the two locations would be by sea, the distance presented no problem.

The initial planning process was completed by 23 March. On the twenty-seventh the last elements of the Royal Naval Division[5] arrived at Port Said, and a day later the first of the ships carrying the 29th Division[6] and the CEO began arriving at Alexandria. It had been found necessary to direct the expeditionary force to a large, friendly port with all the usual facilities in order that the troops, their stores, matériel and animals could be unloaded, sorted and re-embarked 'tactically', so that they would be available according to need. The operation was a massive one, involving a total of eighty-six ships[7] to handle just over 75,000 men, almost 16,500 animals and 3,100 vehicles.[8] The first ships to leave Alexandria – carrying the leading elements of ANZAC[9] – did so on 4 April, and over the following nineteen days the rest of the force followed.[10]

There still remained an enormous amount of work to be done before the operation could commence. Some related to improvising gear and adapting the ships to land men and animals on beaches under fire. That and subsequent engineering works – even basic undertakings such as the construction of piers and jetties – were made no easier by a lack of specialist personnel and basic raw materials. There was a programme of specific training to be organised and carried out, too, focusing on the procedures to be followed in getting from ship to shore. It had been decided that the troops would land from ships' boats,[11] three or four of which, carrying around a hundred and twenty men, would form a 'tow' behind a steam launch. The boats would be cast off when the launch grounded, and would finish their journey under oars; as soon as the men had disembarked, the boats would be towed back out to the waiting transports, and more men would be embarked. Each transport would have four exit points on each side, and the men would be required to descend 'Jacob's ladders' (rope ladders with wooden plank rungs) to reach the boats. Wearing nailed boots and with a 40-kg load this would be no easy undertaking.

There was concern that the number of men it would be possible to land simultaneously on V, W and X Beaches, as the three at Cape Helles were designated, would be insufficient to allow them to carry out their objectives.

The beaches could handle a total of only eighteen tows at any one time, six at V Beach, eight at W Beach (the longest, at 350 metres) and four at X Beach: a maximum of 2,200 men, who would not be reinforced for anything up to an hour. A way to increase the number dramatically was suggested by Cdr. Edward Unwin, the captain of HMS *Hussar*, the minesweepers' depot ship, inspired, he said, by the Trojan Horse.[12] Unwin suggested modifying a collier, the *River Clyde*, to act as a landing ship, by cutting large sally ports into her hull on both sides and rigging wide longitudinal gang planks running towards the bows. She would be accompanied by a steam-powered hopper-barge and three lighters which, as soon as she took the ground (she would be lightened forwards and ballasted aft, to draw only seven feet (2m) at the bow, and the beach was believed to be steep-to), would be run ahead of her to form a bridge to the beach. By that means the first wave could be almost doubled, to at least 4,200 men, and she would be able to give valuable support from machine guns in sandbagged emplacements sited on the fo'c'sle. In addition the ship would later fulfil a number of very valuable extra functions: as a reservoir of drinking water, an ammunition warehouse, a dressing and casualty clearing station and a combined pier and breakwater.[13] As a reward for his inspiration, Unwin, promoted temporarily to the rank of captain, was given command of her.

The adoption of Unwin's scheme brought into focus the vulnerability of V Beach to artillery fire from Kum Kale, and it was decided to land a regiment of French troops there to storm the batteries; these troops were to be withdrawn in due course.

A third modification was to add a fourth landing, Y Beach, three kilometres up the coast from X Beach, at a point adjacent to the village of Krithia. The force to be landed there was to threaten the Turks' line of communication to and from Cape Helles; it was to be held back near the beachhead, and deployed only as necessary.

In addition, any threat from Kum Kale having been eliminated by the French landings there, an earlier decision not to land men within the Straits was now reversed, and a site near Eski Hissarlik Point, on the far side of Morto Bay from Sedd el Bahr, was designated as S Beach.[14] The battalion to land there was later stripped of one of its companies – there were not enough boats available to land all four – which would go ashore at Y Beach instead.

In all, these modifications to the plan would allow the British to put approximately seven thousand men ashore around Cape Helles within about forty minutes, with a further twelve hundred to join them within the next hour. The 29th Division would then advance and capture the Achi Baba (Alçitepe) Ridge.

At Gaba Tepe – Z Beach – the first wave ashore would consist of fifteen hundred men from the 1st Australian Infantry Division, to be followed in two more waves by two thousand five hundred more; they would capture the southern spurs of the Sari Bair, overlooking the beach, and cover the landing of the rest of ANZAC, which would drive eastwards towards Koja Dere (Kocadere) and Boghali in order to support the southern landings by barring the way to the Kilid Bahr Plateau to reinforcements, and also cut the Turks' line of retreat as they were driven back.

The date for the invasion was initially fixed for 23 April, but thanks to bad weather it was subsequently put back to Sunday, 25 April. By chance the day's events were to unroll chronologically from north to south, and it will be convenient to examine them in that order.

During the evening of the twenty-fourth the Royal Naval Division (less the Plymouth Battalion, Royal Marines Light Infantry, which would land at Y Beach, and half the Anson Battalion, assigned to support duties on V Beach), left Trebuki Bay. They arrived off the Gulf of Saros soon after daybreak and began their diversionary demonstration, *Canopus* bombarding the Bulair Lines. Towards dusk ships' boats were swung out and lowered, and men scrambled to fill them. Trawlers each took eight in tow, and began to head for the northern shore. They were decoys; as soon as it was dark they reversed their course, the men re-embarked, and the darkened ships sailed away. The deception played to Liman von Sanders' prejudice, and caused him to keep much of the 5th Division in the area for two days.

The covering force for Z Beach consisted of four thousand men of the 3rd Australian Infantry Brigade. They were to land in darkness on the northern half of the three-kilometre-long beach north of Gaba Tepe and advance on a broad front, the left flank to be anchored on the slopes of Chunuk Bair.

In the very early hours of 25 April, in ideal conditions, the ships carrying the covering force left Mudros. About seven kilometres off Gaba Tepe the three battleships with the first wave aboard hove to, and the men transferred to the boats, twelve tows of three each, a process which took about forty minutes. As the moon set behind Imbros they crept towards the beach, the seven destroyers carrying the second wave, and the transports carrying the third, falling in behind. Three kilometres offshore the ships hove to again, and the steamboats hauling each tow set off in line abreast. Things began to go wrong even as the first tows neared the beach, the launch on the starboard station, which was to set the course for the whole flotilla, missing its mark and heading much too far north, the other boats conforming to its movement. The operation was under the overall command of Cdr. Charles Dix, who had the port station. Seeing the boats' heading change, and realising its consequences, he took drastic action, slowing until the tows to starboard of him had passed, and then speeding up to take the starboard station himself, shouting to the tugs to take their direction from him, in the hope of shepherding his little flock back to their true course.

He had too little time and space in which to work. As the boats slipped their tows to be rowed the last fifty yards to the beach there was a great

deal of confusion, compounded by the fact that the Turkish coast-watchers –
a sizeable position on the knoll above the headland of Ari Burnu, and
outposts on the ridge behind, north and south – had now become aware
of their presence, and had begun firing. Some boats actually beached north
of Ari Burnu, but most came ashore at the point or just to the south of
it, at the northern end of the small curve of beach which became known
as Anzac Cove.[15] Here, instead of the shallow sandy bank backed up by
two hundred metres of flat ground they had been told to expect, they were
met by an almost vertical earth wall up to four metres high, giving on to
a steep slope riven by gullies and covered in scrub and brush, the western
buttress of the Sari Bair Ridge. There was much confusion, the cohesion
of units breaking down, men losing touch with comrades, NCOs and
officers alike as they spilled out of the boats and scrambled to get off the
beach.[16] The second wave, coming in behind, landed on top of the first –
though some tows came in south of Hell Spit, the southern extremity of
Anzac Cove, as intended and had an easier time of it – and only added to
the chaos.

By 0600 local opposition had virtually ceased, save for some sniping from
Second Ridge, though the area was still receiving machine gun and artillery
fire from Gaba Tepe. However, the situation would soon change, for troops
from the 19th Division, held in reserve only seven kilometres away at Boghali,
had begun pouring into the area, led by Mustafa Kemal Bey in person. As
the Australians attempted to move east, off the beach and into the hills, they
met stronger and stronger opposition as they themselves grew steadily weaker
thanks to the sheer effort it took to make any progress in this most unhos-
pitable terrain. Eventually they were stalled and thrown back, notably on the
slopes of Baby 700,[17] where Kemal's 57th Regiment counterattacked most
effectively, but also to the south, along the length of Second Ridge. As darkness
fell they were nowhere more than about a thousand metres from the beach,
their line running the length of the spine of Second Ridge, along Maclaurin's
and Pope's Hills and down Walker's Ridge to the sea, well to the south of
Fisherman's Hut. They held less than two square kilometres (into which
around 20,000 men would soon be packed, the main force having continued
to come ashore throughout the day) and had taken around two thousand
casualties.

At around 2200 Birdwood went ashore to confer with Maj.-Gens. Bridges
and Godley, who 'urged him to contemplate an immediate evacuation' of
the entire beachhead. Birdwood, who had believed the operation to be going
comparatively well, was astounded and refused to even contemplate such a
thing, but was eventually convinced that there was a very real risk of the
position being unable to withstand a counterattack. He reported that to
Hamilton, who arrived offshore aboard HMS *Queen Elizabeth* at around
midnight. From the advice he got from his senior naval commanders Hamilton judged evacuation to be impossible. 'Your news is indeed serious,' he

wrote to Birdwood. 'But there is nothing for it but to dig yourselves right in and stick it out.'

Dig they did, and at daybreak, when the Turkish guns resumed, the men found that the deeper trenches they had been able to fashion gave them much better protection from the shrapnel which had caused so many casualties the previous day. The widespread confusion in the ANZAC ranks still proved impossible to resolve, and units and individuals were still intermixed and intermingled; however, this was less of a problem in static defence than it might have been had the troops been asked to go onto the offensive.[18] In consequence, 26 April passed relatively quietly, the invaders having realised that they could make no progress until they were reinforced, and the defenders content to use the time to strengthen their own positions.

Esad Pasha had been able to convince Sanders that most available reserves should be sent to the southern front, but Kemal had managed to appropriate two extra regiments and some mountain batteries for the northern. They arrived on the evening of the twenty-sixth, and Kemal immediately pushed them up alongside the 72nd Regiment, an Arab unit of his own 19th Division, which had not yet been engaged. This gave him a total of sixteen battalions to face an ANZAC force which counted twenty, but he had a numerical advantage in artillery (if we discount the naval guns, which were sometimes tellingly useful and at others were simply wasting valuable ammunition) and, more particularly, in terms of territory, for not only did he hold the high ground, but he also had space in which to manoeuvre, something the Anzacs never had. However, the Turks, too, found it difficult to advance over such rough terrain, and only once, on the left, early in the afternoon, did Birdwood have cause for concern, when large numbers of Turkish troops were seen descending the slopes of Battleship Hill; presented with targets such as this, the Royal Navy came into its own, and the advance was stopped with heavy gunfire. The following day reinforcements in the shape of the Chatham, Deal and Portsmouth Battalions of the RMLI and the RND's Nelson Battalion landed.

The contrast between the events at Anzac Cove and those at Y Beach, sixteen kilometres away to the south, could not have been more extreme. There, by 0545 the Plymouth Battalion, RMLI, the 1st King's Own Scottish Borderers and a company of the 2nd South Wales Borderers for whom there was no room in the boats which would land on S Beach were ashore, in precisely the right location and without a shot having been fired.

The beach had been chosen specifically for the presence of two gullies which cut through the fifty-metre-high cliffs behind and allowed the troops fairly easy access to the immediate hinterland. Scouts were sent to reconnoitre, and reported no problems, whereupon two companies from the KOSB were sent inland to Gully Ravine – an enormous feature, with banks fifteen metres high and riven by a confusing network of deep tributaries –

which paralleled the beach some three hundred metres inland.

The rest of the morning and much of the afternoon passed with no sign of the Turkish troop movements the force had been landed to interdict or of a planned advance of troops landed at X Beach (the signal for them to move northwards was never received). At around 1500, Lt.-Col. Matthews of the Royal Marines, who was in overall command of the operation,[19] ordered the men to dig in along the cliff-top; he chose a longer-than-necessary line so as to leave no areas of dead ground to his immediate front, and that resulted in the position being thinly held. That seems to have been the signal the Turks were waiting for. The attack, by what was estimated as a battalion, with artillery and machine gun support, was tentative to begin with, but gathered momentum as night fell, when the supporting fire from the ships offshore ceased, and continued right through the hours of darkness, the British soon discovering that the shallow trenches which were all they had been able to excavate in the time with the light tools available gave very little protection.

When the Turkish attack ceased, at daybreak, it was obvious that the situation was dire,[20] for the British had taken over 30 per cent casualties, including many officers, and were short of ammunition. It was clear from the number of bodies left behind when they withdrew that the Turks had suffered heavily, too, but at around 0630 they were seen massing for another attack. Matthews asked for supporting fire from the ships offshore, but it was slow in coming, and at around 0700 the Turks broke through the defensive line; however, they were driven off in hand-to-hand fighting, and it appeared as if the threat had been contained. Then Matthews, touring the position to gauge the situation for himself, discovered that his right-flank trenches were empty of men, the able-bodied having opted to help the wounded down to the beach. All he could do was organise such men as remained to form a rearguard on the cliff-top while the rest of the wounded were recovered and evacuated. When he got to the beach to see how it was proceeding, it was to find unwounded men climbing into the boats alongside the wounded for whom they were intended, and he 'decided to allow it to continue', in the rather laconic words of the British Official History. By midday Y beach was cleared of all British personnel (though not of their kit, most of which was abandoned). Hunter-Weston was not even aware that the evacuation had taken place. It would become clear in the following days that the opportunity lost there was purely golden; had it been properly exploited, and significant numbers of extra troops landed to form a real beachhead and then sent inland, the entire situation at Cape Helles would have been much changed.

The first wave of men to land on V, W and X Beaches around Cape Helles were drawn from the 86th, the 'Fusiliers' Brigade'. As at Z Beach they were divided into a covering force and a main force. The troops of the covering force would be carried to the beaches by HMSs *Implacable* and *Euryalus* and Fleet Sweeper No. 1 (a cross-channel steamer); three more Fleet Sweepers

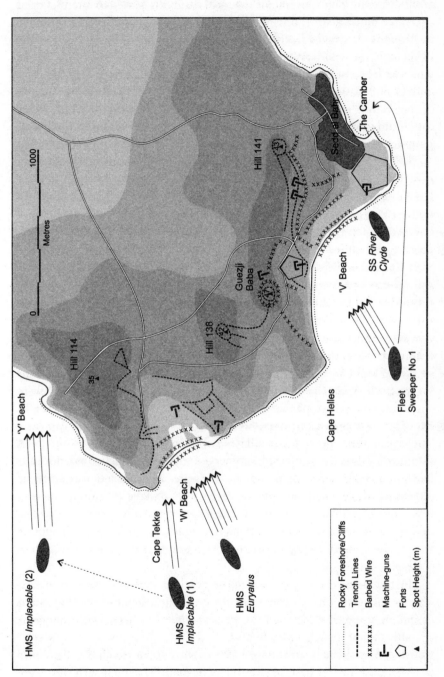

18. *Gallipoli – The Landings at Cape Helles*

'Y' Beach

HMS *Implacable* (2)

HMS *Implacable* (1)

Cape Tekke

'W' Beach

HMS *Euryalus*

Hill 114

35 ▲

Hill 138

Guezji Baba

Hill 141

Hill 138

Cape Helles

'V' Beach

Sedd el Bahr

The Camber

SS *River Clyde*

Fleet Sweeper No 1

1000

Metres

0

Rocky Foreshore/Cliffs

Trench Lines

xxxxxxx Barbed Wire

Machine-guns

Forts

▲ Spot Height (m)

were to stand further off with the second contingent. They were to be in position before daybreak; at 0530 the gun-ships offshore would commence a bombardment which would last for half an hour, and then the first wave would go in. As soon as the tows landed on V Beach, the *River Clyde* would be brought up, beached, and disgorge her troops, and about three-quarters of an hour later the second echelon would be landed, the whole of the covering force to be ashore by 0700. The remaining troops, from the 87th and the 88th Brigades, would begin disembarking at 0830, the two battalions of the former[21] on X Beach, the latter on V Beach, W Beach being reserved for landing two mountain batteries, a howitzer battery and a section of 18-pounders together with the animals necessary to haul them, plus other stores.

The barrage began on schedule, and at a few minutes before 0600 the two tows from *Implacable* which were destined for W Beach were cast off, and the battleship turned to round Cape Teppe and make for X Beach. She held on to within 500m of the shore and, still firing every gun which would bear, released the four tows carrying half the 1st Royal Fusiliers. The Fusiliers were able to land almost unopposed (they were confronted by just one twelve-man section) and scaled the cliffs without loss. By 0730, the entire battalion was ashore and the advance guard was moving inland; by 1100, after the Royals had repulsed a weak counterattack, and with the assistance of troops from W Beach, Hill 114 had been taken. It soon became clear that that position was actually far more valuable than it had been possible to infer from the map, and doubly unfortunate that orders for the troops holding it to advance on the redoubt further east (Hill 138) – which was in part the cause of the troops from W Beach being unable to assist those on V Beach – went astray.

As the leading companies of the Royal Fusiliers were going ashore at X Beach, the six tows from *Euryalus* closed on W Beach, with the two from *Implacable* some way to the rear. Here the situation would be very different, for the beach was well protected; submerged trip-wires attached to landmines had been installed a few metres out into the water, a deep belt of wire extended almost its whole length, and the obstacles were covered by entrenched positions on the flanks and inland on the slope of the hill above, and by two machine guns on the Turks' left flank. In the middle distance, a redoubt on Hill 138 dominated the high ground above the cliffs separating W Beach from V Beach.

The defenders entrenched above the beach waited until the steamboats slipped the tows, then opened up with every gun they had, causing many casualties amongst the men of the 1st Lancashire Fusiliers. Those who were still able to quit the grounded boats to find themselves in waist-deep water[22] were faced by virtually undamaged wire entanglement which stretched from the waterline to the base of the dunes beyond. The men were forced to negotiate it as best they could, tearing it aside and uprooting the stakes which held it while the Turks poured rifle and machine gun fire onto them.

Aboard the tows approaching the beach from *Implacable* was the 86th

Brigade's commander, Brig.-Gen. Hare, who had insisted on going ashore with the first wave. He judged that the water was calm enough to allow a landing on the flat rocks to the north of the beach, and directed the two tows to do just that. As a result D Company of the Lancashires landed virtually unopposed and unscathed, and were able to occupy empty positions on top of the cliff beyond, which looked down on Turkish positions in the dunes from the rear; taken by surprise, their occupants soon abandoned them, easing the situation for the men struggling with the wire on the beach. Hare then took a party of signallers and attempted to link up with the Royal Fusiliers on X Beach, but came under fire from Hill 114, was severely wounded[23] and took no further part in the proceedings. Down on W Beach, a storming party was able eventually to clear the defensive positions on the right flank; by 0715, the situation had improved to the point where the beach itself was now relatively safe and secure, and the second wave of tows, carrying the remainder of the brigade headquarters and support and medical echelons, landed with few casualties.

With just one battalion of fighting troops available, pushing inland to take the primary targets was always going to be problematic; with something like 50 per cent casualties it would be very difficult indeed, especially since the force would have to be split between several objectives. On the right, A Company, now only fifty strong, was to advance along the beach towards the lighthouse, scale the cliffs as and where it could, and then move inland to attack the redoubt on Hill 138, while B Company, to its left, took a more direct route to the same objective; only with that obstacle removed would it be possible for the W Beach force to attempt to link up with that of V Beach. On the left, C and D Companies were to attack Hill 114 in conjunction with Royal Fusiliers from X Beach. The attack on Hill 114 was successful by 1130, and that saw the forces on W and X Beaches joined, but that on the right ran into serious trouble due to a basic misunderstanding: there was indeed a redoubt on the summit of Hill 138, but about three hundred metres to the south-west, on a slightly higher knoll known as Guezji Baba, just inland from the Ertoğrul fort (Fort No. 1), lay another, bigger strongpoint. It was not marked on the British maps, and A Company mistook it for Hill 138; thus, instead of both attacking the same objective from two sides, A and B Companies were in fact divided between the two and were unable to make much progress against either.

If W Beach was a hard nut to crack, V Beach was to prove much, much worse. It was overlooked from both flanks by forts – reduced by naval gunfire but still excellent defensive positions – and the space between them, which Aspinall-Oglander describes as 'a natural amphitheatre which rises by gentle slopes to a height of a hundred feet [30m]', was covered from end to end by two deep barbed-wire entanglements, the first some twenty metres back from the beach, the second fifty metres beyond it. Behind that lay deep trenches and machine gun posts sited in commanding positions.

It had been planned for the six tows of Royal Dublin Fusiliers – five for the beach itself, and one destined for the Camber, just around the point under the old fort of Sedd el Bahr; much store was set by the effect this small force would have on the defenders' flank – to land shortly before 0600, with the *River Clyde* to beach herself and disgorge her forces just minutes later. Insufficient allowance had been made for the current sweeping down the Straits, and the collier found herself amongst the tows and having to take avoiding action, and then loiter while they got ahead of her again, and in the event it was 0622 before she grounded close by a spit of rocks running out into the water near the eastern end of the beach, under the walls of Sedd el Bahr Fort. Here, too, the Turks had remained silent until the men neared the beaches, and then unleashed a storm of rifle and machine gun fire, aimed first at the boats. Heavy pom-pom machine guns – there were two – tore many of the boats to pieces, killing every man in one and causing devastating casualties in the rest; more died as they tried to wade ashore, and just a fortunate few gained the shelter of a sandy bank which marked the limit of the beach.

Aboard the *River Clyde*, Unwin's plan was rapidly unravelling. It had been his intention to bridge the inevitable gap between ship and shore by means of the steam hopper which had been made fast on the port side, but when the hopper was cast loose, instead of forging ahead and filling the gap, her bows swung out to port, and there she remained, broadside-on to the beach and useless. Unwin promptly took matters into his own hands. On the collier's starboard side were three lighters; these were to have been used to make good any gap between beach and hopper. He ordered two of them lashed together thwart-to-thwart and then, together with his orderly, Able Seaman Williams, he jumped into the sea and swam ashore carrying a line attached to the foremost. The two men then hauled them into position, Unwin shouting for the soldiers to begin disembarking.[24]

Covered by fire from machine guns positioned on the collier's foredeck (which were under the command of Josiah Wedgwood, whom we previously encountered as a member of the Mesopotamia Commission; see Chapter 5), the men of the Royal Munster Fusiliers did as they were bade, and died in their droves, Wedgwood's machine guns being unable to locate those of the Turks on the hill above, while the defenders could scarcely miss the press of disembarking men. Soon the gangways and the lighters themselves were choked with the bodies of dead and dying men, and it was decided that no more men should try to land until night fell.

The final landing of the covering force was that of the three companies of South Wales Borderers on S Beach, at the far side of Mortos Bay from Sedd el Bahr; cast loose some distance away from their objective by HMS *Cornwallis*, thanks to the trawlers hauling their tows (of six lifeboats each) being able to make little headway against the current in the mouth of the Straits, it was 0730 before they were ashore. Two companies landed on the beach under fire from defensive positions halfway up the cliff, while the third went ashore at Eski Hissarlik Point, scrambling across the rocks. They outflanked the Turks, who numbered no more than a platoon, and by 0800 the beach was in British hands. The Borderers were to remain in place, sustained by picket boats which took off their wounded, until the arrival of the French on 27 April, but no further calls were made upon them.[25]

At around 0830, Hunter-Weston, convinced that the landings – even, thanks to a message suggesting that 'troops from the collier appear to be getting ashore well', sent at 0730 by an observer offshore, those at V Beach – were proceeding according to plan, ordered the main force sent in, making just one adjustment and sending the 1st Essex to W Beach instead of V. On X Beach the 1st Border Regiment landed without mishap, as, largely, did the Essex on W, but the first detachment to approach the charnel house which was V Beach – two platoons of the 4th Worcestershires and the remaining two companies of the 2nd Hampshires, together with Brig.-Gen. Napier and the 88th Brigade's staff – was confronted by a very different situation. Some of the men in the second wave made it to the beach, but few survived, Napier and his brigade-major being among those shot and killed in the attempt. With that, on Hamilton's 'advice', contained in a signal sent to Hunter-Weston at 1021, further attempts to get men ashore at V Beach were suspended. With the exception of a few of the men who had landed at the Camber and had managed to penetrated into Sedd el Bahr village before being killed, no British soldier got further than the sandy bank at the head of the beach that day.

Following that decision, the remainder of the men waiting to be set ashore on V Beach were diverted to W Beach, where the 1st Essex Regiment were by now all ashore. Two of its companies having been sent to assist with the operation against Hill 114, a third was despatched directly inland to help consolidate the position, while the fourth was sent to assist B Company of the Lancashires, which was still engaged against the redoubts on the right. The already considerable confusion which reigned on W Beach was compounded by the lack of a commanding figure to take control there, in place of Hare, and it was not until 1230, with the arrival of the divisional chief of staff, Col. Owen Wolley-Dod, that any degree of cohesion was restored.

He requested *Euryalus* and *Swiftsure* to bombard Hill 138, and after twenty minutes his men carried it; deprived of its support, the defenders in the second redoubt had little recourse but to abandon it too. The way to the left flank of V Beach now seemed open, but when a detachment of the Lancashires' A Company, together with some of the Worcesters, attempted to advance, they encountered another deep belt of wire dominated by snipers. It cost an hour, and many casualties, to negotiate, and when they did they found themselves exposed to the machine guns which had cut down the Irishmen and the Hampshires on V Beach, and were driven back.

A signal from Hunter-Weston encouraged Wolley-Dod to try again, but once again his troops were stopped by the sheer weight of gunfire from the positions above V Beach, and Lt.-Col. Cayley, the Worcesters' CO, fearing a counterattack under cover of darkness, decided the time had come to consolidate their position before night fell. His line extended from Hill 138 to a point on the cliffs east of the Cape Helles light; running westwards from Hill 138, the line ran back to Hill 114, and then north to X Beach, which had by now been further reinforced by the 1st Inniskilling Fusiliers. Thanks to an error of transcription, a signal sent from W Beach at 1830 reported that the Worcesters had captured Hill 141 (well to the east, above Sedd el Bahr village, see below); it was not until Cayley reported his dispositions at 2115 that Hunter-Weston was told differently, and by then he had made plans for the next morning based on that information, and had hurriedly to amend them.

During the night, wounded men were recovered from V Beach (under extremely difficult conditions; the situation only improved after a makeshift jetty had been constructed from the packs of dead men), and the remaining able-bodied men from the *River Clyde* took their place. In all, the operations that day had secured just a few square kilometres of territory.

Across the Strait, the French landing at Kum Kale was to be a limited affair, restricted to occupying a small neck of land from the cape north of the now ruined village (Kum Burnu) to the neighbouring settlement of Yeni Shehr, about three kilometres to the south, and inland as far as the Mendere River, which there runs parallel to the coast and about five hundred metres from it. It went poorly from the outset, the first boat-load of troops not being ashore until 1000 and the landings not being concluded until 1730, despite being virtually unopposed. That changed when the French began to advance southwards; they soon met with strong resistance, and were halted at a point midway between Kum Kale and Orkanie. With more Turkish troops arriving by the minute, and nightfall imminent, it was decided to dig in, with the intention of resuming the action at first light.

The Turks made four determined attacks through the night; some ended in hand-to-hand fighting, but all were driven off, with significant numbers of casualties. Early the following morning a curious incident took place. A sizeable group of Turks showed they wished to surrender and, weaponless, were taken into the French lines; they were immediately followed by several hundred more who were still armed, and who occupied several houses in Kum Kale. It was mid-afternoon before they were driven out; around sixty were taken prisoner, and some, including the officer leading them, were shot out of hand.

At 0740 on 26 April, Hamilton signalled to d'Amade asking him to bring up the rest of his men – who were at Tenedos by now – and land them on X Beach as soon as possible (Hunter-Weston soon persuaded him to change his mind, and have the French contingent land on W Beach instead).[26]

D'Amade had at least half-hoped that he would be able to convince Hamilton to allow him to reinforce his by now hard-pressed troops at Kum Kale, but on receiving this instruction and realising that possibility was now firmly ruled out, he suggested to Hamilton, when he met him aboard the *Queen Elizabeth* at 1130, that they should be pulled out instead. Hamilton agreed, and d'Amade left to give the necessary orders. The withdrawal was completed before daybreak on 27 April. French casualties during the operation were heavy, at around 780, but the Turks later admitted to having suffered more than twice that, including the men who had deserted.

At the 29th Division's headquarters aboard *Euryalus* the news that the Worcesters had not, in fact, taken Hill 141, and that an immediate advance on Achi Baba was now out of the question, forced Hunter-Weston into a rethink. By this time the troops on V Beach were divided into two main groups. Those, largely on the left, who had now been in place, surrounded by dead and wounded comrades, for twenty-four hours, were both physically and mentally exhausted, and their NCOs and officers were no better; ordered to fight their way off the beach and through the Turkish positions near Fort No. 1, and link up with the men advancing from W Beach, they were incapable of making the required effort. On the right, under the walls of the old fort of Sedd el Bahr, the majority were the much fresher men who had landed from the *River Clyde* during the night; of these men, the main party was to storm the fort and clear it, then move on to the village by way of a postern gate giving onto a steep path which also led down to the Camber, while one company would bypass the fort, passing through a gap cut overnight in the wire above the beach, and make straight for Hill 141. After the village was cleared the main party too was to push on towards Hill 141 and attack from the east while the men from W Beach attacked from the west.

The fort was cleared fairly easily, despite the presence of a Turkish machine gun in the tower overlooking the beach, but on reaching the gate – through which they could pass only one at a time – the troops came under accurate fire from a trench below the village walls and were held up for some time. Clearing the village itself was no easy matter either, the Turks fighting for every house, and it was 1300 before it was done, and they could move on to Hill 141. Their numbers were already beginning to tell, and at 1430, even though promised reinforcements from W Beach had failed to materialise, the hill was taken, and the remaining defenders from there and from the positions around Fort No. 1 withdrew northwards, many of them falling victim to British machine guns in the process.

Tired and depleted, there was no question of the attackers pursuing the retreating Turks into who knew what sort of defended positions. The six hundred or so fresh men of the South Wales Borderers on S Beach would have been invaluable here, but the major in command on the spot – all the officers senior to him having been killed – knew nothing of their presence, and made no attempt to link up with them; they were left twiddling their thumbs for a further twenty-four hours in consequence. Instead the Hampshires and the 'Dubsters', as the combined battalion formed from the survivors of the Dublin and Munster Fusiliers was known, were set to digging defensive positions against a Turkish counterattack which was expected any moment, spurred on, if that is anything like the right term, by Hunter-Weston's instruction that there must be no withdrawal. 'Every man will die at his post rather than retire,' he ordered, signalling the end of offensive operations until reinforcements, in the shape of the French, arrived. In doing so – largely due to circumstances outside his control, but which he should certainly have anticipated – he would give the Turks thirty-six extra hours in which to prepare themselves.

Hunter-Weston had hoped that the French would be ashore before noon on 27 April, and timed his advance on Achi Baba to begin then. However, the (universal) shortage of steamboats delayed their landing, and he was forced to postpone his operation until the next day. In the meantime he reshuffled his command structure; having decided to remain aboard *Euryalus* for the time being, he placed Marshall in temporary command of the division, and promoted three battalion commanders to replace the dead brigadiers. He reorganised his line, too, pulling the depleted 86th Brigade back into reserve and replacing them with the French 175th Regiment, which he ordered to advance on the right as far as S Beach, and ordering the 87th Brigade to push forward on the left, to the mouth of Gully Ravine. In fact, the left-flanking company of the Border Regiment elected to remain where it was, in an entrenched position with a good field of fire on the northern limit of the beachhead at X Beach, around five hundred metres short of the mouth of Gully Ravine, and the other units of the 87th to the right simply swung into line with it. To compensate, in the centre the 88th Brigade's line zigzagged sharply at roughly its midpoint, between the streams called Kirte Dere and Kanli Dere, a four-hundred-metre sector facing north-west, at right-angles to its neighbours. The manoeuvres were completed before nightfall. This, we should recall, was the fourth night most of the men had gone without sleep, and their physical condition was a major source of anxiety,[27] as was the shortage of artillery.

Taking those factors into account, Hunter-Weston decided to restrict his planned advance on Achi Baba, and put just the first stage of his plan – a manoeuvre designed to establish an offensive line to the west of the objective – into effect on 28 April. That would require a right-wheeling advance anchored on Hill 236 on the French right, the left to push forward as far as Hill 472 (Yazy Tepe), about two kilometres north of Krithia, the northern flank halting to form an east–west line running from the hill to Sari Tepe, on the west coast. In the process the line was to extend from a length of roughly three kilometres to roughly eight. Even across forgiving terrain it would have been a complicated procedure for exhausted men to execute; across the tip of the

Gallipoli Peninsula it would be devilishly difficult. Even against five depleted battalions of equally weary Turks it would have been arduous; against nine, four of them fresh, occupying thoughtfully placed and mutually supporting defensive positions which exploited all the natural features of the terrain, there was a distinct danger that it would be little short of murderous.

The engagement which would become known as the First Battle of Krithia opened at 0800 on 28 April with a patchy artillery bombardment, ships offshore joining in with the two batteries of 18-pounders and the four howitzers – before, as the British Official History records glumly, 'the weary troops of the 29th Division climbed out of their trenches and plodded forward in the general direction of Krithia.' Very soon the effect of the zigzag became apparent, and the British line lost cohesion. To make matters worse the Border Regiment, to the west of Gully Ravine, and the Inniskilling Fusiliers to the east were unable to maintain the required pace in the face of stout Turkish defending. Before long companies were fighting independently without any clear idea of their objectives.

Hunter-Weston finally came ashore during the morning, and set up shop on Hill 138. He later sent Marshall with a small staff (but no wireless or telephone) forward to superintend the advance, and in doing so effectively split the command structure and set up a further source of confusion. Marshall arrived at the front at around 1130, and found the advance stalled; he called up the 86th Brigade, which was concentrated near X Beach. Cayley brought his men up, the Lancashires on the left and the Royals on the right, with the Munstermen and the Dubliners to follow in support (the Irishmen were soon lost to him, appropriated by an officer of the 88th Brigade, who rushed them off on his own authority to the right, to support his own beleaguered men, without Cayley's knowledge). They achieved a degree of success, getting within a kilometre of Krithia before being forced to retire when the troops they thought to be supporting them were found to be missing; that marked the limit of the British advance that day, but not, by any means, its final position.

At around 1700 Marshall sent a signal by runner to Hunter-Weston proposing to hold in place until dusk and then retire to a suitable defensive line he had identified some little way to the rear. It took an hour for a reply to reach him, and by that time the 88th and 86th Brigades had in fact retired all the way to their starting line, and there was nothing for it but to pull the 87th back to conform to the west of them. The only useful outcome of the operation was to straighten the line, which now lay north-west to south-east from a point south of Y Beach on the west coast to one about halfway between Esli Hissarlik Point and the mouth of the Kereves Dere. During the day's fruitless fighting the British took around 2,000 casualties, the French perhaps 1,200. Coming on top of the horrendous mess of the landings at V and W Beaches, this was as near catastrophic as made no difference.

*

Even to its most fervent supporters, it was plain as early as the evening of 26 April that the invasion plan had gone so badly awry as to be unrecognisable, and that were it somehow to be rescued, it would only be by very drastic measures, and that meant massive reinforcement in double-quick time. There *were* fresh troops on their way to the area – the 29th Indian Brigade from Egypt, delayed in transit but scheduled to arrive in the next four to five days – but less than four thousand men would hardly make the required difference. If only Sir John Maxwell, the C-in-C, Egypt, had released the 42nd (East Lancashire) Division, back in March ...

Part of the blame for the absence of those troops lies with Hamilton. He had grown up in a school in which one got on with what was given to one, and did not go to the headmaster, bowl in hand, asking for more. Only with the utmost diffidence had he reminded Maxwell that he wanted 'the Gurkhas', as he called Cox's Indians, before he left Egypt (he had never contemplated asking for the 42nd Division because Maxwell had failed to inform him that they were his if he wanted them).²⁸ Eventually, late on 27 April, Hamilton asked Kitchener: 'May I have a call on 42nd East Lancs Territorial Division in case I should need them? You may be sure I shall not call up a man unless I really need him.' Kitchener told Maxwell to embark the 42nd at once. Two days later the French government decided to send a further infantry division to Gallipoli too; its first detachments began to leave Marseilles the following day.

In fact, Maxwell, having originally been reluctant to cut the forces defending the canal, now recognised that 'failure on the part of Hamilton would bring about a critical situation all over the Muslim world', and responded with a will, sending off replacement drafts of officers and men for both ANZAC and the 29th Division immediately and, on 30 April, suggesting that ANZAC's Light Horse and Mounted Rifle Brigades, a total of twelve battalions, should be sent to Gallipoli to serve as infantrymen, as they themselves had never tired of requesting. He worked small miracles with the 42nd Division, too; the first units were on their way on 1 May, and the entire division had left Egypt by 5 May. By about the tenth of the month, if all went according to plan, the Allies would have over eighty thousand men on the Gallipoli Peninsula. In the meantime, Hamilton must fight a holding action using the forces at his disposal while the Turks also rushed additional fighting forces into the region, most of them from Thrace, just a few days away.

While the influx of Turkish troops into the area may have begun slowly, as soon as Sanders knew what he was facing, he took all steps possible to up his numbers, and with all speed. By the evening of 27 April he had pulled all the troops holding the Bulair Lines south into the head of the peninsula, and the transfer of the garrisons from the Asiatic side was already well under way. In addition fresh divisions, the 15th and 16th, of the Second Army's V Corps (with its third, the 13th, to follow, together with the 4th from II Corps), had left Constantinople, and another, the First Army's 12th, had been ordered up from Smyrna to Chanak, to cross the Straits as required. The reinforcements and reorganisations were largely completed even before the majority of Hamilton's own extra troops had left their ports of embarkation; further reinforcements were made over the weeks which followed. If Sanders had a particular concern during this period, it was a shortage of artillery shells, especially for the howitzers which had been used to cover the naval minefields, and which could now be used against the land forces; had he had as many as he wished, it is perfectly feasible that he would have driven the Allies to evacuate before they could have been reinforced.

On the Anzac front, throughout the last week of April the Turks had made a steady encroachment towards the Nek, the narrow spine which separated Russell's Top[29] and Walker's Ridge from the slopes of Baby 700, and by the end of the month they had clear fields of fire over the Top and Monash Gully below. However, the Turks' shell shortage was at its most pressing in this very sector and supplies had now run so low that the already very intermittent bombardment on the New Zealanders' positions ceased entirely. This, coupled with the events in front of Krithia, forty-eight hours earlier, convinced Birdwood that many of the Turks in the zone had been transferred to the southern battlefield, and that Baby 700 was now only lightly held; ambitiously, he decided to take advantage of the lull to launch a night offensive to remove the threat to the Nek.[30]

The plan was to send the Otago Battalion up the western fork of the Monash Gully, and the Australian 13th and 16th up the eastern fork, the 16th to climb the steep slopes on the right past Quinn's Post and hold the ridge from there to the limit of Second Ridge. That done, the 13th would move through their positions and on to the slopes of Baby 700, the Otagos by that time having scrambled up to form their left flank. As soon as they reached the Nek, one company from the Canterbury Battalion entrenched at Walker's Ridge would cross it to extend the line further to the left.

When the preparatory artillery barrage opened up at 1900 on 2 May, some units moved off as prescribed; others were still far out of position and followed as best they could. The Turks' defences were well sited, and the advance soon became fragmented. Those who could seize an advantageous chance did so, and some terrain was gained, including a patch slightly to the north of the original position on Pope's Hill which, unfortunately, was never able to link with neighbouring units on either flank. Around 0130, Godley, believing – for no real reason – the attack was going well, sent the Plymouth and Chatham battalions of the RMLI to reinforce the Anzacs. Bivouacked in Shrapnel Gully, it was daybreak before they reached the top of Monash Gully and the foot of Pope's Hill, and by that time, the stream of wounded coming down from the heights was such that they could make no further progress up the gullies. A few men began to climb the steep slope to the east, but were soon deterred by friendly fire falling short, and retired.

By mid-afternoon on 3 May 'not a man remained in advance of the positions held the day before'. This sort of operation came to characterise the offensive over the next few months: futile but often literally unbelievably courageous attempts to improve a situation which was always desperate, but was deemed until the very last never quite parlous enough to abandon.

Back at Cape Helles, Hamilton had begun planning another advance to Achi Baba as soon as the result of the abortive first attempt was known. There was nothing of any import to be learned from the setback, save that he desperately needed more men, and as a result he would be forced to await the arrival of the Indian 29th Brigade and the first brigade of the 42nd Division, having decided to bring two brigades south from ANZAC, plus all the Corps' field batteries, for which no useful positions had been found, to further augment his numbers. He planned to begin the operation on 6 May.

The Turks pre-empted him. On the night of 1 May they counterattacked with twenty-one battalions of infantry supported by 56 guns. Though there was no preparatory barrage, and the troops were ordered not to load their rifles, they failed to achieve surprise, having begun to yell 'Allah ... Allah-o-Akbar' long before they charged. At just one point – astride the Kirtli Dere – were they successful against the British, but that breakthrough was soon repulsed; they came much closer to breaking the French line across a wider front, but were stopped by artillery. They tried again the next night with no more success; French 75-mm guns, the famed close-support 'soixante-quinze', caught them in the open as they retired, and cut them to pieces. Prisoners revealed that they were eight battalions of the 15th Division, which had landed at Kilia Bay (Kilia Liman), north of Maidos, and had marched thirty kilometres before being sent straight into battle.

As part of his planning for what would be the Second Battle of Krithia, Hamilton took the decision to break up the weakened 86th Brigade and reallocate its battalions to the 87th and 88th, the former receiving the amalgamated Munster and Dublin Fusiliers, the latter the Royals and the 1st Lancashires. To them he added five more brigades: a Composite Division made up of the 2nd Australian Brigade and the New Zealand Brigade, on loan from ANZAC (to which they were returned after the battle), and the Plymouth and Drake Battalions; the 42nd Division's 125th Brigade and the 29th Indian.[31] In all, that amounted to an infantry strength of around 25,000 men. The 125th Brigade – which would come ashore only on 5 May – was to be on the left, allocated the section between the coastal cliffs and Gully Ravine ('Gully Spur'); the 87th and 88th would take up a position from Gully Ravine to Kirte Dere ('Fir Tree Spur'), with the Composite Division to their right ('Krithia Spur'). To the right of Kanli Dere stood the French and their British (naval) reinforcements,[32] spread out across Kereves Spur.[33] The 29th Indian

Brigade was to be in reserve in a central position, about a kilometre back from the firing line.

Once again the advance was to be weighted to the left, but this time the entire force would advance straight ahead for a distance of a mile (1,500m); that was Phase One. The French were then to take up a defensive position and hold it at all costs, while the Composite Division and the 88th Brigade continued forward, pivoting on the junction with the French, taking Krithia and advancing until the line ran north–south, the 125th Brigade continuing to advance on the original axis to fill in the space between the extreme left of the 88th and the sea; that was Phase Two. The 87th and the 29th Brigades would then advance through the north–south line and take Achi Baba, whereupon, the enemy having by now decamped, the French would advance to link up with the British right and straighten the cordon across the peninsula once more, bringing Phase Three to an end. The distance between the start and finish lines was something of the order of five kilometres. No overall timetable was issued, but it was hoped that the operation would be over before dusk.

Delay piled on delay, the majority of the men suffering badly from lack of sleep, and communications being none too reliable, it was 1100 before it was under way. In the centre, the reinforced 88th, with three battalions up and two back, made some progress up Fir Tree Spur until it reached the parcel of woodland which gave it its name, and there it stalled, held up by well-concealed machine guns. Soon that picture was being repeated right across the peninsula, and by early afternoon the entire advance had been stopped by automatic weapons in protected positions which, thanks to the shortage of high-explosive artillery shells, were generally invulnerable and would continue to wreak havoc so long as their own ammunition held out; nowhere had gains exceeded four hundred metres.

Hamilton gave orders for the offensive to be renewed the following morning, by which time fresh men in the shape of the 127th Brigade of the 42nd Division had begun to come ashore. By early afternoon, very little additional progress had been made, however, and when Hunter-Weston ordered a renewed mass attack, at 1630, it, too, failed to make any impression on the defensive line. Ironically, so effective was the Turkish fire that British casualties were very much lighter than might have been expected, simply because any attempt to move forward immediately drew a deadly response, and few were willing to take the futile chance – or even, for once, to insist that others did – and British dead and wounded for the entire day amounted to no more than eight hundred.[34] The French, on the right, fared no better; though an assault in the early afternoon won some ground (and a Turkish trench) and got to within a hundred and fifty metres of the top of the Kereves Spur, the Turks won it all back with a swift counterattack.

By now, it was clear to all concerned that only a miracle could alter the course of the battle, but Hamilton did not dare give up on the hope of one, and that evening he issued orders for the offensive to be renewed yet again on the morning of the eighth. This time it was to be the New Zealand Brigade which would bear the brunt of it, having been ordered to move through the 88th and assault Krithia village by way of Fir Tree Spur: four weak battalions to advance across open ground covered by machine gun emplacements in order to take on at least nine battalions of defenders in prepared positions ... Elsewhere, only the South Wales Borderers and the Inniskillings were to advance, to try to locate a nest of at least five Maxims which had stalled the advance up Gully Spur for forty-eight hours despite the battleships offshore having virtually cut off the top of the cliff with shellfire in a fruitless search for it.

They tried, they tried and they tried again, but each time the machine guns drove them back, until by early afternoon the attack had effectively collapsed. Hamilton's response was one of absolute desperation; at 1600 he ordered the entire Allied line, together with the 2nd Australian Brigade, which was still in reserve (as were the newly arrived 127th and the 29th Indian), to 'fix bayonets, slope arms and move on Krithia at precisely 5.30pm'. The men did as they were bade, and as they rose up and began to move forward, they were mown down in their ranks. Worst hit were the 2nd Australians, advancing along the Krithia Spur, for they had further to go, having started about a thousand metres back from the firing line as it now stood. Within the space of half an hour their 'unrecognised Balaclava', as Aspinall-Oglander described it, cost them half their number.

By the time night fell on 8 May it was over, the men ordered to dig in where they were (save for the 1st Lancashires and the Drake Battalion, RND, which were pushed forward under cover of darkness to bridge the gap left by the fallen 2nd Australians; they were able to do so without losing a single man). The Turks made no attempt to counterattack. Over three days of fighting the Allies had nowhere advanced more than about five hundred metres – and that to no particularly good effect, save that it gave the Allied troops 'much-needed elbow room in the crowded southern zone' – and everywhere the Turkish front-line positions were largely intact. British and French casualties amounted to about 6,500. Turkish losses are thought to have been minimal.

Hamilton cabled Kitchener an appraisal of the overall situation: 'The fortifications and their machine guns were too scientific and too strongly held to be rushed ... Our troops have done all that flesh and blood can do.' Kitchener replied, asking for his proposals, and Hamilton admitted that the only plan he had was 'to hammer away until the enemy gets demoralized', but warned that he feared the situation would 'degenerate into trench warfare with its resultant slowness', and concluded – still diffidently – with a request for two fresh divisions 'if [they] could be spared me'. Kitchener told him next day that he would send him one, the 52nd (Lowland) Division.

*

Over the next few days there were several other developments on the naval front. On 10 May de Roebeck had cabled Churchill, seeming to suggest his ships try to force the Strait once more. In fact he was doing no such thing,[35] and he was very careful to couch the proposal in terms which his professional colleagues at the Admiralty would be bound to reject, pointing out (as if it were negligible; hardly worth considering . . .) the risk of the fleet penetrating to the Sea of Marmara and then being cut off there, doomed to run out of fuel and ammunition, and being forced inevitably to surrender, when the Turks closed the Strait again behind it.

The Board of Admiralty soon delivered the rejection he sought, assuring him on 13 May that 'We think the moment for an independent naval attempt to force the Narrows has passed, and will not arise again under present circumstances.' However, there were two other influential elements to be considered. Firstly, the same day he had cabled Churchill it had been decided to reduce his force by four battleships and four light cruisers, which, as agreed in an adjunct to the secret Treaty of London,[36] were to go to the Adriatic in order to strengthen Italy's position there. In real terms this was not of major importance, since the French had offered to make up the numbers, but there was a second and more important factor: persistent rumours that German submarines were on their way to the Aegean.[37]

These rumours had sent Fisher, for one, into a frenzy of anxiety, particularly in regard to the pride of the fleet, HMS Queen Elizabeth, and he had begun barracking Churchill to agree to her returning to home waters. Churchill was to admit that he was not averse to such a move – reasonably enough; the loss of such an asset was impossible to contemplate, and effective anti-submarine measures were virtually non-existent – but insisted that she be replaced by two more obsolete battleships and the first two of the new 14-in monitors,[38] with more to follow as soon as they were available, and Fisher was quite happy to comply. Orders home were transmitted to Queen Elizabeth on the evening of 12 May, seemingly none too soon, for just hours later the battleship HMS Goliath was torpedoed in Morto Bay. (In fact, though a German ocean-going submarine was indeed on her way to the Aegean, Goliath was sunk by a Turkish destroyer, the German-built Mauvenit-i-Milliye.[39]) Fisher's fears were soon proved justified, however, for when Korvettenkapitän Hersing arrived off Gallipoli on 25 May in U 21 he wasted no time in adding to the score, sinking the battleship Triumph within sight of Anzac Cove that same day.[40] This caused consternation within de Roebeck's staff, and all remaining large warships were immediately sent to Imbros, to shelter in Kefalo Bay. Just one – HMS Majestic – was released the next day to provide artillery support at Cape Helles, and she was promptly torpedoed too, early the next morning, barely 400m off W Beach. This time, boats from the shore were able to rescue most of her crew. From then on, until the monitors and cruisers with anti-torpedo blisters[41] arrived on station, there was no fire support from the Royal Navy save from destroyers' 4-in guns.

*

At the War Office in London, the events of 6–8 May at Gallipoli had to compete for attention with those on both the Western and Eastern Fronts. On the former, where the Second Battle of Ypres was still grinding on, a new offensive had begun in the coalfields of northern France.[42] Its outcome was sufficient to convince Kitchener that the German defences were unbreakable with the resources available, while events in the east – where Austro-German armies had embarked on a rampage of an offensive which would see a fifty-kilometre-wide gap torn through the Russian line, and Przemysl retaken, the Ukrainian city of Lemberg (L'viv) occupied and the Dniester crossed – raised a spectre of Allied vulnerability. If a breakthrough on that scale occurred in France, Kitchener believed the British government would have no choice but to send all available men to assist, and that, in turn, would leave the British Isles vulnerable to a sea-borne invasion. That may seem far-fetched now – it did to many then – but the Secretary of State for War had to at least consider the possibility and how to deal with it.

As a result, when the War Council met on 14 May, in an atmosphere Churchill would describe as 'sulphurous', and the question of reinforcing Hamilton was raised, the Secretary of State for War was adamant that no additional forces (above the division he had promised four days earlier) should be sent to Gallipoli. He went further, his protest turning into something of a diatribe against the perfidious behaviour of the Royal Navy, deserting the army 'when it was struggling for its life with its back to the sea', as Churchill put it.

The meeting then turned to Churchill (*on* him, he thought). By his own account he fought his corner valiantly, pointing out that if it had been known in February that an army of 100,000 men would be made available to take the peninsula, matters would have turned out very differently, and arguing that in the circumstances it was essential to stop futile offensive operations on the Western Front and remain on the defensive there, while resourcing Gallipoli instead. He played down the importance of the *Queen Elizabeth* and stressed the superiority of the ships which would take her place while dismissing Kitchener's invasion fears, reassuring the Council that such a thing was strategically impossible, but that if the Germans did make such an attempt, the Royal Navy could be relied upon to scotch it.

Clearly, no resolution to the problem of whether or not to reinforce Hamilton further was possible at that stage. However, the ever-present third option, that of withdrawing from Gallipoli entirely, was discarded for fear that it would 'throw the Balkan States into the arms of the Germans and might lead to risings all over the Mahommedan world' – and the meeting broke up after instructing Kitchener to demand of Hamilton 'what force you consider would be necessary to carry through the operations upon which you are engaged'. Lest he suffer another fit of diffidence, he was told to 'base this estimate on the supposition that I have adequate forces to place at your disposal'. Needless to say, that flew in the face of Kitchener's true views, and while he was bound to do as he was bidden, he soon made his position clear.

Hamilton told him he wanted three more divisions in addition to the extra one which was already on its way.[43] He got an immediate and depressing response, Kitchener telling him, in effect, not to hold his breath, but instead to make his best efforts to bring the affair to a successful conclusion before the question of it being abandoned was raised. Hamilton made the only reply he could: that he was doing everything possible with the resources at his disposal.

It was as well he was, for he was about to be left to his own devices for precious weeks, Asquith's Liberal government, riven with internal strife caused by the 'shell crisis' (see Chapter 2, Note 26), being about to fall. It would be well into June before the coalition which replaced it (still under Asquith's leadership, but with Tories – and the coming man, David Lloyd George – in Cabinet positions, and with Churchill gone from the Admiralty,[44] to be replaced by Arthur Balfour) would find time to devote to Hamilton's problems.[45] In the meantime, on the Helles front he could only wait as his men sapped forward foot by laborious, arduous foot, towards defensive positions the Turks continued to strengthen and extend.

Even as Hamilton was responding to the War Council's request for clarification of his needs, the Turks were preparing an attack on the ANZAC positions.

Over the three weeks they had been occupied they had been consolidated to a remarkable degree, given the unforgiving nature of the terrain, and four extensive concentrations – at Courtney's, Quinn's and Steele's Posts and on Pope's Hill – had been established; the three Posts were situated in narrow re-entrants near the spine of Maclaurin's Hill, a neck joining Second Ridge with Baby 700, of which Pope's Hill was a spur. Maclaurin's Hill had Monash Gully, at the far side of which was Russell's Top, at its back; to the west of Maclaurin's Hill was Turkish territory: Wire Gully, with Mortar Ridge, the Chessboard and Bloody Angle beyond. Monash Gully was the supply route to the Posts, but its security rested on the degree to which Turkish snipers in commanding positions could be overcome or at least controlled.[46] At some points, ANZAC and Turkish positions were a short stone's – or rather, bomb's – throw apart, more happily for the Turks, who were well supplied with grenades, than for the Antipodeans, who had to make their own, at least to begin with, from jam tins filled with scrap iron and an explosive charge. Many ANZAC positions had their backs to precipitous slopes, and from them there was, quite literally, no retreat.

When the attack came, just before dawn on 19 May, it exhibited no subtlety, but was a straightforward attempt to swamp the defences by weight of numbers, a near-impossibility in such terrain against positions protected by machine guns. The main focus of the attack came on 400 Plateau; the Turks had around two hundred metres of flat, open country to cross, and the result was predictable.[47] Within two hours the Turks had taken so many casualties – 10,000 by their own later account; the Australians counted 3,000 dead, so that would appear to be no exaggeration – that they could not continue, and withdrew.

So great were the numbers of enemy dead that the Australians feared the risk to the men's health would be such as to drive them from their positions, were the corpses not cleared. There was talk of asking for a truce for the purpose; Hamilton forbade it, but by the next evening affairs had reached such a pass that the commander of the 1st Australian Brigade, on his own initiative, hoisted a Red Cross flag. The Turks replied by hoisting the Red Crescent, and recovery parties from both sides were soon at work. The activities ceased at nightfall, but the next day negotiations took place which resulted in a formal truce which lasted from 0730 to 1630 on 24 May.

The Action of 19 May – the only name the brief battle ever had, in British circles – gave Birdwood confidence that his defences would withstand anything the Turks could throw at them, and he began to agitate to be allowed to launch an offensive of his own, in the northern part of the zone. This aroused Hamilton's interest, and he was told to begin outline planning.

At Cape Helles the situation had changed somewhat since the Second Battle of Krithia, the 42nd Division[48] having by now arrived in its entirety and occupied the front line alongside the 29th Indian Brigade, with the two French divisions on the right, allowing the survivors of the 29th Division to be withdrawn to the rear for a much-needed rest. On 24 May the British divisions at Helles were formally organised as VIII Corps, with Hunter-Weston promoted temporarily to lieutenant-general to command. On 4 June Maj.-Gen. Beauvoir de Lisle arrived from France to succeed him in command of the 29th Division.

Despite the very limited progress made up to that point, Hunter-Weston remained confident of success, his 'buoyant spirits, fiery energy and quite unconquerable optimism' sustaining GHQ's hopes that Achi Baba could still be taken. No sooner was the fighting before Krithia on 9 May over than he had started planning a new offensive, based on a systematic advance of the whole of the line by means of sapping and nocturnal movement. An exception was the advance along Gully Spur by 1/6th Gurkhas on the night of 12 May, but not all the progress made was so spectacular, by any means; most involved slogging hard work towards the objective of bringing the Allied front line to within 175m – assaulting distance – of the Turks' positions.

The defenders were not idle during this period. Concentrating on their left flank, since they feared an Allied advance along the shore of the Strait, they had completed two contiguous lines of trenches across the Kereves Spur, with four small redoubts incorporated into the first of them: 'Fortin le Gouez', nearest the sea, 'the Rognon', 'the Haricot' and 'the Quadrilateral', the latter located at the highest point on the Spur. Twice during the latter half of May the Haricot was stormed, but each time so great were the French losses that it proved impossible to consolidate the gain, and it had to be given up. However, on the thirty-first the Fortin le Gouez was taken in a surprise attack, and the French line was extended to incorporate it.

The Allied line was within assaulting distance of the Turks' by the end of May, and Hamilton began to come under pressure from Hunter-Weston and Gouraud, in command of the French corps, to launch another offensive. He would have preferred to wait for additional men (the 52nd Division,[49] but also replacement drafts for the 29th), but, with Kitchener's exhortation to press on still fresh in his mind, and inspired by the Turkish defeat at Anzac, he was convinced, by 31 May, to fight what would become the Third Battle of Krithia. The orders were issued on 2 June, the operation to commence two days later. The following day Kitchener, still undecided as to whether to give his support to enlarging the force at Gallipoli, broke his silence (Hamilton had received no communication from him since 19 May), asking him if he was convinced that with the reinforcements he had requested he could take Kilid Bair 'and thus finish the Dardanelles operation', and he replied, reasonably enough, that he would give him his answer after the forthcoming battle had been fought.

This time the immediate objectives were modest. The first was the Turkish front line, with the reserve positions to be the target of the second wave. Nowhere were troops expected to advance more than about 750m. The total of available troops was 30,000, two-thirds of them British, of whom around 10,000 would be kept back for the second wave. British artillery was still deficient in numbers, with seventy-eight guns and just eight howitzers, and was extremely short of ammunition. Naval gunfire support was provided by two cruisers and four destroyers, with the battleships *Swiftsure* and *Exmouth* also available, but only – for fear of submarines – while they cruised at twelve knots, which reduced their value against point targets to virtually nil.

The attack began with an artillery barrage which wiped out much of the remaining stocks of ammunition but achieved very little. When the infantry went over the top, a few minutes after noon, they found the Turkish positions largely untouched, and the wire before them uncut. Some units fared better than others, with the centre sectors manned by the 42nd Division and the strengthened 88th Brigade making the most ground and penetrating the Turkish lines by as much as a kilometre, while the Indian brigade and the RND,[50] on the left and right respectively, did significantly less well against stronger opposition. These latter – and the French divisions, which had both born the brunt of Turkish artillery and were exposed to dominant machine guns positioned on high ground – were driven back to their start lines by 1330, but the British centre was still holding its gains. Clearly, it was time to throw in reserves, but for Hunter-Weston this posed a problem: should he send them in in the centre, to bolster success, or on the flanks, to reverse failure? He chose the latter.

It has been suggested that Hunter-Weston was already out of his depth, a divisional commander handling a corps, and that he had never been provided with the sort of supporting staff that much larger body required. Be that as it may have been, his decision this day was little short of disastrous. At around 1600 he sent the three reserve RND battalions to join their comrades on the right, and the 1/5th Gurkhas up on the left. At 1700 he added two more battalions on the left, and ordered a third sent up behind the 88th Brigade, not to be committed, but available in an emergency. That accounted for seven of the twelve available battalions; prudence dictated that no more be released.

The six actually sent into action were not enough to tip the balance, no further ground was gained on either flank,[51] and at 1715 Hunter-Weston issued orders to consolidate and hold the ground gained overnight. Until that time he had received nothing but favourable reports from the centre, but it soon became clear that that was where the Turks had chosen to send in their reinforcements, and by 1800 the salient was under attack from three sides and being forced back, notably near a vineyard on the Sedd el Bahr–Krithia road, and astride the two branches of Kirte Dere. By the time night fell, the gains there had been cut back drastically.

The Turks counterattacked the following day, to no particularly good effect, but sent up yet more reserves that night, and made a more determined effort on 6 June, driving the British line back again, across a front a mile wide. With that, the Third Battle of Krithia can be said to have come to an end. Once again, minimal gains had been made, and this time the cost to the British was put at around 4,500 and to the French at 2,000 on the first day alone, when the Turks were thought to have lost up to 10,000. That evening Hamilton replied to Kitchener's signal, saying: 'I am convinced by this action that with my present force my progress will be very slow, but ... I believe the reinforcements asked for ... will eventually enable me to take Kilid Bair.' The following day, when the Dardanelles Committee met for the first time, Kitchener announced that he had quite reversed his earlier position, and now proposed sending Hamilton the three extra divisions (from the volunteer 'New Army'[52]) he had requested. It now remained only to select them, and decide on the means to get them into the theatre as rapidly as possible,[53] and for Hamilton to decide where he would employ them.

As the spring of 1915 turned into summer, the Allies kept battering away at the Turkish defences in the southern zone, increasingly desperate now to break through at least to Achi Baba. During June minor gains were made on the extreme right and the extreme left; at the end of the month Hunter-Weston launched a more extensive offensive on the left to drive the Turks north up Gully and Fir Tree Spurs on both flanks of Gully Ravine. It opened

The *Bab-i Ali*, the 'Sublime Porte' of the Topkapi Palace which gave the Ottoman Government its name in diplomatic circles

The Bashi-Bazouks – literally, 'damaged heads' – were paramilitaries, perfectly suited to the sort of punitive 'security' operations for which they were employed by the Ottoman sultans

The German battlecruiser SMS *Goeben* caused much anxiety at The Admiralty in London when she evaded capture and reached Constantinople in August, 1914; she was then supposedly taken into the Turkish Navy under the name *Yavuz Sultan Selim*

The conditions in which wounded men were evacuated down the Tigris – those who *were* evacuated – gave very serious cause for concern, the river craft pressed into service as hospital ships being totally unsuited to the task; they often arrived at Basra enrobed in faeces

Turkish troops in the Caucasus routinely used skis to get about during the long, harsh winter; note the single pole

Dunsterforce's advance party crossed Persia from Qasr-i-Shirin to Rasht in a fleet of forty-one Ford Model T cars; they are pictured here during the last stages of their journey, north of Qasvin

A 'tow' of ship's boats en route to ANZAC Cove in April, 1915, behind a steam pinnace; as they neared the beach, rowers would take over

Australian troops massed on the deck of HMS *Prince of Wales* prior to entering the boats which would take them to Z Beach

ANZAC wounded being ferried back to Mudros, and hospital
ships which would take them to Egypt

Steam drifters – built in huge numbers for the North Sea herring fishery – became the workhorses of
the Gallipoli and Dardanelles operations, employed first as mine-sweepers and later, like this one, as
ferries

Australian troops charging into action

Men of the Royal Naval Division scramble from their trenches to charge across no-man's land… In fact, this photograph – like many purporting to be taken in action – is believed to have been taken during exercises prior to the Gallipoli landings

An Australian sniper and his observer at Quinn's Post

Dugouts giving onto terraces were home to the men of ANZAC during the periods they spent 'up the line'

Whilst in reserve, the men of ANZAC lived in tented encampments near to the beaches, safe from Turkish shells; this is Outpost No. 2, inland from North Beach, with Ari Burnu visible in the background

Steele's Post, on the heights above Anzac Cove, was typical of the forward positions, many of which were within grenade range of the Turkish front-line trenches

at 0900 on 28 June, and met with some initial success, particularly on Gully Spur; less so to the east of the ravine and markedly less so on the right, the 1/8th Scottish rifles, in particular, suffering very heavy casualties when they advanced without artillery support.[54] For three days and nights the Turks tried to take back the ground they had lost; the third attempt cost them dearly when many of their troops were caught in the open by guns of the Royal Field Artillery, and with that the action seemed to be over. It was not. After a lull of twenty-four hours, and now reinforced and under the personal command of Liman von Sanders, the Turks came on again. Once more the counterattack failed, this time through the gross inadequacy of the preparatory bombardment, which left the defenders largely unscathed; when Turkish infantry appeared, they were confronted by field artillery and machine guns which cut them down in swathes. In all, over the seven days it lasted, the engagement cost the British five thousand casualties (the 156th Brigade alone lost over 1,300 men, and was then reorganised as two composite battalions, one of Royal Scots, the other of Scottish Rifles), while the Turks later admitted to having lost 16,000 killed and wounded. A Turkish request for a short truce in which to bury their dead was refused on the dubious grounds that the presence of so many corpses in front of the defensive line might discourage further Turkish assaults.

It took some time for the British to reorganise after what became known as 'the Action of Gully Ravine', and implement a plan to push forward on the right, to straighten the line, an operation in which the French belatedly decided to participate in a further attempt to gain ground on the Kereves Spur. Originally intended for 7 July, it was postponed eventually for five days, and Hamilton took the unusual step of entrusting it to the inexperienced 52nd Division, while the 29th and the 42nd held the rest of the line and the RND was 'rested'.[55] (He had been told in no uncertain terms that other new formations – the leading elements of the 13th (Western) Division, which had begun embarking in British ports on 16 June, came ashore at Cape Helles on 7 July – were not to be used for offensive operations, but only defensively.[56])

The assault was to be made in the sector stretching from Kanli Dere[57] to the Rognon, a distance of roughly 1500m, two-thirds of the front being allocated to the British. Thanks to the inadequacy of the artillery cover, the British element was to be split in two: the 155th Brigade would assault the right-hand half of the sector in the morning, then fire would be switched to the left-hand half prior to the 157th Brigade attacking in the afternoon, the weakened 156th being held in reserve. The affair lasted forty-eight hours, during which small gains were made, chiefly on the far right, in the French sector – where a section of the Rognon Redoubt was taken and held – and cost around four thousand Allied casualties, but was reckoned a success, for more than twice that number of casualties were inflicted on the Turks, who also lost around 600 men captured.

The fighting at Cape Helles in June and July had drawn in yet more

Turkish troops, large numbers of men of the Second Army having now been despatched to Gallipoli together with Vehip Pasha (Esad Pasha's younger brother), its chief of staff, who took over command of the southern front from the German, Weber. During the fighting of 12/13 July, the southern front had been held by five Turkish divisions. By the end of July they had been joined by the 13th and 14th Divisions from V Corps and the 8th and 10th Divisions from XIV Corps. The Turkish Fifth Army now had just over a quarter of a million men under arms at Gallipoli, the majority of them in the southern zone.

Changes were made in VIII Corps, too. Around 20 July Hunter-Weston succumbed to sunstroke (by the official account; 'nervous exhaustion' was a more common diagnosis), and after a few days' hospitalisation was sent home.[58] Stopford (qv), recently arrived, stepped in as a caretaker commander for a few days and then Maj.-Gen. W Douglas, the commander of the 42nd Division, was given temporary command, with Marshall taking over the division. Douglas was replaced permanently on 8 August by Lt.-Gen. Sir Francis Davies, sent out from France expressly for the purpose.

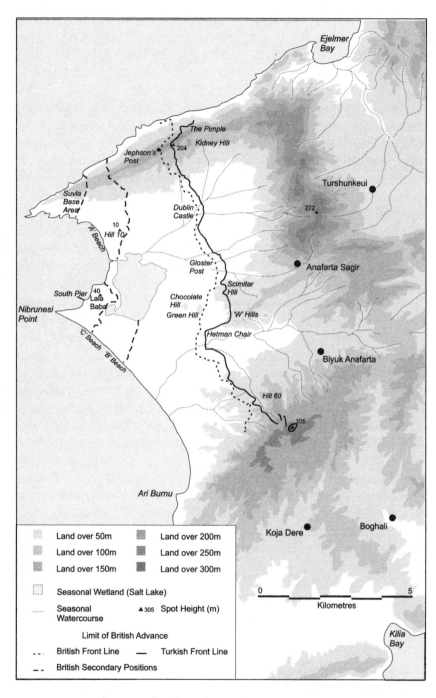

19. Gallipoli – The Suvla Bay Positions

A Failure of Leadership

Birdwood's ambitious plan for breaking the deadlock at Gallipoli, in the making since May, was based on a four-phase assault: the first would take Chunuk Bair; the second, Battleship Hill, Baby 700 and the 400 Plateau; the third, Gun Ridge. The fourth phase – which would almost certainly need further subdivision unless the defenders were routed – would see the attacking forces push through as far as the east coast of the peninsula at a point between Kilia and Ak Bashi Bays. When he submitted a revised version to Hamilton on 1 July, Birdwood had expanded phase one to include the peaks north of Chunuk Bair: Hill Q and Hill 971, the summit of Koja Chemen Tepe itself.

By Birdwood's initial calculations he would require four additional brigades. He later upped this to seven, and the staff at GHQ believed the available space around Anzac Cove could hold no more than three. Clearly, the answer was to land the rest at another location, close enough for the two beachheads to become contiguous. The original objections to a landing anywhere near Gaba Tepe still applied (and were actually stronger than ever, for the beach was vulnerable to the guns the Turks had brought up to cover Anzac Cove), but Suvla Bay, to the north, was only lightly defended and it was known that the salt lake there, if not already dry, would soon be so. Thus, Suvla Bay chose itself as the site of the third disembarkation.

In its topography, the Suvla area is straightforward: a wide cove – which would not serve as a landing beach, for there were shoals across its length – giving onto a coastal plain. Its north and south sides, too, give onto the sea, though the former is bordered by a coastal ridge which continues around the eastern perimeter, the highest points of which are Tekke Tepe and the adjacent Kavak Tepe, to the north, neither of them much more than 250m high but covered with dense, thorny scrub. The coastal ridge, Kiretch Tepe Sirt, runs down to Suvla Point, which forms the northern arm of the bay. To the southeast the plain is dominated by Koja Chemen Tepe, across the Azmak Dere valley, which gives access by way of a low pass (the Anafarta Gap) to the valley of the Ak Bashi Dere, which runs down to the east coast of the peninsula.

The Anafarta Spur, nowhere more than a hundred metres high, protrudes into the plain north of the gap, and terminates in elevated outcroppings the British called the W Hills (Ismail Oglu Tepe). Between the W Hills and the limit of the salt lake are three smaller hills: Scimitar Hill (which is barely more than a rise at the end of a low spur), Chocolate Hill and Green Hill (which are only marginally higher[1]); separating the salt lake from the southern sweep of Suvla Bay, towards Nibrunesi Point which forms its southern arm, is a 40m-high hill known as Lala Baba. The Turks had guns on the W and Chocolate Hills, and maintained outposts there and on Lala Baba; on a rise north of the salt lake known as Hill 10, and at Ghazi Baba, a point near the headland at the western end of Kiretch Tepe, with another detachment on the latter ridge itself.

There were no permanent settlements on the plain, but only occasional labourers' huts. Under the north slope of Koja Chemen Tepe was the village of Biyuk Anafarta (Büyükanafarta); five kilometres north was the area's second village, Anafarta Sagir (Küçükanafarta), occupying a hollow in the hills with Tekke Tepe at its back and the Anafarta Spur to the south. To the north-east, behind Tekke Tepe, was the region's third village, Turshun Keui (Beşyol). None of these settlements would ever become part of the battlefield.

Hamilton believed Turkish forces in the region to amount to five battalions; in fact there were just three, under the command of a Bavarian cavalry officer, Major Wilhelm Wilmers, and by 7 August one of those had been sent to reinforce the positions around Anzac Cove. Wilmers' men came from diverse sources, some from Jandarma units, others from regular infantry; they had no machine guns, but did have a battery of eight mountain guns, and two pairs of field guns on the Tekke Tepe ridge.

By the time Hamilton communicated this plan to Kitchener, he had been offered and had accepted two *more* additional divisions, this time of Territorial Forces[2] (he asked that their departure be delayed briefly, so that the Anzac/Suvla operation would be under way by the time they arrived, his intention being to use them to reinforce it, if it had stalled, or land them at Cape Helles if it had succeeded). Kitchener approved, and detailed planning continued. By now a provisional date had been set: the end of the first week of August.

The second and third New Army divisions left the United Kingdom on the heels of the 13th (Western) Division,[3] the 11th (Northern) Division[4] during the first week of July, and the 10th (Irish) Division[5] the following week. The three divisions were constituted as IX Corps, which was placed under the command of Lt.-Gen. Sir Frederick Stopford. Stopford, who had retired in 1909 without ever having commanded men in battle (he had served in the Boer War, but as military secretary to Sir Redvers Buller[6]), is widely held to have been one of the least competent general officers in the British Army, but that is probably not going far enough. Hamilton had asked for either Sir Henry Rawlinson or Sir Julian Byng, both of whom had commanded corps in France with considerable distinction, but both were junior in the Army List to Sir Bryan Mahon, who commanded the 10th Division, and who would not (then or later) relinquish his seniority. Stopford was a compromise choice, and a disastrously poor one; some of his senior commanders – including Mahon himself – were little better.

In disposing of his forces, Hamilton was forced to weigh inexperience against exhaustion. Should he commit one of the divisions which had seen action at Cape Helles to the Suvla Bay landings? And if so, which one? He first thought of employing the 29th Division, recently brought back up to strength by drafts of fresh men from home, but was eventually dissuaded on the grounds that it would be unfair to ask it to make a second opposed landing. In the process of influencing him, his staff perhaps talked up the qualities of the New Army divisions – that was not uncommon; the New Army was untried, and there were high hopes for it – and as a result, though the exhausted condition of the other Helles divisions surely swayed him too, he decided to employ only fresh troops at Suvla, the 11th Division and two brigades of the 10th.

Most of the troops sent to reinforce ANZAC would be fresh men, too: the 13th Division, which had had the dubious benefit of some weeks in the line at Helles, plus the 29th Brigade of the 10th, though the seasoned Indian 29th Brigade went too. Those reinforcements were to be sent in at night, during the moonless period which began on 3 August. They were to be landed in silence and spirited off the beaches to hiding places prepared for them ahead of time, out of the sight of watching Turks. By that means it was hoped to maintain secrecy and surprise, and the subterfuge succeeded handsomely. On a broader front, however, secrecy would be hard to preserve, given that troopships holding two divisions of infantry had to be moored temporarily off islands which still enjoyed lively if clandestine traffic with mainland Turkey, and where Turkish spies were commonplace. Hamilton's approach was to limit the exposure by taking as few people as possible into his confidence, and discussions as to the newcomers' destination were strongly discouraged, even amongst the ranks of their senior officers. No written orders or maps[7] were issued below corps level prior to the disembarkation (even Stopford was not brought into the picture until 22 July), and this was another factor contributing to the chaos in the invasion beachhead. In fact, Hamilton's efforts at maintaining security were successful; while the Turkish High Command inevitably came to know that *something* was afoot, the place at which any blow would fall was hidden from them. The best Sanders could do was fall back on his original prejudices, and he despatched three divisions to the neck of the peninsula to guard against a landing near Bulair, and three more to the Asian side of the Straits. There was a drawback, however. In the interests of security, Hamilton had forbidden reconnaissance of the Suvla Bay region – and had even restricted overflights – and in consequence he had no up-to-date assessment of local conditions;[8] this applied to the disposition of Turkish troops and even to the state of the salt lake, and it was unclear if it had yet dried completely and would be passable to infantry.

In outline, the proposal Hamilton revealed to Stopford called for the troops to land south of Nibrunesi Point, seize both 'horns' of the bay and the ground between them, then march around the salt lake to approach the Chocolate and W Hills from the north, where they were undefended, and establish positions there and on the Kiretch Tepe and Tekke Tepe ridges. Hamilton stressed the need for the Chocolate and W Hills – presumed to be the site of gun emplacements covering Chunuk Bair and Hill 971 – to be taken before dawn on the first day. Stopford professed himself fully in agreement, but during the days which followed he went over the situation again with his Chief of Staff, Brig.-Gen. HL Reed, who raised some objections, and the plan he presented to GHQ on 26 July was substantially modified. By the time IX Corps headquarters issued its detailed orders for the Suvla Bay landings, on 3 August, they referred to *attacking* the Chocolate Hills and *if possible* (italics added) the W Hills, with no deadline given for their occupation. They did not allude, even, to the original reason the landings were proposed. (The confusion had percolated down to Hammersley, who seemingly believed that the ANZAC offensive on Sari Bair was to be mounted to distract the Turks from the arrival of his 11th Division at Suvla Bay, rather than as the main event.[9] And *his* divisional order stated that his task was 'to secure Suvla Bay for the disembarkation of the 10th Division and stores'.) In addition, de Roebeck's prohibition of a landing inside Suvla Bay itself had been set aside, with disastrous results.

The 13th Division landed at Anzac Cove on 5 August, with the 10th's 29th Brigade and the Indian 29th Brigade to follow in the early hours of the sixth. There were delays; the latter was still coming ashore at daybreak and was heavily shelled, one of the transports being forced to put back to Imbros without disgorging all her passengers. There was some anxiety when the Turks launched an attack on the Anzac right flank an hour later, and it was feared that the massive deception had been rumbled, but it proved to be a nuisance raid.

Birdwood had planned a diversionary operation in the south of his zone, aimed at drawing Turkish forces away from the north, but it was not the only such feint, and before examining it, we should turn our attention to the southern front, where Maj.-Gen. Douglas, still in temporary command of VIII Corps despite the arrival of Lt.-Gen. Davies,[10] was about to mount a limited offensive with the same overall motive.

The local objective of the operation was to straighten out the line by pushing back the salient, centred on the two branches of Kirte Dere (known as the East and West Krithia Nullahs), which had formed during the Third Battle of Krithia. This occupied a front some 1,500m wide, and to eradicate it an advance of three to four hundred metres would be required. The task was to be undertaken by the 29th and 42nd Divisions. Once again there was insufficient artillery to cover the entire front, so it was decided to split the operation into two phases. The 88th Brigade would go in in the western sector on the evening of 6 August. The following morning the 125th and 127th Brigades – far short of full strength – would advance in the eastern. All available artillery assets[11] were to be concentrated on first one, then the other objective. Staff at corps headquarters soon got somewhat carried away with self-generated confidence, and there was rash talk circulating of advancing on Krithia, and even Achi Baba, if all went well.

All went far from well. When the Allied artillery bombardment opened up, Davies, fresh from France, was horrified by the inadequacy of it. The Turks replied with heavy, sustained fire aimed chiefly at the British line, causing numerous casualties among the troops packed, standing, in the trenches. Precisely on time the barrage lifted and the men of the 88th Brigade set out across no-man's-land. Within minutes massed machine guns had stopped the advance and shattered the entire brigade, some two thousand of its three thousand men being killed or wounded.

At divisional headquarters, reports of the disastrous extent of the losses – even from the brigadier himself – were treated with disbelief. Around 1900, de Lisle – unfathomably confident that things were going to plan and to the timetable which was running in his head, and that large stretches of the Turkish line in the centre and left were now in British hands[12] – issued instructions for the Royal Dublin and Royal Munster Fusiliers of the 86th Brigade to be sent in to help consolidate the gains and push the advance further forwards. The attack was timed for 2230, by when few of the men who were to mount it had even reached their start lines. After two postponements the operation was called off at 0315, much to the relief of all concerned. News of the failure of the operation did not reach GHQ on Imbros until 0635, and came with confirmation that the second phase would be going ahead on schedule, which Hamilton's staff took as an indication that things were going well. It also gave further hope that the offensive had achieved its prime objective, of preventing the Turks taking troops from Helles to reinforce Chunuk Bair. Unfortunately, that was not the case; by daybreak, having received reports of troops coming ashore at Suvla Bay, Liman von Sanders had ordered Vehip Pasha to send his reserve division north.

The next day's operations fared no better, and by early evening, with clearer situation reports now to hand, there was real concern at GHQ as to whether the entire Helles zone was vulnerable. Hamilton gave orders that no more offensive operations were to be undertaken. With that, save for a limited offensive by the 52nd Division in November, active operations at Helles ceased, and the opposing lines remained virtually unchanged until the zone was evacuated five months later.

The diversionary operation on the Anzac front was to be mounted on the evening of 6 August across the southern lobe of the 400 Plateau; it was aimed initially at Turkish positions around Lone Pine – Kanli Sirt, 'Bloody Ridge',

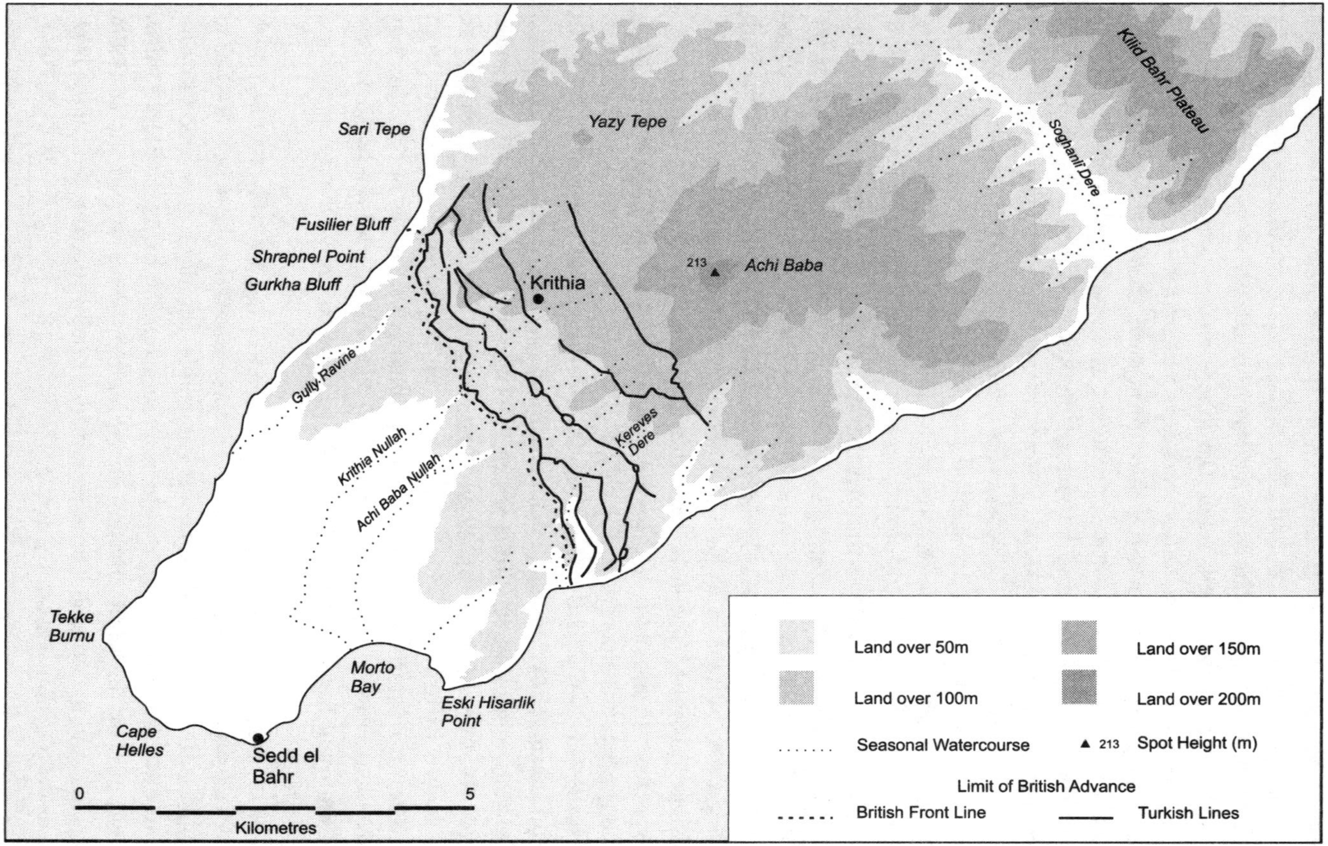

20 *Gallipoli: The Cape Helles Positions*

Kilid Bahr Plateau

Soghanli Dere

Yazy Tepe

213 ▲ Achi Baba

Sari Tepe

Krithia

Kereves Dere

Fusilier Bluff

Shrapnel Point

Gurkha Bluff

Gully Ravine

Krithia Nullah

Achi Baba Nullah

Morto Bay

Eski Hisarlik Point

Sedd el Bahr

Cape Helles

Tekke Burnu

Land over 50m

Land over 100m

Land over 150m

Land over 200m

Seasonal Watercourse

▲ 213 Spot Height (m)

Limit of British Advance

British Front Line

Turkish Lines

0   Kilometres   5

to the Turks – with a second assault planned on German Officer's Trench to the north at around midnight. If all went well, this was to be followed the next morning by an assault on the area further north, at Johnston's Jolly. The Australian lines were no more than 150m from the Lone Pine positions, and since the assault was to be made over a front just 200m wide, and enfiladed on both sides, some of the troops would advance through tunnels dug forward from the vicinity of a strongpoint known as the Pimple.

Just 28 guns were available for the preliminary bombardment, supplemented by the cruiser *Bacchante* and monitors firing on the Turkish batteries north of Gaba Tepe. However, so small was the target area that they were reasonably effective, the heavy timbers covering of the Turkish trenches being destroyed in some places, and some wire cut. The bombardment lifted at 1730, and the troops erupted from their trenches. By 1800 it was clear that the operation had penetrated to the heart of the Turkish defences; the fighting had been hand-to-hand, however, and casualties were heavy. That evening it was decided that the secondary operation to take Johnston's Jolly should be abandoned, and the units earmarked for it used to consolidate the gains at Lone Pine instead (the attempt to take German Officer's Trench went ahead but was repulsed[13]). It was as well the extra troops were on hand, for the battle was far from over, and throughout the night and for the next two days the Turks counterattacked repeatedly though fruitlessly; it was 12 August before it became clear that the Australians had emerged the victors.

The action was not just a local success, but also achieved its wider strategic aim, for both regiments of the Turkish 5th Division in reserve at Koja Dere were rushed forward to bolster the defences during the night of 6 August, and were thus absent when the attack on the Sari Bair ridge was launched. In fact, the Australians may actually have been too successful in that respect, for even after the 5th Division had been committed, Esad Pasha still feared a breakthrough, and ordered up two more regiments, from the 9th Division located south of Gaba Tepe. Their commander, Col. Kannengeisser, arrived with an advance guard during the early hours of 7 August, and his intervention was to be crucial.

The main advance from Anzac onto the Sari Bair ridge was timed to begin as soon as the Turks began committing men to fend off the attack at Lone Pine. The advancing forces would be under the command of the New Zealand and Australian Division's commander, Maj.-Gen. Godley; in addition to his own men he would have the 3rd Australian Light Horse Brigade, the 39th and 40th Brigades from the 13th Division, plus one battalion (the 6th South Lancashire) and its pioneers, the 8th Welch, and the Indian 29th Infantry and Mountain Artillery Brigades; in all that amounted to around 20,000 men.

They would be split into two components. The Right Assaulting Column would itself split to follow the lines of Sazli Beit Dere and Chailak Dere and then recombine to approach the Chunuk Bair summit by way of Rhodo-dendron Spur. The Left Assaulting Column would hug the coast to a point north of Bauchop's Hill then round Walden Point, following the line of Aghyl Dere; it would then split into two, the 4th Australian Brigade crossing Damakjelik Spur and Azma Dere and approaching Hill 971 by way of Abdul Rahman Spur, while the Indian Brigade headed east for Hill Q.

Each Assaulting Column was to have its own Covering Force, which would clear and hold the lower 'foothills'; that on the right would deal with Destroyer Hill, Table Top and the adjacent Old No. 3 Post, and Bauchop's Hill, while that on the left would occupy Damakjelik Bair beyond Walden Point and then advance to link up with the right flank of IX Corps when it landed. The Covering Forces – around two thousand men strong each – were to move out as soon as darkness fell on 6 August, and were expected to have taken their objectives by 2230. The Right Covering Force was successful in taking its objectives but was delayed in doing so both by the terrain and by enemy action. In particular the Turkish post on Bauchop's Hill was only taken – and then at considerable cost – just before 0100. The Left Covering Force made only slightly better time, and was in position by 0030.

The New Zealanders of the Right Assaulting Column (Brig.-Gen. Johnston) postponed their start until 2330; the main body was then further delayed by having to clear an unnoticed Turkish detachment off Table Top, while the Canterbury Battalion lost its way. When the main column reached the rendezvous point, 1,200m short of the summit of Chunuk Bair, there were no Turks in sight. However, there was no sign of the men from Canterbury either, and the brigadier was unwilling to proceed without them. The coming of daylight did not reveal them, and by then the chances of taking the high ground easily were rapidly receding.

The Left Assaulting Column (Maj.-Gen. Cox) moved off at 2300 and almost immediately its advanced guard bumped into the rearguard of the covering force. Monash's Australians then took a wrong turning and ended up in Taylor's Gap, which was home to Turkish snipers and proved to be very hard going. By daybreak on 7 August the leading units of the brigade had progressed no further than a knoll atop Damakjelik Spur, and still had to descend, cross Azma Dere and climb Abdul Rahman Spur before they would even come in clear sight of their objective, Hill 971. By then, the Indian Brigade, deprived of many of its officers by sniper fire, was equally lost. It had managed to follow the planned route during the early part of its march, but before dawn one unit after another took a wrong turning, and daybreak found the scattered companies well short of Hill Q. The actual losses were not heavy in either Assault Column, but by daybreak, at just after 0400, the men were capable of no more and many simply slumped to the ground and fell asleep where they were, exhausted.

*

Though it was known at Birdwood's headquarters that both columns had fallen well behind schedule, it was not clear just how badly. In particular, the position of the New Zealanders, whose advance from Chunuk Bair on to Battleship Hill was to be supported by an assault on Baby 700, was unknown. Birdwood was thus put into a very difficult situation: was he to allow the supporting attack – which was almost certain to be very costly indeed – to go ahead, even though the New Zealanders who were to make the second jaw of the pincer might well be absent, or did he halt it, even though those New Zealanders might be depending on it?

Baby 700 was the most strongly held portion of the entire Turkish defensive position at Anzac, with several lines of trenches across its steep slope; the only direct access to it was by way of the narrow confines of the Nek, and there the Turks held two lines of trenches across its southern end, closest to the Australian positions on Russell's Top, just twenty to sixty metres away, and had it covered by at least five machine guns firing from elevated positions on the hill above. If the Baby 700 positions were not under simultaneous attack from above, any attempt to break out over the Nek would be almost certain to fail at the cost of the lives of the majority of the men committed to it. Nevertheless, such was the potential advantage to be gained if the assault were successful that Birdwood decided it should go ahead.

The principal problem in launching an assault over the Nek was the impossibility of getting enough attackers into the combat zone to overwhelm the defence. The area in front of the Turkish first-line defences was no more than sixty metres wide, flanked by precipitous falls; at best that would accommodate around 150 men, shoulder to shoulder, and such numbers in such confines would not last minutes when confronted by even a pair of well-handled machine guns. The task was allotted to six hundred men from the 8th and 10th Light Horse Regiments, who would attack in four waves, the assault to be preceded by a thirty-minute artillery bombardment. Probably due to a failure to synchronise watches, the bombardment ceased a few minutes too early,[14] and that gave the Turks the time they needed to get back up onto their firesteps. When the first Australians emerged from their trenches they were cut down virtually to a man; the second wave set off two minutes later and was treated in much the same fashion. Seeing the destruction, the commander of the third wave protested to the battalion commander that to send it would be madness. He met with agreement, and the lieutenant-colonel rushed back to brigade headquarters to make the case for abandoning the operation; he was told that men had been seen on the Turkish parapet and must be supported, that the third wave of men must go ... They met the same fate as their fellows, and in the confusion, with the battalion commander still at brigade headquarters, the left wing of the fourth wave – composed this time of men armed with no more than picks and shovels; it was to have been their task to transform the Turkish trenches into defensive positions facing the other way – followed. Within minutes the very few survivors were crawling back the way they had come.

Simultaneously, three diversionary attacks had been mounted, in the left branch of Monash Gully, below the Nek; on Dead Man's Ridge and the Chessboard, and from Quinn's Post. All three met opposition like that at the Nek; many men who survived owed their lives to the fact that they were hit as they climbed over the parapet and fell back wounded into their own trenches.

In all, the cost was over 50 per cent of the total of 1,250 men committed, and it was all for nothing, for the New Zealanders who were supposed to have been advancing from Chunuk Bair to Battleship Hill were still over a kilometre away from their initial objective, on Rhododendron Spur.

In fact, Johnston waited until 0630 for his missing Canterburys, then detached the Otago Battalion to occupy abandoned Turkish trenches on the northern shoulder of Rhododendron Spur, overlooking the Farm, and ordered the Auckland and Wellington Battalions to advance towards the Apex, a rocky hummock, with a similar feature known as the Pinnacle about 100m beyond. Past that lay the Chunuk Bair ridge, rising to the left of the summit. The leading men reached the Apex at around 0730 and came under fire from the ridge, where Kannengeisser had arrived just half an hour earlier with two staff officers to find a small Turkish detachment asleep to a man. The German had barely a score of rifles at his command, but they were enough to halt the New Zealanders' advance.

A personal reconnaissance by a battalion commander brought back the opinion that further progress was impossible without reinforcements and artillery; the brigade-major supported him, and Johnston accepted the view. He reported to Godley, who told him he would order a brief artillery bombardment in which available warships would participate; it would cease at 1030, and he was then to advance on the ridge. Johnston was not at all optimistic, but at that moment two companies of Gurkhas, hopelessly lost, appeared on the northern slopes of the spur and offered to put themselves under his command; he assigned them to assist the Auckland Battalion in the assault.

Long before it began the main body of Kannengeisser's men had arrived and taken up defensive positions. When the artillery bombardment (which was of necessity widely dispersed) lifted, and the assault began, it was met by very heavy rifle and machine gun fire; few men got as far even as the Pinnacle. Further action was halted until nightfall.

Further north, the men of Cox's column, who had had an even more arduous approach march, were clearly in no fit state to resume their advance on Hill 971, and as early as 0800 any thought of trying to make further progress that day had been abandoned. Instead, Godley decided to commit some of his reserves (Cayley's newly arrived 39th Brigade) to an assault on the northern shoulder of Chunuk Bair and Hill Q, and ordered them moved up from their position at No. 3 Post to Cox's headquarters in the valley of the Aghyl Dere. From that location the New Zealanders on Rhododendron Spur were out of sight, and Cayley, when he received his orders at 1100, did not know that Johnston's efforts to reach the ridge south of the summit of Chunuk Bair had failed. He set out on a personal reconnaissance of the spur and was surprised to find the New Zealanders lying there, leaving no room for his own men; that left him no alternative but to advance up the bed of Aghyl Dere and try to take Chunuk Bair from the west, by way of the Farm. However, when he returned to Cox's headquarters, where he expected to find his brigade, he discovered that through some misunderstanding all four battalions had been marched off south towards Chailak Dere; he sent runners after them to call them back, but it was late afternoon before they returned (and the 7th Gloucesters never did; they linked up with the New Zealanders instead). Thus 'the 7th August ended with nothing done', as Aspinall-Oglander noted laconically.

Though twenty-four hours – and surprise – had been lost, Godley still believed that he had an advantageous position and could translate that into a victory. At 1800 he began to set out orders for a renewed offensive the next day. Objectives were unchanged. Johnston, who was to keep the Gloucesters and gain the Maori contingent of the New Zealand force (two companies), the Auckland Mounted Rifles and the 8th Welch, was to make renewed efforts to take Chunuk Bair from the south, while Cox, with the 4th Australian Brigade, the Indian Brigade and the 39th Brigade (with the 6th South Lancashires replacing the Gloucesters; the remainder of the 38th Brigade was to move up to No. 3 Post and become the column's reserve), was to take Hill Q and Hill 971 while approaching Chunuk Bair by way of its northern slopes. They would face 7,000 defenders

For his renewed advance in the early hours of 8 August, Cox had thirteen battalions at his disposal, and he organised them into four columns. Command of the most powerful – comprising the 4th Australian Brigade and the 6th King's Own – he gave to Monash, with instructions to take Hill 971 by way of the Abdul Rahman Spur. He opted to employ the 14th, 15th and 16th Battalions, and keep the 13th and the King's Own back in support. Unfortunately, his line was drawn up at least 800m back from the position it was supposed to be occupying, the advance was further compromised by its 0300 start being delayed by half an hour, and dawn was already beginning to break as his troops breasted the skyline before them. They came under fire from at least four machine guns, and the 14th and 15th Battalions took large numbers of casualties. The 16th, coming up in support, was able to provide some covering fire, and eventually all three formations were able to retire to their start line.

Of the other columns, the individual units of those destined for Chunuk Bair and the northern summit of Hill Q were actually too scattered to ever have been said to form cohesive units, and it seems that they made little attempt to advance on their objectives. Those ordered to take the southern peak of Hill Q made some progress, though the 1/6th Gurkhas, more used to mountain fighting, far outstripped the other two battalions (of the 39th Brigade) and were soon isolated. The Gurkhas' commanding officer, Lt.-Col. Allanson, waited in vain for additional troops to appear, and then, at around 0800, set out to take the objective with just his own battalion. They came under heavy fire about a hundred metres below the crest of the ridge, and Allanson personally went back down to look for reinforcements. He found a company of the 7th North Staffords and some men from the 6th South Lancashires, and the enlarged force was able to make thirty metres' more progress before they were pinned down. They spent the rest of the day on the hillside, and after dark advanced within thirty metres of the crest and dug in.

Over on Rhododendron Spur, after the tragedy of the previous evening,[15] the events of 8 August went somewhat more favourably, though at huge cost. Johnston put his Gloucesters on the left, the Wellington Battalion in the centre and the Welshmen on the right, detailing the Aucklanders and the Maoris to follow up in support and leaving the Otago men to hold the Apex position. So narrow was the spur past the Pinnacle that the men were forced to advance in columns, and could only spread out as they approached the ridge above. Zero hour was set for 0330, and the men steeled themselves for a repeat of the previous day's carnage as they set off. To the amazement of all concerned, not a shot greeted them as they climbed the last slope and breasted the ridge; the defenders had disappeared. We can do worse than leave it to Aspinall-Oglander to describe the scene:

> The men were in high spirits. Away on their right the growing daylight was showing up the paths and tracks in rear of the enemy's lines at Anzac, now at last outflanked. Straight to their front were the shining waters of the narrows – the goal of the expedition. Victory seemed very near.
>   But the triumph was short-lived …

That same growing daylight soon showed them up to the Turks holding Battleship Hill on the right and Hill Q on the left, and they began pouring fire into their positions. Somehow, enfiladed from both sides and being able to dig no more than scrapes in the rocky ground, they saw out the morning; the Turks kept up the pressure throughout the day, and only as night began to fall were the Otago Battalion and two squadrons from the Wellington Mounted Rifles able to come forward and assist in consolidating the position.

By that evening, Godley was rapidly running out of both time and inspiration, the optimism he had briefly felt when told that Johnston's column had secured a foothold on the Chunuk Bair ridge having dissipated when he learned of the failure to make any progress elsewhere. It had been hoped that by now the troops who had landed at Suvla would be making a positive contribution, drawing in Turks to their own battle and reducing the numbers available at Sari Bair, but that had not so far taken effect. He had no alternative but to rely on his own resources, increasingly meagre as they were, and ordered existing positions held at all costs, and a fresh attack at dawn, committing the last of his available reserves to what would almost certainly be a final effort to establish a commanding position on Chunuk Bair and Hill Q and abandoning, at least for the moment, any attempt to take Hill 971.

Those reserves consisted of five New Army battalions under the command of Brig.-Gen. Baldwin. He was to advance up the northern shoulder of Chunuk Bair, take the summit and then stand ready to support the advance by Cox's 39th and Indian Brigades on Hill Q. Johnston in the meantime was to advance on the southern shoulder of Chunuk Bair and then extend his line southwards towards Battleship Hill. Once again all available ships and artillery would join in a preparatory bombardment, scheduled to last for forty-five minutes from 0430. Baldwin had no knowledge of the terrain, and was reliant on the opinion of others even as to which route to take. Godley advised advancing by way of Rhododendron Spur as far as the Apex and the Pinnacle and then angling left for the summit; Johnston was of a different mind, and suggested he advance along Chailak Dere, cross Cheshire Ridge into the valley of the Aghyl Dere, and then approach the summit by way of the Farm. Godley failed to turn up at a meeting called to settle the matter, and Baldwin took Johnston's advice.

Baldwin's column assembled halfway up Chailak Dere, and when darkness fell on 8 August it moved off to begin the ascent of Cheshire Ridge. Before long its cohesion had largely disappeared, its progress interrupted by crowds of wounded men going in the opposite direction. Worse was to come. Around midnight the guides – provided by Johnston from the ranks of his New Zealanders – took a wrong turning; it soon proved to be a dead-end and there was nothing for it but to retire and try again. Daybreak found the men strung out over several kilometres of Aghyl Dere, many of them already exhausted from the strenuous activity after weeks of idleness, far short of what should have been their start line for the assault on Chunuk Bair, and with no hope of reaching it in time to join in what was to have been a concerted rush. It was gone 0600 when Baldwin's column began to advance across the small plateau where stood the Farm, and by that time the Turks had the position covered by fire. Progress was impossible, and Baldwin ordered his men to retreat and dig in.

In the event, since the majority of Cox's and Johnston's troops had been instructed not to set off until Baldwin's arrived, the vital moments following the cessation of the bombardment saw no movement save on the extreme left, where Allanson's mixed force of Staffords, Lancastrians and Gurkhas had passed the night within thirty metres of the Turkish line. Allanson had received notice of the intended attack, but no further orders. Now, as the time for it came and was in danger of slipping away, he decided once more to take matters into his own hands, and ordered his men forward. He timed his rush to perfection. The men reached the ridge itself just as the defenders began to emerge from their shelters, and drove them back in hand-to-hand fighting, gaining a precarious foothold. Moments later disaster struck as a rain of artillery shells began to fall among them,[16] and they were forced back to the positions they had occupied overnight. There they remained all day, fighting off occasional attempts to dislodge them, waiting for support to come up on their right in order to make another attempt to take the ridge. None came, and the next morning they were ordered to retire.

On the left flank, Monash's column had passed the night on Damakjelik Spur, not far to the east of the 4th South Wales Borderers which, with the 5th Wiltshires (withdrawn to join Baldwin's column), had formed the Left Covering Force, and had been in position there since the early hours of 7 August. The Borderers' presence had not gone unnoticed, and Liman von Sanders had formed the impression that the battalion was the spearhead of those which had landed south of Nibrunesi Point, and was probably tasked with advancing on Hill 971. He had taken steps to counter that (and any other attempt the recently landed troops might make to advance into the Azmak Dere/Anafarta Gap), having finally called up two reserve divisions from Bulair, the 7th and the 12th.[17] The 12th would advance along the north side of the valley, the 7th along the south, a path which would bring them into head-on confrontation with Monash's column and the South Wales Borderers. The clash came soon after dawn on 9 August, the Turkish 7th Division moving onto the Damakjelik Spur with four battalions up and two in support. Defensive positions to their rear, on Abdul Rahman Spur, co-operated, and the Australian right took heavy casualties from enfilading machine gun fire at a range of around a kilometre. The main body put up stout resistance, however, and the Turkish attack was driven off, as was a second that evening.

By around 0700 on 9 August it had become clear to Birdwood and Godley that the attempt to take the Sari Bair Ridge had failed fairly dismally. The only glimmers of light were Allanson's grim attempt to hold on to his gains on Hill Q (which, since support could not be sent to him, he would soon be ordered to relinquish) and Johnston's tenure of the area on the ridge below Chunuk Bair.

In strategic terms, Birdwood's overall plan was to be criticised later for having been too ambitious. Had he restricted himself to his original objective – Chunuk Bair – and not expanded his operation to Hill Q and Hill 971, there was a very much greater chance that the plan would have worked. There was no great advantage to be had, his critics would argue, by expanding the plan to include the higher northern peak. It is a criticism difficult to refute. On the other hand, his decision to go ahead with the assault across the Nek was correct under the circumstances. He had no way of knowing that an entire brigade was not poised to descend on the Turks from above and depending on that diversion to give them an even chance of taking their objective. That said, the events on the Nek, in particular, were to have a long-term effect on the Australian soldier, and reduce his previous readiness to expose himself willingly – some would say, far too rashly – to murderous fire.

One of the many imponderables relating to the Dardanelles/Gallipoli campaign is how the Sari Bair offensive would have played out if its essential missing component – support from the large force landed at Suvla Bay – had been present. That force certainly drew in Turkish reinforcements, but that did not materially affect the situation on Sari Bair. More important, given the nature of the terrain over which the men who tried to take the ridge had to fight, was their physical condition.[18] In any event, since the Suvla landings and the operations thereafter were little more than a farce, thanks largely to the incompetence of the men charged with directing them, such speculation is doubly idle.

To recapitulate briefly: the outline plan was straightforward. Land a superior force under cover of darkness and use it to strike a swift killing blow on an unsuspecting enemy known to be present in only relatively small numbers at just a few scattered locations, then take the surrounding high ground and hold it while pushing hard on the right to support the simultaneous attempt to break through to the summits of the Sari Bair ridge. Hamilton, with the experience of two opposed landings under his belt, believed he could get an entire division, with limited artillery,[19] ashore in six hours, with a further two brigades and more substantial artillery, including the all-important howitzers and 60-pounders, to follow. Unfortunately, what should have been an extremely aggressive operation turned into what can only be called a timid, leisurely one, with disastrous results.

In terms of the organisation of the invasion fleet, if nothing else, the lessons on Helles and Anzac had been well assimilated. Far more attention was paid to detail, and – at last – specialist landing craft, powered by oil engines and fitted with armoured shields capable of stopping small-arms fire, were available.[20] These 'beetles' – they were painted black, and the arms from which their bow ramps were lowered were thought to resemble antennae – could carry around five hundred men each; the eleven which had been brought out to the Aegean could comfortably accommodate a brigade at a time. That would still not be sufficient to transport all the men to be landed in the first wave at Suvla, but it would give them at least a fighting chance, were the landings to be opposed. The other noteworthy differences in procedure were that horses and mules were to be landed in significant numbers with the second wave, and that work would begin almost immediately on the construction of an ad hoc port in Suvla Bay, the 1st Australian Bridging Train being landed for the purpose early on 7 August.

*

Just after 2130 on the evening of 6 August ten destroyers, each towing a 'beetle' alongside and a picket boat astern, crept towards the landing beaches, making as little noise as possible as they dropped anchor five hundred metres off. In all they carried over ten thousand men, three thousand destined for A Beach in Suvla Bay itself, the rest for B Beach, south of Nibrunesi Point. At the latter, the four battalions the lighters carried were ashore within thirty minutes, having met no real resistance save for odd rounds of rifle fire; the two on the right – the 7th South Staffs and the 9th Sherwood Foresters from the 33rd Brigade (Brig.-Gen. Maxwell) – immediately extended forward and began to entrench and occupy a defensive line from the sea shore to that of the salt lake, while those on the left, from the 32nd Brigade (Brig.-Gen. Haggard), set off to clear the area as far as the Cut, the channel linking the sea with the lake at its northern extremity, before making contact with the 34th Brigade which was to have landed north of it. The 6th Yorkshires, who like the rest of the division had never seen combat before, took Lala Baba at some cost, but then took up defensive positions instead of pushing on, and were joined in them by the 9th West Yorkshires and subsequently the rest of the brigade.

Sitwell's 34th Brigade had in the meantime run into trouble not of its own making. When the three destroyers carrying the men dropped anchor in line abreast around 500m out from Suvla beach they were a thousand metres south of where they should have been; instead of a clear run in to the beach well to the north of the Cut, the landing craft carrying the first two battalions were faced with a reef. Only one made it all the way to the beach; the others ran aground on the rocks and shoals and either disgorged men in water up to their chests, or waited for smaller craft to assist them, and it was well after midnight before the last men were ashore. Disoriented, the 9th Lancashire Fusiliers failed to locate Hill 10 (which in consequence was still in Turkish hands when the transports entered Suvla Bay after daybreak), while their sister-battalion, the 11th Manchesters, following earlier orders, disappeared into the night heading for Suvla Point (and would then turn to advance along the Kiretch Tepe ridge; they proceeded for three kilometres, then dug in, still not in contact with a formed body of enemy troops). The second wave arrived in penny packets – save for two companies of the Dorsets, which came under accurate shellfire and were diverted to B Beach – the last of them at 0500, and remained on or near the beach while their brigadier prevaricated his way into total inactivity.

Hammersley arrived at B Beach at 0045 and set up his headquarters there. He later moved to within 500m of the Lala Baba position, but not until about 0440 did he learn that the 32nd Brigade had advanced no further than Lala Baba, and that the 34th Brigade was held up short of Hill 10. He ordered Haggard to push his men forward to assist Sitwell; when he reached the 34th Brigade's HQ near the Cut at around 0600, he found chaos, many hundreds of men milling around with no idea of what they were supposed to be doing.

There was some good news, however: Hill 10 had at last been located, and appeared to be lightly held, and it fell soon after to a converging attack from two and a half battalions.

If Hammersley had only minimal information, he was much better informed than his corps commander, who was still aboard his floating head-quarters, HMS *Jonquil*, anchored since midnight just inside Suvla Bay. Stopford was not in touch with the shore (there were no naval signallers ashore until the morning), and at no time did he send to learn how matters were progressing. Indeed, he and Rear.-Adm. Christian, the naval commander, had assumed that all was going according to plan and that, since there had been very little shooting, the landing had been largely unopposed. They then retired, and were woken only at 0400, when Capt. Unwin – in charge of landing craft operations from the naval side, who *had* been ashore, both at B Beach and in Suvla Bay, and had seen the chaotic situation at the latter for himself – came aboard and reported.

His arrival was timely, for six battalions of the 10th Division were even then approaching the bay (this was the 31st Brigade, plus two battalions of Royal Dublin Fusiliers from the 30th), and it had been the intention that they should go ashore on A Beach. In the light of Unwin's report Stopford ordered them landed at C Beach, further down the coast from Nibrunesi Point,[21] instead and instructed the senior officer (Brig.-Gen. Hill) to put himself under Hammersley's command until his own divisional commander, Lt.-Gen. Mahon, arrived from Mudros with the rest of the 30th Brigade. In the event of him failing to find Hammersley he was to march on the Kiretch Tepe ridge by way of Hill 10. Even as Hill was preparing to disembark his men, Cmdr. Keyes, de Roebeck's chief of staff, arrived with the news that a safe landing place did indeed exist south of Suvla Point, but Stopford refused to vary Hill's orders. However, when Mahon arrived, while Hill's men were en route to C Beach, he *was* ordered to land the other two battalions at this new location north of A Beach, then to advance along Kiretch Tepe, to be joined by Hill's detachment once they had marched the seven kilometres from C Beach.

Hill's battalions were just starting to come ashore, at around 0800, when Hammersley heard from one of Maxwell's battalion commanders that patrols had encountered Turkish troops on Chocolate Hill, which perhaps jogged his memory with regard to the original emphasis of his instructions. What followed was a classic case of 'order, counter-order, disorder', as he began to issue a series of mutually contradictory directives for an attack on the Chocolate and W Hills. Sitwell became so befuddled that he preferred to do nothing at all, citing the priorities in Hammersley's original order and the overriding need to protect the beachhead, while Hill and Haggard did their best to make sense of the new instructions and immediately discovered that they were impossible to reconcile, one with the other. Unfortunately, Hammersley had named Sitwell as the commander of the operation, which effectively tied Haggard's and Hill's hands. Hill, whose reading of his orders was that the two objectives were to be attacked simultaneously, and who believed the resources were not adequate to the task, saw nothing for it but to return to divisional headquarters and seek clarification, even though that would mean a considerable further delay. He arrived there at around midday to be told by a staffer that his reading was correct, and was referred to Hammersley, who had gone to the top of Lala Baba to watch the action. When he got there, Hammersley told him that he had sent his chief of staff (Lt.-Col. Malcolm) to Sitwell's HQ to explain matters and that he should rejoin his men, for the advance was to start at once.

When Malcolm arrived at Sitwell's headquarters he found 'a sorry situation', which was compounded by Haggard being seriously wounded by shellfire minutes later. Sitwell declared that his priority was to protect the beachhead, and that he could spare none of the (perhaps thousands) of men now gathered there for offensive action. He and Malcolm argued for some time, but Sitwell was obdurate.

Hill established his own headquarters near the Cut, and in accordance with the most recent of Hammersley's orders, deployed three battalions in line extending north-east from that corner of the salt lake to advance on the Chocolate Hills; the leftmost, the 5th Royal Irish Fusiliers, was harassed by artillery fire from Turkish positions at Baka Baba, west of Anafarta Sagir, and there was no sign of units of the 32nd Brigade, which were to have covered that flank. He went to Sitwell and asked him once more to commit troops in his support; Sitwell told him he would send him two battalions, but it was clear that there would be no urgency about their deployment. He informed Hammersley of this at 1500, and Hammersley now changed his mind yet again, and issued another executive order. The current advance was to be suspended, and would be resumed at 1730; this time the objective was to be the Chocolate Hills only, and the assault was to be mounted by three battalions of the 31st Brigade and two battalions of the 33rd which would come up on their right, the advance to be supported 'by all troops of the 32nd and 34th Brigades which have not suffered heavy casualties', whatever that meant. Artillery support was to be provided by all available ships, and by the three batteries – two of mountain guns, one of 18-pounders – now ashore at Lala Baba. Sitwell was to command overall, and the COs of the 31st, 32nd and 33rd Brigades were to report to him for orders.

This reached its addressees at 1510, Hill and Sitwell agreed that it was too late to stop the advance then in progress, but that made little difference, for it had been halted anyway. It picked up again at around 1700, by which time the two battalions of the 33rd had advanced – across the salt lake – to join the line. The attack lost, then regained, impetus once more, and though the ships had ceased firing as the sun went down beyond Imbros, the batteries on shore continued to do so. Under this shrapnel umbrella the assault troops started up the slopes of the Chocolate Hills, the Irishmen of the 31st Brigade to the fore on the left, the 6th Lincolns and the 6th Borderers on the right. Just as darkness descended they took their objectives; the majority of the Turks withdrew, but a stubborn rearguard held on until the end. The five battalions engaged in the assault became intermingled and the situation confused; as a result no attempt was made to pursue the retreating enemy, nor even to send out patrols to locate his position. Upwards reporting was lax, too. It would be 0100 on 8 August – when Hill moved his headquarters to Chocolate Hill – before Hammersley was informed that it had fallen, and 0800 before he knew that Green Hill was in British hands too.

Progress on the left at Suvla Bay was no more rapid. The three battalions of the 10th Division finally landed at A Beach were not all ashore until late afternoon, due mostly to the refusal of fairly senior officers to use their own initiative; they were then sent off along the Keritch Tepe ridge to find the 11th Manchesters, who had held positions there since early that morning. With no specific objective, on taking over from the Manchesters (who then went back into reserve to join what was still a sizeable pool of unemployed men near Sitwell's headquarters) they extended to right and left athwart the ridge but made no attempt to push on towards the Turkish line, about 700m away, which was held by a quarter their number.

As the clock ticked down to the end of the first day, the British invasion of Suvla Bay could be fairly said to have been something of a shambles. Against perhaps fifteen hundred Turks the 10th and 11th Divisions had lost more than that number of their own, virtually all of them to well-aimed long-range rifle fire, and had failed abjectly in their objective of taking the Tekke Tepe ridge and the Anafarta Spur and its outliers, and securing the Suvla plain.

The landing of animals, guns and supplies, especially water, had been no more efficiently handled. Save for the two batteries of mountain guns and one of 18-pounders landed early on, no more artillery was landed on 7 August, though a total of fifty-six guns and howitzers had been promised by that evening; just 50 of almost a thousand mules had been landed; very few serviceable wells had been located, and supplies of drinking water were running short before midday everywhere save at B and C Beaches, where there was an abundant supply (in lighters) which was not properly distributed.

Early on the morning of 8 August Stopford received reports from his two divisional commanders; both told him their fronts were quiet, Mahon on the basis of not having heard differently from Brig.-Gen. Nicol on Kiretch Tepe, Hammersley because he had been told by both Hill and Sitwell that nothing more could be accomplished until their men had rested; he told Sitwell to move some of the men off the beach and send them inland to occupy a line from Nicol's position to Green Hill, but no more than that.[22] Stopford's greatest concern now, it seems, was to see stores and supplies landed, and he had no intention of ordering a further advance until they were, even though he knew full well that he probably had no more than twelve hours, certainly no more than twenty-four, in which to establish a defensive ring taking in the Tekke Tepe ridge as far as the crest, and the entire Suvla Plain, and linking up with Birdwood's extreme left.

Post-war reports from Turkish sources reveal just how thin were the defences at this point: three companies of gendarmes on Kiretch Tepe; no troops at all on the Tekke Tepe ridge south to Baka Baba,[23] and around eleven hundred men, plus five mountain guns, between the latter and the W Hills.[24] On the way were three battalions sent as an advance guard from Bulair, and a machine gun detachment, four guns, which had just arrived at Anafarta Sagir. Aggressive patrolling, even, would have revealed these deficiencies (and a general advance would simply have walked through the Turkish defences to its objective). Some time after 1100, when he received a report from GHQ that aerial reconnaissance had failed to detect Turkish troops east of Tekke Tepe, Stopford at last ordered a move forwards, but only 'if you find the ground lightly held by the enemy ... in view of want of adequate artillery support I do not want you to attack an entrenched position held in strength'. Both his divisional commanders promptly latched on to that latter, imagining systematic defensive positions where, largely, none existed, and reacted accordingly by ordering that no advance was to be made.

Stopford made his next report to GHQ at around noon, saying 'Heavy fighting yesterday and unavoidable delay landing artillery make me consider it inadvisable to call on troops to attack a strongly entrenched position without adequate support.' Hamilton received the signal an hour later, and finally a suspicion that all was perhaps not quite well stirred in him. He decided to go to Suvla to see the situation for himself, and ordered up the destroyer de Roebeck had put at his disposal for just such eventualities, to be told that she was unserviceable (inexplicably, her fires had been drawn, and it would take six to seven hours to get steam up), and that no other ship would be available until the evening to carry him from Imbros.

He did have eyes at the scene, however, in the shape of Lt.-Col. Aspinall-Oglander of his own staff, who reached Suvla a little before noon in the company of Lt.-Col. Maurice Hankey, despatched from London to report to the Committee of Imperial Defence, of which he was Secretary.[25] To begin with it seemed to the two men that events must have gone exactly according to plan, for all was quiet, the men resting, and none of the frenetic activity that one would expect to find just behind a fighting front. They were soon to be disabused, and we can hardly do better than quote Hankey's own words from a letter to the Prime Minister on the subject, written on 12 August:

A peaceful scene greeted us. Hardly any shells. No Turks. Very occasional musketry. Bathing parties all around the shore. An entire absence of the expected bustle of a great disembarkation. There seemed to be no real-isation of the overwhelming necessity for a rapid offensive, or the trem-endous issues depending on the next few hours ... As an irresponsible

[sic] critic I don't want to be hard, but I must confess I was filled with dismay, as was the G.S. man [Aspinall-Oglander] whom I accompanied. It was a delicate situation for the latter. His message to the C-in-C had to be sent through the corps commander, and it was difficult for him to send an adequate message. He solved the difficulty by doing it through the Vice-Admiral [de Roebeck] ...

When Aspinall-Oglander, who *did* have some executive responsibility, at least to report his findings to Hamilton, discovered the true extent of the lethargy which seemed to be gripping the entire corps, he set out to do something about it. His first stop was the 11th Division's headquarters, where Hammersley told him his men were exhausted and had suffered heavy casualties, and he had received no orders to move forward (which was not the case, of course; he had simply chosen to interpret them thus). He hoped to move forward again the following morning, when his men were rested and guns had been landed.

His next stop was HMS *Jonquil*, where he found Stopford in confident mood. 'Well, Aspinall,' he greeted him, 'the men have done splendidly and have been magnificent.'

'But they haven't reached the hills, sir,' Aspinall-Oglander protested.

'No,' said Stopford, 'but they are ashore!'

Aspinall-Oglander was now in a precarious position, a lieutenant-colonel having to urge a lieutenant-general into action which he was clearly disinclined to take. He suggested that Hamilton would be disappointed that the high ground had not yet been taken, and begged him to order an immediate advance before Turkish reinforcements arrived on the scene. Stopford replied that he fully understood the urgency of the situation, that there was no time to be lost, but that it was simply impossible to move till the men had been rested and more guns had been put ashore. He would order a further advance the next morning ...

Aspinall-Oglander made his excuses and left, to seek out de Roebeck and a wireless transmitter. 'Just been ashore, where I found it all quiet,' he signalled to Hamilton. 'No rifle fire, no artillery fire, and apparently no Turks. IX Corps resting. Feel confident that golden opportunities are being lost and look upon the situation as serious.' So too did Hamilton. He sent a signal to Stopford telling him there was no evidence that the Turks had constructed defensive positions between the coast (at Ejelmer Bay) and the Anafarta Spur (that is, along the breast of the Tekke Tepe); that the trenches in front of the 11th Division were deserted, and that he faced no more than two battalions (all this information derived from aerial reconnaissance), and pointed out that this state of affairs was unlikely to continue. He also told him he was sending two brigades of the 53rd Division that night.

In the meantime, Stopford had at last set foot ashore, if only briefly. He went in search of Hammersley, intending to instruct to advance at once, but found him absent from his headquarters, and was briefed by staff officers. The divisional commander was even then planning an attack on the W Hills, to take place the next morning, he was told; that apparently satisfied him, and he gave his assent to it and returned to HMS *Jonquil.* There he found Hamilton's most recent signal, and began to prepare an executive order to meet the GOC's requirements: the 11th Division would mount an attack aimed at seizing the sector W Hills–Anafarta Sagir, while the 10th Division would take the high ground from the latter to the sea at Ejelmer Bay. He left the timing of the attack up to his divisional commanders, Mahon to conform to Hammersley, and added no indication of urgency. Hammersley received that order at 1800, and began rewriting his own instructions to Maxwell vis-à-vis the attack on the W Hills to include a second brigade and broaden the objective to take in the Anafarta Spur. He did not advance the timetable.

Hamilton was finally able to hitch a lift to Suvla aboard the rear admiral's yacht *Triad* (but had had even so to await her scheduled departure at 1615). He arrived at 1800, and went straight away to consult de Roebeck and be briefed by Aspinall-Oglander. He then crossed over to *Jonquil,* where he was greeted by Stopford with assurances that everything was in hand, that he intended to resume the advance the next morning at a time to be fixed by Hammersley. That, said Hamilton, would not do; could not Hammersley advance at once to take Tekke Tepe? He did not consider a night attack feasible, replied Stopford. Then he would talk to Hammersley himself, said Hamilton. Stopford excused himself from accompanying him – his knee was paining him, after his exertions of the afternoon, he said – and Hamilton left. Stopford immediately sent a personal signal to Hammersley, warning him of the GOC's impending arrival and telling him to be prepared to move at the earliest possible moment.

Hammersley was reading that signal when Hamilton arrived at his headquarters. Advance immediately, Hamilton told him. Impossible to get the men moving before 0800 the next morning, Hammersley replied. Hamilton insisted; even a small force might suffice ... Surely he could do *something* ... Hammersley still resisted. His units were scattered ... No reconnaissance had been carried out ... The terrain was difficult ... The troops were inexperienced ... It was seven o'clock already ...

Hamilton would have none of it. Risks must be accepted and the bold course pursued ... The need was urgent and the moment critical ... The fate of the campaign rested on the events of the next few hours ... Eventually Hammersley conceded that the 32nd Brigade, which he believed was now concentrated near Sulajik (a point north of Scimitar Hill, a long rifle-shot west of Baka Baba), might be able to do something ... 'Then order at least one battalion of it to be at the top of the ridge by daylight,' Hamilton told him. Hammersley agreed, and scribbled an order to Minogue, who had succeeded Haggard, to advance immediately in the sector Anafarta Sagir–Kavak Tepe, one battalion – 'the pioneers,' Hammersley added, as an afterthought, apparently believing them to be fresher than the rest[26] – to be atop Tekke Tepe by dawn.

The orders reached Minogue at 1900, and he immediately sent runners to each of his battalion commanders with instructions to concentrate on Sulajik by 2230. Had he but known it, two of his battalions were actually already better placed than that, the 9th West Yorkshires being a thousand metres east of there, and the 6th East Yorkshires – the pioneers in question; they had been substituted for the 6th Yorkshires, much depleted at Lala Baba, which had remained in reserve at Hill 10 – being on the northern slope of Scimitar Hill (whence their commanding officer had despatched two reconnaissance patrols onto the Tekke Tepe ridge; they had recently returned with news that it was free of Turks to at least halfway to the crest). The runners sent to the other two battalions – the 8th West Riding and the 6th York and Lancasters – located them easily enough, but those sent to the forward pair got hopelessly lost; it was almost seven hours before the men of the East Yorkshires began to arrive at the rendezvous, and of the 9th West Yorkshires there was still no sign. Minogue delayed two further hours, but at 0330 he gave the order to advance, pioneers to the fore.[27] The men, 'dazed with fatigue,' and spread out over a front 800m wide, took time to respond, and by a little before 0400 only one company of the pioneers had assembled. Conscious of the urgency, their battalion commander, Lt.-Col. Moore, led them forward, leaving orders for the others to follow. They had only a little over three kilometres to cover, but though the hill was not steep the scrub was dense, and the advance soon broke up into small pockets of men fighting their way up narrow goat-paths in single file; dawn came as they climbed, the sun as it rose revealing the crest before them in silhouette.

Unfortunately, it also revealed Turkish troops pouring over the ridge, two battalions, part of the advance guard from Bulair, who had been pushed forward not an hour before. Severely depleted by months of fighting at Helles, they numbered less than a thousand men all told, but they were hardened fighters who knew their business, and were quite up to the task of halting exhausted British novices. Soon the men of the East Yorkshires were in flight, and many were shot down as they scrambled back the way they had come. A desperate call for reinforcements brought up two companies of the 6th York and Lancasters, and the Turks' advance was finally checked short of Sulajik; further reinforcements, from the units Sitwell had earlier sent to form a defensive line south from Kiretch Tepe, filled the gaps, and later in the day the entire 159th Brigade of the 53rd (Welsh) Division,[28] which had come ashore at C Beach overnight, was sent into the line.

Further south, Maxwell's 33rd Brigade had been deployed from Green Hill to Kanli Keupru Dere; its advance towards the Anafarta Spur and the W Hills would take it over Scimitar Hill, which the brigadier believed to be in British hands. He also believed that Tekke Tepe, to his left, would be occupied by the time he was to begin his advance, and that his flank would, in consequence, be covered. He was wrong on both counts. As soon as the 6th Lincolns, on the left, and the 7th S Staffords began to advance they came under heavy fire from small-arms and artillery; the Lincolns fared rather better than the Staffords, and managed to retake the northern end of Scimitar Hill and hold it, despite repeated attempts by the Turks to drive them back. On the right the 6th Border Regiment was making progress in the direction of the W Hills. At around 0500, in response to urgent calls from the Lincolns, Maxwell sent in two battalions of Hill's mixed force from the 10th Division, which he had been holding in reserve; they made a difference to begin with, but by 1000 sufficient Turkish troops had been committed against them to drive them back to the western slopes of Scimitar Hill. By then, Maxwell had received further reinforcements in the shape of half the 160th Brigade, and he sent the 2/4th Queen's to bolster the line; the five battalions now deployed were enough to push forward to the top of the hill once more, but by now fire was spreading across the entire area, and by midday they were forced to retire or be burned alive.

During the afternoon, Maxwell's fourth battalion, the 9th Sherwood Foresters (which had been occupying the entrenched line from B Beach to the edge of the salt lake for the previous forty-eight hours), had been pushing forward in an attempt to link up with the 4th South Wales Borderers from Anzac. Their CO had been told that his advance would be unopposed; that might have been true even twelve hours earlier, but was not now, and they soon ran into the left wing of the Turkish 12th Division, advancing along the northern side of Azmak Dere, and were stopped. They resisted the pressure on them to retire, however, and dug in, preventing the spearhead of the Turkish division from breaking through to the sea.

Away to the north, on the Kiretch Tepe ridge, Nicol had been warned that he would be required to push forward the next morning, as far as the eastern end of the ridge and a prominent point named Kidney Hill. His three battalions would be augmented by two from the 11th Division. There was considerable confusion next morning thanks to the failure of these two infantry elements to co-operate. Eventually Nicol was able to instil some order into the situation, but to little profit; none of his men got closer than long rifle-shot to the enemy positions.

Hamilton was now more concerned than ever at the lack of progress Stopford was making; that evening, now back at Imbros, he wrote to him in no uncertain terms. He questioned 'the want of energy and push displayed by the 11th Division', and contrasted that with the 'dash and self-confidence' that the (equally inexperienced) 13th had shown at Anzac. 'Tell me,' he asked frankly, 'what is wrong with 11th Division? Is it the divisional general or brigadiers or both?'

Stopford received the letter around midnight, and replied before dawn, in terms which were prevaricating, self-excusing and in some instances down-right delusional at one and the same time. His first excuse was the want of water. Next he blamed the men's training – they had not had much in-field manoeuvring, he said, though he heard they were quite well grounded in trench warfare – and the lack of artillery, but exonerated his commanders. 'Given water, guns and ammunition,' he wrote, 'I have no doubt of our being able to secure the hills which are so vital to us, but for a success, more water and adequate artillery are absolutely essential.'

Earlier Braithwaite had written to Stopford suggesting that a force of six to eight battalions under a chosen leader would suffice to take the W Hills and the Anafarta Spur. Stopford chose Lindley to lead nine battalions of his 53rd Division, supported by such artillery as was available. He later added the 33rd Brigade, but when Maxwell was told of the plan, he protested that his brigade could not advance until the 53rd had taken Scimitar Hill for fear of enfilading fire from there taking him in the flank. The promised advance opened at 0600, with the available 18-pounders (one battery on Chocolate Hill, two on Lala Baba) shelling Scimitar Hill. It transpired that Lindley would have only eight battalions at his disposal, and he organised them as two brigades. By midday it was clear that the attack had failed. Stopford, watching from Lala Baba, reported that to Hamilton at 1330, adding that he intended to try again at 1700. In the event, it seems that only two companies of the 2/10th Middlesex actually went forward at 1700; they covered around two hundred metres before they realised they had no support, and promptly returned to their starting point.

Errors of judgement and ill-luck had characterised Birdwood's offensive thus far, and the coda to it was no exception. The New Zealanders on Rhododendron Spur and Chunuk Bair required immediate relief, and the 6th Loyal North Lancashires and the 5th Wiltshires of the 13th Division were ordered to take their place as soon as night fell, the Lancashires to lead and the Wiltshires to follow. It was known that there was room for only one battalion in the front-line positions, but it was thought that the Wiltshires, coming up from the Farm, would have time to dig themselves in before daybreak. However, the order to move reached them[29] so late that it was almost 0300 before they arrived on the slopes of Chunuk Bair; there was no hope of them creating adequate defensive positions in the time available, and they were sent down into the Sazli Beit gully to the south of Rhododendron Spur. These men – new to combat, we should recall – had not slept properly for four days, and they promptly stripped off their equipment, piled their rifles and lay themselves down. In their absence the Chunuk Bair position was held by three companies of Lancashires, with the fourth in reserve at the Pinnacle; they were supported by the remnant of the Wellington Battalion, together with the men of the 6th Leinsters sent in the previous evening, and the machine guns of the New Zealand Infantry Brigade, at the Apex.

Immediately to the north of Rhododendron Spur was a very mixed bag of troops. As well as Baldwin and his staff, the commander of the 29th Brigade (Brig.-Gen. Cooper) and his staff were present too, but chains of command, where they could still be said to exist, were tenuous. 'More confusing still was the jumble of units between the Farm plateau and the right of the 4th Australian Brigade on Damakjelik Spur,' says Aspinall-Oglander. This sector was under Cox's command, his Indian units bolstered by men from Cayley's 39th Brigade, and Cox also had command over Monash's 4th Australian Brigade and the South Wales Borderers beyond them. Like the Wiltshires, the great majority of these men had had no sleep for a prolonged period, and were short of water, rations and ammunition, thanks to the gullies behind, the only lines of communication leading down to the beaches, being crammed with wounded men trying to make their own way to the clearing stations.

The next morning, just before daybreak, the Turks counterattacked. The British observation posts on the Chunuk Bair crest were overrun, and from that commanding position the Turks were able to rain grenades down into the trenches on the reverse slopes. At around 0430 the Turkish artillery joined in, and at 0445 the Turkish infantry came storming over the crest, taking the Pinnacle by sheer weight of numbers but being held there by the New Zealanders' machine guns at the Apex. Control of the Pinnacle allowed the Turks to send men down into the Sazli Beit gully, where the 5th Wiltshires were taken completely by surprise and were shot down or scattered as they struggled to pull themselves together. Meanwhile, Kemal's right wing had descended on the Farm plateau, slowly gaining control of it in prolonged hand-to-hand fighting. Attempts to rally stragglers and walking wounded in the Aghyl Dere gully failed, and by 1000 the plateau was in Turkish hands, with the invaders driven back to Cheshire Ridge.

With that, save for a foray by the 5th Connaught Rangers which recovered many wounded men from the Farm plateau, the Battle of Sari Bair was over. Birdwood had taken over 12,000 casualties and had no more reserves to commit.[30] He had achieved little enough in the four days it had lasted, beyond extending his left onto the Damakjelik Spur (though that did allow him to link up with the Suvla front), and though a salient taking in Cheshire Ridge and Rhododendron Spur as far as the Apex had been created and was held, it was tactically useless, dominated by the Turkish positions on Chunuk Bair. To the south, the ground gained at Lone Pine formed another, smaller, salient, while the situation in the centre, below Baby 700, was unchanged.

At Suvla, Hamilton had one more shot in his locker: the 54th (East Anglian) Division, which he ordered landed that same afternoon, 10 August.[31] He recognised that his only chance of saving the situation rested on gaining control of Tekke Tepe ridge before the Turks were able to bring enough troops into the sector to make it impregnable; that done, he would be able to use a further division promised from Egypt (the 2nd Mounted Division), plus elements of the 29th Division from Helles, to reinforce IX Corps for an attack on the Anafarta Gap, to be made in conjunction with a renewed offensive across the northern slopes of the Sari Bair ridge. As Aspinall-Oglander observed, rather archly, 'A sanguine temperament, indomitable courage and a determination to conquer are invaluable qualities in the character of a commander-in-chief.'

Seven of the 54th's battalions were ashore by nightfall. Hamilton had previously warned Stopford that none was to be used without the specific sanction of GHQ, but characteristically he simply ignored that, and immediately sent six of them off to fill an indeterminate gap in the right of the 10th Division's line. Unfortunately, their guide had only the sketchiest knowledge of the area and no map; he soon declared himself lost, and the men passed the night 'marching and counter-marching' to no purpose save to exhaust themselves. Thus, when orders reached IX Corps from GHQ the next morning that the division was to assault the ridge in the central sector between Anafarta Sagir and Kavak Tepe at dawn on 12 August, following a night advance to the foothills and a move through the 53rd Division's positions, they were greeted with consternation. Stopford reacted by writing to Hamilton, ignoring his proposals entirely and instead blaming the 53rd Division for his failure to press home the offensive the previous day. Hamilton, his opinion of Stopford degrading rapidly, had no option but to delay the advance by twenty-four hours.

Following the failure to take the W Hills and the Anafarta Spur, Stopford had ordered Mahon and Hammersley to create an eight-kilometre-long entrenched defensive line, while at the same time sorting the individual units of their forces and reassembling them into their proper brigades and divisions. The Turks had taken advantage of that to push large numbers of snipers into the thick scrub on the lower slopes of Tekke Tepe, and they now posed a serious threat, so much so as to cause Stopford's staff grave doubts that Lindley's much-depleted 53rd Division – ordered to advance onto the lower slopes during the afternoon of the twelfth so as to reduce the distance the 54th would have to cover after moving through its lines – would prove capable of overcoming them. Stopford voiced those doubts at a planning meeting that morning, and Maj.-Gen. Inglefield, the 54th Division's commander, offered to take the task on himself. Stopford accepted, and it was arranged that the 163rd Brigade would carry out the preliminary operation, advancing some two kilometres from Point 28, north-east of Hill 10, across Kuchuk Anafarta Ova to a line of huts roughly the same distance north of Sulajik, whereupon the 53rd Division would come up and consolidate. After dark, the whole of the 54th would then move through the position, advance on the crest of Tekke Tepe, about four kilometres to the east, and take it before dawn on 13 August.

Hardly was the decision made than Stopford got cold feet and changed his mind. When the orders were actually issued, they covered only the afternoon's advance to the forward position, the jumping-off point for the assault on Tekke Tepe. In a covering letter to Hamilton he added that if all went well, the second stage would proceed directly, but in the event of the 163rd being held up, he proposed to impose yet another twenty-four-hour delay. Hamilton immediately saw that there was little chance of Tekke Tepe falling on 13 August.

The action began with the usual lack of co-ordination between the infantry and the supporting artillery, though in the latter's favour it must be said that no one had thought to provide details even of exactly where the 163rd's start-line was located, let alone the co-ordinates of desirable targets, and firing was wild and ineffective as a result. The advance, timed for 1600, was forty-five minutes late in starting; it began steadily enough, the ground over which the troops had to advance initially being clear, much of it cultivated or given over to grazing. That may have been thought an asset, but it soon became apparent that it was a heavy liability, and by the time the 163rd had covered a kilometre so great were its casualties that it had broken up into isolated groups of men seeking such cover as they could find. As night began to fall, the survivors made their way back to their start-line, which was marked by a sunken cart track. Such officers as were left marshalled the men to occupy it; they were able to find only around eight hundred.

Hamilton passed the night in ignorance of the failure of the advance into Kuchuk Anafarta Ova. It was around 0845 on 13 August before the news reached Imbros, and with it came Stopford's estimate that it would be forty-eight hours before the 54th Division was in any fit state to go into action again. Hard on the heels of that signal came another, reporting that a Turkish attack appeared to be imminent, and that the 53rd Division was close to panic 'and may bolt any minute'. Hamilton, perhaps sceptical, by now, of anything emanating from Stopford's HQ, once again called for his destroyer and set off to see for himself.

Aspinall-Oglander describes the meeting between the GOC and his corps commander as momentous, with Stopford insisting that the 53rd Division was finished as a fighting force, and that the 54th was 'incapable of attack'. He must have more time, he said, to rest and reorganise his forces, and his staff agreed. Hamilton was far from convinced and returned to Imbros, mulling three possible courses of action: agree to a further delay, order Stopford to attack anyway, even though he was convinced it would fail, or remove him and appoint a new commander. In the event he chose the first course, but only, as we shall see, as a way of buying time.

Braithwaite passed that decision on to Stopford in a signal which included an instruction to 'Take every opportunity to make as forward a line as possible and make that line impregnable.' Stopford reacted by instructing Mahon to make another attempt to clear the Turks off the Kiretch Tepe ridge and take

Kidney Hill, issuing the appropriate orders at 0845 on 15 August. By this time – for the first time – Mahon had both his available brigades together, Nicol's on the northern slopes and Hill's on the southern, and Stopford also loaned him the 162nd, then bivouacked near A Beach. More effective artillery had been landed by now, and the operation was to be supported by a brigade of 18-pounders, two 60-pounders and four mountain guns, as well as by two destroyers. The operation was timed to begin at 1300; Hill received his orders late, and was able to give his subordinate commanders only the sketchiest of briefings before H-Hour.

Accurate fire from the destroyers' 4-in guns gave Nicol the opportunity to make early gains, but his troops' advance was slow and cautious; as dusk approached, Nicol called on them to be more vigorous, and they stretched themselves, chasing the Turks out of their trenches and taking the strongpoint on the height of the crest. On the right, things went markedly less well, the Inniskillings soon being held up by small-arms and artillery fire. They suffered significant losses, with twenty officers and almost 350 other ranks killed and injured, and at nightfall Hill ordered them to fall back. The lead element amongst the 162nd Brigade was the 1/5th Bedfords, who had been told they were to act as a shielding flank guard and not to expect much fighting. In fact, they soon came under very heavy fire, and their advance slowed; elements of the other two battalions[32] were sent up as reinforcements, the brigadier himself (de Winton) leading, and eventually they succeeded in taking the south-east shoulder of Kidney Hill, and holding it for some hours. Eventually, however, they were withdrawn to prolong the 31st Brigade's line.

The night of 15 August passed in an atmosphere of tension, the British line not being contiguous and the Turks frequently sending out bombing parties. In vain Nicol and Hill asked for reinforcements the next morning, only to be told that none were available. They managed to hold out throughout the day, but at nightfall the two brigadiers took it upon their own authority to retire, and by dawn on 17 August the British battalions were back in the positions they had occupied forty-eight hours earlier, and so were the Turks. The entire affair – which had cost 2,000 British casualties – had been abortive. By Liman von Sanders' account, success there would have had very significant results. 'If ... the British had captured and held the Kiretch Teppe,' he wrote later, 'the whole position of the 5th Army would have been outflanked. The British might then have achieved a decisive and final victory.'

In fact, reserves were at hand, and the situation could have been materially improved without much difficulty. However, both corps and divisional head-quarters were in such a state of confusion that it was impossible to organise even this simple evolution, for on the evening of 15 August the thread holding the sword poised above Stopford's head had been severed, and he was abruptly removed from his command.

As we have seen, Hamilton was slow to accept the possibility that one of his corps commanders was incompetent, even though the evidence of it had

been piling up for a week. During his visit to Stopford's HQ on 13 August he
began to contemplate the possibility of a change of commander, and on his
return to Imbros that afternoon his resolve clearly began to harden. Early on
the morning of 14 August he composed a cable to Kitchener in which he
repeated the choices facing him and, for the first time, expanded on his own
feelings regarding the situation at Suvla, placing the blame for the failure
to capitalise on the surprise achieved on the first night squarely on the
commanders involved. Kitchener's reply arrived the following morning:

> If you deem it necessary to replace Stopford, Mahon and Hammersley,
> have you any competent generals to take their places?[33] From your report
> I think Stopford should come home. This is a young man's war and we
> must have commanding officers who will take advantage of opportunities
> which occur but seldom. If, therefore, any generals fail, do not hesitate to
> act promptly.

Only a short time later a second signal arrived, Kitchener telling Hamilton
that he had asked French to supply a corps commander and two divisional
commanders,[34] adding 'I hope that Stopford has been relieved by you already.'
    Hamilton relieved Stopford of his command that evening, and he left Suvla
the following day. Maj.-Gen. Beauvoir de Lisle was transferred from Helles
(Marshall took over the 29th Division from him) to take temporary charge
of IX Corps. This caused a further problem, for Sir Bryan Mahon – a
lieutenant-general; we may recall that it was his seniority which had neces-
sitated Stopford being appointed to command the corps in the first place –
refused to serve under de Lisle, and demanded to be relieved of his command.
Hill was given the 10th Division temporarily in his place. Hammersley,
somewhat surprisingly, seemed to have weathered the storm, but eight days
later, on direct orders from Kitchener, he, too, was relieved, and replaced by
Maj.-Gen. EA Fanshawe. Meanwhile, on 17 August Lindley resigned his
command of the 53rd Division, to be replaced for the moment by the
commander of the 127th Brigade (Brig.-Gen. HA Lawrence, temporarily
promoted to major-general for the purpose), and the following day, Sitwell,
as culpable as anyone, was sacked as commander of the 34th Brigade, to be
replaced by one of his battalion commanders, Lt.-Col. Hannay of the 5th
Dorsets.
    The bloodletting may have been severe, but as was often the case in such
circumstances, it was far too late. By 10 August at the very latest the Suvla
landings, which represented the only rational means of altering the nature of
the Gallipoli campaign, had failed. The affair would drag on over four more
agonising months, and even more British and Australian troops would be
added to the thirteen Allied divisions already there, but nothing of any value
would be gained beyond tying up twenty Turkish divisions which would
otherwise have been available for use in other theatres, and taking out of the

equation permanently many skilled, hardened fighters which the Turks could ill afford to lose. The implications of that should not be underestimated. Indeed, it is not difficult to demonstrate that this was actually essential to Allied victory in the Middle East; that without the losses the Turks incurred in the eight months' fighting at Gallipoli, the British would not have defeated them in Palestine or in Mesopotamia without committing a great deal more to those campaigns.

De Lisle was whisked away to Imbros aboard a destroyer. There he was briefed by Hamilton and Braithwaite, instructed to pull IX Corps together as quickly as possible and launch it against the Turkish positions on the W Hills and the Anafarta Spur. Within twenty-four hours of assuming command at Suvla, de Lisle had concluded that the situation there was actually far more serious than Hamilton had let on, Aspinall-Oglander tells us. Even after the arrival of 5,000 additional men from Egypt,[35] together with drafts to replace dead and wounded, he would only be able to muster 10,000 men for the renewed attack on the W Hills and the Anafarta Spur. He had also come to a further conclusion: that even if he took these objectives, he would not be able to hold them unless he took Tekke Tepe too. Instead, he proposed to concentrate on the W Hills only, with the objective of straightening the line between Sujalik and Birdwood's northern flank. He put these proposals, together with a candid analysis of the broader situation, in a report to Hamilton on 16 August. Hamilton's immediate reaction was to transfer one of the 29th Division's brigades (the 87th, under the temporary command of Brig.-Gen. Lucas) from Helles to Suvla, and its arrival on the evening of 17 August preceded that of the 2nd Mounted Division from Egypt. No permanent replacement for Mahon had yet been found, and it was decided to place the latter's commander, Maj.-Gen. WE Peyton, in command of the 10th Division, to which his Yeomanry detachment was attached to form a third brigade, with Brig.-Gen. Paul Kenna in Peyton's place. That day, 18 August, Hamilton visited Suvla and found that 'a new spirit was already beginning to pervade the troops' there, the 34th Brigade having succeeded in pushing forward on the right,[36] while the 53rd and 54th Divisions, the morale of which had improved, had filled in the ragged gaps in the line further north.

Despite that, it is clear that de Lisle's report of 16 August brought home to Hamilton just how little chance there was of him turning the affair around with the resources available, and late that night he wrote in extremely pessimistic tones to Kitchener, highlighting his numerical deficiencies – 95,000 Allied troops facing 110,000 Turks – and the strategic shortcomings of the three positions he occupied. In order to go back onto the offensive with any realistic chance of success, he said, he would need 45,000 men to bring his existing formations back up to full strength, and 50,000 additional troops. He concluded by saying, 'I have thought it best to lay the whole truth before you quite plainly. We are up against the main Turkish army, which is fighting bravely and is well commanded.'

At a conference the following afternoon it was agreed that de Lisle's attack on the W Hills would go ahead on 21 August. The new corps commander had high hopes of success, but Hamilton was apparently less sanguine; in particular, he was concerned that the entire Suvla plain was under the eye – and the guns – of the Turks, and urged that the approach to the W Hills should take place under cover of darkness. Both corps and divisional staff officers resisted, on the grounds that the men were not trained to a high enough standard to undertake such an operation at night, and Hamilton allowed himself to be convinced. He was not, however, equally convinced that de Lisle had enough men at his disposal, and he decided to send him the other two brigades of the 29th Division. De Lisle promptly began to expand his plans to include an advance across a much wider front, which had not at all been Hamilton's intention in sending him extra men, and he despatched Braithwaite to clarify his intentions, in particular with regard to any attempt to advance further than the W Hills 'unless the enemy was definitely routed', or along the Kiretch Tepe ridge.

De Lisle's orders for the attack were issued on the afternoon of 20 August. There would be a thirty-minute artillery bombardment, timed to begin at 1430. The main effort was to be made by the 11th Division (against the W Hills; Hammersley, in his last action, placed the 32nd Brigade on the left and the 34th on the right, with the 33rd in reserve near Lala Baba) followed by the 29th Division (with the 87th Brigade on the left to advance on Scimitar Hill, and the 86th on the western extremity of the Anafarta Spur, as far as a point known as 112 Metre Hill; the 88th Brigade was in reserve near Chocolate Hill). If they were successful, an enhanced brigade from the 10th Division (Peyton selected his own Yeomanry) would push through to establish a line further up the Anafarta Spur. The 53rd and 54th Divisions were 'to take advantage of any opportunity to gain ground' in their sectors, but had no specific objectives. Simultaneously with the departure of the 11th, Birdwood's left wing – a composite force of around three thousand men, under Maj.-Gen. Cox[37] – was to advance on and take Hill 60 at the northern extremity of the Damakjelik Spur, and extend to the left to link up with de Lisle's right.

De Lisle was led to believe that the Turks opposing him from the Azmak Dere north to Sulajik amounted to no more than six battalions, with perhaps a division in reserve; the defenders on Kiretch Tepe ridge were known to have been reinforced, but were thought to number not more than three thousand men. In fact, the reserve positions at Bulair had by now been stripped of men, and as well as the 7th and 12th Divisions astride the Azmak Dere, Mustafa Kemal had six battalions in reserve at Turshun Keui (the 9th Division) and six more at Selvili (the 6th Division), while three more were near Ejelmer Bay, in touch with those defending Kiretch Tepe. He also had a total of eighty-four guns, all of them emplaced on the heights overlooking the British positions.

The British bombardment opened on time but proved largely ineffective due to haphazard target data, the battlefield being covered in heat-haze, the inaccuracy of the howitzers, and mechanical defects in the 60-pounders which soon put them all out of commission. The 11th Division began to advance unsupported at 1500, de Lisle and Birdwood having decided to hold the composite force from Anzac back for half an hour. Its primary objective was the first-line trench which ran from Azmak Dere to Hetman Chair, the 34th Brigade to take its southern half, the 32nd the northern. The machine guns massed on Chocolate Hill[38] failed to give the required support, and by 1700, though the 33rd Brigade had been committed to reinforce the 32nd (and had taken many casualties due to shell fire on its approach across the open ground), it was clear that the attack had achieved only very limited local success in the southern sector and had failed completely in the northern.

The 29th Division's 86th Brigade set off towards Scimitar Hill at 1530; here, no-man's-land was considerably deeper than it was to the south, the terrain largely open and flat, studded with isolated patches of scrub which gave no real cover. The forward formations soon found themselves under heavy enfilading fire from the south. Soon patches of scrub were well alight, and though the smoke the fires generated concealed some areas of the advance, that channelled the men into groups, where they were even more vulnerable. To the left, the 87th Brigade had less open ground to cover before it reached the trenches on Scimitar Hill, and was able to close with them. Twice its leading battalions came within reach of the summit only to be driven back.

Even as he watched his four forward battalions being cut to pieces, Marshall received orders from de Lisle that the 2nd Mounted Division was to push through to take the objectives his men had failed to reach, and he instructed his brigadiers to hold their existing positions until the Yeomanry battalions arrived. By this time the division had moved up from its overnight positions behind Lala Baba; thanks to the Turkish shells being fused to burst too soon, it fared better than had the 33rd Brigade in crossing the open ground south of the salt lake, but the respite was short-lived. In the circumstances – heavy shelling and intense machine gun fire; limited visibility due to the haze and the smoke; confusion among wounded men struggling back to the comparative shelter of their own lines – it is surprising they achieved anything at all, but they did manage to maintain a precarious hold on positions on the lower slopes of Scimitar Hill (only to be instructed to withdraw under cover of darkness when Marshall realised the futility of trying to hold them until and unless Hill 112 was taken).

Cox's attempt to take the positions to the south of Azmak Dere and drive the Turks off the Damakjelik Spur ran into trouble from the outset, largely because the attackers knew very little of the nature of the defensive positions.

Cox's advance had two linked objectives: on his right he was to take Hill

60 and extend eastwards towards Hill 100, and on the left he was to advance through Kazlar Chair towards Susak Kuyu and establish a line connecting the 11th Division with Hill 60, seizing the important wells in the narrow Kaiajik Dere gully in the process. When the advance began the men were met by extremely heavy rifle and machine gun fire from both objectives. Many fell trying to cross the Kaiajik Dere gully, where fires soon raged, killing many of the wounded. The Connaught Rangers on the left – the only unit up to anything like strength; they had remained in reserve until the last day of the fighting for Chunuk Bair – took the wells with little opposition, and their success tempted them into a further advance onto the slopes of the hill itself, with the left extending to Susak Kuyu. The wells there, too, were taken with no difficulty, but the main body of the battalion advancing up the slope soon ran into heavy opposition. Despite significant losses in the first wave, they managed to take the first Turkish trench on the north-western side, and here they settled, linking up with the 1/5th Gurkhas when they fought their way up on their left.

By nightfall, little had been achieved elsewhere save for the establishment of a very precarious foothold on the lower slopes of Hill 60. The offensive was renewed on 27 August, and this time positions on the upper slopes were secured. Additional men from the 9th and 10th Light Horse were sent up, and at 0100 on 29 August another attempt was made. By dawn, the belt of interconnecting trenches extending around the hill to the north-west – the original objective of the operation – had been taken, at considerable cost, securing the Susak Kuyu positions, though the summit itself was still in Turkish hands and there it remained.

Meanwhile, there had been developments which would affect the campaign as a whole. To begin with, on 21 August de Roebeck turned down as impractical a plan Keyes had put forward to renew the attempt to force the Dardanelles.[39] Then, that same day, Hamilton received a belated response to his request for massive reinforcements. There were no fresh divisions available, Kitchener told him,[40] and the best that could be done was to send him a total of about 25,000 men, half of them drafts to replace some of those who had fallen, the rest second-line Territorials and Yeomanry to be employed dismounted. There was the prospect of the remaining two brigades of the 2nd Australian Infantry Division, which were now completing their training in Egypt, arriving in Gallipoli, of course,[41] but the total would still fall far short of the minimum he would need to mount another offensive. At that point Hamilton realised that he would now be forced onto the defensive, and began to consider giving up the Suvla position and withdrawing towards Anzac.

On 23 August, Byng arrived in theatre and replaced de Lisle as GOC, IX Corps (de Lisle resumed command of the 29th Division, and Marshall took over the 53rd), while Maude took over from Shaw, who was invalided home, as the commander of the 13th Division, and Fanshawe replaced Hammersley in command of the 11th. The presence of new commanders soon lifted Hamilton's spirits, and he quickly reassessed his abilities to hold on to Suvla, but his new-found optimism did not extend to any idea of going back onto the offensive. It is clear from all reports that by this stage morale in all the zones at Gallipoli had reached rock-bottom, when a day free of shelling, an adequate, uninterrupted meal or a full night's sleep were luxuries and a letter from home was a major landmark. Sickness was endemic – diarrhoea affected everyone from Hamilton down – and was widely thought to have its origins in the rations, particularly tinned 'bully-beef' from Argentina. A small respite – hardly enough to affect the material position, though it did have an effect on morale – saw 'canteens' run by the Army Service Corps,[42] where minor luxury items could be purchased, opened at Helles on 19 August and at Suvla a month later. Others, privately run, were also established at Mudros and Imbros, where troops were sent in small groups for short rest periods, and the YMCA opened branches in both locations.

Then, on 30 August, out of nowhere, news reached Imbros that the French government was contemplating landing six divisions on the Asiatic coast of the Straits. Joy was unconfined in Hamilton's headquarters ('From Bankrupt to millionaire in 24 hours … *Deo Volente* we are saved!' Sir Ian wrote in his diary), and the prospect of opening a new front occupied everyone's attention for the first two weeks of September. When Kitchener and French met their opposite numbers at Calais on 11 September, and it was agreed in principle that the operation should go ahead (in the middle of November, and that the French divisions would be supplemented by two British, the 27th and 28th, from the Western Front; both were subsequently sent to Salonika, where they saw out the war), it really did seem that events in the theatre were about to take a new and very dramatic turn. However, hope took a nose dive when Joffre later took Kitchener aside and told him he believed six divisions to be nowhere near enough, and that Sarrail, who had been named to command the force, was not up to the task.

It soon became clear that the proposal had, in reality, been little more than a political ploy on the part of the French Prime Minister, Raymond Poincaré, designed to curb Joffre's determination to launch his renewed Western Front offensive, but it also involved the continuing employment of Gen. Maurice Sarrail, a contender for Joffre's job, whom the latter had sacked as commander of the Third Army in late July but who had a power-base of his own. The affair casts an interesting light on the machiavellian activities of the French High Command, though an analysis of that has no place here. Sarrail was eventually to command the French troops sent to Salonika, and soon lived down to Joffre's expectations of him.

By that time the British government – and, by extension, Hamilton – had a new cause for concern: on 6 September the Bulgarian government signed a convention allying itself with the Central Powers, and on Sunday 25 September the Bulgarian Army began mobilising for war. There was no doubt whatsoever that its sights would be set on Serbia, its neighbour to the west, and there was every expectation that it would invade in concert with an Austro-German Army crossing the River Save from the north, the operation to commence before the onset of winter. Alarmed by the prospect of Greece being drawn into the conflict, Prime Minister Elefthérios Venizélos 'invited' Britain and France to send troops to Salonika to stand beside the army he himself had ordered mobilised. (This brought Venizélos, who was determinedly pro-British, into conflict with King Constantine, who was equally determinedly pro-German; the King removed the Prime Minister unconstitutionally, which had far-reaching consequences.) No matter that it would be an empty gesture – Churchill called it 'absurd' in military terms – there was general agreement in London and in Paris that it constituted a political necessity, and, on very brief reflection, a recognition that there was but one source of troops to fulfil the commitment rapidly: Gallipoli. The same day on which the Bulgarians called up their reserves, Kitchener cabled Hamilton to tell him that two British divisions and probably one French were to be transferred from Gallipoli to Salonika, and that the Yeomanry units promised and already on their way would also be diverted to Greece. Hamilton should consider withdrawing from Suvla, Kitchener told him.

Hamilton replied by pointing out that a withdrawal from Suvla would send the wrong signals, both to the Bulgarians and to the Turks, and stated his belief that he could hold all his positions if he were permitted to despatch just one British and one French division to Salonika.[43] Kitchener agreed, and Hamilton began making preparations to transfer the 10th Division (which returned to the command of Sir Bryan Mahon in the process) and take over as much of the ground held by the CEO at Cape Helles as was necessary.

The future of the Mediterranean Expeditionary Force was now in the balance, but before any decision could be reached, the British government (in the shape of the Dardanelles Committee, the War Council by another name) resolved to seek the advice of the professionals: the Admiralty War Staff and the General Staff at the War Office. There was a degree of urgency, for winter was well on its way (storms on the exposed Aegean coast had already destroyed piers at Anzac and Suvla and driven lighters ashore). On 9 October the combined body reported. It urged sending no more troops to Salonika, it being too late to save Serbia; was 'unhesitatingly in favour' of continuing the Artois offensive in France, though it wished the government to attempt to persuade Joffre to do nothing for at least three months, and suggested that it would require eight additional divisions to win through in Gallipoli, and that they should be sent to Egypt directly. The Dardanelles Committee was left with the task of deciding between the alternatives, and was not up to it; instead it prevaricated, telling Kitchener to ask Hamilton to estimate how many men he would lose in an evacuation, and Jackson, the First Sea Lord, to ask de Roebeck how many extra men he could support on the peninsula.

The Dardanelles Committee's corporate judgement was clouded by growing mistrust of Hamilton's reliability, stemming from his repeated failure to break through the Turkish defences on any of the three fronts. That was generated – or perhaps compounded – by a fatuous 'report' Stopford had presented to the War Office soon after his return to the United Kingdom, in which he criticised Hamilton by innuendo, protested at himself having been criticised, and suggested that GHQ 'on an island at some distance from the peninsula' was out of touch with the realities of the situation, particularly the numbers of Turks he had faced. Kitchener called on four of the most senior generals in London – Sir Leslie Rundle, Sir James Murray (who had recently resigned as CIGS), Sir Archibald Murray (who had replaced him; the two men were not related) and Sir James Sclater – to examine it. This august group proved no mean hand at prevarication itself, reporting 'We think that the whole series of tasks planned for the IX Corps is open to criticism, but we do not feel justified in suggesting such criticism at this period of the war without much fuller information from those actually on the spot.' Kitchener promptly decoded that according to his own principles, telling the Dardanelles Committee that a number of generals had delivered themselves of 'considerable criticism of Sir Ian Hamilton's leadership'. Hamilton later objected to Stopford's memorandum having been accepted– having been considered, even – without his knowledge, but by that time the damage was done.

Stopford's was not the only document unfavourable to Hamilton doing the rounds in London that October. An Australian journalist named Keith Murdoch[44] presented to the Prime Minister a twenty-five-page letter, a copy of one he had written to his counterpart in Australia 'in the course of which, after cruelly defaming most of the officers and troops (other than Australian) at that time serving on the peninsula or on the lines of communication, he had then levelled a violent attack on the Commander-in-Chief and the Chief of the General Staff', to quote Aspinall-Oglander. Asquith took the unusual step of circulating it 'as was' to members of the government, many of whom passed it on to all manner of interested parties, banging another nail into Hamilton's coffin in the process.

When the Dardanelles Committee next met, it resolved to send 'an adequate and substantial force' to Egypt 'without prejudice as to its final destination', and to despatch a specially selected officer (Kitchener, for choice, largely as a means of getting him out of the way, at least temporarily, for he was fast becoming redundant) to the Eastern Mediterranean 'to advise as to where this force should be employed and what its task should be'. Before that officer could even be selected, events came to a head. Murdoch's letter had been circulated, and 'Every opponent of the Eastern theatre who had seen or heard of [it] was turning it to good account', fanning the flames of dissent within Parliament and without. Clearly, something had to be done, and the obvious course was to sacrifice Hamilton. When the Dardanelles Committee

met on 13 October it considered Hamilton's reply to Kitchener's request for
an estimate of the losses evacuation would cost. He put the figure at up to
half his entire force, or more, for 'with raw troops at Suvla and black [French
colonial] troops at Helles, there might be a real catastrophe'. Perhaps Hamilton was indulging in exaggeration for the sake of effect, in order to take the
possibility of abandoning Gallipoli off the agenda, but if he was, his hyperbole
backfired and sealed his fate.

The next day Kitchener recalled him with immediate effect, placing Birdwood in temporary command, and announced that Sir Charles Monro[45] was
to travel to the region to assess the situation. Were it not for the fact that
Kitchener was solidly in favour of maintaining the Gallipoli operation, from
the choice of Monro we might deduce that London's corporate mind was
made up as to the future for Gallipoli, for he was a dedicated 'Westerner'
who believed that the war would – could only, indeed – be won in France
and that every British soldier possible should be committed there, and would
certainly do everything in his power to see the operation in Turkey closed
down as expediently as possible.

Monro arrived at Imbros on 28 October. His instructions from Kitchener
were to report on the military situation on the peninsula, specifically whether
it would be better to evacuate or again try to win through. Prior to his arrival,
GHQ had been compiling an assessment of the numbers required to achieve
the latter: at least a quarter of a million men was the estimate, and the
operation could not now be undertaken until the spring, so replacing the
existing troops with fresh men would also be necessary. It also looked at
evacuation, and concluded that a retirement undertaken voluntarily would
be much less costly than one forced upon the invaders by the Turks. Monro
made his first report on the afternoon of his arrival; he was noncommittal,
but seemed to come down on the side of continuing the campaign. Though
he was very much in favour of that, it did not satisfy Kitchener, who sent him
a terse signal the following morning: 'Please send me as soon as possible your
report on the main issue at the Dardanelles, namely, leaving or staying.'

Monro decided on a tour of inspection of the three fronts. He met each
divisional commander in turn at Helles, Anzac and Suvla, and asked each
identical questions: were their troops physically and morally fit for a sustained
effort to capture the enemy's positions? And could they maintain their positions throughout the coming winter, unreinforced and with the expected
influx of modern heavy guns and unlimited ammunition turned on them?
To a question couched in such terms there could be but one answer, and to
a man they gave it: the men could not be counted on for more than twenty-
four hours' sustained operations, and as for holding out, they could only
undertake to do their best.

Monro returned to Imbros that night with his mind made up,[46] and the
following morning he cabled Kitchener urging that the operation be wound
up as quickly as possible.

Kitchener clutched at a final straw. He replied, asking Monro if his three corps commanders were of the same opinion. Byng and Davies agreed, but Birdwood did not, citing the likelihood of a severe blow to prestige in the Muslim world (an opinion in which Sir John Maxwell, the C-in-C, Egypt, concurred). If the decision should go in favour of evacuation, he added, he believed it was essential that the troops in question should be immediately employed against the Turks elsewhere, to prevent them reinforcing their armies in the Caucasus and Mesopotamia.

Birdwood could perhaps have been expected to follow the line set by his former chief and mentor – he had been Kitchener's military secretary in South Africa, and had followed him to India when he took up the post of commander-in-chief there – and his dissent gave the War Minister the excuse he needed to hold the matter open. In that he was dealt a helping hand just days later.

On 2 November Asquith finally addressed the administrative problems created by having a committee with twelve members responsible for advising him on strategic decisions. Henceforth, he announced to Parliament, the Dardanelles Committee was disbanded and strategy (for all fronts) would be decided by a War Committee consisting of not less than three or more than five Cabinet Ministers.[47] The Committee sat for the first time the following day, and top of its agenda was the situation in Gallipoli. It considered Monro's two telegrams and Keyes' revised plan for forcing the Straits, towards which Balfour had indeed come to show some favour. In the light of that it was decided not to accept Monro's advice, but instead to send Kitchener to the theatre to assess the situation. The War Minister now had a platform from which to launch a renewed attempt to secure his own way, and he lost no time in mounting it.

On 3 November Monro left Imbros for Cairo, having decided to consult Maxwell and McMahon, the High Commissioner, as to the likely effect of evacuation on Britain's standing in the Muslim world. As soon as he was out of the way, in the early hours of 4 November, Kitchener composed a telegram to Birdwood. In brief, it announced Kitchener's impending visit, told of his espousal of Keyes' plan, and suggested landing at Bulair in order to support the naval operation. 'As regards command,' it went on, 'you would have the whole force ... Work out plans for this or alternative plans as you think fit. I absolutely refuse to sign order for evacuation, which I think would be greatest disaster and would condemn a large percentage of our men to death or imprisonment. Monro will be appointed to command the Salonika force.'

No doubt he expected Birdwood to jump at the chance, but Birdwood would have none of it. Not only did he think the plan to land at Bulair a disaster, but he had no intention of usurping Monro's prerogative, and said so, not in so many words but nonetheless perfectly clearly, in a signal to Kitchener that morning. By the time he received the reply, Kitchener had himself begun to have second thoughts, largely as a result of Keyes also having reacted negatively to the suggestion of landing at Bulair. When he met the commodore again the following afternoon, in company with Balfour, it became clear that the First Lord's enthusiasm for the naval operation was waning, too. Just before leaving for Paris he cabled Birdwood again. 'I fear the Navy may not play up,' he said. 'The more I look at the problem the less I see my way through, so you had better very quietly and very secretly work out any scheme for getting the troops off.'

The jig was finally up. Or so it appeared until Kitchener woke up in Paris the following morning, and learned that the French government – with Briand now at its head, Poincaré having fallen when he failed to support the Serbs adequately; Gen. Gallieni as War Minister (much to the dismay of his arch-rival Joffre), and Lacaze as Minister of the Marine – had no wish to see the Gallipoli operation abandoned, and were now more concerned with the *number* of British troops to be sent to Salonika, rather than their fighting ability . . . He immediately began working on a revised plan, to send the 27th and 28th Divisions (plus whatever other formations he could scrape up from Egypt) to Gallipoli to replace two or three tired or less effective divisions[48] who would go to Salonika, and cabled to Birdwood that he had still not given up hope of keeping the operation alive. To do so, he needed to keep the navy on side, and cabled the Admiralty asking Keyes to join him in Marseilles so that they could work out the details of the operation to force the Straits during the voyage to Mudros; Keyes never received the invitation[49] and, Kitchener said to him later, 'When you didn't turn up at Marseilles, I made up my mind that the naval plan was dead.'

Meanwhile, in Cairo, Monro had consulted McMahon and Maxwell. Both restated their belief that Britain's standing in the Muslim world would suffer as a consequence of evacuation, while the latter insisted that, were Gallipoli abandoned, the question of how best to protect Egypt would have to be settled. The most effective way, he argued, would be to revive the old plan to land troops in the Gulf of Iskenderun to cut the Turks' lines of communication between Anatolia and Syria and Palestine. Discussions were still going on when the trio was summoned to Mudros; by the time they arrived they had all agreed that a landing on the north side of the Gulf of Iskenderun, at Ayas Bay, would provide the optimum solution, Monro assenting chiefly as a means of securing the others' support for evacuation.

They arrived at Mudros on the morning of 9 November, where Monro learned of the proposal Kitchener had made to Birdwood, and his response. Kitchener himself, together with his staff, arrived that evening, and the next twelve days were given over to what was essentially one long conference. As early as the evening of the tenth Kitchener was cabling Asquith with the outline of a plan to land two fresh divisions (the 27th and 28th, which were by now in Egypt) and three thousand cavalry, with two more divisions from France to follow, at Ayas Bay, as a preliminary to evacuating Gallipoli. He had high hopes for the scheme, but they were not shared in Whitehall, where the General Staff's corporate view was that an operation to cut the Turkish lines of communication effectively would require ten to twelve divisions 'who would be chained to the neighbourhood for the duration of the war'. Better, went the Staff view, to meet the Turks just short of Suez, after they had undergone the rigours of a long approach march and had put themselves in proximity to the British power-base.

By now, Kitchener had the bit of Ayas Bay firmly between his teeth, and McMahon and Maxwell chimed in with dire warnings of the effect on the Muslim population of the British (and the French) Empire should the Turks invade Egypt. Over the next five days this provided a persistent side-bar to the main topic of deliberation, but when the War Minister reported to the Prime Minister again on 15 November it was clear that, while he had not yet come round to favouring evacuation, he was at least becoming convinced that it might be feasible without costing the lives or freedom of 50 per cent of the men involved.

During those first five days on Mudros, Kitchener had taken time out to visit the Gallipoli Peninsula and see the conditions there for himself, and what he found had a profound effect on him. 'The country is much more difficult than I imagined,' he wrote to Asquith, 'and the Turkish positions ... are natural fortresses which, if not taken by surprise at first, could be held against very serious attack by larger forces than have been engaged.' (Which prompted Aspinall-Oglander to add, in his commentary, 'Sir Ian Hamilton, in other words, had after all not been so much to blame.')

Having been called away to Greece to resolve grave problems regarding the force in Salonika, Kitchener returned to Mudros on 21 November. By now the French had made it clear that they viewed the plan to land British troops in the Gulf of Iskenderun with mistrust, and would oppose it vehemently,[50] and during Kitchener's absence the proposal had slowly but surely been losing favour. Coincidentally, Kitchener found himself placing more and more trust in Monro's judgement, but on his return he was greeted by a renewed attempt by Birdwood to scotch the evacuation proposals. Supported by the senior Australian officer (Birdwood, we should recall, was British), Maj.-Gen. JG Legge – who maintained that giving up Gallipoli would play very badly in the Antipodes – and by Lt.-Gen. Davies – who had changed his mind when he saw the extent of damage caused to the port installations by the recent storms – Birdwood now made an impassioned plea for staying put, on the grounds that it would be less costly than quitting. He seemed to be borne out that very evening, when the Turks launched an attack at Helles. The 52nd Division was subjected to a fifty-minute bombardment, but it had little real effect, and when the Turkish infantry left their trenches and advanced they were driven back with very heavy losses before they had even passed through their own wire.

Monro was unmoved, and pressed his own case that evening. For some time a compromise option had been under discussion: to evacuate Suvla and Anzac, but to hang on at Helles 'at all events for the present', largely in the hope of keeping the Dardanelles closed to enemy submarines. The following morning Kitchener accepted that view, and said so, finally, in a telegram to Asquith. The Prime Minister replied the next day, saying that the evacuation of the whole of the peninsula had been agreed by the War Committee, and would be submitted to the Cabinet for approval. Kitchener then confirmed Monro as commander-in-chief of all forces in the Eastern Mediterranean, save Egypt, with Mahon at Salonika and Birdwood at Gallipoli reporting to him, the latter to have charge of the evacuation. On 24 November he set sail for Marseilles.

The evacuation of the Gallipoli Peninsula was to proceed in three stages. The preliminary stage saw all non-essential men, animals and material removed; that was already under way by 24 November. The intermediate stage would see all men, guns, animals and stores not required for the tactical defence of Suvla, Anzac and Helles removed, and that would commence as soon as formal approval for the evacuation, by the entire Cabinet, was received. The final stage would be to remove the remaining men,[51] any animals left, and such guns and stores as could be safely got off, over two nights, the date to be established later.

It was widely expected that obtaining Cabinet approval for the evacuation would be little more than a formality, but in the event that proved not to be the case, resistance to it being led by Lord Curzon (who at that time held no office of state, but had very considerable influence). Curzon rehearsed all the old arguments against evacuation, arguing that instead, extra troops should be sent to the peninsula, and to land on the Asiatic shore of the Dardanelles, and that the naval effort to force the Straits should be renewed. His was not a lone voice, for when Hankey, the Cabinet Secretary, was asked to prepare a memorandum on the subject, he too came down heavily in favour of remaining.

The arguments went on through the last week of November with no conclusion in sight, and in the meantime, on the twenty-seventh, nature took a hand. A gale battered the port installations at Anzac and Helles, and so many small craft were lost that any idea of evacuating all three locations simultaneously had to be abandoned. The men suffered, too, a twenty-four-hour downpour which soaked them to the skin, and flooded trenches and dugouts, giving way to a blizzard and heavy snow, with temperatures plummeting to well below freezing and staying there for forty-eight hours. The storm abated on 30 November, but the damage was very extensive, and it was clear that if another struck soon it would have a potentially devastating effect. In the light of the continuing inability of the Cabinet to reach a decision, Kitchener decided to act, and on 1 December he ordered that winter clothing and materials (and ammunition stocks) which had been removed should be landed at Gallipoli once more, and that preparations for overwintering should be resumed.

De Roebeck arrived in London at the beginning of December, and at once put his weight behind the anti-evacuationists' cause. As well as those discussions, the subject of continuing the now moribund operation to assist the Serbs had come up repeatedly, motions to withdraw the troops from Salonika (where the 28th Division had by now arrived from Egypt) had been slowly gathering strength, and Curzon, for one, had been advocating employing those troops to strengthen the Gallipoli garrison. Matters came to a head once more at a War Committee meeting on 2 December. By now, a decision to quit Salonika had been reached in principle (though no orders had been issued), and the prospect of having the four divisions there available to be sent (sent back, in the case of the 10th) to Gallipoli had caused Kitchener to reverse his own position yet again. There was a further factor: Townshend's advance on Baghdad had been stalled at Ctesiphon, and he was withdrawing on Kut with the Turks in pursuit; if Turkish troops were released now, they might very quickly be transferred to Mesopotamia, where they would have a considerable impact ... Wemyss, in command of the Dardanelles Fleet in de Roebeck's absence, was asked how soon he could embark the troops at Salonika and transport them to Gallipoli. He could do so very quickly, he replied.

On 4 December Asquith and Balfour, accompanied by Kitchener and the CIGS, went to Calais to confer with Briand and Lacaze, with both Gallieni and Joffre present to make the army's case. There was just one item on the agenda: Salonika. The French at first refused to countenance a withdrawal, claiming that it would be likely to provoke both Greece and Rumania into entering the war on the side of the Central Powers, but Kitchener was persuasive, and by the day's end, Briand had given his assent.

But that was not that. The next day, having come under pressure when he returned to Paris, he reversed himself, and at a (military) conference at Joffre's headquarters on the sixth, though all present were in favour of evacuating Gallipoli, only Murray was in favour of quitting Salonika. Then, on the seventh, the Russians weighed in, making a formal request (seemingly at the suggestion of the French) that British troops not be pulled out of Greece. This was the last straw. To withdraw from Salonika risked the very fabric of the alliance, it was felt in London, and when the Cabinet met in full session later that day it was finally agreed that the troops would remain there, but that Suvla and Anzac – but not, yet, Helles – were to be evacuated.

Somewhat ironically, at the end of November the number of Allied troops at Gallipoli stood at or near an all-time high: a total of almost 135,000. By 8 December that had been reduced to about 84,000 men, and some guns and considerable quantities of stores had also been removed, and there was a growing optimism that so long as things continued much as normal, the operation could be completed with a considerable measure of success.

On 25 November, Byng and Godley, now named as GOC, Australian and New Zealand Army Corps, in succession to Birdwood, had been told to begin preparing tactical evacuation plans. One overall, general plan would not suffice as the circumstances in the two zones were quite dissimilar: at Anzac the two sides' positions were often in very close proximity, while at Suvla they were normally widely separated.

Godley's approach was to hold his front-line trenches in strength to the end, while getting off all his non-essential men, guns, stores and animals over a ten-day period. The final stage would be carried out over two nights; on the first, support troops would be withdrawn as complete units while men in the front line would be progressively thinned out, a company or even a platoon at a time, assembling behind the piers at Anzac Cove and Ocean Beach, from which they would be taken off in motorised lighters. On the final night selected groups of the remaining men in the first-line positions – known as C Parties – would try to give an impression of normality while the rest – the A and B Parties – made their way to the shore, and then they in turn would make directly for the embarkation points closest to them, some of which would be on open beaches, collapsible trestle piers having been prefabricated and hidden nearby for the purpose. There they would board ships' boats which would be towed out to waiting transports by drifters.

The rearguard would destroy all stores left behind them (by means of explosive and incendiary charges fitted with delayed-action fuses; guns, in particular, were to be so thoroughly destroyed that they would be useless even as trophies; the destruction of large stores dumps which had accumulated on and near the beaches was to be completed by naval gunfire), and to cover their departure devices to fire rifle rounds and detonate bombs mechanically would be used. Prior to departure contact-detonated mines would be laid, and the wire entanglements augmented and strengthened.

Byng's plan was substantially different, for he had decided to follow a more orthodox course and reduce the ground he held by a gradual contraction, withdrawing his troops by stages until he occupied two positions close to the beaches:[52] Reserve Area A, behind what had been A Beach, and Reserve Area B, east and south of Nibrunesi Point and including Lala Baba, which was to be turned into a fortress. However, when those plans were submitted to Birdwood, at a conference on 30 November, it was decided that Byng should continue to hold his first and second lines, the former albeit lightly, while non-essential troops and *matériel* were got off, and then withdraw them in a similar fashion to that proposed by Godley. The navy's opinion was that it would be impossible to get off more than 10,000 men from each zone in the course of one night, and that dictated that all but 40,000 men from both Anzac and Suvla must be evacuated during the intermediate stage.

With so much planning already completed, as soon as the final decision reached Birdwood, on 8 December, he was able to order the intermediate stage of the operation to begin two days later. There was, of course, a variety – sometimes a bewildering variety – of contingencies to be considered and covered, and frankly it is a tribute to the British Army's mastery of bureaucracy that the entire process was wrapped up on time and without significant omission.

Following the late-November storms, there was a three-week period of perfect weather, the sea calm and the wind non-existent. As a result the intermediate stage of the evacuation went exactly as planned. 'Every night the beaches hummed with activity,' Aspinall-Oglander wrote, 'but every morning, before daylight, all was again silence and the sea devoid of ships. Camps, hitherto crowded, were fast emptying, but the appearance of normal activity was produced as far as possible by the maintenance of all fires and the continual moving about of troops in reserve.' Even the Turks seemed to be co-operating, and there was very little hostile activity and no sign of any impending renewal of the offensive, though the level of artillery fire into the Suvla zone increased and its accuracy improved, which led to some speculation that new guns had indeed begun to arrive from Germany and Austria. By the morning of 18 December, the intermediate stage had been completed; just over 40,000 men remained ashore at Anzac and Suvla, with fifty guns, all but sixteen of which were to be taken off that night.

As soon as darkness came,[53] the designated ships from Mudros and Imbros began arriving at the piers at Anzac Cove and North and Ocean Beaches and in Suvla Bay, and men began to file aboard. The vessels, mostly old passenger steamers, Channel packets and the like,[54] would make up to three runs each to the islands, and more would be slotted in as the schedule allowed. The first batch from Anzac took off over four thousand men, and almost six thousand more followed at intervals through the night, and the pattern from Suvla was similar; the entire programme was completed before the first crack of dawn appeared in the sky. There was not a single serious casualty, and not a single hitch.

The arrangements for embarkation at Anzac on the second night of the final stage were perforce rather more complicated, and extended down Brighton Beach (as the strand south of Hell Spit had become known) to almost within rifle-shot of Gaba Tepe in the south, and the whole length of Ocean Beach (north of Ari Burnu) as far as the mouth of the Aghyl Dere in the north. The A Parties, four thousand men in all, began to leave their trenches immediately after dusk. They were off by 2300, by which time the B Parties, similar in size, had left their own positions and were making their way down to the shore. The C Parties,[55] the last two thousand men, began leaving the positions on the extreme left, where the distance to the beaches was at its greatest, at around 0100 on 20 December, and those on the right followed an hour later. The men with the most demanding task, those in the centre, where the Turkish trenches were so close at hand, were not to be clear of their positions until well after 0300. The precise routes they were to take had been mapped out beforehand, and were indicated by trails of flour or salt on the ground, and marked by candles in biscuit tins; men were on hand to act as stewards, each one tallying off the men in his charge as they passed him; when the last had gone, he made good the gap in the wire, then retired himself.

By 0240 Lone Pine was empty of men, some passing within five metres of Turkish troops without raising the alarm. By 0255 the men from Quinn's Post and Pope's Hill had joined them, and only Walker's Ridge and Russell's Top remained occupied; they were clear by 0330, when the signal was given to blow the large mine which had been carefully placed to deny access to the latter from the Nek. At 0400 the lighter carrying the last Diggers cast off; a small party remained behind for ten more minutes in case there were stragglers, then they, too, boarded a boat and moved slowly out into the waiting darkness. There were two casualties from bullet wounds at Anzac that night. Sixteen guns were left behind, all of them obsolete and all of them thoroughly destroyed, plus twenty mules and fifty donkeys.

The operation at Suvla went equally smoothly, and despite the greater distances the men had to cover between front line and beaches, remained largely on schedule. That line had emptied by 0130, the cobbled-together spring-guns keeping up appearances, and in the southern sector the last men were filing through the defensive line linking the salt lake with the sea at the limit of the old B Beach by 0230. By 0315 they had passed through the Lala Baba redoubt lines, the wire had been closed behind them and they were boarding boats at South Pier; Maude and his staff were among the last to leave at around 0400. In Fanshawe's sector to the north the withdrawal went equally smoothly save on the extreme left, where there was some confusion which was rapidly resolved; that caused a short delay, and it was 0500 before the general and his staff boarded the lighter assigned to them at Suvla Cove. Then it was the turn of the Beachmaster, Captain Unwin, still in the forefront of the action after almost eight months, and the Principal Military Embarkation Officer, Lt.-Col. Beynon. At Suvla not a single man was hurt, and no gun, vehicle or animal remained behind when the sun rose on 20 December.

The Turks' suspicions were first aroused by the silence which now emanated from the British trenches; soon after daylight they began bombarding the forward positions and when there was no reply, small parties began to advance. Contact mines and booby-traps encouraged caution, but by around 0700 some had reached the beaches and were ransacking the piles of stores they found there, when cruisers placed offshore for the purpose began to bombard them. Very little *matériel* was left by the end of the day.

There were the dead, of course ... The thousands of dead ... Men had tended their graves to the very end, cleaning, tidying, renewing crosses and markers. As one was heard to say as he contemplated that of a comrade, 'I hope they won't hear us marching back to the beach ...'

That afternoon a severe gale blew up.

*

And then there was Helles. Birdwood's problem there was compounded by uncertainty; was it to be retained for any appreciable length of time, or evacuated as soon as possible? Both he and Monro[56] were in favour of abandoning it at the earliest possible opportunity. In any event, there was a pressing need to relieve the exhausted 42nd Division, the remaining French colonial brigade had to be withdrawn, and there would be an inevitable dip in morale when the Helles garrison learned that those of Anzac and Suvla had gone, yet he had to keep his defences up to a high enough level to deter the Turks from attacking. Sacrifices would have to be made, and as soon as it was withdrawn from Suvla, the 29th Division was returned to the southern zone, despite having suffered very badly in the November blizzard. That came as a considerable blow to the men, many of whom had been at Gallipoli since the very first, and the commander-in-chief undertook that they would remain for as short a period as possible.

On 24 December, Sir William Robertson, the new Chief of the Imperial General Staff – who had made it a condition of accepting the post that all orders were to be issued by him, rather than the War Minister – told Monro to begin making preparations for an immediate withdrawal from Helles. Four days later the definitive order to evacuate 'as soon as practicable' was received. As in the northern zones, the withdrawal from Helles was to be made in three stages, the first of which was already under way, but this time Birdwood, who found it difficult to believe that he could fool the Turks a second time, insisted that the final stage be completed in one night. Accordingly he told Davies that his rearguard – which would still be expected to hold on for up to a week if required – would have to be limited to 15,000 men, that being the number the navy told him could be extracted from V and W Beaches in one lift. In the event, Davies insisted that he could not hold Helles with less than 22,000 men (and 60 guns), and it would be essential to carry the final stage over to a second night, and Birdwood reluctantly agreed.

Davies' plan for the evacuation was approved on 30 December; like those of Godley and Byng, it left nothing to chance and provided for the movement of every unit to a precise timetable. He made one significant change to the earlier arrangements, setting up an embarkation zone between the front line and the beaches, within which all troops would come under the command of Maj.-Gen. Lawrence of the 52nd Division.

On 31 December Monro departed for Alexandria, having reported to CIGS that he could do nothing further, and the following day the intermediate stage of the evacuation began with the withdrawal of the last French brigade. From the first it was dogged by ill fortune and worse weather. Significant progress was made in getting the men off, but by 4 January it was clear that either the timetable must be extended, or large quantities of stores and many animals would have to be left behind.[57] Birdwood opted for the latter course. By the next day things had taken a further turn for the worse, and Davies was forced to reconsider the timetable for the final stage. Was there, he asked de Roebeck (who had returned from leave on New Year's Eve, and had re-assumed command from Wemyss), any way that more than 15,000 men could be taken off in a single night's operations? A sapper captain who had overseen much of the work improving the port facilities suggested modifications to the breakwaters at V Beach, which consisted of two obsolete French warships. By sinking a small collier and linking it to the existing installations by means of a hastily constructed floating bridge, it was calculated, troops could go directly aboard destroyers and transports and two thousand additional troops could be embarked over the available period, as well as more guns. Davies agreed that 17,000 men and 54 guns – seventeen of which were to be destroyed and abandoned – would give him the margin he needed, and the final stage was reduced to a single night once more, that of 8 January.

By the morning of the seventh, the Helles garrison had been reduced to 19,000 men and 63 guns, and everything looked to be on course. Then, around midday, the Turks opened up an artillery bombardment of almost unprecedented violence against Gully Spur, near the left of the line, and on the extreme right, on the Kereves Spur. By 1500 the 13th Division's positions had suffered considerable damage, and far from diminishing, the barrage was actually increasing in intensity. At 1600 two large mines were detonated close to the 13th's first-line trenches, and many bayonets were seen to be massing in the Turkish trenches opposite. By now, every available gun, both ashore and afloat, had been ordered to engage the Turks in this zone; for once there was no limit to the amount of ammunition which could be fired off. Only at two points near Fusilier Bluff did Turkish infantry actually leave their trenches, and they were driven back with heavy losses by the 7th North Staffordshires in the last infantry engagement on the Gallipoli Peninsula.

All went quiet before dark, and that night, as planned, 2,300 men, nine guns and almost a thousand animals were embarked. All that remained now was to pray to the gods of storm and tempest, that their curiosity would not bring them to Cape Helles to participate in the final act of the tragedy which had played out there.

The morning of 8 January dawned clear and bright; there was a gentle breeze from the south and the barometer had fallen marginally, but the meteorologists agreed that the outlook was stable, at least for the next twenty-four hours. Soon after dark, columns of ships began arriving from Mudros and Imbros. In the van were the battleships *Mars* and *Prince George*, which were to carry two thousand men each, and they were followed by six des-troyers, each of which would pack in a thousand more. Channel steamers would take 6,500, and the remaining few – half a battalion from the 13th Division, which would be embarked from Gully Beach – would be accom-modated aboard the cruiser *Talbot*.

By 1900 the wind from the south had freshened. Over the next hour it continued to gather force, but that was insufficient to hamper the lighters on their first trips out to the ships waiting offshore. However, by 2100 it had got up to 35 knots (70km/hr, a Force 8 Gale on the Beaufort Scale) and was still increasing, the sea now pounding the piers and breakwaters. Truly magnificent seamanship was the order of that night, and time after time the sailors overcame tremendous difficulties to bring tired soldiers aboard their vessels, the crews of the destroyers, in particular, working a succession of small miracles as they brought their ships alongside the makeshift breakwaters. Almost unbelievably, the entire second echelon, together with all thirty-seven guns, left the beaches in good order and on schedule.

Just before 0200 the rearguard party of the 13th Division was reported to be leaving Gully Beach aboard two motor lighters. There was a last-minute hitch – one of the lighters ran aground, and the men aboard it, under Maude's command, marched to W Beach and were taken off from there – but by 0345 the last of the boats pushed off into the raging sea. Before they reached the waiting transports the magazine erupted thunderously; behind them the flames of the burning supply dumps lit up the sky, and as the weary men climbed the accommodation ladders the Turks realised they had been hoodwinked once more, and shells began to rain down on the now empty beaches in an empty gesture of vengeful fury.

Once again, the evacuation had gone off almost exactly according to plan, the vicissitudes of the weather notwithstanding, and without loss of life. The Great Adventure of the Gallipoli campaign was over. Now all that remained was to apportion blame for what was seen as a disaster without virtue . . .

Like the catastrophe of Kut, the failure of the Dardanelles operation resulted in a Parliamentary Commission. The Dardanelles Commission's report was not published until 1919; it concluded that the expedition was ill-considered and the difficulties it posed underestimated, and that its execution was hampered by shortages of essential supplies, by personality clashes among its commanders and by all too frequent disagreements and procrastination at the highest levels. It stopped short of condemning any individuals for their incompetence or even their unsuitability and was thus thoroughly devalued.

The entire episode begs a series of interlinked questions, all of them beginning with 'What if . . .' and ending with ' . . . had led to the Allies taking Constantinople?' Turkey would have capitulated, almost certainly; would Germany have acknowledged defeat too, as von Tirpitz suggested she must when deprived of what had become a vital ally? If not, would a thrust up the Danube have taken Austria-Hungary out of the war and had a massive effect on the Eastern Front? Would that have staved off revolution in Russia? There are too many imponderables, but the momentous possibilities, plus the dramatic events, the tremendous hardships and the individual fortitude of the men who took part, combined with the almost miraculous finale, have conspired to turn the Gallipoli campaign into an epic component of the Great War.

IV

EGYPT, PALESTINE AND SYRIA

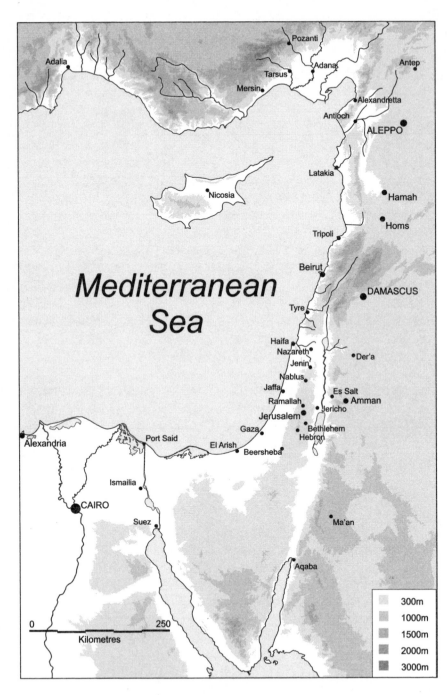

21. Palestine Theatre of Operations

Suez and Sinai

In 1914, Egypt[1] meant just one thing to the British: the Suez Canal. Vital though it was, few enough resources were allocated to its protection in peacetime, but that was to change very rapidly. By the time Britain declared war on Turkey, on 5 November, a Territorial division of the British Army – the 42nd (East Lancashire) – and the Bikaner Camel Corps had arrived to supplement the small indigenous army;[2] and significant numbers of other Indian troops, together with two regiments of Yeomanry from the United Kingdom, were on their way. Late in November it was decided that the Australian and New Zealand Army Corps, then on its way to Europe, would break its journey in Egypt to complete its training. By then overall command of British troops had passed from Maj.-Gen. Julian Byng to Lt.-Gen. Sir John Maxwell;[3] Sir Milne Cheetham was standing in for the Governor-General, Lord Kitchener, as Chargé d'Affaires,[4] and Lt.-Gen. Sir Reginald Wingate remained both Governor-General of the Sudan and Sirdar of the Egyptian Army.

Defence of the canal was entrusted to the Indian divisions, under the command of Maj.-Gen. A Wilson; ANZAC and the East Lancashire Division continued their training in the vicinity of Cairo but were available at need. As well as being a potential target, the canal[5] was a considerable obstacle in its own right (and lay behind one even more formidable: the Sinai Peninsula, sand-desert in the north, and mountainous in the south[6]) and had always figured highly in the overall plan to defend Egypt from an attack from the east; to that end an extensive system of defensive positions was constructed on the west bank. In addition, a total of eighteen defensive positions were constructed on the east bank, mostly to cover ferry crossings or act as assembly points from which counterattacks could be launched. Finally, nine warships, drawn from the navies of both Britain and France, were deployed along the canal, most of them obsolete battleships.

On the outbreak of war, the Turks had no forces in the immediate area. Syria and Palestine (at the time the former referred to the whole of the fertile coastal strip from north of Alexandretta south to the frontier with Egypt at Rafah; the latter was the southern portion of that strip, south from Tyre) were the territory of the Fourth Army, with its headquarters at Damascus; VI Corps was based at Adana, in the north,[7] and VIII Corps at Damascus.[8] Zekki Pasha, the Fourth Army's commander-in-chief, was soon replaced by Ahmed Jemal Pasha, who, having relinquished his post as Minister of the

Marine, arrived at Damascus on 18 November. Jemal *Biyuk* – 'the Great', to distinguish him from the commander of VIII Corps, Mohammed Jemal, who was known as *Kuchuk* ('the Small'); it had nothing to do with physical stature – had a German officer, Col. von Frankenberg und Proschlitz, as his chief of staff, and another, Col. Friedrich Freiherr Kress von Kressenstein, served in the same capacity to Jemal *Kuchuk.*

With the seaways cut, the lines of communication with Constantinople were poor at best, thanks to the gaps in the railway in Cilicia, though internal links within the region were better. A standard-gauge railway ran from Aleppo as far as Rayak; there it gave way to a 1.05-metre-gauge line through Damascus to Der'a, which then split into two, the eastern line running south to the Hejaz, as far as El Medina, and the western to the sea at Haifa. There was also a branch line from Rayak to Beirut. East of Haifa a line to Nablus and Tul el Karm extended from the latter to Lydda, with spurs to Jaffa and Jerusalem, and then to Beersheba and almost to Gaza. Since this entire system was cut off from that of Anatolia, and there were no local coal deposits, as soon as the Allied naval blockade was put into effect, coal for the locomotives was at a premium; when supplies from two colliers in the port of Haifa were exhausted, the operators had to fall back on burning wood.

Throughout December 1914, the Turks assembled troops in the vicinity of Beersheba, and around the turn of the year they began pushing forward into Sinai, occupying Nakhl by 4 January. Kressenstein it was who formulated the plan, which required the main body (which consisted of the 10th and 25th Divisions,[9] accompanied not only by nine batteries of field guns but also by two 15-cm howitzers and at least one 12-cm gun) to cross Sinai from Beersheba by way of El Auja and Ibni, pass between the Jebel el Maghara and Jebel Yelleg, and come to the canal by way of Bir el Jifjafa and Moiya Harab, a distance of over two hundred kilometres.[10] This was an audacious move, for water supplies were by no means guaranteed. A basic quantity was provided, carried by 5,000 camels, but the discovery of wells along the route was most welcome. Simultaneously, smaller parties headed for Qantara by way of El Arish, and through Nakhl towards Suez. By 30 January it was clear that an attack was imminent, and that its main focus was to come in the central sector of the canal, but whether it would fall north or south of Ismailia was still uncertain.

On 1 February there were around three hundred Turks at Bir el Dueidar, opposite Qantara, and twenty kilometres south at Bir el Mahadat were perhaps ten times that number, with a similarly sized force at Bir Habeita, only ten kilometres from the canal. The main body of around 8,000 was at Moiya Harab, and there was no indication whether it would move north-westwards to reinforce the group at Bir Habeita or south-westwards to launch an independent assault near Suez. By now warships had entered the canal from both the north and the south, and the New Zealand Infantry Brigade had been brought up and deployed.

By the following morning, Turkish troops had advanced to within five kilometres of the canal over a wide front between the Great Bitter Lake and Lake Timsah; under cover of a sandstorm they sent parties to cross the canal, but the wind dropped at the critical moment. They came under effective fire and all save three parties were driven back. Most were killed or wounded but a group of men managed to evade capture until later in the day. These were the only Turkish troops to cross the canal of their own volition in the course of the war.

The next day large numbers of troops were again seen approaching the canal, but were driven off by gunfire from the battleship *Requin*, moored in a specially prepared position in Lake Timsah, and the protected cruiser *D'Entrecasteaux*, anchored where the canal debouches into the Great Bitter Lake. Turkish artillery then began bombarding the ships, but was soon stopped by counter-battery fire. Elsewhere, attacks on El Kubri and El Ferdan had been desultory affairs, and a third at Qantara was little more effective, being driven off with heavy losses by machine gun fire.

All concerned expected the offensive to be renewed the following morning, but to universal surprise it was not, save for the occasional ragged volley of rifle fire. Reconnaissance showed that forward positions the Turks had dug were all empty, though reserve positions well to the east were occupied. On 5 February aerial reconnaissance revealed that Turkish forces were massed east of Bir Habeita, and though they threatened to advance, nothing came of that, either. Other organised bodies were located at Moiya Harab and at Rigum, but by 10 February they had all retired;[11] a shortage of fully trained men (and the lack of a provision to keep troops supplied with water) meant that they went unpursued. British losses over the entire period totalled 163, including thirty-two dead; Turkish losses were thought to have numbered around two thousand, including over seven hundred taken prisoner.

Over the next month the British forces in Egypt returned to routine duties. The nearest Turkish forces were at Nakhl[12] and at Bir Hassana, midway between the former and El Arish, and though up to 30,000 troops were thought to be in the vicinity of Beersheba (from which a narrow-gauge railway line was being pushed forward to Kossaima), the atmosphere in the British camp was untroubled. (As was demonstrated by the removal, in March, of most of the battleships stationed in the canal to provide fire support;[13] only *Requin* remained permanently on station.)

Following the attack in early February, the canal front was quiet until 22 March. Turks approached Shallufa Post that day, but withdrew when fired upon. In April two attempts to mine the canal were disrupted, as was another on 30 May. A month later the Turks – or more accurately, Bedouin Arabs – were more successful, and the Holt Line's steamer *Teiresias* hit a mine in the Little Bitter Lake. The ship swung broadside on and blocked the channel, but the obstacle was cleared by that evening.

A further attempt to approach the canal was made late in November, but that too was driven off, and that was the last for many months to come.

In the wake of the decision to abandon the offensive at Gallipoli, Maxwell set out to establish just how many troops would be required to defend the canal against a determined campaign, and his conclusions were alarming: holding a defensive line some 12,000 yards (11km) east of the waterway – which put shipping beyond the range of the heaviest guns – would require twelve infantry divisions, a cavalry division and twenty batteries of heavy artillery. Two further infantry divisions would be required to maintain order and safeguard communications, and another would be necessary to defend against a possible attack from the Senussids in the west (see below). At the War Office, the General Staff made its own calculations and came up with a similar total. It also estimated that the Turks would have the potential to mount such a campaign, and perhaps throw 200,000 men at the canal, by January 1916.

While defence of the canal against an attack from the east was the largest concern by far of the British administration in Cairo, it was not the only one, for potential problems had surfaced in another quarter, in the deserts to the west of the Nile, where a fundamentalist Islamic sect known as the Senussids – named for Sayyid Muhammad ibn Ali as-Senussi, a scholar and teacher who traced his descent to Fatima, the daughter of the Prophet Mohammed, and who had connections to the fundamentalist Wahhabi sect in Arabia – had been gathering adherents since the 1830s. The Senussids, though they had violently opposed the colonisation of Algeria and Libya by the French and Italians, were not natural allies of the Turks, but their shared religion made them potential enemies of the British, and shortly after the outbreak of war with Britain and France, the Turkish government sent Ferik Nuri Bey (Killigil), Enver Pasha's half-brother, to enlist their co-operation.

Within weeks the Senussids,[14] now led by Sayyid Ahmed ash-Sharif, with a Turkish-Arab officer, Jafar el Askeri, as military commander, had attacked Egyptian posts and personnel in the Western Desert, and by 10 December the Western Frontier Force had been established to deal with them. The first major encounter came late in January at Halazin, 35km south-west of Matruh; it was indecisive, but a month later a mixed detachment of infantry and cavalry confronted Senussids in an entrenched, wired position at Agagiya, twenty-five kilometres south-east of Barrani, and achieved a decisive result. Jafar Pasha and two other Turkish officers were captured, though Nuri Bey, who was also present, escaped. The Arabs' losses of around five hundred amounted to about a third of their number. The Senussids never again stood against a British force, but they continued to launch nuisance raids for two more years.

The campaign was brought to a conclusion only in January 1917, when a flying column of armoured cars attacked Senussid forces assembled at Siwa. The arrival of the cars took the enemy by surprise. Though they were not able to penetrate into the camp itself, throughout the night the Senussids could be seen burning stores; by daybreak they had disappeared, heading westwards. With his much-reduced forces scattered, the sheikh's appetite for insurrection disappeared. He remained in the *maghreb* until August 1918, when he was transported to Constantinople aboard an Austrian submarine, but caused no further problems for the Allies. His cousin, Sayyid Idris, formed a genuine relationship with the British. He moved to Egypt in 1923, and remained there until early in 1943, when he returned to recently liberated Libya. He was declared king on 24 December 1951, and ruled until 1 September 1969, when he was deposed in a bloodless coup by Col. Muammar al Qaddafi.

Further south a one-time ally of the British, Ali Dinar, the Sultan of Darfur – he had defected from the cause of the Khalifa Abdullah ibn Muhammad, the successor to the Mahdi (Muhammad Ahmad), on the eve of the Battle of Omdurman, and fled with several thousand followers to El Fasher – had aligned himself with the Senussids, and soon after the outbreak of the war with Turkey he responded to the caliph's call and declared jihad against the British. That was a largely meaningless gesture to begin with, but by late 1915 he had begun to mass men with the object of invading the Sudan. Wingate assembled a sizeable force at El Nahud, around three hundred and fifty kilometres west of Khartoum, and in March 1916 he ordered it forward to occupy the wells at Um Shanga and Jebel el Hilla, just within Ali Dinar's territory. That passed off without serious incident, but by now the Sultan's ragged army had risen to perhaps six thousand men. Murray sent reinforcements, including four aircraft, a wireless section and heavier artillery, and Wingate's troops advanced on El Fasher. On 22 May they met Ali Dinar's forces in a distinctly anachronistic pitched battle reminiscent of Omdurman, which saw machine guns pitted against single-shot rifles, killing or wounding well over a thousand for almost no loss. That broke Ali Dinar's forces; he was cornered in the Jebel Juba, two hundred and fifty kilometres south-west of El Fasher, with perhaps two hundred followers, six months later, and killed.

When we turned our attention away from what a later generation of British servicemen would come to know as the Suez Canal Zone, towards the end of 1915, Sir John Maxwell was turning his energies to organising the defence of the waterway in the expectation that once the Turkish forces on the Gallipoli Peninsula were released, they would descend through Syria upon Sinai. It had already been decided that the British forces evacuated from Gallipoli would be sent to Egypt to rest, recuperate, refit and retrain – not only was it near at hand, but the climate over the winter was ideal – and that these men would provide the manpower for the defence of the canal. Even if the pessimistic expectation that only half the men then garrisoning Gallipoli would be safely evacuated was fulfilled, the influx would clearly put considerable pressure on Maxwell, and it had been decided to install a dual command structure in Egypt, with Maxwell to retain responsibility for the western defences and internal security but with a new appointee to take charge of the canal defences. That job was originally to have gone to Monro, but in the event it would become part of a large reshuffle and go to Sir Archibald Murray after he was succeeded as Chief of the Imperial General Staff by Sir William Robertson.

Murray arrived in Egypt to take up his new command on 9 January 1916, with Maj.-Gen. AL Lynden-Bell as his chief of staff. By that evening it was known that the evacuation of the entire Allied contingent from the Gallipoli Peninsula had gone off without a single man being lost, a possibility which had almost certainly never occurred to anyone on the General Staff. The result was a much larger pool of men than would be required for defence of the canal, and Murray was instructed to establish the Imperial Strategic Reserve, which would provide troops for other theatres as required.[15] With the benefit of hindsight, it is clear that the decision to split Egypt into two commands was a poor one. Maxwell and Murray soon began to jockey for position. Maxwell, by now little more than a quartermaster, stood little chance of success, and on 10 March he was informed that he would be returning home,[16] and that the two commands would be united under Murray. The handover took place on 19 March, when the Force in Egypt (as the British garrison in the country was known, to differentiate it from the indigenous Egyptian Army) was combined with the Mediterranean Expeditionary Force to become the Egyptian Expeditionary Force (EEF).

By the end of March considerable progress had been made in constructing a defensive system to the east of the canal, narrow-gauge railway lines and pipelines for drinking water being laid out to the sites of the entrenched positions. The front was now divided into three sectors, the first from Suez to Kabrit, on the Great Bitter Lake; the second from Kabrit to Ferdan, and the third from Ferdan to Port Said. In addition to constructing static defences, Murray was buying up camels in order to create mobile columns, one from each defensive sector, and was accumulating material to allow the construction of the railway to Qatiya. The permanent way from Qantara was commenced on 10 March. Within four weeks 26km of track had been laid. By mid-April the 5th Mounted Brigade, together with half a company from the 5th Royal Scots Fusiliers, had been deployed to protect the line and the work crews, with posts at Romani, Bir el Dueidar, Hamisah and Qatiya; the Oghratina oasis, eight kilometres east from Qatiya, was then occupied by mounted troops as a forward position.

Reconnaissance had reported the presence of Turkish troops at Bir el Abd, twenty-five kilometres from Qatiya, and on 19 April they raided an outpost at Bir el Mageibra and established a camp of their own there. The British commander on the spot, Brig.-Gen. Wiggin, assembled the Warwickshire and the Worcestershire Yeomanry at Hamisah; they rode out before dawn on 23 April, and arrived at the Turkish camp just after first light, to find it occupied by just a few guards. The camp was destroyed, and the column returned to Hamisah by 0900.

In the meantime Turks from Bir el Abd had attacked Oghratina and forced its garrison's surrender, and then began to advance on Qatiya, and simultaneously the group Wiggin had set out to confront had advanced from Bir el Mageibra to Dueidar. Just after first light, taking advantage of the morning mist, they assaulted the 5th Royal Scots Fusiliers' positions; they were stopped short of the British lines, but remained within rifle shot and kept up a steady fire. At 0625 the commander of the 4th Royal Scots Fusiliers, eight kilometres to the rear, was asked to send up reinforcements, and hurried two companies forward. The augmented force was sufficient to keep the Turks at bay but not to drive them off, and it was not until a squadron of the 5th Australian Light Horse arrived, around noon, that the enemy broke off the engagement.

Wiggin meanwhile had heard the sound of artillery from the direction of Qatiya, but after a march of around thirty kilometres was obliged to water his horses before setting off again, and it was 1000 before Lt.-Col. Coventry led the Worcester Yeomanry to investigate. He found a full-scale attack in process, and threw his men into it, dismounted; this relieved some of the pressure on the British right flank, but only briefly. Wiggin later tried to fight his way through to his aid with the Warwicks, but was forced to fall back on Hamisah, and the Gloucester Hussars, who advanced from Romani, were also driven back.

Around 1500 the Turks overran Qatiya; just eighty men escaped, and a total of three and a half squadrons of Yeomanry were either killed or captured. Later that day and the following morning the 2nd and the rest of the 5th Australian Light Horse moved up from Qantara, but by then the Turks had cleared the area. The incident hardly delayed work on the railway, but it caused the Northern Sector commander, Lawrence, to review and strengthen his forward positions. Post-war, it was discovered that the Turkish forces had been under Kressenstein's command and amounted to a little over 3,500 men with six guns. Kressenstein himself described the operation as a 'fighting reconnaissance', and what he learned certainly stood him in good stead when he came to attack Romani, three months later.

By the first week of June 1916, the 52nd (Lowland) Division had moved up to occupy Romani, which was now the railhead. Living conditions for such a large body were less than ideal; daytime temperatures were regularly over 40°C and every drop of drinking water came from the Nile, by way of a pipeline which had by now reached Pelisium station, and thence by truck or camel. The defensive positions, which were prominent and covered by wire, consisted of eighteen strongpoints, each big enough to accommodate up to half a company and sometimes more. During this period there was little activity on the ground, but both sides used their air forces to effect, a British raid on the Turkish airfield at El Arish, on 18 June, destroying two aircraft and two hangars and damaging several more, though at the cost of three machines.

On 17 July, Turkish activity increased, and aerial reconnaissance showed that up to 2,500 men had assembled at Bir Bayud, south of Bir el Abd, and Gameil, to the west, with evidence of other large bodies at hand; by 20 July a further 3,000 men were at Bir el Abd and Magheira, and 2,000 more as far west as Oghratina. An offensive was clearly about to begin.[17] In response, two battalions of the 42nd Division were moved to Qantara, and the 53rd Division's 158th Brigade to Romani; by the night of 22 July total British strength in the sector was some 14,000 men, all that the water supply could accommodate.

In the event, the threatened offensive was slow in coming, and it was 4 August before it began in earnest, though skirmishes had taken place in the days before. The delay gave Murray all the time he needed to organise his defensive strategy, instructing Lawrence to be ready to deploy mounted infantry to extend his right south-west of Katib Gannit, a prominent sand dune, to Hod el Enna, wagering that the Turks would try to turn that flank. He also pre-positioned naval monitors off Mahamdiya, placed an armoured train in the sidings at Qantara and stationed all available aircraft at Port Said, Ismailia, Qantara and Romani.

Murray's guess proved accurate, and by 0200 two regiments of the 1st Light Horse Brigade were in action south-west of Katib Gannit. When superior numbers told, the Australians retreated to their horse lines, mounted up and retired to their secondary positions. Only with the coming of daylight did the Turks realise how light was the opposition, and they then advanced determinedly.

Lawrence, learning that a Turkish flanking movement was developing, now ordered the New Zealand Mounted Rifles Brigade up to support the Light Horse, with 5th Mounted Brigade – sixteen kilometres back, at Hill 70 – to follow, the 3rd LHB, then at Ballybunnion, being sent up to Hill 70 to replace them. The NZMRB was slow in responding, and by the time it arrived at Dueidar the Turkish advance had swung to the right, its axis now aimed at Canterbury Hill, south of Pelisium Station. Brig.-Gen. Chaytor ordered the NZMRB to attack to forestall them; as they deployed they made contact with the Australians to their left, and were soon joined by the 5th Mounted Brigade, coming up from the south-west, and by Yeomanry units. The Australians and New Zealanders advanced dismounted on the Turkish positions on Mount Royston, but were held back by deep, soft sand, and made only slow progress. It was 1600 before they were within striking distance, but then a well-timed charge by the Yeomanry cleared the southern spur of the objective and simultaneously horse-guns dealt with a troublesome mountain battery on the crest, and they took the hill at the charge. By 1700 it was in their hands, together with around five hundred prisoners, two machine guns and the mountain battery, with the remaining Turks in full flight. Infantry battalions were then sent to advance on Wellington Ridge from the southern positions in the defensive line; they reached a point a hundred metres short of the crest, were halted by heavy rifle fire and took up positions for the night, with orders to stay in contact and keep the Turks pinned down.

With five mounted brigades at his disposal, Lawrence was very well positioned to inflict a considerable defeat on the retreating Turks the following morning, and he wasted no time. As day broke, the 7th and 8th Scottish Rifles on Wellington Ridge attacked the Turkish positions. The Turks' nerve broke; 864 surrendered while the rest fled, only to be corralled by the 7th ALH and the Wellington Mounted Rifles coming up from the south. In all, almost two thousand more prisoners were taken in the space of well under an hour. By 1030 the mounted brigades were in full pursuit of the Turks' main body across a broad front, subduing them with very little effort as they overtook them, until they reached Qatiya, where the Turkish rearguard made a successful stand. This was the first of a series of developed fall-back positions that Kressenstein had constructed along his line of retreat.

By now the troops had been in action for three – and some of them five – days, and fatigue was beginning to tell most severely. However, Maj.-Gen. Chauvel, the commander of the Australia and New Zealand Mounted Division, was loath to give up while there was still a chance of inflicting a still heavier defeat on the Turkish column, and he put a plan for a last all-out effort to Lawrence. He would, he suggested, march the 1st and 2nd LHBs to Qatiya, where they would water, and thence to Hod Hamad, six kilometres north-west of Bir el Abd, where the Turks were now located, to arrive at 0300 on 9 August. There they would rest, then move up to within three kilometres of the objective to rendezvous with the NZMRB for an attack at 0630, the 3rd LHB having worked round the enemy's left in order to cut his line of retreat. The 5th Mounted Brigade would be in reserve. If the Turks put up strong resistance, then the attack would be called off. Frankly, the chances of success were small, but Lawrence accepted the proposal.

The approach went according to plan. By 0500 the NZMRB, in the van, had driven into the Turkish outposts and had reached a rise overlooking the Turkish positions. Joined by the Australians they began to lay down fire on the Turkish trenches, but it soon became obvious to the defenders that their numbers were limited. At 0600 Turkish infantrymen left their trenches and stormed forward in a counterattack; they were held by a combination of machine guns and the Somerset Battery, RHA, and retreated. At 0730 they tried again, and this time penetrated the line between the NZMRB and the 2nd LHB, only to be thrown back once more. That pattern was repeated until early afternoon, and though the smoke from fires indicated that the Turks had begun burning their stores, there was no real possibility of dislodging them with the forces to hand. Chauvel, his men exhausted, was finally compelled to give the order to break off and retreat to Oghratina, leaving the

3rd LHB to watch over the Turks. By 12 August Bir-el Abd had been abandoned, the Turks pulling back to Salamana; a bombardment from the horse batteries followed, and with that Kressenstein withdrew to El Arish. His adventure had cost him over four thousand men taken prisoner and perhaps the same again killed and wounded, as well as much *matériel* and livestock. British casualties amounted to just over 1,100 killed, wounded and missing. The Battle of Romani marked the end of Turkish attempts on the Suez Canal.

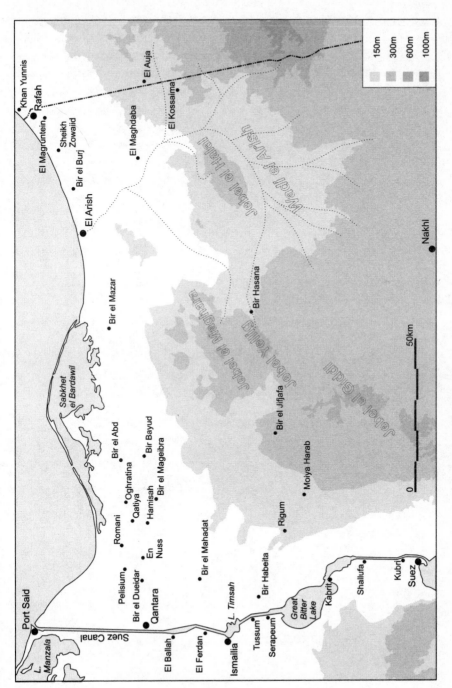

22. *Palestine – The Suez Canal and N. Sinai*

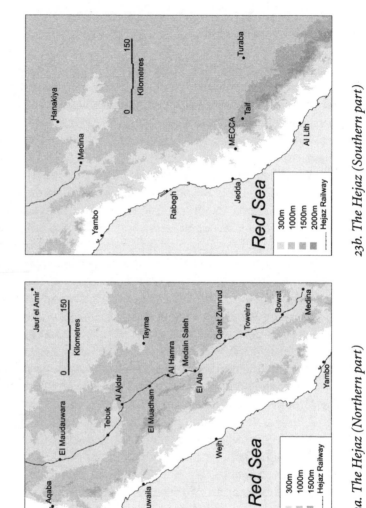

23a. *The Hejaz (Northern part)*

23b. *The Hejaz (Southern part)*

To the Gates of Palestine

By the time Murray defeated Kressenstein's forces at Romani, a minor new front had opened up in the theatre: the Sherif of Mecca, Hussein ibn Ali, had risen in revolt. In military terms his forces were to achieve very little – which is hardly surprising, given their lack of sophistication – but it is nonetheless necessary to look at the causes, and the effects, of the insurrection, for it was to have repercussions after 1918.

In the very early days of the war, the men Kitchener had left behind to manage Egyptian affairs in his absence[1] had hatched a plot to foment a rising in the Hejaz, the all-important – because it included the holy sites of Mecca and Medina – western coastal sector of the Arabian Peninsula. Led by poor intelligence and deliberately misleading information supplied by men who had hidden agendas of their own,[2] they made ill-founded judgements.

While Kitchener's primary concern centred on the Turks taking the Suez Canal, the result of which would have been grave, though possibly not disastrous,[3] he was also apprehensive of the possibility of the caliph – Sultan Mehmet V – proclaiming jihad[4] and his call being answered by the Sunni community of which he was the spiritual head, many millions of whom lived in India.[5] The plot Kitchener's men hatched was aimed at resolving that concern, and centred on replacing Sultan Mehmet as caliph by an Arab who would inspire his people – who represented 40 per cent of the population of the Ottoman Empire – to rise up against the Turks. Its inspiration sprang from Gilbert Clayton's recollection that Abdullah, the son of the Hashemite[6] Hussein ibn Ali, whom Sultan Abdul Hamid had appointed Sherif and Emir of Mecca over the objections of the CUP in 1908, had visited Cairo the previous year, and then again in February and April. He had met both Kitchener and Storrs, and sounded them out as to how Britain would respond if his father's position came under threat from the Young Turks, maintaining that the other strong men of Arabia, Ibn Saud and Ibn Rashid, would rally to his father's cause and submit to his authority if he rose against the Empire. This seemed little short of a gift from heaven, for who better to install as caliph than the man who controlled the holy city of Mecca? Clayton – taken in and his enthusiasm fertilised by shadowy figures such as Muhammed al-Faruqi and Aziz Ali al-Masri[7] – immediately began to evolve a plan to boost Hussein, but crucially there was one element he failed to consider: Abdullah's reliability, or rather the lack of it, there being not a scrap of truth in his assertion that the Saudis or the Rashidis would follow the Hashemite flag.

Over the weeks which followed a plot was hatched, placed and initiated, and the form of it was seductive enough to convince Hussein – who understood the true nature of the caliphate when the British did not, recognising that in the right circumstances, perhaps in the right hands, it conveyed temporal as well as spiritual authority – that he was indeed to become King-in-Waiting, not just of the Hejaz, but of all the Arabs.[8] The folly came to fruition a full year later, on 24 October 1915, in the so-called Hussein–McMahon Correspondence, which promised British support for Arab independence.[9]

When the India Office – in the person of Arthur Hirtzel, then Secretary to the Political Department – belatedly[10] learned of the undertakings given to Hussein, including the suggestion that he might perhaps assume the caliphate, its reaction was one of horror. Primarily, the very notion of a united pan-Arabia went against the India Office's policy for the region, while there was a very real risk that this sort of interference would do what the Ottoman call to *jihad* had so singularly failed to do, and alienate the many millions of Sunni Muslims living under the Raj. And who knew to what that might lead? It was, after all, less than sixty years since the Mutiny in India. And there was another objection, too, and a more practical one: Kitchener's men were backing the wrong horse, for by the Indian Office's estimate, it was Ibn Saud, not Sherif Hussein, who stood the best chance of uniting the Arabian Peninsula,[11] not by persuasion, but by force of arms. When the results were in, long after the coming war was over, Delhi scooped the pool, metaphorically speaking, for Ibn Saud routed first the Rashidis, by 1921, and then the Hashemites, by the end of 1925; by 1932 he was able to proclaim himself King of Saudi Arabia, appending his family name to that of the land, though he had been that in all but name for some years.

Long before the promise to support Arab independence was made, Asquith's government had set up an interdepartmental committee, chaired by Sir Maurice de Bunsen, to define Britain's goals in the Middle East and devise an outline plan for achieving them. Unsurprisingly, the de Bunsen Committee's report judged that it was desirable to establish British influence over the entire region, and it proposed a 'divide-and-rule' strategy, splitting the Ottoman Empire up into five regions: Anatolia, Armenia, Mesopotamia, Palestine and Syria. This would later be refined into the infamous Sykes-Picot Agreement (see Chapter 17) which attempted – well in advance – to form a basis for the distribution of the spoils of the Great War in the Middle East between its victors, Britain and France (which was later extended to include their latecomer allies, Italy and Greece).

Once the committee's findings were in, Asquith's government sent Sir Mark Sykes, Kitchener's personal representative on it, on a wide-ranging mission which took in the Balkans, Egypt, Mesopotamia and India to 'interpret' de Bunsen's recommendations to the men on the spot. Such encounters cannot but be a two-way street, and he returned to London, in December 1915, a much wiser young man than when he had set off, six months earlier. In Egypt, in July 1915, he fell in with an old acquaintance, Storrs, and through him met Clayton, with whom he formed a close bond, the two agreeing in principle that Arab affairs, independent, of course, from the Ottoman Empire, should be guided from Cairo under influence from London.[12] Moving on to India, Sykes soon ran foul of Hardinge, who had a very different view: that India should annex Mesopotamia, that Arab independence was undesirable and Cairo's involvement 'absolutely fantastical'. Naturally, Sykes passed through Cairo once more on his way back to London, and reported the Viceroy's opposition to Clayton; from their discussions the notion of an 'Arab Bureau' was born, and on Sykes' return to London he began to agitate for its creation (under his own leadership . . .). He was a few weeks too late to have a clear run – Austen Chamberlain, now Secretary of State for India, had already begun to urge the creation of an Islamic Bureau, to combat German-funded anti-British propaganda efforts in India, Persia and Afghanistan, and it was felt that the two might interfere with each other – but in the event he won out, with a watered-down proposal: the Bureau would be established, but as a section of the Egyptian government's Intelligence Department (Prop.: G. Clayton).

Many were the objections which were to circumscribe the Bureau's establishment, none of them more important (or, one might add, largely irrelevant) than that of the Director of Naval Intelligence, 'Blinker' Hall; to placate him, the candidate he put forward to head it – David Hogarth, an Oxford University archaeologist serving on his staff – was selected. Hogarth brought in a number of academic protégés, among them one Thomas Edward Lawrence, whom we have already encountered as one of those attempting to buy the freedom of the Kut garrison in April 1916 (see Chapter 3). Lawrence, a postgraduate research student[13] who had travelled widely in the Middle East, pre-war, was turned down for active service on health grounds but obtained a commission late in 1914, and held a variety of junior posts in Clayton's Intelligence Department while working closely with the Bureau. Late in 1916, after Clayton had been superseded by Thomas Holdich, whom Lawrence mistrusted, he joined it full time. During his service with the Bureau, Lawrence acted as one of a team of liaison officers[14] with the Sherifian forces, and expedited deliveries of arms, ammunition and money; he also helped with training, took part in military actions, gathered intelligence, and, perhaps most crucially, worked to forge relationships with tribal leaders. In the spring of 1918, in Aqaba, he fell in with an American cinema news reporter named Lowell Thomas, who later built him up to become Lawrence of Arabia, a character he then further embellished masterfully himself in *Seven Pillars of Wisdom*, his own account of the part he played in the Arab Revolt.

*

When Sherif Hussein declared himself to be in revolt against his Ottoman masters, on 5 June 1916,[15] Clayton et al. naturally claimed the credit for it. They were deluded. In fact, Feisal, the Sherif's third son, had been in Constantinople that spring, and had learned of a plan to depose his father; when, on his return home, he reported signs that additional Turkish troops were moving towards the Hejaz, Hussein wasted no time.[16] He had already begun to receive shipments of rifles and ammunition from Wingate, but without waiting until all his men were equipped[17] he ordered his eldest son Ali, and Feisal, to raise his standard at Medina. Feisal made an unsuccessful attack on the city, while Ali marched to cut the Hejaz railway at Medain Saleh, 290km to the north-west.

These offensives were really no more than demonstrations, announcing Hussein's intentions. His forces were certainly no match for the Turks, especially when the latter were able to deploy even light artillery – which terrified the Arabs, and routinely put them to flight even if poorly aimed – and it was some time before they scored their first victory, at Mecca. Simultaneously irregulars of the Harb tribe attacked the port of Jeddah; with support from RIMS *Hardinge* and the light cruiser *Fox*, together with aircraft from the carrier HMS *Ben-my-Chree*, which bombed targets in the city, the Turks were eventually forced to surrender, giving up sixteen guns and many machine guns. This gave the British a working port of entry, and men and guns from Egypt were soon landed. Rabegh, up the coast, and Yambo (Yanbu), further north still, subsequently fell to the Arabs.

Taif, 115km south-east of Mecca, proved difficult, but the arrival of the guns from Egypt eventually made a telling difference, and the town surrendered on 22 September. Things went less well at Medina. After his demonstration, Feisal had made a half-hearted attempt to invest the city, but on 3 July the Turks sortied and beat his forces convincingly, driving them off. On 3 August, by which time he had been joined by his brother Ali, the Turks attacked again, and this time drove the Arabs back thirty kilometres in a running fight. Clearly little could be done until the Arabs could be armed in greater numbers. Wingate was given the responsibility, and despatched Lt.-Col. EG Wilson, Governor of the Red Sea Province of the Sudan, to Jeddah to act as his representative until a military mission could be established. Wilson set about distributing rifles, and by November, a total of around 20,000 men had been equipped and were organised in three strong bands: 8,000 south of Medina under Ali, and 4,000 under his brother Abdullah, to the north-east of the city, with a mobile column, 8,000 men under Feisal (including, since 23 October, Lawrence, on his first assignment in Arabia) based at Yambo and ready to move inland to operate against the railway.

Hussein had always maintained – to the British – that once his standard was raised, men would flock to it in their hundreds of thousands, including all the Arab troops of the Ottoman army. That defection never took place; no Arab unit ever went over to his side, and neither did any figure of military or political importance save for Jafar el Askeri, qv. In short, there was no support for the so-called Arab Revolt outside the Hejaz, and the claims Hussein, and his son Feisal, later made, to represent the wider Arab community – Hussein declared himself King of the Arab Nation in October 1916, much to the discomfort of his British advisers, who avoided referring to him as such; 'King of the Hejaz' was as far as they would go – were groundless.

The Turks were not idle. Having formally deposed Hussein they proposed to replace him as Sherif by Ali Haidar, brought from Constantinople for the purpose together with eight additional infantry battalions, and had sent other contingents north from the Yemen; in all they had around 15,000 men in and south of Medina and 1,500 more along the line of the railway to the north. It was only a matter of time before they moved on the Sherifian capital, but that move would almost certainly have to come by way of Rabegh, alternative routes being largely waterless.

There had been a proposal, formulated in early September, to land a British brigade at Rabegh; Wingate and McMahon had supported it against determined opposition from Murray, who maintained that the presence of Christian troops so near to Mecca would have a disastrous outcome.[18] His view was finally accepted when Wilson suggested that Hussein be 'invited' to ask for them, and refused to do so. That decision, correct though it undoubtedly was, put a significant strain on the Sherifian forces, and when the Turks began their advance from Medina in early December they soon made significant progress, driving Ali's band back on to Rabegh. Feisal, who was now emerging as the real leader of his father's forces, was advised by Lawrence to ask his brother Abdullah to move to block the railway at Wadi Ais, 115km north of Medina, in an attempt to distract the Turks. In the meantime, Feisal would march north along the coast from Yambo some 320km to establish a new base at Wejh, from where his threat to cut the railway, and in the process isolate Medina, would be much more credible.

By the time the march began on 18 January 1917, Feisal's forces had grown to around 10,000, and now boasted a mountain battery, landed from Egypt but manned by his own fighters, hastily trained. Five days later a five-hundred-man advanced guard was landed from British warships and Wejh was secured, its garrison fleeing south into the arms of Feisal's own vanguard when it arrived two days later. In response to the very successful raids Feisal's men[19] began launching on the railway the Turks gave up any thought of retaking Mecca and retreated to Medina, where, unprepared for a siege, they were soon reduced to eating their pack animals. Elsewhere, the Turkish presence was now restricted to blockhouses along the line of the railway, from which repair parties issued only in significant strength; protected by mountain artillery and machine guns, they went unchallenged, the Arabs allowing them to do their work in peace before returning to the scene under cover of darkness to undo it.

The spring of 1917 found the British in Palestine at last, and with that it became important to extend the Arabs' campaign of armed resistance northwards, out of the Hejaz and into Syria. In early May Lawrence was ordered to gain the confidence of Nuri ibn Shalaan, the fourth of the important Arabian leaders,[20] and one whose influence stretched to Damascus. He delegated the task to one of his companions, Auda Abu Tayi of the Eastern Howeitat, ranked highly amongst the Sherif's men. Auda travelled to meet Nuri at Jauf el Amir, 450km east of Aqaba, while Lawrence went north to Nebk (An Nabk), his objective Ba'albek in the Lebanon, and his task to obtain promises of adherence from local leaders along the way. He was back in Nebk by 19 June and organised a raid on the railway north of Amman before moving south to rejoin Auda.

Together they led a force of around five hundred tribesmen which captured a Turkish *Jandarma* post on the Ma'an–Aqaba road, then retreated to a concealed position in the hills at Abu el Lissal. As expected, a strong force of Turkish infantry sortied from Ma'an. The Arabs watched as they encamped, and engaged them the next morning; imprudently the Turks fired off all the ammunition they had for their one mountain gun, and at dusk the Arabs charged. Within five minutes over three hundred Turks lay dead, and by his account it was only Lawrence's intervention which saved the lives of the rest. Over the following days the Arabs approached Aqaba; on 6 July the important town fell, yielding 600 prisoners with many more killed, and providing the Sherifian forces with a convenient base from which to harry the Turks in Syria and threaten their lines of communications still more effectively.

There was more to come from the Arab Revolt, but at this point we may return to the main narrative and allow it to, as it were, catch up.

Following the defeat of Kressenstein's forces at Romani, Murray, confident that the eastern approaches to the canal were secure, decided to move his headquarters from Ismailia to Cairo. Sir Charles Dobell[21] was appointed GOC, Eastern Frontier Forces. The advance on El Arish – the CIGS having sanctioned in early June the proposal Murray had made back in February – was now to push ahead at full speed, with two basic stipulations: it was to outpace neither the railway nor the pipeline carrying potable water from the Nile. The provision of the latter proved to be the more difficult in execution. The original six-inch pipeline to Romani had proved barely adequate, and was augmented by a twelve-inch pipe, which reached the town on 17 November.

By 7 December the railway and pipeline had advanced to Mazar, and a new force, the 'Desert Column', was constituted from the units which had garrisoned the northern section of the canal defences. It was put under the command of Lt.-Gen. Sir Philip Chetwode, who moved his headquarters up from Bir el Abd. By now, mounted troops had patrolled as far as the outskirts of El Arish, less than fifty kilometres from the frontier of the Ottoman Empire at Rafah, and Murray, ever conservative, had begun expressing concern that his forces – in all he had four under-strength infantry divisions and six cavalry brigades – were insufficient for the task of confronting the Turks on their own borders. On 9 December Sir William Robertson – perhaps spurred on by David Lloyd George, who had just been appointed Prime Minister, and who was known to attach great importance to expelling the Turks from Jerusalem – asked Murray what additional troops he would need to proceed beyond El Arish. Two infantry divisions, he replied, and suggested that they might come from Mesopotamia.[22] There was no chance of that, at least not until the spring, Robertson told him, and added that Lloyd George was taking a personal interest, asking for maximum effort over the winter months. Outgunned, Murray promised to try to reach Rafah with the resources at his command.

When Murray gave the order to advance on El Arish, on 20 December, aerial reconnaissance reported that the 1600 Turks who were thought to have been garrisoning the town had decamped. That changed the nature of the task. Instead of the infantry, it could now be consigned to the cavalry (and camelry; the Imperial Camel Brigade (ICB) had been officially created the previous day, with Brig.-Gen. Smith as its commanding officer), and Chauvel's Australian and New Zealand Mounted Division entered El Arish the next morning. It was joined by the 52nd Division twenty-four hours later, and immediately work was begun on improving the port facilities.

Chetwode learned that the majority of the retreating Turks had gone south-east, towards Magdhaba, heading for the railhead at Kossaima, and instructed Chauvel to pursue. There were no known water sources along the route, and supplies had to be carried by camel, which delayed the operation, but just before dawn on 23 December the Turks' bivouac fires were sighted. Visibility from the air was limited by dense smoke over the target, but eventually enough information came back to provide a picture of the enemy's position. The Turks were occupying a rough pentagon astride the wadi, based on five redoubts, with some linking trenches. Chauvel, whose endurance was limited by his water supply, ordered an immediate attack, employing the 1st and 3rd Australian Light Horse Brigades, the NZ Mounted Rifle Brigade and the Camel Brigade. Support would come from two batteries of the Royal Horse Artillery (Inverness and Somerset) and the Hong Kong Battery of mountain guns which formed part of the ICB.

The 3rd ALHB's 10th Regiment, with two sections of the Machine-Gun Squadron, ordered to loop around to the south to cut off the line of retreat, advanced at the gallop; they took a group of prisoners who reported that the Turks' main body was already moving out. The 1st ALHB was sent directly up the wadi and soon found that the reports of the Turks being in retreat were premature; Cox sent the two remaining regiments of the 3rd ALHB to reinforce the 1st Brigade and they, too, came under heavy fire, as did the ICB, sent around to the north. It was now approaching noon, little progress was being made, and the Camel Brigade, in particular, was taking heavy casualties as it advanced over open ground. Chauvel was faced with the prospect of running out of water – his mounts had had none since leaving El Arish the previous evening – and unless he could penetrate quickly, he would be forced to break off and withdraw. He made the decision to do that at 1350, but even as he was composing the order, he received news that Cox's 3rd Regiment, together with two companies from the Camel Brigade, had taken the redoubt to their front. Within minutes Australians and New Zealanders were pouring into the broken defensive ring, and shortly afterwards the 10th ALHR succeeded in taking the southernmost redoubt. A third was taken at 1600, and with it the garrison commander, Khadir Bey. By 1630 all organised resistance had ceased. In all, almost 1,300 Turks were made prisoner, and most of the rest died on the battlefield; very few escaped. British losses were just under 150.

The relatively easy success of the Magdhaba raid inspired Chetwode, and he was soon lobbying to be permitted to break Murray's golden rule and advance on Rafah without waiting for the railway and pipeline to reach El Arish.[23] Murray accepted his proposal, warning him to run no undue risks, and on 28 December he sent out the first reconnaissance party, to Bir el Burj, twenty kilometres in the direction of Rafah. It found the road perfectly adequate for armoured cars and guns. Two days later the 1st ALHB went further, to Sheikh Zowaiid, just fifteen kilometres from the Turkish positions. At El Arish the character of the countryside had begun to change, with sand giving way to soil and more and more cultivation, but now the improvement was quite dramatic, with plentiful water supplies, good pasturage and crops – and, perhaps more importantly, forage – in the fields and storehouses.

Cox sent patrols as far as high ground overlooking El Magruntein, just a few kilometres short of the frontier, and reported considerable activity there, aerial reconnaissance confirming that the Turks had constructed defensive positions. For all his eagerness to get on, Chetwode made his preparations unhurriedly, content to allow the troops who had fought at Magdhaba time to rest and recuperate, and it was 7 January 1917 before he issued orders for the operation. The brunt of the offensive was to be borne by Cox's 1st and Royston's 3rd Brigades and the ICB, with the 5th Mounted Brigade (Wiggin) and the four Model 'T' Fords of No. 7 Light Car Patrol added. Lt.-Gen. Chetwode decided to command the operation in person.

The force moved off from El Arish at 1600 on 8 January, and by 1100 the following morning had taken Rafah and encircled the objective, having worked up to within 2,000m and come under machine gun and light-artillery fire. Over the hours which followed the attacking troops pressed forward over open terrain which gave very little natural cover, the horse-artillery batteries – and the LCP, which had by now been brought up and was dispersed between El Magruntein and Rafah – keeping pace and providing much-needed support. Progress, however, was slow. At around 1500 Chauvel was informed that at least two battalions of Turkish troops had left Shellal, some fifteen kilometres away in the direction of Beersheba, and were approaching Rafah, and he later learned that more reinforcements were approaching from the direction of Khan Yunis. By 1600 Chetwode was beginning to give serious thought to breaking off the engagement, and by 1630 had issued instructions to Chauvel to do so. Once more the orders were prepared and were actually in the process of being sent out when the breakthrough came. The New Zealand Mounted Rifles Brigade, having advanced over open ground for six to eight hundred metres in a series of rushes, had taken the central redoubt at bayonet point. With that, Turkish resistance began to collapse all across the battlefield, only isolated pockets of men choosing to hold out rather than surrender.

Now the urgency was to gather in wounded and prisoners and retire to the comparative safety of Sheikh Zowaiid – where defensive positions had been prepared with just such an eventuality in mind – before Turkish reinforcements arrived, and that was carried out without further loss, the Turks in fact declining to reoccupy the El Magruntein positions or even the village of Rafah. The following day all available wagons were sent out under the guns of the LCP and much *matériel* was recovered. The force then withdrew to El Arish to await developments. In all almost 1,500 Turks, and not a few Germans, were captured, and an estimated 200 were killed. British losses were 71 killed and around four hundred wounded.

The relative importance of the war he was fighting in Sinai and that which Haig's generals were prosecuting in France and Flanders was brought home to Murray fairly gently at first, on 15 December, when Robertson wrote to him ostensibly to remind him that his prime duty was the defence of Egypt, but also to 'enquire' why he felt it necessary to maintain a division on the canal and another guarding his lines of communication, in addition to the forces now poised just short of the Ottoman frontier. It is fair enough to say that there was a sense in Whitehall at this time that the Turks were, if not a spent force, at least close to the limit of their offensive capacity. They were struggling against the Russians in the Caucasus (though the severe winter had given them something of a respite), and Maude's advance up the Tigris had reached Kut, and there was little doubt that it would fall, probably within weeks. Thus, with the canal safe, there was little real strategic need to apply extra pressure on the third Turkish front. While the prospect of taking Jerusalem and the Holy Land may have had a lively emotional appeal, it could not be considered a first-class war aim, and with the war of attrition on the Western Front constantly demanding fresh gun-fodder, it was only a matter of time before the General Staff began to eye the huge army in Egypt as a source of it. On 11 January Robertson wrote again, and this time he unsheathed a threat: since Murray was reluctant to advance into Palestine with the forces he had, the War Cabinet had decided that he should defer that operation until the autumn, and release an infantry division or two for service in France.[24] Just six days later the threat was realised; he was told to prepare a division to return to Europe.

He chose the 42nd, which was then at El Arish, replacing it with the 53rd from Romani. There were other rearrangements made, too: three Yeomanry brigades which had come from Gallipoli a year earlier and had never been remounted were now officially reclassified as infantry[25] and formed the 74th (Yeomanry) Division, while three unbrigaded Light Horse regiments[26] were assembled into the 4th Australian Light Horse Brigade. This allowed Chetwode's mounted troops to be organised into two divisions of four brigades each: the A & NZ Mounted Division, under Maj.-Gen. Chauvel (1st and 2nd Australian Light Horse; New Zealand Mounted Rifles Brigade and 22nd Mounted Brigade) and the Imperial Mounted Division, under Maj.-Gen. Hodgson (3rd and 4th Australian Light Horse and 5th and 6th Mounted Brigades).

By 5 February the water pipeline had reached El Arish, and the railway was being pushed forward from there. It reached Sheikh Zowaiid by 1 March, and Khan Yunis, from which the Turks had withdrawn on 23 February, before the end of the month. By then the A&NZ Mounted Division's headquarters had advanced to Sheikh Zowaiid, and the 2nd LHB and NZMRB, under Chaytor, had been pushed forward to Khan Yunis. The Turks' withdrawal was strategic rather than forced on them, Jemal Biyuk having decided – against Kressenstein's wishes; he had wanted to fight at Shellal, but accepted reluctantly that he could not hold both it and Gaza – to establish a new defensive line from Gaza, on the coast, to Beersheba. The line was some thirty kilometres long and followed that of a good road; it was manned by approximately 18,000 men, drawn mostly from the 3rd and the newly arrived 16th Division,[27] with two regiments of the reconstituted 3rd Cavalry Division based at Beersheba and elements of the 53rd Division in support to the north.

Despite his force having been reduced to four infantry divisions, Murray had every intention of advancing into the Holy Land without further delay, and planned to take Gaza by means of the sort of cutting-out expedition mounted at Magdhaba and Rafah, the assault force to be withdrawn afterwards if necessary. Even with that proviso, this was an ambitious move, both because of the nature and depth of the defences, and of the distances to be covered.

The centre of Gaza city, one of the most ancient in the region, lay around three kilometres inland, and just over twenty from Khan Yunis. East of the coastal belt of dunes the country was cultivated. Its main feature was the Wadi Ghazze, which cut through it, around eight kilometres south of the city; dry at this season, its bed was sandy, its sides steep and slashed by vertical clefts, some of them running away for considerable distances. North of the wadi the ground rose in two ridges paralleling the coast, the Es Sire, along the western side of which ran the ancient road from Sinai, and the Burjabye, to the east. The city's extensive artificial defences were augmented by a

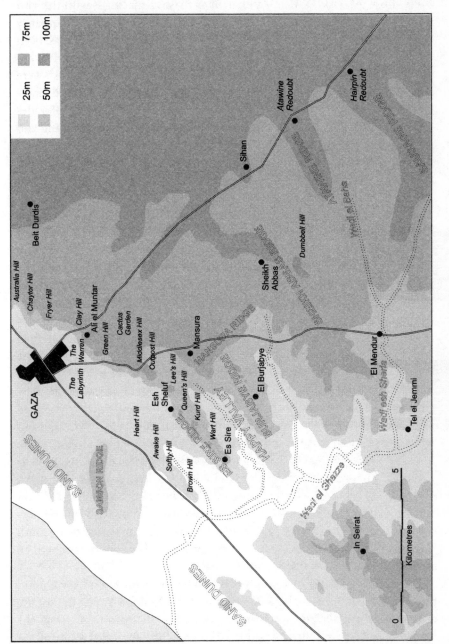

24. Palestine – Southern Approaches to Gaza

centuries-old network of dense hedges of prickly-pear cactus, which has tough spines several centimetres long; these hedges, several metres high and more thick, were completely impenetrable, and could be breached quickly only by the use of explosive charges. They surrounded the city on all sides, bordering tracks and dividing gardens and vegetable plots, but were particularly prolific to the south-east; otherwise, the terrain was completely devoid of cover, and this combination, MacMunn and Falls, co-authors of the *Official History of the Palestine Campaign,* commented dryly, 'gave the position its strength and made of it a little pleasing prospect to infantry attacking from the south and south-east'. The main source of topographical data for the region was a map prepared during the mid-eighteen-seventies for the Palestine Exploration Fund by two young subalterns of the Royal Engineers, one of whom was Herbert Kitchener. That map soon proved to be full of errors, and often more of a liability than an asset.

Dobell's plan of attack called for the Eastern Force to be reorganised; the Desert Column, which would lead, would now consist of the Australia and New Zealand Mounted Division and the Imperial Mounted Division[28] plus the 53rd Infantry Division,[29] the mounted divisions to ring the city and cut the Turks' lines of retreat (and of reinforcement) as they had at El Magruntein, while the infantry attacked from the south-east, through the dominant Ali el Muntar positions. In addition the 52nd and 54th Divisions would be deployed, plus the 229th Brigade, the only formation of the 74th Division yet available. The garrison of Gaza was believed to number around 2,000 men; in fact, it had been increased to 4,000 in the days just prior to the attack.[30]

Dobell's orders to Chetwode were issued on 24 March; reconnaissance of the wadi began immediately and soon moved on to the preparation of crossing points and the examination of the terrain beyond. The mounted units moved up to Khan Yunis, where they were joined by the 53rd Division, and then carried on to Deir el Balah, within striking distance of the wadi, by midnight on the twenty-fifth. The 52nd then moved up to Khan Yunis, and the 54th Division, which was to be in immediate support and screen the Desert Column from the threat of Turkish forces advancing from the direction of Beersheba, moved to In Seirat, three kilometres to the east, its 161st Brigade warned to be ready to move off to join the 53rd Division temporarily.

The mounted divisions reached the wadi in the early hours of 26 March, followed by the infantry and associated artillery. At 0645 Dobell arrived just north of In Seirat, where his forward headquarters had been set up; he was accompanied by Chetwode, who was later to have gone on to Sheikh Abbas.[31] By now Murray had arrived at El Arish, his command post in a railway carriage linked to Dobell's by telephone and telegraph lines.

During the hours of darkness mist had rolled in off the sea, and had thickened as day broke. By 0500 visibility was down to no more than twenty metres. This was extremely unusual in March, and no allowance had been made for it; it is fair to say that its occurrence risked scuppering Dobell's plans before the movement-to-contact had barely begun, yet at the same time made it tactically impossible to cancel the operation for fear of risking the mounted troops who were already moving across bare, open country to envelop the city, and who would be horribly exposed in daylight should the fog suddenly lift.

The A&NZMD's lead unit, the 2nd LHB, crossed the wadi without mishap, set out on a compass bearing and reached Sheikh Abbas around 0800; its vanguard 7th ALH came under fire from Turkish outposts which soon gave ground, falling back across the Gaza–Beersheba road with the Australians in hot pursuit. By 0900 the brigade's headquarters had reached Beit Durdis, and soon thereafter the troops had spread out across what was later known as Australia Hill, to the north-east, occupying the village of Jebaliye with the 7th ALH pushing on towards the sea. The deployment was completed by 1030, by which time the bulk of the 54th Infantry Division had established itself in a screening position on the Sheikh Abbas ridge, with its 161st Brigade – on loan to the 53rd – at El Burjabye.

The 53rd Division, too, left its forming-up position at El Breij and crossed the wadi in darkness, the 158th Brigade moving to Mansura, the 160th to Esh Sheluf on the Es Sire ridge; the 159th remained in the rear, halted near the northern edge of the wadi. It did not receive orders to advance further until 0930, and would thus not be in position to join the assault until noon at the earliest. At 1145, the fog having dispersed, the order to proceed was finally given, and the two forward brigades advanced on the Ali el Muntar positions, the 158th from the south, the 160th along the Es Sire ridge. Of the 159th – which was to move up on the 158th's right, cross the Gaza–Beersheba road and attack the positions on a hillock known as Clay Hill – there was still no sign, nor had the 161st Brigade yet put in an appearance.

By now Chetwode was afraid that if the infantry brigades met stiff resistance, they would not take their objective before dark. Since there were no reports of Turkish reinforcements moving on Gaza, he decided to send them material help in the form of a brigade from each of the mounted divisions, to attack from the north and east, and signalled accordingly to Chauvel and Hodgson just after noon. He changed his mind soon afterwards, when he received intelligence reports doubling the size of the Turkish garrison, deciding to cancel the deployment of the IMD's brigade and commit the entire A&NZMD to the attack instead, sending the IMD northwards to Beit Durdis to fill in the gap left behind it. Chauvel in the meantime had shifted his headquarters to a knoll between Beit Durdis and Gaza; it took some time to locate him and it was 1515 before he issued orders for his brigades to attack.

They met with little resistance at first, the Turks being primarily concerned with countering the threat from the south, but all that changed as the light horsemen – some afoot but others still mounted – neared the outskirts of the city and began to run into the cactus hedges. By nightfall none had penetrated further than the outskirts of the city, by which time it had become clear that Turkish reinforcements in significant numbers were approaching from both the north and the east.

The first infantry units into action were those of the 158th Brigade, but those of the 159th, which had made prodigious efforts to catch up since reaching Mansura at noon, doubling most of the way, were not far behind them. By about 1330 some gains had been made – the Cactus Garden was in their hands, as were two positions near the Ali el Muntar mosque, and Green and Clay Hills were under attack, the artillery attached to the 161st giving support. To the left, the 160th Brigade, with less ground to cover, had taken the Labyrinth, as the maze of hedged gardens on the outskirts of the city came to be known, but the advance up the spine of the Es Sire ridge did not match that progress until 1600, by which time the 161st Brigade had advanced on the right, filling the gap between the 160th and the 158th. Despite heavy fire from the defensive positions, Green Hill was carried by 1730, by which time Clay Hill had also fallen. By 1830 the entire Ali el Muntar position was in British hands, the Turks streaming away back towards Gaza City, which was now almost completely surrounded. To officers and men alike, as they consolidated their positions and began preparing for a night of patrolling and reconnaissance, it seemed inevitable that the city must fall the following day. Dobell and Chetwode, their headquarters still side by side at In Seirat, were less sanguine, the reports of fresh Turkish forces advancing from east and north causing anxiety which was only overshadowed by reports of the condition of the mounted troops' horses, most of which had had no water since the previous evening.[32] Indeed, so grave were the commanders' concerns on that score that it was decided that if Gaza was still holding out at nightfall it would be necessary to withdraw the mounted forces. Chetwode gave the order to do so at 1810,[33] the Camel Brigade being instructed to cover the withdrawal.

That withdrawal went very slowly, even though there was no intervention by the Turks until close to dawn. Chauvel's division passed through Beit Durdis by about 0200 on 27 March, and Hodgson ordered his own to concentrate and follow. The rearguard – the 3rd LHB – came under attack as it crossed the Gaza–Beersheba road at around 0530 but extricated itself under the machine guns of the 7th Light Car Patrol, and the last horsemen were across the wadi by soon after daybreak, the Camel Brigade remaining behind to extend the 54th Infantry Division's flank back to the line of the watercourse.

The withdrawal of the mounted infantry effectively removed Dallas' right-flank protection and left him vulnerable to the Turks advancing from Beersheba, and shortly after Chetwode had ordered Chauvel to pull his men back he instructed Dallas to do the same, to link his right with the forward elements of the two remaining brigades of Hare's 54th Division. Dallas protested, and asked instead for fresh troops to be sent up to fill the gap, but Chetwode refused. The situation was further complicated since in the meantime he had ordered Hare to shift his positions westwards by some three kilometres, to lie along the Burjabye ridge, with his left just north of Mansura; he assumed that Dallas had been informed of that order, but he had not. Thus, Dallas thought that he was being ordered to extend his right out to Sheikh Abbas, where Hare's left *had* been, rather than withdrawing it to the south, to Mansura.

Almost incredibly, it was 2300 before Dobell became aware of exactly how much ground Dallas' men had gained in the last hours before dusk. (It appears that his information came from intercepted enemy radio traffic – between Kressenstein at Tel esh Sheria, twenty-five kilometres south-east of Gaza, on the railway, and Tiller in Gaza – by way of Cairo.) On that basis he told Chetwode that Dallas should 'dig in on his present line', pulling back his left flank and linking his right with the 54th's left. Since this was what Chetwode had told Dallas to do over four hours earlier, he did not bother to repeat it to him.

Even if the order *had* been relayed as Chetwode received it, it would have made no difference, for by this time Dallas' position was already compromised, his men already on the move, his left to retreat for 1,500m down the Es Sire ridge while his right swung and extended almost three times that distance to take up a line from Mansura to Sheikh Abbas. It was nearly midnight before Dallas' staff realised the extent of the confusion, when reports arrived of units of the 54th Division being encountered north of Mansura, at a point close to the Cactus Garden. By then it was too late; the Ali el Muntar positions, along with Green and Clay Hills, taken and held at such cost, had all been given up, and all Dallas could do was order his 159th Brigade into reserve, rather than to occupy the Mansura–Sheikh Abbas sector. The retirement was completed, and a new line established, by 0400 on 27 March.

An hour later Chetwode, still completely out of touch with what was actually going on on the battlefield, learned of the extent of Dallas' withdrawal, and he immediately ordered him to send out patrols to determine if the situation – and the ground gained – could be recovered. Three companies of the 7th Essex were rousted out and pushed back northwards; they found both the Ali el Muntar positions and Green Hill unoccupied and settled in to await the inevitable counterattack. It came just after dawn, but in nowhere near the numbers expected, driving the Essex back but not consolidating the positions, which the battalion and its sister 6th promptly reoccupied once more. Instead of trying again, the Turks then turned their attention on Sheikh Abbas, occupying the high ground there and using the advantage that gave them to shell Dallas' rear echelon.

During the night Dobell had determined to take Dallas' division back under his own direct command, and an order to that effect reached him at 0800. Dallas replied with a situation report which concluded with a request for a counterattack on Sheikh Abbas by the 52nd Division. Dobell had already contemplated bringing it up on Hare's right, but he was still deliberating when a second and much more effective Turkish assault drove the Essex battalions out of Ali el Muntar and surrounded them on Green Hill, from which position they fought their way back to the division's main line only with considerable difficulty. This left Dallas with a hopeless salient, from which he was obliged to withdraw, re-establishing his line through Esh Sheluf.

It soon became clear that even that position was untenable, for all the essential lines of communication across the Wadi Ghazze were now vulnerable to the Turkish batteries on the heights of Sheikh Abbas. The alternative to withdrawal – sending the 52nd Division to take back Sheikh Abbas – appealed to Dobell not at all, and at 1630 on 27 March he ordered Dallas to withdraw his forces. The retreat began at 1900 and was completed before 0400 the following morning, the tired men being greeted by a rather premature *Khamsin*, the hot wind which blows off the desert during the summer months.

British losses were just under four thousand, of whom 78 officers and 445 other ranks were killed and a similar number missing, many of whom were known to have fallen into enemy hands. Turkish casualties were lighter, but included a greater number of prisoners. Leaving aside the matter of the dire handling of Dallas' withdrawal, the events of what was to be the First Battle of Gaza were soon the stuff of controversy. Should the 53rd Division have gone in sooner? Should the mounted infantry have been withdrawn? Should there have been an immediate counterattack to retake Sheikh Abbas? Enough disagreement to power many an argument . . . The situation was not improved by Murray having reported the facts of the matter to the CIGS in a misleading manner, inflating the number of casualties inflicted on the Turks (to between 6,000 and 7,000, with a further 900 taken prisoner), which suggested to Robertson – and the Cabinet – that the battle had ended in victory for the British. That led to a volte-face in the latter's policy. No longer would the invasion of Palestine be put on the back burner until the autumn; instead, Murray was told to advance and capture Jerusalem as soon as possible.

The Turks soon set about reinforcing their defensive positions. Gaza, which had been little more than an outpost, now became the anchoring bastion of a line which stretched from the sea twenty kilometres in the direction of Beersheba, to Abu Hureira; the line was not continuous, but all the terrain in front of it was covered from at least one redoubt, and the fields of fire were excellent. There existed the theoretical possibility of outflanking it to the east – Beersheba was known to be lightly held – but that was practically impossible due to the problems of supplying the necessary force with water. The line was held by the 3rd Division, around Gaza, with the 53rd Division to its left and the 16th beyond that. The British put their total number at around 21,000 infantry, which overestimated their strength by about 15 per cent.

For his part, Murray ordered the railway extended to Deir el Balah, eight kilometres short of the Wadi Ghazze, where the Eastern Force's headquarters were established; there were productive wells there, supplemented by water brought up in tank-trucks. The railway extension also allowed Murray to bring up the full complement of available heavy artillery (twelve 60-pounders and two 8-in and two 6-in howitzers) as well as the two remaining brigades of the 74th Division, the two missing brigades of the mounted divisions (the 1st and 4th Light Horse), and a detachment of eight Tanks, Mark I.[34]

Dobell submitted his new plan of attack to Murray on 3 April. This time he had no option but to mount a frontal assault, and proposed to use his three Territorial divisions, with the 74th in reserve, the 53rd, now under the command of Brig.-Gen. SF Mott,[35] to the west of the Rafah–Gaza road and the 52nd and 54th to the east of it, with the Desert Column's two mounted divisions and the Camel Brigade wide on the right. The action would take place in two phases. The first would be a movement-to-contact to bring the troops up to a line some five kilometres north of the Wadi Ghazze, where they would establish an entrenched, wired position (with a strongpoint capable of holding a brigade at Sheikh Abbas, which would have to be taken in the process); the second, at least twenty-four hours later, would be the assault itself. That delay was designed to allow Dobell to exploit any weakness he perceived in the Turks' response to the initial advance. As well as its own artillery, the force would have fire support from naval assets offshore.[36]

The first phase was to begin well before dawn on 17 April, when the mounted divisions moved out to prevent reinforcements being sent west from Abu Hureira and to screen the open right flank of the 54th Division when it assaulted Sheikh Abbas; some hours later, just as the day began to break, the infantry divisions began to cross the Wadi Ghazze. Dobell's headquarters would remain at Deir el Balah, but this time Chetwode's would move forward, as far as Tel el Jemmi, where the Wadi esh Sheria ran into the Wadi Ghazze. Murray's railway car was installed at Khan Yunis, and once again he would be in direct telephonic and telegraphic contact with his subordinate headquarters throughout the battle.

The 'Eastern Attack' – the advance of the 52nd and 54th Divisions, under the overall command of Maj.-Gen. Smith – went smoothly enough, though one of the tanks allotted to the latter[37] was hit repeatedly by artillery fire and had to be abandoned on the Sheikh Abbas ridge, and the 52nd Division's 157th Brigade came under heavy artillery fire on Mansura ridge. The Desert Column achieved a good measure of success too, the IMD's 5th Mounted Brigade taking Erk completely by surprise and a detachment reaching the Gaza–Beersheba road and cutting the telegraph line, while the A&NZMD's brigades reached Abu Hereira. Before nightfall the mounted brigades withdrew across the Wadi Ghazze, leaving outposts behind. The following day the infantry units consolidated their positions while the artillery bombarded the Turkish lines and the mounted units probed forwards again, failing to provoke a reaction from the Turks.

Dobell had now to choose between two courses of action: either attack Gaza directly from the direction of Ali el Muntar and Sheikh Abbas, or keep the Turkish defences before Gaza pinned in place, and wheel north-east against the Turkish left. He chose the former, with an extension to the right, the 54th Division, with the Camel Brigade attached, to punch a hole in the Turkish line through which reserved units of the Desert Column could pass and fan out to work on the Turkish rear echelons.

The second phase began at 0530 on 19 April with a bombardment, the warships firing on Ali el Muntar, the Labyrinth and the entrenched area known as the Warren behind it, and the army's heavy batteries targeting known enemy concentrations and strongpoints. The barrage lasted two hours, and then pushed back towards the city as the infantrymen began their advance, the divisional 18-pounders now joining in, bombarding the Turkish front lines with shrapnel.[38] The infantry divisions advanced with two brigades up and the third back in reserve, the 54th with the 162nd to the left and the 163rd on the right, making for a redoubt 1500m north-west of Sihan, which was the objective of the Camel Brigade. This was the movement which, if successful, would allow the mounted infantry to get behind the Turkish front lines. To the left the 52nd Division's 155th brigade advanced up the Es Sire ridge with the 156th echeloned out to the right, slightly to its rear, prepared to swing to the left to assault the Ali el Muntar and Green Hill trenches. Beyond the Rafah–Gaza road, in the sand dunes, the 53rd Division had the 159th Brigade up on the left and the 160th beside it on the right, with the 158th in reserve. To the right of the Camel Brigade the Imperial Mounted Division was drawn up, dismounted, spread out across a sector some five kilometres wide spanning the Atawine and Sausage ridges and the Wadi el Baha which separated them, confronting the Atawine and Hairpin redoubts. To its right, echeloned back towards the Wadi Ghazze in the vicinity of Esh Shellal, five of the Australian & New Zealand Mounted Division's battalions formed a dispersed screen, with the rest poised to exploit any breakthrough.

It soon became apparent that the artillery bombardment, directed largely at the trenches, had had very little effect on the Turkish batteries. The 163rd Brigade came under heavy artillery and machine gun fire as soon as it left its positions, but by 0830 had gained a ridge 500m short of the redoubt. A tank – one of five allocated to the Eastern Attack – was sent up, and led elements of the 5th Norfolks into the redoubt, killing or driving out the garrison, and the Turks immediately replied by calling down artillery fire, destroying the tank and reducing the Norfolks so that they could not withstand the counterattack which followed. To the left the 4th Norfolks were pinned down, losing more than half their strength, and the 8th Hampshires, called up to help, could not. In all these three battalions lost 1,500 men, including two commanders and all twelve company commanders. The 162nd Brigade fared no better, though elements of the 10th Londons managed to fight their way across the Gaza–Beersheba road through a gap in the defensive line; becoming isolated in the process, they were eventually forced to withdraw. At 1300, Hare ordered Dodington's 161st Brigade to reinforce the 163rd with the objective of retaking the redoubt the Norfolks had won and lost, but by 1430 it was clear that that was impossible, and their advance was called off. To the right, the Camel Brigade encountered similar opposition. Its 3rd Battalion managed to cross the road and briefly held two small hillocks known as Jack and Jill, east of Sihan, but when the 4th Light Horse Brigade, its neighbour to the right, was forced to give ground, it was obliged to follow. By 1500, Hare was seriously concerned that the IMD would be driven back so far as to uncover his entire right flank, and ordered his division and the Camel Brigade to stand fast and attempt to push forward no more.

On the 54th's left the 52nd Division had a dreadful time of it. The 155th Brigade lost its spearhead tank early on, when the vehicle ditched itself, but the back-up appeared, and led the assault first on Lee's Hill, which fell reasonably easily, and then Outpost Hill, where the attackers came under withering fire from front and flank. Eventually the tank forced a way forward and was followed by men of the 5th King's Own Scottish Borderers. The 4th Royal Scots Fusiliers were less successful on Middlesex Hill to the right, and suffered heavily in the failed attempt to take it. By mid-morning the Turks had retaken Outpost Hill, but over the next hours it changed hands several times, until the 4th KOSB was ordered to retake it after a half-hour bombardment. Reinforced by men of the fifth battalion and from the 5th RSF they succeeded, and held it through the afternoon, but they took many casualties in the process, and eventually had to be withdrawn.

The 156th Brigade, on the right, was stalled before Middlesex Hill and made little progress, its men lying out in the open under fire from Green Hill throughout the morning. The counterattack on the 54th Division to its right forced a withdrawal, and the Turks took advantage of it, though their counterattack from Ali el Muntar was broken up by artillery fire. Across the Rafah road, the 53rd Division made slow progress, held up by machine gun fire from the wooded area to its right (which had been the subject of a gas bombardment which seems to have had little effect). Its primary objective on the right – a line of dunes known as Samson ridge – was taken by the 160th Brigade only at 1300.

Chetwode's orders to Hodgson's Imperial Mounted Division made it clear that its main objective was to be the Atawine Redoubt, where it was 'to pin the enemy in place', Hodgson using his own judgement as to how far he should press his attack if it were successful. In this he would not only secure the 54th Division's eastern flank against attack but also contribute to the chances of breaking through the Turkish line. He pushed the 5th Mounted and the 3rd and 4th Light Horse Brigades forward, holding the 6th Mounted Brigade in reserve. He made steady progress to begin with, Royston's 3rd LHB forging ahead of the others having started off prematurely, and by 0915 was close to the objective. There, however, the advance stalled, under enfilading fire from Sausage Ridge, the 3rd LH and the 5th MB slewing round to the right, creating a gap between the former and the 4th. Chaytor sent his Wellington Regiment to assist the 5th, to no effect, the Hairpin Redoubt being unassailable. On the right Cox's 1st LHB, moving towards Abu Hureira, occupied Baiket es Sana.

By early afternoon the tide of the battle nearer to Gaza had turned in the Turks' favour; a series of counterattacks was launched against the mounted divisions, forcing them back right across the battlefield. The 3rd and 4th Light Horse, in particular, were seriously threatened, and only the arrival of the 6th Mounted Brigade at the gallop saved the situation. Towards Abu Hureira, the Turks made a determined attempt to drive the 1st LHB out of Baiket es Sana without notable success. When Dobell ordered the infantry to dig in, at 1600, the mounted divisions were withdrawn to a line from Dumb-bell Hill, at the south of the Sheikh Abbas ridge, through Munkheile to Hiseia; to their left, the Camel Brigade withdrew to Charing Cross, south-west of Sheikh Abbas.

During the course of the evening Dobell issued an order to renew the attack the next day, but on reflection, and particularly in view of the casualty roll – which stood at around 6,000 – and the state of the ammunition supply, especially of artillery rounds, he later postponed it, recommending to Murray that it be abandoned. Murray concurred, and thus ended the Second Battle of Gaza. The line finally occupied and held was very close to that reached on the evening of 17 April; only on the far left, at Samson ridge, was any appreciable gain made. The Turks made no effort to counterattack save in the Wadi Sihan, where they were driven back by artillery fire. Two days later Dobell – one of relatively few Canadians to reach senior rank in the British Army – was relieved of his command and returned to the United Kingdom; he was later given command of a division in India, which was a serious demotion. Chetwode took over as GOC, Eastern Force. Chauvel took over the Desert Column from Chetwode, and his place at the head of the A&NZMD was taken by Chaytor. Murray himself, criticised widely for what was usually described as indecisiveness, was recalled on 11 June, to be replaced by General Sir Edmund Allenby.[39] Allenby – 'The Bull', as he was known both for his manner and his stature – assumed command of the Egyptian Expeditionary Force on 28 June. Murray, who had briefly been Chief of the Imperial General Staff, spent the rest of the war commanding reservists at Aldershot. However, Allenby himself said that his careful preparations 'formed the cornerstone of my successes'.

21 Palestine, Southern Part (Philistia and Judaea)

Through Gaza to Judaea

The final months of Sir Archibald Murray's period in command of the Egyptian Expeditionary Force – and indeed, the first of Allenby's – were characterised by consolidation and force-building in the grinding heat of the desert summer. Following Allenby's arrival this included extending the railway by means of branch lines to the south-east of Gaza, the new commander-in-chief having decided that his first attempt to defeat the Turks would be made well away from the city – which by now was a 'strong modern fortress, heavily entrenched and wired, offering every facility for protracted defence' – save for what was intended as a diversionary attack on its western side, which actually resulted in its capture.

Allenby's proposal, which he forwarded to the War Office in the second week of July, was to mount an offensive in the sector Abu Hureira–Tel esh Sheria, an essential precursor of which would be the capture of Beersheba in an encircling move reminiscent of the 'cutting-out' operations which had succeeded at Magdhaba and Rafah and failed in the First Battle of Gaza.

Much of Allenby's planning was based on work Chetwode, an accomplished strategist, had done before he arrived. In particular Chetwode made the point that it would be no good simply driving the Turks back from the Gaza–Beersheba line; they would have to be comprehensively beaten and then pressed hard, allowing them no opportunity to regroup and stand on the reserve positions they had created. To achieve this, he argued, it would be necessary, in addition to three mounted divisions, to field seven full-strength infantry divisions: the 52nd, 53rd and 54th, 'of poor rifle strength . . . and with no drafts to keep them up', would not suffice.' It was Chetwode, too, who focused Allenby's attention on the eastern sector of the front. 'Once established on the high ground between Beersheba and Hureira,' he wrote in the appreciation which awaited the new commander-in-chief upon his arrival, 'and with Beersheba in our possession, we can attack north and north-westwards, always from higher ground, always with observation, with water at Beersheba, with water at Esani, with water at Shellal, Fara and Qamle . . . and with the only prospect, which no alternative course affords, of finding a flank on which we can use our great preponderance in mounted troops.' Surprise would be of the essence, of course, and it would be vital to mount a diversionary operation designed to convince the Turks that the British were willing to batter themselves senseless against Gaza city once more.[2]

It was a seductive, well-grounded proposal, and Allenby bought into it

wholeheartedly. The Chief of the Imperial General Staff recommended compliance to the War Cabinet, even though it would mean bringing in substantial numbers of men and much *matériel* from other theatres. In the event
Allenby did not get all the extra resources he had asked for,[3] but on 10 August
he did get the War Cabinet's approval to proceed.

Two days later Allenby made significant changes to his table of organisation. The cavalry would now become the Desert Mounted Corps,[4] while
the infantry was reorganised into XX Corps[5] and XXI Corps.[6] In addition
there was a 'Composite Force' formed in September.[7] He made staff changes,
too; having brought Maj.-Gen. Louis Bols with him from France, he installed
him as his chief of staff in place of Lynden-Bell, with Brig.-Gen. Guy Dawnay,
formerly Dobell's and then Chetwode's senior staffer, as his deputy.

The plan was distributed to senior officers in outline on 15 August, to be
put into effect as soon as seven effective infantry divisions were to hand. XXI
Corps would mount the diversionary attack on the Turkish right, while XX
Corps and elements of the Desert Mounted Corps attacked Beersheba; the
latter's infantry component would then advance to drive the Turks out of Tel
esh Sheria and Abu Hureira, creating a gap through which the cavalry would
push on to Tel el Nejile, about thirty kilometres north of Beersheba on the
railway. From then on, further advances would be predicated on results, with
the hope that the Turks in and around Gaza would be isolated and cut off.
Initially Allenby hoped to be able to go onto the offensive in September, but
in the event supply problems proved difficult to surmount, and it would be
late in October – perilously close to the start of the rainy season – before he
was able to commence.

Perhaps the most serious concern facing the EEF staff was that of transportation. Soon after the Second Battle of Gaza, Murray had decided to build
an extension to the railway from Rafah to the Wadi Ghazze.[8] This line reached
Bir Qamle by the end of June, and a loop to Shellal was soon completed. In
view of Allenby's intention to attack Beersheba, it was decided to extend it
ten kilometres to Kharm, but only at the last possible moment, and then to
carry it on a further three kilometres as a light railway. The possibility of
using motor vehicles was also investigated. There were a considerable number
in Cairo – four transport companies with a total of 180 lorries – but there were
doubts as to how practical they would be in the terrain. In fact, experiments
showed that they would operate quite happily, not only on the existing tracks,
but also across open country, and arrangements were made to bring three of
the companies to the front. 134 Holt 'caterpillar' tractors were also available;
most of these would be required to move the big guns and transport ammunition for them, but twenty-four, with trailers, were made available to carry
rations and engineering stores for the DMC. Together with all the camels,
mules and horse-wagons available – XXI Corps was temporarily denuded of
all its transport; this would create problems of mobility for it later on – it
was hoped that this would prove sufficient.

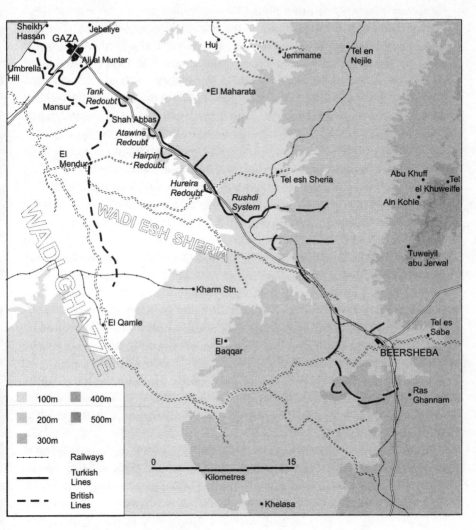

26. *Palestine – Prior to the Third Battle of Gaza*

When Allenby arrived in the theatre, the situation vis-à-vis the Air Force was unchanged since the operations at Gaza had begun, and the Germans – there *were* Turkish aircrew, but in very small numbers – enjoyed air superiority. That changed quite dramatically in mid-September when an additional squadron of the Royal Flying Corps, equipped with Bristol Fighters, arrived; within days this had swung the balance firmly in Allenby's favour. Crucially, this was to prevent reconnaissance flights over the British assembly areas during the build-up to the battle, and allowed work on the extension of the railway spur to Kharm to continue undetected.

During this period the Turks were not idle, though quite how effective – on any level – their activity was is moot. We have touched already on the *Yildirim* Group (see Chapter 5), but now we must look at it in more detail, for it was during this period it was created and, despite opposition at the highest level, designated for Palestine, not Mesopotamia.

Even as Allenby was crossing the Mediterranean, on 24 June Enver Pasha, having visited the Palestine front, convened a conference at Aleppo, to which Ahmet Izzet Pasha, in overall command in the Caucasus, Mustafa Kemal, then commanding the Second Army in the vicinity of Lake Van, Jemal Pasha, commanding the Fourth Army in Syria, and Halil Pasha, commanding the Sixth Army in Mesopotamia, were summoned, with the German Chief of the General Staff, Bronsart von Schellendorf, in attendance. The main item on the agenda was the role of the Yildirim Ordular Grubunu, the Thunderbolt Army Group, the creation of which had already been ordained and which the German Erich von Falkenhayn[9] had been appointed to command. Army Group F, as it was known to the Germans, would be made up of an entirely new army, the Seventh, composed of III Corps (the 24th, 27th and 50th Infantry Divisions plus the little more than skeletal 3rd Cavalry) and XV Corps (the 19th and 20th Divisions), plus the German Asienkorps, also known as 'Pascha II'.[10]

Enver's original plan had been to employ the Yildirim force alongside Halil Pasha's Sixth Army to retake Baghdad; when he unveiled this proposal at the Aleppo meeting, Jemal – who knew its outline in advance – objected. Instead, he suggested, the force should be concentrated at Aleppo, where it would form a strategic reserve, available for use to the north, in the Caucasus, to the east, in Mesopotamia, or to the south, in Syria, as required. Izzet supported the suggestion. Enver refused to countenance any change to his plan. Jemal was not content to let the matter rest. He appealed to Talaat, who had taken over as Grand Vizier from Said Halim on 4 February, but was told that the decision was that of the Council of Ministers, and would not be overturned. Still he refused to accede, and in mid-August travelled to Constantinople to attempt to bring the matter up once more. Perhaps surprisingly, given Enver's dislike of dissent, he succeeded in convening another conference, at which Enver, Falkenhayn, Schellendorf and his own Chief of Staff, Ali Fuad Bey, were present. To his surprise, Falkenhayn, concerned about the fitness of the Fourth Army and wishing to drive the British back across Sinai and make another attempt to seize the Suez Canal, supported him. This was not much to Jemal's liking; it threatened his position as regional Commander-in-Chief, but having seemed to have got his way, there was little he could now do ... [11]

It was the end of August before the German component of the Yildirim Group arrived in Constantinople, and by then the 19th Division had reached Aleppo, with the 20th set to follow. III Corps had been activated, but the 24th Division proved to be in very poor shape. Kressenstein noted that of the 10,000 men who left Haydarpaşa Station, across the Bosporus from Constantinople, only 4,634 had arrived in Aleppo fit for duty. On 6 September there was a massive explosion at Haydarpaşa Station, which destroyed much of the supplies stockpiled there for the Yildirim Group. The cause was never established, or if it was, was never made public, and quite how much damage was done is unclear – the Turkish government kept a very tight grip on the news – and to what degree the operation was set back is not known, but it must be assumed to have been considerable.

Mustafa Kemal had been placed in charge of the Seventh Army, and was not at all happy with the situation. He complained to Enver that this was no time to be going onto the offensive; Turkey's reserves of men were now exhausted, he pointed out, and each unit must be safeguarded and committed only when absolutely necessary (this conservatism was a regular feature of Kemal's behaviour off the battlefield, in contrast to the way he led his men on it). He also complained about the 'Germanification' of Turkey's strategic policy, and that was very much what Enver did not want to hear. Just weeks later he resigned his command, to be replaced by Fevzi Pasha. He would return to Palestine to assume command of all Ottoman forces there at the end of August 1918, too late to affect the outcome of the war in the theatre.[12]

It was the end of September before the army assembled at Aleppo began to move, though not all units went to Palestine (the 50th Division, for example, was sent to Mesopotamia), and those which did were not in the best of condition; some were so reduced that the 59th Division, still at Gallipoli, was deactivated and its men used to bring the numbers up to something like establishment, and other units were also ordered to the region.

The majority of units facing Allenby on the Gaza–Beersheba line were those of the newly constituted Eighth Army under Kress von Kressenstein: on the left XX Corps, under the command of Ali Fuad Bey, had its head-quarters at Huj and comprised the 26th and 54th Divisions, while XXII Corps, under Refet Bey, had its headquarters at Jebaliye and held the sector from the sea to Tel esh Sheria with the 3rd and 53rd Divisions, with the 7th Division in reserve at Deir Sneid. The only Seventh Army divisions yet at the front were those reallocated to III Corps: the 27th and the 3rd Cavalry, at Beersheba under the command of Ismet Bey, and the 24th Division at Jemmame, east of Huj, though the 19th was at Iraq el Menishiye, forty kilometres north of Beersheba on the railway, and the 16th was in transit; total effective strength was around 33,000 infantry and 260 guns, with around 1,100 cavalry. Like the British, the Turks had worked through the stifling heat of the summer, improving their positions as best they could despite a shortage of materials, particularly one of the simplest: barbed wire.[13] Behind the line they succeeded in extending the branch railway from Et Tine as far as Beit Hanun, about eight kilometres north-east of Gaza, and ran a spur to Deir Sneid.

By mid-October it had been decided that the offensive should start on the last day of the month. Allenby's staff had originally thought a week enough for the concentration of forces, but decided to allow three extra days, largely so that the water supply situation could be improved, and the build-up began on 21 October. It is clear that by 28 October Kressenstein's staff was well informed as to the build-up; it was at that point that the effects of the 'haversack' ruse (see Note 2) were felt, the German commander persisting in the belief that what he was seeing was a feint aimed at drawing his attention away from Gaza, a belief which was reinforced when the heavy artillery batteries in the sector began bombarding the city on 27 October and the warships off the coast joined in, two days later.

By the morning of 30 October the build-up of forces was complete, though the positions the mounted infantry occupied – the A&NZMD at Asluj and the AMD at Khelasa – left them long approach marches. As soon as night fell the columns set off, under the light of a one-day-past-full moon. The 7th ALH, designated as the advanced guard of the force which was to envelop Beersheba, moved off first, followed by the rest of the A&NZ Mounted Division, along the line of a track which ran generally north-eastwards; so well timed was the operation that the last units had just cleared the site when the AMD, coming up from Khelasa, hove into view and followed in their wake.

The infantry divisions of XX Corps were drawn up with the 60th on the right and the 74th on the left, to the south-west of the town, with the 53rd, less two battalions but augmented by a brigade from the 10th, dug in along the Wadi Hanafish to the west. The rest of the 10th was in reserve at Shellal, together with the Yeomanry Mounted Division, which also linked XX Corps with XXI Corps' right by means of a series of outposts.

The preliminary artillery bombardment opened at 0555 on 31 October. After sixty-five minutes the guns were silenced to allow the dust the settle; there was little improvement in visibility, but it became evident eventually that the wire in front of the Turkish positions had survived intact. Brig.-Gen. da Costa, in command of the lead brigade, believed that a further protracted bombardment would probably have no better effect, and asked Shea's permission to carry out an immediate assault at Point 1069, a redoubt and trench system in front of the main line; he was held back until 0830, but his 181st Brigade then took the position swiftly. The leading elements of the 74th

Division then came up on the left; machine gun fire slowed them, and they took significant casualties, but they forced their way forward to within five hundred metres of the main line by 1040. In the meantime the artillery batteries had been moved forward, and now they opened up once more, hoping again to cut the defensive wire. Once again the bombardment failed to have the desired effect – it seldom did – but Chetwode ordered the assault in anyway, at 1215, the artillery to continue firing until the men were within touching distance of the enemy line. The four forward brigades – the 60th's 179th and 181st, and the 74th's 230th and 231st – moved off into the curtain of dust the shells had put up. Screened by it they dealt with the wire and went on. By 1300 their objectives were taken. Chetwode's orders were that the infantry divisions should now halt, and not become involved in the fighting for the town itself until specifically instructed.

Chetwode had decided to divide the mounted force. The A&NZMD was to pass right around the eastern perimeter of Beersheba to a point near Bir el Hammam, twelve kilometres away. The AMD was to follow it as far as Iswaiwin, where it could either advance westwards, directly into the town, or move north to assist its sister-division. The 7th Mounted Brigade was to operate independently, to monitor defensive positions at Ras Ghannam, five kilometres south of Beersheba, and maintain contact with the Turks if and when they retired. The horsemen had a considerable distance to cover before they would even come into the proximity of the enemy – it was forty kilometres from Asluj to Bir el Hammam, and fifty from Khelasa to Iswaiwin – but by 0900 all were in position; the Turks remained ignorant of their approach.

At 0910 the NZMRB began its advance on a hill known as Tel el Sabe, south of the Hebron road and around four kilometres from Beersheba, which was held by a battalion of Turks and a machine gun company. Meldrum put the Canterbury Regiment on the right, on the far side of the Hebron road, and the Auckland on the left, with the Somerset Battery, RHA, in support, keeping the Wellington in reserve. As they turned towards the hill the 2nd LHB advanced on Bir es Sqati, further up the road to Hebron, with the intention of screening the New Zealanders from a counterattack from the north, and was soon in contact with the two diminished regiments of the Turkish 3rd Cavalry Division.

The New Zealand Mounted Rifles Brigade's regiments made little progress, and first the 3rd and then the 2nd ALH were sent to reinforce them, together with the Inverness Battery, RHA; this enhanced force was still not able to approach the hill close enough to risk an assault, and at 1330 Chauvel told Hodgson to lend Chaytor his 3rd LHB to reinforce it further. However, by the time they moved up from Iswaiwin and got into position on the right, the New Zealanders had done the job for themselves, capturing an outlying hillock and using it as a fire-base. A little after 1500 the hill fell to the Aucklands, and the Turks immediately began to bombard it.

The stout resistance the Turks put up on Tel el Sabe set Chauvel's timetable back severely. Allenby, who had moved up to Chetwode's headquarters at El Baqqar, ordered him – perhaps rather unnecessarily, for he needed little urging – to take the town by nightfall, and Chauvel responded by telling Hodgson to commit the 4th LHB. Its 11th Regiment was astride the Beersheba–Iswaiwin road, with the 4th and 12th to the east; they were well dispersed to protect against attack from the air, and it was some time before Grant could assemble them, but at 1630 they moved off, with the 7th Mounted Brigade following on the left and the 5th Mounted Brigade bringing up the rear. The 4th and 12th ALH advanced at the trot and then broke into a gallop, the men with their rifles slung across their backs and their bayonets – a poor substitute for the sabres with which the British Yeomanry units were armed, their blades just seventeen inches long – in their hands, each regiment on a squadron frontage (thus, no more than about two hundred metres wide). They came under machine gun fire from the Ras Ghannam trenches, but the Notts Battery, RHA, which had come up in support, soon disposed of that threat. Between them and Beersheba there were now just two rows of shallow trenches; they took the first at the gallop, and at the second the 4th dismounted and took on the defenders in hand-to-hand fighting while two squadrons of the 12th Regiment swept on into the town, carrying all before them, with the 11th in hot pursuit. The 4th Light Horse Brigade was in effective control of Beersheba by 1800. The only avenue of retreat left to the Turks was the Gaza road, and they fled up it to take cover behind fall-back positions which Izzet Bey had had prepared on the high ground to the west of the Hebron road. Over 1500 were taken prisoner, to add to the more than four hundred XX Corps had taken, and much *matériel* was seized, as were the wells. However, the Turks had had time to destroy much of the pumping gear, and that would cause severe problems in the days to come. Total casualties amongst the Desert Mounted Corps were extraordinarily light: 53 dead and 144 wounded, the majority of them in the fighting for Tel el Sabe. The charge of the 4th Light Horse Brigade had cemented a crucial victory, and not only wrote another chapter in that unit's short but illustrious history, but also caused a further rethink in British tactics. From then on, where conditions demanded it, the horsemen would be employed as true cavalry, and not 'just' as mounted infantry.

The following morning, 1 November, the 53rd Division, with the Imperial Camel Brigade on its right, moved up to Tuweiyil abu Jerwal, ten kilometres to the north of Beersheba, deploying westwards from there for five kilometres. Meanwhile, the A&NZMD advanced and occupied the line Bir el Marruneh-Tuweiyil abu Jerwal to screen the infantry's right, meeting some opposition on the way and failing to find the sources of water it had hoped for. The following day the advance northwards continued, the mounted units on the western side of the Hebron road, now with the 7th Mounted Brigade added, pushing towards Tel el Khuweilfe, their progress slowing as the going became steeper and the resistance increased. It was still unclear whether the Turks moving eastwards in the face of the advance were concentrating to counter-attack at Beersheba, trying to prevent the British from rounding their flank, or simply trying to escape.

On 3 November 53rd advanced towards a track running through Ain Khole in the direction of Tel esh Sheria (which roughly followed the line of the Wadi Abu Khuff), with the objective of being in position to launch an attack on the Turks' left flank south of Tel esh Sheria the following day. The day was hot, the going difficult, and the advance was slow, and the 160th Brigade, on the right, got no further than a point south of Tel el Khuweilfe, which was strongly defended, though the 159th Brigade[14] reached Abu Khuff. Neither found water, which was by now in short supply. It later transpired that the stiffer-than-expected resistance was due to reinforcements from the 19th Division having arrived on the scene. The delay made it impossible to carry out Allenby's order to attack the 16th Division on 4 November, and Bols agreed to a 24-hour postponement, which was later extended until 6 November.

The Turks counterattacked that afternoon, engaging the 5th Mounted Brigade, which had replaced the 7th the previous afternoon. The Yeomanry regiments held them, but at considerable cost. The fifth of November saw further Turkish counterattacks, and it was becoming clear that the remaining divisions of XX Corps would have to assault the Tel esh Sheria positions without the benefit of support from the eastern flank.

The objective of the attack was to break through the defensive line which ran for something over twelve kilometres eastwards from Abu Hureira in order to reach the wells at Tel esh Sheria.[15] This was a well-prepared defensive system which spanned the railway to Beersheba; east of the permanent way it consisted of closely spaced redoubts, while to the west it was a contiguous trench line, with a secondary line to the rear. However, thanks to the shortages of materials there was no wire to the east of the line, and little to the west.

The attack would be mounted by the 74th Division on the right, the 60th in the centre, facing some isolated positions north of Bir Abu Irqaiyiq, and the third brigade of the 10th deployed to its left and slightly forward. Rather than attempting to participate directly, Mott argued, the 53rd would be better employed continuing to hammer away at Khuweilfe in order to keep as many Turkish troops as possible engaged there, and Allenby, having seen the situation for himself, agreed. In addition to the infantry divisions' embedded field batteries, two heavy batteries and three siege batteries would be available to support the assault.

The 74th Division had a longish march to its jumping-off point, and its task was complicated by that having been shifted by three kilometres to the south-east at dusk on the fifth. However, most units were in position on time, at 0330 on 6 November, and the advance began thirty minutes later, without any preamble. After some initial resistance, several redoubts and short trench sections fell in quick succession, those which showed stronger resistance being bypassed and cleared out later (methods reminiscent to a limited degree of the 'stormtrooper' tactics the German, von Hutier, had first employed to break the siege of Riga, two months earlier). A final push saw the railway line reached at 1330.

The attack of the 10th and 60th Divisions was not to begin until the 74th had reached this objective, but the active brigades began advancing to contact at 0800. Supporting artillery opened up a preparatory barrage at 1030, hoping to cut gaps in the wire. In the event, when Brig.-Gen. Edwards saw Turkish troops retiring to the front of his 179th Brigade, at around 1230, he anticipated the order to attack, and his men were followed into action by those of the 180th.[16] Both came under heavy artillery and machine gun fire, but their own artillery now lifted its aim and was able to suppress much of it, allowing the men to break through the front line. Seeing this, Brig.-Gen. Morris ordered his 31st Brigade forward at 1300; by 1430 significant gains had been made, and the enemy could be seen retiring in the direction of the large redoubt at Abu Hureira on the far side of the Wadi esh Sheria. The 179th Brigade then pushed forward rapidly, and soon held all the positions east of the wadi.

Chetwode's subsequent orders, issued at 1505, instructed the 31st Brigade to hold its line while its two sister-brigades (which had been in reserve earlier) moved up on the left and the lead units of the 60th forged ahead, allowing the division to turn its axis through ninety degrees to face north towards Tel es Sheria, a shift the 74th was also required to make. Those two would then sweep on, the 60th to move through the objective and take up a defensive line there, the 74th to be angled more to the north-east to meet the threat still posed by the Turkish 19th if it should succeed in throwing back the 53rd and was still in any fit state to advance.

Neither made much progress. Nonetheless, there was considerable optimism at Chetwode's and Allenby's headquarters that the wadi would be crossed sometime that night, and that as soon as that happened, the Turks would break. Accordingly, Allenby issued orders to Chauvel, who had brought the AMD up onto the 10th Division's southern/western flank, to prepare to pursue them, putting the 74th division under his orders for the purpose.

It had been Allenby's intention to delay the attack on Gaza, feint though it chiefly was, until he had seen the outcome of the offensive to take Beersheba. He would then launch the diversionary attack on the city and when it was in full swing, begin the main event: the attack on the Abu Hureira–Tel esh Sheria position which was designed to smash through the Turkish line and give his troops free rein to advance through northern Philistia and into Judaea. Having held to the belief that the attack on the central positions would go ahead by 4 November, he ordered the attack on Gaza to begin on the second; even when it became clear that the Esh Sheria offensive would be delayed, he held to that decision.

As we have noted, the preparatory artillery bombardment had begun on 27 October, with two counter-battery groups and the general 'Bombardment Group' bringing a total of 68 heavy guns to bear.[17] When the ships offshore joined in on 29 October, the effect was devastating.[18]

The 54th Division, with the 52nd Division's 156th Brigade on the right, was to attack the Turkish line on a front stretching from Sheikh Hassan on the shore to the Rafah road; on the right no-man's-land was no more than six hundred metres wide, but to Sheikh Hassan the distance from the British line was almost four kilometres, the defensive positions running almost parallel with the natural line of advance, with trenches extending across no-man's-land to the shore from the Rafah Redoubt and then paralleling the beach. Umbrella Hill, a large dune just west of the Rafah road, was to be the first objective. As a consequence of the great distances to be covered in no-man's-land, Lt.-Gen. Bulfin, XXI Corps' commander, suggested that a night attack would, for once, be justified, weighing the dangers of disorganisation against those presented by machine guns with interlocking fields of fire, and the GOC agreed.

The terrain over which that advance would take place – indeed, on which virtually all of the battle would be fought – was infernal: soft sand into which men sank up to their ankles and which offered no protection (all defensive positions had to be heavily revetted and topped off with sandbags, and were very vulnerable indeed to artillery bombardment).

The offensive began at 2300 on 1 November, with the attack on Umbrella Hill. Though an advanced party had been spotted by a Turkish outpost, an intense ten-minute bombardment subdued the defenders, and the position was soon in the hands of the 156th Brigade. It proved very difficult to consolidate, however, the trenches, especially the communications trenches, having been largely destroyed by the artillery, and when the Turks themselves began shelling the position the men of the Scottish Rifles who had taken it suffered badly.

Zero hour for the main attack was 0300. On the right, the El Arish Redoubt fell quickly, and counterattacks, including a strong one at 0630, failed to win it back. Two tanks of the 8th Palestine Tank Detachment fielded supported the attack; both passed through the redoubt, though one was ditched and the other hit in the process.[19] To the west of the El Arish Redoubt there was considerable disorganisation and some units lost direction (the moon was of less help than had been hoped, for the night was hazy, with some cloud cover, and the Turkish artillery kicked up a great deal of dust), setting up a tidal flow of gains and losses in the face of counterattacks, but overall the attackers proved too strong. Triangle and Burj Trenches fell to the 8th Hampshires, then, after some confusion, Zowaiid Trench and the Rafah Redoubt and the trenches running north were taken by two battalions of the Essex

Regiment, and the Sea and Beach Posts and the transverse trenches linking them also fell. Finally the Cricket Redoubt and then Gun Hill were taken, and these last opened the way to Sheikh Hassan; a brief, intense bombardment completed the demoralisation of its defenders, almost two hundred of whom were taken prisoner when it was stormed, and by 0615, almost all the objectives had been attained.

Allenby intended to exploit that success by loosing the Imperial Service Cavalry Brigade[20] to drive deep into the region to the north of the city, but first it would be necessary to clear the defenders out of Lion Trench, about a kilometre to the north-east. The task was given to a company of the 4th Northamptons; they had succeeded by 0730, and were in the process of removing wire when they came under strong counterattack and were forced to retire. Over the next hour, increasing numbers of Turks were observed moving towards Sheikh Hassan from the north-east, and a contingency plan was put into effect, the whole of the British artillery park laying down a barrage which covered a zone three kilometres long running roughly north–south, and approximately that same distance inland. The ships offshore joined in, and Turkish losses were very heavy.

The Turks, in their turn, shelled the occupied area, particularly Sheikh Hassan itself, throughout the day, but as the gains were consolidated, and it became possible to move artillery up, their batteries were driven back until, during the following night, they were removed out of range altogether. The next day an attempt was made to push through into the outskirts of the city, south of Sheikh Hassan, but the Yunis Trench proved impossible to hold, the 4th Essex which took it losing heavily in the counterattack which followed, while Turtle Hill, to the north, was unapproachable. That night the Turks switched their attention to the east side of the city, launching repeated assaults on the Sheikh Abbas heights which were driven off by the 75th Division.

The troops who had carried out the Gaza offensive were rested briefly, but following the capture of Tel esh Sheria and the Hureira Redoubt a renewed effort would be necessary if Allenby's plan to drive through from there to the sea, and isolate the Turks who remained in and around Gaza, was to be brought to a successful conclusion. It was timed to begin on 7 November, but was too late, for by then the Turks had cut their losses and slipped away; by the evening of 6 November, Gaza was deserted.[21] The 54th Division moved through the devastated, empty city to take up a line from the Jaffa road to the sea, while the 157th Brigade of the 52nd Division, from the corps reserve and thus far not involved, advanced along the shore to turn the defensive line on the Wadi el Hesi, the next major natural obstacle, and one which had already been partially fortified.

As soon as Allenby heard that the Qawuqa trench system, to the west of the railway at Tel esh Sheria, had been taken, he ordered Chauvel to assemble all available mounted units (save the Yeomanry Mounted Division and the New

Zealand Mounted Rifles Brigade, which would remain in the hills north of Beersheba with the 53rd Infantry and the Camel Brigade) in preparation for a speedy advance on Jemmame and Huj;[22] that would provide them with a forward water supply and permit them to proceed to the sea and cut off the Turks left to the south. In the event, the attack Shea launched at 0330 on the morning of 7 November, designed to secure the railway viaduct and cross the Wadi esh Sheria, was held up by determined defenders (who had been reinforced by fresh men rushed down from the north), and it took a considerable effort by the 180th and 181st Brigades to dislodge them and establish a defensive perimeter north of Tel esh Sheria. It remained now to take the Hureira Redoubt on the Gaza–Beersheba road, the task given to the 10th Division's 31st Brigade. It was carried out speedily and with minimal casualties despite no artillery support being available save for a brief initial bombardment, and later the 31st Brigade was able to extend to the left and make contact with the Composite Force, on XXI Corps' extreme right.

The mounted infantry was released on the morning of 7 November; the A&NZMD took Ameidat Station easily, but as the horsemen approached Tel el Nejile and Jemmame they began to run into opposition. The next day the AMD, held up by the delay in clearing the Wadi esh Sheria, began its own advance, and it, too, was soon in action against small, determined bodies of Turkish infantrymen with well-placed machine guns, and made only slow progress. Even so, on 8 November Allenby still believed he would be able to destroy the Gaza garrison as it withdrew northwards and pressed Chauvel to speed up his advance, but in fact the combination of stiff resistance by rearguard units and the sheer number of prisoners to be dealt with as the advance broke through them and got in amongst the tail of the fleeing army was already proving too much for the light horse battalions. By the afternoon of 9 November, despite prodigious efforts by the horsemen, it was clear that the race to cut off the retreating Turks had largely been lost, and that attempts at envelopment would now, like it or not, have to give way to pursuit.

As we noted, the advanced guard of XXI Corps – the 52nd Division's 157th Brigade – had been pushed northwards along the coast early on 7 November. Bulfin had despatched his own corps cavalry[23] ahead of it, to cross the Wadi el Hesi if possible. The Wadi el Hesi is the most northerly of its kind on that coast (from then on the watercourses are rivers proper), and water was almost always to be found there, though it was sometimes necessary to dig for it. It entered the sea about twelve kilometres north of Gaza City as it then was, and a similar distance south of the ruins of Ashkelon. Sand dunes extended inland for seven or eight kilometres around the wadi's mouth, but less so immediately to the north, where there were numerous settlements: Herbie and Deir Sneid, in proximity to the wadi, and Burbera, further north; there the Turks had begun to construct defensive works, though they were thought to be limited to short stretches of trench.

The 157th Brigade crossed the wadi near its mouth, and deployed north-wards for a further three kilometres to face the high ground to the east. In the event, not only did the ridge prove to be both broader and considerably higher than had been estimated, but the Turks were present in much greater strength than had been supposed, too. The Turkish positions in the dunes fell easily enough to the 157th Brigade the following morning, but when it came to assault the ridge beyond, the 155th was held, and only cool heads kept its flanks secure. After some delay the 157th was sent up in support, but by the time its men were in position, night had fallen. They gained the crest under heavy fire, and took the positions there in hand-to-hand fighting, but were driven off almost immediately by a Turkish counterattack. Four times the Scots tried to retake the ridge, and four times they were defeated, much of the fighting on each occasion being at very close quarters. Eventually Moore sent up his brigade reserve. Together with a renewed attack from the flank this was enough to carry the position. Some Scots had been bayoneted where they lay wounded, and few if any Turkish prisoners were taken.

Before midnight Allenby ordered Bulfin to send another division forward, to advance to the line Julis–Hamame, about thirty kilometres north-east of Gaza, to support the A&NZMD. The 75th Division was selected, and was readied to move forward from its positions around Sheikh Abbas, but its departure was delayed for lack of transport, its own – and most of the rest of the corps' – having been loaned to XX Corps for the deployment towards Beersheba and not yet having arrived back. It was returned during the course of the morning of 9 November, but was in no fit state to proceed immediately; the 75th managed to send one brigade group – the 275th, with some support troops – forward to Beit Hanun and subsequently to Deir Sneid, where the water supply was accessible, but it was the following day before the bulk of the division was able to follow.

Bulfin's objective now was Junction Station in the Wadi es Sarar, where the railway line from Beersheba joined that linking Jerusalem with Jaffa and points north. This accomplished, the Turkish Seventh and Eighth Armies would be split apart, the former cut off from any easy resupply route and dependent on material brought to Jerusalem either by road from Nablus or across the Jordan from the Hejaz railway. Allenby, the bulk of his effort now centred in the coastal plain, expected Falkenhayn to attempt to launch a counteroffensive on the right, but was confident that the Seventh had neither the *matériel*, the organisation nor the spirit for the sort of fight that would require, and merely ordered the now rested Camel Brigade to move up from Beersheba to Tel Abu Dilakh, north of Sheria, and the 60th Division, now at Jemmame, to be prepared to advance and take the Turks in the flank if they tried to move on Tel el Nejile.

By this juncture Allenby's forces had started to outrun their supply train. The Royal Navy began landing supplies at the mouth of the Wadi el Hesi, which eased the situation but did not solve the problem entirely. Water, too, was still in short supply, for though wells were now more numerous, the Turks had had more time to render them unusable. However, the Australian Mounted Division was still moving ahead, the 3rd LHB passing through Iraq al Menshiye and the 4th through Faluja, to the west, the two linking up by dusk. The Australian & New Zealand Mounted Division, its horses exhausted by the exertions of 9 November, made little progress that day, and by the evening it had been decided that the Yeomanry Mounted Division should relieve it.

The infantry's advance was still continuing too, with the 75th Division now ordered to send a brigade group up to Suafir el Gharbiye and the 52nd to despatch one to Sdud. The 157th Brigade drew that latter duty, but when it arrived in the vicinity and met up with the 1st LH Brigade it was to learn that, while Sdud itself had been taken, the Turks were ensconced on a ridge five kilometres to the east and were using their artillery to deny the Australians access to the wells there. Moore decided on an immediate assault, even though his men had marched over twenty kilometres through heavy sand into the teeth of an unseasonal *Khamsin*, and there remained no more than half an hour of daylight. The defenders put up a stubborn resistance, their machine guns, positioned in advance, covering the approaches with inter-locking fields of fire, but the Scots were able to subdue them eventually with their Stokes mortars. The enemy positions on the ridge were taken, and held against a determined counterattack, the Highlanders leaving the trenches and meeting the Turks in the open, but it soon became clear that there was a reserve position on a second ridge, and it was decided to leave that until daylight returned. When it did it revealed that the Turks had withdrawn. This was the second time in forty-eight hours that the 157th Brigade had carried out a successful night attack across unknown terrain.

That morning, 11 November, Allenby told Bulfin, who had by now moved his headquarters up to Deir Sneid, to close up his two forward divisions on their advanced brigades and Chauvel to move the Yeomanry Division from the right flank through to the coast, the AMD to remain as a covering force on the right. He still thought it likely that the Turks would attempt a counteroffensive there, but paid the prospect little heed.[24]

Late on 10 November, in the only advance the A&NZMD had made that day, the 1st LHB had forced a crossing of the Nahr (river) Suqreir north of Sdud. It had been unable to develop more than a bare hold on the right bank, and now the 52nd Division was to enlarge the bridgehead and drive the Turks back from their positions east of Burka, while the AMD advanced on its right. The 9th ALH, following a tributary of the Suqreir up the Wadi el Burshein, passed through Barqusya unopposed, and at noon occupied the hilltop hamlet of Tel es Safi, the Castle Blanchegarde of the crusader King Fulk of Jerusalem,[25] while the Gloucesters of the 5th Mounted Brigade found Balin unoccupied and the 4th LHB sent a squadron across the Huj branch of the railway at Qastine. Early in the afternoon, from the vantage point of

Tel es Safi three separate Turkish columns were sighted, advancing from the north and north-east.

Fitzgerald ordered the Warwicks and Worcesters up to join the Gloucesters on the ridge north of Balin while his horse artillery opened fire in a vain attempt to slow the advance; meanwhile the 9th ALH gave up Tel es Safi and rejoined the rest of its brigade at Barqusya, while the 4th LHB occupied high ground north of Summeil towards Jelediye, on the 5th Mounted Brigade's left. It soon became clear that the Turks had committed most of the remains of the Eighth Army, the three columns seen from the hilltop vantage-point being the 26th, 53rd and 54th Divisions, with the 16th – which had marched from Beit Jibrin during the night – still out of sight to the rear.[26]

The Turks quickly drove an outpost off the high point of the ridge north of Balin, which allowed them to enfilade the rest of the position, forcing the 5th Mounted to withdraw to the next ridge south, roughly in line with the 3rd LHB at Barqusya (that withdrawal was a close-run thing, the unit's wounded being evacuated from the dressing station at Balin on horseback at the gallop). It was soon apparent that that ridge, too, was untenable, thanks to Turkish artillery, and the entire line withdrew to extend that occupied by the 4th LHB north of Summeil.

In fact, the steps necessary to stop the Turkish advance had already been taken, when Leggett's 156th Brigade crossed the Nahr Suqreir, but there was to be a fierce fight before they won through and demonstrated that. The first task was to clear the Turks out of Burqa; the brigade crossed the river at 1100 and fanned out on the right bank. The first line of defences, amongst cactus hedges on the outskirts of the village, fell relatively easily, but not so the second and third, on a ridge beyond, and it was only as night fell that the settlement was in their hands. To the east, towards the village of Yazur, lay a steep-sided knoll known as Brown Hill (Hill 220). Ordered to clear it, the 4th Royal Scots advanced but made slow progress against the fire of several howitzers located behind the hill, and took many casualties. When it did finally succeed in taking the position, at around 1600, the battalion was not strong enough to hold it against an immediate counterattack. Seeing this, the officer commanding a nearby field battery obtained permission to use the two companies of infantry covering his guns to support the Scots, and men of the 2/3rd Gurkhas and the 2/5th Hampshires doubled across the intervening ground to assist them. Together they took the hill once more, and this time were able to consolidate their gain.

Even as the Scots were fighting for Burqa, Allenby was meeting with Bulfin and Chauvel at the latter's forward headquarters at Julis to plan the following day's operation to take Junction Station and, if possible, begin the advance to Jerusalem. There was a certain air of urgency, since the previous day Allenby had received a somewhat discursive signal from London reminding him that he would perhaps soon be called upon to send some of his divisions to France, with a warning not to occupy positions he would not be able to hold with depleted forces. There was some anxiety lest a heavy storm on the night of 11 November had presaged the coming of the wet season, but the twelfth had dawned fine and continued that way, the roads drying out satisfactorily.

Bulfin's XXI Corps was to carry out the attack, Palin's 75th Division on the right, its exposed flank screened by the AMD, and Hill's 52nd on the left, with the rest of the Desert Mounted Corps outside it. The 75th was to advance astride the road from Gaza and attack the Turkish line Tel et Turmus–El Qastine–Yazur, then take the twin villages of Mesmiye el Gharbiye and Mesmiye esh Sherqiye; the 52nd's objective was the line from Yazur to Beshshit, about eight kilometres north-east of Burqa, and then Qatra and the adjacent village of El Maghar. The advance would then halt for the artillery to catch up before fresh troops pushed through to Junction Station and Mansura, about four kilometres beyond. The attack would commence at 0800 the next day, and be preceded by an hour's bombardment by such heavy artillery as was available. In addition to the four Turkish divisions which had advanced, the 3rd and 7th of XX Corps were lined up, roughly north–south, from a point south of Qatra to El Qubeibe, north of Yibna; Turkish numbers were estimated to be around 13,000 spread out across twenty kilometres of front. The terrain was generally clear of obstacles, the villages themselves, with their cactus hedges, being the only ones of note.

Tel et Turmus and Qastine were occupied by Colston's 233rd Brigade, and the 232nd extended the line to Yazur with no opposition save from the Turkish artillery, but when the 233rd pressed on to Mesmiye the shelling became heavier, and machine guns on the southern flank joined in. The brigade reached Mesmiye el Gharbiye by noon, but found it strongly held, and it was well over an hour before the Turks were compelled by accurate shelling to fall back to high ground north of the line of advance, whence their machine guns made further progress impossible. Colston was obliged to detach the 4th Wiltshires, with two companies of the 5th Somerset LI and two sections of his machine gun company, to secure the ridge, but it was 1600 before that was accomplished, by which time the 232nd on the left had forged ahead, creating a wide gap between the two battalions; it was filled by bringing up the 232nd's reserve battalion, the 5th Devons, and the line was able to continue its advance until held by flanking fire from Qatra.

Meanwhile, the 234th Brigade's 58th Rifles had come up on the right, following the line of the railway, and was making slow progress towards Mesmiye esh Sherqiye, its leftmost company being stalled by machine gun fire from another ridge-top position before it reached the outskirts of the village. Trying to take the ridge by storm, the Indians took many casualties, but were ultimately successful when two troops of the 11th ALH appeared and outflanked the defenders.

By now the sun had set and the light was fast going, but Palin's men were still short of their third-phase objective, and he ordered the 234th, of which only small numbers of men had yet been engaged, to continue towards Junction Station. Two of the brigade's battalions had now reached Mesmiye esh Sherqiye, but the other two were still at Qastine, and it was some hours before they could be brought up. Thus it was 2230 before the advanced guard – the 123rd Rifles – set out, and another hour before the main body followed. Unsure of his ground, Brig.-Gen. Anley had given instructions to proceed cautiously. Twice the lead battalion was surprised when it came upon bodies of Turkish troops; the first proved to be a supply column, and was dealt with swiftly, but the second was a formed body of infantry, at least a battalion strong, and it was some time before they could be driven off. With that Anley concluded that any chance he'd had of taking the station by surprise was gone, and ordered a halt. A demolition party made an attempt to cut the line north of the station but was unsuccessful, and in the hours which followed many Turks, Kress von Kressenstein reportedly amongst them, were able to escape by train.

Palin only received a report of Anley's activities at 0615 on 14 November, and he sent two armoured cars then at Mesmiye to assist him. They arrived at brigade headquarters and were sent straight on to support the 123rd Rifles; at around 0830 they came within sight of the station. Turkish troops were milling around in confusion and were put to flight up the Ramle road by the cars' guns, and minutes later the advanced company of the 123rd Rifles was able to occupy the area.

There was considerable criticism levelled at Anley for the delay in taking the station, but in the event it proved that the Turks had been more interested in escape than in destroying the vast quantities of supplies stockpiled there, or even in disabling much of its infrastructure.[27] The steam-powered water pumping station was still operative, and two rather tired but serviceable locomotives and sixty trucks were taken intact.

On the northern flank, the 52nd Division's 155th Brigade had been ordered to take Beshshit, then advance on Qatra and El Maghar, the 156th Brigade to its right having no specific responsibility beyond remaining in contact with the 75th Division's left, and the 157th Brigade being ordered to occupy Yibna, to the north-west, after it had been taken by the Yeomanry Mounted Division. The 155th was then to move on to El Mansura, a few kilometres north of Junction Station, in the wake of the Yeomanry Division. Beshshit was occupied without much opposition, but reconnaissance patrols found Qatra and El Maghar being reinforced. Speed was clearly of the essence, and Pollock-McCall immediately ordered the 5th Royal Scots Fusiliers to attack Qatra, with the 4th Battalion in support, and the 4th King's Own Scottish Borderers, with the 5th in support, to focus on El Maghar.

The two villages were sited on a ridge line, separated by a depression, the Wadi Qatra; both were surrounded by walled and hedged gardens, and south of Qatra was a large orange grove. Between the ridge and Beshshit there was open country, with very little cover. The positions were held by the remains of the 7th Division, a total of perhaps 3,000 effectives, backed up by a substantial number of guns.

Those guns, and machine guns on the ridge, took a toll of the Scots as they crossed the open plain, but by 1130 the two leading battalions had reached the comparative shelter of broken ground at the foot of the hill, around five hundred metres short of their objectives, where they stalled. The support battalions were sent in, the 4th RSF to try to round the right flank south of Qatra, but achieved very little, and an attempt to work up the Wadi Qatra also proved a failure. Pollock-McCall met with Hill at around 1300, and the latter offered an artillery bombardment on Qatra, but not before 1530.

Coincidentally, the Bucks Yeomanry of the 6th Mounted Brigade was already concentrating in the Wadi Jamus (as the Wadi Qatra became known to the west of the ridge it bisected), preparing the attack on the Maghar ridge as a precursor to advancing on Aqir, beyond. It was accompanied by a horse-artillery battery, which began to shell the village at a range of 3,000m. The Dorset Yeomanry was ordered forward to assist, and as soon as the (rather narrow) wadi was cleared, the Berkshires, held back in reserve, were to move up. The brigade's machine gun squadron was to deploy on the right, with a clear field of fire until the charge neared its objectives.

The horsemen, with three and a half kilometres to cover, moved out at the trot, and at once came under sporadic artillery fire. Having covered about half the distance they quickened to the gallop. When they neared the crest, the Turks turned and fled to a man, but perhaps two hundred were taken anyway, plus two guns and twelve machine guns, which were quickly turned on Maghar, where there was still opposition.

As the Yeomanry began its advance, Pollock-McCall made his way towards the forward positions of his Borderers. Seeing the guns which had previously pinned them down shift over to the horsemen, he picked up a rifle and led them forward himself. They reached the village just as the Berkshires came up, and between them, cavalry and infantry cleared the village, taking four hundred more prisoners. Later, units of the 22nd Mounted Brigade, ordered to secure it, ascended the ridge; beyond 'the whole eastern slope was covered with the running figures of many hundreds of Turks converging on Aqir, which lay in full view below'. An attempt was made to seize the village, but the task proved beyond the Yeomanry's resources and as night fell the squadrons withdrew to the ridge.

To the south, the Fusiliers waited out the promised artillery bombardment and then, as the last shells were falling on Qatra, began to advance. They took heavy casualties in the process, for some of the Turkish machine gunners remained at their posts until they were overrun, but by 1600 the village was in their hands, along with a further four hundred prisoners.

The Action of El Maghar, as it became known, broke the already under-strength Turkish Seventh Division as a fighting force; over a thousand of its men were taken prisoner and over four hundred dead were removed from the battlefield. It was to achieve a small place in history as an exemplar of how infantry, cavalry and artillery could combine successfully in a small-scale action. It was clear, however, that a very much heavier defeat could have been inflicted on the Turks had the entire 22nd Mounted Brigade been able to combine to take Aqir, for that would effectively have closed the roads north to Ramle. The village was not occupied until 0600 the following morning, by which time it and the countryside south to Junction Station were largely clear of Turks.

By the morning of 14 November the Turks were in full retreat right across Philistia. The remains of the Eighth Army took up a line Jaffa–Lydda (Lod), with detachments covering Ramle and Latron (Latrun). On this front only the New Zealand Mounted Rifles Brigade were engaged, at Nes Ziyona, in the coastal strip. This was one of many recently established Jewish settlements, all of them constructed within the previous quarter-century and very different in character from the older Arab settlements with which they were intermingled. Some were little more than extended farms, but others, such as Rehovoth, south of Ramle, were prosperous modern villages. At Nes Ziyona the NZMRB found itself opposed by what seems to have been virtually all that remained of the 3rd Division, and was held up for most of the day, the surviving Turks retreating only as darkness fell, giving up Rishon le Ziyon as well. The following day Godwin's 6th Mounted Yeomanry was given the task of taking the Abu Shushe ridge, which protected Ramle's eastern flank, together with the 22nd. It fell to a two-axis mounted/dismounted attack before nightfall, whereupon the Camel Brigade took over and consolidated the territory gained. This was the second successful mounted action in two days. The 2nd ALH entered Ramle at around 1100, and Lydda was occupied without resistance some hours later.

The result of the push on Junction Station and beyond had been exactly as Allenby had foreseen: the Turkish Seventh and Eighth Armies were now separated, the Eighth contained in the coastal strip, the Seventh driven into the hills of Judaea. It remained now only to continue to push the Eighth Army northwards while the advance on Jerusalem was planned in detail.[28]

The days which followed were spent in consolidation and reorganisation. The railway from Beit Hanun to Junction Station was brought back into working order (and by 5 December was operative to Ramle and Lydda), and a new landing-place was established at the mouth of the Nahr Suqreir, which allowed XXI Corps to move its supply depot up from Deir Sneid to Yibna. Jaffa was occupied without opposition, but a reconnaissance towards Amwas on the Jaffa–Jerusalem road found it held in some force.

Allenby's plan was to cut the arterial Nablus–Jerusalem road at Bire, just to the east of Ramallah, well to the north of the Holy City, then hold his front on the plain with XXI Corps and a mounted division while the rest of the Desert Mounted Corps, supported by one of XX Corps' infantry divisions, moved into the Judaean hills. This distribution of forces proved impossible to support logistically, and instead he used the 54th Division and the A& NZMD as his holding force while the Australian and Yeomanry Mounted Divisions and the 52nd and 75th Infantry Divisions advanced.

The offensive was to have started on 18 November with an operation by the AMD to capture Amwas, but at the last minute that was cancelled, and the 75th Division was ordered up the Ramle–Jerusalem road instead,[29] while the 52nd Division took the (unmetalled) Lydda–Jerusalem road further north. Meanwhile the YMD was to advance on Bire by way of Beit Ur et Tahta; the road proved impassable to wheeled vehicles, and it was sent back to Ramle, the Hong Kong Mountain Battery being sent up in place of its horse artillery. During the course of 19 November the 75th Division made speedy progress, and by dark its advanced units were ten kilometres south-east of Amwas, while the 52nd's vanguard reached Beit Liqya that evening after a difficult march over a road which had soon been reduced to a poor track and, in places, disappeared altogether. By now the wet season had begun in earnest, the rain heavy and almost incessant, which exacerbated the situation considerably, and the YMD, crossing some of the worst country in the region, had a very poor time of it. Ordered to be at Beitunye, five kilometres south-west of Bire, by nightfall, it had failed even to reach Ain Arik, west of Ramallah.

The next day the 75th encountered its first resistance, at Saris; it was overcome by the 2/4th Somerset LI with armoured-car support, and the village taken before noon, and the advance moved on to Qaryet el Inab. Turkish forces were cleared out of the hills north of the road and the village was occupied by nightfall. The deterioration in the route the 52nd Division was following continued, its troops now being forced down to a single file. However, Beit Duqqu, north of the road, was captured by 1030, and by 1300 most of the enemy had been cleared from the high ground south-east of Beit Anan, where the Division passed a second miserable night on iron rations.

That morning, while the 22nd Brigade struggled onwards to Ain Arik, Barrow ordered Godwin's 6th Mounted Brigade to head south-eastwards towards its original objective, Beituniye. It soon struck an even more serious obstacle, the so-called Zeitun Ridge, east of Beit Ur el Foqa. Narrow from north to south and three kilometres long, the steep-sided, flat-topped ridge rises 300m above the surrounding terrain; it was to be the scene of heavy fighting on a number of occasions, and was not taken until close to the year's end.

On 21 November, Bulfin ordered the 52nd Division to stand fast while the 75th left the main road and head across its front, from Qaryet el Inab to Buddu and thence to El Jib, by way of a poor track. Buddu was cleared of Turks, and then the advanced guard, the 233rd Brigade's 2/4th Dorsets, came under fire from the hill of Nabi Samweil. The 123rd Rifles and the 1/4th Duke of Cornwall's LI of the 234th Brigade[30] went straight into the attack. In failing light the Indians and the Cornishmen advanced into machine gun fire; by the time they reached the summit of the hill, the site, tradition says, of the Prophet Samuel's tomb, it was quite dark, and they took possession of it with little difficulty.

Barrow, his attack on Bire by now already a day overdue, continued to batter away at the obstacles between him and his objective. The East Riding Yeomanry moved on Ramallah and were soon halted by Turkish guns in a dominant position; by 1400 substantial Turkish reinforcements were seen advancing against them.[31] At that point Barrow was forced to admit defeat; he could make no further progress without the artillery which was denied him by the terrain, and ordered his men to retire to Beit Ur el Foqa and (the 22nd Brigade) to Beit Ur et Tahta. Had the unremitting bad weather not made aerial reconnaissance impossible, it would perhaps have become apparent earlier that he had actually reached the Turkish main line of resistance, the line at which they meant to try to hold Jerusalem, as, soon, would the infantry divisions.

When the 75th Division continued towards the Nablus–Jerusalem road the following day, only four of its battalions were available.[32] Their first task was to take El Jib, and in order to do that it was necessary to drive the Turks off the high ground east of Beit Izza. That they failed to do, and by nightfall they were back where they had started, in the valley north-west of Buddu. During the course of the day the four battalions holding Nabi Samweil faced four successive attempts to dislodge them. The fourth wave, at 1530, almost surrounded the mosque, where the wounded had been brought, and where most of the defenders were now located. Things were going so badly that all the able-bodied men were sent out in a desperate charge, leaving the walking wounded to defend the ruined building with their rifles and just one Lewis gun; the 1/4th DCLI and the 3/3rd Gurkhas drove the Turks back down the terraced hillside with bayonet and *kukri*, killing many by the simple expedient of throwing boulders down on them. How desperate was the action can be gauged by the casualty figures. In all, British killed, wounded and missing on Nabi Samweil that day amounted to over 750 officers and men, 261 of them within the ranks of the Gurkhas.

Another attempt to cut the Nablus road was made the following morning, the original four battalions made up to six by the addition of the 2/3rd Gurkhas and 1/5th Devonshires. From the jumping-off point near Buddu, they had around two kilometres of open plain to cross to reach their objective, and came under machine gun fire from three separate locations as soon as they emerged. Without artillery support it was useless.

Clearly, it was necessary to clear the Turks off the adjoining high ground if El Jib was to be taken, and greater efforts were made to get artillery up, the guns being double-teamed while the engineers did all they could to improve the roads. The onslaught began again on the morning of the twenty-fourth; this time the 52nd Division would carry out the assault, and as well as El Jib would attempt to clear the dominant positions to the north and north-east, across the Nabi Samweil ridge to Bir Nebala and Er Ram. This time, with artillery support and the enfilading positions under direct attack, the assault was more successful than previously, though casualties were still high. The 5th Scots Fusiliers and 5th KOSB had reached the outskirts of El Jib, and were about to embark on a new attack when, at 1600, the order was given to stand fast.

The problem lay on Nabi Samweil, where the Turks had by now established very strong positions in a maze of walled gardens below the mosque. They were covered by artillery at Er Ram and Ramallah, and proved unassailable, and the failure led to the 157th Brigade not being able to fulfil its own commitment to advance on Er Ram. Hill reported to Bulfin that the task was beyond him with the means at his disposal, and the corps commander was forced to accept that. At 1950 Allenby ordered the offensive to cease. At last the Turks had found the means – and the concentrated manpower – to slam the door to Jerusalem in the invaders' faces.

Allenby's army had been in action continuously for over three weeks; the men were extremely tired, and few units had received drafts to help bring them back up to strength. Within the ranks of the infantry, XXI Corps had borne the brunt of the fighting, and it was now time to withdraw it and bring up XX Corps to take its place. As Cyril Falls remarked, this was just the time of vulnerability which 'provides the quick-thinking and resolute defender with a chance to turn on the offensive', and Falkenhayn did just that.

His greatest coup was to march the 19th Division north from Jerusalem to Nablus (where he now had his own headquarters; he decamped from Jerusalem on 19 November, leaving a somewhat aggrieved Ali Fuad in command there), then west to Tul Karm, Kressenstein's base, then south to Abud, fifteen kilometres north-east of Lydda, where it was nicely positioned to penetrate the gap between the Yeomanry Mounted Division and the 54th Infantry Division. This march of 160km, which took seven days, went unnoticed by British Intelligence officers.

Allenby's orders for the changeover were issued on 25 November. Bulfin's first priority was to exchange his 52nd Division for Chetwode's 60th, which was already in position (with the 74th on the march to Majdal, and the 10th at Deir Sneid preparing to follow; they were thus four and five days respectively from the front), the handover to be completed by dawn on 28 November. By the morning of the twenty-seventh the 179th Brigade was astride the Ramle–Jerusalem road, from Soba to near Beit Surik, with the 180th to its left, its own line curving eastwards to take in Nebi Samweil; on its left, its line bent far back towards the west, were the exhausted Highlanders of the 157th. Next to them was the Yeomanry Mounted Division, now down to no more than eight hundred effectives and virtually at its last gasp. Two RHA batteries stood west of it, covering Foqa and Tahta, but then there was a yawning gap, eight kilometres wide, to the rightmost posts of the 54th Division at Shilta. It was this gap that the Turkish 19th Division was so well placed to exploit.[33]

The first signs of a Turkish counteroffensive were manifest further east, at Beit Surik, when an attempt was made to infiltrate the narrow zone between the 179th and 180th at around 0230 on the morning of 27 November. That came to nothing, but twelve hours later there was a more concerted – but ultimately no more successful – attack on the mosque on Nabi Samweil. That evening the 157th Brigade was relieved by the 181st, and Shea took over command of the sector from Hill. Meanwhile the Yeomanry had come under attack too. Forward posts at City Hill in front of Et Tire, and at Sheikh Abu ez Zeitun, on the western end of the ridge, neither of them held in great strength, were attacked simultaneously at around 1400. The men at City Hill were forced to withdraw to Signal Hill, half a mile to the north-west, a considerably stronger position. The party on Zeitun Ridge managed to hold out all day, though their numbers were reduced by half.

Well to the west, out on the plain near El Yehudiye, just north of the Jaffa–Lydda road, units of Hare's 54th Division had been in action since dawn. When the 10th Londons, at Deir Tureif, and the 5th Bedfords at Beit Nabal came under attack, both held, but some hours later, a company of the Imperial Camel Brigade on Bald Hill was driven back a quarter-mile, which forced other posts in the vicinity to pull back too. Chaytor, in command in that sector, ordered Bald Hill retaken, but later accepted that denying it to the Turks by means of artillery fire would suffice. That was a mistake; by not occupying the hill he exposed the 4th Northamptons, on the immediate right, who were holding the line from El Yehudiye through a pre-war German settlement at Wilhelma to the railway at the small station which served it. The station was the first to fall, soon after midday, but was recovered by a counterattack; meanwhile Turkish forces were increasing in strength in front of Wilhelma, which had now come under an artillery bombardment, but it was 1700 before they showed signs of being ready to try an all-out assault. The Northamptons' commander, afraid of being overwhelmed in the approaching darkness, decided to launch a pre-emptive strike of his own, using three platoons from each of the companies holding his flanks, at the station and El Yehudiye. They surprised the Turks and drove them back to Rantye, two kilometres to the north.

That evening Barrow considered the implications of the gap in the line between Tahta and Shilta. He had been informed that the 7th Mounted Brigade was being sent to support him, and signalled Chauvel asking that its departure be accelerated. Hill was ordered to send a battalion of his 155th Brigade – the 4th Royal Scots Fusiliers – up to El Burj before dawn, and Chauvel also ordered the 4th Light Horse Brigade to move up to Berfilya, three kilometres west of El Burj, but later told Grant to continue on to Tahta.

The 7th MB – not a 'full strength' brigade by any means, we should recall, consisting of just the Sherwood Rangers and the S. Nottingham Hussars – arrived in the gap at 0445, having passed within little more than half a kilometre of the Turkish 19th Division's cavalry squadron. A kilometre west of Tahta (thus, just in the rear of the Lincolns of the 22nd MB) it halted, the mounts were unsaddled and the troopers began preparing breakfast in the first light of day. Brisk firing broke out, and a line of Turkish infantry could be seen advancing against the Lincolns at Hellabi. For some time the situation was touch-and-go, the Turks working steadily around the 7th MB's left flank, which was held by just one armoured car. However, by 0800 the 4th RSF had arrived in the vicinity of El Burj, and the rest of the 155th Brigade was hard on its heels, Pollock-McCall, ordered to send up another battalion, having taken it upon himself to bring his entire command back into the line. With the help of his Scots the situation was eventually stabilised, though the Turks were still firmly in control of the valley, and a battery of mountain guns they had brought up caused considerable problems in the rear echelons, particularly amongst the 7th MB's horse-holders.

The Turks assailing Zeitun Ridge had not been idle either; they maintained their onslaught right through the night and by mid-morning it was necessary to withdraw the 6th Mounted Brigade, the Berks and Bucks pulling back to cover Foqa and the Dorsets onto Jonquil Hill to the south-east. In mid-afternoon the Dorsets were driven back, most retiring to Foqa; some, however, were forced down the Wadi Zeit, where, extremely hard pressed, they suddenly found themselves under covering fire from the 4th LHB. The light horsemen had followed the route the 7th MB had taken to El Burj, but had then skirted the village to the south; those of its troops who had saved the retreating Dorsets were men of the 11th ALH, who now occupied the wadi.

The loss of Jonquil Hill exposed the 8th MB's left flank, and the 1st County of London pulled back to Beit Duqqu. The Yeomanry Mounted Division was in no fit state to stand an attack of this intensity; inevitably, something had to give, and when Godwin warned Barrow that his men at Foqa were facing annihilation, the divisional commander ordered him to pull them back to a line east and south-east of Tahta, where they could link up with the 22nd MB.

A second infantry brigade from the 52nd Division, the 156th, had by now also been ordered to make a volte-face and return to the line, and it arrived at Beit Liqya at 1130. Its 1/4th Royal Scots were sent up to the west of El Burj, to make contact with the right wing of the 54th Division, and by nightfall a semblance of order had been restored in that sector too. By dawn on 29 November it seemed that the counteroffensive had been held, if only narrowly, with additional troops coming up to overcome the (very local) superiority in numbers the enemy had briefly enjoyed and complete the delayed handover of the front to XX Corps. That, however, is not to say that the battle was yet concluded: it was to continue until 3 December, with the Turks' chances of real success diminishing with every day that passed.[34]

At 0900 on 29 November the Turks resumed shelling the mosque on Nebi Samweil, bringing up troops into the houses and gardens which crowded the slopes around it, and at 1330 tried to rush it. They were repulsed once more, this time by the 2/20th Londons. North of Tahta, too, the fighting had intensified again, but with the aid of the 7th Scottish Rifles, the last reserve element of the 156th Brigade, the battered defenders there withstood an onslaught which began in the small hours of the morning and lasted until 1000. That same morning there was more fighting in the vicinity of El Yehudiye, too, the Turks first taking, and then losing, ground west of Beit Nebala and making a late incursion south-west of Bald Hill, digging themselves in overnight. That proved to be a mistake, for when the sun came up they found themselves enfiladed from both flanks, and the entire party – three officers and 147 men – was forced to surrender.

When 30 November dawned, the situation was still far from stable in the hills of Judaea, difficulties around Foqa being exacerbated by the lack of a reliable map and even of accurate intelligence: the 231st Brigade was ordered that morning to take over there 'if still in British hands', when it had actually been evacuated thirty-six hours earlier. When the 25th Welch Fusiliers attempted to carry out that instruction, with assistance from the 10th Shropshires, it found it held by a reinforced battalion of Turks. Fortunately for the Welshmen, their adversaries were uncharacteristically relaxed – they found them with arms piled and cooking fires going – and an immediate attack secured the village without opposition, capturing around 450. However, there were more Turks in the vicinity, and the (much-reduced) company left to hold Foqa soon came under counterattack and was forced to retreat by the way they had come, rejoining elements of the Shropshires at Signal Hill before being forced back from that position, which required that Et Tire be abandoned too. Over the next twenty-four hours the Turks also retook a section of the ridge near Tahta, albeit only temporarily, but were held at El Burj and driven back. Prisoners taken during this fighting were wearing German-style steel helmets and carried the new model of Mauser rifle; interrogation established that they belonged to the 19th Division's 'Storm Battalion', a unit not previously encountered. On 3 December a renewed attempt was made by the 74th Division to reoccupy Foqa, the 16th Devonshires succeeding but then being forced to withdraw under heavy machine gun fire from positions on neighbouring high ground. As Barrow had earlier learned to his cost, Girdwood was forced to accept that Foqa was untenable while Zeitun Ridge and Jonquil Hill, in particular, were in enemy hands.

That afternoon Chetwode – who had by now accepted that the situation in the hills west of the Nablus road would not be resolved by piecemeal action – outlined to his senior commanders his plan to take Jerusalem. He intended to extend his right to Ain Karim, south of the Ramle–Jerusalem road, and then advance north-eastwards with the 60th and 74th Divisions skirting the western edges of the city while 'Mott's Detachment' (the 53rd Division, XX Corps' cavalry, a heavy-artillery battery and one of armoured cars) advanced up the Hebron road and threatened it from the south. Mott sent a pair of armoured cars to reconnoitre; they reported that there were no Turkish troops south of Hebron, and the following day advanced to the Dilbe Valley, with instructions to proceed to the Sur Bajir–Sherafat line (five kilometres south of Jerusalem) by the morning of 8 December, when the attack was scheduled to begin. Mott's men made steady progress, and on the evening of 7 December, in the last of the daylight, the Holy City could be seen from a vantage point near Ras esh Sherife. By then it had become clear that the Turkish defensive line was located north of Bethlehem; what was not clear, however, was whether Mott would be in place to challenge it by the next morning, for the weather had taken a distinct turn for the worse, with roads washed out and his men in considerable difficulties.

According to the plan, that morning the 60th and 74th Divisions would be established on a front from Ain Karim to Nabi Samweil, the left pivoting on the latter, the advance continuing in four phases so that the right ended up at Ras et Tawil, five kilometres north of Jerusalem, cutting the city off from Turkish forces to the north. Forces would then be sent to seize Ramallah and Bire. All went well to begin with, Deir Yesin and the two nearby redoubts falling before 0700 and the 74th taking Beit Iksa before it was checked. On the right the 60th took Ain Karim before dawn and El Jura soon afterwards, but the failure of the 53rd Division to come up on schedule on the right made a further advance in that sector out of the question, and Chetwode, in consultation with Shea, decided to postpone it until the following day.

In fact, in keeping with Falkenhayn's instructions, the Turkish defences around Jerusalem were withdrawn during the early hours of 9 December. The first the British knew of this was a report from two mess cooks of the 2/20th Londons, wandering in search of water, who stumbled into the southern suburbs and upon a party led by the Mayor of Jerusalem, looking for someone to whom he could surrender his city. They declined to accept, and returned to their lines. Next the mayoral party happened upon two sergeants of the 2/19th Londons, on outpost duty, but they likewise declined the honour. Next it came upon two officers from the 60th Division's artillery, who promised to telephone the news to their headquarters but respectfully refused to take a more active part in the proceedings . . .

Finally the mayor made contact with the commander of the 303rd Brigade, RFA, himself out on a reconnaissance mission, and managed to convince him of his bona fides. Lt.-Col. Bayley sent back for additional personnel, and was eventually joined by Brig.-Gen. Watson, the 180th Brigade's commander. Some while later Shea arrived and formally took the surrender in Allenby's name. British troops were henceforth confined to the suburbs, outside the city walls, until the commander-in-chief had made his own entrance. He did so – on foot, with no pomp and little ceremony – on 11 December.

*

Though the Turkish XX Corps had proved unequal to the task of defending the Holy City, there was still a danger of Falkenhayn launching a counter-attack, to which both Jerusalem and Jaffa were in theory vulnerable. Thus, Allenby could not rest on his laurels (much as his troops might have liked him to have done; the weather was uniformly atrocious, both cold and extremely wet), but needed to push both his flanks forward. By now XXI Corps, on the left, had the 52nd Division in the coastal strip, the 54th astride the railway and the 75th on its right. Bulfin ordered a brigade (the 232nd) pushed forward to secure artillery positions on a ridge north-east of Beit Nebala, which dominated Lydda and the surrounding plain, and which would have presented an obstacle to the combined advance of the 75th and 54th Divisions. They moved up to a line Ibanne–Et Tire on 15 December, and were then in a position to threaten the Nahr el Auja.

It was 20 December before sufficient bridging material – much of it impro-vised – had been brought up, but then the operation went ahead smartly; the crossings began soon after nightfall, and by daybreak on the twenty-first the 52nd Division was established on the right bank, its casualties remarkably light. The rest of the corps then pushed north and north-east, to drive the Turkish artillery which still threatened Jaffa out of range of the city, and this was accomplished by nightfall on 22 December, by which time elements of the 52nd Division had advanced as far as Arsuf, on the coast, sixteen kilo-metres north of Jaffa. From there the British line ran south-eastwards to Rantye, a similar distance to the east of the city. With Jaffa secure the task of resupplying Allenby's army by sea was much simplified, and attention turned to the other flank, to driving the Turks back from Jerusalem, towards the Jordan and northwards towards Nablus.

The weather had deteriorated in earnest, and a general advance scheduled to begin on Christmas Eve had to be postponed until 27 December. There was considerable Turkish activity in the early hours of that morning, particularly around Tel el Ful and Beit Hannina, astride the Nablus road, but nonetheless when the 53rd and 60th Divisions, to the east and north, respectively, of the city, began their advance at 0600 they made good progress from the outset, and by 0900 the latter had reached the western end of the Zeitun Ridge. There they met heavy machine gun and artillery fire, and it was not until after dark that it was finally taken. By early afternoon – by which time the 53rd's 158th Brigade had taken Anata; even though the units to left and right of them had been unable to make similar gains this secured the 60th's right flank from an attack from the direction of Jericho, where the Turks had been gathering in strength – the momentum had clearly passed to the attackers. The 74th and elements of the 10th Division to the west had further to go, pushing north-eastwards towards Ramallah, the former taking Hill 2450 (by early on the morning of the twenty-eighth) and subsequently Beituniye. By that afternoon it was possible to bring artillery up to bombard the Turks who were now evacuating Ramallah, and by the next morning the 159th Brigade was able to push through Hizmeh, Jaba and eventually Burqa. The 74th Division finally took Ramallah and Bire on the afternoon of 29 December, while the 60th Division pushed on to the line Beitun–El Burj and the 10th Division's 30th Brigade, having fought its way through Deir Ibzia and Ain Arik, secured the Et Tireh ridge to their left.

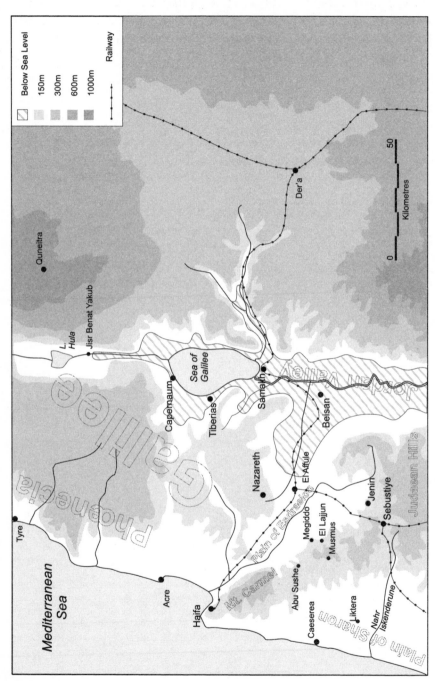

27. *Palestine – Northern Part (Galilee)*

By Way of Armageddon

With Jerusalem secure Allenby was able to relax the pressure he had maintained on his army over a period of two months. It had been a close-run thing, the weather, which had been deteriorating steadily ever since the winter rains had begun, now having very much the upper hand. Resupply operations were badly hit, and men and mounts alike had celebrated Christmas on short rations.

Far away in London, however, the weather in Palestine was of little interest. More pressing, particularly in the mind of the Prime Minister, was the continuing need to prove his belief in the theory that Germany could be brought to her knees – or at least the negotiating table – by 'knocking out the props' supporting her, and in this context that meant demolishing her ally, Turkey.[1] With the U-boat campaign in the Atlantic still having a profound effect on morale at home, with the Americans on whom both British and French pinned so many of their hopes proving very slow off the mark, and with the collapse of the Eastern Front bringing the certainty of the German army in the west being hugely increased in size, and with it the inevitability of a renewed and perhaps overwhelming offensive, Lloyd George badly needed a hat, and a rabbit to pull from it. The hat was the Middle East, and the rabbit the defeat of the Turks in Palestine.

Even as he was walking in sedate triumph into Jerusalem, news was on its way to Allenby that an infantry division from Mesopotamia – the 7th Indian – was to be transferred to reinforce his army,[2] together with a request that he outline his plans for the immediate future. He replied on 14 December; he could do nothing before the end of January, he said, when the worst of the rains would have finished, but even then would be reliant on the railway. However, as soon as possible he intended to advance his right, to straighten the line from the sea at Arsuf to the point where the Wadi el Auja[3] meets the Jordan, and then turn his attention to the Trans-Jordan, to operate against the 20,000 Turks who were said to remain south of Amman.

That was far from good enough for Lloyd George. His knowledge of the geography of the Holy Land informed by his reading of the Old Testament, he told Allenby that the entire country, 'from Dan to Beersheba', was to be occupied as soon as possible, but only as a secondary objective if the primary – an advance to capture Aleppo, cut Turkey's communications with Mesopotamia and eliminate her as a meaningful military force at a stroke – failed. Allenby, rather more down to earth, replied innocently that he believed

Dan to have been located approximately halfway between Nazareth and Damascus, and that, provided the enemy did not oppose him with more than 60,000 men, and he made the expected progress with his railway construction programme, he might reach it in his present strength by June or July ... Were he, on the other hand, to be directed to advance on Aleppo, which would inevitably require him to take Damascus first, he would need at least sixteen infantry divisions in addition to his mounted corps.

In fairness, there was a certain truth in the Prime Minister's assumption of Turkish vulnerability: the war had taken a hard toll on a nation which had no industrial base to speak of, little in the way of logistical infrastructure, a relatively small (and scattered) population which included many dissenters, and a hopelessly inefficient and still inexperienced government. It was true, too, that with Russia out of the war (and the way), and unable to press her claims, it would be very much easier to advance armistice proposals which the government in Constantinople might find acceptable. However, Turkey had proved both doughty and stubborn, and showed no signs of imminent collapse through war fatigue; would it actually be possible to inflict on her a defeat of sufficient proportions to bring her to a position where those proposals might even be discussed? The CIGS – perhaps influenced by a conviction that the new year would see a massive German offensive on the Western Front – thought not, and he was far from alone when he pointed out that 'It would seem very difficult for Turkey to shake off the German grip even if she wished to do so' in a paper he circulated on 26 December.

With the easterners and the westerners in Westminster and Whitehall unable to agree, the obvious course was a consultative process which took place, nominally at least, under the auspices of the Supreme War Council at Versailles (in fact, the French – westerners almost to a man, despite their involvement in Macedonia – played very little part, and the dialogue, which Falls likens to Greek drama, was largely between British politicians and British soldiers). The politicians won a pyrrhic victory, and on 21 January a decision 'to stand on the defensive in France, Italy and the Balkans and to "undertake a decisive offensive against Turkey with a view to the annihilation of the Turkish armies and the collapse of Turkish resistance"' was issued.

All this was fancy, of course, but very soon a character with his feet very firmly on the ground would be reintroduced to the dramatis personae: Lt.-Gen. Jan Smuts, the South African lawyer-turned-soldier who had very nearly defeated the British in his homeland more than a decade earlier, but who had by now become one of Britain's staunchest allies.[4] In February Smuts was sent to consult Allenby, his naval commander, Rear-Adm. Jackson, and Maj.-Gen. Gillman, Marshall's chief of staff in Mesopotamia, in an attempt to work out a strategy. He quickly concluded that neither Allenby nor Marshall had sufficient forces at his disposal to win the necessary sweeping victory, and that in consequence one should go over to the defensive, and hand its surplus divisions to the other. Marshall was further from Aleppo –

acknowledged to be the key – than Allenby, so his should be the force put onto the back foot; he should transfer two (more; the 7th Indian had arrived in Egypt in early January) of his infantry divisions to Allenby, including the 13th, plus a cavalry brigade; and an Indian cavalry division should be sent to him from France, where it was of little real use. Smuts' proposal met with approval in London, but before it could be translated into operational orders, the initiative collapsed under the weight of events on the Western Front.

Allenby's first action after the successful advance to establish a permanent defensive line north of Jerusalem was to send most of the Desert Mounted Corps into reserve, retaining the Australian Mounted Division to fill the gap between XX and XXI Corps temporarily.[5] Simultaneously the 74th Infantry Division was withdrawn into reserve near Buddu.

The first week of what would be the last year of the war brought a temporary improvement in the weather; hasty repairs were made to roads and permanent ways and the extension of the latter was put in hand once more. In early February, as the weather deteriorated again, Chetwode turned his attention to ways and means of carrying out Allenby's intention to push his right up to El Auja on the Jordan. He decided that the 60th Division would advance as far as the terminus of the Judaean highlands before they gave way to the Jordanian plain, with two mounted brigades (the 1st Light Horse and the New Zealand Mounted Rifles) to be given free rein to proceed as far as the river. To the north the 53rd Division would cover the right.

The operation began early on 14 February and concluded seven days later. The 1st Light Horse occupied Jericho by 0800 on 28 February, while the New Zealanders headed for Rujm el Bahr, near where the Jordan flows into the Dead Sea, which they found deserted and stripped of boats and supplies. Reconnaissance revealed no Turkish troops south of Ghoraniye, which seemed to be held in some strength, and on 22 February most of the combat units were withdrawn.

Successful though it was, the advance to Jericho had not established a broad enough base to allow operations to be launched east of the Jordan; for that it would be necessary to push the line north to El Auja. Allenby unveiled his plan to do so at a conference on 26 February, announcing that he intended subsequently to cross the river and occupy Es Salt, which he would use as a base from which to cut and keep out of commission the Hejaz railway north of Amman. That accomplished, he continued, he intended to push northwards towards Nablus and Tul Karm, which he hoped to reach by mid-April.

By this time there had been significant changes in the Turkish military hierarchy. By his actions at Gaza, where he insisted that the blow would fall on the Turkish right, Kress von Kressenstein had forfeited any remaining confidence the Turkish General Staff had in him, and he was replaced as commander of the Eighth Army by Javed Pasha. Later, Falkenhayn too was to go, supplanted as Turkey's commander-in-chief in Syria by Liman von Sanders[6] on 8 March. The change of command did not have the desired effect, though it is not unfair to say that it came too late to have made a real difference. Falls notes, quoting an unnamed Turkish officer who had served with Sanders in Gallipoli and followed him to Palestine, that 'The policy of Falkenhayn was defence by manoeuvre; that of Liman defence by resistance in trenches. Falkenhayn never fully realised how difficult manoeuvre was to troops short of transport on bad roads; Liman never realised that ground in Palestine had not the value it had had at Gallipoli.' Though Liman's strategy would seem to have paid off during the summer of 1918, in truth it succeeded only because Allenby had been denuded of the troops he needed to push forward as he wished; had he not been forced to give up so much to the Western Front, there can be little doubt that the war in the Palestinian theatre would have been effectively concluded long before – perhaps five or even six months before – it eventually was. Whether that would have taken Turkey out of the war at that point is, of course, another matter.

To return to the narrative: as we know, Allenby's plans for a brisk advance to and beyond Nablus came to naught thanks to forces well outside his control, but he did have time to execute the second phase of his plan to consolidate his right beyond the Wadi el Auja, and then carry out his stated intention of crossing the Jordan to attack the Hejaz railway. On the night of 2 March the 53rd Division pushed forward over a five-kilometre front, the 10th, on the left, advancing to conform. Four nights later the 52nd pushed on again, and on the night of 8 March the general advance of XX Corps began.[7] No opposition was encountered south of the Wadi el Auja, the Turks having withdrawn across the Jordan, blowing the bridge at Ghoraniye behind them. The wadi was crossed by three battalions of the 181st Brigade Group – which included most of the Auckland Rifles – before dawn, in order to attack Abu Tulul, which was in British hands by 1430. The next – the main – objective was Tel Asur, the highest point of the Judaean hills north of Jerusalem, at an elevation of just over 1,000 metres. It fell to the 5th Royal Welch Fusiliers at around 0930, and the 1st Herefords then went on to capture Chipp Hill to the north, but were soon driven back off it. The Turks briefly retook the main summit, too, but were driven back almost immediately by the 6th RWF which had advanced through its sister-battalion. During the course of the day the Turks tried four more times to retake the vantage point – from which one could see Mount Hermon, 150km away, in the north, eastward to Gilead and Moab and across most of the Dead Sea, southward to Hebron and westward to the Mediterranean – but with no success and at considerable cost.

To the left the 74th Division's advance followed the axis of the Nablus road; it, too, found the resistance tenacious, and was stopped at the gorges of the Wadi el Jib and the Wadi el Nimr, the further lips of which were held by the Turks. The 10th Division, further to the west, was operating in two groups, the 29th Brigade on the left and the 30th and 31st, less two battalions in reserve, on the right. The objective of the latter was the twin villages of Atara and Ajul, which commanded a crossing of the Wadi el Jib, while the former was to cross the wadi between Deir es Sudan and Nabi Salih. Atara was taken by 0930, but Ajul held out until after noon. On the left resistance was lighter but the distance to be covered greater; Deir es Sudan was reached in mid-afternoon, and Nabi Salih occupied. The advance continued after night fell, and by early the following afternoon, 10 March, Kufr Maliq was occupied. The 74th's 231st Brigade succeeded in crossing the Wadi en Nimr under cover of darkness and then assaulted the Lisane Ridge, carrying the summit at 0300 and holding it against counterattacks. To the left, the 230th had a much harder time of it in trying to cross the Wadi el Jib gorge, gaining its northern lip, from which the defenders had laid down heavy fire throughout the night, only at dawn (but then took Es Salat and Et Tell, south of the village of Sinjil, without further ado). The 10th, its objectives taken on the ninth, had expected no further demands made on it, but during the night it was decided that it should advance further, to take two hills south and south-west of Jiljliya. That proved impossible in the darkness, but met with limited success following a long-range bombardment the next morning.

The 53rd Division pushed on again the following morning, and attempted, but failed, to cross the Wadi el Kola, being defeated, once again, by the combination of precipitous slopes and enemy gunfire. However, its 160th Brigade, on the left, succeeded in forcing a passage, and then fought its way through to the outskirts of Abu Fala. By now, resistance was slackening; villages and erstwhile strongpoints fell one after another, the defenders pulling back, and by the morning of 12 March Chetwode settled on holding a line from Kufr Maliq to a point south-west of Sinjil with the 53rd and 74th, while the 10th held from Jiljliya to a point north of Nabi Salih. In all, the operation had pushed the Turks back some eight kilometres across a front over twenty kilometres wide. Far on the left XXI Corps was able to advance to bring itself into line with XX Corps without any of the problems the latter had encountered, not only because the going was considerably easier, but also because it was better supplied with artillery in consequence of that. The two corps' respective casualty figures demonstrate the imbalance most dramatically: XX Corps' came to over 1,300, while those of XXI Corps were just 104.

Allenby now judged that his hold on the west bank of the Jordan was sufficiently strong to allow him to cross the river and mount an expedition to cut the Hejaz railway at Amman.[8] The operation was to be carried out by 'Shea's Force': the 60th Division, reinforced by the A&NZMD, the Imperial Camel Brigade and the Light Armoured Car Brigade, plus artillery and support troops. Shea was to cross the Jordan on the night of 19 March, occupy Es Salt with his infantry and push his cavalry on to Amman, where they would target a ten-arch viaduct which carried the railway south from the city, and a tunnel south of that.

In the event, the predicted improvement in the weather failed to materialise, and on the given date the Jordan was still in full flood; Allenby ordered a delay of two days, by which time the situation had improved, but only marginally. On the night of 21 March the 180th Brigade, which was to force crossings at two points, approached the river. At Ghoraniye – where the Jericho–Es Salt road, which the Turks had metalled after a fashion, crossed the river – the 2/17th Londons were to install three bridges; and at Hijla, five kilometres to the south – where an older track, which led to Amman by way of Na'ur, crossed by means of a ford – the 2/19th Londons were to establish another. In the event, it proved impossible to cross at Ghoraniye, where resistance was heavy, but at Hijla the attempt was successful. Additional troops were sent across there, and a column moved northwards up the left bank and suppressed the opposition at Ghoraniye by noon on the twenty-third. An infantry footbridge was in place there by 1630, by which time the 2/21st had crossed on rafts, and by 2130 the other two bridges were also completed, and an additional pontoon bridge had also been installed at Hijla. By 2200 all three of the 60th's brigades were on the east bank, strung out between the two crossing points; two mounted regiments were across and the rest were poised to follow. The crossing had cost relatively little – twenty-six lives, with about twice that number wounded – but, unfortunately, had taken far too long; this gave the Turks ample time to reinforce the defences of Amman, with significant results.

The advance of the infantry to Es Salt, some thirty kilometres away, began in driving rain on the morning of 24 March. The 181st followed the 'main road' by way of Shunet Nimrin, where Shea made his headquarters, and El Huweij, while the 179th took a minor but more direct track to the north. The mounted men separated into three columns, the 2nd Light Horse Brigade and the Camel Brigade taking the track through Na'ur, the NZMRB following the main road as far as a track leading to Ain es Sir (where the wheeled transport was unloaded and the contents transferred to pack animals; this further delayed the operation) and then branching off to the south, and the 1st LHB – whose 3rd Regiment had crossed the Jordan by a ford just below El Auja – covered the left flank. Es Salt was occupied on the evening of the twenty-fifth. There had been very little resistance on the line of march and none in the town. That night the 2nd Light Horse bivouacked just short of Na'ur, and the following morning pushed on towards Ain es Sir, where the New Zealanders had made their own camp. In the heavy going it was impossible to make Amman before nightfall on the twenty-sixth – though raiding parties were sent to cut the railway north and south of the city – and it was the following morning before Chaytor issued orders for an attack, the New Zealanders to take the dominant hills to the south, concentrating on Hill 3039; the Camel Brigade, much reduced by the conditions encountered on the approach march, to attack the city from the west, and the 2nd LH from the north-west. It was found to be no easy matter, thanks chiefly to the large number of machine guns the German contingent located at Amman deployed, and very little progress was made that day.

On the morning of 26 March Brig.-Gen. da Costa's 181st Brigade had set out from Es Salt expecting to reach Amman by the evening of the following day. Along the way he became embroiled in a dispute between Christian peasants and Circassian irregulars at Suweile; he was forced to bivouac for the night of the twenty-seventh well short of the city as a result, and only came up on the morning of the twenty-eighth. Chaytor ordered him to lead his men straight into the attack. He suggested it would be better left until after dark, but the cavalry commander was adamant; his two forward battalions were to advance up the north side of the main road with the 2nd LH protecting their flanks and the other units renewing the attacks they had made the previous day.

They met with little success; once again the artfully sited German-manned machine guns dominated the battlefield, and the infantry could not get closer to the outskirts of the city than about six hundred metres. That evening da Costa learned from Shea's headquarters that his reserve battalion, left at Es Salt, together with two from the 180th, were on their way up to join him. Chaytor asked him whether he preferred to renew his attack with the two battalions already in place the following morning, or wait for his reinforcement. He would wait, he said, and repeated his advice that an attack under cover of darkness was the preferable course. This time Chaytor agreed, and 0200 on 30 March was set as the time for it. During the day the Turks sent troops under Essad Bey across the Jordan from Jisr ed Damiye, and more from the north, via the Hejaz railway; thirteen aircraft bombed Shunet Nimrin, killing 119 and wounding 39 more.

Rain was falling heavily once more as the attack recommenced; it was soon halted by machine gun fire from the Citadel. It was clear that this was the key to the entire situation; it was impervious to the light artillery which was all that was available to Shea's force, and while it was manned by machine gunners was impossible to approach: the 2/18th Londons mounting an attack on it failed to get within a thousand yards (900m). The Turks began counterattacking at dawn and were generally held, but the situation was hopeless; Chaytor ordered another attack on the Citadel at 1400, but when it failed was forced to confront the realities of the situation. Shea asked him, by wireless, if there was any hope of taking the city, and when he replied that there was not, he ordered him to break off, and the entire force to withdraw across the Jordan, leaving a detachment at Ghoraniye.

Even as Shea's Force was approaching the Jordan, Ludendorff unleashed the first phase of his offensive in France; the effect was near-immediate, even as far away as Palestine, and two days later Allenby was ordered to move Fane's

7th (Lahore) Indian Division into the line and relinquish one of his 'British' divisions, with another soon to follow. The 52nd was withdrawn, and sailed from Egypt early in April,[9] and shortly thereafter Allenby was deprived of the 74th too.[10] Nonetheless, he decided to push XXI Corps forward through Et Tire, with Tul Karm, the headquarters of the Turkish Eighth Army, as its objective. This would require an advance up the coastal Plain of Sharon, where Turkish defences were at their strongest, Sanders having ordered a trench system constructed in considerable depth to add to the natural obstacles of lakes and marshes. It was here that the Asienkorps (less the 703rd Battalion, in Amman) was positioned, together with five Turkish divisions.[11]

Bulfin's plan was ambitious but straightforward: the 75th Division, on the British right, would take the village of Berukin with the adjacent higher ground; then the 7th Division, on the left, would advance by two thousand yards (1800m) to a point where artillery could be brought to bear on the enemy line from Tabsor to Jaljulye, the guns being supported by ships offshore. The 159th Brigade group, on loan from Longley's 10th Division, would then come up and occupy the ground to the right of the railway, freeing the 75th and the 54th Divisions to make the main push up the centre, the latter to turn left and roll up the Turks' lines as far as the coast. That would open a breach through which the Australian Mounted Division would pour, advancing on Et Tire and Tul Karm before the Turkish rear echelons had time to react.

The 75th Division went into action just before dawn on 9 April, but did not achieve its primary objectives until late in the afternoon (and its secondary objectives not at all), and that delay had a knock-on effect on the rest of the operation. When the advance resumed at first light on the tenth it was soon stalled, attack and counterattack carrying the notional line of advance backwards and forwards; by the end of the day little if any real further progress had been made, and the 75th still stood well short of the line it was to have occupied twenty-four hours earlier. Further counterattacks that night actually drove it back, and by the morning of the eleventh it was clear that things could not proceed as they were. Bulfin ordered a halt to give his men time to recuperate, but the order to recommence never came; instead, on 15 April Allenby ordered the offensive called off. For some unfathomable reason the tide of war in the theatre seemed to have changed, and none too subtly at that.[12]

Far to the south, following the capture of Aqaba, Feisal's Arab irregulars continued their campaign against the Hejaz railway, as did detachments of Egyptian, French-Algerian and Indian troops imported for the purpose. (It was a force of the latter, under Newcombe and Davenport, which mounted what was the most successful operation of the entire campaign, destroying five kilometres of track at Qal'at Zumrud in July 1917.) Raids too numerous to catalogue were made on the railway north to Ma'an but very little real

French colonial troops – many of them, like these men, from Sénégal – played an important role in the Cape Helles Campaign at Gallipoli; two divisions were deployed on the right of the line

A 'soixante-quinze', the renowned 75mm field gun by which the French Army set such store; they were much more effective than their British counterparts chiefly because they were supplied with shrapnel shells in adequate quantities

The scene at V Beach, below Sedd el Bahr Fort, after the landings; it continued to be the main conduit for men, animals and supplies right up until the evacuation in January, 1916

Members of a British machine gun team at Gallipoli taking considerable care not to expose themselves to their opposite numbers, who were often disconcertingly close

One of the few pleasures of life at Gallipoli was the proximity of the sea; bathing parties were a daily occurrence during the summer months

The ridge bordering the Suvla Plain to the north, Kiretch Tepe, was typical of the terrain facing the invading Allies

A German-made Turkish field gun in action against Allied positions at Suvla Bay

An Australian dressing station at Anzac Cove during the blizzards of November, 1915

Suvla Point, north of the bay, became the location of an enormous depot and supply dump; evacuating it in December, 1917 was a massive undertaking, but passed off without a hitch

HMS *Cornwallis* firing in support of land operations near Anzac Cove

Games of cricket were played out as part of the elaborate operation to deceive the Turks into believing it was 'business as usual' in the final days before the evacuation of the Gallipoli bridgeheads

Turkish troops manning the trenches of the Hureira Redoubt, a strongpoint in the defensive line linking Gaza with Beersheba

Turkish machine gunners on the Gaza–Beersheba Line. Note the use of a hand-held stereoscopic range-finder

With the German troops sent to Palestine as part of the Yildirim force came the use of recently-developed 'stormtrooper' tactics. The German general Friedrich Freiherr Kress von Kressenstein is seen here inspecting picked Turkish soldiers in Palestine; note the German-style steel helmets

Turkish infantry in exposed positions in the rough country of the Judaean Hills, north of Jerusalem

Men of the Australian Light Horse passing through Damascus on the morning of 1 October, 1918, on their way to establish blocking positions on the Homs road, north of the city

Some of the twenty thousand Greek troops who landed at Smyrna on 15 May, 1919, and precipitated what was to become the Turkish War of Independence

effort was made to support Allenby's offensive at Gaza in November, the one serious attempt – an operation led by Lawrence to destroy an important bridge over the River Yarmuk between Der'a and Shamakh – coming to nothing.

The British entry into Jerusalem in December saw a resurgence of the Arab fighting spirit, and a succession of way-stations, villages and towns south of Ma'an – including Jurf ed Darawish, Kerak, Madeba, Shobek and most importantly Tafila – were either raided or even occupied, albeit briefly. By the spring of 1918 the Anglo-French cadre was better equipped and manned (with armoured cars, artillery and a flight of reconnaissance/ground-attack aircraft), and some raids saw very considerable damage done to the permanent way and its support installations. On 19 April Dawnay led a raiding party which managed to destroy many kilometres of line, including no less than seven stations, between Ramla and Ma'an but was driven off when it attempted to attack Mudauwara. Destruction of the railway aside, the greatest contribution the tribes of the Hejaz made prior to the autumn of 1918 was in tying down up to 12,000 Turkish troops, not all of them second-rate by any means, at a time when every man counted. After that time their involvement was more important, as we shall see in due course.

On 18 April Allenby decided to make a demonstration in the Jordan Valley hoping to convince the Turks he was planning another raid on Amman, with the object of keeping their troops off the irregulars; Chaytor organised it, sending his A&NZMD across the river under cover of bombardment, with instructions to follow the Turks if they retreated but not as far as Es Salt. In the event the Turks stayed put and defended strongly; the operation was terminated at dusk and the horsemen brought back to the west bank. It alerted the Turks to the possibility of the east bank coming under renewed attack, if they needed such a reminder, with serious consequences when Allenby did decide to launch a second raid at the end of the month.

This time he would content himself with isolating the Turkish forces now located at Shunet Nimrun and seizing or destroying as much as possible of the wheat and barley harvest of the fertile upland plains to prevent it falling into Turkish hands. That dictated the timing of the raid, but as well as denying the Turks the harvest Allenby was also alive to the benefits of pushing his 'eastern front' onto the high ground of the plateau east of the Jordan. If he could hold that line, the conditions his troops would have to face during the coming summer would be much easier than down in the valley, where the hot season was notorious. He also had a third, and more subtle, reason for wishing to operate on the east bank: while he knew that it would be some time before he could resume his drive north, when he did, he intended the blow to fall in the Plain of Sharon. By threatening Amman now he might well convince the Turks to transfer to the region forces he would otherwise be obliged to fight.

The operations were to be carried out by Chauvel's Desert Mounted Corps, and he took over command in the Jordan Valley from Chetwode. He would employ the A&NZMD and the AMD, and would have two brigades of the 60th Division and the 20th Indian Brigade for infantry, supported by a heavy battery of 60-pounders, two field artillery brigades and one of mountain guns. He would be opposed, he believed, by 'the motley collection of troops now known as the VIII Corps', totalling perhaps six thousand men, who were astride the main road at Shunet Nimrin. He proposed to use the infantry to contain them while he sent the AMD around to the north, leaving detachments to cover the crossing places on the Jordan and forbid them to reinforcements; the horsemen would then take Es Salt from the west and north-west, send a blocking detachment to Suweile and then move down the main road to take the Turkish positions at Shunet Nimrin in the rear. The tracks through Ain es Sir and Na'ur would, he was assured, be held by Arabs advancing from Madeba.

The operation commenced in the early hours of 30 April. Chauvel's dismissal of the force opposing him at Shunet Nimrin was soon exposed as optimistic; the 60th Division's 179th and 180th Brigades singularly failed to make any lasting impact on them and were never able to penetrate onto the plateau, with devastating results for the expedition as a whole. The blocking force the Australian Mounted Division left east of the Jordan crossings (the 4th ALHB) was soon in trouble, too, and was able to extricate itself, the following day, only with great difficulty and at the cost of all but three of its guns. The advance on Es Salt went off as planned, and the town was occupied on the first evening, but that was as far as the light horse regiments were to get; when they tried to push on up the road towards Amman the next day they were stopped at Suweile and driven back. Worse was to come; first they came under attack from the Turks who had crossed the river and brushed the 4th ALHB aside, and then, when they attempted to assist the infantry by attacking the Shunet Nimrin positions from the rear they were stopped at El Howeij and forced to retire themselves. By the evening of 2 May it was clear that the situation was grave, and with the benefit of hindsight the sensible course would have been to disengage, beginning with the light horse. Shea, however, still believed that it would be possible to salvage a victory of some sort if only the 60th Division could break through the opposition, and he ordered yet another frontal attack on the Shunet Nimrin positions.

On 3 May Allenby himself became involved; he sent the 181st Brigade up to the Jordan valley in lorries, and then went to see for himself. Within hours he had judged the situation hopeless, and told Chauvel to break off and withdraw. By midnight on 4 May most of Shea's battalions were west of the river once more, having been preceded by the mounted units, the 181st Brigade having remained behind to defend the Ghoraniye bridgehead. In all, British casualties were 214 killed, 1,298 wounded and 137 missing, the majority of them amongst the infantry. Turkish casualties were believed to have been substantially greater; almost a thousand prisoners were taken, and that allowed Allenby's staff to put a positive spin on it, and present the episode as a victory of a sort, but in fact it was a singularly dismal coda to a winter campaign which had achieved so much.

It would be many months before Allenby could go onto the offensive again, the cream of his infantry having been skimmed off to bolster the armies on the Western Front.[13] As spring turned to summer, the troops of both armies sweltered in the heat and suffered on a grand scale. Daytime temperatures in the Jordan Valley often exceeded 50°C in the shade, and unlike the desert the climate there was extremely humid thanks to the presence of the Dead Sea, which, of course, has no outlet, and relies on evaporation to maintain its level; the uplands of Judaea and the Plain of Sharon were mild in comparison.

By September, as the weather cooled and his drafts of replacements reached something akin to combat-readiness, Allenby was ready to go back onto the offensive.[14] He had issued his first preliminary instructions to his corps commanders on 1 August; essentially, Bulfin's XXI Corps was to break through in the coastal Plain of Sharon, on a front which would bring it to a line from Tul Karm to the sea north of the Nahr Iskanderune. Chauvel was then to push through the gap thus created with three cavalry divisions, hook around to the east and advance on Sebustiye (Samaria) and Nablus to get astride the Turkish lines of communication, cutting the railway to Nablus and also the road joining the city with Tiberias and Damascus. The infantry would then move through in its turn, both hooking to the right and driving northwards towards Haifa, while Chetwode's XX Corps attacked up the Nablus–Jerusalem road.

That plan was subsequently refined and became considerably more ambitious as the month wore on: instead of the DMC advancing on Sebustiye and Nablus, the infantry would now take over that responsibility, freeing the cavalry to penetrate much further to the north, to Liktera and El Affule (Afula), a vital railway junction only ten kilometres south of Nazareth, in the Plain of Esdraelon or Megiddo, and extend into the Jezreel Valley to the east, to Beisan, near the Jordan, just south of the Sea of Galilee. The virtue of the new plan over the original was not so much its depth of penetration, but the extra width it allowed, which would make it impossible for the retreating Turks to stand on any line south of Nazareth even if they could somehow withdraw and regroup speedily enough.

Allenby's orders were issued on 9 September.[15] As well as virtually all the available infantry and cavalry, every artillery piece in the theatre, 380 guns and 172 howitzers, would be employed, and ammunition was to be available on a scale hitherto unknown. In all, over six hundred lorries and tractor/trailer combinations would be available to haul ammunition and supplies and move heavy guns as required, and in order to facilitate their passage in the all-important coastal strip a total of ten bridges – all but two

of them capable of taking 60-pounder guns – had been constructed over the
Nahr el Auja between its mouth and Ferrikhiye, eleven kilometres inland. All
six of the Royal Air Force's squadrons would be employed, and great store
was set on securing German/Turkish aerodromes – especially that at Jenin –
for their use as soon as possible.

The assembly of such a force – around 70,000 fighting men, plus all the
associated support troops – in secrecy stretched the capabilities of the British
to the limit. However, by 18 September the concentration was complete. On
the left stood the 60th Division, then the 7th, the 75th and the 3rd, with the
54th on XXI Corps' right (to their rear the Desert Mounted Corps was drawn
up, ready to move through their lines as soon as the infantry commanders
considered it safe to do so). Then came the Détachement Français de Palestine
et Syrie (DFPS), and to its right the 10th and the 53rd Divisions, separated
by a gap over ten kilometres long which was lightly held by Watson's Force,[16]
with Chaytor's Force deployed along the Wadi el Auja at the right of the line,
as far as the Jordan. When a Turkish map of the British dispositions as
Sanders' staff believed them to be on 17 September was captured later, at the
Yildirim HQ in Nazareth, it demonstrated that Allenby's efforts to maintain
security had paid off handsomely; the Turks had no idea that the 60th had
moved across to the far left of the battlefield, and believed it still to be between
the 10th and 53rd, in the Judean hills.[17] Though an Indian NCO defected to
the enemy on the very eve of the attack, Sanders studiously ignored the
intelligence he brought, believing him to be a 'plant'.

The Battle of Megiddo – as the Battle Nomenclatures Committee later
decided it should be known, for no very good reason other, one suspects,
than its connection with (biblical) Armageddon; to the Turks it was the Battle
of Nablus – began with a brief artillery bombardment, just fifteen minutes
long. At 0445 on 19 September the infantry began to move; only the 75th
Division met strong opposition, as it approached Et Tire, and it was soon
clear that the pace of the advance was beating even the most optimistic
predictions. During the course of the day the 60th Division advanced thirty
kilometres, and occupied Tul Karm before dark, with the other divisions
keeping well up. By midnight XXI Corps' front ran in a shallow arc from Tul
Karm to Bidya in the south. As early as 1535 the order for XX Corps to
advance – which was conditional on the 75th Division having reached its
objectives – was passed, to be put into effect as soon as night fell.

The cavalry, too, exceeded all expectations. At 0700 the 5th Cavalry Division was given leave to pass through the infantry's lines, and by 0730 was
crossing the Nahr Falik; before noon it was across the Iskenderune too, and,
proceeding parallel to the Turks' flank, had reached Liktera, where, having
covered over forty kilometres, it rested until 1815. Moving more slowly now,
and chiefly in single file along rough upland tracks, it crossed the Carmel
Spur by way of J'ara and Abu Sushe and dropped down onto the plain,
reaching the Haifa–El Affule railway at 0300 on 20 September. Its Field

Squadron, Royal Engineers, blew a hundred-yard gap in the permanent way, and then it proceeded to what a native guide swore was Nazareth, but which patently was not. (It was El Mujeidil, but yielded two hundred Turkish prisoners in any event.) A force the equivalent of a weak brigade reached the Son of God's home town at 0430, and the Gloucester Hussars, in the lead, charged up the winding highway with swords drawn, hoping to surprise the German commander-in-chief. They were disappointed, but soon found themselves embroiled in a long-drawn-out street fight with headquarters staff who had been unable to find transport to allow them to escape.[18] It became clear by early afternoon that they could not take the town with the forces to hand – though the headquarters of the Yildirim general staff were searched, and such papers as remained taken away – and withdrew to El Affule.

Elsewhere, the 4th Cavalry Division had been equally busy. Barrow had obtained Fane's permission to pass through the 7th Division at 0840, and it then advanced without hindrance, crossing the Nahr Falik at Zerqiye and moving towards Jelame, driving dispirited Turkish third-line troops before it. It crossed the Carmel Spur by way of the Musmus Pass, reaching Kerkur at around 2030. The advanced guard reach El Lajjun at 0330, still without having met any opposition, and despite some confusion and missed directions, the head of the column – the 2nd Lancers, with a section of armoured cars – reached El Affule, where the first serious resistance was encountered, at 0530. Here the Turks were in considerable force. A frontal attack on the forward positions by the 2nd Lancers was halted, and instead two squadrons made a looping charge into the right flank, resulting in a complete rout; the outcome of the action was a foregone conclusion thereafter, and El Affule was in British hands by 0800. Some hundreds of prisoners were taken, together with ten locomotives and fifty trucks, and three aircraft on the landing field; the armoured cars pursued a convoy of a dozen lorries and caught them well short of Beisan, which town was in the 4th Division's hands by nightfall.

The Australian Mounted Division, which advanced behind the 4th and 5th, moved first to El Lajjun, arriving there around noon. At 1445 Chauvel, who had received aerial reconnaissance reports of large numbers of Turkish troops leaving Jenin, asked Hodgson to investigate and also to make contact with the 5th LH Brigade, which had been attached directly to XXI Corps, and was supposed to be advancing up the Damascus road (it had in fact returned to Tul Karm after cutting the railway at Ajje); Hodgson sent the 3rd LHB to occupy Jenin and take any fleeing Turks it found into captivity. Some 1,800 were made prisoner about five kilometres short of the town; perhaps 1,200 more were taken in Jenin itself. Later, 2,800 more prisoners were taken on the road north out of the town and more followed; by the following morning the total had risen to around 8,000.

On the morning of 20 September the DFPS and the 75th Division (which alone of XXI Corps did not conform to the general wheel to the right) were halted in place (and would soon be withdrawn into reserve) while the 60th continued its push towards Nablus, and the 3rd, the 7th and the 54th Divisions kept pace over the rough tracks of the Carmel Spur, pushing the Turks' rearguard before them as they went. On the left, the 60th had the lightest workload that day; the 179th Brigade, which had been in reserve on the 19th, bearing the brunt of it, carried the village of Anebta and then took control of the nearby railway tunnel, which had been prepared for demolition but left untouched. The 181st Brigade later took up positions on its right, as far as Shuweike.

On its right the 7th Division advanced in two columns, with the 19th and 21st Brigades up and the 28th back in reserve; little opposition was encountered. On the right the 21st found it hard going and was halted at Kufr Zibad; on the left the 19th hit opposition at Kufr Sur, brushed it aside and proceeded towards Beit Lid, where it ran into a heavy machine gun barrage from a gully short of the village and, its mountain guns being far in the rear, was stalled. Even with the assistance of the 21st Brigade, Beit Lid proved a tough nut to crack, and it was 1815 before it was taken, and with that the 28th marched through towards Masudiye and Sebustiye.

To the south the 3rd Division's opponents that day would be the German reserve, under von Oppen. The 8th Brigade's first objective was a ridge running north-west from Kefar Thilth, where it met well-placed opposition. Only when a solitary howitzer was brought up, and audaciously positioned very close to the front line, so that it could clear the high banks of the wadi at the required range, was the brigade able to take its objective and move on to Janisfut, where it halted that evening. On its left the 7th Brigade had as its first objective the village of Azzun, which had until the day before been the headquarters of the Asienkorps. It too was held up before the defensive positions there until the 8th made its breakthrough and cleared the flank, whereupon the 91st Punjabis were able to enter the village. Skilfully, the 1st Connaught Rangers were diverted a little way southwards, passed through the sector the 8th was holding and were able to reach a road junction near El Funduq before von Oppen's artillery column, capturing five guns, many waggons and horses, and some prisoners. Further north, the 9th Brigade advanced through Jiyus and bypassed Azzun to make for Baqa and other villages grouped south of the Tel Karm–Nablus road; it was thus well placed to intercept more of the German troops fleeing Azzun, capturing some four hundred in a number of separate engagements.

On the right, the convergent attacks of the 10th and 53rd Divisions, which had begun in darkness in the small hours, met more sustained opposition in the Judaean Hills, the latter's 160th Brigade actually having to fight off a Turkish counterattack at Jibeit, near Mughaiyir, during the course of the morning. By mid-afternoon, having advanced beyond the range of its supporting artillery, its progress had slowed measurably (though the 159th

Brigade managed to push on as far as Ras et Tawil). In the course of their withdrawal up the Nablus road the Turks had managed to do less damage to it than had been foreseen. Watson's Force of pioneers – placed astride the road to deal with this eventuality – made rapid progress; by the evening, a mobile heavy battery and a siege battery had been able to move up as far as El Lubban, and give invaluable support the next day. On the left, the 10th, too, was held up by mid-afternoon, short of Kefar Haris, by well-placed machine guns; here, however, the RFA managed to get up batteries of 18-pounders, which soon overcame the opposition and allowed the 54th Sikhs to smash through and carry the ridge – then, with the 2nd Royal Irish Fusiliers in support, swarm down the hillside beyond to take Haris at bayonet point. The day ended with the division holding the line from there to Iskaka, where a metalled road to Nablus began and where, until that morning, the Turkish III Corps had had its headquarters.

Chetwode, who believed the enemy would not stand, gave orders for the two divisions to press on after dark, and to attempt to exploit the break-through the cavalry had made in the Turks' rear. The 10th was to advance directly on Nablus, the 53rd to work on the flank, advancing to cut the first of three routes from the city into the Jordan Valley at Majdal Beni Fadl, where the Turkish XX Corps HQ was located. Chetwode's belief proved correct; however, the going was not easy, and it was dawn before Majdal Beni Fadl was occupied, without resistance, by the 158th Brigade. Mott himself rode up to a nearby crossroads to meet with his two forward brigadiers, and sent the 158th on, to occupy Aqrabe. It met little resistance, a field battery which had by now come up to Qusra putting a column of retreating Turks to flight, inflicting heavy losses. By 1045 it had taken Aqrabe, and proceeded to El Qerum and later Beit Dejan. With that, Chetwode ordered the 53rd to stand fast.

The 10th had resumed its advance at 2330, the 29th and 31st Brigades now spearheading the movement, with the 30th following the former with orders to move through it when it reached the Jerusalem–Nablus road at Quza. Before they moved off, Longley called his brigadiers to him and asked for a final great effort which would take them into Nablus before the twenty-first was out. As the battalions descended towards the city, at the northern extremity of the Judean Hills, the going got easier and their progress faster, despite a considerable weight of long-range machine gun fire. By noon they had reached a position on high ground at Nabi Belan, some seven kilometres north-east of Nablus, from which point artillery could dominate the main escape route from the city: the road through the Wadi el Far'a to the Jordan Valley. A stream of Turkish transport of all kinds was already on this road, but by evening the vehicular traffic had stopped, the Royal Air Force having bombed the head of the column and created a blockage which could not be circumnavigated except on foot, the roadway being located halfway up the side of a ravine. That effectively ended the 10th Division's – and thus XX

Corps' – role in the Battle of Meggido, and from then on Chetwode's men were put to consolidating, organising and moving the thousands of prisoners taken, and salvaging as much usable *matériel* as possible. In all they took over 6,800 prisoners, 140 guns and 1,345 automatic weapons. The corps' total casualties during the course of the battle were just in excess of 1,500, 225 of whom were killed.

On the XXI Corps front, during the course of 20 September the 54th Division had advanced to a line from the higher ground to the north of the Wadi Qana south to Bidya, with the attached DFPS on the right extending to Ez Zawiye and Arara, on the Rafat Ridge, and there the division held. The next day the 60th, 3rd and 7th Divisions crossed the Tel Karm–Nablus road and moved into positions covering Sebustiye, Masudiye and Tel Karm. Once again, considerable numbers of prisoners were taken, the entire garrison of Sebustiye surrendering en masse, and at Masudiye one locomotive and sixteen waggons were seized. During the afternoon the 5th Light Horse Brigade, with a detachment of armoured cars, finally forced its way into Nablus, the 14th ALH continuing to link up with the left flank of the 10th Division at Balata.

During the course of the Battle of Meggido XXI Corps – which had been the key to Allenby's success – incurred 3,378 casualties in all, of whom a relatively small proportion, 446, were killed in action or died of wounds (though a further 310 were reported as missing). The corps took well over 10,000 prisoners and almost 150 guns, together with very large quantities of small arms and ammunition.

The Desert Mounted Corps was still active on 21 September, the 13th Brigade finally rousting the last defenders out of Nazareth, but the main problem facing Chauvel that day concerned the prisoners now being held at Jenin and the horde of Turkish fugitives trying still to flee the battlefield. Exhausted, and with little or nothing in the way of food or water, most of these men were quite literally staggering away northwards and eastwards with little idea of where they were going, even, but here and there there were still formed, disciplined bodies of troops which had to be treated cautiously.

On the morning of 22 September Chauvel gave orders that Haifa and Acre, the last remaining Turkish positions in the region, should be taken, by the 5th Cavalry Division, the following day; however, just hours later reconnaissance flights reported that Haifa was being evacuated, and Allenby instructed Chauvel to despatch a force of armoured cars to occupy it and install a military governor. This proved to be wildly optimistic; five kilometres short of the city the vehicles came under artillery and machine gun fire from the high ground to the south – the northern slopes of Mount Carmel – and were forced to retire.

The following morning Chauvel's plan to take Haifa and Acre by force was put into effect. The 5th Cavalry advanced in two columns, the weaker – the 13th Cavalry Brigade Group, less a horse-artillery battery but with the 11th

Light Armoured Motor Battery's armoured cars – advanced on Acre by way of Saffurye and Shafa Amr, and took possession of the city with scarcely a shot being fired. The rest of the division moved up the road to Haifa, the 15th Cavalry Brigade in the lead with a spearhead of armoured cars from the 1st Light Car Patrol. All went well until the head of the column reached Balad esh Sheikh, at around 1000, but there it came under machine gun fire, to which was soon added artillery fire from Mount Carmel. The brigade deployed to the left of the road, onto the foothills of Carmel, and to the right, towards the Nahr el Muqatta (the River Kishon), into the marshy ground to be found there, additional regiments being sent up to reinforce it. These included the Jodhpore and Mysore Lancers, who were to approach from the direction of Acre and attack across the river. However, the estuary of the Kishon soon proved an insurmountable obstacle, and that plan had to be abandoned, the troops being redirected further east to a point were the river was fordable. In the confusion the lancers took casualties, many of their horses being shot down by machine guns on the lower slopes, but were eventually able to regroup and charge the guns which had plagued them. That in turn opened up a gap through which more of the cavalrymen were able to pass. Soon the vanguard was in the streets on the outskirts of the city, but the guns on Mount Carmel were still manned and still taking a toll, and it was only when two squadrons of the Mysore Lancers made an arduous up-hill charge, assisted at the death by a half-squadron of Sherwood Rangers, that they were silenced. By early afternoon the city was in British hands; around seven hundred prisoners were taken, along with 16 guns.

Chaytor's prime responsibility during the Battle of Meggido was to secure the British right flank; but if, as was hoped, the defeat of the Turkish Seventh and Eighth Armies in Judea prompted the Fourth Army in the Trans-Jordan to withdraw along the line of the Hejaz railway, Chaytor would be permitted to cross the river and engage its rearguard.

That, it was assumed, would be no easy task. Since Allenby had launched the second Trans-Jordan raid the Turks had established a powerful defensive line, entrenched positions covered with wire along the foothills of the plateau from a point opposite Hijla to about seven kilometres north of the Jericho–Es Salt road, with strongpoints on their left flank at Qabr Said, El Kufrein and Qabr Mujahid, and on the right a broken defensive line stretching to the river at Umm esh Shert. That latter was continued on the west bank of the Jordan, following the line of the Wadi Mellaha as far as the foot of the Judaean Hills, and then running south-west to a spur known as Bakr Ridge. The infantry force on the west bank consisted of the 53rd Division (part of the Seventh Army's XX Corps), with the 3rd and 24th Cavalry Divisions in the valley, astride the river; on the east bank stood VIII Corps, with the 48th Division and what the British referred to as the Composite Division, with the Caucasian Cavalry Corps and a mule-mounted infantry regiment on its left. To the rear of VIII Corps was II Corps – primarily the 62nd Infantry Division – whose chief responsibility was the security of the Hejaz railway south from Damascus, and which was spread out over three hundred kilometres.

The British front was divided into two sectors. South of El Auja was the responsibility of Ryrie's 2nd Light Horse Brigade, with the 20th Indian Brigade attached; to the north Meldrum had a mixed infantry force comprising the 38th Royal Fusiliers – one of the two volunteer Jewish battalions – and the two battalions of the British West Indies Regiment, with the New Zealand Mounted Rifles Brigade and the 39th Royal Fusiliers in reserve. The force reserve consisted of the 1st LH Brigade.

Chaytor's Force went onto the offensive on the west bank in the early hours of 20 September, the 2nd BWI driving the Turks off Bakr Ridge and Chalk Ridge to the north, while its sister-battalion took the outlying outposts of Grant's Hill and Baghalat. The 38th R Fusiliers had less success north of the Mellaha, and were driven back, and two regiments of light horse and the Patiala Infantry crossed the river and probed the left-flanking outposts, but found them strongly held. Chaytor then exploited his success on the left and sent the Auckland Regiment to take Fasail, three kilometres north of Baghalat on the track leading to the crossing at Damiye, before dawn the following morning. The New Zealanders' patrols soon discovered Turkish troops descending the Wadi el Far'a and crossing the river. Chaytor took this to be the sign that the Turks were abandoning the eastern margins of the Judaean Hills, and gave orders for the remainder of the NZMRB and the two West Indian battalions to advance that night to Fasail and take the Damiye crossing the next morning. Chaytor perhaps underestimated the enemy's numbers, or perhaps his determination; the fighting which followed was stiff, and the Aucklanders, in the van, were held at Ain Jozele. Cox's 1st Light Horse Brigade was called up to clear the area to the west of the force aimed at Damiye – and captured a Turkish column in the process – while Meldrum's men pushed forward. By 1050 on 22 September the bridge at Damiye was in sight and the resistance was lessening, and Meldrum released the Auckland Regiment to charge the perimeter dismounted; supported by a squadron of the Canterburys and some West Indians it broke through, and had soon secured the crossing. Further south the 3rd ALH and the 2nd BWI took the crossing at Mafid Jozele and secured the right flank. Later, news came that the Jewish volunteers, sensing a weakening of the enemy's resolve north of the Mellaha, had gone back onto the offensive also, and had taken the crossing at Umm esh Shert.

The river crossings further north, to the east of Beisan, were also in British hands,[19] but it soon became apparent that the Turks had been able to exploit the considerable – more than fifty-kilometre – gap between the two formations, and that significant numbers of men were escaping to the east bank. It was too late in the day by then to advance the 4th Cavalry Division to intervene, but Chauvel ordered it to do so the following morning, and the 29th Brigade descended both banks of the river.[20] Over the course of the day the cavalry regiments fought a series of engagements against large bodies of Turkish troops; only a few succeeded in crossing the river and evading capture. By the evening of 24 September, reconnaissance patrols reported that there were now no Turks left at liberty west of the river between the Dead Sea and the Sea of Galilee, and the operation concluded.

It now remained only to occupy Samakh, at the southern tip of the Sea of Galilee, which the railway from Der'a to Beisan and El Affule served in a loop, and the Australian Mounted Division was given the task, which was passed down to Grant's 4th Light Horse Brigade. Though his command was weakened by the detachment of several units, including the 4th ALH and much of the 12th, he decided to press on without waiting for the latter to be returned to him, aware that simultaneously, orders had gone out to the 3rd Brigade to move on Tiberias from Nazareth. His troops crossed the Jordan, and its tributary the Yarmuk at 0230 on 25 September, so as to arrive at the objective by dawn. Reconnaissance was not possible, but Grant learned that the ground south of Samakh was a flat plain, four kilometres wide, devoid of obstacles, and he decided on a mounted assault covered by machine guns on his left, on the far side of the railway line to Beisan.

At 0430 intense machine gun fire broke out from positions in front of Samakh; Grant ordered his own machine guns to fire on the flashes while he deployed two squadrons of the 11th ALH beside the railway line to Der'a, to the east. With day just beginning to break they charged on either side of the line, breaking through the left flank of the defences with ease; two troops of 'A' Squadron were detached to enter the village and the rest dismounted to assault the railway station. Its stone buildings offered excellent protection to the defenders, and the fighting was both hard and long drawn out; by the afternoon all the Australian troops had been committed to the attack, which was all over by 1730, leaving a hundred Germans dead and two hundred in captivity. Tiberias was occupied that afternoon, too, with much less opposition.

With no meaningful Turkish positions left on the west bank, the time was now right for Chaytor's Force to cross the river in strength. At an orders group on the evening of 22 September it was decided that the 2nd LHB was to advance against Qabr Said and Qabr Mujahid; a substantial part of the 20th Indian Brigade[21] was to take the main road towards the enemy positions at Shunet Nimrin, with all available artillery in support; the 1st LHB was to cross at Mafid Jozele and strike eastwards from there, and the NZMRB, less one squadron to provide security at Damiye, was to cross there, with the 1st BWI, and move up the Damiye track to attempt to take Es Salt. The two Jewish battalions, now constituted as 'Patterson's Column', under the senior battalion commander, were to wait at the Auja bridgehead and be prepared to support the Indians.

Chaytor's careful preparations proved unneccesary. 'Directly the sun was up [on 23 September],' Falls tells us, 'it became clear that the enemy would make no stand in the valley; before darkness fell it was shown that he dared not fight even upon the eastern scarp.' During the course of the day Chaytor's Force advanced on a front almost twenty-five kilometres wide, each column finding its objectives deserted by their defenders. Only the New Zealanders met resistance – a rather desultory rearguard action on the Damiye track – and when a strongpoint just short of Es Salt was outflanked and surrounded, and its garrison surrendered, resistance in the town crumbled, and it was occupied without further fighting.

During the night Allenby instructed Chaytor to press on to Amman with all speed. The retreating Turks having had time to destroy whole sections of it at well-chosen locations, the main road was impassable, and it was neces- sary to advance by way of minor tracks, leaving the wheeled transport behind at Shunet Nimrin. Nonetheless, the 1st and 2nd Light Horse Brigades were at Es Salt by the afternoon, by which time the New Zealand Mounted Rifles Brigade had pressed on to Suweile (from where that night a party a hundred strong rode to the railway some ten kilometres north of Amman, and put it out of action). At 0600 on 25 September the advance on Amman itself began; the 2nd LHB, on the right, was held up temporarily, but the New Zealanders on the left pressed on, the Canterbury Regiment taking the Citadel on foot. By 1330 the resistance was giving way. The first troops into the city were men of the 5th ALH; there was some fighting in the streets, but white flags began to appear, and Ryrie took the surrender soon afterwards. Over 2,500 prisoners were taken, and ten guns, but it became clear that the bulk of the Turkish forces – and all the remaining Germans – had been able to make their escape by train to the north just before the line had been cut the previous night.

Chaytor's task now was to prevent the northward movement of troops from Ma'an and points south, and he called up the 20th Indian Brigade, which had reached Es Salt, to take over at Amman while the 2nd LHB moved south down the railway as far as Libban, encountering Turkish troops for the first time on 27 September. A prisoner gave up the information that the Ma'an garrison had left the town and was moving northwards, with the head of its column already at El Qastel, just a few kilometres away. The following day an aircraft located it, and dropped a message informing the commander that all water sources were now in British hands, and that he should surrender forthwith. He did so the next morning, 29 September, expressing a very reasonable fear that his men would come under attack from the hundreds of mounted bedouin who had by now ringed their position. The British position was by no means a strong one: just one regiment, the 5th ALH, was present, and it was reduced to two squadrons. Its commander, Lt.-Col. Cameron, assured the Arabs' leaders that he would fire on them if they approached the

Turkish lines, and to his relief they heeded his warning. At 1700 Chaytor himself arrived and took charge of the situation, instructing the Turkish commander that his men must look to their own defence that night. In the event the rest of the 2nd LHB arrived before dark and reinforced Cameron's positions, but this did little to still the Turks' anxieties, and all night long bursts of machine gun fire came from their lines. The following morning they were disarmed, save for the two best battalions which provided flank guards for the rest as they were marched off to Amman, where their arrival, fully armed, caused considerable consternation.

Megiddo was a success perhaps even beyond Allenby's expectations – he had destroyed the Turkish Seventh and Eighth Armies as fighting forces and put the Fourth to flight. Compelled to march, thanks to Feisal's Arab irregulars having looped around to the east and cut the railway definitively south of Der'a, that latter would be hard put to to reach Damascus before the British cavalry, and if it were caught short of the Syrian capital, it, too, might yet be destroyed.

Allenby left it until 26 September to hold a corps commanders' conference at which he outlined his plans for the advance into Syria. He would, he announced, move on to Damascus and Beirut employing the Desert Mounted Corps and two divisions of Bulfin's XXI Corps. The latter were to march via Haifa and Acre to Beirut, the cavalry was to depart for Damascus at once, two divisions to pass to the west of the Sea of Galilee and cross the Upper Jordan at Jisr Benat Yakub, passing through El Quneitra and proceeding up the Roman road – the final stretch of the Via Maris, which had its beginnings at Heliopolis, on the Nile – to take up positions around Damascus, and the third (the 4th Cavalry Division) to go by way of Samakh and Der'a, north of which it would hopefully meet and deal with the Fourth Army, before rejoining the corps. The main difficulties Allenby's staff foresaw involved keeping the mounted troops (and indeed, their mounts) supplied with rations – a perennial problem in cavalry operations, of course – and in the event the men of the 4th Cavalry Division were forced to fall back on the always risky requisitioning of food as they went, supplementing what they could obtain by 'iron rations' carried with them. By the time they arrived in Damascus they had not a scrap remaining for horse or man.

The advance on Der'a was to be made in conjunction with a demonstration by the Arab irregulars – the 'Sherifian Forces' as they were by now known – with Lawrence now 'determined that in this, probably the last task of the war, the Arabs should pull their weight, that, for the sake of their self-respect and political future, they should contribute grandly to the coming victory', as Cyril Falls was to put it. The plan was for a force of 450 'regular Sherifal Camel Corps', with a French mountain battery, two armoured cars, a detachment from the Egyptian Camel Corps and another of Gurkhas, to march to Qasr el Azraq, a Roman fort in the desert a hundred kilometres south-east of Der'a, where there was an abundant supply of fresh water. There their ranks were to be swollen by the men of Nuri esh Shalaan, the Howeitat bedouin under Auda Abu Tayi, and Talal el Hareidhun with the villagers from the Hauran, around Der'a. It was hoped that this force would amount to five thousand men by 16 September, when it was planned to surround Der'a. In the event the railway bridges at Jabir, south of Der'a, were taken that day, and more damage was done to the permanent way north of the town the next, but it was decided not to attack Der'a itself since a strong contingent of German troops had arrived there from El Affule.

The Arabs finally began to live up to the promises Lawrence had continued to make for them through thick and thin on 26 September, when they left Azraq en masse for Shaikh Sa'ad, twenty-five kilometres NNW of Der'a, Auda Abu Tayi's men capturing a train, with two hundred Turks aboard, at Ghazale, and Talal el Hareidhun's taking the station at Izra on the way. By now Der'a had largely been abandoned, and at dusk on 27 September the tribesmen swept down upon the town. When, the following day, the vanguard of the 4th Cavalry Division, which had hoped to find supplies in the town, came up, they found only the results of wanton destruction.

The Australian Mounted Division left Tiberias on the morning of 27 September, the 5th Cavalry following in its tracks. It was known that the four-teenth-century bridge over the Upper Jordan at Jisr Benat Yacub had been blown up, and the 3rd LH Brigade was ordered to find suitable alternative crossing points. The vanguard regiment (9th ALH) found the left bank of the river defended between Jisr Benat Yacub and the shallow Lake Hula (the biblical Waters of Merom). The 3rd Brigade was then ordered to hold the enemy in place, and if possible locate a crossing near the lake, while the 5th Brigade attempted to force a crossing further south. The latter found a suitable site at El Min but was unable to envelop the Turkish defenders on the east bank, who escaped during the night. The next day the fallen span of the bridge was replaced by a wooden construction and the division was able to move on towards Quneitra, where a force four regiments strong under Brig.-Gen. Grant was left to provide security,[22] the local Circassians being extremely hostile.

During the afternoon of 29 September the Rolls-Royce cars of the spear-head 11th Light Armoured Motor Battery ran into heavy opposition near Sa'sa, some thirty kilometres north of Quneitra; by the time the 9th ALH had come up it had become clear that this would be a serious check to the advance, the machine guns being very numerous and well sited, and in fact it was after 0300 before the opposition was overcome thanks to a flanking attack by the 9th and a direct assault by the 8th ALH. The next blocking position was found at Kaukab and east from there, along the ridge of the Jebel el Aswad. In the event the defenders' right flank was found to be uncovered, thanks to a complete lack of artillery support, and the French cavalry was sent to exploit that. Attacking mounted over very rough terrain they put the defenders to flight with very little opposition, a dozen machine guns being abandoned, and the advance was able to continue once more, this time with the *Régiment Mixte de Marche de Cavalerie* in the van. It encountered more opposition at El Mezze, little more than three kilometres from the centre of Damascus, and this time attacked dismounted, supported by the 14th ALH. Progress was slow, and by 1300 the horse-artillery batteries were brought up; under bombardment the Turkish fire slackened and eventually died away, the defenders having broken off the action in favour of a retreat on Ba'albek by way of the Barada Gorge, to the north-west. In the circumstances – though they actually had little choice, for this route had the only water in the region, and standing was no longer an option – this proved a poor decision, for the pursuing French and six machine gun teams of the NZMG Squadron, sent to support them, scrambled up the reverse slope, lined its rim and began pouring fire down on the column, causing very numerous casualties. The Turks thus trapped to the east – they included many men who had by now fled Damascus – had no option but to surrender to the Australians coming up the road behind them; around four thousand prisoners were taken.

What followed was to cause both a diplomatic incident, of a sort, and very considerable confusion, both then and later. Allenby had decided – or had been told[23] – that his troops were to stay out of Damascus until Feisal's Arabs had entered the city. He thus instructed Hodgson, by way of Chauvel, who, when he ordered the 3rd Light Horse Brigade take up a blocking position on the Homs road, running north-eastwards out of the city, instructed it to by-pass Damascus to the west. The leading regiment (the 9th ALH) got no further than a point overlooking the village of Dummar, some three kilo-metres west of the point where the RMMC had halted the Turkish column. Below it the road was packed with men who had been in the forefront of the retreat, and it immediately opened fire, killing at least four hundred and causing a roadblock which took days to clear. By now night was falling, and the prospect of a cross-country march in the darkness was hardly appealing. Instead Brig.-Gen. Wilson proposed, and Hodgson agreed, to rest his men until first light on 1 October and then pass through Damascus instead of skirting it. Thus his men were the first Allied forces into the Syrian capital and were welcomed warmly by one of a pair of brothers who could have been said to be in control there, Mohammed Said Abd el Kader.[24] That may seem inconsequential, and though the Australians did not remain, but passed through to the Homs road, in military law it gave the British, and not their Arab allies, right of conquest, much as Lawrence sought to deny it and demonstrate to the contrary.

Meanwhile, the 5th Cavalry Division had followed the AMD from Quneitra to Sa'sa and had then been ordered east, to the 'Pilgrims' Road', where reports had it that a column of around 2,000 Turks were retiring on

Damascus. The 14th Brigade arrived in the outskirts of the city by around 1500 and bivouacked, having been on the move for twenty-one hours, fighting a series of actions and capturing around six hundred Turks in the process. The 13th Brigade spent the night at Kaukab and moved on to Damascus the following morning; it, too, took large numbers of prisoners, though it failed to prevent the destruction of the railway or a radio station at Qadem.

The 4th Cavalry Division marched out of Beisan, the 10th Brigade in the lead, on the morning of 26 September, ordered to reach Irbid, where water was available and where it was believed it would make contact with Arab irregulars that night. The road proved to be in very poor repair, and the leading regiment, the 2nd Lancers, were still climbing to the plateau where Irbid was located, with only a few hours' daylight remaining, when it came under machine gun fire. The Lancers' commander decided on an attempt to break through before night fell, the three squadrons attacking Irbid from different directions, but the ground was too rough and too steep to allow a mounted attack. The brigadier came up to see the situation for himself and ordered up the Berkshire Battery, but it arrived too late to be of any real assistance, as did the Central Indian Horse. A renewed attempt to take the village was made, but had to be abandoned when the light failed. However, next morning the Turks – whose strength the villagers who remained put at some five thousand – were discovered to have decamped in the night.

The 12th Brigade bivouacked that night at Esh Shuni, four kilometres east of the Jordan, with the 11th and brigade headquarters at Jisr el Majami, the river crossing south of the confluence of the Jordan and the Yarmuk. Barrow's orders, the next morning, were for the 12th Brigade to move off to the Wadi esh Shelale and there to await the 10th, which was to advance to Er Remta. This latter village was erroneously declared free of Turks by the RAF, but when the Dorset Yeomanry approached it, it was met by machine gun fire. A flanking mounted attack from the right suppressed it, and after some hand-to-hand fighting the village was in British hands. The Central Indian Horse then passed through the Dorsets, and soon came up with a group of Turks, perhaps 150 strong, who had elected to retreat rather than assist in holding the village; they were quickly rounded up, as was a further group detected withdrawing from a defensive position astride the Der'a road.

The next morning, 28 September, the brigade entered Der'a. 'A grim spectacle was needed to shock the troops of a cavalry division which for ten days had been harrying the retreat of a routed army,' wrote Falls; 'but the sight of Der'a Station and its encampments that met the 10th Cavalry Brigade as it rode in that morning was ghastly beyond aught that any man there had witnessed.'

Barrow arranged with Nuri as-Said, Feisal's chief of staff, that the Arabs would cover his right flank the following day, when they would march north, and sent the 11th and 12th Brigades to bivouac at Muzeirib, away from the carnage at Der'a, which the men of the 10th dealt with as best they could, extinguishing the almost ubiquitous fires, burying the dead and clothing and caring for the few wounded Turks the Arabs had left alive.

The division set out as planned, up the Pilgrims' Road towards Damascus, the 10th Brigade, less a regiment left to guard the wounded at Der'a, rejoining at Sheikh Miskin in the early afternoon. It reached Dilli that night, and Zeraqiye late in the afternoon of 30 September; there it received reports from the advanced guard of the 11th Brigade, now at Khan Deinun, of a substantial column to the east of the road. At first it was assumed that this was the Sherifial army, but soon Lawrence arrived, saying it was the rearguard of the Turkish Fourth Army, which the Arabs had been harassing since the twenty-seventh, and requesting assistance. The Hampshire Battery was moved up and shelled the column until it was too dark to see, and the 29th Lancers attempted to head it off but failed, and it appeared to have escaped, but the next morning Lawrence reappeared with news that the Howeitat had decimated it during the night.[25]

The morning of 1 October found the three divisions of the Desert Mounted Corps in sight of Damascus; Chauvel's instructions had been for the AMD to remain in place west of the city (save for the 3rd Light Horse Brigade, as noted above), the 5th Cavalry Division to take up positions to the east and the 4th astride the Pilgrims' Road from the south. He had a fairly clear idea of the situation of the Turks left in the city, for their military commander – an Arab-born Turkish officer, Gen. Ali Riza Pasha el Rikabi – had defected to his headquarters the previous afternoon. He reported that the population had turned against (but rarely actually on) the Turks, and that those who had failed to escape were now thoroughly demoralised, with any will to resist which might have remained in them evaporated.

Chauvel's instructions from Allenby were to hold back and permit the Sherifial forces to enter Damascus ahead of his own men, thereby establishing the fiction that it was the Hashemites who had liberated Syria from Ottoman rule. In this, though he did not yet know it, he was about to be frustrated by Wilson's decision to send his light horsemen *through* the city to reach his appointed place on the Homs road, instead of around it. When the 10th ALH entered the city they were greeted with an explosion of popular feeling. The leader of the spearhead squadron was ushered into the presence of Mohammed Said Abd el Kader, who declared (quite falsely) that he had been installed as governor[26] the previous afternoon, and wished to surrender the city to him. Maj. Olden, perhaps overwhelmed, but with the imperative to get to the Homs road and block it, was eventually able to extricate himself and his men and proceed on his way, but by then the damage had been done.[27]

At 0640 Bourchier received orders from Wilson to send men into western Damascus; a squadron of the 4th ALH approached the barracks on the Beirut road and was greeted with some desultory rifle fire, which ceased when the rest of the regiment arrived on the scene; no less than 265 officers and 10,481 other ranks, many of them sick or wounded and all of them half-starved, surrendered (and another 2,500 were later discovered in hospitals and lazarettos, too sick to move; unsurprisingly, the diseases to which they had fallen ill were soon transmitted to British troops, but see below).

At 0730[28] Lawrence arrived, in a state of acute anxiety, accompanied by 'officials' of the Sherifial forces, including Sherif Nasir of Medina and Nuri as-Said, Feisal's chief of staff. They were greeted with scenes of exultation (at least, according to TEL's account in *Revolt in the Desert*. In the much more comprehensive *Seven Pillars of Wisdom* he had spoken of 'the quietness and emptiness of the streets', the people standing almost silently, 'joy shining in their eyes' as he passed by in 'Blue Mist', his Rolls-Royce armoured car). When his party arrived at the city hall it was to find the Abd el Kader brothers still in authority, and he immediately ordered them removed and 'the good-hearted' Shukri al Ayyubi, a Damascene supporter of Hussein, installed in their place.[29] When Chauvel later asked on what authority he had done that he lied brazenly, and told him that it had been by popular acclaim of the citizens. It was a textbook example of striking while the iron was hot, of course, and one has to admire Lawrence's presence of mind, but there was absolutely no legal basis for it, and it was to be the source of much suffering to come, when the French insisted on the terms of the Sykes-Picot Agreement of 1915 (see Chapter 17) being fulfilled, and Syria falling into their bailiwick, and expelled Feisal, who had in the meantime been declared king.

In any event, and whatever the legality of the situation, with the Arabs installed, the real conquerors could now enter the city formally, and on 2 October Chauvel, with Barrow, Macandrew and Hodgson, each with representatives of their staffs, one squadron per regiment and one horse-artillery battery per division, marched through its streets. The next day Feisal himself, with his large entourage, arrived outside the city, and Lawrence requested that he be allowed to enter in triumph. Allenby himself had by now arrived, and his schedule did not allow for ceremonials. Instead he summoned Feisal et al. to the Hotel Victoria and informed him that the procedures laid down in the Sykes-Picot Agreement would be followed; in other words, that the French were to have Syria, and that the 'prince' would administer it on behalf of his father under their guidance (and that he would have no say over the affairs of the Lebanon). Feisal objected in the strongest terms, and when Allenby turned to Lawrence and enquired why he was so incensed, Lawrence simply dissembled. He had no idea that the French were to have the protectorate over Syria, he said, nor that the Lebanon was to be specifically excepted from any sphere of influence Feisal might have. Feisal and his retinue then withdrew, leaving Lawrence behind. He was unwilling to serve under a French 'adviser', he told Allenby, and requested permission to take his accumulated leave and return to London. Allenby agreed.

Later that afternoon Feisal had his triumphal entry into Damascus, and then, on Lawrence's advice, sent a group of picked men hurrying to Beirut, to enter the city before Allenby's army arrived. They hoisted the flag of the Hejaz and proclaimed the city liberated on 5 October; this alarmed the French, who sent warships and a contingent of troops the next day. On 8 October Allenby's men arrived, ordered the flag taken down, and took control; later Picot, long ago selected to become the de facto ruler of Syria, arrived. From that time on, Syrian affairs took on a new murkiness, characterised by the murder of Ali Abd el Kader by pro-Feisal police, 'while attempting to escape'.

In all, between 26 September and 1 October, almost twenty thousand Turks and Germans had been taken prisoner (making a total of around 47,000 since the nineteenth); in the advance on Damascus the Desert Mounted Corps had taken just over five hundred casualties. However, its men had also acquired a variety of infections, not least among them a new strain of influenza, the results of which were to be little short of devastating.

With that, the Egyptian Expeditionary Force with which Allenby had taken Gaza, eleven months earlier, had arrived halfway to its eventual destination, Aleppo. There were no natural obstacles in its way, and it was confidently expected that the occupation of the Syrian ports – Beirut, Tripoli, Tartus and Latakia chief amongst them – would ease its supply problems. However, it was a very long way to Aleppo – over three hundred and twenty kilometres by the most direct route, through Homs and Hama – and already there was a disturbing rise in the incidence of malaria within the ranks of Allenby's army: cases doubled between the first and the second weeks in October. Pneumonia was also on the rise, as were typhoid, enteric fever and influenza among the huge prisoner population, while supply problems were never less than acute until the long viaduct over the Yarmuk, which the Turks had blown during their retreat, was reopened on 26 October, and the railway from Haifa by way of El Affule and Beisan could be brought back into use.

On 3 October Allenby ordered Chauvel to capture Riyaq, some fifty kilometres north-west of Damascus, on the Litani River in the Beka'a Valley, as soon as possible. Chauvel readied the 5th Cavalry Division to leave on 5 October, with the 4th following hard on its heels. By then Fane's 7th Division had reached Tyre on its march up the littoral plain. The 5th bivouacked at Khan Meisalun, about halfway to Riyaq, that night, and was joined by two detachments of armoured cars. That night Macandrew received reports of matériel and rolling stock being destroyed at Riyaq (which was the terminus of the standard-gauge line from Constantinople via Aleppo and Homs; this rolling stock was thus vital), and ordered the 14th Cavalry Brigade to push on immediately with the armoured cars and put a stop to the destruction. Before it could saddle up he learned that the Turks had quit Riyaq, and reversed his orders, much to the horsemen's relief. The brigade reached the town at 1400 the next afternoon, and amidst great destruction found much matériel – and several standard-gauge locomotives, as well as a considerable quantity of rolling stock – undamaged; at the airfield outside the town the retreating Germans had been more thorough, however, and had left only the burnt-out remains of around thirty aircraft. The following day, 7 October, the armoured cars were sent on to Beirut, and reported the Lebanese capital unoccupied; twenty-four hours later the advanced guard of the 7th Division arrived, its engineers having worked wonders improving the road north from Tyre so that artillery tractors and the guns they towed could pass.

The Beka'a Valley and the two mountain ranges it separates dominated the topography of the Lebanon; only the road from Damascus to Beirut via Riyaq cut across the country in those days. Allenby's subsequent advance was thus constrained, and on 9 October he ordered the 7th Division to push on up the coast to Tripoli, and the DMC to occupy Homs by way of Riyaq, the route the retreating Germans had taken.[30] Chauvel told Macandrew to be in Homs by 16 October, and Barrow to stay hard on his heels, despite more and more of his men reporting sick each day. Macandrew split his division into two columns and sent them off a day apart; the leading formation – the 13th Cavalry Brigade and 'B' Battery, HAC – arrived on schedule, finding the city – home to around 70,000, in the fertile plain of the short but significant Orontes River – deserted of Turks. Meanwhile the 4th Division had halted at Ba'albek, and that same day the forward brigade of the 7th Division reached Tripoli. Allenby then called a brief halt to the advance, and turned his attention to the problems of governing the territory he now occupied, dividing it into three zones: East (of the Jordan and a line following the old trade route north through Baniyas towards Antioch), to be governed by Ali Riza Pasha el Rikabi; North (of a line running roughly from Tyre to Baniyas), to be governed by Col. de Piépape, and South, to be governed by Sir Arthur Money.

On 18 October Allenby ordered Chauvel to advance on Aleppo, the 5th Cavalry Division to leave Homs on 20 October and reach its objective by the twenty-sixth. Macandrew would have additional mechanised reconnaissance units, bringing those at his disposal to six: three LAMBS and three LCPs.[31] The 4th Division was to move up to Homs. By now the latter's casualty role was alarming: it could muster just 1,200 fit men, half the number available to the 5th Division, and Chauvel, realising that he would not be able to call on it to support the 5th at need, petitioned Allenby, who halted the latter's advance at Hama. On 22 October Macandrews' armoured cars were sent to probe enemy positions and caught the rearguard, after a brief chase, north of Khan es Sebil. It bivouacked that night at Seraqab, just fifty kilometres from Aleppo, and the following day pressed on, discovering the Turks, with a good stiffening of Germans, holding an entrenched line five kilometres south of the city. One of the LCPs' commanders sent a note under a flag of truce demanding their surrender. 'The Commander of the Turkish Garrison does not find it necessary to reply to your note,' Mustafa Kemal's chief of staff responded.

The cars then dropped back to Zibre, twenty kilometres south-west of Aleppo, where they were joined by the 15th Cavalry Brigade on 25 October. By now the Arabs were abreast of the British forward elements, and Nuri as-Said had promised to push forward to the east of the city to co-operate in the attack which was to come. In the event, the Arabs launched an attack of their own on the blocking force; they were driven back, but that same evening got into the city from the east, whereupon Sanders – who had himself by now retired to Adana – ordered a general withdrawal, not only of his forces in the city, but also those holding the positions to the south, regrouping fifteen kilometres to the north-west, near Haritan. The next morning Brig.-Gen. Harbord took his 15th Cavalry Brigade to clear the area west of Aleppo and get astride the road to Alexandretta. He found the area unoccupied, but began to receive reports of a formed body of Turks to the north. He moved northwards cautiously himself, but when two squadrons of the Jodhpore Lancers breasted a rise overlooking Haritan and were met by machine gun fire, he decided to attack at once, the Mysore Lancers to round the eastern end of the ridge with the remaining Jodhpores to follow, while the units which had made contact, reinforced by the Machine-Gun Squadron, kept the enemy's attention from the south. Even though the defenders' left flank turned out to be much further to the east than had been thought, the Mysore Lancers charged, three squadrons abreast and one in reserve, in what, though they could not know it, would be the last engagement of the war in the Palestine theatre. The Mysores were unable to make a dent in the enemy line, and though they tried once more, this time with the Jodhpores in close support, the Turks drove them back. It soon became evident that the defenders actually numbered three thousand or more men, and the lancers withdrew out of rifle range to await the outcome of events. At one point the Turks seemed to be assembling for an attack, but it came to nothing, and instead they began to dig in; by midnight they had begun to withdraw.

In the meantime, Macandrew had entered Aleppo with his armoured cars at 1000 that morning, to general acclaim. The Turks, under the personal command of Mustafa Kemal, continued to fall back in something like good order though pursued by Arabs, reports all proclaimed, and it was clear that the war in Palestine – in fact, the entire war in the Middle East, for the army in Mesopotamia was reporting a similar lack of real resistance – would very soon be over.

V
AFTERMATH AND CONCLUSIONS

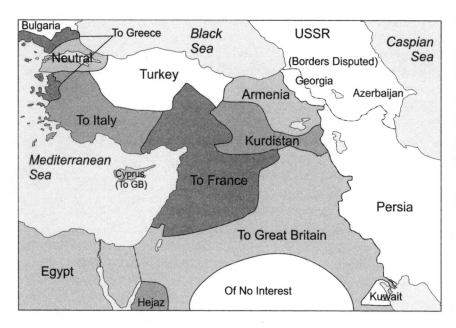

28. The Middle East as proposed by the Treaty of Sèvres

Defeat and Victory;
Dismemberment and Renewal

British Intelligence learned on 4 October 1918 that the Ottoman government had told the German that it was about to sue for a separate peace, citing the Central Powers' inability to keep it supplied with the *matériel* necessary to continue with the war. Further signs of impending collapse came the following week, with the news that Talaat Pasha's Cabinet had resigned, Talaat being replaced as Grand Vizier initially by Ahmet Tewfik Pasha, who failed to form a government, and then by Ahmet Izzet Pasha.

On 7 October – the day Allenby's forces reached Beirut, and while Marshall's were still south of the Fat-ha Gorge and fighting their way up the Tigris – the Council of Allied Premiers, meeting at Versailles, decided that Allied troops from Salonika should march into Thrace to threaten Constantinople. That same day Lloyd George instructed Sir Eric Geddes, the First Lord of the Admiralty, to ensure that Vice-Adm. Sir Somerset Gough-Calthorpe, the Commander-in-Chief, Mediterranean Fleet, would take the leading role in surrender negotiations when they took place. Calthorpe arrived at Mudros on 12 October.

Some weeks earlier, Lt.-Col. Stewart Newcombe, who had surrendered his raiding party unwillingly to a much superior Turkish force during the fighting for Beersheba a year earlier,[1] had succeeded on his third attempt in escaping from custody. By 22 September he was in hiding at the home of a Greek family in Pera, Constantinople's diplomatic quarter, and there he began to hear rumours that certain Ottoman politicians were determined on an armistice. That, given that Bulgaria was showing every sign of wishing to reach a separate peace,[2] was not inconceivable, he thought, and began to write to senior figures in the Ottoman government. Some took him very seriously, and there are suggestions that his notes caused a split in the Ottoman leadership, though frankly, by that time greater schismatic forces were already at work. In any event, by the time Izzet Pasha (Izzet Furgaç, as he later became) took over as Grand Vizier, on 14 October, Newcombe was out of hiding, his words dropping into very receptive ears; two days later Izzet proposed sending him to Salonika to broker a ceasefire, but no aircraft could be found to fly him there.

Enter another, and far more distinguished, if perhaps less honourable, prisoner of war: Sir Charles Townshend, as he now was, whom we last saw disappearing up the Tigris in some comfort following the fall of Kut, while

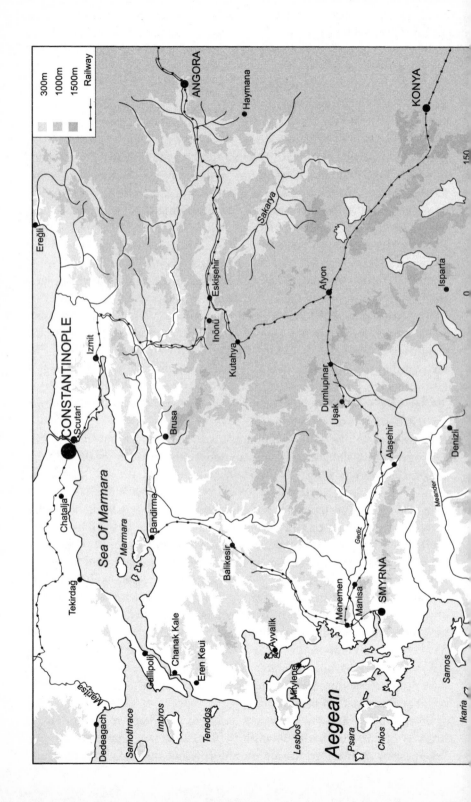

Legend:
- 300m
- 1000m
- 1500m
- Railway

Eregli

ANGORA

Haymana

Sakarya

Eskişehir

İnönü

Kütahya

Afyon

Konya

Isparta

İzmit

CONSTANTINOPLE

Scutari

Brusa

Dumlupınar

Uşak

Alaşehir

Denizli

Chatalja

Bandirma

Meander

Gediz

Tekirdağ

Sea Of Marmara

Marmara

Balıkesir

Menemen

Manisa

SMYRNA

Gallipoli

Chanak Kale

Eren Keui

Ayvalık

Maritsa

Samothrace

Imbros

Tenedos

Mitylene

Lesbos

Aegean

Psara

Chios

Samos

Ikaria

150

0

0

his men struggled and died on their way to their own miserable captivity. On or about 15 October Townshend wrote to Izzet Pasha from his luxurious prison-villa on Büyükada, the largest of the Prinkipo Islands in the Bosporus, asking for an interview, and was received on the seventeenth. He suggested that in return for peace Britain might now be willing to allow Turkey to retain control of Syria, Mesopotamia and even the Caucasus so long as the regions were allowed a degree of autonomy, though as he later acknowledged, that ridiculous notion sprang solely from his own imagination.[3] Not surprisingly, Izzet jumped at the chance of obtaining such a favourable settlement, and so, when he met Townshend that evening, did Hussein Rauf Bey, who was now serving as Minister of the Marine.[4] Townshend was escorted to Smyrna, and there boarded a tugboat. Off the Greek island of Lesbos the vessel was stopped by a British patrol craft. By the evening of 20 October he was ensconced with Calthorpe at Mudros and the pair were busy preparing cables to be transmitted to London. Firstly, Townshend stressed that the Turks wished to deal only with the British.[5] He then presented a series of terms very generous to the Turks and blandly suggested that were they not accepted the Turks would fight on.

The outcome was a marathon Cabinet meeting which resulted in Calthorpe being authorised to negotiate an armistice – not a surrender, because that would require the consultation of those of the allies who were also at war with Turkey – based on the Turks giving up control of the Dardanelles and allowing the Royal Navy free passage through the Straits and into the Black Sea.[6] When the French government learned of this there was uproar, not just because Lloyd George had given Calthorpe the go-ahead to negotiate without consulting it,[7] but out of a creeping belief that the British were now seeking to go back on the Sykes-Picot Agreement for the distribution of the spoils. Lloyd George sent Milner, the Secretary of State for War, to Paris to placate Clemenceau. He succeeded, but the French blew up again when they learned that the British intended to implement one point of the original draft of the armistice proposal which now worked very much in their favour: that negotiations should be conducted by the first member of the alliance the Turks contacted. The British wilfully misconstrued that to mean that they *alone* would conduct the negotiations, and Calthorpe was instructed to exclude the French from the negotiating table by any means in his power. He achieved that by manoeuvring the Turks into explaining (by letter) to the only French representative even remotely at hand – Vice-Adm. Aget, who was not aboard the battleship HMS *Agamemnon*, in the security of which Calthorpe had decided to hold the talks – that since they were accredited only to the British, they could treat only with them. Inasmuch as the Turks accepted all the provisions of the draft Agreement it was an entirely needless provocation.

The armistice negotiations began at 0930 on 27 October, Turkey being represented by Rauf Bey, an army officer named Sadullah, who was Chief of Staff of the Eighth Army, and a senior functionary from the Foreign Ministry.

By the evening of 30 October negotiations were over. Rauf Bey accepted all the proposals of the draft armistice – which included a provision that the Allies could occupy any location in the Empire where security was deemed to be threatened; since they alone would be the arbiter of what represented a security threat, this was a wide-open remit – and signed himself into history[8] on behalf of his government and people. The war between the Ottoman Empire and Britain, France, Italy, Greece and lists of other less important allies who had never been directly involved in the conflict was effectively over. Two weeks later, on 12 November, Calthorpe led a squadron of warships through the Dardanelles, into the Sea of Marmara and then on into the Bosporus, to keep the Ottoman capital under its guns.

That same day French troops arrived in Constantinople, to be followed the next by British (who had occupied both shores of the Dardanelles, as well as the port of Iskenderun in the Gulf of Alexandretta, four days earlier). Little more than a fortnight later the city had been divided into zones of responsibility and Calthorpe had been appointed military 'adviser'. In this capacity he later ordered the arrest of prominent Turkish politicians, civil servants and military personnel (the first was Ali Ihsan, on 29 March 1919) and their internment at Malta, while the archives were examined for any indication that they had committed war crimes. Others were put on trial by Turkish authorities from 28 April, the sultan – Mehmet VI Vahideddin, who had succeeded to the throne on 4 July 1918 – seeking to curry favour with the forces of occupation. Few of those either interned or put on trial were significant figures, the three principal Young Turks having fled Turkey for Germany on 2 November 1918 (aboard a German submarine which took them to the Crimea). All three were dead within four years, Talaat[9] and Jemal[10] at the hands of Armenian assassins and Enver[11] at the head of a cavalry charge (by some accounts; at the hand of an assassin paid by Moscow or by others) near Baldzhuan, in the present-day Republic of Tajikistan, while fighting the Red Army. Mustafa Kemal, scheduled for internment by the British, escaped, and in the first days of May 1919, the Grand Vizier, Damat Ferid Pasha,[12] appointed him Inspector-General of the Ninth Army in Ana-tolia, an area unoccupied by Allied troops[13] and where he would have complete freedom of action. He boarded the SS *Bandirma* for Samsun on the sixteenth, and set up his headquarters in the Mintika Palace Hotel. He soon became a potent rallying point for resistance to the Allied occupation and the terms proposed for the peace settlement, as we shall see in due course.

Even as Kemal was setting out on the journey which would take him to the leadership of his nation, others were beginning a process which would drag Turkey into further turmoil. However, to trace their reasons and their objectives we have to return to 1915, and examine the decisions the Allied governments had taken as to what it was they hoped to gain out of the war with the Ottoman Empire.

As we have seen, the British government set up the de Bunsen Committee to formulate its war aims in the Middle East. Kitchener's representative on that committee was 37-year-old Sir Mark Sykes, a Yorkshire landowner and Member of Parliament for Hull Central. When Sykes returned to London from a protracted trip to Egypt and India to explain the Committee's recommendations, he was immediately co-opted to negotiate with a representative of the French government, François Georges-Picot,[14] to establish a means to integrate those war aims with those of Britain's principal ally.[15] The Sykes-Picot Agreement, as it was known, was accepted on 16 May 1916, with the knowledge and approval of the Russians who, by a separate accord – the Constantinople Agreement of 18 March 1915, which actually hinged on the success of the operation to force the Dardanelles and take Turkey out of the war – were to have their own war aims – control of Constantinople and the Straits, plus Turkey's Armenian provinces – satisfied.

The Agreement gave Britain direct control over Lower Mesopotamia and the western/southern Persian Gulf littoral, and 'influence' over a swathe of territory to the west (but not as far as the Mediterranean coast save at the ports of Haifa and Acre), while the French got direct control over the southern coast of Anatolia and the coastal region of Syria, including the Lebanon, and of a large portion of south-eastern Anatolia, and 'influence' over the remainder of Syria and northern Mesopotamia. Palestine was to be under joint administration pending further consultations with interested parties. There was provision in the Agreement to clarify the April 1916 Treaty of London (which brought Italy into the war on the side of the Triple Entente) with respect to Italy's entitlement to a share of the spoils, and this was effected by the St Jean de Maurienne Agreement of April 1917. Under it, Italy was to receive a large chunk of south-western Anatolia.

Sykes-Picot was supposed to remain secret, of course, but after the second Russian revolution brought the Bolsheviks to power its text was published by *Izvestia* and *Pravda* on 23 November 1917 (as was that of the Constantinople Agreement, and all other accords to which the tsarist government had been a party), and was printed in Britain by the *Manchester Guardian* three days later. The Hashemite Revolt was in full swing at the time, and members of the Ottoman government wasted no time in trying to convince any Arab who would listen that the existence of the Agreement demonstrated that any promises of Arab independence the British, in particular, had made were false. As it was British gold, not British promises, which was actually holding the revolt together, their protestations fell on deaf ears.

When the time came to try to put the provisions of Sykes-Picot into effect, the real situation had changed out of all recognition.[16] By then Lloyd George had become convinced that it should be scrapped, and a plan which better recognised Britain's dominant role in winning the war against the Turks put up in its place. He said so in Cabinet on 3 October 1918, and by the month's end was ready to go public; when Georges Clemenceau protested at his attitude at a meeting in Paris on 30 October (ostensibly at him having made unilateral decisions regarding the armistice), Lloyd George tore into him. According to his own memoirs, he pointed out that:

> Except for Britain no one had contributed anything more than a handful of black troops to the expedition in Palestine . . . The British had now some 500,000 men on Turkish soil. The British had captured three or four Turkish armies and had incurred hundreds of thousand of casualties in a war with Turkey. The other governments had only put in a few nigger policemen to see that we did not steal the Holy Sepulchre! When, however, it came to signing an armistice, all this fuss was made.

By the time Lloyd George and Clemenceau met in London on 1 December, 'The Tiger' seemed to have forgotten – or at least forgiven – 'The Welsh Wizard' for his intemperate outburst, and was now compliant. When Clemenceau asked him what variations to the Agreement he would like to see made, he replied, 'Mosul.' 'Agreed,' said Clemenceau. 'What else?' 'Palestine,' said Lloyd George. 'You shall have it,' replied Clemenceau, and stuck to his word as best he could in the negotiations which followed. Clemenceau expected a quid pro quo in the shape of Lloyd George's support for his overarching claims upon Germany, and Lloyd George played on that unmercifully until Clemenceau, provoked by a campaign against him in the French press mounted by disgruntled functionaries from the Foreign Ministry, eventually snapped, calling him a cheat and promising no more concessions.

On 12 January 1919 the Paris Peace Conference opened. Attended by representatives of over thirty nations, its purpose was to settle all the questions raised at the end of hostilities: essentially, who got what from whom, and how to ensure that the peace would endure. It was in session, on and off, for a little over a year, ending on 16 January 1920, with the inaugural General Assembly of the League of Nations, the establishment of which was US President Woodrow Wilson's cherished aim.[17] There is no proposal here to describe how the conference proceeded, either in public or in private, but only to examine the outcome as it related to the division of the Ottoman Empire and the effect that had.[18]

In the event, Lloyd George manipulated the agenda so skilfully as to put the question of the occupation of Middle Eastern territories beyond discussion. It was not until February of 1920 that the matter was addressed substantially, at a conference in London, called to agree a response to the decision of the newly elected Ottoman parliament to implement the six-point *Missak-I Milli* (National Pact or Oath), published on 12 February,[19] and to revise formally the status of Palestine and the Mosul *vilayet* as suggested in Sykes-Picot. The French had by now accepted reluctantly that control of the latter should be decided by the League of Nations and that the former should fall into the British sphere of influence. The London Conference thus established the framework for what would become the Treaty of Sèvres, and that was confirmed when the conference reconvened – in response to Feisal having been named King of Syria, see below – in the Italian riviera town of San Remo, in a resolution passed on 25 April.[20] In addition the resolution incorporated the terms of the Balfour Declaration regarding Palestine, saying: 'The Mandatory [Britain] will be responsible for putting into effect the declaration originally made on November 8 1917, by the British Government, and adopted by the other Allied Powers, in favour of the establishment in Palestine of a national home for the Jewish people, it being clearly understood that nothing shall be done which may prejudice the civil and religious rights of existing non-Jewish communities in Palestine, or the rights and political status enjoyed by Jews in any other country.' The treaty itself was signed at Sèvres by all parties[21] on 10 August; it was never presented to the Ottoman parliament for ratification, for it had by then been dissolved, and neither did the Greek government ratify it. In the event it served as an outline only, and was superseded by the Treaty of Lausanne.

In simplified terms, the Treaty of Sèvres recognised the Kingdom of the Hejaz; recognised the Democratic Republic of Armenia;[22] awarded Syria and neighbouring south-east and east-central Anatolia, as far north as Sivas and west to Mersin (İçel), to France; awarded Mesopotamia and Jordan, including Palestine, to Britain; awarded Smyrna and its hinterland, and eastern Thrace save for Constantinople, to Greece (to administer; a referendum was to be held five years later to determine the matter definitively); awarded a large area of southern and west-central Anatolia, including Adalia (Antalya) and Konya to Italy. A small rump of Kurdistan was reserved for the Kurds, but was to be subject to a referendum. The Straits – not just the Dardanelles but also the Bosporus and the Sea of Marmara, including the capital – were to be an internationalised, demilitarised zone. All these 'awards' were to be ratified by the League of Nations in the form of mandates. Outside the specified zones the Turks were to be left to their own devices; their economy would be under the effective control of Britain, France and Italy, their army would be limited to 50,000 men and they would be allowed only a handful of small warships.

Long before the treaty was signed, in mid-March 1919, the Italian government had begun landing troops in Anatolia and then re-embarking them, ostensibly to restore and keep order, but actually to establish its right to do so. Within months isolated operations had run into one another, and Italian troops had occupied Adalia (on 29 April) and Fethiye, Bodrum and Marmaris (11 May). Lloyd George suspected this to be the precursor to an occupation of the entire area Italy was now claiming – which was larger than had been envisaged – and enlisted Wilson's aid. Wilson, characteristically undiplomatic, went over the heads of the Italian delegation at Versailles and appealed to the Italian people in an attempt to convince Prime Minister

Vittorio Orlando to modify his demands, whereupon Orlando withdrew the Paris delegation. In its absence the USA, Britain and France turned on the Italians, causing their attitude to harden still further and Orlando to order warships sent to Smyrna. This in turn further provoked Wilson, and soon rumours of the USA's readiness to go to war with Italy in order to curb its aggression and prevent its forces committing acts of atrocity began to circulate. Then Lloyd George stepped in once more, and invited the Greek Prime Minister, Eleftherios Venizélos,[23] to land troops at Smyrna to pre-empt the Italians; 20,000 Greek troops went ashore there on 15 May, and a fortnight later troops also landed at Ayvalik, a hundred kilometres to the north, adjacent to the island of Lesbos.

The presence of Greek forces was satisfactory both to Lloyd George and to Wilson, for rather different reasons: to Lloyd George because he was Hellenistic and anti-Turk; to Wilson because Smyrna was historically Greek,[24] and he believed passionately in a population's right of self-determination. To the Turks, however, it was anathema; it would be impossible to overstate their hatred and distrust of the Greeks, and that was soon to be proved justified.[25]

There was never a chance that the occupation of Smyrna would go off peacefully. In the first moments a Turkish nationalist shot and killed the Greek standard-bearer, and with that the Greeks opened fire on the army barracks and the offices of the city's governor, killing three to four hundred. Turks returned their fire and killed perhaps a third of that number. That gave the Greeks licence to outrage, and they did (but carefully, not until Lloyd George and Millerand had given them the go-ahead). On 16 June the invaders entered the town of Menemen, 33km from Smyrna, and in the space of twenty-four hours killed several hundred Turkish men, women and children; soon most had fled into the hinterland. Over the next three months Greek forces spread out into the Meander (Büyük Menderes) Valley to the south and east, and towards Alaşehir to the north, primarily to establish a defensive perimeter, but in October they began to expand further into north-western Anatolia, towards the Sea of Marmara, and to move eastwards. By December they had reached Eskişehir, heading for Angora (Ankara), where a substitute, unofficial Turkish parliament – the Grand National Assembly – had set up shop and where Kemal was rapidly gathering support and would soon (on 23 April 1920) form a de facto government.

In the meantime, not only had the Treaty of Sèvres been signed, but there had been profound changes in the Greek government. The pro-German king, Constantine, deposed by the Allies[26] in June 1917, had been succeeded by his younger son Alexander. Alexander died – of sepsis contracted from a monkey-bite – on 25 October 1920. Venizélos lost a general election in a landslide the following month, and with power went his hopes of turning Greece into a republic. His great rival Dimitrios Gounaris returned from exile to become the real authority in the country (though he was not named as Prime Minister until the following April), and Constantine was returned to the throne by a rigged plebiscite; he promptly dismissed pro-Venizélist army officers, denuding the command structure, and appointed Gen. Anastasias Papoulas as commander-in-chief in Anatolia.

To this point the Greeks had met little or no resistance in their advance into Anatolia, and now occupied a region which stretched from Izmit, at the eastern end of the Sea of Marmara in the north, to the mouth of the Meander in the south, the Turkish force, poorly equipped and outnumbered, having been content to fall back before them. They encountered organised opposition for the first time at Eskişehir, in the last days of December, and retreated to regroup, moving forward again, now in divisional strength, a week later. Once again they met with resistance, but tried to fight their way through. By 9 January 1921, they were involved in a pitched battle at Inönü and, much to their surprise, were checked by forces under the command of Mustafa Ismet, who had shown no real aptitude as a leader in Palestine (where he had commanded the 3rd Cavalry Division and later XX Corps).

The following month another conference was called in London, and this time members of the Ottoman government in Constantinople and the breakaway group in Ankara were invited, the latter protesting the former's presence and refusing to accept the Treaty of Sèvres as the basis for discussion. The conference dragged on from 21 February to 12 March 1921, achieving nothing of note.

A fortnight after it closed the Greeks attacked at Inönü again, and were defeated once more by the last day of the month. (In celebration of his victories, when Kemal later instituted the practice of using surnames, Ismet took Inönü for his own.) The Greeks were in the process of reinforcing their troops – to around 100,000, in nine divisions, four on the northern front around Brusa (Bursa), five on the southern – and pushed forward again, aiming to establish themselves on a line Afyonkarahisar–Kutahya–Eskişehir. That was achieved by late July, Ismet's forces being defeated, though not conclusively, in the process. Ismet wished to throw all his men into the battle in a fight to the finish, but was restrained by Kemal, who now took personal command with Fevzi (Çakmak) Pasha as his chief of staff but instead of pressing the retreating Turks the Greeks, now under the command of Gen. Georgios Hatzianestis,[27] then stopped, giving them time to establish a defensive line east of the Sakarya River. In the event, it would be 23 August before the Greeks, who still enjoyed a significant numerical advantage, attacked the Turkish positions on the high ground of the Haymana Plateau, forty kilometres south of Ankara. They achieved local success, taking the Mangal Dağ and Çal Dağ, but never managed to push the Turks back across a wide front or to break through. The battle turned into one of attrition, lasting for three weeks, until 13 September, and weak though the Turks were, at least in material terms, the Greeks were weaker, their lines of communication cut repeatedly by well-handled cavalry, and they were forced to retreat to the Afyonkarahisar–Eskişehir line.

There they stayed, seemingly incapable of summoning the will to regroup and launch another campaign, for almost twelve months, appealing for assistance from Allied powers who were not at all disposed to support Constantine. Perhaps more importantly, those same powers were also beginning to suspect that the terms of the Treaty of Sèvres, at least with regard to the Turkish heartland, were unenforceable. That suspicion was reinforced at yet another London Conference round in March 1922, when they proposed modifying its terms marginally and the Turkish nationalists made it clear that they would accept nothing but its abandonment.

All the while the Turks, now receiving substantial material support from the Soviet government in exchange for Kemal having seceded to it the port of Batum,[28] were growing stronger, while the Greek position was weakened significantly by Constantine's decision, in July, to withdraw two divisions, send them to Thrace and threaten to occupy Constantinople. On 26 August 1922 Kemal launched an offensive of his own, having previously feinted both north, towards Brusa (Bursa), and south into the Meander Valley, and drawn off significant numbers of Greek troops. The Greek positions at Afyonkarahisar were overrun the next day, and three days later they were very decisively beaten at the Battle of Dumlupinar, losing perhaps half their entire force killed, wounded or captured, along with much irreplaceable *matériel*. Just how chaotic was the situation in the Greek camp by this time is demonstrated by the fact that Gen. Nikolaos Trikoupis, who was captured in the aftermath of the battle, was named commander-in-chief to succeed Hatzianestis when he had already been in captivity for twenty-four hours.

On 1 September Kemal ordered his men on to the Mediterranean coast, and they chased the Greeks to Smyrna (while their forces in the north fell back on the Sea of Marmara, abandoned their transport and heavy weapons and were taken off by ships sent to Bandirma). Though they pressed the Greeks hard in retreat – covering some 400km in just over a week; the Turkish vanguard entered the outskirts of the city on 9 September – the Turks failed to prevent them killing and burning indiscriminately as they went, destroying entire communities. Unsurprisingly, that only infuriated them all the more, and with Smyrna in their hands by 11 September, they set about taking their revenge, systematically massacring its Greek population. The *Megali Idea* had been transformed into the *Megali Katastrophia*.

Much of the responsibility for the massacre at Smyrna has been put on Nurettin Pasha, who had, we may recall, beaten Townshend at Ctesiphon and then been dismissed when he retired from Shaikh Sa'ad. Restored to favour, he commanded the Turkish First Army at the Battle of Dumlupinar and was then appointed Military Governor of Smyrna for a crucial ten-day period. He ordered unlimited reprisals against the Christian population, making an example of the Greek Orthodox Metropolitan, Chrysostomos, who was handed over to the mob and brutally mutilated – tied to a barber's chair, his ears, nose and hands were cut off, and his eyes gouged out – before being killed. In the process the Christian quarters of the city burned – for five days and nights – while the Greek government frantically rounded up every seaworthy vessel it could find in an attempt to rescue as many of its people as possible. Nurettin moved on to Izmit, where a further five thousand ethnic Greeks were killed, and later to the Pontus, the Black Sea coast east of Trebizond, where men under his command are thought to have murdered at least ten thousand and perhaps significantly more. There was a move to put Nurettin on trial later, but nothing came of it after Kemal intervened on his behalf and it became clear that to do so would open the Turks to renewed accusations of systematic brutality as an instrument of policy.

In addition to the campaign against the Greeks in western Anatolia, the Turks were fighting simultaneously on two other fronts: in the Caucasus and in Cilicia (Çukurova).

In the Caucasus the principal enemy was the Democratic Republic of Armenia, now under the leadership of Tovmos Nazarbekian, assisted by Andarnik Ozanian, with 'Dro' (Drastomat Kanayan) – who had proved his mettle north of Erevan in May 1918 – in command of its armed forces. Though the Treaty of Batum, signed on 4 June 1918, had brought an uneasy peace between the Armenians and the Ottoman forces, the Turks had insufficient time to consolidate their position in the west of the region, and on 16 June 1920, given heart by US President Wilson's having forced the inclusion of the establishment of an enlarged homeland for them in the treaty which would be signed at Sèvres, Armenian troops occupied Oltu. The Turkish nationalists were slow to react, but on 3 September four battalions of troops led by Kazim Karabekir – appointed to command XV Army Corps at Erzurum on 13 March 1919 – appeared and forced the Armenians to withdraw. Karabekir advanced in pursuit, and the Democratic Republic of Armenia declared war on Turkey on 24 September.

By 28 September Karabekir's forces had occupied Sarikamiş, and then took Kağizman and Merdenik, killing many civilians in the process in an organised campaign which the Armenians still maintain amounted to yet more ethnic cleansing. The government of the DRA appealed to the Allied powers but received no response (though the Greeks were vocal in their support; the only other encouragement came from the government of the Soviet Union, which signed a friendship agreement on 24 October). Karabekir, still advancing, arrived at Kars, which was given up without a fight and occupied on 30 October. He then continued to Aleksandropol, and occupied it in turn, on 7 November. A ceasefire was negotiated on 18 November, but by then the Soviet government had intervened, as doubtless it had intended to all along, VI Lenin having sent JV Stalin, the Commissar for Nationalities 'Affairs, to the region as his representative. Stalin ordered the Soviet Eleventh Army to

invade the DRA (from Azerbaijan) with the objective of establishing a Bolshevik republic, but it was slow in coming, and fearing further depredation
by the Turks, Nazarbekian signed a treaty with Turkey (the Treaty of Aleksandropol of 2 December) agreeing to give up the territory awarded to
Armenia by the Treaty of Sèvres. The agreement was never ratified by the
Armenian parliament, for the same day the Soviets arrived. A popular rising
followed; by 5 December 1926 a Revolutionary Committee had taken control
and soon afterwards the Armenian Soviet Socialist Republic was proclaimed.[29] The fate of Western Armenia was sealed by the Treaty of Kars,
signed on 23 October, which saw most of the territory seized by Russia during
the 1877–8 war finally returned to Turkey, and the present-day boundary
established.

Meanwhile, to the south, in Cilicia, the Turks were fighting the French.
Troops were landed first at Antakya, south of Iskenderun, on 7 December,
and at Mersin on 17 December 1918. Two days later they were in Tarsus, and
later that same day shots were exchanged in a brief engagement at Dörtyol. A
headquarters was established at Adana on 20 December, and by 27 December,
when they occupied the key strategic location of Pozanti in the Gülley Pass,
the entire Cilicia region was under French control.

There was little manifest opposition to the French presence until October
and November of the following year, when French troops took over the
cities of Urfa (Şanliurfa), Antep (Gaziantep), Maraş and Birecik, which
had been under British control since the spring. The region had been quiet
in British hands, but following the arrival of the French forces there was
friction between Armenians in their ranks[30] and the Muslim population,
and fighting soon broke out, at Antep where it was to continue for over a
year, and at Maraş, where it lasted for three weeks from 20 January to 10
February 1920, and resulted in the French quitting the town. From then
on the Turkish resistance grew in both strength and determination. A truce
negotiated in May proved fragile, and a running battle between Tarsus and
Pozanti towards the end of the month saw over five hundred French troops
captured. Two days later Kazan, north-west of Adana, was evacuated,
Birecik followed on 11 July, and Saimbeyli was given up on 22 October. On
8 February 1921, the French finally succeeded in overcoming nationalist
forces who had been holding out at Antep, but that was against the run
of things. Some weeks later Kadirli was abandoned, and Feke, Düziçi and
Bahçe soon followed. For some time representatives of Aristide Briand's
government had been in talks with Kemal's administration, and on 9
March a treaty was signed in London which should have put an end to
the matter. In the event, the drafting of the agreement was faulty, and it
was not until the Treaty of Ankara was signed on 20 October 1921, that
the Turks achieved the result they wanted, and the French agreed to give
up any and all claims to territory in Anatolia.[31] As a quid pro quo the
Turkish provisional government acknowledged the French mandate to

govern Syria. The last French troops left Cilicia during the first week of January 1922.

French troops had also been sent to two locations on the north Turkish coast, the coal-producing regions of Karadeniz Ereğli and Zonguldak, which were occupied on 18 March 1919. The former was evacuated on 8 June 1920, but Zonguldak, the more important coalfield, and the one which supplied most of Constantinople's needs, was not given up until 21 June the following year.

By the summer of 1922 there was a growing conviction in both London and Paris that it was time to leave the Turks to their own devices, now that the accessible parts of their empire had been detached and handed over into British and French care. There was still Lloyd George's residual personal antipathy towards the Turks – something his (succession of) French counterparts did not share – to be considered, but the impact of that was reduced as he allowed his Foreign Secretary, Lord Curzon, increasingly to set policy with regard to them. There was, however, a further factor: Kemal's clear intention to take matters into his own hands ...

From Smyrna his First Army moved northwards, heading for the Neutral Zone, and on 11 September was warned by the Allied High Commissioners not to violate it. He made no response. When Lloyd George's Cabinet met on 15 September to consider its reaction, it soon became clear that while there was a general wish to be done with the whole affair, there was an equally general determination to resist anything which smacked of a threat, even at the risk of going to war with Turkey once more. Churchill, who had moved from the War Office and the Air Ministry[32] to become Colonial Secretary the previous year, spoke on the subject of obtaining the support of the Commonwealth governments for the use of force, should it come to that.[33] He was instructed to draft a cable to go out to all the appropriate prime ministers over Lloyd George's signature, informing them that Britain intended to resort to military force if necessary to defend the Neutral Zone – the Strait and Constantinople, essentially – in Turkey, and asking for their assistance in that eventuality. The Cabinet also decided that the British public should be informed, and a press communiqué was issued, making it clear that while Britain was ready to convene a new round of peace talks, it would not do so under threat from the Turkish Army, and was considering military action along with the French, the Italians and the Dominions.

That statement appeared in the London papers the following morning, and caused uproar, first in Paris and then in the Dominions, whose leaders had not yet received decoded versions of the warning telegram. The first reaction came from Poincaré, who was furious at Lloyd George's presumption and on 18 September ordered his troops withdrawn immediately from frontline positions east of the Dardanelles, the Italians following suit. Next came cables from the prime ministers of Canada (Mackenzie King) and Australia

(Billy Hughes), informing the British government that they would not follow its line. Jan Smuts, by now the South African premier, remained silent; only William Massey of New Zealand and Richard Squires of Newfoundland replied positively. The eventual outcome of the affair was the dissolution of the coalition government Lloyd George had managed to sustain for so long, and with it his own fall from power. The Conservative parliamentarians met at the Carlton Club on 19 October, and Andrew Bonar Law, a former leader of the party – somewhat reluctantly, but prodded on by press baron Lord Beaverbrook – spoke out against the coalition; a vote was taken, and by a very considerable majority it was resolved to fight the next general election on party lines. When Lloyd George heard of this he resigned, and Bonar Law took his place as Prime Minister. He called an immediate election, which the Conservatives won with a comfortable majority. Lloyd George never held office again. (Churchill was one of those who lost his seat, and was out of politics once more, but only until November 1924, when – after two defeats and having 're-ratted', in his words, quitting the Liberals in favour of the Conservatives[34] – he returned as the member for Epping and was promptly enrolled as Chancellor of the Exchequer in Stanley Baldwin's government.)

Churchill was given personal charge of settling the matter on 22 September and deputised Curzon, who travelled to Paris to attempt to repair the damage. The next day he was able to convince Poincaré (and Count Carlo Sforza, Italy's ambassador, who was also strongly supportive of Turkish nationalism) that Britain was prepared to accede to Kemal's demands so long as it appeared, at least, to stem from a negotiated settlement and was not simply a climb-down in the face of threat. That same day the first of Kemal's troops arrived in the vicinity of the Dardanelles, a strong detachment of cavalry crossing into the Neutral Zone at Eren Keui, near Kum Kale. The British were reinforcing feverishly, and by 28 September the contingent at Chanak Kale had been strengthened to six battalions, with three howitzer batteries across the Narrows on the Gallipoli Peninsula and with thirty-six medium-calibre guns and sixteen 8-in howitzers on the way. A strong naval flotilla, including two aircraft carriers, was anchored out in the Straits, and a fighter squadron of the RAF was on hand, with three more on the way. Things came to a head that day, Harington, the British commander in the theatre, reporting to London that the Turks were 'grinning through the wire' at his men. The Cabinet's response was to instruct him to deliver an ultimatum to the Turks, and back it up with military action as he saw fit. Harington was a good choice; he kept the threat to himself and a cool head, and allowed the situation to develop; within two days the Turks had backed off of their own accord.

Meanwhile, Curzon's travails in Paris had resulted in an invitation being extended to Kemal to attend a conference at Mudanya, a resort on the Sea of Marmara, near Brusa. With the invitation went an undertaking to restore Eastern Thrace, as far as the Maritsa River and including Adrianople, to Turkey; to evacuate Constantinople as soon as a peace accord was ratified, and support Turkey's admission to the League of Nations. Kemal agreed, and 3 October was set as the date for the conference to begin.

Its delegates – Ismet Pasha for the Turks and the Allied military commanders, each with a retinue of advisers – deliberated until 5 October and then talks broke down, thanks, by Churchill's account, to 'the ineffable M. Franklin-Bouillon [who had brokered the Treaty of Ankara], whose efforts were directed towards leading the Turks to hope for more than they would ever get from Great Britain, and to believe that the British were unable or unwilling in the last resort to fight'. That may indeed have been the case, but it certainly did not appear to be so, for British forces in the Neutral Zone had by now been further reinforced, and the British Ambassador in Constantinople, Sir Horace Rumbold, had made it known that the terms of the (undelivered but understood) 23 September ultimatum still went. The conference reconvened on 10 October, and at 0730 the following morning a convention was signed, under the terms of which the Greeks would be required to withdraw all their forces in Thrace behind the Maritsa,[35] and the Turks would recognise the neutrality of the Strait. That led to a definitive peace conference being convened at Lausanne in Switzerland; it met for the first time on 21 November, having been delayed by the general election in the United Kingdom and by Benito Mussolini having seized power in Italy. By that time the Grand National Assembly had established the state of Turkey, which was defined as the Turkish-speaking region of the old empire, and abolished the sultanate. Mehmet VI Vahideddin left Constantinople on 17 November, a private citizen, having renounced the caliphate, bound for Malta aboard the British battleship HMS *Malaya*. He later settled in San Remo, where he died in May 1926. He was succeeded as caliph by Abdul Mejid, the eldest son of Abdul Aziz, though briefly, only, for the caliphate itself was abolished by the Turkish parliament – though by what right is unclear, for it was relevant to all Sunni Muslims, and not just to their own people[36] – on 3 March 1924.[37]

Curzon, Britain's chief negotiator at Lausanne, believed from the outset that France and Italy would sabotage his position at Lausanne if they could by that means cement their own. He was not, however, prepared for the intransigence of Ismet, by now Turkey's Foreign Minister, who he described as 'a true born son of the bazaars'. Negotiations fell into three categories: territorial and military matters, financial and economic questions (primarily the Ottoman debt and reparations) and the judicial status of foreigners in Turkey. Three working groups were set up, Curzon reserving the first for himself to chair and allocating the others to Camille Barrère, the principal French delegate (he was France's ambassador in Rome), and the Marquis Garroni, Italy's High Commissioner in Constantinople.[38] By 4 February 1923, the territorial and military questions – the status of the Strait, the Greek presence in Western Thrace, a provision for a population exchange, the status of Constantinople and the size of the Turkish Army – had been settled. It had been agreed that the disposition of the Mosul *vilayet* should be left for the League of Nations to decide, but the matter of how interest on the national debt was to be paid, and on the capitulations (reintroduced in 1918), remained alive, as did a Turkish demand for reparations from Greece for the damage done by her armed forces in Anatolia. As a result Ismet refused to sign a draft treaty, Curzon walked out in disgust, not to return, and the proceedings broke down.

The conference reconvened on 23 April, with Rumbold in Curzon's place, and it soon became clear that there were now additional barriers to agreement. The French had decided to renew a claim for reparations from the Turks (which had earlier been set aside), and the Greeks talked of advancing their armed forces to the Chatalja Lines if the Turks insisted on them making reparations, but offered the border locality of Karaağaç in full settlement instead. Eventually, largely due to quiet diplomacy on the part of Rumbold (and the edge that being able to read all Turkey's signals gave him, the British government's newly established Code and Cypher School having proved adept at breaking their code), an agreement was reached and, despite the almost obligatory last-minute prevarications, a treaty was signed on 24 July. The Turkish Grand National Assembly ratified the treaty on 23 August, and on 2 October the last contingent of Allied troops ceremoniously quit Constantinople. Turkish troops moved in four days later, and on 29 October the Turkish Republic was proclaimed, with Kemal as its first president and, since the thirteenth, Ankara as its capital.

There was no mention in the treaty of a homeland for the Kurds, and the matter of the borders of Armenia having been settled by other means, and Wilson's proposals in that direction having gone by the board, neither did it attempt to address that matter. It did, however, provide for an exchange of Christian and Muslim populations; it is thought that up to 1.25 million Greeks were expelled from Turkey and around 100,000 from neighbouring countries, and around 450,000 were expelled from Greece, 60,000 of them to Bulgaria. Muslims living in Western Thrace were exempt, as were Greeks living in Constantinople and on the islands of Imbros (Gokçeada) and Tenedos (Bozcaada); however, the Turkish government soon took steps to make life difficult for those Greeks who had remained, and a Greek population of perhaps 250,000 in the erstwhile capital in 1924 had dwindled to less than 5,000 by the end of the century.

The other consequences of the defeat of the Ottoman Empire – the detachment of its possessions outside Anatolia and Thrace – were less bloody than the war of independence had been, but that does not by any means signify that they passed off peacefully or without dispute. In summary:

The Hashemite Feisal ibn Hussein was declared King of Syria on 7 March 1920, by a self-selected congress. On 14 July he was given an ultimatum by the French, to abdicate or be deposed; he tried to negotiate,

30. Eurasia by 1939

the French sent a colonial division with artillery, armour and air support and routed a makeshift army led by his War Minister, an ex-Ottoman officer named Yusuf al-Azmah, at Maysalun, twenty kilometres west of Damascus, on 24 July. Feisal was expelled, and Gen. Henri Gouraud, who had commanded French forces at Gallipoli, was installed as High Commissioner. The presence of a substantial (Maronite) Christian population in the Lebanon, as well as Druzes and both Sunni and Shia Muslims, inevitably meant there was scope, at least, for unrest, and so it proved. Five years later, the Druzes rose in open rebellion, which took two years to suppress, and there were to be further insurrections in later years. Syria – with the Lebanon hived off as a separate entity in September 1926 – remained under French control until 1946. During 1941 the region was the scene of fighting which pitted Frenchman against Frenchman when Free French forces, with considerable assistance from the British, expelled those loyal to Pétain's puppet government after almost six months of bitter combat.

Following independence, Syria experienced continued unrest; in the decade to 1956 it had twenty different administrations and four constitutions, and then fell under the influence of the Soviet Union. Two years later it entered into a short-lived pact with Egypt which brought the two nations together as the United Arab Republic, and later came under military rule. In March 1963, a Ba'athist government was installed with, from 1970, Hafiz al-Assad at its head. He was to remain in power for thirty years, and when he died in 2000 was succeeded as president by his son, Bashar al-Assad.

Feisal quit Syria for Jordan, where his brother Abdullah was later installed as emir, but his contribution to the unfolding story was by no means over, for on 21 August 1921 he was installed as king of Iraq. When the war ended, an Indian Army officer, Arnold Wilson, had been put in as a temporary civil commissioner. (Percy Cox, the obvious candidate for the job, was appointed acting minister in Teheran, where he was central to the (failed) Anglo-Persian Agreement;[39] Cox returned to take the reins back from Wilson in June 1920.) Wilson warned of the dangers of insurrection, and was to be proved right; by the summer of 1919 British personnel were being murdered with a disturbing regularity, and twelve months later, coincidental with Cox's return, the entire region rose against the British, jihad being proclaimed within the Shi'ite community at Karbalah and spreading to the Sunni community. At the height of the revolt the active rebels numbered about 130,000, perhaps half of whom were armed with modern rifles. The Delhi government ordered reinforcements sent, and slowly order was restored, but not before perhaps five hundred British soldiers had perished along with as many as ten thousand Arabs. No sooner was the Arab revolt over than the Kurds in the north embarked on a sustained uprising of their own.

Churchill took on the overall responsibility for the affairs of the fledgling

British Middle Eastern territories on 13 February 1921, and was to hold the post of Colonial Secretary until October the following year. He had served two years as War (and Air) Minister, and had overseen very drastic cuts in British military spending. He brought the same agenda to the Middle East; in eighteen months he cut spending across the region by 75 per cent, with the British military commitment in Iraq, as Mesopotamia was now being called, reduced from thirty-two infantry battalions to six, plus native levies. Instead, he increased the size of the air force there, and by 1922, when responsibility for the country's security was devolved to it, had eight squadrons in place. They played a major part in keeping the civilian population docile, bombing communities – including the city of Sulaimaniya, the Kurdish capital – whenever they showed signs of unrest. As one British politician (Leo Amery) was to remark the following year: 'If the writ of King Feisal runs effectively throughout the Kingdom, it is entirely due to British aeroplanes. If the aeroplanes were removed tomorrow, the whole structure would immediately fall to pieces.' It is sometimes suggested that the Royal Air Force employed chemical weapons against insurgent Kurds during this period, but there is no real evidence that it did (though Churchill, while Air Minister, certainly argued in favour of the use of tear gas). However, the use of mustard gas does seem to have been discussed, and white phosphorus was employed as an incendiary agent.

Within weeks of taking office, Churchill had convened a conference in Cairo, which disquieted Curzon. After almost four decades of British rule there was considerable unrest in Egypt by this time, and within twelve months that would have resulted in the Allenby Declaration which gave Egypt limited independence. The outcome was the decision to offer Feisal the throne of Iraq and his brother Abdullah the emirate of Jordan (to prevent him from leading an uprising in Syria; not out of altruism, but to prevent the French retaliating by invading Palestine), which territory was construed as being bounded on the west by the River Jordan.

Feisal arrived in Basra on 24 June, and was received as a guest of the nation, an important first step. On 16 July it was announced that a plebiscite – a simple yes-or-no vote – would be held; on 18 August it was announced that Feisal had won convincingly (he took 96 per cent of the votes cast; there were allegations of vote-rigging, but the reality was less crude: as Cox's biographer put it: 'the results of all such operations . . . owe much to official prompting'), and five days later he was crowned king, and at the same time the state of Iraq came officially into being. Soon, he too was making waves, protesting that the League of Nations mandate status on which Britain was depending was inappropriate, and that there should be instead a negotiated treaty between the British government and his own. That treaty was long in the negotiation, and it was 22 October 1922 before it was signed.[40] It allowed for British rule to continue for twenty years. The *vilayet* of Mosul was formally added to the kingdom in 1926 when the League of Nations finally decided its fate in Britain's favour.

In November 1930, with over half the mandate period still to run, the British gave notice that they would grant Iraq partial independence and support its application to join the League of Nations, to which it was admitted on 3 October 1932. Feisal died – peacefully, in Switzerland – the following year, to be succeeded by his 21-year-old son Ghazi, who was unsuited to the task; his weakness encouraged strong men to attempt to seize power, and over the next three years, in an atmosphere of intrigue exacerbated by tribal rebellions, the government changed five times. In October 1936 Hikmat Sulayman, the strongest of the politicians, incited a divisional commander in the Iraqi Army, Gen. Bakir Sidqi, to stage a coup. Sulayman became Prime Minister with the army very much the power behind his office, a situation which was to remain unchanged until 1941. In 1939, Ghazi was killed in a motoring accident; his four-year-old son Feisal II succeeded to the throne, but Ghazi's brother Abdullah was appointed Regent, and ruled until Feisal, British-educated, came of age in 1953 and then continued to exercise considerable influence from behind the scenes.

On the outbreak of the Second World War, Gen. Nuri as-Said, Feisal I's old chief of staff was Prime Minister. He wanted to declare war on Germany, but was dissuaded by his Cabinet, members of which doubted Britain's capacity to win, and had to be content with the breaking of diplomatic relations with Berlin. By June 1940, as-Said was Rashid Ali al-Gaylani's Foreign Minister, but this time he was unable even to secure the sundering of diplomatic ties, while extremist pan-Arab elements around al-Gaylani wanted to declare for the Axis. The situation deteriorated over the following year, and Nuri and Abdullah were forced to flee the country. In the spring of 1941 the British moved in to re-establish control. Fighting was sporadic for a month, but by the beginning of summer order – and the monarchy – had been restored, Abdullah and as-Said had returned, and al-Gaylani had been sent into exile; Iraq declared war on Germany in January 1942.

Abdullah called for the establishment of a parliamentary system at the war's end; some of his proposals were implemented, but older, conservative, elements were able to prevent more than partial compliance. In 1947 as-Said, by now Prime Minister once more, called an election, which was largely boycotted. He resigned, and was replaced by Salih Jabr, the first Shi'ite to hold the position. Jabr had been Minister of the Interior during the war, and had made a good many enemies; he entered into negotiations with Britain aiming at cementing his own position, but like many such attempts, his failed. He signed a new alliance with Britain (at Portsmouth, in January 1948) under the terms of which, among other things, Iraq gained sovereignty over the two large bases the RAF maintained in the country (though agreed to Britain using them in time of war), British troops were to be withdrawn and a truly independent Iraqi Army created and rearmed. But that was not enough: rioting broke out, as-Said returned to power, and the treaty was repudiated.

There was widespread unrest over the next four years, and it came to a head again in 1952 in another popular uprising; Abdullah called on the army to restore order. Civilian rule was restored at the end of 1953, but there was no sign of conservative elements being prepared to share power. Feisal's rule – partially overshadowed by Abdullah, now Crown Prince but very much the power behind the throne – was characterised by continuing strong ties with the United Kingdom.

Before the decade's end, the younger elements in Iraq's murky political world had begun to despair of ever being able to force their way to its forefront, and their mood had communicated itself to the so-called Free Officers, led by a Shi'ite, Brigadier Abd al-Karim Qasim. Qasim decided to act in July 1958. The king and his entire household were assassinated during the course of the coup (as was Nuri as-Said, attempting to flee the country dressed as a woman; his men's shoes gave him away. The degree of popularity he enjoyed by then can perhaps be gauged by the fact that his body was subsequently dug up, dragged through the streets of Baghdad, hung up, mutilated and burned). Iraq then became a republic, and British influence over its affairs effectively ceased for good. Qasim, who found a power base within the (largely Shi'ite) Iraq Communist Party, was to remain in power for just five years, during which time he managed to alienate the entire world, save for the Soviet bloc, before the US Central Intelligence Agency motivated the (Sunni) Ba'ath ('Renewal' or 'Renaissance') Party into launching the coup which was eventually, after several more bloody interludes, to bring Saddam Hussein to power sixteen years later.

At the conclusion of the Cairo Conference, Churchill travelled to Jerusalem, where he met with Abdullah ibn Hussein and offered him the emirate of Trans-Jordan, the territory to the east of the Jordan River (which comprised 77 per cent of the whole, by area), the territory to the west to be under direct British control with Sir Herbert Samuel as High Commissioner. The British mandate to administer the territory was later amended to that effect. Transfer of administrative authority to Abdullah began in 1923, and was largely completed by 1928, though as with Egypt (and Iraq), the British retained control of defence and foreign policy. That remained the case until the British mandate expired in 1946, and the Hashemite Kingdom of Trans-Jordan was created, with Abdullah as king. During the first quarter-century of its existence, Trans-Jordan was stable and peaceful, at least compared to its neighbours; only after 1948, when it involved itself in the Israeli War of Independence (and was the only Arab party to that war to make significant inroads into the territory the Jewish state wished to retain for itself), did dissident forces make their presence felt.

Abdullah was shot and killed – by a Palestinian Arab who was fearful that he was about to make a deal with the Israeli government regarding the territory the kingdom had seized on the west bank of the Jordan – while attending Friday prayers at the al-Aqsa Mosque in Jerusalem on 20 July 1951; he was succeeded by his son Talal, a schizophrenic, and the real power lay with his eighteen-year-old grandson, Hussein. Talal abdicated the following year, and Hussein became king; he ruled until 1999, and was succeeded by his son Abdullah. Jordan, as the kingdom had become, allied itself with Egypt and Syria during the disastrous (for the aggressors) Six-Days War of 1967, and lost the west bank territory, together with east Jerusalem, in consequence.[41]

Samuel's appointment as High Commissioner in Palestine on 1 July 1920 was technically illegal, of course, since the British had no mandate to govern the territory at that point. Many people expressed serious concern that his primary allegiance would be to his co-religionists, rather than to the British government. In fact, Samuel's Zionism was manifested only in his determination to see British policy put into effect with regard to the establishment of a Jewish homeland, as embodied in the Balfour Declaration and reaffirmed in the San Remo resolution. That was no more or less than would have been expected of any incumbent. In his efforts to placate the Palestinian Arabs he went so far as to install a known militant with pronounced anti-British sentiments – Muhammed Amin al Husseini, who had fought against the British during the war – as Grand Mufti of Jerusalem.[42]

The British mandate to administer Palestine was agreed on 24 July 1923, coincidentally the day the Lausanne Treaty was signed, and came into effect on 29 September. Until 1939 immigration was unrestricted, and during that period the Jewish population of Palestine increased substantially. To begin with there was little opposition from the Palestinian Arabs, but as anti-Semitism in Europe increased, during the 1930s, and immigrant numbers grew, it became more marked. While the population increase (and the Jews' determination to prosper though their industry) was not the sole reason for Arab disaffection, there was significant intercommunal violence. Events came to a head in 1936, which saw the start of a three-year-long Arab revolt; it took the intervention of 20,000 extra British troops to put down, and led to calls[43] for the partition of Palestine into separate Jewish and Arab states. It is estimated that around 5,000 Arabs died during the insurrection, together with four hundred Jews and perhaps half that number of British servicemen. In addition to British forces, Jewish 'self-help' groups such as the Haganah, which was later to form the nucleus of the emerging nation's armed forces, came into being, as did shadowy organisations such as the Special Night Squads, the brainchild of Orde Wingate,[44] Sir Reginald Wingate's nephew, which saw British soldiers operating alongside Jewish civilians. The period also witnessed the birth of organisations such as the Irgun (Etel) and the Lehi (more widely known perhaps as the Stern Gang). The British labelled these as terrorist organisations, and they did, indeed, rely on tactics such as assassination and bombing which a later generation of Israelis would come to revile when they were used against them by Palestinian Arabs and their sympathisers.

On 30 November 1947, the United Nations, successor to the League of Nations, voted in favour of terminating the British government's mandate to administer Palestine; the British responded by undertaking to give it up no later than 1 August 1948. From the date of the UN vote, a de facto civil war broke out in Palestine, and became increasingly militarised from January. As the date for the British pull-out neared, both sides redoubled their efforts to consolidate their hold over as much territory as possible, the focus being Jerusalem, which both claimed as the site of the capital of their respective states. On 14 May, a day before the date set for the termination of the mandate, the independent State of Israel was proclaimed, and with that came the First Arab-Israeli War, often known as the War of Independence. It lasted until February 1949, when the first armistice agreement was reached between Israel and Egypt. Similar agreements were reached over the next six months with the other combatants. The outcome saw Israel left in possession of 78 per cent of the territory of mandatory Palestine, the rest being composed of two blocks: the West Bank (of the Jordan), including east Jerusalem, and the 'Gaza Strip', which remained under Egyptian control. Both were subsequently seized by Israel during the 1967 war and incorporated into her territory, though her right to hold them was immediately disputed.

Britain and France, Italy and Greece, were not the only notional winners in the war against the Ottoman Empire, of course, and it could very well be held that another interested party – the Arabs – had the best of the entire affair, but certainly not in the way anyone had envisaged. Even while San Remo was under way, the Hashemite Arab element – which was not invited to attend, having made a thoroughgoing nuisance of itself in Paris, with the very active encouragement and participation of TE Lawrence – was already proving troublesome, insisting that McMahon's undertaking to Hussein, and not Sykes-Picot, was the agreement which should stand. In the event, the only part of the old empire they were allowed to retain was the Hejaz, their original 'kingdom', and here they came under attack from a different direction.

Ibn Saud was just a child when, together with the rest of his (fundamentalist Wahhabi) family which had ruled much of the Najd (the central Arabian Peninsula, east of the Hejaz) since the eighteenth century, he was exiled to Kuwait in 1890 by the Rashidis, who had gained control of the region with the assistance of the Ottoman Empire. Grown to manhood, just, he returned to his native Riyadh with a small band of followers in 1902, and in an astonishing personal feat of arms, succeeded in taking the city. Two years later his forces defeated a Rashidi/Ottoman army, and by 1906, after widespread fighting across the region, he had regained much of his ancestral territory, controlling it by means of the Ikhwan (Brotherhood), established in small desert colonies. He defeated the Turks in Al Hasa province in 1913, but was forced to acknowledge Ottoman suzerainty afresh the following year. He accepted subsidies from the British during the First World War, but retained his independence, and in 1919 struck his first blow against the Hejaz. His Ikhwan army soundly defeated Sherif Hussein's men; the following year his son Feisal won control of Asir province, between the Hejaz and the Yemen, and in 1921 Ibn Saud defeated the last of the Rashidis and annexed the whole of northern Arabia. This brought the Saudis into conflict with the British in Iraq and Trans-Jordan, and also in their capacity as protectors of Kuwait; Saud's army blockaded Kuwait, and there were numerous incidents there and on the (implicit; demarcation was more a matter of tribal suzerainty than of lines in the sand) borders with the Hejaz, Trans-Jordan and Iraq.

In 1923 the British called all concerned to attend a conference in Kuwait. It ended in disarray, even though the border dispute was settled in the Saudis' favour, and in September 1924 the Wahhabis attacked the Hejaz. They captured Taif after a brief struggle, massacring much of its male civilian population; occupied Mecca without opposition, and then laid siege to Jedda and Medina. Sherif Hussein, in an attempt to retain popular support for his regime, responded by abdicating his throne in favour of his third son, Ali. By the end of 1925 both Medina and Jedda had surrendered to the Saudis, and the area around Aqaba was occupied by British-dominated Trans-Jordan to prevent its falling into Wahhabi hands. On 8 January 1926 Ibn Saud, who had adopted the title of Sultan of Najd in 1921, was proclaimed King of the Hejaz in the Great Mosque of Mecca. In 1927 he was also proclaimed King of Najd and its dependencies, the two parts of his dual kingdom being administered for the time being as separate entities. In the same year the Treaty of Jedda placed his relations with Great Britain on a permanent footing when the British acknowledged Saudi independence.

Ibn Saud soon found himself in difficulties with hard-line religious elements among his people, angry at the way he had dealt with the Christian powers and at his complaisant attitude to the British-protected regimes in Iraq, Kuwait and Trans-Jordan. Incidents on their frontiers created a state of undeclared war, in which British aircraft played an important role in discouraging Wahhabi incursions. Ibn Saud tried to suppress political and military opposition by the Ikhwan, and in 1928, accusing him of betraying the cause – essentially, Wahhabi dominance of the entire region – for which they had fought, they rose against him. The majority of the population rallied to the king's side, and civil war dragged on into 1930, when the rebels, now based in Kuwaiti territory, were rounded up by the British and their leaders were handed over to the king. With their defeat, power passed definitively into the hands of townspeople rather than the tribes, and the two kingdoms were unified into Saudi Arabia in September 1932. Saud remained neutral throughout most of the Second

World War, but received considerable assistance from the Allies, and in 1945 declared war on Germany, which paved the way for Saudi Arabian membership of the United Nations.

Saudi Arabia's economy is almost entirely based on oil. The first exploratory oil concession was granted, to Standard Oil of California, in 1933; oil was discovered in Al Hasa province, bordering the Persian Gulf, in 1938, but it was 1941 before it was exploited in any meaningful way, at the hands of Aramco (the Arabian-American Oil Company; the name is somewhat misleading, for until 1973 it was 100 per cent American-owned). Prior to that, despite its size Saudi Arabia was one of the poorest nations in the world, based on simple, tribal economy; many of the people were nomads, engaged in raising camels, sheep, and goats. Agricultural production was localised and subsistent, and by far the greatest part of national revenues, such as they were, were derived from pilgrims coming to Mecca. Even after the oil had begun to flow, little benefit found its way back to the kingdom until 1950, when Ibn Saud levied a tax of 50 per cent on Aramco's income. Ibn Saud died three years later, to be succeeded by his ultra-conservative elder son, Saud II. His younger son, Feisal, was more popular with the 'sophisticated' town-dwelling Arabs, and the next eleven years saw power switch backwards and forwards between the two brothers until eventually, in November 1964, Saud was deposed and Feisal mounted the throne. The rise of 'modern' Saudi Arabia can be dated from that time.

The Saudi government gained control of one quarter of Aramco in 1973, and the company later passed fully into Saudi ownership. Feisal was assassinated in 1975, and his half-brother Khalid ascended to the throne, with another half-brother, Fahd, named as Crown Prince; Fahd in fact held the reins of power. He in turn came to the throne in 1982, by which time the evolution of Saudi Arabia into a modern (albeit an elitist, despotic and non-democratic) nation-state can be said to have been completed.

With the resilation from the mandates, formal British and French participation in Middle Eastern affairs came to an end, at least temporarily.[45] That is not to say that the region found peace after more than three decades of disturbance and uncertainty – religious intolerance saw to that – but at the very least the states created from the ruins of the Ottoman Empire now had the power of self-determination. If they could but resist others' efforts to intervene in their affairs for their own nefarious motives, they would be able to blossom and grow into full members of the international community of nations.

Notes

1. And, technically speaking, reached as far as the island of Lundy, off the North Devon coast, at one point, through a rather convoluted network of allegiances running by way of the Barbary pirates and the Dey of Algiers.

2. This was the grandiloquent name accorded in diplomatic circles to the government of the Ottoman Empire; it is a French translation of the Turkish *Bab-i Ali*, the official name of the ornate arched gateway giving access to the block of buildings within the Great Seraglio at Topkapi, overlooking the Bosporus, which housed the principal departments of state.

3. Though Serbia had gained a sort of independence in 1817, and Greece had done so definitively, with the assistance of all the Great Powers, in 1832.

4. Domestically produced cotton and reprocessed imports from further east – of commodities such as silk, transformed into carpets and textiles – dominated the empire's exports. However, there was no other manufacturing base, and virtually all non-agricultural commodities had to be imported; thus, as soon as a taste for such goods developed the stage was set for economic disaster.

5. Anything up to £13 trillions by today's standards, depending on the basis used for calculation. The debt had accumulated over twenty years and comprised a number of individual loans, the first (in 1854; it was raised to fund in part the Crimean War) of £3m; fresh loans had been used in part to pay the interest on earlier borrowings.

6. Turkey's creditors in the financial centres of London and Paris were left to pick up the pieces, and later (in 1881) set up the Ottoman Public Debt Administration to run the country's economy at arm's length in order to ensure that things got no worse. Not everyone suffered, however: lions, as well as jackals, will take wounded prey. Thanks to the Porte's attention being focused elsewhere, in November the Prime Minister of the United Kingdom, Benjamin Disraeli, was able to persuade Ismail Pasha, the Khedive of Egypt, the sultan's suzerain – who had similar money worries of his own – to sell his personal holding of 176,602 shares in the Compagnie Universelle du Canal Maritime de Suez to the British government for £3,976,582, making it the largest shareholder in the company, with 44% of the capital. The French, who held the remainder of the equity, but not in one block, were furious, and to many, in those pre-Entente Cordiale days, that was the best part of the entire affair.

7. From the Turkish *başıbozuk*, literally 'damaged head'. Noted for their lack of discipline, the bashi-bazouks were armed and maintained by the government; they did not receive pay (but were allowed to keep what they stole) and did not wear uniforms or distinctive badges. They were thus ideally suited to what we might now call 'deniable' paramilitary operations.

8. He was deposed on 30 May 1876 (and murdered three days later), not because he had behaved barbarically in Bulgaria but because he had ruled while the economy

crumbled. He was replaced by his nephew Murat. An alcoholic with severe psychological problems, he lasted just three months and was superseded by his brother Abdul Hamid. In consequence, 1876CE – 1292 by Islamic reckoning – became known as the Year of the Three Sultans.

9. Curiously, there was one episode in which Russia came to the Ottomans' aid: in 1832, when the dissident Viceroy of Egypt, Mehemet Ali, invaded Anatolia and got to within a few days' march of the Sea of Marmara, Sultan Mahmud appealed to Britain and to France and was rebuffed, and eventually went to Tsar Nicholas I, who agreed to send an army to support him.

10. Largely as a result of the Turks, most fortuitously, having armed themselves with Winchester repeater rifles, while the Russians had nothing better than obsolete single-shot Berdans.

11. The Tory government of Benjamin Disraeli – not exactly pro-Ottoman, but ready to support the empire on the principle that Palmerston had established, in this case that Britain needed it to prevent Russia from actively pursuing its ambitions regarding India – decided as early as 21 July 1877 to declare war on Russia if she occupied Constantinople. Popular sentiment in Britain was summed up by a ditty which was doing the rounds:

> We don't want to fight,
> But by Jingo, if we do,
> We've got the ships,
> We've got the men,
> We've got the money, too!

introducing a new word into the language in the process. By late March the following year, with the situation still volatile, despite armistices having been agreed and treaties signed, Disraeli went so far as to order the reserves mobilised and moved Indian troops to Malta. It was not until 1907 that Britain's fear of Russia's ambitions towards India was settled, by treaty.

12. It was united with the (ethnically Bulgarian) southern part – Eastern Rumelia, as it was known – in 1885.

13. Four years later, in 1882, when widespread rioting broke out in Egypt, it, too, was occupied. Both Cyprus and Egypt became British Protectorates in due course, in November and December 1914, respectively.

14. It had little enough effect on the Turks' behaviour, though. The success the Balkan Christians had had in shaking off Turkish rule inspired the Armenians to attempt something similar; things came to a head in 1894, and Abdul Hamid responded by imposing taxes he knew they could not raise with the intention of provoking open rebellion. The Armenians duly rose, and he put them down with a degree of brutality alongside which that in Bulgaria paled. Up to 300,000 are believed to have died, and Gladstone, now retired from active politics, was driven to fury. He attempted to persuade Lord Salisbury, the prime minister of the day, to declare war on Turkey, but failed.

15. The elder von Moltke had been despatched to Turkey as a military adviser to the first of the westernised sultans, Mahmud II, in 1835, and entered Turkish service, fighting in the internecine war against the renegade Egyptian viceroys. He returned to Germany after four years, very pro-Ottoman. Within less than two decades he was chief of the Prussian General Staff, and remained so, a very influential figure indeed, for three more.

16. Culminating, from 1884, with territorial claims in Africa and the Pacific, Germany's

'place in the sun'. She was a latecomer even to neo-colonialism, but all the more determined for that, at least in government circles; her people saw things differently, and preferred, when they emigrated – and they did so in their millions – to go to the fast-growing, dynamic United States rather than roughing it in Tanganyika, Namibia, the Cameroons or New Guinea.

17. His grandson; Wilhelm I's successor, his son Friedrich III, came to the throne terminally ill with cancer, and ruled for only three months, from 9 March to 15 June.

18. A phrase first coined by the American naval officer and geostrategist, Rear Adm. Alfred Mahan, only in 1902, to characterise the region from Turkey to India.

19. The first railway constructed in Turkey was a 120km line linking Aydin to the port of Smyrna (Izmir) on the west coast of Anatolia, built in 1856 by British interests who wished to simplify the process of exporting the cotton for which the region was famous. Other short lines linking centres of production with ports followed, and then, in 1871, more ambitious plans were drawn up for a line to penetrate into Anatolia. Since 12 August 1888, it had been possible to travel by train from Berlin to Constantinople via Vienna, where one could join the celebrated Orient Express from Paris, and – at German prompting – a plan to extend the Turkish system as far as Baghdad and eventually to Basra and the Persian Gulf had been formulated. There were enormous problems to be overcome, of course, but by 1915 the line extended to within eighty kilometres of Diyarbakir, with gaps where tunnelling work had not been completed, and a section ran east from Aleppo as far as Nisibin (Nusaybin); some line had been laid north from Baghdad as far as Samarra, leaving a gap of approximately 500 kilometres. At that time the journey from Constantinople to Baghdad took 22 days. Prisoners of war were used to extend the line up to 1918, and it was finally completed in the 1920s, with American financing, as part of the so-called Chester Concession, by which time British Army engineers had already constructed a line from Baghdad to Basra, which was later extended to Kuwait. In the meantime a substantial network had also been constructed in Syria, reaching as far as Medina in the Hejaz (see Chapter 13).

20. 'Young Turks' – so-called because they were the successors to the earlier Young Ottoman movement – has come to mean the triumvirate which dominated during the Great War: Ismail Enver Pasha, the War Minister; Mehmet Talaat Pasha, the Minister of the Interior and later Grand Vizier, and Ahmet Jemal Pasha, who first served as Minister of the Marine and was later commander-in-chief in Syria. Enver and Jemal were both career army officers, Talaat – said to be the intellectual leader – an employee of the Post Office. Other notables included Javed Bey, the Finance Minister, and Said Halim, Grand Vizier until 1917. Enver became the spiritual leader of the group when he led the raid on the War Ministry which returned the Young Turks to power in 1913 (see Note 27, below), and cemented that position by leading the force which retook Adrianople. That same year he married Emine Naciye, a granddaughter of Sultan Abdul Mejid.

21. The *madrassas* were – and are, but not in Turkey – schools run by the *Ulema*, the religious establishment, outside the control of a government. They focused on the study of the Qur'an, which was customarily committed to memory in its entirety, and on other aspects of Islam including Sharia law and the *Haditha*, the recorded deeds and sayings of the Prophet, which are accorded the same degree of respect as the Holy Book itself.

22. The *Kafes*, the original gilded cage, was established in 1618, when Osman II succeeded his mentally retarded uncle, Mustafa I, and consigned him to it; it then served as a holding cell for one who might conceivably succeed to the throne, a desirable alternative to the customary fratricide (succession in the empire was to the next-oldest

male member of the dynasty, not necessarily from father to son). By the 1870s the *Kafes* took the physical form of a grand apartment in the Dolmabahche Palace.

23. 'Pasha', probably derived from 'Padishah', was a title, a degree of nobility; there were four ranks, of which the highest was reserved for the sultan. 'Bey' was a lower degree.

24. However, their writ ran no further than the reach of their battleships' guns, the Senussi under Sayyid Ahmed ash-Sharif (see Chapter 13) having waged a campaign of resistance which endured for many years.

25. Because they were unable to send an army; they had no means to transport one by sea, and the British in Egypt blocked the land route.

26. Greece had gone to war with Turkey as recently as 1897, an inconsequential affair which sprang out of a revolt by ethnic Greeks against the Turkish rulers of Crete. The war lasted thirty-two days and was characterised by the total ineptitude of both Crown Prince Constantine and the Turkish commander-in-chief, Edhem Pasha; it achieved precisely nothing.

27. The loss of Libya to Italy had had a deleterious effect on the CUP, and it had been forced out of office in July 1912, to be replaced by the Liberal Union, an expedient political coalition which was neither liberal nor even remotely united. The interregnum was brief, for six months later, when it became known that the Liberal Union was ready to cede Adrianople to Bulgaria, the most ambitious of the Young Turks, Enver Pasha (personally; he led a raid on the War Ministry during the course of which the minister, Nazim Pasha, was shot dead, and Kamil Pasha, the Grand Vizier, was threatened with the same if he did not resign his post), launched a *coup d'état* and the CUP came back to power, this time with Şevket Pasha at the head of the government as Grand Vizier and with Enver in Nazim's place. Şevket was assassinated in retaliation for the murder of Nazim just hours after the Treaty of London was signed. The Young Turks' coup of 23 January has become known as the Sublime Porte Incident *(Bab-i Ali Baskini).*

28. Which she subsequently lost (to Greece) in the aftermath of WW1.

29. Some argue for a different, simpler and more conventional, cause: that Britain, having by now finally settled any differences it may have had with Russia in a treaty signed in 1907, no longer needed to keep Turkey even, so to speak, on the back burner as a potential counterweight, which begs several questions of its own as to quite what weight the British government thought the Turks now carried.

30. Enver served as Military Attaché in Berlin from 1909 to 1911; his pro-German position was established then.

31. Indeed, it is said that in late May Talaat had approached a very unlikely would-be ally: Sergei Sazonov, Russia's Foreign Minister. Nothing came of it, and it is generally thought that the approach was no more than a smokescreen. However, the British Official History of the Gallipoli campaign adds an interesting footnote: it suggests that on 5 August, the day after Britain declared war on Germany (and three days after the Turks had signed their treaty with Germany), Enver Pasha renewed this approach, suggesting a Russo-Turkish alliance to the Russian military attaché in Constantinople, Gen. Leontev. Leontev and de Giers, the ambassador, were convinced of his sincerity, and pleaded with the Russian government to accept, to no avail. The Russian government did not see fit to inform its allies of this approach; it became common knowledge only in 1924.

32. This time, rather than a simple mutually supportive treaty, the suggestion was that the Entente should back Turkey's claim to the Aegean islands which Italy – still, if increasingly shakily, aligned with Germany and Austria-Hungary – had annexed, and that as a quid pro quo, the empire would formally ally itself with Britain, France and Russia.

33. It stemmed from the fact that the Ottoman navy had been instrumental in the deposition of his predecessor, Abdul Aziz; his preferred residence – the Beylerbey Sarayi which Abdul Aziz had built – fronted onto the Bosporus, and was thus horribly vulnerable to hostile warships.

34. And the Imperial Russian navy, alive to the fact that Turkish battleships were as likely to operate in the Black Sea as in the Aegean, joined in too, ordering three dreadnoughts of the Imperatritsa Mariya class built at Nikolayev (Mikolayiv), its main ship-building centre on the Black Sea; none were completed prior to the start of WW1.

35. A second ship, to have been known as the *Fatik*, was ordered from Vickers on 29 April 1914, for delivery three years later; her keel was laid on 11 June, but work was suspended when war broke out. She was later broken up on the slipway.

36. Her guns were to come from Bethlehem Steel in the United States. *Salamis* remained incomplete when the Great War began; the project was abandoned, the guns were sold to the Royal Navy and monitors – shallow-draught gun platforms designed for shore bombardment – were built to accommodate them. They soon found their intended targets, for all four ships – named after generals: *Abercrombie, Havelock, Raglan* and *Roberts* – were to see action against the Ottomans in the Dardanelles campaign.

37. *Crna Ruka*; Officially, 'Unification or Death', *Ujedinjenje ili smrt.* Founded in 1901, it embraced assassination as a means of reaching its political goals.

38. Individual declarations of war came sporadically as the conflict became global, the last coming on the the penultimate day of the conflict, 10 November 1918, when a new government in Rumania declared war on Germany, rather unnecessarily.

39. It is to be presumed that Wangenheim was fully up-to-date with the German government's position, vis-à-vis the Turks and war; he had returned from a visit to Berlin, to settle a recalcitrant mistress, only days before.

40. Though by some accounts they did, late on 1 August, offer to turn over to the *Kaiserliche Marine* one of the battleships due for delivery by Britain, and that may have been enough to sway Wangenheim. In fact, there was no question that the Turks actually meant to go ahead with the transfer of a ship which had, quite literally, been paid for by taking the bread from children's mouths; they were already aware, if not officially, that the ships had been seized.

41. Not only was the mobilisation premature, it was impossibly badly handled. Men were ordered to turn up forthwith at their appointed barracks with three days' rations; no arrangements had been made to feed or accommodate them, and within a week many – perhaps most – had drifted away in search of food and a place to sleep. They thus became de facto deserters, afraid to return to their homes or to their barracks, and only slowly and belatedly were arrangements made to re-accommodate them. Additionally, their call-up – and that of thousands of draught animals – seriously affected the agricultural community's ability to get in what should have been a bountiful harvest, and thus everybody suffered. This same ineptitude in conscripting men into the army was continued and, as David Fromkin has it, in his analysis of the origins and outcomes of the war in the Middle East, *A Peace to End All Peace*, 'set a terrible pattern [and] brought famine in good years as well as bad'.

42. Rear Adm. Ernest Troubridge's First Cruiser Squadron, loitering off Cephalonia with just that end in mind, could have intercepted them, but would almost certainly have been annihilated in the process; Troubridge chose the prudent path into which he believed he had been directed by a signal from Churchill. He was court-martialled as a result, but was acquitted of negligence in failing to pursue 'an enemy then flying'.

43. That was a fiction, too; *Goeben* remained on the German navy list, and her crew in

German pay, until 2 November 1918 when she was transferred to Ottoman ownership; *Breslau* never did become Turkish property, for she was lost when she sortied from the Dardanelles into the Aegean in *Goeben*'s company on 20 January, 1918.

44. And won substantial concessions. Germany agreed to assist in abolishing the capitulations (a protocol under which foreign nationals who committed crimes – of any sort – in the Empire were tried not under Ottoman law, but by consular courts applying their own nations' judicial standards and sanctions); mediate in Turkey's favour in the distribution of any spoils of war; not conclude any peace treaty unless any Turkish territory which might have been occupied was liberated; see to it that the Aegean islands were returned to Turkey should Greece enter the war and be defeated; ensure a redrawing of Turkey's border with Russia which would facilitate direct contact with Russian Muslims, and ensure that Turkey received a war indemnity.

45. It comprised most of the ships which had chased *Goeben* from one end of the Mediterranean to the other, now under the command of Vice-Adm. Sackville Carden.

46. The British Official History of the Gallipoli campaign attributes the action to the Turkish regional commandant, Col. Javad Bey, acting on the advice of his German mentor, Vice-Adm. Merten.

47. This was a lasting fear of Kemal's; as late as 1917, when he voiced his objections to Falkenhayn being given command of the Yildirim force, qv, it was based on his objections to Turkey's war being managed by German interests.

48. These were the first instalments of a loan totalling 100m marks (5m lire).

CHAPTER 2

1. Hulagu – a Christian – sacked Baghdad and Damascus, and was largely responsible for the locus of Arab civilisation shifting to Cairo.

2. The first European power to interest itself in the region was Portugal which, by the early seventeenth century, had established fortified trading posts on both shores of the Persian Gulf. The British appeared in 1622 and in 1763 established a Residency at Bushire. Later, when Napoléon led his army out of Egypt into Syria, the British became concerned that he would attempt to emulate Alexander the Great, and advance on India by way of Persia, but nothing came of it, and little more of a subsequent attempt by Tsar Paul, but following that latter 'diplomatic' pressure on the Persian rulers increased, and the state became a useful buffer.

3. 'Harboured' is exactly the right word; Russian hopes centred on obtaining access to an all-season port on the Persian Gulf.

4. APOC had been in private ownership until, on 17 June 1914, having secured conditional Treasury approval for the deal a month earlier, First Lord of the Admiralty Winston Churchill successfully put forward to the House of Commons the case for His Majesty's government obtaining a controlling interest in it; the necessary Act of Parliament received royal assent on 10 August. It acquired 51% of the company for £2.2m, and later paid £3.8m to purchase the rest of its equity. It subsequently merged it into British Petroleum (BP), another acquisition, this time by dint of wartime confiscation from Deutsche Bank, which used it as a vehicle for the sale of Rumanian oil in the UK. By the end of the century, and by then back in private ownership once more, BP would be the world's third-largest oil company.

5. The Royal Navy began experimenting with oil-firing in 1898. By October 1914 it had a total of 205 oil-fired surface warships either in commission or in construction – 10 battleships, 18 cruisers and 177 destroyers – as well as 83 diesel- or petrol-engined submarines. No other navy had oil-fired capital ships or cruisers, though most had oil-

fired destroyers, though the battleship *Nevada* was then in construction for the United States Navy.

6. Coal production in the Ottoman Empire (826,000 tons in 1914) was minuscule in comparison with that of Britain (292m tons) or Germany (277m tons).

7. While the official capital had been moved to Delhi (from Calcutta (Kolkotta) in 1911, the climate there was such that during the summer, everyone, from the Viceroy down, decamped to Simla (Shimla), in the foothills of the Himalayas, for as long as five to six months. Since its actual location matters not in the least, this account uses 'Delhi' throughout to mean either.

8. Somewhat surprisingly, Churchill was reluctant to see troops he believed were more urgently needed elsewhere allocated to the defence of the Abadan works. On a minute from the naval staff urging the despatch of such troops to the head of the Gulf, on 1 September, he had noted: 'Indian troops must be used at the decisive point. We shall have to buy our oil from elsewhere. The Turk can also be dealt with better at the centre. I have told Lord Crewe that Europe and Egypt have greater claims than we have on the Indian Army.'

9. That, at least, is the generally accepted version. There are other motives advanced: Sir Edmund Barrow, military secretary to the India Office, said (on 26 September) the operation was '*ostensibly* [italics added] to protect the oil installation, but in reality to notify the Turks that we mean business', as Paul K Davis points out in *Ends and Means – The British Mesopotamian Campaign and Commission.*

10. During the Great War the Indian Army sent seven expeditionary forces abroad: Force A – two infantry and two cavalry divisions – to Europe; B – two brigades – and C – five battalions – to East Africa; D to Mesopotamia; E – two divisions – and F – a mixed bag of reinforcements – to Egypt, and G to Gallipoli.

As initially constituted Force D was a single infantry division, which consisted of three infantry brigades, each of four battalions (three Indian, one British; each brigade had given up at least one battalion from its peacetime establishment); a field artillery brigade of three batteries and a mountain artillery brigade of two; a cavalry regiment; sappers and miners (and signallers, the Royal Engineers then having that additional responsibility); pioneers and medical services including four field ambulances, a clearing hospital and base hospitals, for a total of almost 15,000 men plus camp followers.

Nominally, each Indian battalion had 13 British officers, 17 Indian officers – even the most senior of whom was subordinate to the most junior British officer – and 840 other ranks, up from the peacetime establishment of 723; British battalions were somewhat larger (a British infantry company of this period was much larger than that of modern times, comprising four platoons each of sixty-six riflemen plus a small headquarters; four companies, plus a headquarters, made up a battalion), with a nominal total of 32 officers and 991 other ranks. A cavalry regiment consisted of three or four squadrons (Indian regiments) each of 162 officers and men, organised into four troops of thirty-eight under a subaltern.

11. Under the command of Brig.-Gen. Walter Delamain, it comprised 2nd Dorset Regiment, 20th Duke of Cambridge's Own Infantry (Brownlow's Punjabis; henceforth, 20th Punjabis), 104th Wellesley's Rifles and 117th Maharattas, together with 1st Indian Mounted Artillery Brigade.

12. Under the command of Maj.-Gen. CI Fry, it consisted of 2nd Norfolk Regiment, 7th Duke of Connaught's Own Rajputs, 110th Maharatta Light Infantry and 120th Rajputana Infantry, together with 48th Pioneers, 10th Brigade, Royal Field Artillery, and two squadrons of light cavalry. This contingent also included the divisional commander and his staff and divisional and support troops. There were supernumerary

British personnel present too, notably Sir Percy Cox, the Political Officer, and his staff.

13. Under the command of Brig.-Gen. WH Dobie, it comprised 1st Oxfordshire and Buckinghamshire Light Infantry, 22nd Punjabis, 103rd Maharatta Light Infantry and 119th Infantry (the Multan Regiment).

14. *Ocean* had been allowed to remain in the Persian Gulf after she had delivered her charges for fear that the German commerce raider SMS *Emden*, then active in the Indian Ocean, had been ordered to Basra. When *Emden* was sunk, by HMS *Sydney* off the Cocos Islands on 9 November, *Ocean* was withdrawn. With curious symmetry, some of the first British troops to become involved in ground operations during Operation Iraqi Freedom, the invasion of Iraq in 2003, were men of 40 and 42 Commando, Royal Marines, who came ashore near the tip of the Al Fao Peninsula from a recently commissioned helicopter assault ship, HMS *Ocean*.

15. *Miner* had previously been the yacht of HM Consul-General at Baghdad. She was now armed with one 12-pounder, one 3-pounder and a Maxim. The other armed vessels of the riverine force at this time were: *Comet* (one 3-pounder and 'three old Nordenfelts'); *Lewis Pelly* (two 3-pounders and one Maxim); *Shaitan* and *Sirdar-i-Naphte* (both steam paddle-tugs, with one 12-pounder and one Maxim) and the smaller *Mashona* (one 3-pounder). They were joined later by a number of tugs and three stern-wheelers, *Massoudieh*, *Muzaffri* and *Shushan*, the two former lightly armed, the latter with the weapons taken from *Miner*, which was decommissioned.

16. In all, the fighting between 6 November and the year's end cost the Turks perhaps as many as three thousand officers and men dead, wounded or taken prisoner. British losses totalled no more than five hundred dead and wounded.

17. 'So [the Lord God] drove out the man, and he placed at the east end of the Garden of Eden Cherubim, and a flaming sword which turned every way [surely, a good naive description of a Maxim gun on a swivel mount . . .], to keep the way of the tree of life.' Genesis IV, 24.

18. Under the command of Maj.-Gen. C Davison, it comprised 2nd Queen's Own Royal West Kent Regiment from the Julunder Brigade, 44th Merwaras and 90th Punjabis from the Mhow Brigade and 4th Rajputs; it arrived in theatre – together with the 16th Cavalry, which had already embarked at Bombay with Europe as its destination, and was simply rerouted – in the first week of February.

19. It was not just Turks who were moving east from Amara. Amongst their number was a German agent, Wilhelm Wassmuss, 'Wassmuss of Persia' or 'The German Lawrence', as he was perhaps inevitably to become known later. He was a career officer, who had joined the German Diplomatic Service in 1906 at the age of twenty-six. Appointed Consul-General at the Gulf port of Bushire (Bushehr) in 1913 (where Percy Cox was then also based), he had already spent some years in Persia, spoke Farsi, and had made the acquaintance of local tribal leaders. Wassmuss, convinced of the feasibility of inciting jihad amongst the Shia communities and nomads of southern Persia, was on his way back to the region from a series of meetings in Constantinople at which he had been given carte blanche – and a considerable sum in gold – to initiate an anti-British campaign among the local tribes. Cox had crossed swords with Wilhelm Wassmuss before, during his own time at Bushire, and apparently had a healthy respect for him. It would prove to be well merited, for he went on to become a most convincing thorn in the side of the British in southern Persia; within months it would prove necessary to divert troops to the region to combat his efforts, and eventually to mobilise a dedicated force, the South Persia Rifles (see Chapter 3, Note 22) to do so. Cox wasted no time in attempting to neutralise Wassmuss. He had learned of his impending return to Persia when British agents had raided the German Consulate in Bushire, and had

spread the word that he would pay good money for his capture. On his way south from the oilfields Wassmuss passed through Behbehan, where he and two companions were captured and held for ransom by the local headman. This khan sent word to Cox's people, who despatched a posse under Captain Edward Noel to bring the Germans in; when they reached Behbehan, it was to learn that Wassmuss had escaped. The affair was not a complete waste of time, however, for in the luggage he'd left behind was found a copy of a German Diplomatic Cypher, which eventually came into the possession of Rear Adm. Sir Reginald 'Blinker' Hall, the British Director of Naval Intelligence. (In fact, there is compelling evidence that the book was not found amongst Wassmuss' possessions, but amongst those of Dr Helmuth Listemann, the then German Consul at Bushire, who had been arrested, quite illegally, by Cox's successor, CJ Edmonds. The story of Wassmuss' involvement was put about as a smoke screen.) In any event, Hall's staff used the key to good effect, most famously in decoding 'the Zimmerman Telegram', an act which played a pivotal role in finally bringing the United States of America into the war. See Barbara Tuchman's justly acclaimed study under that title.

20. Under the command of Brig.-Gen. R Wapshare, it consisted of 1/4th Hampshire Regiment from the Rawalpindi Brigade, 11th Rajputs from the Presidency Brigade in Calcutta, 66th Punjabis from Rangoon in Burma (Myanmar), and the 67th Punjabis from 2nd Quetta Infantry Brigade; it began arriving in theatre during the third week of March (save for the Rajputs, who were delayed for some weeks), and its 'pick-up' nature reflected the difficulties facing the Indian Army in meeting the demands being placed on it.

21. Under the command of Maj.-Gen. Charles Melliss, it consisted of 24th and 76th Punjabis and 2/7th Gurkhas. It arrived in theatre on 6 April. Its fourth battalion, 126th Baluchis, drawn mostly from Pathans from the North-West Frontier, had shown signs of being reluctant to fight co-religionists, and was not sent to Mesopotamia.

22. Gorringe was a favourite of Kitchener, who had promoted him in 1911, aged just forty-three, to be the youngest major-general in the Indian Army. By one description he was 'a large, arrogant, tactless, officious man', who was 'often loathed and distrusted', but was equally 'a relentless commander, cool under pressure and calm in a crisis'.

23. Askeri was succeeded as the Turkish commander in Iraq by Colonel Yussef Nurettin Bey, lately chief of police of the Basra *vilayet*, who remained in charge until command of the Sixth Army – reconstituted after the defeat at Shaiba – passed to the German Field Marshall Colmar von der Goltz (qv) in mid-October 1915, though he remained in effective day-to-day command until January 1917.

24. After the British Army failed to capitalise on initial success at the Battle of Neuve Chapelle in the Artois sector of the Western Front, in March, the British Commander-in-Chief, F.M. Sir John French, told Col. Charles Repington, the influential War Correspondent of *The Times*, anti-Liberal as always, that a shortage of artillery shells was to blame. *The Times* then mounted a massive campaign which resulted in the fall of Herbert Asquith's Liberal government, and its replacement (under the same Prime Minister) by a coalition, with David Lloyd George as Minister of Munitions.

25. The first aircraft, two Maurice Farman MF 11 Shorthorns, gifts from the Maharajah of Gwalior, arrived in Iraq in May 1915, together with a battered MF 7 Longhorn which had seen service in Egypt and was good for very little; the first operational flights were made on 1 June. They were operated chiefly by Australians who had volunteered for the assignment at the request of the Indian government and formed what was known as the Mesopotamian Half Flight of the Australian Flying Corps.

26. *Marmaris* was the only purpose-built Turkish warship of any size in Mesopotamia; the other armed vessels were no more than launches. She was armed with four 9-

pounder QF guns and two pom-poms, and mounted one 18-in torpedo tube.

27. In the entire operation, 1,773 prisoners were taken, together with 17 guns and large quantities of small arms and over a million rounds of ammunition, and four river steamers and several smaller craft were also secured, and two more destroyed.

28. Actually, just Melliss' 30th Brigade, plus divisional troops including one mountain-, one field- and one heavy battery, and some of the 33rd Brigade's Hampshires, with the 12th Brigade in reserve.

29. Capt. Wilfred Nunn, commander of HMS *Espiègle*, had been named the expeditionary force's Senior Naval Officer (SNO).

30. The 16th, 17th and the two battalions of the 30th, all the cavalry and most of the artillery.

31. The cavalry was accompanied by the two light armoured cars, the first time such vehicles had been deployed operationally in the Mesopotamia theatre. They proved their worth, both as mobile machine gun posts and also as impromptu ambulances, but also demonstrated their limitations; both were out of action by mid-afternoon on 28 September, with bent or broken axles.

32. The Official History suggests that the statistically unlikely proportion of dead to wounded was the result of the firing loopholes in the Turkish positions being designed to stop the defenders firing high; many of the wounded had been shot in the legs.

33. The descriptions of the conditions the men had to endure are horrific, and everyone concerned did everything in his power to prevent the situation coming to the notice of the British public. Eventually, however, reports reached the United Kingdom, and there was very considerable public outcry which resulted in a commission being sent to Mesopotamia to investigate. It comprised two men initially, Sir William Vincent, an Indian civil servant, and Maj.-Gen. AH Bingley; they were joined later by EA Rudsdale, a Red Cross Commissioner. Their report was published as an appendix to that of the Mesopotamia Commission, qv, Nixon and his Director of Medical Services – Maj.-Gen. William Babtie – coming in for the lion's share of the (very sturdy) criticism contained in it.

CHAPTER 3

1. The 34th Infantry Brigade (Brig.-Gen. EC Tidswell) comprised 1/5th Queen's Royal Regiment (West Surreys), 31st Punjabis, 112th Infantry and 114th Maharattas. The 35th Infantry Brigade (Brig.-Gen. GBH Rice) comprised 1/5th Buffs (East Kent Regiment), 37th Dogras, 97th Infantry and 102nd Grenadiers.

2. *Firefly* was the first of the new 'Fly' class river gunboats, fabricated in sections in the United Kingdom by Yarrow on the Clyde and assembled at Abadan. Known as China Gunboats to camouflage their destination, twelve were ordered initially, and four more were built later. They displaced ninety-eight tons and drew just 0.6m; armed with one 4-in, one 12-pounder, one 6-pounder, one 3-pounder and four or five machine guns, they were driven by single-screw propellers operating in a tunnel and could make 19km/h.

3. The point where the defensive line on that bank descended to the river lay at an artificial 'cut' dug in 1912, which eliminated a horse-shoe bend to the south; the defences were sited along the banks of this now dry watercourse.

4. The British remained unaware that the enemy had aircraft available to him until 1 January.

5. Including the guns' breech-blocks; unfortunately, the spare for *Firefly*'s 4-in gun, kept below decks, was overlooked in the confusion; this was to have serious repercussions

later when the Turks repaired her and put her back into commission.

6. According to a signal Townshend sent around noon on 5 December. 'Of infantry alone I have only about 7500 combatants,' he added. His tally did not include camp followers, of whom there were over four thousand.

7. His quartermaster disagreed. They had sixty days' rations for British troops, he said (but tea only for thirty-four).

8. He did not, at least not immediately – thinking, he claimed, by that means to keep up morale – and British troops continued to receive the full daily scale: 1lb of meat, 1lb of bread, 3oz of bacon, butter and cheese, 6oz of potato, 4oz of onion, 2½oz of sugar, 3oz of jam, 1oz of tea and ½oz of salt. By 8 March this had been reduced to 12oz of bread, 20oz of horse- or mulemeat and 1oz of jam; all else was exhausted. The bread ration was subsequently reduced further; by 18 March it stood at 8oz per day, and by 10 April at 6oz. By that time the ration for Indian troops was 5oz of barley meal and 4oz of whole barley plus 12oz of meat, which latter many refused to eat on religious grounds, despite the British government in India having gone to considerable lengths to obtain dispensations from religious leaders.

9. Once again, he did not, or at least not at that juncture, and that failure to put all foodstuffs under military control was clearly a very serious oversight. There was an alternative: expelling the native population; he suggested doing so, but Cox persuaded him against it on the grounds that if evicted, the women and children at least would experience serious hardship and perhaps die of exposure. Townshend said later that he regretted following Cox's advice – 'I always bitterly regretted my clemency' – for the Arabs proved extremely troublesome. Early on he had twelve men caught looting shot 'pour encourager les autres', and held more hostage, but that did little to settle his anxiety that the Arabs might rise against him.

10. They dug in shifts, night and day. The total length of trench, including communications trenches, is difficult to estimate; the straight-line length totalled perhaps six kilometres, and communications trenches accounted for considerably more, but none were straight lines, of course, and traverses and dugouts would have at least doubled the amount of material which had to be shifted. In addition, the four existing blockhouses had to be replaced by artillery-proof redoubts. Work began in earnest on 5 December, and was finished, in the main, by Christmas Day. Many of the positions were subsequently abandoned when the river rose.

11. The 36th Infantry Brigade (Brig.-Gen. G Christian) comprised 1/6th Devonshire Regiment and 26th, 62nd and 82nd Punjabis.

12. The 28th (Frontier Force) Brigade comprised 2nd Leicestershire Regiment, 51st and 53rd Sikhs and 56th Rifles.

13. Latterly Adjutant-General in India, he was sent to Mesopotamia to command the 3rd Division, its original commander, Lt.-Gen. Sir Henry Watkis (and his staff) having remained in France. On 8 December he was appointed to command the Tigris Corps: all British forces on the Tigris above Ezra's Tomb, including those besieged at Kut. He and Townshend were friends of long standing, and, with ironic symmetry, it had been Aylmer who had relieved Townshend at Chitral.

14. Younghusband was elevated to command the 7th Division, his place at the head of the 28th Brigade was taken by Nixon's GSO1, Kemball, who was himself replaced by Maj.-Gen. AW Money, drafted in from India.

15. Severe problems with the system had become evident as soon as Force D had begun to push upriver from Basra. It was not until Sir George Buchanan, who had run the port of Rangoon for many years, was appointed Director-General of Port Administration in December 1915 that the situation improved at all, and then it did so only very slowly.

As the Official History notes, there were some 10,000 troops at Basra on 21 January, the day Aylmer fought and lost at Hanna (see below); they could not be sent up to the front because there was no transport to keep them supplied there. It is probably safe to surmise that their presence would have made all the difference to the outcome. For the want of a nail ...

16. Its composition was soon to change. When fully assembled, the 7th (Meerut) Division, under the command of Maj.- Gen. Sir George Younghusband, comprised the 19th Brigade (Brig.-Gen. EC Peebles; 1st Seaforth Highlanders, 28th Punjabis, 92nd Punjabis, 125th Rifles), the 21st Brigade (Brig.-Gen. CE Norie; 2nd Black Watch, 6th Jats, 9th Bhopal Infantry, 41st Dogras), the 28th Brigade (Maj.-Gen. GV Kemball; 2nd Leicestershire Regiment, 51st Sikhs, 53rd Sikhs, 56th Rifles) and divisional troops. The 35th (and the 36th) were held as corps troops until May, and were then combined with the 37th Brigade to form the 14th Division.

17. The 3rd (Lahore) Division was under the command of Maj.-Gen. H d'U Keary; it comprised the 7th Brigade (Maj.-Gen. RG Egerton; 1st Connaught Rangers, 27th Punjabis, 89th Punjabis, 128th Pioneers), the 8th Brigade (Lt.-Col. FPS Dunsford; 1st Manchester Regiment, 2nd Rajputs, 47th Sikhs, 59th Rifles), the 9th Brigade (Brig.-Gen. LWY Campbell; 1st Highland Light Infantry, 1/1st Gurkhas, 11/9th Gurkhas, 93rd Infantry) and divisional troops. It was not completely assembled in Mesopotamia until mid-January, six weeks later than planned.

18. Previously he had relied on buying up food stocks, with – perhaps predictably – poor results.

19. These were the 37th, 41st and 42nd Infantry Brigades. They were expected to leave India as soon as the twelve additional 'garrison' battalions to replace them – eight of them Indian units then in Egypt – arrived, and to be in theatre by mid-March. In the event, only the 37th arrived on – in fact, actually slightly ahead of – schedule; the 41st and 42nd were not in the theatre until April.

20. In practice the new arrangement soon proved to be unworkable, and India's last vestige of responsibility for Mesopotamian operations was transferred to Whitehall six months later, on 18 July.

21. The Turkish defeat there is usually given as the reason more troops freed at Gallipoli were not sent to Mesopotamia.

22. The task was entrusted to Sir Percy Sykes, a brigadier-general in the Indian Army, who had excellent connections in Persia, having served there in a variety of capacities on and off since 1893. Sykes landed at Bandar Abbas in March 1916, with three British and three Indian officers, twenty picked NCOs and a troop of cavalry, and began recruiting men to form what would become the South Persia Rifles. By this time the Swedish-officered, German-leaning Persian gendarmerie had lost cohesion and its remaining men were on the point of taking to banditry; Sykes took the bold step of taking them into his force. He never was able to capture Wassmuss, but most of his agents were neutralised. The Qashqai, a nomadic tribe whose territory lay astride the trade route between Bushire and Shiraz, were another matter. Sykes managed to keep them in check until the spring of 1918, chiefly by means of bribery, but then a short, sharp tribal war, fomented by the Teheran government, broke out; Sykes brought in additional troops from Baluchistan, and eventually prevailed.

23. In fact, Turkish accounts, gathered after the war's end, show that the Turks were unaware of the British advance until the artillery barrage opened up.

24. The 13th, commanded by Maj.-Gen. Stanley Maude, was a division of Kitchener's 'New Army'. It comprised the 38th Infantry Brigade (Brig.-Gen. JW O'Dowda; 6th King's Own (Royal Lancashire Regiment), 6th East Lancashire Regiment, 6th Prince of

Wales's Volunteers (the South Lancashire Regiment) and 6th Loyal North Lancashire Regiment), the 39th Brigade (Brig.-Gen. W de S Cayley; 9th Royal Warwickshire Regiment, 9th Worcestershire Regiment and 7th Prince of Wales's (the North Stafford-shire Regiment); the brigade lacked its fourth battalion (7th Gloucestershire Regiment) until 19 April; it had been quarantined at Basra) and the 40th Brigade (Brig.-Gen. AC Lewin; 8th Cheshire Regiment, 8th Royal Welch Fusiliers, 4th South Wales Borderers and 5th Duke of Edinburgh's (the Wiltshire Regiment)), plus divisional troops. As in all the New Army divisions they included a pioneer battalion (8th Welch Regiment).

25. *Mantis* was the first of the Insect-class, known, for purposes of deception, as the Large China Gunboats. Twelve were ordered in February 1915, from five small British shipbuilders, for service on the Danube. Designed by Yarrow, they were in effect small monitors, armed with two 6-in QF guns, one forward and one aft, two 12–pounders and six machine guns. They were twin-engined, driven by propellers in tunnels, and could make fourteen knots (28km/h). Four operated on the east coast of the United Kingdom; four went to Port Said, and the remaining four – *Gnat*, *Mantis*, *Moth* and *Tarantula* – were sent to the Persian Gulf for service in Mesopotamia.

26. In fact, what Lake ordered was the effort to be stepped up, for the Royal Flying Corps' 30 Squadron had been attempting to supply the besieged garrison since 4 January. BE2Cs were used, the Lewis guns and ammunition in the observer's cockpit having been removed, to fly the first air supply operations in British military aviation history. During March and April, supplies of all kinds were air-lifted from the field base at Al Ora, a distance of thirty-seven kilometres, the packages being dropped from an altitude of 5,000ft. The consignments included flour, sugar, salt, dates, medical stores, wireless parts, engine parts, maps and even a mill stone weighing 32kg (70lbs). Corn was free-dropped by placing the full sack in a larger sack which received the grain when the smaller burst on impact. The effort was prodigious. During the last two weeks of April, when it was at its most intense, forty flights delivered eight tons, some 1,500kg (3,300lbs) being dropped on the first day alone. The RNAS also participated in the relief effort, two of its aircraft less suitable being shot down and the pilots killed in the process.

27. He hoped to strike the sort of deal Junot had made at Lisbon in 1808, he said, or Masséna at Genoa, eight years earlier. By negotiating with the British – notably Dal-rymple and Burrard, who were later pilloried for the decision, as, temporarily, was Wellesley, who had nothing to do with it – Andoche Junot secured the release of his 20,000 men with their arms and kit intact. Under the Convention of Cintra they were taken off in British ships and landed in France, to fight another day (and, largely, die during the retreat from Moscow). One cannot help but think Lisbon a rather more attractive bargaining chip than Kut . . .

28. Despite over two hundred tons of more suitable rations being available aboard the *Julnar.*

29. One successful – albeit bizarre – attempt is documented in *The Road to En-Dor.*

30. And was even knighted whilst in captivity as a reward for the tenacity he showed in commanding the 6th Division during the siege. Others thought less well of his conduct, and he came in for much negative criticism for an attitude which was widely characterised as supine, if not actually collaborative.

CHAPTER 4

1. Sir William Robertson was still minded to order a withdrawal to Amara as late as 12 September, and reiterated on 30 September, in a cable to Duff, that Lake's mission

remained 'to protect the oilfields and pipelines in the vicinity of the Karun River and maintain our occupation and control of the Basra *vilayet*, and to deny hostile access to the Persian Gulf and Southern Persia'.

2. The 14th Division, under the command of Maj.-Gen. Sir Raleigh Egerton, comprised the 35th Brigade (Brig.-Gen. WM Thomson; 1/5th Buffs (East Kent Regiment), 37th Dogras, 3rd Brahmans, 2/14th Gurkhas); the 36th Brigade (Brig.- Gen. LB Walton; 1/4th Hampshires, 26th Punjabis, 62nd Punjabis, 82nd Punjabis) and the 37th Brigade (Brig.-Gen. FJ Fowler; 1/4th Devonshire Regiment, 36th Sikhs, 45th Sikhs, 1/2nd Gurkhas).

3. The 15th Division, under the command of Maj.-Gen. Sir Harry Brooking, comprised the 12th Brigade (Brig.-Gen. FPS Durnford; 1/5th Queen's Royal Regiment (West Surrey), 43rd Infantry, 90th Punjabis), the 34th Brigade (Brig.-Gen. EC Tidswell; 2nd Queens Own Royal West Kent, 31st Punjabis, 112th Infantry, 114th Maharattas) and the 42nd Brigade (Brig.-Gen. FG Lucas; 1/14th Dorsets, 2/5th Gurkhas, 2/6th Gurkhas).

4. The 41st Infantry Brigade (Brig.-Gen. A Cadell) comprised 1/4th Somerset Light Infantry, 6th Jats, 2/103rd Maharattas and 2/10th Gurkhas.

5. 1st Ox and Bucks LI; 2/7th Gurkhas; 2/119th Infantry; 20th Punjabis.

6. Gorringe returned to Europe, and the Western Front, where he proved to be a less than inspiring commander of the 47th (2nd London) Division. He was the only officer in the British Army who began WW1 as a major-general and ended it as such (his temporary promotion to lieutenant-general having expired; he was promoted substantively postwar, however, and finished his career in that rank), in command of a division. However, in his autobiography Field-Marshal Bernard Law Montgomery, who served as his senior staff officer in 1918, attributed the success of his own system of battle-management to the experience he gained with Gorringe's division.

7. I Indian Army Corps consisted of the 3rd and 7th Infantry Divisions with their associated divisional artillery and support echelons.

8. III Indian Army Corps consisted of the 13th and 14th Infantry Divisions with their associated divisional artillery and support echelons. Marshall had commanded at brigade (and briefly a variety of divisions) at Gallipoli.

9. Drowned when the cruiser HMS *Hampshire*, aboard which he was travelling to Russia, hit a mine laid by the German submarine *U 75* off the Orkneys. Kitchener's mission to Russia was quite unnecessary, and had been devised by Asquith as a way of sidelining his War Minister, who had gone into a decline, many of his duties having been taken over by Robertson as CIGS. There had been warnings of enemy mine laying off the Orkneys, Naval Intelligence having broken the German code, but Adm. Jellicoe's staff misread them and their commander subsequently covered the fact up. It was not until 1985 that the truth came out.

10. Including an average of 11,000 officers and men *per month* invalided out of the country during June, July and August. Reinforcing drafts were particularly vulnerable, and many men found themselves back in India without ever having seen action.

11. Lake had asked for more heavy artillery but had to make do with twenty-four 4.5-in howitzers to replace his antiquated 5-in, plus an additional battery of 60-pounder guns. Maude was later sent extra field batteries of 18-pounders and some anti-aircraft guns, together with motor tractors, some of them of the new 'caterpillar' type, to improve the mobility of the heavy batteries. He was also sent additional and improved aircraft and crews to redress the balance of air power, which had fallen temporarily into Turkish hands with the arrival of modern machines including Albatrosses and Fokkers. The shortage of machine guns was corrected too; by the time Maude was ready to go onto the offensive once more, each infantry brigade had a machine gun

company (made up exclusively of British personnel) armed with sixteen Vickers guns, and each battalion had eight of the lighter Lewis guns. Stokes and lighter two-inch mortars were also deployed, the former at brigade and the latter at battalion level.

12. The 36th and 45th; of a total of 17 British officers, 30 Indian officers and 1,180 ORs engaged, 16, 28 and 988 respectively were killed or wounded.

13. The three large gunboats *Mantis*, *Moth* and *Tarantula*, and the smaller *Gadfly* and *Butterfly*.

14. It was that of the Prophet Mohammed's barber and confidant, who was buried there.

15. Enver, taking a personal hand in the affair, had ordered Halil to employ XIII Corps on the left bank of the Tigris before Baghdad, and place XVIII Corps on the right, ignoring the fact that the former could never hope to reach the region in time, and that the latter was but a shadow of what it had been.

16. The lake has long been drained and built over, and no trace remains, but the course of the Mahsudiya Canal which linked it to the Tigris can still be discerned in modern aerial photographs.

17. Kazim Karabekir had advised retreating directly to Istabulat, to cover Samarra, and fight no intermediate actions along the way; Halil disagreed. Kazim's preferred course was certainly the more sound, but Halil, having surrendered Baghdad, was unwilling to give up more territory, and ordered him replaced by Şevket Pasha, who was his inferior as a tactician but would follow orders. Events were to prove Kazim right; all the two actions the Turks fought between Baghdad and Istabulat really achieved was to diminish their strength without materially delaying the British advance.

18. He had some 4,600 infantry and 46 guns. Maude seems to have believed Keary's column numbered around 8,000, having 'overlooked the weak strengths of the units composing it', as the Official History has it; they were at little more than 50 per cent of establishment. That misunderstanding was to have important consequences.

19. The Official History refers to 'his well-known habit – disinterested and altruistic though it undoubtedly was – of personally controlling details generally left to subordinates'.

20. Alexeyev later told Robertson that the VII Caucasian Corps' advance towards Mosul – which, of course, had made very little headway – was also to be abandoned, and that it would attempt to hold the line Ruwandiz–Sulaimaniya–Qizil Ribat instead.

21. One regiment arrived at Samarra on 6 April, a second joined it a week later, and a third was close behind.

22. The British were unable to use the line, the Turks having removed all the locomotives and rolling stock when they evacuated Baghdad, until 30 wagons were taken at Balad, and were harnessed to mules.

23. He was isolated, having chosen to remain in his headquarters at Sindiya, and was out of direct touch with the battlefield due to a shortage of telegraph cable.

24. It had a further effect: as AJ Barker noted, 'on the rock-strewn plain the shrapnel and shell splinters soon proved to be much more lethal than ever they had been on the yielding clay of the Tigris valley.'

25. Maude had also heard from Radatz that the water level in the Diyala had risen to the point that it was now unfordable, and would remain so for at least a month; this gave the Turks a measure of security from attack by the Russians, should they recover and go onto the offensive, and allowed Ali Ihsan Pasha some leeway in his own manoeuvring.

26. The Dujail Canal was a formidable obstacle in its own right; six to eight metres wide and holding two metres of water, it had steep banks twelve metres high in places.

27. This, of course, was the railhead.

28. Which achieved some notoriety as the location of the last hiding place of the deposed President of Iraq, Saddam Hussein, in 2004.

29. It is worth noting that all their senior officers had been killed or disabled early in the action.

CHAPTER 5

1. Wedgwood was a serving officer in the Royal Navy, and had acquitted himself with distinction at Gallipoli. See Chapter 11.

2. The charge against Gen. Sir Edmund Barrow was quietly dropped after he resigned his post.

3. Whose conduct had been the subject of a separate inquiry; see Note 33, Chapter 2.

4. Later Field Marshal Sir Archibald Wavell, British commander-in-chief in first the Middle East and then India during WW2.

5. Its 35th Brigade had now been replaced by the 50th Brigade (Brig.-Gen. AW Andrew; 1st Oxfordshire and Buckinghamshire Light Infantry, 6th Jats, 24th Punjabis and 1/97th Infantry), and the others made up to full strength, the 12th by the addition of the 2/39th Garhwal Rifles and the 42nd by the 1/5th Gurkhas.

6. Though in early June he had requested nine extra batteries of six 18-pounders, one of four 60-pounders and two four-gun 6-in howitzer batteries; these were promised before the end of August. In addition, at the end of the month Monro had promised six extra infantry battalions, out of twenty-four then being raised and trained in India in response to a request from London. They were 13th Rajputs, 49th Bengalis, 83rd Infantry, 85th Burma Infantry, 104th Rifles and 126th Baluchistan Infantry; they, too, reached Basra in August, but required substantial extra training before they could be presumed to be ready for combat.

7. Under the command of Maj.-Gen. W Gilman (who became Marshall's chief of staff, and was replaced by Brig.-Gen. GAJ Leslie), it comprised the 34th Brigade from the 15th Division, now under the command of Brig.-Gen. AG Wauchope; the 51st Brigade (Brig.-Gen. RJT Hildyard; 1st Highland Light Infantry, 1/2nd Rajputs, 14th Sikhs and 1/10th Gurkhas) and the 52nd Brigade (Brig.-Gen. FA Andrew; 1/6th Hampshire Regiment, 45th Sikhs, 84th Punjabis and 1/113th Infantry).

8. Light Armoured Motor Batteries (LAMBs). A total of six saw service in Mesopotamia (though some did not reach the theatre until early 1918) and another went to Persia later, to accompany Dunsterforce; they were normally equipped with eight Rolls-Royces, modified versions of the Silver Ghost touring car. With 9mm steel armour the cars weighed 3.5 tons and carried a crew of four; a 50bhp engine gave them a top speed of 95km/h. They mounted a single Vickers gun in a revolving turret.

9. Bringing the total to fifteen, each equipped with eight 3in mortars. These recently developed weapons – simple tubes with a base-plate and a steadying bipod – gave individual infantry units a close-support capability which could be deployed from the front-line trenches; they fired a 4.8-kg high-explosive bomb to a maximum of just over 700 (and a minimum of under 100) metres, variations in range being achieved by a combination of changes in the projectile charge and the angle of the tube.

10. In this he was doubtless much influenced by Robertson's injunction to hold the Baghdad *vilayet* and not commit himself to further offensive action. Whether this was actually the right strategy is open to some doubt; Erickson, for one, suggests in his history of the Ottoman Army in WW1, *Ordered to Die*, that had he pursued Halil past Tikrit, even to Mosul, there was every likelihood of the Turkish Sixth Army having

collapsed. He describes Maude's decision as a godsend to Halil and the Turkish General Staff, and 'one of the great windfalls of the First World War'.

11. Including compiling accurate maps of the areas he held and those in which he would in future have to fight, from aerial photographs covering several hundred square miles taken by the RFC. During the period the corps' presence in the theatre was augmented by a further squadron, No. 63, and was reorganised as the 31st Wing.

12. If one discounts his occupation of Balad Ruz, to threaten Mandali, in late June, which was accomplished without resistance.

13. Troops and supplies were moved downriver on roughly constructed flat-bottomed craft called *shakturs*, and rafts *(keleks)*; timber was so scarce that these crude craft were then broken up and carried overland back to Jerablus for reuse. It took up to six weeks to reach Ramadi from there – a distance of over seven hundred kilometres – by this method, and considerably more for the return journey.

14. This was of particular importance since Brooking's force, like Haldane's, was partially mechanised, with ten Fiat lorries and 350 Ford vans. It also had fifty motor ambulances.

15. The course of the Diyala as it ran in 1917 is now impossible to discern, a large artificial lake having been created by damming the river north of Al Mansuriya

16. The British ration strength in Mesopotamia then stood at almost 255,000 all-ranks, plus 158,500 followers; on the Baghdad front combatants numbered 3,500 cavalry, 66,000 infantry and 302 guns. At this time, we should not forget, British strength on the Western Front was short by around a hundred thousand men, by Haig's estimate, and there was the ever-present danger, now that the Bolshevik government had replaced the Provisional in Russia, of as many as forty German divisions being switched to the war in France. This would be offset to a degree by the arrival of twelve divisions of American troops, promised by the following May (and a further twelve by December), but that would still leave a very significant shortfall.

17. The 18th Infantry Division comprised the 53rd Infantry Brigade (Brig.-Gen. GAF Sanders; 1/9th Middlesex Regiment, 1/89th Punjabis, 1/3rd Gurkhas and 1/7th Gurkhas); the 54th Infantry Brigade (Brig.-Gen. RW Nightingale; 115th Royal West Kent Regiment, 1/39th Garhwalis, 25th Punjabis and 52nd Sikhs) and the 55th Infantry Brigade (Brig.-Gen. GM Morris; 115th East Surrey Regiment, 1/10th Jats, 1/94th Infantry and 116th Mahrattas), each with a machine gun company and a supply and transport company, plus the usual complement of cavalry, field artillery (with both 18-pounder guns and howitzers) and support troops.

18. And, under severe pressure from Haig, he persisted in that view even when news came of the Bolshevik government in Russia having sued for a separate peace, with all the dangers of Turkish reinforcement in Mesopotamia that posed.

19. There was a political element to that change; Wilson was brought back to London from France, where he had commanded a corps, to take over Eastern Command in September 1917; this gave him the ear of the Prime Minister, David Lloyd George, with whose view – that the Allies should mark time on the Western Front until the Americans arrived – he agreed, unlike Robertson.

20. As it still was, for the moment; the Royal Air Force came into being on 1 April 1918, when the Royal Flying Corps was amalgamated with the Royal Naval Air Service.

21. 'It is related that an Indian officer of the 21st Cavalry charged a Turkish officer, who was bombing our men, and took his head clean off with one stroke (Cut Three on the right)', the Official History notes, matter-of-factly.

22. During the Ludendorff Offensives, employing troops released from the Eastern Front.

23. In addition, before Marshall went onto the offensive again, in September, he had been instructed to give up twelve battalions to be transferred to Salonika; each infantry brigade in the 14th, 15th, 17th and 18th Divisions gave up one, and they were thus reduced to three battalions each.

24. This was probably a considerable overstatement. Erickson, quoting Turkish official archives, tells us that less than nine thousand Turkish soldiers and around 2,250 civilians actually returned home from Russian PoW camps.

25. On 30 July 1918, just prior to a War Cabinet meeting on the subject of war aims, that body's Secretary, Sir William Hankey, wrote to Sir Eric Geddes, First Lord of the Admiralty, to make a very important point, saying: 'The retention of the oil-bearing regions in Mesopotamia and Persia in British hands, as well as a proper strategic boundary to cover them, would appear to be a first-class British war aim.' Foreign Secretary Arthur Balfour took that line during the meeting which followed, and Hankey's suggestion was adopted. From then on, the occupation of Mosul before hostilities in the theatre came to an end became a matter of high priority; when it was found to be impossible, Marshall – at the insistence of the War Cabinet – simply bent the rules, and occupied the city anyway, after the armistice was in force.

26. Allenby's troops had reached Damascus on 1 October, and he was now gearing up for an advance on Aleppo.

27. The Darb-al-Khail Pass is approximately twenty kilometres south-east of the Fatha Gorge, the Ain Nukhaila roughly twice that distance.

28. This was no simple undertaking. Even at this season, when the river was at its lowest, the water was deep and fast-flowing, and the ford itself consisted of a narrow submerged causeway covered by a metre and a half of water; during the crossing several men drowned and horses were lost.

29. It proved to be the 13th Infantry Regiment.

30. It is evident from the conflicting accounts in individual battalions' war diaries that the attack had lost cohesion if, indeed, it ever had any on 29 October. Units were separated and out of contact with their neighbours, their own men scattered and uncoordinated. In consequence it was very difficult to organise any concerted effort, even in terms of artillery bombardment. During the night and the early hours of 30 October order was gradually restored, and the infantry battalions brought back into mutual contact.

31. Clause 7, which gave the Allies the right to occupy any strategic point, and Clause 16, by which the Ottoman government agreed to surrender all garrisons in Hejaz, Asir, Yemen, Syria and Mesopotamia to the nearest Allied commander.

32. Clause 7 failed to define a strategic point; the Turkish Sixth Army was a *field* army, not a garrison, and thus did not fall into the category defined by Clause 16.

CHAPTER 6

1. And in the Crimean War, a quarter-century earlier. They included Ardahan; Artvin; the important port of Batum; Kars, Oltu and Sarikamiş, a nondescript barely-a-village which took on a new significance when it was chosen as the terminus for a branch line of the Trans-Caucasian Railway.

2. Nikolai Nikolaevich Yudenich, unarguably the most competent general on either side of the conflict in the Caucasus, graduated from the Aleksandrovsky Military Academy at the age of 19, in 1881, and the General Staff Academy six years later. He attained regimental command in 1902, and fought and was wounded in the Russo-Japanese War. He was promoted to General and given command of a brigade in 1905,

and in 1907 was appointed Deputy Chief of Staff of the Caucasus region. In the
aftermath of the March Revolution he fell out of favour. Some accounts state he resigned
his post, others that he was dismissed for insubordination, transferred to a meaningless
post in central Russia and then resigned. He was succeeded by Przevalski, whose tenure
was short-lived.

3. The Plastun Brigades were Cossack infantry. Fighting dismounted was looked down
upon – with no pun intended – by the Cossacks, and the Plastun Brigades were drawn
from the poorer peasants, though that proved to be no barrier to combat efficiency.
Bergmann had a total of 37 battalions of infantry, 36 *sotni* (squadrons) of cavalry and
120 guns of all types.

4. 14 infantry battalions, 36 *sotni* and 52 guns.

5. Infantry divisions consisted of four regiments, each of four battalions. Turkistanski
brigades also consisted of four regiments, but only two or three (smaller) battalions
strong. Plastun Brigades had six battalions each.

6. By the Gregorian calendar in use in the West; by Russian reckoning, and the Julian
calendar, it was 19 October. Gregorian dates are used throughout.

7. And his disbelief became difficult to contain, apparently, as Enver went on to describe
how this was but the first step towards the union, under Turkish leadership, of the
entire Turan, a Persian term for a region which encompasses the whole of Central Asia,
from the Urals to the borders of China.

8. The *Top Yol* was known to the Russians – the Caucasian Army's Topographical Dept.
had described it in a paper of 1908 – but it was not thought practicable for the movement
of large bodies of troops, and was kept under surveillance only, by patrols of the border
guards from Bardiz.

9. It is unclear whether this is nominal roll, 'ration strength' or a mixture of both; for
instance, Erickson quotes the strength of X Corps and IX Corps in round figures, while
giving that of XI Corps as a much more precise 22,274.

10. The Jandarma had been created – under French tutelage, as the name suggests –
after the 1877–8 war with Russia. Units were to be found right across the Ottoman
Empire, but in greatest strength in the frontier areas of Eastern Anatolia and Kurdistan,
where they shared internal and border security duties with Frontier Guards units.
Essentially a militarised police force, they were well trained and disciplined, but were
armed with nothing heavier than mountain artillery and machine guns.

11. Returns from the Turkish General Staff put the actual figure at 118,660 regular
troops, with 218 artillery pieces and 73 machine guns.

12. Kazim Orbay, as he became. (He should not be confused with the Kazim Bey who
was then serving as II Corps' chief of intelligence, Kazim Karabekir; the latter had a
very illustrious career subsequently, though he was eventually to run foul of Enver's
ambitions, and we shall encounter him later in consequence.) Kazim Orbay had
married Enver's younger sister Mediha. Post-WW1 he served as Chief of Staff of
Afghanistan's army and later of the Army of the Turkish Republic. Hussein Rauf, qv,
was his brother.

13. Hafiz Hakki had been a contemporary of Enver Pasha at the Imperial Military
Academy; he had graduated top of the class, with Enver placed second. Hakki was
serving on the General Staff as deputy to Schellendorf on the outbreak of war (at which
point both men were actually in Berlin for 'consultations') and had produced a version
of the Primary Campaign Plan of his own the previous month. It was based on two
presumptions of global dimensions – that the Russians were paralysed by their defeat
in East Prussia, and that the Anglo-French were too busy on the Western Front to turn
their attentions elsewhere – and was very ambitious indeed, calling for a force three

corps strong to be landed on the Pontic coast of the Black Sea and advance along the littoral to take Batum and then turn on Tiflis, while the Third Army, in similar strength, would mount an offensive on Ardahan and – in conjunction with a further corps from Mesopotamia, and gendarmerie and reserve cavalry from east of Lake Van – into Azerbaijan. He added existing plans to attack Egypt with a two-corps force based in Syria to his own, but extended them to include an attack on the British coaling base at Aden, at the mouth of the Red Sea. His plan was deemed too ambitious, and was shelved. Hakki arrived in Erzurum two days before Enver, on 10 December, as a supernumerary with no position in the Third Army's command structure; however, he clearly had instructions from Enver, for he immediately began putting his plans for the Sarikamiş offensive into place, using Izzet's chief of staff, the German Lieutenant-Colonel Guse, as his medium.

14. Ahmet Fevzi should not be confused with another Fevzi Pasha, Mustafa – who went on to become Marshal Fevzi Çakmak, chief of the Turkish General Staff – whom we shall encounter elsewhere. Those who study Turkish affairs during this period tend to wish someone had anticipated Kemal Atatürk's initiative and introduced surnames earlier ...

15. The opening salvoes of the offensive were 'blue-on-blue', two of the Turkish columns which had approached Oltu from different directions firing on each other. Over a thousand casualties resulted, and Istomin was able to profit from the confusion.

16. Or, conceivably, gorging themselves ... The town's main claim to fame is as the birthplace of the *döner kebab.*

17. In fact, he refused to believe that X Corps was in the region at all.

18. He had also (just) heard of the defeat, by Stange's notionally inferior expeditionary force, of three battalions of Russian infantry at Ardahan on 25 December. Even though Stange failed to follow up on his victory, and merely sat, inactive, at Ardahan, rather than heading north into the Rioni Valley as he feared, this was enough to convince Myshlayevski that the entire hinterland of Batum was now in Turkish hands, and that an offensive into southern Georgia would follow.

19. Przevalski was probably the most competent of Yudenich's senior commanders, and eventually succeeded him. He was the son of an eminent explorer, NM Przevalski, who travelled extensively in Asia and came close to reaching Lhasa, then a forbidden city. The elder Przevalski gave his name to a proto-horse, a gazelle, a partridge and a redstart, amongst others, but not, if rumours which began circulating in Moscow in the 1950s are to be believed, to the illegitimate son he fathered on an employee, twenty-year-old Ekaterina Geladze, at his home in Gori, Georgia. The boy took the name and patronymic of his mother's husband, Vissarion Dzhugashvili, but subsequently changed it to Stalin.

20. Who, by then known as Şerif Köprülü, was critical, particularly of Hafiz Hakki but also of Enver, in the handling of the battle in his book *Sarikamiş Ihata Maneuvrasi* (The Sarikamiş Encirclement), published in 1922. 'The most unfortunate thing,' he wrote, 'was that nobody was asking: "What if these plans fail?"'

CHAPTER 7

1. Even from his own senior personnel. Mustafa Kemal, who had by then returned from his enforced exile as Military Attaché in Sofia, described in his memoirs how he asked Enver how it had gone at Sarikamiş. 'We fought,' said Enver. 'That's all.' 'What is the situation now?' asked Kemal. 'Very good,' was the reply.

2. From his existing formations he lost the 3rd Caucasian Infantry Division, the 20th

Infantry Division and two Plastun Brigades, a total of forty-three battalions, and was able to raise only seventeen infantry battalions, together with some cavalry formations, to replace them. His situation was improved when the Caucasian Cavalry Division – which included three regiments of dragoons – and the 2nd and 3rd Transbaikal Cavalry Brigades were returned to his command from the Eastern Front. By the late spring he had a total of 98 infantry battalions available to him, ten less than he had had in December 1914, but substantially more cavalry, and more artillery, too.

3. The division comprised the 37th, 40th and 43rd Infantry Regiments plus three battalions of cavalry and mountain and field artillery; its paper establishment was 248 officers and 10,920 other ranks. Its commander, Lt.-Col. Halil Bey, later known as Halil Kut, Enver's uncle – though he was a year younger than the War Minister – was serving as Military Governor of Constantinople at the time.

4. The troops travelled by train from Haydarpaşa to Pozanti, in the Taurus mountains, then marched for four days before boarding trains to Osmaniye; then there were five days of foot-slogging to Katma, another brief train journey, and then ten more days (at least) on foot to Diyarbakir.

5. 102 men had died, 1,041 had deserted, and 1,040 had been left behind in hospitals along the way, Erickson tells us, while 2,708 were sick but had remained with their units.

6. Kazim Karabekir; he later commanded a division at Gallipoli and XVIII Corps in Mesopotamia. Post-WW1 he was instrumental in winning the War of Independence in eastern Anatolia.

7. Perhaps by ships sent to threaten the port of Alexandretta, the (Turkish) military commander of which was holding British subjects hostage. The *Pearl*-class light cruiser HMS *Philomel*, by then on loan to the Royal New Zealand Navy, was certainly in the area, and landed at least one party, losing three of her crew. The *Eclipse*-class light cruiser *Doris* was also operational in the area, and landed two parties north of Alexandretta on 18 and 19 December 1914, destroying two stretches of railway line, a station and a bridge, derailing one locomotive and blowing up two others.

8. The British government, for example, instigated an inquiry, much of it carried out by the eminent historian Arnold Toynbee, the findings of which were published as the Bryce Report in October 1916. Viscount Bryce had some experience of producing what some (almost exclusively Turkish) historians have called unvarnished propaganda, having previously been responsible for a similar report into German atrocities committed during the invasion of Belgium in 1914. The US Ambassador in Constantinople published his own account as *Ambassador Morgenthau's Story* in October 1918. Morgenthau employed a ghost-writer, a journalist named Burton J Hendrick, though that does not detract from his important account of life in Turkey in the run-up to, and during, WW1. Both these documents are available on the internet courtesy of Brigham Young University's library. A great deal more material on the subject can be located online, too, and Armenian assertions and Turkish denials are exhaustively rehearsed.

9. Malazgirt, known in an earlier age as Manzikert, had been the site of a landmark battle which had seen the Seljuk Turks, precursors of the Ottomans, defeat the Byzantine Empire in 1071 CE (Ahlat, qv, had been the scene of an earlier encounter).

10. Where, at Seyhin, there was a rarity: a bridge spanning the river.

11. In visualising the region's topography, we should recall that Lake Van itself lies at an altitude of over 1,700 metres.

12. All things are relative, however. Erickson tells us that IX Corps' strength was 11,338 on 4 June, still ten thousand down on what it had been six months earlier, and little more than a third of its establishment; X Corps stood at just under five thousand at

that time, XI Corps at a little over. Those numbers had almost certainly increased before IX Corps was committed to battle once more, over a month later, but not significantly, and when the 29th Division went into action at the Mirgemir Pass on 6 August, it actually amounted to little more than the equivalent of a single regiment.

13. The Swedish mission was led by General Harald Hjalmarsson, and by 1914 numbered 36, with some six thousand men under arms; those Swedes, all of them serving army officers or NCOs, were ordered home at the start of 1915, but roughly half, all of them solidly pro-German, elected to remain. Swedish police officers were also sent to Persia, to organise a civilian police force in Teheran.

14. The Grand Duke Nicholas, a first cousin of the tsar, had been appointed Commander-in-Chief of Russia's forces on the outbreak of WW1 despite never having led an army in the field. He was nonetheless successful in holding the Russian Army together on the Eastern Front in the face of adversity. Deeply religious, with mystical tendencies, he made a confirmed enemy of the tsarina's favourite, the charlatan 'mad monk' Rasputin, who proclaimed that the Russian Army would never be successful until the tsar himself stood at its head, and on 21 August 1915, Tsar Nicholas took on the responsibilities of supreme commander and despatched his cousin to the Caucasus to replace Count Vorontsov-Dashkov.

15. The young shah, Ahmad, had been taken into custody in the Russian Embassy in Teheran, 'for his own protection', and his advisers neutralised.

CHAPTER 8

1. He had narrow-gauge tracks on the Décauville system run along the existing roads.

2. Both Przevalski and Kalitin had been appointed to command their respective corps as soon as Yudenich took overall command, after Sarikamiş, having performed to his satisfaction there.

3. Three each in IX, X and XI Corps, plus the 36th and 37th; the 51st and 52nd, as the two Expeditionary Forces despatched from Thrace a year earlier had become, had by this time been relocated to Mesopotamia. There were also perhaps a score of Frontier Guards and Jandarma battalions, and the 2nd Cavalry Division, available.

4. Yudenich quickly despatched the Siberian Cossack Brigade to support them and exploit their breakthrough; cavalry was generally of little use in the mountains in winter, but this unit was an exception.

5. The campaign also saw the first effective use of motor transport in the theatre; the Russians had had such a detachment at Tiflis since before the start of the war, but it was not until the build-up before Erzurum that it was actually employed close to the front line.

6. If 8 million rounds sounds a lot, one should bear in mind that just one battery of ten Vickers machine guns of the British 100th MG Coy expended 999,750 in a continuous barrage lasting twelve hours on the night of 24 August 1916, at High Wood on the Somme.

7. No one saw any reason to hurry. Even the Third Army's commander, Mahmut Kamil, dawdled in Constantinople; it was 29 January before he returned to Erzurum and took back control from Abdul Karim.

8. A Turkish division, the 10th, had indeed been sent to Samsun, on the Black Sea coast, by sea, but it had many days of hard marching ahead of it before it reached Erzurum.

9. Known, say Allen and Muratoff, as 'elpidiphores', after a saint of the Orthodox church.

10. Who had made a name for himself at Gallipoli. He was known later as Vehip Kaçi.

11. Ahmet Izzet (Furgaç) was Turkey's most senior general; a generation older than Enver, he had over twenty years' service under his belt by the time WW1 began, and had served as Chief of the General Staff from August 1908 to January 1914. Despite a disparity in their ranks – Vehip was nominally a brigadier-general, Izzet a marshal – they served as equals, with neither subordinate to the other. Rank in the senior echelons of the Ottoman Army counted for less than command responsibility.

12. V Corps went to the Third Army, the rest to the Second. It soon became clear that it would be June at the very earliest before the Second Army could become even marginally effective; in fact, it was to be August before it was committed to battle.

13. *U*33, which sank a Russian hospital ship (the French steamer *Portugal)* on 30 March. It was later rammed – but not sunk – by a Russian coastal destroyer.

14. The IRN had six such in operation in the Black Sea by 1916.

15. The Russian headquarters had withdrawn to Mogilev (Mahilyow), Baranovichi having become uncomfortable following the massive German advances in 1915.

16. In consequence of the Brusilov Offensive the German High Command asked Enver to send Turkish troops to the Eastern Front, and he complied. In all, some 120,000 Turks were despatched, XV Corps (two divisions) to Galicia, VI Corps (three divisions) to Rumania, and XX Corps (two divisions) to Macedonia.

17. II Corps, with the 11th and 12th Inf. Divs.; III Corps, with the 1st, 14th and 53rd Inf. Divs.; IV Corps, with the 47th Inf. Div. – its sister-divisions, the 48th and 49th, were still on their way from Thrace, where they had formed and trained; these three were the Second Army's only untried units – and XVI Corps with the 5th, 7th and 8th Inf. Divs.

CHAPTER 9

1. If one reckons the European operations to constitute a single front (which they did not, of course; the Turks were in three quite separate locations, but see below), and discounts the Persian expedition, and the ongoing campaign to subdue the Christian Armenians, which still required considerable manpower, as sideshows. In addition, the Ottoman Army maintained a four-division corps in the Yemen, as it did throughout the war.

2. Save for the ultimately abortive second expedition into Southern Persia, but see below.

3. In other words, a return to the frontier established at the Congress of Paris which ended the Crimean War in 1856; the arrangement was to have been the subject of a plebiscite.

4. Ending the Trans-Caucasian Federative Republic. Armenia and Azerbaijan – which latter was already slipping into a civil war of its own which pitted Christians against Muslims – subsequently proclaimed their own independence. This is said by some to have provoked the Bolsheviks to join forces with the Armenians (especially in Baku) on the premise that 'my enemy's enemy is my friend'; like many thus inspired, the alliance was short-lived.

5. Plus the Turkish 36th Division. In the event the Azeris proved to be of only limited value, though their presence was useful for propaganda purposes and to subdue local Christian communities.

6. Azerbaijani oil, not explosives, was the source of the Nobel family fortune, and funded the eponymous prizes. By the 1890s the Baku oilfield was satisfying around 50 per cent of world needs; in 1904 it produced 11 million tons, and even after the start of

WW1, when production there was limited by external factors, it was still producing 7 million tons annually. During that period (1914–17) British interests controlled 60% of Baku's production.

7. The Musavat Party was established in 1911 as a secret organisation under the leadership of Mammad Ali Rasulzade. By 1913 its leadership had been taken over by Mammad Amin Rasulzade, cousin of the founder. It was he who merged the Musavat with right-wing Azeri nationalist elements and made it a force to be reckoned with in Azerbaijan's confused political climate.

8. More than a political party, the Dashnaktsutiun, 'the Armenian Revolutionary Federation', was a movement which existed to free Armenians from Turkish rule and influence. It came into existence formally in 1892.

9. Not to be confused with the Ali Ihsan (Sokmen) who commanded IX Corps at Sarikamiş, was captured by the Russians towards the battle's end and spent the rest of the war in captivity. *This* Ali Ihsan, a class-mate of Halil Pasha, saw out the war in Mesopotamia.

10. The 35th was disbanded too, in the second week of May, and its troops allocated to the other divisions.

11. This, of course, was long before the Germans had made allies of the former and the Turks had made friends with the latter.

12. Dunsterforce was one of two essentially similar missions. The other was to operate east of the Caspian under the command of Maj.-Gen. Sir Wilfrid Malleson; it did not commence until mid-June 1918, and was to make for Ashkhabad (Ashgabat), on the Transcaspian Railway, by way of Mashhad in Persia's north-eastern Khorasan province.

13. Forty-one of them; as well as a driver for each, the party consisted of eleven officers, four NCOs and four officers' servants. As an indication of how bad the conditions were at times, the last forty-kilometre stretch to Hamadan, including the Asadabad Pass, took a week to negotiate.

14. Somewhat surprisingly, there were British consular officials in all the major Persian cities throughout this period, and most had branches of the Imperial Bank of Persia managed by Britons. Dunsterville was lavish in his praise for the men and women of these tiny expatriate communities, though not all was always quite as it might have been: the consul in Rasht, McLaren, later killed Maj. Sir Walter Bartellot, one of the men Dunsterville had sent on ahead to reconnoitre the route before setting out himself from Baghdad, 'for making love to his wife', evidence of the malign influence of 'the atmosphere of lilies and languor and love' which Dunsterville had detected, perhaps . . .

15. By mid-July they had recruited around eight hundred.

16. The departure of the Red Guards was a considerable bonus; it removed the main threat to Dunsterville's security in Enzerli, and allowed him to take control of the port later.

17. They got as far as loading thirteen ships, with the intention of sailing them north to Astrakhan, at the mouth of the Volga. The Centro-Caspian Dictatorship had two small gunboats at its disposal; they forced the ships to return to Baku and to unload what proved to be a very mixed cargo 'including perambulators, gramophones, sewing machines and other miscellaneous rubbish', which demonstrated, as far as Dunsterville was concerned, that the Bolsheviks' action 'was only a cloak to cover a general looting of the town'.

18. But he also blamed Marshall for refusing him more troops. The size of his force – no matter what its origins – was the real consideration.

19. It was actually the Imperial Russian ensign, but flying it upside-down, as the remaining Red Guards in Enzeli insisted, turned it into the Serbian . . .

CHAPTER 10

1. Duckworth's objective was to induce the sultan, Selim III, to make peace with Russia (then allied with Britain against France) and dismiss the French ambassador, Sebastiani, whose influence over the Sublime Porte was considerable. With seven ships of the line, two frigates and two bomb ketches he entered the Dardanelles on 19 February, suffered some damage from gunfire from the guardian forts, engaged and largely destroyed a Turkish flotilla in Sari Siglar Bay and then proceeded to Constantinople, where he delivered an ultimatum which the Turks ignored. Deterred from bombarding the city by the presence of forty-two very large cannon, manufactured almost three hundred and fifty years earlier but still very effective, he withdrew after ten days, and was mauled by the Dardanelles forts on the way out.

2. Field Marshal Earl Kitchener of Khartoum, lately Britain's Agent and Consul-General (effectively, Viceroy) in Egypt and the Sudan, knew a thing or two about Middle Eastern affairs, at least by his own reckoning, most of his career having been spent there. As luck would have it, he was in London in July 1914, to be ceremoniously invested into the earldom to which he had been elevated on 29 June. In the first days of August, with war now certain, Kitchener – who professed ignorance in European ways of war-making – attempted to return to Egypt but was forestalled when a group of fairly eminent parliamentarians decided he was needed in London and so persuaded Asquith. At an hour-long meeting with him on the morning of 4 August, he told the Prime Minister that if obliged to remain in the United Kingdom he would accept nothing less than the War Office, which Asquith himself was then holding in addition to the premiership. The next day he got his way, and became the first serving military officer to hold an office of state since Monck was appointed a Gentleman of the Bedchamber in 1660, after he had restored the monarchy.

Given his antecedents, it is not surprising that Kitchener was to play a very active role in the management of the war in the Middle East; as well as controlling government policy regarding the Dardanelles offensive, he also kept a very close eye on Egyptian affairs and was prevented from taking a leading role in Mesopotamia only by reason of the war there being run from India until February 1916. In Egypt he was assisted by the chosen men he left behind in Cairo, who continued to do his bidding even if they did allow their own ambitions to run away with them, particularly with regard to Arab affairs, and especially those concerning the self-styled King of the Arabs, Sherif Hussein ibn-Ali; the ramifications of their actions are addressed in Chapter 14.

3. Essentially, the Russians would have no truck with putting a Greek army into Constantinople; if anyone was going to occupy the Ottoman capital, it would be them.

4. The Majestics – there were nine – were 15,000-ton ships mounting the usual combination of four 12-inch and twelve 6-inch guns and capable of 17 knots (34km/h) on a good day. The last was delivered in January 1898. The six Canopuses were their successors, with similar armament but 30 per cent more power, which gave them an extra knot.

5. That is not an exaggeration; had all the available vessels been 'rafted-up' like that, they would have presented a front over 1.3 kilometres wide.

6. In essence, Carden's plan was: A – Reduce the defences at the entrance, first by long-range indirect fire, then by direct fire; B – Clear the defences up to Kephez Point; C – Reduce the defences at the Narrows by indirect fire from battlecruisers standing off the west coast of the peninsula near Gaba Tepe; D – Clear a passage through the minefields, advance through the Narrows, reducing the forts above them, then advance into the

Sea of Marmara. Simultaneously with A and B the Bulair Lines would be bombarded and a battery near Gaba Tepe would be reduced. Carden estimated that the operation would take a month (without making allowance for interruption due to weather conditions), and stuck to that estimate thereafter. In the event it was adopted with few amendments: Phase C was to be undertaken from within the Straits, and the Bulair Lines were not to be bombarded. It called for the deployment of 12 battleships, 3 battlecruisers, 3 light cruisers, 16 destroyers and a leader, 6 submarines, 12 minesweepers and a seaplane tender. Three extra British battleships were later added to the force, as were four French capital ships.

7. The Queen Elizabeths were built to an entirely new design, to accommodate a gun – the 15in/42-calibre Mkl – which was still on the drawing board at the time. It was the need to fire these ships with oil, in order to achieve the required performance characteristics, which inspired the decision to buy the Anglo-Persian Oil Co. for the nation (see Chapter 2, esp. Note 4). In fact, they were all over-weight, and the Admiralty's refusal to accept small-tube boilers reduced their power output, but they could still produce 72,000shp with forced draught when called upon in an emergency, and touch 24 knots.

The 15in Mkl gun proved to be capable of throwing a 1,938-pound (881kg) shell to a range of 28,732 yards (26.3km) with impressive accuracy. The Queen Elizabeths carried eight, in paired, superimposed 'A' and 'B' and 'X' and 'Y' turrets.

8. The biggest guns the Turks deployed were short-barrelled 28-cm rifles, with a maximum range of 11,400m; the 12in guns mounted aboard the obsolete British battleships, effective out to around 14,000 yards (13km), outranged them, but by no great margin. The best guns the Turks had were modern 24-cm rifles from Krupp, which ranged out to around 20km.

9. Churchill noted that Fisher and Adm. of the Fleet Sir Arthur Wilson were both present and remained silent, which traditionally signified assent.

10. The commission set up to enquire into the affair in June 1916; see Chapter 12 below.

11. On the grounds that German submarines were reported heading for the Dardanelles; at the time there was no effective way of protecting against them.

12. Which latter is curious, since on learning that the 29th Division was to go to the Eastern Mediterranean the French government, too, ordered a division detached and sent there. Joffre, the commander-in-chief, resisted, whereupon the War Ministry ordered a new division constituted from Legionnaires and colonial troops in depots in France and North Africa. It was to be known as the Corps Expéditionnaire d'Orient and was placed under the command of Gen. d'Amade; it was to form on 1 March, and sail for Lemnos a few days later. Almost astoundingly, given the complexity of the task and the limited time available, it did just that. The British Official History of the Gallipoli Campaign – there is also an Australian version, and the two are by no means congruent – was the work of Brig.-Gen. Cecil Aspinall-Oglander, who served on Hamilton's staff; it was published in two volumes in 1929 and 1932.

13. The Australian and New Zealand Army Corps.

14. It is widely held that Kitchener sorely needed a competent General Staff to advise him, and this episode is often advanced as evidence of that; all the men who would have constituted such a body had been hurried off to France in the first months of the war which was, of course, going to be over by Christmas . . .

15. Kitchener had selected Hamilton for the post, should it require filling, as early as 3 March; only on 12 March was Hamilton himself informed, and the following day he was on his way to the Mediterranean with a very small staff (the administrative component would not arrive in the theatre until 1 April, and it was sorely missed in

the intervening period). At Marseilles a fast cruiser, HMS *Phaeton*, awaited him; he arrived at Tenedos on the afternoon of 17 March.

16. As early as mid-December, Lt. Norman Holbrook's submarine *B 11* had penetrated as far as Sari Siglar Bay, sinking the forty-year-old central-battery ironclad battleship *Messudieh* and getting away scot-free. That was by no means the only – or even the most daring – penetration, and over the course of the Gallipoli campaign Allied submarines reached the Sea of Marmara on a number of occasions, the most successful being those of Boyle and Nasmith. The latter ventured there twice, and even entered the Bosporus and despatched a munitions ship off the Golden Horn. In all, the seven boats employed sank two battleships, a destroyer, five gunboats, seven ammunition ships and nine transports. Three were lost.

17. Times are local, which in this region was two hours ahead of Greenwich Mean Time.

18. When British battleships bombarded Bulair from the Gulf of Saros. Later – on 28 March, 6 April and 22 April – they also bombarded Smyrna.

19. Keyes, later Admiral of the Fleet Lord Keyes, was one of the Royal Navy's authentic twentieth-century heroes. His career began with anti-slavery operations off East Africa in the 1880s and ended as Director of Combined Operations in 1941, by way of the Boxer Rebellion (he was the first man into Beijing, having previously led boarding parties which took four Chinese destroyers by storm), the Dardanelles, the Dover Patrol, the raids on Zeebrugge and Ostend, and Norway in 1940. He also found time to be an active member of parliament.

20. Which accusation was ill deserved; the North Sea trawlermen who had been recruited were perfectly willing to sweep mines, which was a dangerous enough pastime in itself, but had never been told they would be expected to do so under a perfect barrage of artillery fire at close range.

21. And then their transports were not loaded tactically, to be disembarked in the order they would be required, and had to be diverted to Alexandria for that to be rectified; see below.

22. Two from ANZAC, the 29th, the Royal Naval Division and the French.

23. De Roebeck went on to command the Grand Fleet's 2nd Battle Squadron until 1919, when he became High Commissioner at Constantinople; he later commanded the Atlantic Fleet.

24. Wemyss, later Admiral of the Fleet Lord Wester Wemyss, went on to command the Mediterranean Fleet and was eventually appointed First Sea Lord in succession to Sir John Jellicoe. He was Britain's naval representative at the Paris Peace Conference.

25. Previously ships had bombarded forts from the mouth and across the peninsula, with very little success due to their inability to spot where their shots fell and correct their aim.

26. *Agamemnon* and *Lord Nelson* were the last British pre-dreadnoughts, with four 12in/50cal guns (with significantly better characteristics than those of the older ships) in their main battery and ten 9.2in in the secondary.

27. Sister-ships *Charlemagne* and *Gaulois* were the first French capital ships to carry their main armament of four 12in/40cal guns in paired mountings, as had long been the case in other navies.

28. *Bouvet* was the oldest of the French ships assigned to the Dardanelles operation. She entered service in 1898, and was the last French capital ship to carry both 12in and 10.8in guns in single mounts, the former fore and aft, the latter amidships in turrets rising out of the very considerable tumblehome which characterised French capital ship design of the period.

29. *Suffren* was a development of the *Charlemagnes*, 10 per cent bigger and better protected but with the same armament.

30. *Inflexible* was one of the Invincible class, the first so-called battlecruisers, armed like a dreadnought with eight 12in and sixteen 4in guns but forgoing armour for speed. *Inflexible* had led the fruitless hunt for *Goeben*; in the meantime she had been involved in the Battle of the Falkland Islands, where she and *Invincible* easily dealt with *Scharnhorst* and *Gneisenau*, just as they had been designed to do. From Tenedos she was towed to Malta and repaired.

31. *Gaulois* was badly holed below the waterline just abaft the bow on the port side; she had later to be beached at Rabbit Island (Tavşanada), off Tenedos, but was patched, pumped out and rejoined the fleet.

32. This was the last time the Council met until 14 May.

33. HMSs *Queen* and *Implacable* were already on their way, and Fisher had ordered *London* and *Prince of Wales* to join them; the French had despatched *Henri IV* to make up for the loss of *Bouvet*.

34. That was the widely held opinion, then and even long after the war (though Erickson, quoting Turkish sources, says that just one-sixth of the available ammunition had been expended on 18 March). An official German account, written by Sanders' staff officer (Mühlmann), says the five remaining 35.5-cm guns had fifty rounds each, the eleven 23-cm (sic) guns had thirty to fifty; long-range high-explosive shells – the only ones effective against the battleships' armour – were in particularly short supply, with the forts on the Chanak Kale side having just seventeen, and those at Kilid Bahr only ten.

CHAPTER 11

1. Erickson insists that the defensive arrangements were entirely the work of Turkish minds, the plans implemented having been evolved to counter a Greek invasion during the Balkan War of 1912–13.

2. Otto Liman von Sanders is said to have felt the isthmus to have been the most likely site for the landings, believing that the Royal Navy's long-range guns could easily close the northern entrance of the Dardanelles to Turkish shipping which, in any event, would be vulnerable to submarine attack.

3. The Corps Expéditionnaire d'Orient consisted of the 1st Metropolitan Brigade (175th Infantry Regiment; 1st Régiment de Marche d'Afrique), made up of a battalion of Zouaves (recruited originally from the French community in Algeria and one of the Foreign Legion, and a further half-battalion of the Legion) and the 2nd Colonial Brigade (4th and 6th Colonial Regiments, recruited in North Africa and Senegal with European officers and one battalion of European troops each) plus eight batteries of light field artillery.

4. Less its Light Horse mounted units.

5. Under the command of Maj.-Gen. Archibald Paris; the RND, composed of reservists surplus to requirements as seamen, was a division in name only, with just two brigades (the 1st, with Drake, Hawke, Hood and Nelson Battalions, and the 2nd, with the Anson and Howe Battalions plus the 1st and 2nd Battalions, Royal Marine Light Infantry) and no artillery.

6. Under the command of Maj.-Gen. Aylmer Hunter-Weston (until early June, when he was replaced by Maj.-Gen. H de B de Lisle), the 29th Division comprised the 86th Brigade (2nd Royal Fusiliers, 1st Lancashire Fusiliers, 1st Royal Munster Fusiliers and 1st Royal Dublin Fusiliers); the 87th Brigade (2nd South Wales Borderers, 1st King's

Own Scottish Borderers, 1st Royal Inniskilling Fusiliers and 1st The Border Regiment) and the 88th Brigade (4th Worcestershire Regiment, 2nd Hampshire Regiment, 1st Essex Regiment and 1/5th Royal Scots). All save the last-named were regular battalions. The division had one brigade of the Royal Horse Artillery, two brigades of field artillery and a howitzer battery, and two batteries of Royal Garrison Artillery.

7. There were also other units in the support fleet; including all the warships, there were well over two hundred vessels involved in the operation.

8. To begin with, few vehicles were taken to Gallipoli; eventually, though the conditions on the peninsula made their use problematic, significant numbers were landed. They included four armoured cars – three Rolls-Royces and a Seabrook – from the RNACD's 3 and 4 Squadrons; they were accommodated in special dugouts at Cape Helles, and rarely sortied from them, though they did attempt to approach and drag away defensive wire, a task they had earlier undertaken in France, without much success. The rest of the squadrons' vehicles remained aboard ship, and their crews fought as dismounted machine gun teams.

9. The Australian and New Zealand Army Corps (Lt.-Gen. Sir William Birdwood) consisted of two divisions. The New Zealand and Australian Division (Maj.-Gen. Sir Alexander Godley) comprised the New Zealand Brigade with four battalions (Auckland, Canterbury, Otago and Wellington); the 4th Australian Brigade (13th, 14th, 15th and 16th Battalions); the 1st and 2nd NZ Field Artillery Brigades each with two four-gun and one four-howitzer batteries; the New Zealand Mounted Rifles Brigade (Auckland, Canterbury, Otago and Wellington Regiments); the 1st Australian Light Horse Brigade (1st, 2nd and 3rd Light Horse Regiments), plus engineers and medical and support echelons. The 1st Division, Australian Imperial Forces (Maj.-Gen. William Bridges), comprised the 1st, 2nd and 3rd Australian Brigades, each with four battalions, numbered 1 to 12; three field artillery brigades, each with twelve 18-pounder guns in three batteries; the 4th Light Horse Regiment and the 2nd Australian Light Horse Brigade (5th, 6th and 7th Light Horse Regiments), plus engineers and medical and support echelons. The 7th Indian Mountain Artillery Brigade was attached to ANZAC. The Light Horse units were left behind in Egypt when the rest of the force embarked for Gallipoli, but later volunteered en masse to fight as dismounted infantry. A third division, the 2nd Division, Australian Imperial Forces, similar in composition to the first, but with just one regiment of cavalry, was raised later and sent to Gallipoli under the command of Maj.-Gen. JG Legge, the 5th Brigade arriving in August, the 6th and 7th in September.

10. The French contingent and the Royal Naval Division were assembled in Trebuki Bay on the island of Skiros, 130 kilometres from Lemnos, the harbour at Mudros having filled up by mid-April. This dispersal further complicated the co-ordination of the invasion.

11. The boats used included 42ft (12.8m) launches, 36ft (11m) pinnaces and 32ft (9.75m) cutters, just some of the bewildering variety of small craft carried by the capital ships of the period. The ships also carried 45ft and 50ft steam pinnaces, and these were employed to tow the boats.

12. The site of ancient Troy lies just behind Kum Kale, on the Asian side of the Straits.

13. Birdwood, in charge of the landings at Z Beach, was offered a similar arrangement, but declined it.

14. There would be no T Beach or U Beach, it was decided, for fear of confusing them with V and W in spoken communications.

15. Unsurprisingly, there is considerable disagreement over the reason for the covering force having landed where it did, in Anzac Cove, and not where it was supposed to

have done, well to the south of it. Much of it centred on the fact that the current along the coast – if it existed at all on 25 April – is certainly not strong enough to have caused the tows to have been carried 'a full mile to the north of the selected landing place' (as the British Official History suggests) in the course of covering just twice that distance at what we can assume to be something less than ten knots (20km/h). The Turkish Navy's Oceanographic Department estimates that the current in that area runs at a rate of 0.25 to 0.5 knots; the Royal Navy's HMS *Humber*, which operated in that area for six months, reported that a current running at 1.5 knots could be produced by a high wind such as had been blowing only 24 hours before. It is more likely that the misdirection came about due to a lack of precision in the way the orders for the operation were framed. Birdwood was instructed to land his divisions 'on the beach between Gaba Tepe and the fisherman's hut', which latter was about 1,500 metres north of Ari Burnu, and six kilometres from Gaba Tepe, and by his own account intended that his right wing should land 'about a mile north of Gaba Tepe'. (Or 'opposite the K in Kurija Dere [Koja Dere]' as it appeared on the map he was using, by another account, which indicates a point just south of Hell Spit, the southern extremity of Anzac Cove.) However, it seems that precise instructions as to where they should drop the tows were not given to the battleships or the destroyers which took station on them, and it may well be that they interpreted the general instructions in such a way as to position themselves halfway between Gaba Tepe and Fisherman's Hut (ie, almost directly off Anzac Cove, as the sketch map in the Australian Official History indicates), and that may account for the displacement. In any event, whatever the explanation, the responsibility for the landings at Z Beach going so badly wrong lies with the Royal Navy.

Birdwood later tried to make the best of it, saying 'As subsequent events turned out, I cannot help thinking that the hand of Providence directly guided us, for it so happened that the beach on which we landed, and which we have since held, is one of the few places where the steepness of the cliffs has made us to a great extent immune from shell fire. Almost everywhere else we should probably have had to vacate owing to the heavy shell fire which would most certainly have been poured on us.' While it is impossible to speculate on what the outcome might have been had things gone differently, it seems clear that had the force landed as planned, it would have made very much faster progress, and would have met the Turkish reinforcements on very much more favourable terrain, where its superiority in numbers would surely have told.

16. Many men failed to find their units that day; throughout it, many, demoralised because leaderless, began returning to Anzac Cove, some – considerably more than was strictly necessary, though that was commonplace – helping wounded mates, but more of them simply because they had no idea of what else to do; they were made up into ad hoc companies and sent back out, but they kept returning. This became a cause for serious concern, and led to a growing feeling among senior officers that, should the Turks launch a strong counterattack, it was likely to succeed.

17. As was the British Army's custom, hills were commonly referred to by their 'spot height' (in feet); in many cases it had been misconverted from the metric markings on the (French) maps which were the best available, and they should not be taken as accurate elevations.

18. When some were told to straighten the line near McKay's Hill an impromptu local advance did begin, and led to many casualties.

19. That was disputed by Lt.-Col. Archibald Koe of the KOSB, who believed himself to be in overall command; it is suggested by some that the tension between the two

was, at least in part, the cause of the confusion which wrecked the operation. Matthews had led the 'commando' raid on Kum Kale on 4 March.

20. In truth, it had been extremely shaky all night long; as early as 2355 Matthews had asked for an additional battalion to be landed before dawn (and had been ignored) and he repeated his request at around 0600, with a similar outcome.

21. The other two were the KOSB and SWB battalions landed at S and Y Beaches.

22. The boats carrying the battalion's four machine guns grounded on shoals in such deep water that the men had to swim to land; three of the guns were lost in the process of trying to unload them.

23. This was a significant loss, for Hare was in overall command of the covering force. His brigade-major sent word to the Royals' commanding officer that he must assume command of the brigade; before he could do so, he too was badly wounded. A second brigade commander, Napier, was killed later, as were two brigade-majors and several battalion commanders; the shortage of senior officers was to have serious consequences throughout the day.

24. Unwin and Williams were both awarded the Victoria Cross, as were four other men aboard the *River Clyde*.

25. Their commander, Lt.-Col. Casson, was convinced by a prisoner who told him that two full battalions of Turks lay between him and Sedd el Bahr (when the real figure was one platoon), and decided not to risk an attempt to take the village from the rear with his remaining able-bodied men.

26. It had been Hamilton's intention that the French should advance northwards from X Beach to link up with Matthews' beleaguered men on Y Beach. This begs the question why the British reserve battalions there – the Borderers and the Inniskillings – had not been employed for the same purpose. It appears that Hunter-Weston – who had operational command, we must recall – did not share Hamilton's enthusiasm for the landing on Y Beach, or his optimism regarding the possibilities it might present, and, more concerned with events around Cape Helles, 'he had decided that the Y Beach detachment must be left to its fate', in the words of Aspinall-Oglander.

27. It was compounded by the fact that many had discarded their packs, which contained reserves of ammunition as well as rations.

28. Kitchener's signal to Maxwell read: 'You should supply [Hamilton with] any troops in Egypt which can be spared, or even selected officers or men that Sir Ian Hamilton may want, for Gallipoli. You know that Peyton's Mounted Division [the 2nd Mounted Division; this was a yeomanry formation intended to make good any shortfall, which left England on 8 April] is leaving for Egypt. This telegram should be communicated by you to Sir Ian Hamilton.' It was not.

29. Russell's Top was one of the keys to the Anzac position; if the Turks could take and hold it, they would command Anzac Cove and the southern end of Ocean Beach to the north, and also (and from the rear) the precarious positions on Maclaurin's Hill.

30. His original over-ambitious plan had been to take the whole of Mortar Ridge and 400 Plateau too, but he soon realised that was a good few many steps too far.

31. Under the command of Maj.-Gen. HV Cox, the 29th Indian Brigade comprised the 16th Sikhs, 69th and 89th Punjabis and 1/6th Gurkhas. The two Punjabi battalions each had two companies of Muslim troops, who were held back from combat duties against their co-religionists. Those battalions were later returned to Egypt and were replaced by 1/5th and 2/10th Gurkhas.

32. On 4 May Hamilton had sent d'Amade three battalions of the RND (Anson, Hood and Howe), which took over the western sector of his line.

33. These 'Spurs' were the low, south-west-facing extensions of the Achi Baba Ridge;

the names were fabrications on the part of the staff, and just to confuse matters the Australians used different ones: Ravine Spur, Krithia Spur, Central Spur and Kereves Spur, respectively, from the north.

34. The untried 125th Brigade had the worst of it; over the first two days of the battle it lost 23 officers and 626 men, and on the evening of 7 May was withdrawn into reserve, its place to be taken by the 87th Brigade.

35. The suggestion emanated from lower down the chain of command; de Roebeck passed it on, but, significantly, failed to recommend it.

36. By this treaty, signed on 26 April in fulfilment of an agreement reached the previous September, Italy agreed to renounce the Triple Alliance and join the war on the side of the Allies. She declared war on Germany and Austria-Hungary on 23 May. The battle-ships which were to quit the Dardanelles Squadron were *Queen, London, Implacable* and *Prince of Wales.*

37. Submarine warfare was in the forefront of public attention, for on 8 May the Cunard liner RMS *Lusitania* had been torpedoed and sunk off the southern coast of Ireland en route from New York.

38. *Abercrombie* and *Roberts.* The battleships selected were the *Venerable* and the *Exmouth.*

39. She was under the command of Kapitänleutnant Rudolph Firle. He evaded the destroyers *Beagle* and *Bulldog* and put three torpedoes into *Goliath*; at least one hit a magazine and she sank almost immediately with the loss of 570 of her 700-strong crew. *Mauvenit-i-Milliye* escaped in the confusion, which made her victory even sweeter.

40. Thanks to the skill of the captain and crew of the destroyer *Chelmer*, which came up under the *Triumph's* stern-walk and took off most of the crew before she capsized, few lives were lost.

41. Essentially, hollow tanks conforming roughly to the shape of the hull, fitted at and below the waterline along much of the ship's length. Their purpose was to detonate torpedoes' warheads without damage to the integrity of the ship itself.

42. Fighting was on two fronts, the British being active north of the city of Lens – first at Neuve Chapelle (in March), then at Aubers, and later at Festubert – and the French to the south, near Souchez (Vimy Ridge). The efforts came to nothing at considerable cost.

43. The 52nd (Lowland) Division, a Territorial force, was to set out from Britain within days. Hamilton made the caveat that if the Greeks or Bulgarians joined the war on the side of the Allies, or if the Russians landed a force at the Bosporus, he would make do with two more divisions in total.

44. His demotion was the price the Tories extracted for joining the coalition; they had not forgiven him for 'ratting' (his word) on them by crossing the floor of the House of Commons to join the Liberals eleven years earlier (he later 're-ratted', of course; his words again). He remained in the Cabinet as Chancellor to the Duchy of Lancaster, with a voice but no real power. Fisher went first, walking out on Churchill with a prima donna-ish display of self-justification which the First Lord first tried to deflect and finally accepted. Churchill persuaded Sir Arthur Wilson to replace him as First Sea Lord, but when Churchill was ousted Wilson stood down and the ineffectual Sir Henry Jackson took his place; thus the Admiralty had new professional and political heads simultaneously.

45. Asquith's Liberal government fell on 25 May; the reconstructed War Council, now known as the Dardanelles Committee, met for the first time on 7 June.

46. It was while attempting to climb Monash Gully under fire that Maj.-Gen. William Bridges was shot and mortally wounded on 15 May.

47. Said Aspinall-Oglander: ' ... line after line of Turks came steadily forward, while the Australians, standing or sitting on their parapets to get a better view, mowed them down with their fire.'

48. The 42nd Division was under the command of Maj.-Gen. W Douglas; it comprised the 125th Brigade (1/5th, 1/6th, 1/7th and 1/8th Lancashire Fusiliers), the 126th Brigade (1/4th and 1/5th East Lancashire Regiment and 1/9th and 1/10th Manchester Regiment) and the 127th Brigade (1/5th, 1/6th, 1/7th and 1/8th Manchester Regiment) with nine 18-pounder batteries and two of howitzers.

49. The 52nd (Lowland) Division, under the command of Maj.-Gen. GGA Egerton, began arriving at Gallipoli in the first week of June. It comprised the 155th Brigade (Brig.-Gen. F Erskine; 1/4th and 1/5th Royal Scots Fusiliers and 1/4th and 1/5th King's Own Scottish Borderers); the 156th Brigade (Brig.-Gen. W Scott-Moncrieff; 1/4th and 1/7th Royal Scots and 1/7th and 1/8th Scottish Rifles) and the 157th Brigade (Col. WH Millar; 1/5th, 1/6th and 1/7th Highland Light Infantry and 1/5th Argyll and Sutherland Highlanders), with very limited artillery, most going no further than Egypt. Half the 1/7th Royal Scots were aboard a train to Liverpool which crashed at Quintinshill near Gretna on 22 May (when a signalman made a fateful error which resulted eventually in no less than five trains colliding; the fire which engulfed the wreck and burned for three days was responsible for most of the deaths); all but seven officers and fifty-seven men were killed or injured. The last brigade to be deployed, the 157th, arrived in Gallipoli only during the first week of July.

50. The RND had lately been augmented, the Collingwood, Hawke and Benbow Battalions, and 500 men to replace some of those lost by the others, arriving in theatre in the last days of May. The Collingwood and Benbow Battalions were disbanded after the Third Battle of Krithia (though the latter had played no part in it; the Collingwood had been virtually annihilated early on in the action) and their men used to replenish the ranks of other units.

51. On the left, astride Gully Ravine, the 14th Sikhs suffered particularly heavily, losing twenty-three out of twenty-nine officers and 380 of 514 men. The Gurkhas sent to reinforce them lost heavily too.

52. Kitchener's New Army was a volunteer force raised to supplement the British Army's regular and Territorial divisions; its units down to company level were led by regular officers and most senior NCOs were also regular soldiers. In the case of the officer corps, this meant that elderly retired men had often been recalled to the colours; they were by no means universally of the highest standard, and as the British Official History notes 'some were men who would never have attained command in times of peace.' Slowly the chaff was winnowed from the wheat, but to begin with, at least, poor leadership was a major problem, and one which went all the way to the top. In all, thirty divisions were raised, a total of around two and a half million men having volunteered. The first of them went into action at Gallipoli in August.

53. It was decided to employ the Cunard liners *Aquitania* and *Mauretania* (which latter was even then transporting a brigade of the 52nd Division to the Eastern Mediterranean) and White Star's *Olympic* (the sister-ship to the ill-fated *Titanic* and the less well known but equally doomed HMHS *Britannic*, mined in the Mediterranean on 21 November 1916, while on her way to Lemnos for the fifth time to carry wounded to hospitals in the United Kingdom), which could each carry six to seven battalions.

54. Hunter-Weston, who was known for his disregard for the lives of his men, claimed he had sent the 156th into action (for the first time) without a preliminary artillery barrage as a means of 'blooding the pups'.

55. In the loosest possible sense. The rest areas were near the tip of the peninsula and

well within range of Turkish guns on Achi Baba and across the Straits at Kum Kale; accommodation consisted of unroofed trenches. The only recreations were those the men organised for themselves. As acute diarrhoea was endemic, there was little interest. The British Official History notes that casualty figures in the rest areas were virtually identical to those in the line when no 'push' was in progress.

56. When Hamilton had asked for three additional divisions, on 17 May, he had undertaken not to land them on the peninsula until he could advance 'another 1000 yards and so free the beaches from the shelling to which they are subjected on the western side'; until then, he said, they would remain on adjacent islands, handy, but out of harm's way. He broke that undertaking in respect of the 13th Division. When the last of its units arrived on 17 July, he sent it into the line at Krithia to replace the 29th and the 42nd, which were sent off to Imbros and Lemnos to rest; the former was hastily recalled just four days later, when it appeared that the Turks were about to launch an offensive.

57. Which at this time was still known as Achi Baba Nullah; the fighting became known officially as the Action of Achi Baba Nullah in consequence, though the French knew it as the Fifth Action of Kereves Dere. In fact, the left-hand boundary of the operation was to be the point at which the new front line, established at the Third Battle of Krithia, bent back.

58. He recovered soon enough, to wreak his share of havoc on the Western Front. He commanded VIII Corps at the Battle of the Somme, distinguishing himself by his incompetence once more.

CHAPTER 12

1. Prior to the landing the name Green Hill was not used, and the features were paired as 'the Chocolate Hills'; this resulted in some confusion later, as did the fact that on captured Turkish maps they were also referred to by two names: Mastan Tepe and Yilghin Burnu, used interchangeably.

2. These would be the 53rd (Welsh) and 54th (East Anglian) Divisions. Territorial Forces, which came into being in 1908, as an offshoot of Haldane's far-reaching reforms, were something of an anomaly; they were operated by County Territorial Associations, and in some instances (notably in Ireland) resembled private armies. The War Office had very little control over them to begin with (they could not be forced to serve overseas, for example), and Kitchener so mistrusted them that he created an entirely new system, the New Army, qv, rather than exploit them as a cadre for the expansion of the regular army.

3. The 13th (Western) Division, raised as part of Kitchener's New Army, was under the command of Maj.-Gen. FC Shaw; it comprised the 38th Brigade (6th King's Own; 6th East Lancashire Regiment; 6th South Lancashire Regiment and 6th Loyal North Lancashire Regiment); the 39th Brigade (9th Royal Warwickshire Regiment; 7th Gloucestershire Regiment; 9th Worcestershire Regiment and 7th North Staffordshire Regiment) and the 40th Brigade (4th South Wales Borderers; 8th Royal Welch Fusiliers; 8th Cheshire Regiment and 5th Wiltshire Regiment). It had the 8th Welch Regiment as pioneer battalion (an innovation). Like the 52nd Division, most of its artillery went to Egypt, where it remained.

4. The 11th (Northern) Division, raised as part of Kitchener's New Army, was under the command of Maj.-Gen. Frederick Hammersley; it comprised the 32nd Brigade (9th West Yorkshire Regiment; 6th Yorkshire Regiment; 8th West Riding Regiment and 6th York and Lancaster Regiment); the 33rd Brigade (6th Lincolnshire Regiment; 6th Border

Regiment; 7th South Staffordshire Regiment and 9th Sherwood Foresters) and the 34th Brigade (8th Northumberland Fusiliers; 9th Lancashire Fusiliers; 5th Dorsetshire Regiment and 11th Manchester Regiment). Its pioneer battalion was the 6th East Yorkshire Regiment. One of its three field artillery brigades remained in Egypt.

5. The 10th (Irish) Division, raised as part of Kitchener's New Army, was under the command of Lt.-Gen. Sir Bryan Mahon; it comprised the 29th Brigade (10th Hampshire Regiment; 6th Royal Irish Rifles; 5th Connaught Rangers and 6th Leinster Regiment); the 30th Brigade (6th and 7th Royal Munster Fusiliers and 6th and 7th Royal Dublin Fusiliers) and the 31st Brigade (5th and 6th Royal Inniskilling Fusiliers and 5th and 6th Royal Irish Fusiliers). Its pioneer battalion was the 5th Royal Irish Regiment. It too had limited artillery.

6. Who was, of course, famously relieved of his command after Colenso, when he advocated giving up Ladysmith.

7. Indeed, maps of the Asian coast around Kum Kale were issued instead, as part of the security arrangements.

8. A patrol had landed on the northern side of Kiretch Tepe and crossed the plain to the W Hills during the night of 20 June; it reported a good supply of water on the former and guns – which may have been dummies – on the latter, but little more.

9. Says Aspinall-Oglander in the Official History.

10. Hamilton decided to postpone the change of command until the planned action had run its course.

11. A total of ten 15-pounders, eighty-four 18-pounders, four 60-pounders and sixteen howitzers, plus six French howitzers and a brigade of 75s. They would be augmented by the guns of the First Division of a naval Special Squadron consisting of HMS *Edgar* (an obsolete first-class protected cruiser, the protection of which was improved by the addition of 'blisters'; she mounted twelve 6-in guns, her two 9.2s having gone to arm M 15-class monitors; three of her sister-ships, *Endymion, Grafton* and *Theseus*, similarly modified, were also in Eastern Mediterranean waters by this time), five monitors (the two *Abercrombies* and three of the smaller M 15 class; of shallow draught in any event, these ships had been fitted with anti-torpedo blisters as standard) and six destroyers.

12. His misapprehension was reinforced by observers reporting they could see the sheet-metal circles the advancing troops were wearing on their backs as indicators of their position in the enemy trenches; indeed they could, but the men wearing them were dead. Similar devices had been tried before, with equally misleading results, and the continuing reliance on the practice begs a few questions of its own.

13. This operation had a specific aim: to reduce the enfilade fire which would meet the men assaulting the Turkish positions on the Nek (see below) at dawn. It was undertaken from Steele's Post, and was a complete failure; the Turkish lines being less than twenty metres from the Australian, men who emerged from the latter were cut down by rifle and machine gun fire before they had gone but a few paces. Such was the importance placed on this mission that a second attempt was made some hours later, with essentially similar results.

14. Seven, says the Australian Official History, which in such circumstances would surely have seemed an eternity; some Australian officers seem to have expected the bombardment to recommence, to 'give them a heavy burst at the finish', but they were disappointed.

15. Just before dark Johnston ordered the Canterbury and Otago Battalions up to the Apex; the Otagos made their way forward a few at a time, and arrived safely, but the Canterbury Battalion's commander formed them up in close order on the exposed hillside. Intense rifle and machine gun fire soon scattered them, killing and wounding

many, and just 37 men of the battalion reached the area where they were to bivouac for the night.

16. So accurate was this fire from the very first that it is almost certain that it was the work of British batteries already registered on the target, though all concerned denied it.

17. The two divisions marched the thirty kilometres from Bulair non-stop; as a result they arrived (on the afternoon of 8 August) in no fit state to go straight into battle, and the corps commander, Feizi Pasha, gave in to his divisional commanders' requests that they be allowed to rest until the next morning. When he heard of this, Sanders dismissed Feizi, and gave command of the corps to Mustafa Kemal, who had already distinguished himself in his efforts to halt the ANZAC advance with limited forces during the days after the April landings.

18. The newcomers were totally unprepared for the rigours of what was, in effect, mountain warfare, while the men who had been at Anzac for over three months were worn out by it, and by endemic sickness.

19. Eight 10-pounder mountain guns and a battery of four 18-pounders.

20. These landing craft had been constructed for an amphibious operation aimed at the Baltic or the German North Sea islands. Some had in fact been available as early as March, but the Admiralty had kept them a secret from Hamilton; he learned of their existence from one of his staff, and requested the use of some for the April landings, but was turned down. It is possible to imagine how many lives might have been saved at W and V Beaches had that not been the case.

21. In the event, as the last battalion was approaching the beach, its landing craft came under accurate artillery fire, and diverted to A Beach instead.

22. Sitwell took him very literally, telling Minogue, who now led the 32nd Brigade, which he had selected for the task, that the men were not intended to fight, but merely to create a defensive line.

23. Guns which had been placed on the western slope, and had been shelling the beach and anchorage, had been pulled back behind the crest, for fear that they would fall into enemy hands.

24. These troops were a mixed bunch: 450 infantrymen from the 1st Battalion of the 31st Regiment; 300 gendarmes; 200 dismounted cavalry, and a pioneer company.

25. Despite his lowly rank, Hankey was a very powerful man indeed thanks to his position, a post he had taken up in 1912 and would hold for twenty-six years, twenty-two of them (from 1916) in parallel with that of Secretary to the Cabinet.

26. The addition of a pioneer battalion to an infantry division was a recent innovation in the British Army; Hammersley apparently considered them as just an extra fighting unit. In this case, there was no justification whatsoever for his assumption that this unit – the 6th East Yorkshires – was fresher than any other available; in fact, the very reverse was true. His action here – which, as we shall see, resulted in the essential Scimitar Hill position being abandoned to the Turks – was later cited as an example of his poor grasp of the situation and the inferior quality of his staff work.

27. Minogue had originally selected the 8th W. Riding to lead the advance, but had then recalled Hammersley's injunction to 'send the pioneers'.

28. The 53rd (Welsh) Division was a unit of the Territorial Force. It had lost most of its best battalions since formation, sent to France as reinforcement drafts (hence the distinctly non-Welsh character of its third brigade). Under the command of Maj.-Gen. JE Lindley, it comprised the 158th Brigade (1/5th, 1/6th and 1/7th Royal Welch Fusiliers and 1/1st Herefordshire Regiment); the 159th Brigade (1/4th and 1/7th Cheshire Regiment and 1/4th and 1/5th Welch Regiment) and the 160th Brigade (2/4th Queen's (Royal

W. Surrey Regiment), 1/4th Royal Sussex Regiment, 2/4th Royal W. Kent Regiment and 2/10th Middlesex Regiment). The division had no artillery or support troops save two field companies of sappers and a company of cyclists.

29. In fact, only rather more than half of them; only two and a half companies were alerted. In the circumstances, that proved to be a blessing in disguise.

30. Hamilton had offered him the 54th Division, but he reluctantly declined, recognising that he could not keep them supplied, particularly with water. The division was landed at Suvla Bay instead.

31. The 54th (East Anglian) Division was a unit of the Territorial Force. Under the command of Maj.-Gen. FS Inglefield, it comprised the 161st Brigade (1/4th, 1/5th, 1/6th and 1/7th Essex Regiment), the 162nd Brigade (1/5th Bedfordshire Regiment, 1/4th Northamptonshire Regiment and 1/10th and 1/11th London Regiment) and the 163rd Brigade (1/4th and 1/5th Norfolk Regiment, 1/5th Suffolk Regiment and 1/8th Hampshire Regiment). It too lacked artillery and had just two field companies of Royal Engineers and a company of cyclists in support.

32. The Northants did not land until that afternoon.

33. It is not clear whether Hamilton had in fact suggested replacing Hammersley at this stage, and he did not do so until later, and then on Kitchener's instruction. He had not wished to replace Mahon, but see below.

34. He asked Sir John French to release Lt.-Gen. Sir Julian Byng to command IX Corps; he arrived on 23 August, together with Maj.-Gens Maude and Fanshawe.

35. Composed mainly of the 2nd Mounted Division, a yeomanry unit, which was to be operated as infantry, of course. Kitchener had ordered it sent to Egypt in late April, intended as a reinforcement for Gallipoli 'if Sir Ian Hamilton needs it'. 5,000 of its men, organised as five battalions in a reinforced brigade, had been despatched from Alexandria on 9 August; they were now ready to disembark.

36. Though an attempt to make yet more ground, the following day, saw the 8th Northumberland Fusiliers lose almost half their number.

37. It consisted of the remnants of his own 29th Indian Brigade, the 4th Australian Brigade, the 5th Connaught Rangers, the 10th Hampshires and the 4th South Wales Borderers, and two regiments of the New Zealand Mounted Rifles Brigade. This sounds like an impressive force, but in reality these units were at far from full strength, and though they had had some rest since the Battle of Sari Bair, were in very poor physical condition.

38. A total of twenty-two; they had been hurriedly collected, and there had been no time to develop a proper fire plan.

39. Though he permitted Keyes to go to London, to put it before Balfour at the Admiralty. If Balfour favoured it, de Roebeck intended to ask to be relieved of his post. Keyes' proposal was based on the situation in the Dardanelles being much changed from that which had applied on 18 March, particularly since many of the movable guns which had been used to harass the fleet to such good effect then had been transferred in order to be brought to bear on the Helles and Anzac beachheads. That, combined with much-improved arrangements to sweep for mines (and the elimination of those in Eren Keui Bay, which had done the real damage to the fleet) and the presence in the fleet of specialist bombardment ships, meant that a determined effort now had a good chance of success, Keyes argued, and in that he was supported most solidly by Wemyss.

40. This decision was informed by that of the French Commander-in-Chief, Joffre, to mount an offensive on the Western Front in September. Joffre did not have the support even of his own government, but was prepared to go ahead anyway. The offensive, which began on 25 September and continued until 6 November, encompassed the

Second Battle of Champagne, where the French lost 100,000 and the Germans 75,000, the Third Battle of Artois, a continuation of the attempt to take Vimy Ridge, and the Battle of Loos, which cost the British perhaps 60,000. That latter was to be the downfall of Sir John French, who was replaced in command of the British Expeditionary Force by Sir Douglas Haig on 17 December.

41. The 6th and 7th Brigades arrived early in September.

42. They were the predecessor of the Navy, Army and Air Force Institute, NAAFI, which began operating in 1921.

43. The French troops withdrawn from Helles were not all from the same division; rather they were selected from both, and included both metropolitan regiments, the Zouaves and the Légion Étrangère. From early October the only French troops at Gallipoli were the twelve battalions of Senegalese and Colonial Infantry, plus the field and heavy artillery batteries.

44. Father of Rupert, founder of News International. The twenty-eight-year-old Murdoch had high hopes of being appointed Australia's official war correspondent at Gallipoli, but was beaten to it by CEW Bean. Instead, he found work with a cable service providing material for the Sydney *Sun* and the Melbourne *Herald* from the offices of *The Times* in London. On his way to the United Kingdom, in August 1915, he stopped in Egypt, and wrote to Hamilton asking permission to visit Gallipoli. Hamilton, who had little time for journalists, reluctantly agreed, and Murdoch spent four days at Anzac. There he met the English newspaperman Ellis Ashmead-Bartlett, who was fiercely critical of Hamilton, and whose opinions seemed to confirm reports he had heard in Cairo. Ashmead-Bartlett played a leading role in creating the stalwart image of the ANZAC trooper which persists in the public imagination, particularly in Australia, to this day. The Australian war correspondents Bean, Schuler and Smith also helped to foster 'Australia's sense of nationhood through the Gallipoli experience', in the words of the National Library of Australia, though often in terms which, were it not laughable, might almost appear homoerotic. Ashmead-Bartlett persuaded Murdoch to smuggle a letter highly critical of Hamilton and GHQ to London, bypassing the censorship regulations. In the event, the letter's existence became known, Murdoch was arrested by French military intelligence at Marseilles, and the letter confiscated, but he retained enough of the sense of it to write a lengthy 'report' of his own in a similar, though much more emphatic, vein to the Australian Prime Minister, Andrew Fisher, with whom he was on personal terms. A copy of this document found its way to Asquith (at Lloyd George's suggestion), and despite its acknowledged factual errors, Asquith took the most unusual step of having it reprinted by His Majesty's Stationery Office, giving it official standing. There is no doubt that it was influential in having Hamilton recalled. The tone of the letter can be judged by quoting Murdoch on the subject of the General Staff:

What I want to say to you now very seriously is that the continuous and ghastly bungling over the Dardanelles enterprise was to be expected from such General Staff as the British Army possesses, so far as I have seen it. The conceit and self-complacency of the red feather men are equalled only by their incapacity. Along the line of communications, and especially at Mudros, are countless high officers and complacent young cubs who are clearly only playing at war. What can you expect of men who have never worked seriously, who have lived for their appearance and social distinction and selfsatisfaction [sic] and are now called on to conduct a gigantic war? Kitchener has a terrible task in getting pure work out of these men, whose motives can never be pure for they are unchangeably selfish. I want to say frankly that it is my opinion, and that without exception of Australian officers, that appointments to the General Staff are made from motives of friendship and personal influence. Australians now loathe and detest any Englishman wearing red. Without such a purification of motive as will bring youth and enthusiasm to the top we cannot win.

45. Monro had made a name for himself in France, having commanded first the 2nd Division, then I Corps, then the Third Army.

46. Churchill, who knew exactly what Monro's recommendation would be, and deprecated it, maintained that 'he familiarised himself in the space of six hours with the conditions prevailing on the 15-mile front of Anzac, Suvla and Helles, and spoke a few discouraging words to the principal officers at each point. He came, he saw, he capitulated,' he said.

47. Its inaugural membership was Asquith, Balfour, Lloyd George and Grey. Bonar Law (who was both Colonial Secretary and Leader of the Conservative Party) was added some days later after pressure had been applied by the Tories. Kitchener was its secretary. Churchill, who had missed no opportunity to champion the cause of remaining in Gallipoli, had no place on it, and his reaction to being bypassed was characteristic: he resigned his office as Chancellor of the Duchy of Lancaster ('a well-paid sinecure', he called it) and retired first to France for four months (reviving his army commission and taking command of the 6th Royal Scots Fusiliers), and then to the backbenches. He returned to the Cabinet the following year, first as Minister of Munitions and later as Secretary of State for War, under Lloyd George.

48. Those tentatively selected were the 53rd, the 54th and the RND.

49. Apparently because it was believed there was no chance of him reaching the Mediterranean port in time, rather than due to any conspiracy to scupper Kitchener's plan. When he, in turn, reached Paris he learned that so keen were the French on the Allies remaining in Gallipoli that they would contribute six more obsolescent battleships to the naval operation. By the time he reached Mudros, via Naples, it was too late, however, for Kitchener had by then given his assent to evacuation.

50. Their objection was a political one. The subject comes in for a more detailed analysis in the British Official History of the Palestine campaign, in which a translation of a letter from the Military Attaché at the French Embassy in London to the CIGS is reproduced. 'French public opinion could not be indifferent to any operations attempted in a country *which it considers as destined to form part of the future Syrian state ...*' (italics added). This correspondence pre-dates the Sykes-Picot Agreement (qv) by six months.

51. The strength of the garrison required to hold the three zones – for a week, if necessary, in the event of prolonged bad weather – was put at 26,000 men and forty guns for Suvla, the same for Anzac, and 18,500 men and 60 guns for Helles. Those levels were subsequently reduced.

52. By now, the salt lake having reformed, the only communication between the northern and southern sectors of the zone was at the front line and by means of a bridge across the Cut, close to the beach.

53. In fact, the moon was two days before full; with the sky clear, there was a good degree of illumination.

54. But included the old battleship HMS *Mars*.

55. Each one consisted of nine officers and ninety-four picked men. They were divided into three groups: C1 parties consisted of four officers and twenty-six men, and were the first to leave; C2 Parties left half an hour later, and consisted of two officers and thirty-four men, and fifteen minutes later the remainder would follow.

56. The day after the northern zones were cleared, on 21 December, Monro received orders to return to Europe, to take command of the First Army. Sir William Robertson had been appointed CIGS to replace Murray, who had been ordered to Egypt to take over the Mediterranean Expeditionary Force, and would have overall responsibility for Helles and Salonika too. Monro signalled Kitchener on 23 December that he intended to sail three days hence, leaving Birdwood in temporary charge, but the War Minister instructed him to remain until Murray arrived.

57. The embarkation of mules was much affected by the loss of a transport, the *St Oswald*, which sank after a collision with the battleship *Suffren*.

CHAPTER 13

1. Still a province of the Ottoman Empire, though it had been under de facto British control since 1882; Britain declared it a Protectorate on 18 December 1914.

2. Seventeen infantry battalions, a small cavalry/mounted infantry detachment, six batteries of field and mountain artillery and one of machine guns; the majority of the units were located in the Sudan, where the British had fought an on-and-off – but extremely bitter – war from 1883 to 1898, and which still required a garrison to keep the populace in check.

3. Who had served in that same role in 1908–12; on the outbreak of war Maxwell had been liaison officer with the French High Command.

4. Cheetham was named High Commissioner when Britain declared the protectorate, and was replaced in that post by Sir Henry McMahon just twenty-three days later, on 9 January 1915.

5. The canal is 163km long and was, at that time (it has since been enlarged considerably), around 100m wide. It is a sea-level canal, and itself accommodates the marginal difference in the levels of the Red Sea and the Mediterranean without the need of locks. It passes through three lakes – Timsah (11km long) and the (contiguous) Great and Little Bitter Lakes (together 35km in length) – on its way from Port Said at the northern end, by way of Ismailia, to Suez at the southern. A railway and a sweet-water canal followed the line of the waterway on its west bank.

6. There were just three viable routes across the Sinai from Palestine. The best, with the most abundant wells and oases, paralleled the coast from Gaza to El Arish, Qatiya and Romani to Qantara; another ran from Aqaba to Suez by way of Nakhl (where the only important watering-point was located) and a third ran north of there, from Aqaba through the central highlands to Ismailia. The border between Egypt and Syria ran from Rafah to the Gulf of Aqaba; thus the whole of Sinai was notionally under British control.

7. And was soon ordered to Thrace, to be replaced, in part, by the 35th and 36th Divisions of XII Corps, transferred from Mesopotamia.

8. VIII Corps was brought up to a strength of five infantry divisions: the 8th, 10th, 23rd, 25th and 27th. The 8th, 10th and 25th were later transferred to Gallipoli, and the 24th arrived from Thrace. VIII Corps was later brought back up to four- division strength by the addition of the 3rd, following the evacuation of Gallipoli, and more divisions followed.

9. Of which each regiment had left its third battalion in Palestine, perhaps having taken the strongest individuals to make up numbers in the others. The expeditionary force which advanced into Sinai totalled around 25,000 by Jemal's account.

10. As they neared the canal they came within range of aircraft based at Ismailia (five Farmans and a BE2a), which had very limited capabilities. French seaplanes operating

from the converted captured cargo steamer *Aenne Rickmers* also participated, flying as far as Aqaba and Beersheba. The aircraft not only kept tabs on the advancing Turks but also attacked them with rudimentary bombs, to little effect. The *Aenne Rickmers* was taken into British service as HMS *Anne* in January 1915, and continued to operate in the Eastern Mediterranean and the Red Sea until 1917. A second German merchantman, the *Rabenfels*, was also taken up by the Royal Navy for similar purposes, and was commissioned as HMS *Raven II*.

11. On the orders of Jemal Pasha, and against the initial advice of Kressenstein, who wished to continue the operation; the German later changed his mind but remained in Sinai, with three infantry battalions, some guns and a cavalry squadron, to cause as much mischief as possible and act as a focus for any renewed attempt on the canal.

12. This was Kressenstein's sizeable force.

13. They formed the nucleus of the squadron which tried to force the Dardanelles on 18 March.

14. The hard core numbered around 2,500, organised as seven battalions (accompanied by numerous Bedouin irregulars who were mostly in it for the loot, and tended to disappear when things went against them); they had at least nine mountain guns and a dozen or more machine guns. They were under the military command of a 'Turkish' Arab, a native of Baghdad, named Jafar el Askeri, who proved to be a very effective trainer and combat commander. Jafar, captured and imprisoned, later changed sides and led a force of Arab 'regulars' (largely composed of other ex-PoWs) in Syria, distinguishing himself at the Battle of Talifa.

15. The Imperial Strategic Reserve amounted to fourteen divisions (though not all were present in Egypt at the same time). In the event, four remained in Egypt beyond the end of June 1916 (and one of those was later sent to France); nine went to France and one to Mesopotamia; of those ten, the last had left before the end of June 1916. As well as the divisions from Gallipoli, two new ones (the 4th and 5th) were formed from men sent from Australia (and the New Zealand and Australian Division was broken up, the men from New Zealand being combined with new drafts to form the New Zealand Division, the Australians to be combined with others of their countrymen), and two (the 31st and 46th) came from the United Kingdom; these latter were to remain in Egypt only briefly, and before the end of February both had received orders for France.

16. On his return to the United Kingdom he was posted to Dublin as Commander-in-Chief. He is perhaps best known for his role in putting down the Easter Rising there soon afterwards.

17. Turkish prisoners soon revealed that the forces at hand were men of the 3rd Division, veterans of Gallipoli, who had been transferred to Palestine the previous April. Kress von Kressenstein was in command. Erickson, quoting Turkish sources, puts their overall strength at almost 12,000.

CHAPTER 14

1. Kitchener left Cairo, never to return, in July 1914: see Chapter 10, esp. Note 2. Chief amongst the men he left behind were Sir Milne Cheetham, who stood in for him until 18 December, when Sir Henry McMahon was appointed High Commissioner, and Lt.-Gen. Sir Reginald Wingate, a career soldier who had succeeded him as Sirdar of the Egyptian Army and Governor-General of the Sudan at the end of 1899. Behind Wingate was Gilbert Clayton, another career soldier, who was at one and the same time the Agent for the Sudan in Cairo and Director of Intelligence of the Egyptian Army, to which responsibilities he was to add those of Director of

British Intelligence in Cairo on 31 October 1914. Also present was Ronald Storrs, Wingate's Oriental Secretary.

2. The likes of Muhammed al-Faruqi, a junior officer in the Turkish Army who had deserted at Gallipoli and had then insinuated himself into intelligence circles in Cairo, and Aziz Ali al-Masri; see Note 17 below.

3. In that it would have slowed, but not prevented, communication between Britain and her eastern dominions.

4. Jihad is a much-misunderstood term outside the Islamic community. Its original and perhaps purest meaning is 'struggle', in the sense of one's internal struggle to live a moral and virtuous life, and this is known as the Greater Jihad or Jihad of the Soul (*jihad bin qalb*). The so-called Lesser Jihad is usually defined as the (armed, if necessary) struggle for the defence or advancement of Islam, some suggesting that it is legitimate to go as far as to force it on the entire population. It is in this sense, that of 'holy war', that the term is (mis)used here.

5. Muslims made up around 25 per cent of the entire population of 'British' India, which then stood at perhaps 300 million. Kitchener's fears proved to be largely groundless. The call came on 11 November, six days after Britain declared war on the Ottoman Empire, and went largely unheeded save in Mesopotamia and amongst some fundementalists in the *maghreb*. A similar declaration of jihad against Allied forces was made by the Grand Mufti of Jerusalem on 25 November 1941, and met with a similar unenthusiastic response.

6. From Banu Hashim, a subgroup or clan of the Quresh tribe, from which the caliph had traditionally come until the caliphate was transferred to Constantinople by Sultan Selim in 1517CE and combined with the Osmanli sultanate.

7. Al-Masri was a former officer in the Ottoman Army, of Circassian descent but brought up in Cairo. A class-mate of Enver Pasha, he had advanced no further than the rank of major, and, dissatisfied, had begun to meddle in Arab politics, joining (perhaps forming) a secret society known as al-Ahd. Al-Masri actually aspired to supplant Enver, but had to content himself with a lesser role as *agent provocateur*. He convinced Clayton, for one, that he could function at a high level in Arab circles, and that he had significant influence over Hussein and his circle. David Fromkin describes his role and that of al-Faruqi (and indeed, the general mood of Britain's administration in Cairo) most convincingly in A Peace to End All Peace, and it serves little purpose to do more than précis his account here.

8. He declared himself to be just that, without much noticeable effect outside the Hejaz, in 1916, but see below.

9. The correspondence was drafted not by McMahon – 'notoriously dull-witted and ineffectual' – but rather by Ronald Storrs, following the line dictated to him by Kitchener. The promise was unsustainable, of course, but worse was to come when it was contradicted in Balfour's eponymous declaration to the Zionists two years later; see Chapter 17.

10. Not, apparently, until 12 December, long after the message had gone out to Hussein.

11. Ibn Saud had already risen in revolt against the Ottomans once, in the coastal al-Hasa province, the previous year, and had defeated a Turkish army, but had not been able to hold on to his gains. He had also been probing to try to determine which way the British would jump if he rose against the Ottomans again, to be told, by Capt William Shakespear, an officer of the Indian Political Service who was then Britain's Political Agent in Kuwait, that his government was not prepared to interfere in Ottoman domestic affairs.

12. It soon became clear that Clayton was a very much more adept operator than Sykes;

the traffic between the two was certainly weighted in his favour, and he made far better use of Sykes than Sykes ever did of him.

13. Hogarth had obtained for him a four-year 'demyship', a travelling scholarship, from Magdalen College, after he came down from Jesus College with a first-class honours degree in Modern History in the summer of 1910.

14. Amongst them Alan Dawnay, Pierce Joyce, Alec Kirkbride and Stewart Newcombe, the operation's original commander; Lawrence was the group's self-appointed 'intelligence officer', and as such spent more time than the others in the company of Prince Feisal, building a relationship he fostered assiduously post-war.

15. The day of Kitchener's death, coincidentally.

16. There are suggestions that the troops in question were in fact bound for the Yemen, with the objective of protecting German technicians led by Freiherr Othmar von Stotzingen, or perhaps proceeding to Somaliland, where the ruler was said to have designs on Italian Eritrea. Stotzingen was apparently tasked with establishing a radio station at or near Sana'a in the Yemen. In the event, his men – and one woman, the Kurdish wife of a German adventurer named Neufeld, who served as his translator – got no further than Yambo, and scattered when Feisal's band arrived; the troops – 3,500 of them – were used to bring the garrison at Medina back up to full strength.

17. He had around 30,000 men assembled near Medina; only 6,000 of them had rifles, and they had no heavier weapons, not even machine guns.

18. Particularly at that moment, for the Hajj, the annual pilgrimage to the Holy Places, took place in September. The British government assisted many pilgrims from Egypt and India to attend, and generated considerable goodwill in the process.

19. Led, for the most part, by British officers trained in the use of explosives; where before the Arabs had contented themselves with removing a rail or two, which the Turks would replace within hours, raiding parties now demolished whole stretches of the line – and occasionally, trains too – culverts and bridges being prime locations for substantial charges. Elsewhere, French officers from colonial regiments performed similar duties alongside Ali's and Abdullah's men, a French military mission under Col. E Bremond having arrived in September.

20. Along with Hussein ibn Ali, Abdul Aziz ibn Saud and Ibn Rashid. Ibn Shalaan was an ally of ibn Saud.

21. Dobell had been in command of the Western Frontier Force since June; he was now promoted lieutenant-general.

22. His suggestion was poorly timed, if nothing else; this was just days before Maude began advancing on Kut.

23. The Royal Navy filled in; in the fortnight following 23 December, some 1,500 tons of stores were landed at El Arish.

24. He would retain all his mounted troops, he was told, and 'there was no intention of curtailing such activities as he considered justified by his resources'.

25. And, under the command of Maj.-Gen. ES Girdwood, became the 229th, 230th and 231st Infantry Brigades. At this point, the latter two were in the Western Desert. The 229th Brigade consisted of the 16th Devonshire Regiment, the 12th Somerset Light Infantry, the 14th Royal Highlanders and the 12th Royal Scots Fusiliers; the 230th Brigade consisted of the 10th East Kent Regiment, the 16th Sussex Regiment, the 15th Suffolk Regiment and the 12th Norfolk Regiment; the 231st Brigade consisted of the 10th Shropshire Light Infantry, the 24th Welsh Regiment and the 24th and 25th Royal Welch Fusiliers.

26. The 4th, 11th and 12th ALHR.

27. From Thrace, where it had been sent to rebuild itself after Gallipoli.

28. Each of them less one brigade, the 1st Light Horse from the former and the 4th from the latter, which remained at Khan Yunis.

29. The 53rd (Welsh) Division had been under the command of Maj.-Gen. AE Dallas since the previous spring; its constitution was unchanged since Gallipoli (see Chapter 12, Note 28) save that, as with other divisions, a machine gun company had been added to each brigade.

30. The garrison was made up of the 79th and 125th Regiments and a battalion from the 81st, supported by five artillery batteries. It was under the command of a German major named Tiller.

31. The British Official History is at pains to point out that while Dobell had forces considerably greater than those of a corps at his command, his staff was not commensurate, and that Chetwode had a staff equivalent in size to that of a single division. MacMunn and Falls attribute many of the command errors made, especially during the latter part of the battle, to this shortage of staff officers.

32. Water had been found in limited quantities in the wadi running north from Gaza and to the east of the city, but for substantial amounts it would be necessary to withdraw to the Wadi Ghazze, where engineers had been digging productive wells since early that morning.

33. Thus, some twenty minutes before the infantry had secured Ali el Muntar. Chetwode did not learn of that success until some time later, but it is not clear whether it would have influenced his decision had he known earlier.

34. They had been used for instruction, and were more than a little tired, though they performed better than had been expected as soon as the crews learned not to grease the tracks, as they had been accustomed to do in Europe.

35. Dallas resigned his command – for reasons of ill-health – in the last days of March.

36. The *Requin* and the monitors *M 21* and *M 31*. Warships had not been employed during the first battle out of fear of their fire falling on British positions. The monitors were M 15-class ships, hastily constructed (some took just three months from their keels being laid to their being commissioned) in 1915 and mounting single 9.2in guns originally intended for use aboard heavy cruisers of the *Edgar* and *Drake* classes. They were undistinguished ships with a lively motion which diminished their effectiveness as gun platforms.

37. Two tanks were told off to accompany each division; those with the 52nd were not required and did not go into action.

38. In all, the 60-pounders and 6-in howitzers had 500 rounds per gun, the 8-in howitzers 400; the 4.5-in howitzers and the 18-pounders had 600 rounds each. As early as mid morning it had become clear that the provision of shells had been nowhere near enough for the task at hand. For the first forty minutes of the initial barrage, the 4.5-in howitzers fired gas-filled shells, 4,000 rounds of which had been brought up for the purpose; this was the first time gas had been used in the theatre. They were to be directed at enemy batteries and the wooded area south-west of Ali-el Muntar.

39. Prime Minister Lloyd George had wanted the South African, Jan Smuts, for the job, but he declined. Allenby, then commanding the Cavalry Corps in France, is said to have thought the posting a demotion at first.

CHAPTER 15

1. Chetwode based his estimates on intelligence which suggested that the Turks now had five infantry and one cavalry division in the front line, and at least another infantry division south of Jerusalem, with an effective strength of 46,000 rifles, 2,100 sabres (in

fact, the Turkish cavalry was armed with the lance, not the sword), 250 machine guns and 200 artillery pieces of all types. This estimate was vastly inflated; the real effective infantry strength was half the quoted figure, and that of the cavalry no more than a third.

2. Allenby's staff went to considerable lengths to perpetuate that deception. One of the simplest, and apparently most successful, operations involved an intelligence officer riding out into the desert on a reconnaissance patrol which carefully brought him within range of Turkish cavalry. He was fired on, appeared to be wounded, and dropped a haversack convincingly splashed with (horse's) blood, which contained documents including the agenda for a staff meeting, all of which pointed to Gaza being the objective of the next offensive; the attack on Beersheba, they warned, would be a feint. It seems that while Turkish staff officers were suspicious – the British had, in fact, rather over-egged the pudding – Kressenstein was inclined to believe what he read, and work on defensive positions on the left, around Beersheba, was reduced in favour of those near Gaza, including some along the coast north of the city, where the 'lost' documents had indicated an amphibious landing would take place. Richard Meinertzhagen claimed the credit for having developed and executed the plan, but he lied; the author was Lt-Col. JD Belgrave, and it was carried out by Capt. ACB Neate. Kressenstein, writing in 1928, claimed never to have been taken in.

3. He asked for two additional infantry divisions on top of the 60th, then in the process of equipping, and the 75th, in formation (the 60th was a Territorial division, recruited exclusively in London, which had seen service in France and was then at Salonika. The 75th was a mixed division of Territorials and native battalions from India), which he had been promised; this would bring the total to eight. In the event he got one additional division, the 10th (Irish).

4. The Desert Mounted Corps (DMC) was under Lt.-Gen. Sir Harry Chauvel's command; it consisted of the Australia and New Zealand Mounted Division (Chaytor), with the 1st Australian Light Horse Brigade (Cox; 1st, 2nd and 3rd ALH Regiments), the 2nd Australian Light Horse Brigade (Brig.-Gen. GL Ryrie; 5th, 6th and 7th ALH Regiments) and the New Zealand Mounted Rifles Brigade (Brig.-Gen. W Meldrum; Auckland, Canterbury and Wellington MR Regiments); the Australian Mounted Division (Hodgson), with the 3rd Australian Light Horse Brigade (Brig.-Gen. LC Wilson; 8th, 9th and 10th ALH Regiments); the 4th Australian Light Horse Brigade (Brig.-Gen. W Grant; 4th, 11th and 12th ALH Regiments) and the 5th Mounted Brigade (Brig.-Gen. PD Fitzgerald; 1/1st Warwickshire Yeomanry, 1/1st Gloucestershire Yeomanry and 1/1st Worcestershire Yeomanry); the Yeomanry Mounted Division (Maj.-Gen. Sir George Barrow), with the 6th Mounted Brigade (Brig.-Gen. CAC Godwin; 1/1st Buckinghamshire Hussars, 1/1st Berkshire Yeomanry and 1/1st Dorset Yeomanry); the 8th Mounted Brigade (Brig.-Gen. CS Rome; 1/1st City of London Yeomanry, 1/1st and 1/3rd County of London Yeomanry) and the 22nd Mounted Brigade (Brig.-Gen. FAB Fryer; 1/1st Lincolnshire Yeomanry, 1/1st Staffordshire Yeomanry and 1/1st E. Riding Yeomanry). The Imperial Camel Corps Brigade (Brig.-Gen. CL Smith; 2nd (Imperial) Battalion, 3rd and 4th (A&NZ) Battalions) and the 7th Mounted Brigade (Brig.-Gen. JT Wigan; 1/1st Sherwood Rangers and 1/1st S. Nottinghamshire Hussars) were attached.

5. Commanded by Lt.-Gen. Sir Philip Chetwode, it consisted of the 10th Division (unchanged except in detail since its arrival in Gallipoli; see Chapter 12, Note 5. Maj.-Gen. JR Longley was in command), the 53rd Division (Mott), the 74th (Yeomanry) Division (Girdwood) and the 60th (London) Division. The latter was commanded by Maj.-Gen. JSM Shea and consisted of the 179th Brigade (Brig.-Gen. FM Edwards; 2/13th, 2/14th, 2/15th and 2/16th London Regiment); the 180th Brigade (Brig.-Gen. CF

Watson; 2/17th, 2/18th, 2/19th and 2/20th London Regiment) and the 181st Brigade (Brig.-Gen. EC da Costa; 2/21st, 2/22nd, 2/23rd and 2/24th London Regiment), plus a pioneer battalion (the 1/12th Loyal North Lancashire Regiment).

6. Commanded by Lt.-Gen. Sir Edward Bulfin, it consisted of the 52nd Division (Maj.-Gen. J Hill), the 54th Division (Hare) and the 75th Division. The latter was commanded by Maj.-Gen. PC Palin and consisted of the 232nd Brigade (Brig.-Gen. HJ Huddleston; 1/5th Devonshire Regiment, 2/5th Hampshire Regiment, 2/4th Somerset Light Infantry and 2/3rd Gurkhas); 233rd Brigade (Brig.-Gen. EM Colston; 1/5th Somerset Light infantry, 1/4th Wiltshire Regiment, 2/4th Hampshire Regiment and 3/3rd Gurkhas) and the 234th Brigade (Brig.-Gen. FG Anley; 1/4th Duke of Cornwall's Light Infantry, 2/4th Dorset Regiment, 123rd Outram's Rifles and 58th Vaughan's Rifles).

7. The Composite Force consisted of Indian troops on Imperial Service, the 1st Battalion, the British West Indies Regiment, and detachments from the French contingents (qv); it amounted to 3,000 rifles and six mounted squadrons.

8. One of Allenby's early decisions was to act on Murray's suggestion and order the line from Qantara to Rafah doubled; the existing single line would be enough to supply the army he was building to take Gaza and Beersheba – just – but not to sustain that which would be necessary to advance beyond Jerusalem, and it was believed that the enlargement would take at least six months to accomplish. In fact, by the time the offensive began the second track had reached Mazar, halfway to the front, a mile (1,500m) a day having been laid during September and October.

9. Erich von Falkenhayn had succeeded von Moltke as the German Chief of Staff after the Battle of the Marne in 1914. It was he more than anyone who settled on the policy of fighting a battle of attrition at Verdun, and when it did not have the effect he hoped, his detractors – principally von Hindenburg and Ludendorff, who had all along favoured a strategy of focusing German pressure on Russia, and whom he had forestalled – succeeded in ousting him. He was first named as commander of the Ninth Army in Rumania, and launched a campaign which saw Bucharest captured in four months, and was then seconded to the Ottoman Army, arriving in Constantinople to take up his post in late July.

10. The Asienkorps (Asya Kolu to the Turks) was under the command of Col. von Frankenberg und Proschlitz (he was later succeeded by Col. von Oppen). It consisted initially of three battalions raised from volunteers on the Western Front, the 701st, 702nd and 703rd, each with six heavy and eighteen light machine guns. To each battalion was attached a machine gun company with a further six Maxims, a troop of cavalry, an 'infantry-artillery platoon' with two mountain guns, and a trench-mortar section with four mortars. Attached was the 701st Artillery detachment, with two batteries of four 7.7-cm guns and one of four 10.5-cm howitzers, and the machine gun detachment Hentig. It also brought with it four flights of aircraft, three for reconnaissance and one for pursuit, as well as communications specialists. It was assembled at Neuhammer (Świętoszów) in Silesia in April or May 1917. The Asienkorps was also known by the codename Pascha II, Pascha having been that given to a much smaller detachment of German troops sent to Sinai to assist the Turks in the abortive attack on the Suez Canal. Pascha II was later increased in size, augmented by the 146th Masurian Infantry Regiment (three battalions) and the 11th Reserve Jäger (Mountain) Battalion, a mountain artillery detachment with three batteries of four 10.5-cm howitzers, and a mountain machine gun detachment of four companies. Each battalion, together with its attached support troops, was trained to operate independently if necessary. The Turks, who had expected a much larger force, were not impressed, but were wrong to underestimate what was always intended to be a 'cadre' force of highly skilled men.

11. He was right to be concerned. Soon thereafter he was invited to visit Germany as the guest of the Kaiser. When he arrived at the General Staff's headquarters at Bad Kreuznach, he found a cable from Enver waiting. It informed him that he had been relieved of his command in Palestine, which Falkenhayn would take over. From then on he was restricted to 'providing logistical support to von Falkenhayn', as Edward Erickson puts it, from his headquarters in Damascus. He later resigned his command and returned to Constantinople.

12. During the interim period Kemal accompanied the Crown Prince, Mehmet Vadhettin, on a visit to Germany; in the course of it he fell ill, and spent some months in Vienna and Carlsbad in recovery. Thus, the man held by many to be the Ottoman Army's most competent general was unavailable to it during a crucial period. He returned to active service only in April 1918.

13. Such wire as there was available was allocated to the Gaza defences and to the positions south-west of Beersheba. It was never enough, and the quality of the Beersheba positions, in particular, suffered as a result.

14. Now under the command of Brig.-Gen. NE Money (sic).

15. Still crucial, even though by now the wells at Beersheba were back in full production and were delivering 400,000 gallons (1.9m litres) of water a day.

16. Now under the command of Brig.-Gen. CF Watson. Brig.-Gen. Carleton had relinquished command in August 1917, and was replaced by Brig.-Gen. Hill, who was soon elevated to command the 52nd Division.

17. With the addition of the ships offshore, this was the heaviest artillery bombardment of the entire war outside the European theatres.

18. The bombardment fleet consisted of the 14-in monitor *Raglan* (qv); the *Requin* with her two 27.4-cm guns; the 9.2-in monitor *M 29*; the heavy cruiser HMS *Grafton*, with two 9.2-in; three 6-in monitors; the river gunboats *Ladybird* and *Aphis*, which each mounted two 6-in, and seven destroyers, all of which had multiple 4-in guns. Not all ships were present throughout the action.

19. Four more tanks were allocated to the 161st and 163rd Brigades, and two were held in reserve. Overall they proved to be of limited value, and this was the detachment's last deployment in the theatre.

20. A 'pure' cavalry unit, as opposed to mounted infantry (and armed with the lance, not the sword), it was something of an anomaly by this time; it consisted primarily of the Jodhpore, the Mysore and the 1st Hyderabad Lancers.

21. Falkenhayn arrived in Jerusalem on the evening of the fifth; one of his first acts was to consent to Kressenstein's request to be allowed to evacuate his heavy artillery from Gaza, and the bulk of it was moved, some by rail, that night. The infantry followed the following day.

22. Allenby returned the Australian Mounted Division to Chauvel's command now; even so, the number of horsemen he would be able to field on 7 November – four complete brigades – fell short of the GOC's hopes.

23. A composite regiment made up of one squadron each from the Royal Glasgow Yeomanry, the Duke of Lancaster's Yeomanry and the 1/1st Hertfordshire Yeomanry.

24. In fact, he was in greater danger than he knew on that flank, for under Kressenstein's guidance the Turks had stabilised and reorganised the 16th, 26th and 53rd Divisions, which were now lined up on a front of ten kilometres from the railway to Beit Jibrin.

25. Built around 1145 as one of a ring of fortifications designed to keep the Egyptian Fatimids in their place at Ashkelon. It is also held that it was the Gath of the Philistines, home to Goliath.

26. Falkenhayn had also sent the Seventh Army's 3rd Cavalry and 19th Infantry Divi-

sions to Beit Jibrin during the night, but had yet to order their forward deployment.

27. The destruction was planned in detail but not carried out, those responsible electing to save their own skins.

28. Unbeknown to Allenby, on the evening of 13 November Enver had visited Falkenhayn's headquarters in the city; they agreed that there was to be no siege, and that if the defensive screen before it was broken, the garrison would fall back.

29. The 9th ALH was not told of the change of plan; it proceeded to carry out its orders and entered the Wadi es Salman, north of Amwas, reaching the village of Yalo. In consequence the Turks evacuated the town, and when the 75th Division arrived the following morning (19 November) it found it abandoned.

30. Now under the command of Brig.-Gen. CAH Maclean.

31. Barrow was actually opposed by the 3rd Cavalry Division and half the 24th Infantry Division. They may have been weakened and depleted, but so was his own Yeomanry Mounted Division – by this stage the fighting strength of the YMD was no more than 1,200 – and this was no country for heavy horsemen.

32. Palin having felt it necessary to leave four – the 123rd Rifles, the 3/3rd Gurkhas, the 2/4th Hampshires and the 1/4th Duke of Cornwall's LI – to hold Nabi Samweil, and three on the Ramle road with the 2/4th Dorsets nearby, on the spur which led towards Buddu, until a brigade of the 52nd Division arrived to take over.

33. In detail, the situation was even more uncomfortable. The 22nd Mounted Brigade, which formed the eastern doorpost of the gap, was itself far too widely deployed. The E. Riding and Staffordshire Yeomanries were on the right, holding the high ground north-north-west of Foqa, while the Lincolnshire was at Hellabi, well to the left, north-west of Tahta; thus there was a two-kilometre gap between them.

34. Falls puts the Turks' inability to land a really telling blow down to the fact that 'Falkenhayn's ... scheme mainly depended [on the 19th Division having made] long marches over unknown and difficult country, with indifferent maps, and [he] was unaware of the golden opportunity within its grasp.' Be that as it may have been, Turkish sources suggest that, to the contrary, the field-marshal knew exactly what he was doing, but had been over-ambitious in thinking that he could march already weary men over that sort of distance and expect them to fight a battle immediately.

CHAPTER 16

1. Lloyd George had always adhered to the theory that Germany's greatest vulnerability lay outside France and away from the Western Front. In consequence he fought running battles with the 'Westerners' who continued to insist that only there could she be defeated definitively. It is worth repeating that he retained a visceral hatred of the Turks which he had acquired from William Ewart Gladstone.

2. The 7th (Indian) Division was indeed intended to reinforce Allenby's army, and not, as turned out to be the case, to replace one of his existing divisions.

3. Not to be confused with the Naur el Auja which flows into the Mediterranean north of Jaffa.

4. Smuts, who had fought successfully against the Germans in East Africa, arrived in London in March 1917, as a delegate to the Imperial War Conference called to settle the by now thorny question of the involvement of the Dominions' governments in the running of the war. Lloyd George persuaded him to stay behind after its business was concluded, and gave him a seat in the Cabinet. He had been offered command of the Allied forces in Palestine, and was tempted to accept, but turned it down when Robertson made it clear to him that the sort of manpower and weaponry he believed

necessary would not be made available to him, and Allenby was appointed instead.

5. It was to be replaced by the A&NZMD as soon as the latter had caught its breath, so to speak; the third of Chauvel's divisions, the Yeomanry, was the one in most need of rest.

6. In the days prior to his removal, Falkenhayn had moved his staff from Nazareth to Damascus and had ordered the headquarters of the Seventh Army moved from Nablus to Amman, and that of the Eighth from Tul Karm to Nablus. Immediately on being appointed, Sanders countermanded those orders, returning the staff to Nazareth.

7. Though only one of the 60th Division's brigades, the 181st, was involved, and that only on day one.

8. He was influenced by the successes Feisal's Arabs had had following their capture of Aqaba on 6 July 1917; using the port as a base they raided the Wadi Araba (as the Ghor, the Great Depression, is known, south of the Dead Sea), threatening Ma'an and the Hishe region from which the Turks derived food supplies and the wood which kept the railway operating. Late in 1917 they had reached Tafila, 75km north of Ma'an, stimulating the Turks to send a strong force to drive them back (to Shobek) in early March. Allenby reasoned that that force – which included the German 703rd Battalion – could not have returned to Amman by the time he would arrive there, but he was wrong.

9. Having exchanged its artillery for that of the 7th Division.

10. The 74th would be replaced by the other Indian Army Division from Mesopotamia, the 3rd (Lahore), under Maj.-Gen. Hoskins (though it would quit the line in Palestine long before its replacement arrived). The Yeomanry Division of the Desert Mounted Corps also underwent reorganisation, its brigades each giving up two 'British' regiments and receiving two from India in their place. Before long it would be split in two, becoming the 4th and 5th Cavalry Divisions, the former under Maj.-Gen. Barrow, the latter under Maj.-Gen. Macandrew. See below for the revised order of battle.

11. The 19th and 20th, forming XXII Corps, on the right, the 7th, 16th and 46th Divisions, together with the Germans, on the left. The boundary between them was the railway, running north–south.

12. Conventional wisdom has it that it was the presence of the Asienkorps, with its predominance of machine guns, both at Amman and opposing the 75th Division on the edge of the Plains of Sharon, that swung the affairs in the Turks' favour. In the latter, Sanders' insistence on creating strong defensive positions certainly played a part.

13. In all, Allenby sent over 60,000 officers and men to France. As well as losing the 52nd and 74th Divisions in their entirety, and nine Yeomanry regiments, Allenby was told at the end of April to send fourteen more battalions from his remaining divisions to France, the deficit to be made up by troops from India. By the beginning of summer, all seven divisions in the EEF (with the exception of the 54th) consisted of three British and nine Indian battalions – that is, the same make-up as the divisions of the 'old' Army of India.

By the end of the summer, when the offensive recommenced, Allenby's infantry consisted of XX Corps, under the command of Lt.-Gen. Sir Philip Chetwode, and XXI Corps, under the command of Lt.-Gen. Sir Edward Bulfin. XX Corps consisted of the 10th Division, under the command of Maj.-Gen. JR Longley, which comprised the 29th Brigade (Smith; 1st Leinster Regiment, 1/101st Grenadiers, 1/54th Sikhs, 2/151st Indian Infantry), the 30th Brigade (Greer; 1st R Irish Regiment, 1st Kashmir IS Infantry, 38th Dogras, 46th Punjabis) and the 31st Brigade (Morris; 2nd R Irish Fusiliers, 2/101st Grenadiers, 74th Punjabis, 2/42nd Deoli Regiment) and the 53rd Division, under the command of Maj.-Gen. FS Mott, which comprised the 158th Brigade (Vernon; 5/6th R Welch Fusiliers, 4/11th Gurkha Rifles, 3/153rd and 3/154th Indian Rifles), the 159th

Brigade (Money; 4/5th Welch Regiment, 3/152nd Indian Infantry, 1 and 2/153rd Indian Infantry).

XXI Corps consisted of the 3rd (Lahore) Division, under the command of Maj.-Gen. A R Hoskins, which comprised the 7th Brigade (Davidson; 1st Connaught Rangers, 2/7th Gurkha Rifles, 27th and 91st Punjabis), the 8th Brigade (Edwardes; 1st Manchester Regiment, 47th Sikhs, 59th Scinde Rifles and 2/124th Baluchistan Infantry) and the 9th Brigade (Luard; 2nd Dorsetshire Regiment, 1/1st Gurkha Rifles, 93rd (Burma) Infantry, 105th Maharatta Light Infantry); the 7th (Meerut) Division, under the command of Maj.-Gen. V B Fane, which consisted of the 19th Brigade (Weir; 1st Seaforth Highlanders, 28th and 92nd Punjabis and 125th Napier's Rifles), the 21st Brigade (Kemball; 2nd R Highlanders, 1st Guides Infantry, 20th Punjabis, 1/8th Gurkha Rifles) and 28th Brigade (Davies; 2nd Leicestershire Regiment, 51st and 53rd Sikhs and 56th Punjabi Rifles); the 54th (East Anglian) Division, under the command of Maj.-Gen. S W Hare, which comprised the 161st Brigade (Orpen-Palmer; 1/4th, 1/5th, 1/6th and 1/7th Essex Regiment), the 162nd Brigade (Mudge; 1/5th Bedfordshire Regiment, 1/4th Northamptonshire Regiment and 1/10th and 1/11th London Regiment) and the 163rd Brigade (McNeill; 1/4th and 1/5th Norfolk Regiment, 1/5th Suffolk Regiment and 1/8th Hampshire Regiment); the 60th Division, under the command of Maj.-Gen. J S M Shea, which comprised the 179th Brigade (Humphreys; 2/13th London Regiment, 3/151st Punjabi Rifles, 2/19th Punjabis, 2/127th Baluch Light Infantry), the 180th Brigade (Watson; 2/19th London Regiment, 2nd Guides Infantry, 2/30th Punjabis, 1/50th Kumaon Rifles) and the 181st Brigade (Da Costa; 2/22nd London Regiment, 130th Baluchis, 2/97th Deccan Infantry, 2/152nd Indian Infantry) and the 75th Division, under the command of Maj.-Gen. P C Palin, which comprised the 232nd Brigade (Huddleston; 1/4th Wiltshire Regiment, 72nd Punjabis, 2/3rd Gurkha Rifles, 3rd Kashmir IS Infantry), the 233rd Brigade (Colston; 1/5th Somerset Light Infantry, 29th Punjabis, 3/3rd Gurkha Rifles, 2/154th Indian Infantry) and the 234th Brigade (Maclean; 1/4th Duke of Cornwall's Light Infantry, 123rd Outram's Rifles, 58th Vaughan's Rifles, 1/152nd Indian Infantry).

The 54th (East Anglian) Division had attached to it the Détachement Français de Palestine et Syrie, under the command of Col. P de Piépape, which comprised the Régiment de Marche de Tirailleurs (7me Bn 1er Tirailleurs Algériens, 9me Bn 2me Tirailleurs Algériens) and the Régiment de Marche de la Légion d'Orient (1er and 2me Bns Arméniens).

Of the mounted formations, the Australia and New Zealand Mounted Division remained unchanged, as did the Australian Mounted Division (which was now armed with the 1908-Pattern cavalry sword, with its 35in (89cm) blade), with the exception of the 5th Australian Light Horse Brigade (which now had attached the Régiment Mixte de Marche de Cavalerie, made up of two squadrons of Spahis and two of Chasseurs d'Afrique) having been substituted for the 5th Mounted Brigade. The Yeomanry Mounted Division was transformed into the 1st Mounted Division and subsequently the 4th and 5th Cavalry Divisions were created (see below).

The Desert Mounted Corps, under the command of Lt.-Gen. Sir Harry Chauvel, comprised the Australian Mounted Division (unchanged except as noted above); the 4th Cavalry Division, under Maj.-Gen. Sir George Barrow, which comprised the 10th Cavalry Brigade (Howard-Vyse; 1/1st Dorset Yeomanry, 2nd Lancers, 38th Central Indian Horse), the 11th Cavalry Brigade (Gregory; 1/1st County of London Yeomanry, 29th Lancers, 36th Jacob's Horse), the 12th Cavalry Brigade (Wigan; 1/1st Staffordshire Yeomanry, 6th Cavalry, 19th Lancers) and the 5th Cavalry Division, under Maj.-Gen. H J Macandrew, which comprised the 13th Cavalry Brigade (Kelly; 1/1st Gloucestershire

Yeomanry, 9th Hodson's Horse, 18th Lancers), the 14th Cavalry Brigade (Clarke; 1/1st Sherwood Rangers, 20th Deccan Horse, 34th Poona Horse) and the 15th (Imperial Service) Cavalry Brigade (Harbord; Jodhpore IS Lancers, Mysore IS Lancers and 1st Hyderabad IS Lancers).

Two battalions of Jewish men (of many nationalities) were recruited in the United Kingdom following the publication of the Balfour Declaration (see Chapter 17) in November 1917; they were mustered as the 38th and 39th Battalions, the Royal Fusiliers, and arrived in theatre in March and April respectively. (The 40th Battalion also formed, but was retained in Egypt.) They comprised part of Chaytor's Force with the Australia & New Zealand Mounted Division (Chaytor; unchanged), the 20th Indian Brigade (Murray; Alwar IS Infantry, Gwalior IS Infantry, Patiala IS Infantry, 110th Maharatta Light Infantry) and the 1st and 2nd British West Indies Regiments.

14. As he had indicated he would as early as July to Sir Henry Wilson, who had taken over as Chief of the Imperial General Staff from Robertson in February after the latter – always a staunch 'Westerner' and thus at odds with the Prime Minister's 'Eastern' predilection – had finally provoked Lloyd George into removing him. Allenby only revealed his plans to his superiors in London after Wilson had suggested he might be able to 'lend' him three or four divisions from France over the winter, and had asked to what use he might put them. The offer was withdrawn only weeks later, when it became clear that the men would be required in France after all, but Allenby had perhaps never taken it entirely seriously anyway, and proceeded with the force he had at hand.

15. Though considerable detail was still missing; for security reasons, brigadiers, even, were not informed of their precise objectives until two or three days before the attack was launched.

16. 'Watson's Force' was composed mainly of pioneers (those of the 53rd and 10th Divisions), and was intended to repair the roads to enable the artillery to advance. Chetwode planned a convergent attack which would bring his two divisions together along a line Aqrabe–Jemma'in, about twelve kilometres north of his jumping-off point, without attacking the Turkish positions on the Nablus road south of that line, which were the strongest in the sector. The lines of march of the 10th and 53rd Divisions would thus use all the features of the terrain to their advantage.

17. The map also shows the 6th Indian Division, which was actually in Mesopotamia, located inland of Jaffa.

18. It seems that the 5th Cavalry did, in fact, miss an opportunity to capture Sanders; had it been possible to find a guide to lead even a small detachment by a roundabout path to enter Nazareth from the north, he could perhaps have been surprised. Alerted by firing south of the town at around dawn, he thought of immediate flight (and some reports say he resorted to it, clad in pyjamas, but returned later), but then became convinced that the situation was not dire, and oversaw the defence of Nazareth until 1315. Sanders reached Tiberias that afternoon, but without his General Staff.

19. Those of the 4th Cavalry Division, which was by this time stretched very thinly, for it had the responsibility not only of guarding many thousands of Turkish and German prisoners but also of holding the road from Beisan towards El Affule.

20. It is held that the failure to close the gap earlier was the only major shortcoming of the entire battle from the British perspective.

21. The remainder, about a third of the entire force, was to remain to provide security at the crossings.

22. His own 11th ALH; the 15th, of the 5th Brigade, and the Sherwood Rangers and Hyderabad Lancers of the 5th Cavalry Division. The remaining two regiments of the

4th LHB were placed under the command of the senior lieutenant-colonel and became known as Bourchier's Force.

23. See Fromkin, *A Peace to End All Peace*, for an analysis of the situation and an account of the political shenanigans which followed. As he says, 'Evidence is scanty as to who made the decision [that British – not French – troops were to be the first to enter Damascus] and why', but it was perhaps the work of Gilbert Clayton, who was by now Allenby's Chief Political Officer.

24. For whom, incidentally – or perhaps not – Lawrence nurtured something like hatred, believing him and his rather more powerful brother, the Emir Ali, to be supporters 'of Hussein and Islam rather than of Feisal and [Arab] nationalism' (Fromkin). There is also the suggestion – but it is only one of many alternative reasons put forward – that the Abd el Kader brothers knew details of Lawrence's private affairs. The Abd el Kader brothers (also known as Al Jazairi) were of Algerian origin, and had accompanied their father, one of the chief obstacles to French rule there, into exile in 1847, arriving in Damascus – where he, and later they, wielded considerable power – in 1855.

25. That, in any event, is the account given in Lawrence's *Revolt in the Desert*. In fact, while the Arabs had certainly killed many Turks, the column was still an organised, disciplined body when it was cut off by the 9th ALH two days later.

26. By Mohammed Jemal Pasha (Jemal *Kuchuk*, the ex-commander of VIII Corps and more recently that of the Fourth Army, not Jemal *Biyuk* the Young Turk triumvir, who had long returned to Constantinople), when he quit the city for Ba'albek in company with Liman von Sanders. That same day Mustafa Kemal, who had been reappointed to command the Seventh Army on 16 August, and had singularly failed, on this occasion, to stem the British advance, was ordered to Rivaq (qv), to take command there.

27. The 3rd LHB then began a lengthy chase up the Homs road, being checked by the Fourth Army's German rearguard – men of the 146th Regiment – at virtually every turn. The Australians bivouacked at Duma that night, and early the following morning the 9th ALH set out in pursuit once more. Luck, which had deserted the Australians the previous day, was with them now, and they managed to intercept the head of the Turkish column at Khan Ayash, just where the road entered the hills, taking around 1,500 prisoners.

28. By Falls' account; at 0900 by his own. The difference is probably immaterial. Lawrence insisted that Sherifial troops had been in Damascus since the previous evening; that may have been the case, but if so, they had not made their presence known in any way, to either friend or foe, and so it was largely irrelevant.

29. Shukri al Ayyubi lasted just days before he was replaced, at Chauvel's orders, by Ali Riza Pasha el Rikabi! By then, history had been (re)written to Lawrence's satisfaction.

30. Sanders understood there was no natural line south of Aleppo on which he could stand; he had ordered von Oppen to retreat there with the remains of the Asienkorps (and Mustafa Kemal, with what little was left of the Seventh Army, to join him) while Jemal Kuchuk organised a rearguard defence at Homs to buy them time. Allenby had asked Feisal to send 1,500 men up the direct road to Homs to cover the DMC's advance up the Beka'a Valley and then to operate between Hama and Aleppo.

31. One of which latter, the 2nd, had an epic journey to join Macandrew; it left Sollum, in Libya, on 11 October, and ten days later was in action north of Homs, having covered two thousand kilometres, half of it on its own wheels and the remainder on a railway flatcar, in the interim.

CHAPTER 17

1. He had led a small force into enemy territory hoping to foment an uprising; he failed, and had to content himself with cutting the Beersheba–Hebron road instead.

2. Bulgaria petitioned for a cessation of hostilities on 26 September and signed an armistice agreement three days later.

3. By his own later account: 'In the cabin of the launch, which took me across from Prinkipo to the Sublime Porte, I jotted down in my pocketbook the conditions which I proposed. They were as follows:

 1 The opening of the Dardanelles and the Bosporus to the British fleet.
 2 Autonomy of Mesopotamia and Syria under the sovereignty of the Sultan, and evacuation of those territories by the troops of the Entente.
 3 Frontier settlement as in the Treaty of London.
 4 Immediate release of all British and Indian prisoners of war.'

These formed the basis of his proposal to lzzet Pasha, who made no demands of his own 'for he knew that the terms I would suggest would be honourable', and who was more than happy to see them put to the British government by one of its own.

4. Hussein Rauf had captained the cruiser *Hamidieh*, the Ottoman Navy's only effective asset during the Balkan Wars, and had been captain-designate of the battleship *Sultan Osman I*. During the last days of the war he replaced Jemal Pasha as Minister of the Marine, and signed the 30 October armistice; see note 8 below.

5. Whether he knew it or not – and one can imagine he did not – he was mistaken. The Turks had tried initially to open a channel to the (neutral, with respect to them) Americans, on 13 October, via the two nations' embassies in Madrid, but got no reply (the request was passed up to the President, but Wilson prevaricated, and by the time he was ready to act, Townshend had appeared on the scene); they then tried the French, but failed to make contact; it was only then that Izzet Pasha turned first to Newcombe and later to Townshend. However, Townshend's claim certainly muddied the waters – many sources still suggest that the Turks would talk only to the British – and emboldened London to insist to Calthorpe that he take every possible step to exclude the French from any subsequent negotiations.

6. The Allies had already accepted a draft armistice agreement (composed by the British) to be used in negotiations with Turkey. It had some two dozen points in all, but Lloyd George instructed Calthorpe to focus on only those which would see hostilities cease and allow the navy access to the Black Sea. In the event, all were accepted.

7. Just as Franchet d'Esperey, the (French) commander-in-chief in the Balkans, had negotiated unilaterally with the Bulgarians, it was pointed out. The comparison was a poor one; d'Esperey really did not have the time to consult the Council of Allies if he was to make the most of his opportunities.

8. And, later, ignominy, Mustafa Kemal holding that in doing so he had betrayed his country. He put him on trial in 1926 (by which time, now known as Rauf Orbay, he had emerged as a leader of the party opposed to the Father of the Turks), and exiled him for ten years, though he later returned to favour. Ever an anglophile, he served as Turkey's ambassador to Britain during WW2.

9. He was shot and killed by Soghomon Tehlirian in Berlin on 14 March 1921 (Tehlirian was acquitted by a German court). His remains were returned to Turkey in 1943 as part of Hitler's campaign to seduce her government out of its neutrality in WW2. There are rumours of the involvement of the British and Soviet Russian intelligence services in his assassination, but it is difficult to take them seriously. Armenians claim that both

he and Jemal died as a result of 'Operation Nemesis', set in train by the Armenian Revolutionary Federation. The same organisation also claims to have assassinated Said Halim Pasha; he, too, died in Berlin, on 5 December 1921, at the hand of Arshavir Shiragian.

10. He accompanied Enver to Moscow (see Note 11) but soon realised that the Bolsheviks were merely stringing him along, and subsequently travelled east to Afghanistan to assist in training its army. On his way back to Moscow he died, together with two aides, in Tiflis on 21 July 1922, at the hands of Armenian assassins Stepan Dzaghikian, Bedros Der Boghosian and Ardashes Kevorkian (by one account; by another he was murdered on the orders of the Georgian secret police by one Sergo Lobadze; by yet another his killers were Armenians named Karakin Lalaian and Sergo Vartanyan).

11. Influenced by the German Communist Karl Radek and, following Talaat's assassination, the unrivalled leader of the Young Turks in exile, he developed a plan to remove and supplant Mustafa Kemal with the aid of the Soviet government. He convinced Jemal of the viability of his scheme and the pair travelled – with no little difficulty; Enver was forced to break his journey and spent four months in a Lithuanian prison, charged with spying – to Moscow, where they met Lenin. The Bolshevik leader seemed to see some merit in his plan, and despatched him to Batum, on the Black Sea coast of Georgia, close to its border with Turkey, to be sent back into the country at the head of an exile army should Kemal's campaign fail. When it did not, and realising that the Bolsheviks had no real intention of backing him by force in any other circumstances, he reverted to his original ambition: to establish a pan-Turania state/confederacy. He died on 4 August 1922, aged only 41. His remains were returned to Turkey in 1986.

12. Izzet had lasted only until 8 November, and was then replaced by Tewfik; he, in turn, was replaced by Ferid on 10 March. He lasted until October 1919, and was replaced by Ali Riza, who gave way to Hulusi Salih the following March. Salih lasted just three weeks; Ferid replaced him until October, and then Tewfik returned as the last Ottoman Grand Vizier, the office being abolished on 17 November 1922.

13. It was never the Allies' intention to occupy all of Anatolia.

14. A confirmed imperialist; his father, a noted jurist and amateur historian, had created the Comité de l'Afrique Française and was a member of the Comité de l'Asie Française, of which his brother was also a member. He was a close associate of Pierre-Étienne Flandin, the leader of the domestic movement to ensure that Syria fell into the French bailiwick, post-war. Just as the British Arabists in Egypt had convinced themselves that the Arabs looked towards London for their salvation, so this group had convinced themselves that they looked towards Paris.

15. The negotiations had already started prior to Sykes' return, but Sir Arthur Nicholson, the Permanent Under-Secretary at the Foreign Office, had soon locked horns with Picot.

16. Specifically, Britain's government had decided that it wished to hang on to northern Mesopotamia, it being clear that there were considerable deposits of oil to be found both at Mosul and at Kirkuk. On 30 July 1918, just prior to a War Cabinet meeting on the subject of war aims, Hankey wrote to Sir Eric Geddes, First Lord of the Admiralty, to make precisely that point, saying: 'The retention of the oil-bearing regions in Mesopotamia and Persia in British hands, as well as a proper strategic boundary to cover them, would appear to be a first-class British war aim.' Foreign Secretary Arthur Balfour took that line during the meeting which followed, and Hankey's proposal was adopted.

17. Ironically, the USA never joined the League, Wilson's domestic enemies, who were many and varied, and who controlled the US Senate, having combined to prevent it.

Wilson's other contributions to the proceedings at Versailles were often either nugatory or downright obstructive, and he was routinely outsmarted by Lloyd George, for one.

18. Again, David Fromkin addresses the political elements of the conference as it related to Middle Eastern affairs in *A Peace to End all Peace*.

19. The *Missak-I Milli* proposed that the non-Arab areas of the Empire should be considered the 'Turkish homeland', and that the status of the rest should be determined by referendum, as should that of Kars, Ardahan and Batum. The security of the Constantinople region, extending to the Sea of Marmara, should be guaranteed, and the status of the Bosporus and the Dardanelles should be determined by Turkey 'and other interested parties'. Mustafa Kemal said of the decision, 'It is the nation's iron fist that writes the Nation's Oath, the main principle of our independence.' The Allies responded directly by altering the status of the de facto occupation of Constantinople on 16 February, giving it a legal basis where before none had existed.

20. An annex to the resolution gave the Compagnie Française des Pétroles 25 per cent of any oil found in the Mosul *vilayet*. By means of this palliative, French opposition to the inclusion of the region within the British mandate to govern Iraq was removed. The formal agreement which established the Iraq Petroleum Company was not finally signed until 31 July 1928, by which time oil had been found in enormous quantities at Kirkuk. It allocated the rest of the production equally to Royal Dutch/Shell, US interests (Standard Oil of New Jersey and Socony (later Mobil), under an umbrella known as the Near East Development Company) and the Anglo-Persian Oil Co.; each party contributed 1.25 per cent from its share to Calouste Gulbenkian, who had brokered the deal; in turn he contracted to sell his 5 per cent of the Iraqi field's output to France at the prevailing price, and became one of the richest men in the world as a result.

21. That is, the Ottoman government, Britain, France, Italy and Greece, plus sundry others including the British dominions, Belgium and Japan.

22. This provision was largely the work of Wilson, and the area was described at the time as 'Wilsonian Armenia'; as originally defined it included regions which had no significant Armenian population, such as Trebizond and its hinterland.

23. Since the inception of the Paris Conference Venizélos had been promoting the *Megali Idea* (the Great Idea) to anyone who would listen. The Great Idea had been a major plank of Greek ambition ever since the country gained its independence from the Ottoman Empire in 1831. Essentially it involved the Greeks regaining control of any part of Ottoman territory which was or ever had been ethnically Greek, including Thessaly, Epirus, Macedonia and all of Thrace including Constantinople and the southern portion of Bulgaria, all the islands, the Aegean coast from a point east of Rhodes and the Black Sea coast too.

24. Before WW1 it had a population of around a quarter of a million, of whom perhaps half were Greek.

25. Some commentators were to go so far as to suggest that, had Greek forces not set foot on Anatolian soil, the Turkish Nationalist Movement would not have sprung up in the form it did.

26. In fact, by the actions of the Allied commander in Macedonia, Gen. Maurice Sarrail, who, with the aid and connivance of Venizélos, made his position untenable. Sarrail's actions almost led to civil war in Greece, and he himself was removed five months later, to be replaced by the more diplomatic Louis Franchet d'Esperey.

27. The post had been offered to Ioannis Metaxas, Greece's foremost general, who had refused, saying he believed the war unwinnable.

28. The British occupied Batum and the surrounding area until June 1920.

29. Georgia soon followed, the Georgian Soviet Socialist Republic replacing the Demo-

cratic Republic of Georgia on 25 February 1921. Azerbaijan had become a Soviet Socialist Republic on 28 April 1920. Armenia, Azerbaijan and Georgia were united into the Transcaucasian Socialist Federative Soviet Republic in March 1922.

30. These were men who had joined the Légion d'Orient, a component of the Légion Étrangère established in November 1916, after they had been rescued from the Gulf of Alexandretta region by French warships during the concerted Turkish campaign against their people. This unit was renamed the Légion Arménienne, on 1 February 1919.

31. And also, by Churchill's account (in *The World Crisis*; he had previously made the point in a Cabinet memorandum), to supply the Turkish Nationalists with weapons.

32. He had taken up this dual responsibility in January 1919, having returned to the government as Minister of Munitions eighteen months earlier.

33. Following their participation in the Paris Peace Conference in their own right, the Dominion leaders had been put in a much stronger position, and had effectively secured for themselves the right to remain neutral in the event of Britain going to war, something which had been unthinkable in 1914.

34. Though he did not immediately rejoin the party (or its bastion, the Carlton Club).

35. By then the situation in Athens had changed dramatically. On 26 September the Gounaris government resigned en masse, and the following day Constantine abdicated again, to be replaced by his elder son George. Real power lay in the hands of a triumvirate of relatively junior military officers, two colonels – Nikolaos Plastiras and Stylianos Gonatas, both of whom later served as Prime Minister on various occasions – and a naval captain named Phokas. On 13 November Gounaris and seven of his colleagues were arrested, and were later tried by what was little more than a kangeroo court motivated by a desire to be revenged for the catastrophe which had befallen Greece. Two of the accused were sentenced to life imprisonment; the rest, including Gounaris and Hatzianestis, were shot without further ado. The deposed king's brother, Prince Andrew (father of Prince Philip, the Duke of Edinburgh), was sent into exile.

36. A conference was organised to address the issue of the pan-Islamic importance of the caliphate; it met in Cairo in May 1926, and declared it to be 'a necessity', but failed to carry the matter forward. Two further conferences were held, in Mecca the same year, and in Jerusalem in 1931, but failed to reach a consensus, and with that the issue rested.

37. Kemal's further reforms included the closing of the *madrassas* (religious schools run by the *Ulema*) in 1924 and the substitution of westernised headwear for the fez (with the Hat Law of 1925; the policy was continued with the Law Relating to Prohibited Garments in 1934, which outlawed turbans, and veils for women). He outlawed multiple marriage and divorce-by-renunciation in 1926; introduced a westernised (and logically structured) alphabet to replace Arabic script in May 1928, and that same year proclaimed Turkey a secular state. He gave full political rights to women in 1934, when he also promulgated the Law of Surnames, taking Atatürk (Father of the Turks) as his own, by public demand.

38. Curzon was seconded by Rumbold, who later took over from him. Barrère was seconded by Maurice Bompard, who took over from him, and by Gen. Pellé, the French High Commissioner in Constantinople, who later took Bompard's place. Montagna later took over from Garroni. Venizélos, now back in favour in Athens, was the principal Greek delegate. The government of the Soviet Union was invited to send a delegation to attend those elements of the conference which were to deal with the Straits Convention, which was to be redrafted.

39. Primarily, it was concerned with oil concessions.

40. It gave Iraq roughly the same degree of autonomy that Egypt enjoyed: Britain

reserved the right to set foreign policy, and had unfettered military access to bases and installations.

41. Syria lost the Golan Heights; Egypt lost the Sinai Peninsula but subsequently recovered it. The military power of all three of the Arab nations was substantially reduced. Jordan did not participate in the later and almost equally disastrous Yom Kippur War of 1973.

42. He never wavered in his anti-British stance, and served with the Waffen-SS during WW2.

43. Including one from the Palestine Royal Commission (the Peel Commission) which the British government set up to consider the causes of the revolt.

44. Who later came to prominence as the leader of the Chindit expeditionary forces in Burma during WW2.

45. To be renewed briefly, with catastrophic consequences, in Egypt in 1956, and again, more substantially and this time alongside the USA instead of in opposition to it, in Iraq in 1991 and again from 2003. The British retained a residual presence in the area, remaining in Cyprus until 1960 (and even then held on to two 'Sovereign Base Areas' at Akrotiri and Dhekelia), and in Aden, at the tip of the Arabian Peninsula, until November 1967.

Index